Augustus John Cuthbert Hare

Walks in Rome

Vol. II.

Augustus John Cuthbert Hare

Walks in Rome
Vol. II.

ISBN/EAN: 9783744778275

Printed in Europe, USA, Canada, Australia, Japan

Cover: Foto ©ninafisch / pixelio.de

More available books at **www.hansebooks.com**

WALKS IN ROME

By AUGUSTUS J. C. HARE
AUTHOR OF "MEMORIALS OF A QUIET LIFE," "WANDERINGS IN SPAIN," ETC

TWO VOLUMES.—II.

FOURTH EDITION

W. ISBISTER & CO.
56, LUDGATE HILL, LONDON
1874

[*All rights reserved.*]

JOHN CHILDS AND SON, PRINTERS.

CONTENTS.

CHAPTER XI.
THE NEIGHBOURHOOD OF THE BATHS OF DIOCLETIAN . . 7

CHAPTER XII.
THE ESQUILINE 46

CHAPTER XIII.
THE BASILICAS OF THE LATERAN, SANTA CROCE, AND S. LORENZO 94

CHAPTER XIV.
IN THE CAMPUS MARTIUS 148

CHAPTER XV.
THE BORGO AND ST. PETER'S . . . 223

CHAPTER XVI.
THE VATICAN 282

CHAPTER XVII.

THE ISLAND AND THE TRASTEVERE . . 360

CHAPTER XVIII.

THE TRE FONTANE AND S. PAOLO 392

CHAPTER XIX.

THE VILLAS BORGHESE MADAMA, AND MELLINI . . . 410

CHAPTER XX.

THE JANICULAN 432

CHAPTER XI.

THE NEIGHBOURHOOD OF THE BATHS OF DIOCLETIAN.

The Cappuccini—S. Isidoro—S. Niccolo in Tolentino—Via S. Basilio—Convent of the Pregatrici—Villa Massimo Rignano—Gardens of Sallust—Villa Ludovisi—Porta Salara—(Villa Albani—Catacombs of Sta. Felicitas and Sta. Priscilla—Ponte Salara)—Porta Pia—(Villa Torlonia—Sant' Agnese—Sta. Costanza—Ponte Nomentana—Mons Sacer—S. Alessandro)—Villa Torlonia within the walls—Via Macao—Pretorian Camp—Railway Station—Villa Negroni—Agger of Servius Tullius—Sta. Maria degli Angeli—Fountain of the Termini—Sta. Maria della Vittoria—Sta. Susanna—S. Bernardo—S. Caio.

OPENING from the left of the Piazza Barberini, is the small *Piazza of the Cappuccini*, named from a convent suppressed since the Sardinian occupation, but which was one of the largest and most populous in Rome.

The conventual church, dedicated to *Sta. Maria della Concezione*, contains several fine pictures. In the first chapel, on the right, is the magnificent *Guido* of the Archangel Michael trampling upon the Devil,—said to be a portrait of Pope Innocent X., against whom the painter had a peculiar spite.

"Here the angel, standing, yet scarcely touching the ground, poised on his outspread wings, sets his left foot on the head of his adversary; in one hand he brandishes a sword, in the other he holds the end of a chain, with which he is about to bind down the demon in the bottomless pit. The attitude has been criticised, and justly; the grace is somewhat mannered, verging on the theatrical; but Forsyth is too severe when he talks of 'the air of a dancing master': one thing, however, is certain, we do not think about the attitude when we look at Raphael's St. Michael (in the Louvre); in Guido's it is the first thing that strikes us; but when we look farther, the head redeems all; it is singularly beautiful, and in the blending of the masculine and feminine graces, in the serene purity of the brow, and the flow of the golden hair, there is something divine; a slight, very slight expression of scorn is in the air of the head. The fiend is the worst part of the picture; it is not a fiend, but a degraded prosaic human ruffian; we laugh with incredulous contempt at the idea of an angel called down from heaven to overcome such a wretch. In Raphael the fiend is human, but the head has the god-like ugliness and malignity of a satyr; Guido's fiend is only stupid and base. It appears to me that there is just the same difference—the same *kind* of difference—between the angel of Raphael and the angel of Guido, as between the description in Tasso and the description in Milton; let any one compare them. In Tasso we are struck by the picturesque elegance of the description as a piece of art, the melody of the verse, the admirable choice of the expressions, as in Guido by the finished but somewhat artificial and studied grace. In Raphael and Milton we see only the vision of a 'shape divine.'"—*Jameson's Sacred Art*, p. 107.

In the same chapel is a picture by *Gherardo della Notte* of Christ in the purple robe. The third chapel contains a fresco by *Domenichino* of the Death of St. Francis, and a picture of the Ecstasy of St. Francis, which was a gift from the same painter to this church.

The first chapel on the left contains The Visit of Ananias to Saul, by *Pietro da Cortona*.

"Whoever would know to what length this painter carried his style in his altar-piece should examine the Conversion of St. Paul in the Cappuccini at Rome, which though placed opposite to the St. Michael of Guido, cannot fail to excite the admiration of such judges as are willing to admit various styles of beauty in art."—*Lanzi*.

On the left of the high-altar is the tomb of Prince

Alexander Sobieski, son of John III., king of Poland, who died at Rome in 1714.

The church was founded in 1624, by Cardinal Barberini, the old monk-brother of Urban VIII., who, while his nephews were employed in building magnificent palaces, refused to take advantage of the family elevation otherwise than to endow this church and convent. He is buried in front of the altar, with the remarkable epitaph—very different to the pompous, self-glorifying inscriptions of his brother—

"Hic jacet pulvis, cinis, et nihil."

This Cardinal Barberini possesses some historical interest from the patronage he extended to Milton during his visit to Rome in 1638.

"During his sojourn in Rome Milton enjoyed the conversation of several learned and ingenious men, and particularly of Lucas Holsteinius, keeper of the Vatican library, who received him with the greatest humanity, and showed him all the Greek authors, whether in print or MS.—which had passed through his correction; and also presented him to Cardinal Barberini, who, at an entertainment of music, performed at his own expense, waited for him at the door, and taking him by the hand, brought him into the assembly. The next morning he waited upon the Cardinal to return him thanks for these civilities, and by the means of Holsteinius was again introduced to his Eminence, and spent some time in conversation with him."—*Newton's Life of Milton.**

Over the entrance is a cartoon (with some differences) for the Navicella of Giotto.

From this church is entered the famous cemetery of the

---

* "At Rome, Selvaggi made a Latin distich in honour of Milton, and Salsilli a Latin tetrastich, celebrating him for his Greek, Latin, and Italian poetry; and he in return presented to Salsilli in his sickness those fine Scazons or Iambic verses having a spondee in the last foot, which are inserted among his juvenile poems. From Rome he went to Naples."—*Newton.*

Cappuccini (not subterranean), consisting of four chambers, ornamented with human bones in patterns, and with mummified bodies. The earth was brought from Jerusalem. As the cemetery was too small for the convent, when any monk died, the one who had been buried longest was ejected to make room for him. The loss of a grave was supposed to be amply compensated by the short rest in the holy earth which the body had already enjoyed. It is pleasant to read on the spot the pretty sketch in the "Improvisatore."

"I was playing near the church of the Capuchins, with some other children who were all younger than myself. There was fastened on the church door a little cross of metal; it was fastened about the middle of the door, and I could just reach it with my hand. Always when our mothers had passed by with us they had lifted us up that we might kiss the holy sign. One day, when we children were playing, one of the youngest of them inquired, 'why the child Jesus did not come down and play with us?' I assumed an air of wisdom, and replied that he was really bound upon the cross. We went to the church door, and although we found no one, we wished, as our mothers had taught us, to kiss him, but we could not reach up to it; one therefore lifted up the other, but just as the lips were pointed for the kiss, that one who lifted the other lost his strength, and the kissing one fell down just when his lips were about to touch the invisible child Jesus. At that moment my mother came by, and when she saw our child's play, she folded her hands, and said, 'You are actually some of God's angels, and thou art mine own angel,' added she, and kissed me.

"The Capuchin monk, Fra Martino, was my mother's confessor. He made very much of me, and gave me a picture of the Virgin, weeping great tears, which fell, like rain-drops, down into the burning flames of hell, where the damned caught this draught of refreshment. He took me over with him into the convent, where the open colonnade, which enclosed in a square the little potato-garden, with the two cypress and orange-trees, made a very deep impression upon me. Side by side, in the open passages, hung old portraits of deceased monks, and on the door of each cell were pasted pictures from the history of the martyrs, which I contemplated with the same holy emotions as afterwards the masterpieces of Raphael and Andrea del Sarto.

"'Thou art really a bright youth,' said he; 'thou shalt now see the dead.' Upon this, he opened a little door of a gallery which lay a few steps below the colonnade. We descended, and now I saw round about me skulls upon skulls, so placed one upon another, that they formed walls, and therewith several chapels. In these were regular niches, in which were seated perfect skeletons of the most distinguished of the monks, enveloped in their brown cowls, their cords round their waists, and with a breviary or withered bunch of flowers in their hands. Altars, chandeliers, bas-reliefs, of human joints, horrible and tasteless as the whole idea. I clung fast to the monk, who whispered a prayer, and then said to me, 'Here also I shall some time sleep; wilt thou thus visit me?'

"I answered not a word, but looked horrified at him, and then round about me upon the strange grizzly assembly. It was foolish to take me, a child, into this place. I was singularly impressed with the whole thing, and did not feel myself easy again until I came into his little cell, where the beautiful yellow oranges almost hung in at the window, and I saw the brightly coloured picture of the Madonna, who was borne upwards by angels into the clear sunshine, while a thousand flowers filled the grave in which she had rested. . . . .

"On the festival of All-Saints I was down in the chapel of the dead, where Fra Martino took me when I first visited the convent. All the monks sang masses for the dead, and I, with two other boys of my own age, swung the incense-breathing censer before the great altar of skulls. They had placed lights in the chandeliers made of bones, new garlands were placed around the brows of the skeleton monks, and fresh bouquets in their hands. Many people, as usual, thronged in; they all knelt and the singers intoned the solemn Miserere. I gazed for a long time on the pale yellow skulls, and the fumes of the incense which wavered in strange shapes between me and them, and everything began to swim round before my eyes; it was as if I saw everything through a large rainbow; as if a thousand prayer-bells rung in my ear; it seemed as if I was borne along a stream; it was unspeakably delicious—more, I know not; consciousness left me,—I was in a swoon."—*Hans Ch. Andersen.*

The street behind the Piazza Cappuccini leads to the *Church of S. Isidoro*,* built 1622, for Irish Franciscan monks.

* A holy hermit of Scete, who died 391.

The altar-piece, representing S. Isidoro, is by *Andrea Sacchi.* This church contains several tombs of distinguished Irishmen who have died in Rome.

Opposite are the recently founded convent and small chapel of the *Pregatrici*—nuns most picturesquely attired in blue and white, and devoted to the perpetual adoration of the Sacrament, who sing during the Benediction service, like the nuns of the Trinità di Monti.

The *Via S. Niccolo in Tolentino* leads by the handsome *Church* of that name, from the Piazza Barberini to the railway station. In this street are the hotels " Costanzi " and " Del Globo."

Parallel with, and behind this, the *Via S. Basilio* runs up the hill-side. At the top of this street is the entrance of the *Villa Massimo Rignano*, containing some fine palm-trees. This site, with the ridge of the opposite hill, and the valley between, was once occupied by the *Gardens of Sallust* (Horti Pretiosissimi), purchased for the emperors after the death of the historian, and a favourite residence of Vespasian, Nerva, and especially of Aurelian. Some vaulted halls under the cliff of the opposite hill, and a circular ruin surrounded by niches, are the only remains of the many fine buildings which once existed here, and which comprised a palace, baths, and the portico called Milliarensis, 1000 feet long. These edifices are known to have been ruined when Rome was taken by the Goths under Alaric (410), who entered at the neighbouring Porta Salara. The obelisk now in front of the Trinità di Monti, was removed from hence by Pius VI. The picturesque old casino of the Barberini, which occupied the most prominent position in the gardens, was pulled down in 1869, to make way for a house belonging to Spithover the librarian. The hill-side is supported by long picturesque buttresses, beneath which are remains of the huge masonry of Servius Tullius, whose *Agger* may be traced on the ridge of the hill running towards the present railway station. Part of these grounds are supposed to have formed the Campus Sceleratus, where the vestal virgins suffered who had broken their vows of chastity.

"When condemned by the college of pontifices, the vestal was stripped of her vittæ and other badges of office, was scourged, was attired like a corpse, placed in a close litter, and borne through the forum, attended by her weeping kindred with all the ceremonies of a real funeral, to the Campus Sceleratus, within the city walls, close to the Colline gate. There a small vault underground had been previously prepared, containing a couch, a lamp, and a table with a little food. The Pontifex Maximus, having lifted up his hands to heaven and uttered a secret prayer, opened the litter, led forth the culprit, and placing her on the steps of the ladder which gave access to the subterranean cell, delivered her over to the common executioner and his assistants, who conducted her down, drew up the ladder, and having filled the pit with earth until the surface was level with the surrounding ground, left her to perish deprived of all the tributes of respect usually paid to the spirits of the departed. In every case the paramour was publicly scourged to death in the forum."—*Smith's Dict. of Antiquities.*

"A Vignaiuolo showed us in the Gardens of Sallust a hole, through which he said those vestal virgins were put who had violated their vows of chastity. While we were listening to their story, some pretty Contadini came up to us attended by their rustic swains, and after looking into the hole, pitied the vestal virgins—'*Poverine*,' shrugged their shoulders, and laughing, thanked their stars and the Madonna, that poor Fanciulle were not buried alive for such things now-a-days."—*Eaton's Rome.*

A turn in the road now leads to the gate of the beautiful *Villa Ludovisi*, to which it has been very difficult to obtain admittance since the Sardinian occupation. The excellent proprietors, the Duke and Duchess Sora, have lived at

Foligno in complete seclusion, since the change of government.

The villa was built early in the last century by Cardinal Ludovisi, nephew of Gregory XV., from whom it descended to the Prince of Piombino, father of Duke Sora. The grounds, which are of an extent extraordinary when considered as being within the walls of a capital, were laid out by Le Nôtre, and are in the stiff French style of high clipped hedges, and avenues adorned with vases and sarcophagi. Near the entrance is a pretty fountain shaded by a huge plane-tree; the Quirinal is seen in the distance.

To the right of the entrance is the principal casino of sculptures, a very beautiful collection (catalogues on the spot). Especially remarkable are,—the grand colossal head, known as the "Ludovisi Juno" (41);

"A Rome, une Junon surpasse toutes les autres par son aspect et rappelle la Junon de Polyclète par sa majesté: c'est la célèbre Junon Ludovisi que Goethe admirait tant, et devant laquelle dans un accès de dévotion païenne,—seul genre de dévotion qu'il ait connu à Rome,—il faisait, nous dit-il, sa prière du matin.

"Cette tête colossale de Junon offre bien les caractères de la sculpture de Polyclète; la gravité, la grandeur, la dignité; mais ainsi que dans d'autres Junons qu'on peut supposer avoir été sculptées à Rome, l'imitateur de Polyclète, on doit le croire, adoucit la sévérité, je dirai presque la dureté de l'original, telle qu'elle se montre sur les médailles d'Argos, et celles d'Elis."—*Ampère, Hist. Romaine,* iii. 264.

"No words can give a true impression of the colossal head of Juno in the Villa Ludovisi: it is like a song of Homer."—*Goethe.*

—the *Statue of Mars* seated (1), with a Cupid at his feet, found in the portico of Octavia, and restored by Bernini;

"Il y avait bien un Mars assis de Scopas, et ce Mars était à Rome; mais un dieu dans son temple devait être assis sur un trône et non sur un rocher, comme le prétendu Mars Ludovisi. On a donc eu raison, selon moi, de reconnaître dans cette belle statue un Achille, à l'expression pensive de son visage, et surtout à l'attitude caractéristique que le sculpteur lui a donnée, lui faisant embrasser son genou avec ses deux mains, attitude qui, dans le langage de la sculpture antique, était le signe d'une méditation douloureuse. On citait comme très-beau un Achille de Silanion, sculpteur grec habile à rendre les sentiments violents. D'après cela, son Achille pouvait être un Achille indigné ; c'est de lui que viendrait l'Achille de la villa Ludovisi. L'expression de dépit, plus énergique dans l'original, eût été adoucie dans une admirable copie.'—*Ampère, Hist. Rom.* iii. 437.

—and No. 28 ;

"Le beau groupe auquel on avait donné le nom d'Arria et Pætus ; il fallait fermer les yeux à l'évidence pour voir un Romain du temps de Claude dans ce chef barbare qui, après avoir tué sa femme, se frappe lui-même d'un coup mortel. Le type du visage, la chevelure, le caractère de l'action, tout est gaulois ; la manière même dont s'accomplit l'immolation volontaire montre que ce n'est pas un Romain que nous avons devant les yeux ; un Romain se tuait plus simplement, avec moins de fracas. Le principal personnage du groupe Ludovisi conserve en ce moment suprême quelque chose de triomphant et de théâtral ; soulevant d'une main sa femme affaissée sous le coup qu'il lui a porté, de l'autre il enfonce son épée dans sa poitrine. La tête haute, l'œil tourné vers le ciel, il semble répéter le mot de sa race : 'Je ne crains qu'une chose, c'est que le ciel tombe sur ma tête.'"—*Ampère, Hist. Rom.* iii. 207.

At the end of the gardens, to the left, is another casino, from whose roof a most beautiful view may be obtained. Here are the most famous frescoes of *Guercino*. On the ceiling of the ground-floor, Aurora driving away Night and scattering flowers in her course, with Evening and Daybreak in the lunettes ; and, on the first floor, "Fame" attended by Force and Virtue. Smaller rooms on the ground floor have landscapes by *Guercino* and *Domenichino*, and some groups of Cupids by *T. Zucchero ;*

on the staircase is a fine bas-relief of two Cupids dragging a quiver.

"The prophets and sibyls of Guercino da Cento (1590—1666), and his Aurora, in a garden pavilion of the Villa Ludovisi, at Rome, almost attain to the effect of oil paintings in their glowing colouring combined with the broad and dark masses of shadow."—*Kugler.*

"In allegorising nature, Guercino imitates the deep shades of night, the twilight grey, and the irradiations of morning, with all the magic of *chiaroscuro;* but his figures are too mortal for the region where they move."—*Forsyth.*

In B.C. 82, the district near the Porta Collina, now occupied by the Villa Ludovisi, was the scene of a great battle for the very existence of Rome, between Sylla, and the Samnites and Lucanians under the Samnite general Pontius Telesinus, who declared he would raze the city to the ground if he were victorious. The left wing under Sylla was put to flight; but the right wing, commanded by Crassus, enabled him to restore the battle, and to gain a complete victory; fifty thousand men fell on each side.

The road now runs along the ridge of the hill to the Porta Salara, by which Alaric entered Rome through the treachery of the Isaurian guard, on the 24th of August, 410.

Passing through the gate and turning to the right along the outside of the wall, we may see, against the grounds of the Villa Ludovisi, the two round towers of the now closed *Porta Pinciana,* restored by Belisarius. This is the place where tradition declares that in his declining years the great general sat begging, with the cry, "Date obolum Belisario."

"A côté de la Porta Pinciana, on lit sur une pierre les paroles célèbres : 'Donnez une obole à Bélisaire'; mais cette inscription est moderne, comme la légende à laquelle elle fait allusion, et qu'on ne trouve dans nul historien contemporain de Bélisaire. Bélisaire ne demanda jamais l'aumône, et si le *cicerone* montre encore aux voyageurs l'endroit où, vieux et aveugle, il implorait une obole de la charité des passants, c'est que près de ce lieu il avait, sur la colline du Pincio, son palais, situé entre les jardins de Lucullus et les jardins de Salluste, et digne probablement de ce double voisinage par sa magnificence. Ce qui est vrai, c'est que le vainqueur des Goths et des Vandales fut disgracié par Justinien, grâce aux intrigues de Théodora. La légende, comme presque toujours, a exprimé par une fable une vérité, l'ingratitude si fréquente des souverains envers ceux qui leur ont rendu les plus grands services."—*Ampère, Emp.* ii. 396.

A short distance from the gate, along the Via Salara, is, on the right, the *Villa Albani* (shown on Tuesdays by an order), built in 1760 by Cardinal Alessandro Albani,—sold in 1834 to the Count of Castelbarco, and in 1868 to Prince Torlonia, its present possessor. The scene from its garden terrace is among the loveliest of Roman pictures, the view of the delicate Sabine mountains—Monte Gennaro, with the Montecelli beneath it—and in the middle distance, the churches of Sant' Agnese and Sta. Costanza, relieved by dark cypresses and a graceful fountain.

The *Casino*, which is, in fact, a magnificent palace, is remarkable as having been built from Cardinal Albani's own designs, Carlo Marchionni having been only employed to see that they were carried out.

"Here is a villa of exquisite design, planned by a profound antiquary. Here Cardinal Albani, having spent his life in collecting ancient sculpture, formed such porticoes and such saloons to receive it as an old Roman would have done : porticoes where the statues stood free upon the pavement between columns proportioned to their stature ; saloons which were not stocked but embellished with families of allied statues, and seemed full without a crowd. Here Winckelmann grew into an antiquary under the cardinal's patronage and instruction ; and here he projected his history of art, which brings this collection continually into view."—*Forsyth's Italy.*

The collection of sculptures is much reduced since the French invasion, when 294 of the finest specimens were carried off by Napoleon to Paris, where they were sold by Prince Albani upon their restoration in 1815, as he was unwilling to bear the expense of transport. The greater proportion of the remaining statues are of no great importance. Those of the imperial family in the vestibule are interesting—those of Julius and Augustus Cæsar, of Agrippina wife of Germanicus, and of Faustina, are seated; most of the heads have been restored.

Conspicuous among the treasures of this villa, are the sarcophagus with reliefs of the marriage of Peleus and Thetis, pronounced by Winckelmann to be one of the finest in existence; a head of Æsop, supposed to be after Lysippus; and the bronze "Apollo Sauroctonos," considered by Winckelmann to be the original statue by Praxiteles described by Pliny, and the most beautiful bronze statue in the world,—it was found on the Aventine. But most important of all is the famous relievo of Antinous crowned with lotus, from the Villa Adriana (over the chimney-piece of the first room to the right of the saloon), supposed to have formed part of an apotheosis of Antinous:

"As fresh, and as highly finished, as if it had just left the studio of the sculptor, this work, after the Apollo and the Laocoon, is perhaps the most beautiful monument of antiquity which time has transmitted to us."—*Winckelmann, Hist. de l'Art,* vi. ch. 7.

Inferior only to this, is another bas-relief, also over a chimney-piece,—the parting of Orpheus and Eurydice.

"Les deux époux vont se quitter. Eurydice attache sur Orphée un profond regard d'adieu. Sa main est posée sur l'épaule de son époux, geste ordinaire dans les groupes qui expriment la séparation de ceux qui s'aiment. La main d'Orphée dégage doucement celle d'Eurydice, tandis que Mercure fait de la sienne un léger mouvement pour l'entraîner. Dans ce léger mouvement est tout leur sort ; l'effet le plus pathétique est produit par la composition la plus simple ; l'émotion la plus pénétrante s'exhale de la sculpture la plus tranquille."—*Ampère, Hist. Rom.* iii. 256.

The villa also contains a collection of pictures, of which the most interesting are the sketches of *Giulio Romano* for the frescoes of the story of Psyche in the Palazzo del Te at Mantua, and two fine pictures by Luca Signorelli and Perugino, in compartments, in the first room on the left of the saloon.* All the works of art have lately been rearranged. The *Caffè* and the *Bigliardo*—(reached by an avenue of oaks, which, being filled with ancient tombstones, has the effect of a cemetery)—contain more statues, but of less importance.

Beyond the villa, the Via Salara (said by Pliny to derive its name from the salt of Ostia exported to the north by this route) passes on the left the site of Antemnæ, and crosses the Anio two miles from the city, by the *Ponte Salara*, destroyed by the Roman government in the terror of Garibaldi's approach from Monte Rotondo, in 1867. This bridge was a restoration by Narses, in the sixth century, but stood on the foundations of that famous Ponte Salara, upon which Titus Manlius fought the Gaulish giant, and cutting off his head, carried off the golden collar which earned him the name of Torquatus.

"Manlius prend un bouclier léger de fantassin, une épée espagnole commode pour combattre de très-près, et s'avance à la rencontre du Barbare. Les deux champions, isolés sur le pont, comme sur un théâtre, se joignent au milieu. Le Barbare portait un vêtement bariolé et une armure ornée de dessins et d'incrustations dorées, conforme au caractère de sa race, aussi vaine que vaillante. Les armes du Romain étaient bonnes, mais sans éclat. Point chez lui, comme chez son adversaire, de chant, de transports, d'armes agitées avec fureur, mais un cœur plein de courage et d'une colère muette qu'il réservait tout entière pour le combat.

"Le Gaulois, qui dépassait son adversaire de toute la tête, met en avant son bouclier et fait tomber pesamment son glaive sur l'armure de son adversaire. Celui-ci le heurte deux fois de son bouclier, le force à reculer, le trouble, et se glissant alors entre le bouclier et le corps du Gaulois, de deux coups rapidement portés lui ouvre le ventre. Quand le grand corps est tombé, Manlius lui coupe la tête, et, ramassant le collier de son ennemi décapité, jette tout sanglant sur son cou ce collier, le *torques*, propre aux Gaulois, et qu'on peut voir au Capitole porté par celui qu'on appelle à tort le gladiateur mourant. Un soldat donne, en plaisantant, à Manlius le sobriquet de *Torquatus*, que sa famille a toujours été fière de porter."—*Ampère, Hist. Rom.* iii. 10.

Beyond the ruins of the bridge, is a huge tomb with a tower, now used as an Osteria. Hence, the road leads by the Villa of Phaon (Villa Spada) where Nero died, and the site of Fidenæ, now known as Castel Giubeleo, to Monte Rotondo.

The district beyond the Porta Salara, and that extending between the Via Salara and the Monte Parioli, are completely undermined by catacombs (see Ch. IX.). The most important are—1. Nearest the gate, the *Catacomb of St. Felicitas*, which had three tiers of galleries, adorned by Pope Boniface I., who took refuge there from persecution,—now much dilapidated. Over this cemetery was a church, now destroyed, which is mentioned by William of Malmesbury. 2. *The Catacomb of SS. Thraso and Saturninus*, much decorated with the usual paintings. 3. *The Catacomb of Sta. Priscilla*, near the descent to the Anio. This cemetery is of great interest, from the number of martyrs' graves it contains, and from its peculiar construction in an ancient *arenarium*, pillars and walls of masonry being added throughout the central part, in order to sustain the tufa walls. Here were buried—probably because the entrance to the Chapel of the Popes at St. Calixtus was blocked up to preserve it in the persecution under Diocletian—Pope St. Marcellinus (ob. 308), and Pope St. Marcellus (ob. 310), who was sent into exile by Maxentius. On the tomb of the latter was placed, in finely cut type, the following epitaph by Pope Damasus:—

> "Veredicus Rector, lapsos quia crimina flere
> Prædixit, miseris fuit omnibus hostis amarus.
> Hinc furor, hinc odium sequitur, discordia, lites,
> Seditio, cædes, solvuntur fœdera pacis.
> Crimen ob alterius Christum qui in pace negavit,
> Finibus expulsus patriæ est feritate tyranni.
> Hæc breviter Damasus voluit comperta referre,
> Marcelli ut populus meritum cognoscere posset."

"The truth-speaking pope, because he preached that the lapsed should weep for their crimes, was bitterly hated by all those unhappy ones. Hence followed fury, hatred, discord, contentions, sedition, and slaughter, and the bonds of peace were ruptured. For the crime of another, who in (a time of) peace had denied Christ, (the pontiff) was expelled the shores of his country by the cruelty of the tyrant. These things Damasus having learnt, was desirous to narrate briefly, that people might recognise the merit of Marcellus."*

Several of the paintings in this catacomb are remarkable; especially that of a woman with a child, claimed by the Roman Church as one of the earliest representations of the Virgin. The painting is thus described by Northcote:—

"De Rossi unhesitatingly says that he believes this painting of our Blessed Lady to belong almost to the apostolic age. It is to be seen on the vaulted roof of a *loculus*, and represents the Blessed Virgin seated, her head partially covered by a short light veil, and with the Holy Child in her arms; opposite to her stands a man, clothed in the pallium, holding a volume in one hand, and with the other pointing to a star

---

* See Roma Sotterranea, p. 174.

which appears above and between the figures. This star almost always accompanies our Blessed Lady, both in paintings and in sculptures, where there is an obvious historical excuse for it, *e.g.*, when she is represented with the Magi offering their gifts, or by the side of the manger with the ox and the ass; but with a single figure, as in the present instance, it is unusual. The most obvious conjecture would be that the figure was meant for St. Joseph, or for one of the Magi. De Rossi, however, gives many reasons for preferring the prophet Isaias, whose prophecies concerning the Messias abound with imagery borrowed from light."—*Roma Sotterranea*.

This catacomb is one of the oldest, Sta. Priscilla, from whom it is named, being supposed to have been the mother of Pudens, and a contemporary of the apostles. Her granddaughters, Prassede and Pudenziana, were buried here before the removal of their relics to the church on the Esquiline. With this cemetery is connected the extraordinary history of the manufacture of Sta. Filomena, now one of the most popular saints in Italy, and one towards whom idolatry is carried out with frantic enthusiasm both at Domo d'Ossola and in some of the Neapolitan States. The story of this saint is best told in the words of Mrs. Jameson.

"In the year 1802, while some excavations were going forward in the catacomb of Priscilla, a sepulchre was discovered containing the skeleton of a young female; on the exterior were rudely painted some of the symbols constantly recurring in these chambers of the dead; an anchor, an olive branch (emblems of Hope and Peace), a scourge, two arrows, and a javelin: above them the following inscription, of which the beginning and end were destroyed:—

——LUMENA PAX TE CUM FI——

"The remains, reasonably supposed to be those of one of the early martyrs for the faith, were sealed up and deposited in the treasury of relics in the Lateran; here they remained for some years unthought of. On the return of Pius VII. from France, a Neapolitan prelate was sent to congratulate him. One of the priests in his train, who wished to create a sensation in his district, where the long residence of the French had probably caused some decay of piety, begged for a few relics to carry home, and these recently discovered remains were bestowed on him; the inscription was translated somewhat freely, to signify *Santa Philumena, rest in peace.* Another priest, whose name is suppressed *because of his great humility*, was favoured by a vision in the broad noon-day, in which he beheld the glorious virgin Filomena, who was pleased to reveal to him that she had suffered death for preferring the Christian faith and her vow of chastity to the addresses of the emperor, who wished to make her his wife. This vision leaving much of her history obscure, a certain young artist, whose name is also suppressed, perhaps because of his great humility, was informed in a vision that the emperor alluded to was Diocletian, and at the same time the torments and persecutions suffered by the Christian virgin Filomena, as well as her wonderful constancy, were also revealed to him. There were some difficulties in the way of the Emperor Diocletian, which *incline* the writer of the *historical* account to incline to the opinion that the young artist in his wisdom *may* have made a mistake, and that the emperor may have been not Diocletian but Maximian. The facts, however, now admitted of no doubt; the relics were carried by the priest Francesco da Lucia to Naples; they were enclosed in a case of wood resembling in form the human body; this figure was habited in a petticoat of white satin, and over it a crimson tunic after the Greek fashion; the face was painted to represent nature, a garland of flowers was placed on the head, and in the hands a lily and a javelin with the point reversed to express her purity and her martyrdom; then she was laid in a half-sitting posture in a sarcophagus, of which the sides were glass, and, after lying for some time in state in the chapel of the Torres family in the Church of Sant' Angiolo, she was carried in grand procession to Mugnano, a little town about twenty miles from Naples, amid the acclamations of the people, working many and surprising miracles by the way. . . . . Such is the legend of Sta. Filomena, and such the authority on which she has become within the last twenty years one of the most popular saints in Italy."—*Sacred and Legendary Art*, p. 671.

It is hoped that very interesting relics may still be discovered in this Catacomb.

"In an account preserved by St. Gregory of Tours, we are told that under Numerianus, the martyrs Chrysanthus and Daria were put to death in an *arenaria*, and that a great number of the faithful having been seen entering a subterranean crypt on the Via Salara, to visit their tombs, the heathen emperor caused the entrance to be hastily built up, and a vast mound of sand and stone to be heaped in front of it, so that they might be all buried alive, even as the martyrs whom they had come to venerate. St. Gregory adds, that when the tombs of these martyrs were re-discovered, after the ages of persecution had ceased, there were found with them, not only the relics of those worshippers who had been thus cruelly put to death, skeletons of men, women, and children lying on the floor, but also the silver cruets (*urcei argentei*) which they had taken down with them for the celebration of the sacred mysteries. St. Damasus was unwilling to destroy so touching a memorial of past ages. He abstained from making any of those changes by which he usually decorated the martyrs' tombs, but contented himself with setting up one of his invaluable historical inscriptions, and opening a window in the adjacent wall or rock, that all might see, without disturbing, this monument so unique in its kind—this Christian Pompeii in miniature. These things might still be seen in St. Gregory's time, in the sixth century; and De Rossi holds out hopes that some traces of them may be restored even to our own generation, some fragments of the inscription perhaps, or even the window itself through which our ancestors once saw so moving a spectacle, assisting, as it were, at a mass celebrated in the third century."—*Roma Sotterranea*, p. 88.

Returning to the Porta Salara, and following the walls, we reach the *Porta Pia*, built, as it is now seen, by Pius IX.—very ugly, but appropriately decorated with statues of St. Agnes and St. Alexander, to whose shrines it leads. The statues lost their heads in the capture of Rome in 1870 by the Italian troops, who entered the city by a breach in the walls close to this. A little to the right was the *Porta Nomentana*, flanked by round towers, closed by Pius IV. It was by this gate that the oppressed Roman people retreated to the Mons Sacer—and that Nero fled.

"Suivons-le du Grand-Cirque à la porte Nomentane. Quel spectacle ! Néron, accoutumé à toutes les recherches de la volupté, s'avance à cheval, les pieds nus, en chemise, couvert d'un vieux manteau dont la couleur était passée, un mouchoir sur le visage. Quatre personnes seulement l'accompagnent ; parmi elles est ce Sporus, que dans un jour d'indicible folie il avait publiquement épousé. Il sent la terre trembler, il voit les éclairs au ciel : Néron a peur. Tous ceux qu'il a fait mourir lui apparaissent et semblent se précipiter sur lui. Nous voici à la porte Nomentane, qui touche au Camp des Prétoriens. Néron reconnaît ce lieu où, il y a quinze ans, suivant alors le chemin qu'il vient de suivre, il est venu se faire reconnaître empereur par les prétoriens. En passant sous les murs de leur camp, vers lequel son destin le ramène, il les entend former des vœux pour Galba, et lancer des imprécations contre lui. Un passant lui dit : 'Voilà des gens qui cherchent Néron.' Son cheval se cabre au milieu de la route : c'est qu'il a flairé un cadavre. Le mouchoir qui couvrait son visage tombe ; un prétorien qui se trouvait là le ramasse et le rend à l'empereur, qu'il salue par son nom. A chacun de ces incidents son effroi redouble. Enfin il est arrivé à un petit chemin qui s'ouvre à notre gauche, dans la direction de la voie Salara, parallèle à la voie Nomentane. C'est entre ces deux voies qu'était la villa de Phaon, à quatre milles de Rome. Pour l'attendre, Néron, qui a mis pied à terre, s'enfonce à travers un fourré d'épines et un champ de roseaux comme il s'en trouve tant dans la Campagne de Rome ; il a peine de s'y frayer un chemin ; il arrive ainsi au mur de derrière de la villa. Près de là était un de ces antres creusés pour l'extraction du sable volcanique, appelé *pouzzolane*, tels qu'on en voit encore de ce côté. Phaon engage le fugitif à s'y cacher ; il refuse. On fait un trou dans la muraille de la villa par où il pénètre, marchant quatre pieds, dans l'intérieur. Il entre dans une petite salle et se couche sur un lit formé d'un méchant matelas sur lequel on avait jeté un vieux manteau. Ceux qui l'entourent le pressent de mourir pour échapper aux outrages et au supplice. Il essaye à plusieurs reprises de se donner la mort et n'y peut se résoudre ; il pleure. Enfin, en entendant les cavaliers qui venaient le saisir, il cite un vers grec, fait un effort et se tue avec le secours d'un affranchi."—*Ampère, Emp.* ii. 65.

Immediately outside the Porta Pia is the entrance of the beautiful *Villa Patrizi*, whose grounds enclose the small *Catacomb of St. Nicomedus*. Then comes the *Villa Lezzani*, where Sta. Giustina is buried in a chapel, and where her festa is observed on the 25th of October.

Beyond this is the ridiculous *Villa Torlonia* (shown with an order on Wednesdays from 11 to 4, but not worth seeing), sprinkled with mock ruins.

At little more than a mile from the gate the road reaches the *Basilica of St' Agnese fuori le Mura*, founded by Constantine at the request of his daughter Constantia, in honour of the virgin martyr buried in the neighbouring catacomb; but rebuilt 625—38 by Honorius I. It was altered in 1490 by Innocent VIII., but retains more of its ancient character than most of the Roman churches. The polychrome decorations of the interior, and the rebuilding of the monastery, were carried out at the expense of Pius IX., as a thank-offering for his escape, when he fell through the floor here into a cellar, with his cardinals and attendants, on April 15, 1855. The scene is represented in a large fresco by *Domenico Tojetti*, in a chamber on the right of the courtyard.

The approach to the church is by a picturesque staircase of forty-five ancient marble steps, lined with inscriptions from the catacombs. The nave is divided from the aisles by sixteen columns, four of which are of "porta-santa" and two of "pavonazzetto." A smaller range of columns above these supports the roof of a triforium, which is on a level with the road. The baldacchino, erected in 1614, is supported by four porphyry columns. Beneath is the shrine of St. Agnes surmounted by her statue, an antique of oriental alabaster, with modern head, and hands of gilt bronze. The mosaics of the tribune, representing St. Agnes between Popes Honorius I. and Symmachus, are of the seventh century. Beneath, is an ancient episcopal chair.

The second chapel on the right has a beautiful mosaic

altar, and a relief of SS. Stephen and Laurence of 1490. The third chapel is that of St. Emerentiana, foster-sister of St. Agnes, who was discovered praying beside the tomb of her friend, and was stoned to death because she refused to sacrifice to idols.

"So ancient is the worship paid to St. Agnes, that next to the Evangelists and Apostles, there is no saint whose effigy is older. It is found on the ancient glass and earthenware vessels used by the Christians in the early part of the third century, with her name inscribed, which leaves no doubt of her identity. But neither in these images, nor in the mosaics, is the lamb introduced, which in later times has become her inseparable attribute, as the patroness of maidens and maidenly modesty."—*Jameson's Sacred Art*, p. 105.

St. Agnes suffered martyrdom by being stabbed in the throat, under Diocletian, in her thirteenth year (see Ch. XIV.), after which, according to the expression used in the acts of her martyrdom, her parents " with all joy " laid her in the catacombs. One day as they were praying near the body of their child, she appeared to them surrounded by a great multitude of virgins, triumphant and glorious like herself, with a lamb by her side, and said, " I am in heaven, living with these virgins my companions, near Him whom I have so much loved." By her tomb, also, Constantia, a princess sick with hopeless leprosy, was praying for the healing of her body, when she heard a voice saying, " Rise up, Constantia, and go on constantly ('Costanter age, Constantia ') in the faith of Jesus Christ, the Son of God, who shall heal your diseases,"—and, being cured of her evil, she besought her father to build this basilica as a thank-offering.*

On the 21st of January, a beautiful service is celebrated here, in which two lambs, typical of the purity of the virgin

* Une Chrétienne à Rome.

saint, are blessed upon the altar. They are sent by the chapter of St. John Lateran, and their wool is afterwards used to make the pallium of the pope, which is consecrated before it is worn, by being deposited in a golden urn upon the tomb of St. Peter. The pallium is the sign of episcopal jurisdiction.

"Ainsi, le simple ornement de laine que ces prélats doivent porter sur leurs épaules comme symbole de la brebis du bon Pasteur, et que le pontife Romain prend sur l'autel même de Saint Pierre pour le leur adresser, va porter jusqu'aux extrémités de l'Eglise, dans une union sublime, le double sentiment de la force du Prince des Apôtres et de la douceur virginale d'Agnes."—*Dom Guéranger.*

Close to St' Agnese is the round *Church of Sta. Costanza,* erected by Constantine as a mausoleum for his daughters Constantia and Helena, and converted into a church by Alexander IV. (1254—61) in honour of the Princess Constantia, ob. 354, whose life is represented by Marcellinus as anything but saintlike, and who is supposed to have been confused in her canonization with a sainted nun of the same name. The rotunda, seventy-three feet in diameter, is surrounded by a vaulted corridor; twenty-four double columns of granite support the dome. The vaulting is covered with mosaic arabesques of the fourth century, of flowers and birds, with scenes referring to a vintage. The same subjects are repeated on the splendid porphyry sarcophagus of Sta. Costanza, of which the interest is so greatly marred by its removal to the Vatican from its proper site, whence it was first stolen by Pope Paul II., who intended to use it as his own tomb.

"Les enfants qui foulent le raisin, tels qu'on les voit dans les mosaïques de l'église de Sainte Constance, les bas-reliefs de son tombeau et ceux de beaucoup d'autres tombeaux chrétiens sont bien d'origine païenne, car on les voit aussi figurer dans les bas-reliefs où paraît Priape."—*Ampère, Hist. Rom.* iii. 257.

Behind the two churches is an oblong space, ending in a fine mass of ruin, which is best seen from the valley below. This was long supposed to be the Hippodrome of Constantine, but is now discovered to have belonged to an early Christian cemetery.

The Catacomb of St' Agnese is entered from a vineyard about a quarter of a mile beyond the church. It is lighted and opened to the public on St. Agnes' Day. After those of St. Calixtus, this, perhaps, is the catacomb which is most worthy of a visit.

We enter by a staircase attributed to the time of Constantine. The passages are lined with the usual *loculi* for the dead, sometimes adapted for a single body, sometimes for two laid together. Beside many of the graves the palm of victory may be seen scratched on the mortar, and remains of the glass bottles or *ampullæ*, which are supposed to indicate the graves of martyrs, and to have contained a portion of their blood, of which they are often said to retain the trace. One of the graves in the first gallery bears the names of consuls of A.D. 336, which fixes the date of this part of the cemetery.

The most interesting features here are a square chamber hewn in the rock, with an arm-chair (*sedia*) cut out of the rock on either side of the entrance, supposed to have been a school for catechists,—and near this is a second chamber for female catechists, with plain seats in the same position. Opening out of the gallery close by is a chamber which was apparently used as a chapel; its *arcosolium* has marks of an altar remaining at the top of the grave, and near it is a credence-table; the roof is richly painted,—in the central compartment is our Lord seated between the rolls of the Old and New Testament. Above the arcosolium, in the place of honour, is our Saviour as the Good Shepherd, bearing a sheep upon his shoulders, and standing between other sheep and trees;—in the other compartments are Daniel in the lions' den, the Three Children in the furnace, Moses taking off his shoes, Moses striking the rock, and —nearest the entrance—the Paralytic carrying his bed. A neighbouring chapel has also remains of an altar and credence-table, and well-preserved paintings,—the Good Shepherd, Adam and Eve, with the tree between them, Jonah under the gourd, and in the fourth compartment a figure described by Protestants merely as an Orante, and by Roman Catholics as the Blessed Virgin.* Near this chapel we can look down through an opening into the second floor of the catacomb, which is lined with graves like the first.

In the further part of the catacomb is a long narrow chapel which has received the name of the *cathedral* or *basilica*. It is divided into three parts, of which the furthest, or presbytery, contains an ancient episcopal chair with lower seats on either side for priests—probably the throne where Pope St. Liberius (A.D. 359) officiated, with his face to the people, when he lived for more than a year hidden here from persecution. Hence a flight of steps leads down to what Northcote calls "the Lady Chapel," where, over the altar, is a fresco of an orante, without a nimbus, with outstretched arms,—with a child in front of her. On either side of this picture, a very interesting one, is the monogram of Constantine, and the painting is referred to his time. Near this chapel is a chamber with a spring running through it, evidently used as a baptistery.

---

* The reasons for this belief are given in "The Roman Catacombs of Northcote," p. 78.

At the extremity of the catacomb, under the basilica of St. Agnes, is one of its most interesting features. Here the passages become wider and more irregular, the walls sloping and unformed, and graves cease to appear, indicating one of the ancient *arenaria*, which here formed the approach to the catacomb, and beyond which the Christians excavated their cemetery.

The graves throughout almost all the catacombs have been rifled, the bones which they contained being distributed as relics throughout Roman Catholic Christendom, and most of the sarcophagi and inscriptions removed to the Lateran and other museums.

"Vous pourriez voir ici la capitale des catacombes de toute la chrétienté. Les martyrs, les confesseurs, et les vierges, y fourmillent de tous côtés. Quand on se fait besoin de quelques reliques en pays étrangers, le Pape n'a qu'à descendre ici et crier, *Qui de vous autres veut aller être saint en Pologne?* Alors, s'il se trouve quelque mort de bonne volonté, il se lève et s'en va."—*De Brosses*, 1739.

Half a mile beyond St' Agnese, the road reaches the willow-fringed river Anio, in which " Silvia changed her earthly life for that of a goddess," and which carried the cradle containing her two babes Romulus and Remus into the Tiber, to be brought to land at the foot of the Palatine fig-tree. Into this river we may also recollect that Sylla caused the ashes of his ancient rival Marius to be thrown. The river is crossed by the *Ponte Nomentana*, a mediæval bridge, partially covered, with forked battlements.

"Ponte Nomentana is a solitary dilapidated bridge in the spacious green Campagna. Many ruins from the days of ancient Rome, and many watch-towers from the middle ages, are scattered over this long succession of meadows ; chains of hills rise towards the horizon, now partially covered with snow, and fantastically varied in form and colour by the shadows of the clouds. And there is also the enchanting vapoury vision of the Alban hills, which change their hues like the chameleon, as you gaze at them—where you can see for miles little white chapels glittering on the dark foreground of the hills, as far as the Passionist Convent on the summit, and whence you can trace the road winding through thickets, and the hills sloping downwards to the lake of Albano, while a hermitage peeps through the trees."—*Mendelssohn's Letters.*

The hill immediately beyond the bridge is the *Mons Sacer* (not only the part usually pointed out on the right of the road, but the whole hillside), to which the famous secession of the Plebs took place in B.C. 549, amounting, according to Dionysius, to about 4000 persons. Here they encamped upon the green slopes for four months, to the terror of the patricians, who foresaw that Rome, abandoned by its defenders, would fall before its enemies, and that the crops would perish for want of cultivation. Here Menenius Agrippa delivered his apologue of the belly and its members, which is said to have induced them to return to Rome; that which really decided them to do so being the concession of tribunes, to be the organs and representatives of the plebs as the consuls were of the patricians. The epithet Sacer is ascribed by Dionysius to an altar which the plebeians erected at the time on the hill to Ζεὺς Δειμάτιος.

A second secession to the Mons Sacer took place in B.C. 449, when the plebs rose against Appius Claudius after the death of Virginia, and retired hither under the advice of M. Duilius, till the decemvirs resigned.

Following the road beyond the bridge past the castle known as *Casale dei Pazzi* (once used as a lunatic asylum) and the picturesque tomb called Torre Nomentana,—as far as the seventh milestone—we reach the remains of the unburied *Basilica of S. Alessandro*, built on the site of the place where that pope suffered martyrdom with his companions Eventius and Theodulus, A.D. 119, and was buried on the same spot by the Christian matron Severina.* The plan of the basilica, disinterred 1856-7, is still quite perfect. The tribune and high altar retain fragments of rich marbles and alabasters; the episcopal throne also remains in its place.

The "Acts of the martyrs Alexander, Eventius, and Theodulus," narrate that Severina buried the bodies of the first two martyrs in one tomb, and the third separately—"Theodulum vero alibi sepelivit." This is borne out by the discovery of a chapel opening from the nave, where the single word "martyri," is supposed to point out the grave of Theodulus. A baptistery has been found with its font, and another chapel adjoining is pointed out as the place where neophytes assembled to receive confirmation from the bishop. Among epitaphs laid bare in the pavement is one to a youth named Apollo "votus Deo" (dedicated to the priesthood?) at the age of 14. Entered from the church is the catacomb called "ad nymphas," containing many ancient inscriptions and a few rude paintings.

Mass is solemnly performed here by the Cardinal Prefect of the Propaganda on the festival of St. Alexander, May 3, when the roofless basilica—backed by the blue Sabine mountains and surrounded by the utterly desolate Campagna—is filled with worshippers, and presents a striking scene. Beyond this a road to the left leads through beautiful woods to *Mentana*, occupying the site of the ancient Nomentum, and recently celebrated for the battle between the papal troops and the Garibaldians on Nov. 3, 1867. The conflict took

* The bodies were removed to Sta. Sabina in the fifth century by Celestine I.

place chiefly on the hillside which is passed on the right before reaching the town. Two miles further is *Monte Rotondo*, with a fine old castle of the Barberini family (once of the Orsini), from which there is a beautiful view. This place was also the scene of fighting in 1867. It is possible to vary the route in returning to Rome from hence by the lower road which leads by the (now broken) Ponte Salara.

If we re-enter Rome by the Porta Pia, immediately within the gates we find another Villa belonging to the Torlonia family. The straight road from the gate leads by the Termini to the Quattro Fontane and the Monte Cavallo. On the left, if we follow the *Via de Macao*, which takes its strange name from a gift of land which the princes of Savoy made to the Jesuits for a mission in China, we reach a small piazza with two pines, where a gate on the left leads to the remains of the *Pretorian Camp*, established by Sejanus, the minister of Tiberius. It was dismantled by Constantine, but from three sides having been enclosed by Aurelian in the line of his citywall, its form is still preserved to us. The Pretorian Camp was an oblong of 1200 by 1500 feet; its area was occupied by a vineyard of the Jesuits till 1861, when a "Campo Militare" was again established here, for the pontifical troops.

"En suivant l'enceinte de Rome, quand on arrive à l'endroit où elle se continue par le mur du Camp des prétoriens, on est frappé de la supériorité de construction que présente celui-ci. La partie des murs d'Honorius qui est voisine a été refaite au huitième siècle. Le commencement et la fin de l'empire se touchent. On peut apprécier d'un coup d'œil l'état de la civilisation aux deux époques : voilà ce qu'on faisait dans le premier siècle, et voilà ce qu'on faisait au huitième, après la conquête de l'empire Romain par les Barbares. Il faut songer toutefois que cette époque où l'on construisait si bien a amené celle où l'on ne savait plus construire."—*Ampère, Emp.* i. 421.

Hence a road, three-quarters of a mile long, leads—passing under an arch of Sixtus V.—to the Porta S. Lorenzo (Ch. XIII.).

The road opposite the gateway leading to the Camp is bordered on the left by the buildings belonging to the *Railway Station*, beyond which is the entrance to the grounds of the *Villa Massimo Negroni*, which possessed a delightful terrace, fringed with orange-trees—a most agreeable sunny walk in winter—and many pleasant shady nooks and corners for summer, but which has been mutilated and stripped of all its beauties since the Sardinian rule. In a part of this villa beyond the railway but still visible from hence, is a colossal statue of Minerva (generally called "Rome"), which is a relic of the residence here of Cardinal Felix Perretti, who as a boy had watched the pigs of his father at Montalto, and who lived to mount the papal throne as Sixtus V. The pedestal of the statue bears his arms,—a lion holding three pears in its paw. Here, with her husband's uncle, lived the famous Vittoria Accoramboni, the wife of the handsome Francesco Perretti, who had been vainly sought in marriage by the powerful and ugly old Prince Paolo Orsini. It was from hence that her young husband was summoned to a secret interview with her brothers on the slopes of the Quirinal, where he was cruelly murdered by the hired bravos of her first lover. Hence also Vittoria went forth—on the very day of the installation of Sixtus V.—to her strange second marriage with the murderer of her husband, who died six months after, leaving her with one of the largest fortunes in Italy—an amount of wealth which led to her own barbarous murder through the jealousy of the Orsini a month afterwards.

Here, after the election of her brother to the papacy, lived

Camilla, the sister of Sixtus V., whom he refused to recognise when she came to him in splendid attire as a princess, but tenderly embraced when she reappeared in her peasant's wimple and hood. From hence her two granddaughters were married,—one to Virginius Orsini, the other to Marc-Antonio Colonna, an alliance which healed the feud of centuries between the two families.

In later times the Villa Negroni was the residence of the poet Alfieri.

The principal terrace ends near a reservoir which belonged to the baths of Diocletian.

"As one looks from the Villa Negroni windows, one cannot fail to be impressed by the strange changes through which this wonderful city has passed. The very spot on which Nero, the insane emperor-artist, fiddled while Rome was burning, has now become a vast kitchen-garden, belonging to Prince Massimo (himself a descendant, as he claims, of Fabius Cunctator), where men no longer, but only lettuces, asparagus, and artichokes, are ruthlessly cut down. The inundations are not for mock sea-fights among slaves, but for the peaceful purposes of irrigation. In the bottom of the valley, a noble old villa, covered with frescoes, has been turned into a manufactory for bricks, and part of the Villa Negroni itself is now occupied by the railway station. Yet here the princely family of Negroni lived, and the very lady at whose house Lucrezia Borgia took her famous revenge may once have sauntered under the walls, which still glow with ripening oranges, to feed the gold fish in the fountain,—or walked with stately friends through the long alleys of clipped cypresses, or pic-nicked *alla Giornata* on lawns which are now but kitchen-gardens, dedicated to San Cavolo."—*Story's Roba di Roma.*

The lower part of the Villa Negroni, and the slopes towards the Esquiline, were once celebrated as the *Campus Esquilinus*, a large pauper burial-ground, where bodies were thrown into pits called *puticoli*,* as is still the custom at Naples. There were also tombs here of a somewhat pre-

* Cramer's Ancient Italy, i. 389.

tentious character: "those probably of rich well-to-do burgesses, yet not great enough to command the posthumous honour of a roadside mausoleum."* Horace dwells on the horrors of this burial-ground, where he places the scene of Canidia's incantations:—

> "Nec in sepulcris pauperum prudens anus
> Novemdiales dissipare pulveres."
> *Epod.* xvii. 47.
>
> 'Has nullo perdere possum
> Nec prohibere modo, simul ac vaga luna decorum
> Protulit os, quin ossa legant, herbasque nocentes.
> Vidi egomet nigrâ succinctam vadere pallâ
> Canidiam, pedibus nudis passoque capillo,
> Cum Saganâ majore ululantem ; pallor utrasque
> Fecerat horrendas aspectu,
> *   *   *   *
> Serpentes atque videres
> Infernas errare canes ; lunamque rubentem,
> Ne foret his testis, post magna latere sepulcra."
> *Hor. Sat.* i. 8.

The place was considered very unhealthy until its purification by Mæcenas.

> "Huc prius angustis ejecta cadavera cellis
> Conservus vili portanda locabat in arcâ.
> Hoc miseræ plebi stabat commune sepulcrum,
> Pantolabo scurræ, Nomentanoque nepoti.
> Mille pedes in fronte, trecentos cippus in agrum
> Hic dabat ; heredes monumentum ne sequeretur.
> Nunc licet Esquiliis habitare salubribus, atque
> Aggere in aprico spatiari ; quo modo tristes
> Albis informem spectabant ossibus agrum."
> *Hor. Sat.* i. 8.

> "Post insepulta membra different lupi,
> Et Esquilinæ alites."
> *Hor. Ep.* v. 100.

"The Campus Esquilinus, between the roads which issued from the

---

* Cic. Phil. ix. 7. See Dyer's Rome, p. 215.

Esquiline and Viminal gates, was the spot assigned for casting out the carcases of slaves, whose foul and half-burnt remains were hardly hidden from the vultures. The *accursed field* was enclosed, it would appear, neither by wall nor fence, to exclude the wandering steps of man or beast; and from the public walk on the summit of the ridge, it must have been viewed in all its horrors. Here prowled in troops the houseless dogs of the city and the suburbs; here skulked the solitary wolf from the Alban hills, and here perhaps, to the doleful murmurs of the Marsic chaunt, the sorceress compounded her philtres of the ashes of dead men's bones. Mæcenas (B.C. 7) deserved the gratitude of the citizens, when he obtained a grant of this piece of land, and transformed it into a park or garden. . . . The Campus Esquilinus is now part of the gardens of the Villa Negroni."—*Merivale, Romans under the Empire.*

Within what were the grounds of the Villa Negroni until they were encroached upon by the railway, but now only to be visited with a "lascia passare" from the station master, are some of the best remains of the *Agger of Servius Tullius*. In 1869—70, some curious painted chambers were discovered here, but were soon destroyed,—and the foolish jealousy of the authorities prevented any drawings or photographs being taken. The Agger can be traced from the Porta Esquilina (near the Arch of Gallienus), to the Porta Collina (near the Gardens of Sallust). In the time of the empire it had become a kind of promenade, as we learn from Horace.*

Opposite the station are the vast, but for the most part uninteresting, remains of the *Baths of Diocletian*, covering a space of 440,000 square yards. They were begun by Diocletian and Maximian, about A.D. 302, and finished by Constantius and Maximinus. It is stated by Cardinal Baronius, that 40,000 Christians were employed in the work; some bricks marked with crosses have been found

* Sat. i. 8, 15.

in the ruins. At the angles of the principal front were two circular halls, both of which remain; one is near the modern Villa Strozzi, at the back of the Negroni garden, and is now used as a granary, the other is transformed into the Church of S. Bernardo.

The Baths are supposed to have first fallen into decay after the Gothic invasion of A.D. 410. In the sixteenth century the site was sold to Cardinal Bella, ambassador of Francis I. at Rome, who built a fine palace among the ruins; after his death, in 1560, the property was re-sold to S. Carlo Borromeo. He sold it again to his uncle, Pope Pius IV., who founded the monastery of Carthusian monks. These, in 1593, sold part of the ruins to Caterina Sforza, who founded the Cistercian convent of S. Bernardo.

About 1520, a Sicilian priest called Antonio del Duca came to Rome, bringing with him from Palermo pictures of the seven archangels (Michael, Gabriel, Raphael, Uriel, Santhiel, Gendiel, and Borachiel), copied from some which existed in the Church of S. Angiolo. Carried away by the desire of instituting archangel-worship at Rome, he obtained leave to affix these pictures to seven of the columns still standing erect in the Baths of Diocletian, which, ten years after, Julius II. allowed to be consecrated under the title of Sta. Maria degli Angeli; though Pius IV., declaring that angel-worship had never been sanctioned by the Church, except under the three names mentioned in Scripture, ordered the pictures of Del Duca to be taken away.* At the same time he engaged Michael Angelo to convert the great oblong hall of the Baths (Calidarium) into a church. The church then arranged was not such as we now see, the present

* See Hemans' Catholic Italy, Part I.

entrance having been then the atrium of the side chapel, and the main entrance at first by what is now the right transept, while the high altar stood in what is now the left transept. In 1749, the desire of erecting a chapel to the Beato Nicolo Albergati, led to the church being altered, under Vanvitelli, as we now see it.

The *Church of Sta. Maria degli Angeli*, still most magnificent, is now entered by a rotunda (Laconicum) which contains four monuments of some interest; on the right of the entrance is that of the artist Carlo Maratta, who died 1713; on the left that of Salvator Rosa, who died 1673, with an epitaph by his son, describing him as " Pictorum sui temporis nulli secundum, poetarum omnium temporum principibus parem !" Beyond, on the right, is the monument of Cardinal Alciati, professor of law at Milan, who procured his hat through the interest of S. Carlo Borromeo, with the epitaph " Virtute vixit, memoria vivit, gloria vivet," —on the left, that of Cardinal Parisio di Corenza, inscribed, " Corpus humo tegitur, fama per ora volat, spiritus astra tenet." In the chapel on the right are the angels of Peace and Justice, by *Pettrich;* in that on the left Christ appearing to the Magdalen, by *Arrigo Fiamingo*. Against the pier on the right is the grand statue of S. Bruno, by *Houdon*, of which Clement XIV. (Ganganelli) used to say, " He would speak, if the rule of his Order did not forbid it."

The body of the church is now a perfect gallery of very large pictures, most of which were brought from St. Peter's, where their places have been supplied by mosaic copies. In what is now the right transept, on the right, is the Crucifixion of St. Peter, *Ricciolini;* the Fall of Simon Magus, a copy of *Francesco Vanni* (the original in St. Peter's); on the left, St. Jerome, with St. Bruno and St. Francis, *Muziano* (1528—92) (the landscape by *Brill*); and the Miracles of St. Peter, *Baglioni*. This transept ends in the chapel of the Beato Nicolo Albergati, a Carthusian Cardinal, who was sent as legate by Martin V., in 1422, to make a reconciliation between Charles VI. of France and Henry V. of England. The principal miracle ascribed to him, the conversion of bread into coal in order to convince the Emperor of Germany of his divine authority, is represented in the indifferent altar-piece. In the left transept, which ends in the chapel of S. Bruno, are: on the left, St. Basil by the solemnity of the Mass rebuking the Emperor Valens, *Subleyras*; and the Fall of Simon Magus, *Pompeo Battoni*;—on the right, the Immaculate Conception, *P. Bianchi*; and Tabitha raised from the Dead, *P. Costanzi*.

In the tribune are, on the right, the Presentation of the Virgin in the Temple, *Romanelli*; and the Martyrdom of St. Sebastian, a grand fresco of *Domenichino*, painted originally on the walls of St. Peter's, and removed here with great skill by the engineer Zabaglia;—on the left, the Death of Ananias and Sapphira, *Pomarancio*; and the Baptism of Christ, *Maratta*.

On the right of the choir is the tomb of Cardinal Antonio Serbelloni; on the left that of Pius IV., Giovanni Angelo Medici (1559—1565), under whose reign the Council of Trent was closed,—uncle of S. Carlo Borromeo, a lively and mundane pope, but the cruel persecutor of the Caraffa nephews of his predecessor, Paul IV., whom he executed in the Castle of S. Angelo.

Of the sixteen columns in this church (45 feet in height, 16 feet in diameter), only the eight in the transept are of ancient Egyptian granite; the rest are in brick, stuccoed in imitation, and were additions of Vanvitelli. On the pavement is a meridian line, laid down in 1703.

"Quand Dioclétien faisait travailler les pauvres chrétiens à ses étuves, ce n'était pas son dessein de bâtir des églises à leurs successeurs ; il ne pensait pas être fondateur, comme il l'a été, d'un monastère de Pères Chartreux et d'un monastère de Pères Feuillants. . . . C'est aux dépens de Dioclétien, de ses pierres et de son ciment qu'on fait des autels et des chapelles à Jesus-Christ, des dortoirs et des réfectoires à ses serviteurs. La providence de Dieu se joue de cette sorte des pensées des hommes, et les événements sont bien éloignés des intentions quand la terre a un dessein et le ciel un autre."—*Balzac.*

The Carthusian convent behind the church (ladies are not admitted) contains several picturesque fountains. That in the great cloister, built from designs of Michael Angelo, is surrounded by a group of huge and grand cypresses, said to have been planted by his hand.

"Il semble que la vie ne sert ici qu'à contempler la mort—les hommes qui existent ainsi sont pourtant les mêmes à qui la guerre et toute son activité suffirait à peine s'ils y étaient accoutumés. C'est un sujet inépuisable de réflexion que les différentes combinaisons de la destinée humaine sur la terre. Il se passe dans l'intérieur de l'âme mille accidents, il se forme mille habitudes, qui font de chaque individu un monde et son histoire."—*Madame de Staël.*

On a line with the monastery is a Prison for Women— then an Institution for Deaf, Dumb, and Blind—then the ugly *Fountain of the Termini* (designed by Fontana), sometimes called Fontanone dell' Acqua Felice, (Felice, from Fra Felice, the name by which Sixtus V. was known before his papacy,) to which the Acqua Felice was brought from Colonna 22 miles distant in the Alban hills, in 1583, by Sixtus V. It is surmounted by a hideous statue of Moses by *Prospero*

Bresciano, who is said to have died of vexation at the ridicule it excited when uncovered. The side statues, of Aaron and Gideon, are by *Giov. Batt. della Porta* and *Flaminio Vacca*.

Opposite this, in the Via della Porta Pia, is the *Church of Sta. Maria della Vittoria*, built in 1605, by Carlo Maderno, for Paul V. Its façade was added from designs of Giov. Batt. Soria, by Cardinal Borghese, in payment to the monks of the adjoining Carmelite convent, for the statue of the Hermaphrodite, which had been found in their vineyard.

The name of the church commemorates an image of the Virgin, burnt in 1833, which was revered as having been instrumental in gaining the victory for the Catholic imperial troops over the Protestant Frederick and Elizabeth of Bohemia, at the battle of the White Mountain, near Prague. The third chapel on the left contains the Trinity, by *Guercino;* a Crucifixion, by *Guido;* and a portrait of Cardinal Cornaro, *Guido*. The altar-piece of the second chapel on the right, representing St. Francis receiving the Infant Christ from the Virgin, is by *Domenichino*, as are two frescoes on the side walls. In the left transept, above an altar adorned with a gilt bronze-relief of the Last Supper, by Cav. d'Arpino, is a group representing Sta. Teresa transfixed by the dart of the Angel of Death, by *Bernini*. The following criticisms upon it are fair specimens of the contrast between English and French taste.

"All the Spanish pictures of Sta. Theresa sin in their materialism; but the grossest example—the most offensive—is the marble group of Bernini, in the Santa Maria della Vittoria at Rome. The head of Sta. Theresa is that of a languishing nymph, the angel is a sort of Eros; the whole has been significantly described as 'a parody of Divine love.' The vehicle, white marble,—its place in a Christian church,—enhance all its vileness. The least destructive, the least prudish in matters of art, would here willingly throw the first stone." — *Mrs. Jameson's Monastic Orders*, p. 421.

"La sainte Thérèse de Bernin est adorable ! couchée, évanouie d'amour, les mains, les pieds nus pendants, les yeux demiclos, elle s'est laissée tomber de bonheur et d'extase. Son visage est maigri, mais combien noble ! C'est la vraie grande dame qui a séché dans les feux, dans les larmes, en attendant celui qu'elle aime. Jusqu'aux draperies tortillées, jusqu'à l'allanguissement des mains défaillantes, jusqu'au soupir qui meurt sur ses levres entr'ouvertes, il n'y a rien en elle ni autour d'elle qui n'exprime l'angoisse voluptueuse et le divin élancement de son transport. On ne peut pas rendre avec des mots une attitude si enivrée et si touchante. Renversée sur le dos, elle pâme, tout son être se dissout ; le moment poignant arrive, elle gémit ; c'est son dernier gémissement, la sensation est trop forte. L'ange cependant, un jeune page de quatorze ans, en légère tunique, la poitrine découverte jusqu'au dessous du sein, arrive gracieux, aimable ; c'est le plus joli page de grand seigneur qui vient faire le bonheur d'une vassal trop tendre. Un sourire demi-complaisant, demi-malin, creuse des fossettes dans ses fraîches joues luisantes ; sa flêche d'or à la main indique le tressaillement délicieux et terrible dont il va secouer tous les nerfs de ce corps charmant, ardent, qui s'étale devant sa main. On n'a jamais fait ce roman si séduisant et si tendre."—*Taine, Voyage en Italie.*

Close by is the handsome *Church of Sta. Susanna*, rebuilt by *Carlo Maderno*, for Sixtus V., on the site of an oratory founded by Pope Caius (A.D. 283), in the house of his brother Gabinus, who was martyred with his daughter Susanna because she refused to break her vow of virginity by a marriage with Maximianus Galerus, adopted son of the Emperor Diocletian, to whom this family were related. The bodies of these martyrs are said to rest beneath the high altar. The side chapel of St. Laurence was presented by Camilla Peretti, the sister of Sixtus V., together with a dowry of fifty scudi, to be paid every year to the nine best girls in the parish, on the festival of Sta. Susanna. The frescoes of the story of Susanna and the Elders, painted here on the side walls, from the analogy of names, are by *Baldassare Croce;* those in the tribune are by *Cesare Nebbia.*

Opposite this, is the Cistercian convent and *Church of S. Bernardo,* a rotunda of the Baths of Diocletian, turned into a church in 1598, by Caterina Sforza, Contessa di Santa Fiora.

Hence the Via della Porta Pia leads to the Quattro Fontane. On the left is the small *Church of S. Caio,* which encloses the tomb of that pope, inscribed " Sancti Caii, Papæ, martyris ossa." Further, on the left, is the great recently suppressed convent of the Carmelites, and the *Church of Sta. Teresa.* The right of the street is bordered by the orange-shaded wall of the Barberini garden.

Between S. Caio and Sta. Teresa, is the *Studio of Overbeck,* the venerable German devotional painter, who died 1869. His daughter allows visitors to be admitted on Sunday afternoons.

CHAPTER XII.

THE ESQUILINE.

Golden House of Nero—Baths of Titus and Trajan—S. Pietro in Vincoli — Frangipani Tower — House of Lucrezia Borgia — S. Martino al Monte—Sta. Lucia in Selce—Sta. Prassede—Santissimo Redentore—Arch of Gallienus—Trophies of Marius—Sta. Bibiana — Temple of Minerva Medica—S. Eusebio—S. Antonio Abbate—Sta. Maria Maggiore.

THE ESQUILINE, which is the largest of the so-called 'hills of Rome,' is not a distinct hill, but simply a projection of the Campagna. "The Quirinal, Viminal, Esquiline, and Cœlian stretch out towards the Tiber, like four fingers of a hand, of which the plain whence they detach themselves represents the vast palm. This hand has seized the world." *

Varro says that the name Esquiline was derived from the word *excultus*, because of the ornamental groves which were planted on this hill by Servius Tullius,—such as the Lucus Querquetulanus, Fagutalis, and Esquilinus.† The sacred wood of the Argiletum long remained on the lower slope of the hill, where the Via Sta. Maria dei Monti now is.

The Esquiline, which is still unhealthy, must have been so in ancient times, for among its temples were those

* Ampère, Hist. Rom. i. 38. † Varro, de Ling. Lat. iv. 8.

dedicated to Fever, near Sta. Maria Maggiore—to Juno Mephitis,* near a pool which emitted poisonous exhalations —and to Venus Libitina,† for the registration of deaths, and arrangement of funerals. As the hill was in the hands of the Sabines, its early divinities were Sabine. Besides those already mentioned, it had an altar of the Sabine sun-god Janus, dedicated together with an altar to Juno by the survivor of the Horatii,‡ and a temple of Juno Lucina, the goddess of birth and light.

> "Monte sub Esquilio multis incæduus annis
> Junonis magnæ nomine lucus erat."
> *Ovid, Fast.* ii. 435.

This hill has two heights. That which is crowned by Santa Maria Maggiore was formerly called *Cispius*, where Servius Tullius had a palace; that which is occupied by S. Pietro in Vincoli was formerly called *Oppius*, where Tarquinius Superbus lived. It was in returning to his palace on the former (and not on the latter height, as generally maintained) that Servius Tullius was murdered.

The most important buildings of the Esquiline, in the later republican and in imperial times, were on the slope of the hill behind the Forum, and near the Coliseum, in the fashionable quarter called Carinæ,—the "rich Carinæ,"

> ' Passimque armenta videbant
> Romanoque Foro et lautis mugire Carinis."
> *Virgil, Æn.* viii. 361.

of which the principal street probably occupied the site of the present Via del Colosseo. At the entrance of this

---

* Fest. *v.* Septimone.   † Ampère, Hist. Rom. i. 65.   ‡ Fest. p. 297.

suburb, where the fine mediæval Torre dei Conti now stands, was the house of Spurius Cassius (Consul B.C. 493), which was confiscated and demolished, and the ground ordained to be always kept vacant, because he was suspected of aiming at regal power. Here, however, or very nearly on this site, the *Ædes Telluris*, or temple of Tellus, was erected *c.* B.C. 269,*— a building of sufficient importance for the senate, summoned by Antony, to assemble in it. The quarter immediately surrounding this temple acquired the name of *In Tellure*, which is still retained by several of its modern churches.† Near this temple—"in tellure," lived Pompey, in a famous though small historical house, which he adorned on the outside with rostra in memory of his naval victories, and which was painted within to look like a forest with trees and birds, much probably as the chambers are painted which were discovered a few years ago in the villa of Livia.‡ Here Julia, the daughter of Julius Cæsar, and wife of Pompey, died. After the death of Pompey this house was bought by the luxurious Antony. The difference between its two masters is pourtrayed by Cicero, who describes the severe comfort of the house of Pompey contrasted with the voluptuous luxury of its second master, and winds up his oration by exclaiming, " I pity even the roofs and the walls under the change." At a later period the same house was the favourite residence of Antoninus Pius. Hard by, in the Carinæ, the favourite residence of Roman knights, lived the father of Cicero, and hence the young Tullius went to listen in the forum to the orators whom he was one day to

* Cicero pro doma sua, 38; Dionysius, viii. 79; Livy, ii. 41.
† See Dyer's City of Rome, p. 65. The Acts of the Martyrs mention that several Christians suffered " In tellure."
‡ See Ampère, Hist. Rom. iv. 421.

surpass.* Also in the Carinæ, but nearer the site of the Coliseum, was the magnificent house of the wealthy Vedius Pollio, which he bequeathed to Augustus, who pulled it down, and built the portico of Livia on its site:

> "Disce tamen, veniens ætas, ubi Livia nunc est
> Porticus, immensæ tecta fuisse domûs.
> Urbis opus domus una fuit; spatiumque tenebat,
> Quo brevius muris oppida multa tenent.
> Hæc æquata solo est, nullo sub crimine regni,
> Sed quia luxuriâ visa nocere suâ.
> Sustinuit tantas operum subvertere moles,
> Totque suas heres perdere Cæsar opes."
> Ovid, Fast. vi. 639.

At its opposite extremity the Carinæ was united to the unfashionable and plebeian quarter of the *Suburra*, occupying the valley formed by the convergence of the Esquiline, Quirinal, and Viminal—which is still crowded with a teeming population. In one of the small streets leading from the Vicus Cyprius (between the Esquiline and Viminal) towards the Carinæ, was the *Tigellum Sororis*, which was extant—repaired at the public expense—till the fifth century. This, "the Sister's Beam," commemorated the well-known story of the last of the Horatii, who, returning from the slaughter of the Curiatii, and being met by his sister, bewailing one of the dead to whom she was betrothed, stabbed her in his anger. He was condemned to death, but at the prayer of his father his crime was expiated by his passing under the yoke of "the Sister's Beam." On one side of the Tigellum Sororis was an altar to Juno Sororis; on the other an altar to Janus Curiatius.†

* See Ampère, Hist. Rom. iv. 431. † Liv. i. 26; Dionysius, iii. 22.

During the empire several poets had their residence on the Esquiline. Virgil lived there, near the gardens of Mæcenas, which covered the slopes between the Esquiline and Viminal. Propertius had a house there, as we learn from himself—

> "I, puer, et citus hæc aliqua propone columna
> Et dominum Esquiliis scribe habitare tuum."
>
> *Propert. Eleg.* iv. 23.

It is believed, but without certainty, that Horace also lived upon the Esquiline. He was constantly there in the villa of Mæcenas, where he was buried, and which he has described in his poems both in its original state as a desecrated cemetery, and again after his friend had converted it into a beautiful garden.

> "Nunc licet Esquiliis habitare salubribus, atque
> Aggere in aprico spatiari, quo modo tristes
> Albis informem spectabant ossibus agrum."
>
> *Sat.* i.

The house of Mæcenas, the great patron of the poets of the Augustan age, probably occupied a site above the Carinæ, where the baths of Titus afterwards were. It was a lofty and magnificent edifice, and is described by Horace, who calls it—

> " Fastidiosam desere copiam, et
> Molem propinquam nubibus arduis :
> Omitte mirari beatæ
> Fumum et opes strepitumque Romæ.'
>
> *Od.* iii. 29.

Mæcenas bequeathed his villa to Augustus, and Tiberius at one time resided in it.

Another, though less well-known poet of this age, who lived upon the Esquiline, was Pedo Albinovanus, much extolled by Ovid, who lived at the summit of the Vicus Cyprius (probably the Via Sta. Maria Maggiore), in a little house:

> "Illic parva tui domus Pedonis
> Cælata est aquilæ minore penna."
> *Martial*, x. *Ep.* 19.

Near this was the *Lacus Orphei*, a fountain, in the centre of which was a rock, &c., surmounted by a statue of Orpheus with the enchanted beasts around him. The house of Pedo was afterwards inhabited by Pliny. On *Septimius*, as the furthest slope of the Esquiline towards the Viminal was called, lived Maximus—of whom Martial says:—

> "Esquiliis domus est, domus est tibi colle Dianæ,
> Et tua Patricius culmina Vicus habet:
> Hinc viduæ Cybeles, illinc sacraria Vestæ,
> Inde Novum, Veterem prospicis inde Jovem."
> *Mart.* vii. *Ep.* 72.

Only the northern side of the Esquiline is now inhabited at all; the southern, and by far the larger portion, is clothed with vineyards and gardens, sprinkled over with titanic masses of ruin. On most parts of the hill, one might imagine oneself far away in the country. According to Niebuhr, the dweller amid the vines of the Esquiline, when he descends into the city, still says, "I am going to Rome."

Nero (A.D. 54—68) purchased the site of the villa of Mæcenas, and covered the whole side of the hill towards the Carinæ with the vast buildings of his Golden House, which also swallowed up the Cœlian and a great part of the Palatine ; but he did not destroy the buildings which already existed, and "the Golden House was still the old mansion of Augustus and the villa of Mæcenas connected by a long series of columns and arches."* Titus (A.D. 79—81) and Trajan (A.D. 98—117) used part of the same site for their baths, and the ruins of all these buildings are now jumbled up together, and the varying whims of antiquaries have constantly changed the names of each fragment that has been discovered.

The more interesting of these ruins are on the southern slope of the Esquiline towards the Coliseum, and are most easily approached from the Via Polveriera. They are shown now as the *Baths of Titus*, or Camere Esquiline, and occupy a space of about 1150 feet by 850. That the chambers which are now visible were to be seen in the time of Leo X. (1513—22) we learn from Vasari, who says that Raphael and Giovanni da Udine were wont to study there and copy the arabesques to assist their work in the Vatican Loggie. After this, neglect and the falling in of the soil caused these treasures to be lost till 1774, when they were again partially unearthed, but they were only completely brought to view by the French, who began to take the work in hand in 1811, and continued their excavations for three years.

The principal remains, which are now exhibited by the dim torch of a solitary cicerone, are those of nine chambers, extending for 300 feet, and having on the north a kind of corridor, or cryptoporticus, whose vault is covered with

* Merivale, Romans under the Empire, ch. liii.

paintings of birds, griffins, and flowers, &c. In two of these halls are alcoves for couches, and in one is a cavity for a fountain with a trench round it, like that in the nymphæum of the Palace of the Cæsars. In one of the halls is a group representing Venus attended by two Cupids, with doves hovering over her. Near this a pedestal is shown as that occupied by the Laocoon, though it was really found in the Vigna de Fredis, between the Sette Sale and Sta. Maria Maggiore. A set of thirty engravings, published by Mirri, from drawings taken in 1776, show what the paintings were at that time, but very few now remain perfect. A group of Coriolanus and his mother, represented in Mirri's work, is now inaccessible. All the paintings are Pompeian in character, and for some time were considered the best remains of ancient pictorial art in Rome, but they are inferior to those which have since been discovered on the Latin way and at the Baths of Livia. The chambers which open beyond the nine outer halls are considered to be part of the Golden House. In one of these the Meleager of the Vatican was found. A small chapel, dedicated to Sta. Felicitas and her seven sons (evidently engrafted upon the pagan building in the sixth century), was discovered in 1813. It is like the chapels in the catacombs, and is decorated with the conventional frescoes of the Good Shepherd, Daniel in the lions' den, &c. There are also some faint remains of a fresco of the sainted patrons.

Behind the convent of S. Pietro in Vincoli, in the open vineyards, are other ruins called the *Sette Sale*, being remains of the reservoirs (in reality nine in number) for the Baths. In these vineyards also are three large circular ruins, adorned on the interior with rows of niches for statues. One of them is partly built into the Polveriera, or powder maga-zinc. These have been referred alternately to the Baths of Titus and those of Trajan.

Immediately behind the forum of Nerva stands the colossal brick tower, known as the Torre dei Conti, and built by Innocent III. (1198—1216) as a retreat for his family, now extinct. Its architect was Marchione d'Arezzo, and it was so much admired by Petrarch that he declared it had "no equal upon earth;" he must have meant in height. Four of the Conti have mounted the papal throne, Innocent III., Gregory IX., Alexander IV., and Innocent XIII. The last-named pope (1721—24) boasted of having " nine uncles, eight brothers, four nephews, and seven great nephews;" yet—a century after—and not a Conti remained.

If we turn to the left close to this, we shall find, in a commanding position, the famous Church of *S. Pietro in Vincoli*, said to have been originally founded in A.D. 109 by Theodora, sister of Hermes, Prefect of Rome, both converts of the then pope, who was the martyr St. Alexander of the basilica in the Campagna. A bolder legend attributes the foundation to St. Peter himself, who is believed to have dedicated this church to his Divine Master. History, however, can assign no earlier foundation than that in 442, by the Empress Eudoxia, wife of Valentinian III., from whom the church takes its name of the *Eudoxian Basilica*, and who placed there one of the famous chains which now form its great attraction to Roman Catholic pilgrims.

"The chains, left in the Mamertine Prisons after St. Peter's confinement there, are said to have been found by the martyr Sta. Balbina, in 126, and by her given to Theodora, another sainted martyr, sister to

S. PIETRO IN VINCOLI.

Hermes, Prefect of Rome, from whom they passed into the hands of St. Alexander, first pope of that name, and were finally deposited by him in the church erected by Theodora, where they have since remained. Such is the legendary, but the historic origin of this basilica cannot be traced higher than about the middle of the fifth century, subsequent to the year 439, when Juvenal, Bishop of Jerusalem, presented to the Empress Eudoxia, wife of Theodosius the younger, two chains, believed to be those of St. Peter, one of which was placed by her in the basilica of the apostles at Constantinople, and the other sent to Rome for her daughter Eudoxia, wife of Valentinian III., who caused this church, hence called Eudoxian, to be erected, as the special shrine of Peter's chains."—*Hemans*.

One chain had been sent to Rome by Eudoxia the elder, and the other remained at Constantinople, but the Romans could not rest satisfied with the possession of half the relic; and within the walls of this very basilica, Leo I. beheld in a vision the miraculous and mystical uniting of the two chains, since which they have both been exhibited here, and the day of their being soldered together by invisible power, August 1, has been kept sacred in the Latin Church!

The church is at present entered by an ugly atrium, which was the work of Fontana in 1705; but Bacio Pintelli had already done almost all that was possible to destroy the features of the old basilica, under the Cardinal Titular of the church, Giulio della Rovere, the same who, as Pope Julius II., destroyed the old St. Peter's and eighty-seven tombs of his predecessors. By Pintelli the present capitals were added to the columns in the nave, and the horizontal architrave above them was exchanged for a series of narrow round-headed arches.

But, in spite of alterations, the interior is still imposing. Two long lines of ancient fluted Doric columns (ten on each side), relics of the Baths of Titus or Trajan, which once covered this site, lead the eye to the high altar, supposed to cover the remains of the seven Maccabean brothers, and to the tribune, which contains an ancient episcopal throne, and is adorned with frescoes by *Jacopo Coppi*, a Florentine of the sixteenth century, illustrative of the life of St. Peter. Beneath these is the tomb of G. Clovis, a miniature painter of the sixteenth century, and canon of this church.

On the left of the entrance is the tomb of Antonio Pollajuolo, the famous worker in bronze, and his brother Pietro. The fresco above, which is ascribed to Pollajuolo, refers to the translation of the body of St. Sebastian, as " Depulsor Pestilitatis," from the catacombs to this church,—one of the most picturesque stories of the middle ages. The great plague of A.D. 680 was ushered in by an awful vision of the two angels of good and evil, who wandered through the streets by night, side by side, when the one smote upon the door where death was to enter, unless arrested by the other. The people continued to die by hundreds daily. At length a citizen dreamt that the sickness would cease when the body of St. Sebastian should be brought into the city, and when this was done, the pestilence was stayed. In the fresco the whole story is told. In the background the citizen tells his dream to Pope Agatho, who is seated among his cardinals. On the right the angels of good and evil (the bad angel represented as a devil) are making their mysterious visitation, on the left a procession is bringing in the relics, and the foreground is strewn with the corpses of the dead. The general invocation of St. Sebastian in Italy, and the frequent introduction of his figure in art, have their origin in this story.

At the entrance of the left aisle is a fine bas-relief of St. Peter throned, delivering his keys to an angel, who acknowledges his supremacy by receiving them on his knees. This work was executed in 1465, and serves as a monument to the Cardinal de Cusa, Bishop of Brixen, whose incised gravestone lies beneath.

Over the second altar is a most interesting mosaic of 680, representing, in old age, the St. Sebastian whom we are accustomed to see as a beautiful youth, wounded with arrows,—which he survived :—

"A single figure in mosaic exists as an altar-piece in S. Pietro in Vincoli. It is intended for St. Sebastian, who was removed to the church by Pope Agathon, on occasion of the plague in 680, and doubtless executed soon after this date. As a specimen of its kind it is very remarkable. There is no analogy between this figure and the usual youthful type of St. Sebastian which was subsequently adopted. On the contrary, the saint is represented here as an old man with white hair and beard, carrying the crown of martyrdom in his hand, and dressed from head to foot in true Byzantine style. In his countenance there is still some life and dignity. The more careful shadowing also of the drapery shows that, in a work intended to be so much exposed to the gaze of the pious, more pains were bestowed than usual; nevertheless, the figure, upon the whole, is very inanimate; the ground is blue."—*Kugler.*

The first altar in the right aisle has a picture of St. Augustine by *Guercino;* then come tombs of Cardinals Margotti and Agucci, from designs of *Domenichino,* who has introduced a portrait of the former in his monument. At the end of this aisle is the beautiful picture of St. Margaret and the Dragon by *Guercino;* the saint is inspired, and displaying no sign of fear,—an earthly impulse only appearing in the motion of her hand, which seems pushing back the dragon.

"St. Margaret was daughter of a priest of Antioch named Theodosius, and was brought up as a Christian by her nurse, whose sheep she watched upon the hills, while meditating upon the mysteries of the gospel. The governor of Antioch fell in love with her and wished to marry her, but she refused, and declared herself a Christian. Her friends thereupon deserted her, and the governor tried to subdue her by submitting her to horrible tortures, amid which her faith did not fail. She was then dragged to a dungeon, where Satan, in the form of a terrible dragon, came upon her with his inflamed and hideous mouth wide open, and sought to terrify and confound her; but she held up the cross of the Redeemer, and he fled before it. She finally suffered death by decapitation. Her legend was certainly known in the fifth century: in the fourteenth century she was one of the favourite saints, and was specially invoked by women against the pains of child-birth.

"'Mild Margarete, that was God's maide;
Maid Margarete, that was so meeke and milde.'"
See *Jameson's Sacred and Legendary Art*, v. 1.

Here is the glory of the church—the famous Moses of *Michael Angelo*, forming part of the decorations of the unfinished monument of Julius II.

"This pope, whom nature had intended for a conqueror, and destiny clothed with the robe of a priest, takes his place by the side of the great warriors of the sixteenth century, by the side of Charles V., of Francis I., of Gonsalvo, of Cortes, of Alba, of Bayard, and of Doria. It is difficult to imagine Julius II. murmuring prayers, or saying mass in pontifical robes, and performing, in the midst of all those unmanly functions and thousand passive forms, the spirit-deadening part which is assigned to the popes, while his soul was on fire with great-hearted designs, and while in the music of the psalms he seemed to hear the thunder of cannon. He wished to be a prince of the Church; and with the political instinct of a prince he founded his state in the midst of the most difficult wars against France, and unhesitatingly conquered and took possession of Bologna, Piacenza, Parma, Reggio, and Urbino. . . . .

The greatest pope since Innocent III., and the creator of a new political spirit in the papacy, he wished, as a second Augustus, to glorify himself and his creation. He took up again the projects of Nicholas V. Rome should become his monument. To carry out his designs he found the genius of Bramante and Raphael, and, above all, that of Michael Angelo, who belonged to him like an organ of his being. St. Peter's, of which he laid the foundation-stone, the paintings of the Sistine, the loggie of Bramante, the stanze of Raphael, are memorials of Julius the Second."—*Gregorovius, Grabmaler der Papste.*

Most of all Julius II. sought immortality in his tomb, for which the original design was absolutely gigantic. Eighteen feet high, and twelve wide, it was intended to contain more than forty statues, which were to include Moses, St. Peter and St. Paul, Rachel and Leah, and chained figures of the Provinces, while those of the Heaven and the Earth were to support the sarcophagus of the pope. This project was cut short by the death of Julius in 1513, when only four of the statues were finished, and eight designed.* Of those which were finished, three statues, the Moses, the Rachel, and the Leah, were afterwards used for the existing memorial, which was put together under Paul III. by the Duke of Urbino, heir of Julius II.—in this church of which his uncle had been a cardinal.

"The eye does not know where to rest in this the masterpiece of sculpture since the time of the Greeks. It seems to be as much an incarnation of the genius of Michael Angelo, as a suitable allegory of Pope Julius. Like Moses, he was at once lawgiver, priest, and warrior. The figure is seated in the central niche, with long-flowing beard descending to the waist, with horned head, and deep-sunk eyes, which blaze, as it were, with the light of the burning bush, with a majesty of anger which makes one tremble, as of a passionate being, drunken with fire. All that is positive and all that is negative in him is equally

---

* "Des huit figures ébauchées il y en a deux aujourd'hui au musée du Louvre (les deux esclaves). Lorsque Michel-Ange eut renoncé à son plan primitif il en fit don à Roberto Strozzi. Des mains de Strozzi elles passèrent dans celles de François 1er, et puis dans celles du connétable de Montmorency, qui les plaça à son château d'Ecouen, d'où elles sont venues au Louvre. Quatre autres *prisonniers* sont placés dans la grotte de Buontalenti au jardin du Palais Pitti, à Florence. Un groupe, représentant une figure virile en terrassant une seconde, se voit aujourd'hui dans la grande salle del *Cinquecento*, au Palais vieux de Florence, où elle fut placé par Côsme 1er.—*F. Sabatier.*

dreadful. If he were to rise up, it seems as if he would shout forth laws which no human intellect could fathom, and which, instead of improving the world, would drive it back into chaos. His voice, like that of the gods of Homer, would thunder forth in tones too awful for the ear of man to support. Yes! there is something infinite which lies in the Moses of Michael Angelo. Nor is his countenance softened by the twilight of sadness, which is stealing from his forehead over his eyes. It is the same deep sadness which clouded the countenance of Michael Angelo himself. But here it is less touching than terrible. The Greeks could not have endured a glance from such a Moses, and the artist would certainly have been blamed, because he had thrown no softening touch over his gigantic picture. That which we have is the archetype of a terrible and quite unapproachable sublimity. This statue might take its place in the cell of a colossal temple, as that of Jupiter Ammon, but the tomb where it is placed is so little suited to it, that regarded even only as its frame it is too small."—*Gregorovius.*

On either side of the principal figure are niches containing Michael Angelo's statues of Rachel and Leah,—emblematic of active and contemplative life. Those above, of the Prophet and the Sibyl, are by Raphael da Montelupo, his best pupil; on the summit is the Madonna with the Infant Jesus by Scherano da Settignano. The worst figure of the whole is that, by Maso dal Bosco, of the pope himself, who seems quite overwhelmed by the grandeur of his companions, and who lies upon a pitiful sarcophagus, leaning his head upon his hand, and looking down upon the Moses. He is represented with the beard which he was the first pope to reintroduce after an interval of many centuries,—and it is said to have been from his example that Francis I., Charles V., and others, adopted it also.

After all, Julius II. was not buried here, and the tomb is merely commemorative. He rests beneath a plain marble slab near his uncle Sixtus IV., in the chapel of the Sacrament at St. Peter's.

Close to the Moses is the entrance to the chapel in which the chains are preserved, behind a bronze screen—the work of Pollajuolo. They are of unequal size, owing to many fragments of one of them (first whole links, then only filings) having been removed in the course of centuries by various popes and sent to Christian princes who have been esteemed worthy of the favour!* The longest is about five feet in length. At the end of one of them is a collar, which is said to have encircled the neck of St. Peter. They are exposed on the day of the "station" (the first Monday in Lent) in a reliquary presented by Pius IX., adorned with statuettes of St. Peter and the angel—to whom he is represented as saying, "Ecce nunc scio vere." † On the following day a priest gives the chains to be kissed by the pilgrims, and touches their foreheads with them, saying, "By the intercession of the blessed Apostle Peter, may God preserve you from evil. Amen."

" Peter, therefore, was kept in prison : but prayer was made without ceasing of the church unto God for him. And when Herod would have brought him forth, the same night Peter was sleeping between two soldiers, bound with two chains : and the keepers before the door kept the prison. And, behold, the angel of the Lord came upon him, and a light shined in the prison : and he smote Peter on the side, and raised him up, saying, Arise up quickly. And his chains fell off from his hands."—*Acts* xii. 5—7.

Other relics preserved here are portions of the crosses of St. Peter and St. Andrew, and the body of Sta. Costanza.

The sacristy, opening out of this chapel, contains a number of pictures, including, very appropriately, the Deliverance of St. Peter from Prison, by *Domenichino*. Here, till a few

---

* The wife of Oswy, king of Northumberland received a golden key containing filings of the chains from Pope Vitalianus, in the sixth century.
† Acts xii. 11.

years ago, was preserved the famous and beautiful small picture, known as the Speranza of *Guido*. It has lately been sold by the monks to an Englishman, and is replaced by a copy.

In this church Hildebrand was crowned pope as Gregory VII. (1073). Stephen IX. was also proclaimed here in 939. The adjoining convent was built from designs of Giuliano San Gallo. Its courtyard contains a picturesque well (with columns), bearing the arms of Julius II., by *Simone Mosca*. The arcades were decorated in the present century with frescoes by *Pietra Camosci*, as a votive offering for his recovery from cholera, to St. Sebastian, " depulsori pestilitatis."

Opposite S. Pietro in Vincoli is a convent of Maronite monks, in whose garden is a tall palm-tree, perhaps the finest in Rome. In the view from the portico of the church it forms a conspicuous feature, and the combination of the old tower, the palm-tree, and the distant capitol, standing out against the golden sky of sunset, is one very familiar to Roman artists.

The tall machicolated *Tower* on the right was once a fortress of the Frangipani family, who obtained their glorious surname of " bread-breakers " from the generosity which they showed in the distribution of food to the poor during a famine in the thirteenth century. The tower is now used as a belfry to the adjoining Church of *S. Francesco di Paola*, being the only mediæval fortress tower applied to this purpose. The adjoining building is known as the *House of Lucrezia Borgia*, and the balcony over the gateway on the other side is pointed out as that in which she used to stand meditating on her crimes. Here Cæsar Borgia and his unhappy brother, the Duke of Gandia, supped with Lucrezia and their mother Vanozza, the evening before the murder of the duke, of which Cæsar was accused by popular belief. It is worth while to descend under the low-browed arch from the church piazza, and look back upon this lofty house, with its steep, dark, winding staircase,—a most picturesque bit of street architecture, which looks better the further you descend. The Via S. Francesco di Paola is considered by Ampère* to have been the place where the house of the Horatii and the Tigellum Sororis once stood.

Following the narrow lane behind S. Pietro, we reach, on the left, *S. Martino al Monte*, the great church of the Carmelites, which, though of uninviting exterior, is of the highest interest. It was built in A.D. 500 by S. Symmachus, and dedicated to the saints Sylvestro and Martino, on the site of an older church founded by St. Sylvester in the time of Constantine. After repeated alterations, it was modernised in 1650 by P. Filippini, General of the Carmelites. The nave is separated from the aisles by twenty-four ancient Corinthian columns. The aisles are painted with landscapes by *Gaspar Poussin*, having figures introduced by his brother Nicholas. The roof is an addition by S. Carlo Borromeo.

The pillars of different marbles are magnificent, and the effect of the raised choir, with winding staircases to the crypt below, is highly picturesque. On the walls are frescoes by *Cavaluccio* (ob. 1795), who is buried in the left aisle. The collection of incised gravestones deserves attention, they comprise those of a knight in mail armour of 1349; Cardinal Diomede Caraffa, with a curious epitaph; and various generals and remarkable monks of the Carmelite Order.

* Hist. Rom. i. 464.

Beneath the high altar rest the bodies of Popes Sergius, Sylvester, Martin I., Fabian, Stephen I., Soter, Ciriacus, Anastasius, and Innocent I., with several saints not papal, removed hither from the catacombs. In the curious crypt, part of the Baths of Titus, the early Council of Sylvester and Constantine was held, as represented in the fresco in the left aisle of the upper church. The back of the ancient chair of Sylvester still remains, green with age and damp. In the chapel on the left, where St. Sylvester used to celebrate mass, is an ancient mosaic of the Madonna. In front of the papal chair is the grand sepulchral figure of a Carmelite, who was General of the Order in the time of Sta. Teresa. An urn contains the intestines of the "Beato," Cardinal Giuseppe-Maria de Tommasis, who died in 1713. His body is preserved beneath an altar in the left aisle of the upper church, and is dressed in his cardinal's robes.

"In 1650 was reopened, beneath SS. Martino e Sylvestro, the long-forgotten oratory formed (according to Anastasius) by Sylvester among the halls of Trajan's Thermæ—or, more probably, in an antique palace adjacent to those imperial baths—and called by Christian writers 'Titulus Equitii,' from the name of a Roman priest then proprietor of the ground. Now a gloomy, time-worn, and sepulchral subterranean, this structure is in form an extensive quadrangle, under a high-hung vault, divided into four aisles by massive square piers; the central bay of one aisle adorned with a large red cross, painted as if studded with gems; and ranged round this, four books, each within a nimbus, earliest symbolism to represent the Evangelists. Among the much-faded and dim-seen frescoes on these dusky walls, are figures of the Saviour between SS. Peter and Paul, besides other saints, each crowned by a large nimbus."
—*Hemans' Ancient Sacred Art.*

Here is preserved a mitre, probably the most ancient extant, and said to be that of St. Sylvester, who lived in the fourth century, and who was the first Latin bishop to wear the mitre originally worn by the priests of pagan temples. This ancient mitre is so low as to rise only just above the crown of the head.

This church was dedicated to St. Martin, the holy Bishop of Tours, within a hundred years after his death, showing the very early veneration with which that saint was regarded.

Leaving S. Martino by the other door, near the tribune, we emerge at the top of the steep street called *Sta. Lucia in Selci*, which is the same with that described by Martial in going to visit the younger Pliny as—

"Altum vincere tramitem Suburrae." *Lib.* x. *Ep.* 19, 5.

And again—

"Alta Suburrani vincenda est semita clivi." *Lib.* v. *Ep.* 23, 5.

Here is a whole group of convents. In the hollow is the convent of S. Francesco di Paola, with several others. Just above (in the Via Quattro Cantone) is the convent of the Oratorians, or S. Filippo Neri. At this point also are two mediæval towers, one enclosed within the convent walls of Sta. Lucia in Selci, the other on the opposite side of the street, supposed by some to be the tower of Mecænas, celebrated by Horace. On the left of the street is the house of Domenichino (Domenico Zampieri), whose residence here is commemorated by an inscription.

Mounting the street we soon reach, on the right, the picturesque tenth century west gate (a high narrow arch upon Ionic columns, modernized and plastered over under the Sardinian government) of the *Church of Sta. Prassede*, which leads into the atrium of the church. This is seldom open, but we can enter by a door in the north aisle.

Sta. Prassede was sister of Sta. Pudenziana, and daughter

of Pudens and his wife Claudia, with whom St. Paul lodged, and who were among his first converts (see Ch. X., Sta. Pudenziana). She gave shelter in her house to a number of persecuted Christians, twenty-three of whom were discovered and martyred in her presence. She then buried their bodies in the catacombs of her grandmother, Sta. Priscilla, but, collecting their blood in a sponge, placed it in a well in her own house, where she was afterwards buried herself. An oratory is said to have been erected on the site by Pius I., A.D. 160, and was certainly in existence in A.D. 499, when it is mentioned in the acts of a Council. In A.D. 822 the original church was destroyed, and the present church erected by Pascal I., of whose time are the low tower, the porch, the terra-cotta cornices, and the mosaics. During the absence of the popes at Avignon, Sta. Prassede was one of the many churches which fell almost into ruin, and it has since suffered terribly from injudicious modernisations, first in the fifteenth century from Rosellini, under Nicholas V., and afterwards under S. Carlo Borromeo in 1564.

The interior is a basilica, the nave being separated from the aisles by sixteen granite columns, many of which have been boxed up in hideous stucco pilasters, decorated with frescoes of apostles; but their Corinthian capitals are visible, carved with figures of birds (the eagle, cock, and dove) in strong relief against the acanthus leaves. The nave is divided into four compartments by arches rising from the square pilasters; the roof is coffered.

In the right aisle is the entrance to the famous chapel, called, from its unusual and mysterious splendour, the *Orto del Paradiso*—originally dedicated to S. Zeno, then to the Virgin, with the invocation " Libera nos a pœnis inferi," and finally to the great relic which it contains. Females are never allowed to enter this shrine except upon Sundays in Lent, but can see the relic through a grating. Males are admitted by the door which is flanked by two columns of rare black and white marble, supporting a richly-sculptured marble cornice, above which are two lines of mosaic heads in circlets—in the outer, the Saviour and the twelve apostles; in the inner, the Virgin between St. Stephen and St. Laurence, with eight female saints; at the angles St. Pudens and St. Pastor. In the interior of the chapel four granite columns support a lofty groined vault, which, together with the upper part of the walls, is entirely covered with mosaic figures, which stand out distinctly from a gold ground.

"Here are SS. Peter and Paul before a throne, on which is the cross, but no seated figure; the former apostle holding a single gold key,[*] the latter a scroll; St. John the Evangelist, with a richly-bound volume; SS. James and Andrew, the two daughters of Pudens, and St. Agnes, all in rich vestments, and holding crowns; the Virgin Mary (a veiled matronly figure), and St. John the Baptist standing beside her; under the arch of a window, another half-figure of Mary, with three other females, all having the nimbus, one crowned, one with a square halo to indicate a person still living; above these, the Divine Lamb on a hill, from which the four rivers issue, with stags drinking of their waters; above the altar, the Saviour, between four other saints,—figures in part barbarously sacrificed to a modern tabernacle that conceals them. On the vault a colossal half-figure of the Saviour, youthful but severe in aspect, with cruciform nimbus, appears in a large circular halo supported by four archangels, solemn forms in long white vestments, that stand finely distinct in the dim light. Within a niche over the altar is another mosaic of the Virgin and Child, with the two daughters of Pudens, in which Rumohr (Italienische Forsch.) observes ruder execution, indicating origin later than the ninth century."—*Hemans' Ancient Christian Art.*

[*] "Ciampini gives an engraving of this figure without the key : a detail, therefore, to be ascribed to restorers :—surely neither justifiable nor judicious."—*Hemans.*

The relic preserved here (one of the principal objects of pilgrimage in Rome) is the column to which our Saviour is reputed to have been bound, said to have been given by the Saracens to Giovanni Colonna, cardinal of this church, and legate of the crusade, because, when he had fallen into their hands and was about to be put to death, he was rescued by a marvellous intervention of celestial light. Its being of the rarest blood jasper is a reason against its authenticity; the peculiarity of its formation having even given rise to the mineralogical term, "Granito della Colonna." A disk of porphyry in the pavement marks the grave of forty martyrs collected by Paschal I. The mother of that pope is also buried here, and the inscription commemorating her observes an ancient ecclesiastical usage in allowing her the title of "episcopa:" "*Ubi utique benignissimæ suæ genitricis, scilicet Dominæ Theodoræ, Episcopæ corpus quiescit.*" In this chapel Paschal I. saw the spirit of his nephew dragged to heaven by an angel, through the little window, while he was saying a mass for his soul.

The high altar covers the entrance to a small crypt, in which are two ancient sarcophagi, containing the remains of the sainted sisters Prassede and Pudenziana. An altar here, richly decorated with mosaic, is shown as that which existed in the house of Prassede. Above is a fresco, referred to the twelfth century, representing the Madonna between the sainted sisters. At the end of the left aisle is a large slab of granite (nero-bianco), upon which Sta. Prassede is said to have slept, and above it a picture of her asleep. In the centre of the nave is the well where she collected the blood, with a hideous statue of her squeezing it out of a sponge.

The chapel at the end of the left aisle is that of S. Carlo Borromeo, who was cardinal of this church, and contains his episcopal throne (a wooden chair) and a table, at which, like St. Gregory, he used to feed and wait upon twelve poor men daily. The pictures in this chapel, by *Louis Stern*, represent S. Carlo in prayer, and in ecstasy before the Sacrament. In the cloister is an old orange-tree which was planted by him, but is still flourishing.

Opposite the side entrance of the Orto del Paradiso is the tomb of Cardinal Cetive (1474), with his sleeping figure and statuettes of SS. Peter and Paul, Sta. Prassede, and Sta. Pudenziana. This will recall Browning's quaint forcible poem of 'The Bishop who orders his tomb at Saint Praxed's church.'

> "Saint Praxed's ever was the church for peace.
> . . . .
> And there how I shall lie through centuries,
> And hear the blessed mutter of the mass,
> And see God made and eaten all day long,
> And feel the steady candle flame, and taste
> Good strong thick stupefying incense-smoke!"

Other tombs of interest are those of Cardinal Ancherus, assassinated in 1286 outside the Porta S. Giovanni, and of Monsignor Santoni, a bust, said to have been executed by Bernini when only ten years old.

Two pictures in side chapels are interesting in a Vallombrosan church, as connected with saints of that order,—one representing S. Pietro Aldobrandini passing through the furnace at Settimo; and another the martyrdom of Cardinal Beccaria, put to death at Florence (whither he was sent by Alexander IV. to make peace between the Guelfs and Ghibellines)—and consigned to hell by Dante.

>   —"Quel di Beccaria
>   Di cui segò Fiorenza la gorgiera."
>   *Inferno*, xxxii.

Steps of magnificent rosso-antico lead to the tribune, which is covered with mosaics of A.D. 817—824. Those on the arch represent the heavenly Jerusalem; within is the Saviour with a cruciform halo—the hand of the first person of the Trinity holding a crown over his head—and St. Peter and St. Paul bringing in the sainted sisters of the church; on the right, Pope Paschal I.,* with a model of his church; on the left, St. Zeno (?). Above these figures, is the Adoration of the spotless Lamb, and beneath their feet the Jordan; below all is the Lamb again, with the twelve sheep issuing from the mystic cities of Jerusalem and Bethlehem, and verses recording the work of Paschal I.

> "The arrangement of saints at Sta. Prassede (817) is altogether different from that at Ravenna, but equally striking. Over the grand arch which separates the choir from the nave is a mosaic, representing the New Jerusalem, as described in the Revelations. It is a walled enclosure, with a gate at each end, guarded by angels. Within is seen the Saviour of the World, holding in his hand the orb of sovereignty, and a company of blessed seated on thrones: outside, the noble army of martyrs is seen approaching, conducted and received by angels. They are all arrayed in white, and carry crowns in their hands. Lower down, on each side, a host of martyrs press forward with palms and crowns, to do homage to the Lamb, throned in the midst. None of the martyrs are distinguished by name, except those to whom the church is dedicated—Sta. Prassede and her sister Pudenziana."—*Mrs. Jameson.*

While Pope Gelasius II. was celebrating mass in this church, he was attacked by armed bands of the inimical houses of Leone and Frangipani, and was only rescued by the assistance of his nephew Gaetano, after a conflict of

---

* With a square nimbus, denoting execution in his lifetime, as at Sta. Cecilia and Sta. Maria in Navicella.

some hours. Hence in 1630, Moriandi, abbot of Sta. Prassede, was suddenly carried off and put to fearful tortures, which resulted in his death, ostensibly on account of irregularities in his convent, but really because he had been heard to speak against Urban VIII.*

In the sacristy is preserved a fine picture by Giulio Romano of the Flagellation—especially appropriate in the church of the Colonna.

Hence the curious campanile of the old church (built 1110) may be entered, and a loggia whence the great relics of the church are exhibited at Easter, including: portions of the crown of thorns, of the sponge, of the Virgin's hair, and a miniature portrait of our Saviour which is said to have belonged to St. Peter and to have been left by him with the daughters of Pudens.

The *Monastery* attached to the church, founded by Paschal I., was first occupied by Basilian, but since 1198 has belonged to Vallombrosan monks. Nothing remains of the mosaic-covered chapel of St. Agnes, built by the founder within its walls.

Where the Via Sta. Prassede crosses the road leading from Sta. Maria Maggiore to the Lateran, is the modern gothic church of *Il Santissimo Redentore*, built by Father Douglas within the last few years.

A little beyond this, attached to the Church of S. Vito, from which it has sometimes been named, is the *Arch of Gallienus* (supposed to occupy the site of the Esquiline gate in the wall of Servius), dedicated to Gallienus (A.D. 253—260) and his Empress Salonina, by Marcus Aurelius Victor, evidently a court-flatterer of the period, who was prefect of

* See Hemans' Catholic Italy.

Rome, and possessed gardens on this spot. It is of very inferior execution; the original plan had three arches; only that in the centre remains, but traces of another may be seen on the side next the church. Gallienus was a cruel and self-indulgent emperor, who excited the indignation of the Romans by leaving his old father, Valerian, to die a captive in the hands of the Persians, so that the inscription, " *Clementissimo principi cuius invicta virtus sola pietate superata est*," is singularly false, even for the time.

"Il arrivait à Gallien de faire tuer trois ou quatre mille soldats en un jour, et il écrivait des lettres comme celle-ci, adressée à un de ses généraux : 'Tu n'auras pas fait assez pour moi, si tu ne mets à mort que des hommes armés, car le sort de la guerre aurait pu les faire périr. Il faut tuer quiconque a eu une intention mauvaise, quiconque a mal parlé de moi. Déchire, tue, extermine : *lacera, occide, concide.*' Entré dans Byzance en promettant leur pardon aux troupes qui avaient combattu contre lui, il les fit égorger, et les soldats ravagèrent la ville au point qu'il n'y resta pas un habitant. Voilà pour la clémence. Tandis que Valérien, son père, était prisonnier du roi des Perses Sapor, qui pour monter à cheval se servait du dos du vieil empereur comme d'un marchepied, en attendant qu'il le fit empailler, l'indigne fils de Valérien vivait au sein des plus honteuses voluptés, et ne tentait pas un seul effort pour le délivrer. Voilà pour la vaillance et la piété."—*Ampère, Emp.* ii. 334.

Close to this Gallienus had ordered a statue of himself to be erected, which was to be double the height of the colossus of Nero, but it was unfinished at the time of his death, and destroyed by his successor. From the centre of the arch hung, from the thirteenth century, the chain and keys of the gates of Viterbo, removed at the same time as the great bell of the Capitol. These interesting memorials of middle-age warfare were taken down in 1825.

Passing under the arch we enter upon the Via Maggiore, the main artery leading to Santa Croce. On the left is the humble convent of the *Monache Polacche*, where the long-suffering Madre Makrena, the sole survivor of the terrible persecution of the nuns of Minsk, has lived in the closest retirement since her escape in 1845.

The story of the cruel sufferings of the Polish-Basilian nuns of Minsk reminds one of the worst persecutions of the early Christians, under Nero and Diocletian. Makrena Miaczylslawska was abbess of a convent of thirty-eight nuns, whom the apostate bishop Siemasko first tried to compel to the Greek faith in the summer of 1838. Their refusal led to their being driven, laden with chains, to Witepsk, in Siberia, where they were forced to hard labour, many of them being beaten to death, one roasted alive in a hot stove, and another having her brains beaten out with a stake by the abbess of the Czernice (apostate nuns), on their persisting in their refusal to change their religion. In 1840 the surviving nuns were removed to Polock, where they were forced to work at building a palace for the bishop Siemasko, and where nine of them perished by a falling scaffold, and many others expired under the heavy weights they were compelled to carry, or under the lash. In 1842 their tortures were increased tenfold, eight of the sisters having their eyes torn out, and others being trodden to death. In 1843 those who still survived were removed to Miadzioly, where the "protopope Skrykin" said that he would "drown them like puppies," and where they were dragged by boats through the shallows of the half-frozen Dwina, up to their necks in water, till many died of the cold. In the spring of 1845, Makrena, with the only three nuns who survived with the use of their limbs (Eusebia Wawrzecka, Clotilda Konarska, and Irene Pomarnacka,) scaled the walls of their prison, while the priests and nuns who guarded them were lying drunk after an orgie, and, after wandering for three months in the forests of Lithuania, made good their escape. The nuns remained in Vienna ; the abbess, after a series of extraordinary adventures, arrived in Rome, where she was at first lodged in the convent of the Trinità de' Monti. The story of the nuns of Minsk was taken down from her dictation at the same time by a number of eminent ecclesiastics, authorized by the pope, and the authenticity of her statements verified ; after which she retired into complete seclusion in the Polish convent on the Esquiline, where she has long filled the humble office of portress. Her legs are eaten into the bone by the chains she wore in her prison life. The story of the persecution at Minsk may be read in " Le Récit de Makrena Miaczylslawska," published at Paris, by Lecoffre, in 1846 ; in a paper by Charles Dickens, in the " Household Words," for May, 1854; and in " Pictures of Christian Heroism," 1855.

Nearly opposite this convent is the picturesque ruin of a nymphæum, probably of the time of Septimius Severus, erroneously called *The Trophies of Marius*, from the trophies, now on the terrace in front of the Capitol, which were found here.

Beyond this, on the right, is the entrance of the *Villa Palombara*, occupying a great part of the site of the Baths of Titus.

"This villa once belonged to Queen Christina of Sweden, who has left upon the little doorway exactly opposite the ruin called the Trophies of Marius, a curious record of her credulity. It consists of a collection of unintelligible words, signs, and triangles, given her by some alchymist, as the rule to make gold, and which, no doubt, he had found successful, having obtained from her, and probably from many other votaries, abundance of that precious metal in exchange for it. But as she could make nothing of it, she caused it to be inscribed here, in case any passenger, wiser than herself, should be able to develope the mystic signs of this golden secret."—*Eaton's Rome.*

Though the existing ruin is misnamed, the trophies erected in honour of the victories which Marius gained over the Cimbri were really set up near this; and, curiously enough, on this site also Marius was defeated at the "Forum Esquilinum" by Sylla, who suddenly descended upon Rome from Nola with six legions, and entering by the Porta Esquilina, met his adversary here, and forced him to fly to Ostia.

Behind the Trophies of Marius a lane branches off on the left to the desolate *Church of Sta. Bibiana.*

In the time of Julian the Apostate, there dwelt in Rome a Christian family, consisting of Flavian, his wife Dalfrosa, and his two daughters, Bibiana and Demetria. All these died for their faith. Flavian was exiled, and died of starvation; Dalfrosa was beheaded; the sisters were imprisoned (A.D. 362) and scourged, and Demetria died at once under the torture. Bibiana glorified God by longer sufferings. Apronius, the prefect of the city, astonished by her beauty, conceived a guilty passion for her, and placed her under the care of one of his creatures named Rufina, who was gradually to bend her to his will. But Bibiana repelled his proposals with horror, and her firmness excited him to such fury, that he commanded her to be bound to a column, and scourged to compliance. "The order was executed with all imaginable cruelty, rivers of blood flowed from each wound, and morsels of flesh were torn away, till even the most barbarous spectators were stricken with horror. The saint alone continued immoveable, with her eyes fixed upon heaven, and her countenance radiant with celestial peace,—until her body being torn to pieces, her soul escaped to her heavenly bridegroom, to receive the double crown of virginity and martyrdom." *

After the death of Bibiana, her body was exposed to dogs for three days in the Forum Boarium, but remained unmolested; after which it was stolen at night by John the priest, who buried it here.

The church, founded in the fifth century by Olympia, a Roman matron, was modernised by Bernini for Urban VIII., and has no external appearance of antiquity. The interior is adorned with frescoes; those on the right are by *Agostino Ciampelli*, those on the left are considered by Lanzi as the best works of *Pietro da Cortona*. They pourtray in detail the story of the saint :—

1. Bibiana refuses to sacrifice to idols.
2. The death of Demetria.
3. Bibiana is scourged at the column.
4. The body of Bibiana is watched over by a dog.
5. Olympia founds the church, which is dedicated by Pope Simplicius.

The statue of the saint at the high altar is considered the masterpiece of *Bernini*. It is dignified and graceful, and would hardly be recognised as his work.

"This statue is one of his earliest works; and it is said that when Bernini, in advanced life, returned from France, he uttered, on seeing it, an involuntary expression of admiration. 'But,' added he, 'had I

---

* Croiret, Vie des Saints.

always worked in this style, I should have been a beggar.' This would lead us to conclude, that his own taste led him to prefer simplicity and truth, but that he was obliged to conform to the corrupted predilection of the age."—*Eaton's Rome.*

The remains of the saint are preserved beneath the altar, in a splendid sarcophagus of oriental alabaster, adorned with a leopard's head. A column of rosso-antico is shown as that to which Sta. Bibiana was bound during her flagellation. The *fête* of the martyred sisters is observed with great solemnity on December 2.

"Il est touchant de voir, le jour de la fête, le Chapitre entier de la grande et somptueuse basilique de Sainte-Marie-Majeure venir processionellement à cette modeste église et célébrer de solennelles et pompeuses cérémonies en l'honneur de ces deux vierges et leur mère: C'est que si ces trois femmes étaient faibles et ignorées selon le monde, elles sont devenues par leur foi, fortes et sublimes ; et l'Église ne croit pouvoir trop faire pour glorifier une pareille grandeur."—*Impressions d'une Catholique à Rome.*

On or near this site were the *Horti Lamiani*, in which the Emperor Caligula was hastily buried after his assassination, A.D. 41, though his remains were shortly afterwards disinterred by his sisters and burnt. These gardens were probably the property of Ælius Lamia, to whom Horace addressed one of his odes.* At an earlier period Elius Tubero lived here, celebrated for his virtue, his poverty, and his little house, where sixteen members of the Elian Gens dwelt harmoniously together.† He married the daughter of L. Emilius Paulus, "who," says Plutarch, "though the daughter of one who had twice been consul and twice triumphed, did not blush for the poverty of her husband, but admired the virtue which had made him poor."

* l. 26.   † Ampère, Hist. Rom. iii. 177.

On the other side of the Trophies of Marius, the Via Porta Maggiore leads to the gate of that name (see Ch. XIII.). Approached by a gate on the left of this road, most desolate, until the making of the railway amid its vineyards and gardens, and crowned with lentiscus and other shrubs, is the picturesque ruin generally called the *Temple of Minerva Medica*, from a false impression that the Giustiniani Minerva, now in the Vatican, had been found here.* It is now generally decided to be a remnant of the bath built by Augustus in honour of his grandsons Caius and Lucius Cæsar (sons of Agrippa and Julia. It is a decagon, with a vaulted brick roof, and nine niches for statues; those of Æsculapius, Antinous, Hercules, Adonis, Pomona, and (the Farnese) Faun, have been found on the site.

Near this is a curious *Columbarium of the Arruntia Family*, and a brick-lined hollow, supposed to be part of the Naumachia which Dion Cassius says that Augustus constructed "in the grove of Caius and Lucius."

Just where the lane turns off to Sta. Bibiana is the entrance to the courtyard of the *Church and Monastery of S. Eusebio*, built upon the site of the house of the saint, a priest of noble family, martyred by starvation under Constantius, A. D. 357. His body rests under the high altar, with that of St. Orosus, a Spanish priest, who suffered at the same time. The ceiling of the church is painted by *Mengs*, and represents the apotheosis of the patron saint. The campanile dates from 1220. In this convent (which was conceded to the Jesuits in 1825 by Leo XII.) English clergymen about to join the Roman Catholic Church frequently "make a retreat" before their reception; Archdeacon Wilber-

* It was found in the gardens of the convent of Sta. Maria sopra Minerva.

force is one of many converts who have been received here.

Turning towards Sta. Maria Maggiore, on the left is a *Cross* on a pedestal formed by a cannon reversed, and inscribed " In hoc signo vinces,"—a memorial of the absolution given by Clement VIII. in 1595 to Henry IV. of France on his being received into the Roman Catholic Church.

Opposite this is a peculiar round arched doorway—unique in Rome—forming the entrance to the *Church of S. Antonio Abbate*, said to occupy the site of a temple of Diana. The church is decorated with very coarsely-executed frescoes of the life of the saint,—his birth, his confirmation by a bishop who predicted his future saintship, and his temptation by the devil in various forms.

"S. Antonio, called 'the patriarch of monks,' became a hermit in his twentieth year, and lived alone in the Egyptian desert till his fifty-fifth year, when he founded his monastery of Phaim, where he died at the age of 105, having passed his life in perpetual prayer, and often tasting no food for three days at a time. In the desert Satan was permitted to assault him in a visible manner, to terrify him with dismal noises ; and once he so grievously beat him that he lay almost dead, covered with bruises and wounds. At other times the fiends attacked him with terrible clamours, and a variety of spectres, in hideous shapes of the most frightful wild beasts, which they assumed to dismay and terrify him ; till a ray of heavenly light breaking in upon him, chased them away, and caused him to cry out, ' Where wast thou, my Lord and Master ? Why wast thou not with me ? ' And a voice answered, ' Anthony, I was here the whole time ; I stood by thee, and beheld thy combat : and because thou hast manfully withstood thy enemies I will always protect thee, and will render thy name famous throughout the earth.' "—*Butler's Lives of the Saints.*

"Surely the imagery painted on the inner walls of Egyptian tombs, and probably believed by Anthony and his compeers to be connected with devil-worship, explains his visions. In the ' Words of the Elders ' a monk complains of being troubled with 'pictures, old and new.' Probably, again, the pain which Anthony felt was the agony of a fever, and the visions which he saw its delirium."—*Kingsley's Hermits.*

In the chapel of S. Antonio is a very ancient mosaic, representing a tiger tearing a bull.

"Le tigre en mosaïque conservé dans l'église de St. Antoine, patron des animaux, est, selon toute apparence, le portrait d'un acteur renommé."—*Ampère, Hist. Rom.* iv. 28.

Hither, on the week following the feast of St. Anthony (January 17), horses, mules, and cows are brought to be blest as a preservative against accidents for the year to come. On the 23rd, the horses of the pope, Prince Borghese, and other Roman grandees (about $2\frac{1}{2}$ P.M.) are sent for this purpose. All the animals are sprinkled with holy water by a priest, who receives a gift in proportion to the wealth of their master, and recites over each group the formula,—

"Per intercessionem beati Antonii Abbatis, hæc animalia liberantur a malis, in nomine Patris et Filii et Spiritus Sancti. Amen!"

"Les bergers romains faisaient la *lustration* de leurs taureaux ; ils purifiaient leurs brebis à la fête de Palès (pour écarter d'eux toute influence funeste), comme ils les font encore asperger d'eau bénite à la fête de Saint Antoine."—*Ampère, Hist. Rom.* ii. 329.*

"'Long live St. Anthony,' writes Mabillon (in the 17th century) as he describes the horses, asses, and mules, all going on the saint's festival to be sprinkled with holy water, and receive the benediction of a reverend father. 'All would go to ruin,' say the Romans, 'if this act of piety were omitted.' So nobody escapes paying toll on this occasion, not even Nostro Signore himself."—*Stephens' French Benedictines.*

"S. Antonio Abbate is the patron of the four-footed creation, and his feast is a saturnalia for the usually hard-worked beasts and for their attendants and drivers. Gentlefolks must be content on this day to stay at home or go on foot, for there are not wanting solemn tales of how the unbelievers who had obliged their coachmen to drive out on this day

---

* This pagan benediction of the animals is represented in a bas-relief in the Vatican (Museo Pio-Clementino, 157). A peasant bearing two ducks as his offering, brings his cow to be blessed by a priest at the door of a chapel, and the priest delaying to come forth, a calf drinks up the holy water. Ovid describes how he took part in the feast of Pales, and sprinkled the cattle with a laurel bough. (*Fasti*, iv. 728.)

have been punished by great misfortunes. The church of S. Antonio stands in a large piazza, usually looking like a desert; but to-day it was enlivened by a varied throng: horses and mules, with tails and manes splendidly interlaced with ribbons, are brought to a small chapel standing somewhat apart from the church, where a priest armed with a large asperge plentifully besprinkles the animals with the holy water which is placed before him in tubs and pails, sometimes apparently with a sly wish to excite them to gambols. Devout coachmen bring larger or smaller wax-tapers, and their masters send alms and gifts, in order to secure to their valuable and useful animals a year's exemption from disease and accident. Horned cattle and donkeys, equally precious and serviceable to their owners, have their share in the blessing."—*Goethe, Römische Briefe.*

"At the blessing of the animals, an adventure happened, which afforded us some amusement. A countryman, having got a blessing on his beast, putting his whole trust in its power, set off from the church door at a grand gallop, and had scarcely cleared a hundred yards before the ungainly animal tumbled down with him, and over its head he rolled into the dirt. He soon got up, however, and shook himself, and so did the horse, without either seeming to be much the worse. The priest seemed not a whit out of countenance at this; and some of the standers-by exclaimed, with laudable steadfastness of faith, 'That but for the blessing, they might have broken their necks.'"—*Eaton's Rome.*

"Un postilion Italien, qui voyait mourir son cheval, priait pour lui, et s'écriait: O, Sant' Antonio, abbiate pietà dell' anima sua!"—*Madame de Staël.*

"The hog was the representative of the demon of sensuality and gluttony, which Anthony is supposed to have vanquished by the exercise of piety and by the divine aid. The ancient custom of placing in all his effigies a black pig at his feet, or under his feet, gave rise to the superstition, that this unclean animal was especially dedicated to him and under his protection. The monks of the Order of St. Anthony kept herds of consecrated pigs, which were allowed to feed at the public charge, and which it was a profanation to steal or kill; hence the proverb about the fatness of a 'Tantony pig.'"—*Jameson's Sacred Art,* p. 750.

We now enter the Piazza of Sta. Maria Maggiore, in front of which stands a beautiful Corinthian column, now called *Colonna della Vergine.* This is the last remaining column of the Basilica of Constantine, and is forty-seven feet high without its base and capital. It was brought hither by Paul V. in 1613. The figure of the Virgin on the top is by Bertelot.

The *Basilica of Sta. Maria Maggiore*, frequently named from its founder the *Liberian Basilica*, was founded A.D. 352, by Pope Liberius, and John,* a Roman patrician, to commemorate a miraculous fall of snow, which covered this spot of ground and no other, on the 5th of August, when the Virgin appearing in a vision, showed them that she had thus appropriated the site of a new temple.† This legend is commemorated every year on the 5th of August, the festa of La Madonna della Neve, when, during a solemn high mass in the Borghese chapel, showers of white rose-leaves are thrown down constantly through two holes in the ceiling, " like a leafy mist between the priests and worshippers."

This church, in spite of many alterations, is in some respects internally the most beautiful and harmonious building in Rome, and retains much of the character which it received when rebuilt between 432 and 440, by Sixtus III., who dedicated it to Sta. Maria Mater Dei, and established it as one of the four patriarchal basilicas, whence it is provided with the "porta santa," only opened by the pope, with great solemnity, four times in a century.

The west front was added under Benedict XIV. (Lambertini) in 1741, by Ferdinando Fuga, destroying a portico of the time of Eugenius III., of which the only remnant is an architrave, inserted into which is an inscription, quoted

---

* His flat tombstone is in the centre of the nave.
† This story is the subject of two of Murillo's most beautiful pictures in the Academy at Madrid. The first represents the vision of the Virgin to John and his wife,—in the second they tell what they have seen to Pope Liberius.

by its defenders in proof of the existence of Mariolatry in the twelfth century :—

> "Tertius Eugenius Romanus Papa benignus
> Obtulit hoc munus, Virgo Maria, tibi,
> Quæ Mater Christi fieri merito meruisti,
> Salva perpetua Virginitate tibi.
> Es Via, Vita, Salus, totius Gloria Mundi,
> Da veniam culpis, Virginitatis Honos."

In this portico is a statue of Philip IV. of Spain by *Lucenti*. In the upper story are preserved the mosaics which once decorated the old façade, some of them representing the miracle which led to the foundation of the church.

"To 1300 belong the mosaics on the upper part of the façade of Sta. Maria Maggiore (now inserted in the loggia), in which, in two rows, framed in architectural decorations, may be seen Christ in the act of benediction, and several saints above, and the legend of the founding of the church below—both well-arranged compositions. An inscription gives the name of the otherwise unknown master, 'Philippus Rusuti.' This work was formerly attributed to the Florentine mosaicist Gaddo Gaddi, who died 1312."—*Kugler*.

Five doors, if we include the walled-up Porta Santa, lead into the magnificent nave (280 feet long, 60 broad), lined by an avenue of white marble columns, surmounted by a frieze of mosaic pictures from the Old Testament, of A.D. 440—unbroken, except where six of the subjects have been cut away to make room for arches in front of the two great side chapels. The mosaics increase in splendour as they approach the tribune, in front of which is a grand baldacchino by Fuga, erected by Benedict XIV., supported by four porphyry columns wreathed with gilt leaves, and surmounted by four marble angels by Pietro Bracci. The pavement is of the most glorious opus-alexandrinum, and its crimson and violet hues temper the white and gold on the walls. The flat roof (by Sangallo), panelled and carved, is gilt with the first gold brought to Spain from South America, and presented to Alexander VI. by Ferdinand and Isabella.

"The mosaics above the chancel arch are valuable for the illustration of Christian doctrine : the throne of the Lamb as described in the Apocalypse, SS. Peter and Paul beside it (the earliest instance of their being thus represented) ; and the four symbols of the Evangelists above ; the Annunciation ; the Angel appearing to Zacharias ; the Massacre of the Innocents ; the Presentation in the Temple ; the Adoration of the Magi ; Herod receiving the head of St. John the Baptist ; and, below these groups, a flock of sheep, type of the faithful, issuing from the mystic cities, Bethlehem and Jerusalem. We see here one curious example of the nimbus, round the head of Herod, as a symbol of power, apart from sanctity. In certain details these mosaics have been altered, with a view to adapting them to modern devotional bias, in a manner that deserves reprobation ; but Ciampini (Monumenta Vetera) shows us in engraving what the originals were before this alteration, effected under Benedict XIV. In the group of the Adoration the child *alone* occupied the throne, while opposite (in the original work) was seated, on another chair, an elderly person in a long blue mantle veiling the head—concluded by Ciampini to be the senior among the Magi : the two others, younger, and both in the usual Oriental dress, with trousers and Phrygian caps, being seen to approach at the same side, whilst the mother *stood* beside the throne of the child,—her figure recognisable from its resemblance to others in scenes where she appears in the same series. As this group is now before us, the erect figure is left out ; the seated one is converted into that of Mary, with a halo round the head, though in the original even such attribute (alike given to the Saviour and to all the angels introduced) is *not* assigned to her."—*Hemans' Ancient Christian Art*.

The vault of the tribune is covered with mosaics by Jacopo da Turrita, the same who executed those at the Lateran basilica.

"A general affinity with the style of Cimabue is observable in some mosaics executed by contemporary artists. Those in Sta. Maria

Maggiore are inscribed with the name of Jacobus Torriti, and executed between 1287 and 1292. They are surpassed by no contemporary work in dignity, grace, and decorative beauty of arrangement. In a blue, gold-starred circle is seen Christ enthroned with the Virgin; on each side are adoring angels, kneeling and flying, on a gold ground, with St. Peter and St. Paul, the two St. Johns, St. Francis, and St. Anthony (the same in size and position as at St. J. Lateran), advancing devoutly along. The upper part is filled with graceful vine-branches, with symbolical animals among them. Below is Jordan, with small river gods, boats, and figures of men and animals. Further below are scenes from the life of Christ in animated arrangement. The group in the centre of the circle, of Christ enthroned with the Virgin, is especially fine: while the Saviour is placing the crown on His mother's head, she lifts up her hands with the expression both of admiration and of modest remonstrance.* The forms are very pure and noble; the execution careful, and very different from the Roman mosaics of the twelfth century."—*Kugler.*

In front of and beneath the high altar Pius IX. has lately been preparing his own monument, by constructing a splendid chamber approached by staircases, and lined with the most precious alabaster and marbles.

On the right of the western entrance is the tomb of the Rospigliosi pope, Clement IX. (1667—69), the work of Ercole Ferrata, a pupil of Bernini. His body rests before the high altar, surrounded by a number of the members of his family. Left of the entrance is the tomb of Nicholas IV., Masci (1288—92), erected to his memory three hundred years after his death by Sixtus V. while still a cardinal. He is represented giving benediction, between two allegorical figures of Justice and Religion,—a fine work of Leonardo da Sarzana.

* This mosaic will bring to mind the beautiful lines of Dante:—
"L' amor che mosse già l' eterno padre
Per figlia aver di sua Deità trina
Costei che fu del figlio suo poi madre
Dell' universo qui fa la regina."

"It is well to know that this pope, a mere upstart from the dust, sought to support himself through the mighty family of Colonna, by raising them too high. His friend, the Cardinal Giacomo Colonna, contributed with him to the renewal of the mosaics which are in the tribune of Sta. Maria Maggiore, and one can see their two figures there to this day. It was in this reign that Ptolemais, the last possession of the Christians in Asia, fell into the hands of the Mohammedans; thus ended the era of the Crusades."—*Gregorovius.*

Behind this tomb, near the walled-up Porta Santa, is a good tomb of two bishops, brothers, of the fifteenth century, and in the same aisle are many other monuments of the sixteenth century, some of them fine in their way.

Nearly on a line with the baldacchino is the entrance of the *Borghese Chapel*, built by Flaminio Ponzio for Paul V. in 1608, gorgeous with precious marbles and alabasters. Over its altar is preserved one of the pictures attributed to St. Luke (and announced to be such in a papal bull attached to the walls!), much revered from the belief that it stayed the plague which decimated the city during the reign of Pelagius II., and that (after its intercession had been sought by a procession by order of Innocent VIII.) it brought about the overthrow of the Moorish dominion in Spain.

"On conserve à Sainte Marie Majeure une des images de la Madonne peintes par St. Luc, et plusieurs fois on a trouvé les anges chantant les litanies autour de ce tableau."—*Stendal.*

The "Scheme of decorations in this gorgeous chapel is so remarkable, as testifying to the development which the theological idea of the Virgin, as the Sposa or personified Church, had attained in the time of Paul V.—the same pope who in 1615 promulgated the famous bull relative to the Immaculate Conception"—that the insertion of the whole passage of Mrs. Jameson on this subject will not be considered too much.

"First, and elevated above all, we have the 'Madonna della Concezione,' 'Our Lady of the Immaculate Conception,' in a glory of light, sustained and surrounded by angels, having the crescent under her feet, according to the approved treatment. Beneath, round the

dome, we read in conspicuous letters the text from the Revelation:—
SIGNUM . MAGNUM . APPARAVIT . IN . CŒLO . MULIER . AMICTA . SOLE .
ET . LUNA . SUB . PEDIBUS . EJUS . ET . IN . CAPITE . EJUS . CORONA .
STELLARUM . DUODECIM. Lower down is a second inscription expressing the dedication. MARIÆ . CHRISTI . MATRI . SEMPER . VIRGINI .
PAULUS . QUINTUS . P.M. The decorations beneath the cornice consist of eighteen large frescoes, and six statues in marble, above life size. We have the subjects arranged in the following order:—

"1. The four great prophets, Isaiah, Jeremiah, Ezekiel, and Daniel, in their usual place in the four pendatives of the dome.

"2. Two large frescoes. In the first the Vision of St. Gregory Thaumaturgus, and Heretics bitten by Serpents. In the second, St. John Damascene and S. Ildefonso miraculously rewarded for defending the majesty of the Virgin.

"3. A large fresco, representing the four Doctors of the Church who had especially written in honour of the Virgin: viz., Irenæus and Cyprian, Ignatius and Theophilus, grouped two and two.

"4. St. Luke, who painted the Virgin, and whose gospel contains the best account of her.

"5. As spiritual conquerors in the name of the Virgin, St. Dominic and St. Francis, each attended by two companions of his Order.

"6. As military conquerors in the name of the Virgin, the Emperor Heraclius, and Narses, the general against the Arians.

"7. A group of three female figures, representing the three famous saintly princesses, who in marriage preserved their virginity, Pulcheria, Edeltruda (our famous Queen Ethelreda), and Cunegunda.

"8. A group of three learned Bishops, who had especially defended the immaculate purity of the Virgin, St. Cyril, St. Anselm, and St. Denis (?).

"9. The miserable ends of those who were opposed to the honour of the Virgin. 1. The death of Julian the Apostate, very oddly represented; he lies on an altar, transfixed by an arrow, as a victim; St. Mercurius in the air. 2. The death of Leo IV., who destroyed the effigies of the Virgin. 3. The death of Constantine IV., also a famous iconoclast.

"The statues which are placed in niches are—

"1—2. St. Joseph, as the nominal husband, and St. John the Evangelist, as the nominal son, of the Virgin; the latter, also, as prophet and poet, with reference to the passage in the Revelation, xii. i.

"3—4. Aaron, as priestly ancestor (because his wand blossomed), and David, as kingly ancestor, of the Virgin.

"5—6. St. Dionysius the Areopagite, who was present at the death of the Virgin, and St. Bernard, who composed the famous 'Salve Regina' in her honour.

"Such is this grand systematic scheme of decoration, which, to those who regard it cursorily, is merely a sumptuous confusion of colours and forms, or at best a 'fine example of the Guido school and Bernini.' It is altogether a very complete and magnificent specimen of the prevalent style of art, and a very comprehensive and suggestive expression of the prevalent tendency of thought in the Roman Catholic Church from the beginning of the seventeenth century. In no description of this chapel have I seen the names and subjects accurately given : the style of art belongs to the *decadence*, and the taste being worse than questionable, the prevailing *doctrinal* idea has been neglected, or never understood."— *Legends of the Madonna*, lxxi.

On the right is the tomb of Clement VIII. (1592—1605), the Florentine Ippolito Aldobrandini, the builder of the new palace of the Vatican, and the cruel torturer and executioner of the Cenci. He is represented in the act of benediction. The bas-reliefs on his monument commemorate the principal events of his reign,—the conclusion of peace between France and Spain, and the taking of Ferrara, which he seized from the heirs of Alphonso II.

On the left is the tomb of Paul V. (1605—1621), Camillo Borghese,—in whose reign St. Peter's was finished, as every traveller learns from the gigantic inscription over its portico, —who founded the great Borghese family, and left to his nephew, Cardinal Scipio Borghese, a fortune which enabled him to buy the Borghese Palace and to build the Borghese Villa.

"It is a truly herculean figure, with a grandly developed head, while in his thick neck, pride, violence, and sensuality seem to be united. He is the first pope who wore the beard of a cavalier, like that of Henry IV., which recalls the Thirty-years' War, which he lived through ; as far as the battle of the White Mountain. In this round, domineering, pride-swollen countenance, appears the violent, imperious spirit of Paul, which aimed at an absolute power. Who does not remember his famous quarrel with Venice, and the rôle which his far superior adversary Paolo Sarpi played with such invincible courage? The bas-reliefs of his tomb represent the reception given by the pope to the envoys of Congo and Japan, the building of the citadel of Ferrara, the sending of auxiliary troops to Hungary to the assistance of Rudolph II., and the canonization of Sta. Francesca Romana and S. Carlo Borromeo."—*Gregorovius*.

The frescoes in the cupola are by *Cigoli;* those around the altar by the Cav. D'Arpino ; those above the tombs and on the arches by *Guido*, except the Madonna, which is by *Lanfranco*. The late beloved Princess Borghese, *née* Lady Gwendoline Talbot, was buried in front of the altar, all Rome following her to the grave.

> The funeral of Princess Borghese proved the feeling with which she was regarded. Her body lay upon a car which was drawn by forty young Romans, and was followed by all the poor of Rome, the procession swelling like a river in every street and piazza it passed through, while from all the windows as it passed flowers were showered down. In funeral ceremonies of great personages at Rome an ancient custom is observed by which, when the body is lowered into the grave, a chamberlain, coming out to the church door, announces to the coachman, who is waiting with the family carriage, that his master or mistress has no longer need of his services ; and the coachman thereupon breaks his staff of office and drives mournfully away. When this formality was fulfilled at the funeral of Princess Borghese, the whole of the vast crowd waiting outside the basilica broke into tears and sobs, and kneeling by a common impulse, prayed aloud for the soul of their benefactress.

The chapel has been lately the scene of a miraculous story, with reference to a visionary appearance of the Princess Borghese, which has obtained great credit among the people, by whom she is already looked upon as a saint.

The first chapel in the right aisle is that of the Patrizi family, and close by is the sepulchral stone of their noble ancestor, Giovanni Patricino, whose bones were found beneath the high altar, and deposited here in 1700. A little further is the chapel of the Santa Croce, with ten porphyry columns. Then comes the *Chapel of the Holy Sacrament*, built by Fontana for Sixtus V. while still Cardinal of Montalto. Gregory XIII., who was then on the throne, visited this gorgeous chapel when it was nearly completed, and immediately decided that one who could build such a splendid temple was sufficiently rich, and suppressed the cardinal's pension. Fontana advanced a thousand scudi for the completion of the work, and had the delicacy never to allow the cardinal to imagine that he was indebted to him. The chapel, restored 1870, is adorned with statues by Giobattista Pozzo, Cesare Nebbia, and others. Under the altar is a presepio—one of the best works of Bernini, and opposite to it, in the confession, a beautiful statue of S. Gaetano (founder of the Theatines, who died 1547*), with two little children. On the right is the splendid tomb of Pius V., Michaele Ghislieri (1566—72), the barefooted, bareheaded Dominican monk of Sta. Sabina, who in his short six years' reign beheld amongst other events the victory of Lepanto, the fall of the Huguenots in France, and the massacre of St. Bartholomew, events which were celebrated at Rome with *fêtes* and thanksgivings. The figure of the pope, a monk wasted to a skeleton (by Leonardo de Sarzana), sits in the central niche, between statues of St. Dominic and St. Peter Martyr. A number of bas-reliefs by different sculptors represent the events of his life. Some are by the Flemish artists Nicolas d'Arras and Egidius.

On the left, is the tomb of Sixtus V. (1585—90), Felice

---

* See Sta. Dorothea, ch. xvii.

Perretti, who as a boy kept his father's pigs at Montalto; who as a young man was a Franciscan monk preaching in the Apostoli, and attracting crowds by his eloquence; and who then rose to be bishop of Fermo, soon after to be cardinal, and was lastly raised to the papal throne, which he occupied only five years, a time which sufficed for the prince of the Church who loved building the most, to renew Rome entirely.

"If anything can still the spectator to silence, and awaken him to great recollections, it is the monument of this astonishing man, who, as child, herded swine, and as an old man commanded people and kings, and who filled Rome with so many works, that from every side his name, like an echo, rings in the traveller's ear. We never cease to be amazed at the wonderful luck which raised Napoleon from the dust to the throne of the world, as if it were a romance or a fairy story. But if in the history of kings these astonishing changes are extraordinary accidents, they seem quite natural in the history of the popes, they belong to the very essence of Christendom, which does not appeal to the person, but to the spirit; and while the one history is full of ordinary men, who, without the prerogative of their crown, would have sunk into eternal oblivion, the other is rich in great men, who, placed in a different sphere, would have been equally worthy of renown."—*Gregorovius.*

In a little chapel on the left of the entrance of this—which is as it were a transept of the church—is a fine picture of St. Jerome by *Spagnuoletto*, and in the chapel opposite a sarcophagus of two early Christian consuls, richly wrought in the Roman imperial style, but with Christian subjects,— Daniel in the den of lions, Zaccheus in the sycamore-tree, Martha at the raising of Lazarus, &c.

At the east end of the right aisle, near the door, is perhaps the finest gothic monument in Rome,—the tomb of Cardinal Gonsalvi, bishop of Albano, c. 1299.

"A recumbent statue, in pontifical vestments, rests on a sarcophagus, and two angels draw aside curtains as if to show us the dead; in the background is a mosaic of Mary enthroned, with the Child, the apostle Matthias, St. Jerome, and a smaller kneeling figure of Gonsalvi, in pontifical robes; at the apex is a tabernacle with cusped arch, and below the epitaph 'Hoc opus fecit Joannes Magister Cosmæ civis Romanus,' the artist's record of himself. In the hands of St. Matthias and St. Jerome are scrolls; on that held by the apostle, the words, 'Me tenet ara prior'; on St. Jerome's, 'Recubo presepis ad antrum', these epigraphs confirming the tradition that the bodies of St. Matthias and St. Jerome repose in this church, while indicating the sites of their tombs. Popular regards have distinguished this tomb; no doubt in intended honour to the Blessed Virgin, lamps are kept ever burning, and vases of flowers ranged, before her mosaic image."—*Hemans' Mediæval Christian Art.*

At the west end of the right aisle is the entrance of the *Baptistery*, which has a vast porphyry vase as a font. Hence we reach the *Sacristy*, in the inner chamber of which are some exceedingly beautiful bas-reliefs by *Mino da Fiesole.*

One of the greatest of the Christmas ceremonies is the procession at 5 A.M., in honour of the great relic of the church—the Santa Culla—*i.e.*, the cradle in which our Saviour was carried into Egypt, not, as is frequently imagined, the manger, which is allowed to have been of stone, and of which a single stone only is supposed to have found its way to Rome, and to be preserved in the altar of the Blessed Sacrament. The "Santa Culla" is preserved in a magnificent reliquary, six feet high, adorned with bas-reliefs and statuettes in silver. On the afternoon of Christmas eve the public can visit the relic at an altar in a little chapel near the sacristy. On the afternoon of Christmas Day it is also exposed, but upon the high altar, where it is less easily seen.

"Le Seigneur Jésus a voulu naître dans une étable; mais les hommes ont apporté précieusement le petit berceau qui a reçu le salut du monde, dans la reine des cités, et ils l'ont enchâssé dans l'or.

"C'est bien ici que nous devons accourir avec joie et redire ce chant triomphant de l'Eglise: *Adeste, fideles, læti triumphantes; venite, venite in Bethleem.*"—*Une Chrétienne à Rome.*

Among the many other relics preserved here are two little bags of the brains of St. Thomas à Becket.

It was in this church that Pope St. Martin I. was celebrating mass in the seventh century, when a guard sent by the Exarch Olympius appeared on the threshold with orders to seize and put him to death. At the sight of the pontiff the soldier was stricken with blindness, a miracle which led to the conversion of Olympius and many other persons.

Platina, the historian of the popes, was buried here, with the epitaph : " Quisquis es, si pius, Platynam et sua ne vexes, anguste jacent et soli volunt esse."

Sta. Maria Maggiore was the scene of the seizure of Hildebrand by Cencius :

"On Christmas Eve, 1075, the city of Rome was visited by a dreadful tempest. Darkness brooded over the land, and the trembling spectators believed that the day of final judgment was about to dawn. In this war of the elements, however, two processions were seen advancing to the Church of Sta. Maria Maggiore. At the head of one was the aged Hildebrand, conducting a few priests to worship at the shrine of the Virgo Deipara. The other was preceded by Cencius, a Roman noble. At each pause in the tempest might be heard the hallelujahs of the worshippers, or the voice of the pontiff, pouring out benedictions on the little flock which knelt before him—when Cencius grasped his person, and some yet more daring ruffian inflicted a wound on his forehead. Bound with cords, stripped of his sacred vestments, beaten, and subjected to the basest indignities, the venerable minister of Christ was carried to a fortified mansion within the walls of the city, again to be removed at daybreak to exile or death. Women were there, with women's sympathy and kindly offices, but they were rudely put aside ; and a drawn sword was already aimed at the pontiff's bosom, when the cries of a fierce multitude, threatening to burn or batter down the house, arrested the aim of the assassin. An arrow, discharged from below, reached and slew him. The walls rocked beneath the strokes of the maddened populace, and Cencius, falling at his prisoner's feet, became himself a suppliant for pardon and for life. . . . . In profound silence, and with undisturbed serenity, Hildebrand had thus far submitted to these atrocious indignities. The occasional raising of his eyes towards heaven alone indicated his consciousness of them. But to the supplication of his prostrate enemy he returned an instant and a calm assurance of forgiveness. He rescued Cencius from the exasperated besiegers, dismissed him in safety and in peace, and returned, amidst the acclamations of the whole Roman people, to complete the interrupted solemnities of Sta. Maria Maggiore."—*Stephens' Lectures on Eccles. Hist.*

Leaving the church by the door behind the tribune, we find ourselves at the top of the steep slope of the Esquiline and in front of an *Obelisk* erected here by Fontana for Sixtus V.,—brought from Egypt by Claudius, and one of two which were used to guard the entrance to the mausoleum of Augustus. The inscriptions on three of its sides are worth notice :—" Christi Dei in æternum viventis cunabula lætissime colo, qui mortui sepulchro Augusti tristis serviebam."—" Quem Augustus de vergine nasciturum vivens adoravit, sed deinceps dominum dici noluit, adoro."—" Christus per invictam crucem populo pacem præbeat, qui Augusti pace in præsepe nasci voluit."

CHAPTER XIII.

THE BASILICAS OF THE LATERAN, SANTA CROCE, AND S. LORENZO.

Via S. Giovanni—The Obelisk and Baptistery—Basilica and Cloisters—Mosaic of the Triclinium—Santa Scala—Palace of the Lateran—Villa Massimo Arsole—SS. Pietro e Marcellino—Villa Wolkonski—(Porta Furba—Tombs of the Via Latina—Basilica of S. Stefano)—Santa Croce in Gerusalemme—Amphitheatrum Castrense—Porta Maggiore—(Tomb of Sta. Helena—Torre dei Schiavi—Cervaletto—Cerbara)—Porta and Basilica of S. Lorenzo—Catacomb of S. Hippolytus.

BEHIND the Coliseum the Via S. Giovanni ascends the slope of the Esquiline. In mediæval times this road was always avoided by the popes, on account (as most authorities state) of the scandal attaching to the more than doubtful legend of Joan, the famous papessa, who is said to have horrified her attendants by giving birth to a child on this spot, during a procession from the Lateran, and to have died of shame and terror immediately afterwards. Joan is stated to have been educated at Athens, to have skilfully obtained her election to the papal throne, disguised as a man, between the reign of Leo IV. and that of Benedict III. (855), and to have taken the name of John VIII. In the cathedral of Siena the heads of all the popes in terra-cotta (down to

Alexander III.) decorate the frieze above the arches of the nave, and among them was that of Pope Joan, inscribed "Johannes VIII. Femina de Anglia," till 1600, when it was changed into a head of Pope Zacharias by the Grand Duke, at the request of Pope Clement VIII.

On the left of this street is S. Clemente (described Ch. VII.). On the right, a long wall flooded by a cascade of Banksia roses in spring, and a villa inlaid with terra-cotta ornaments, are those of the favourite residence of the well-known Marchese Campana, the learned archæologist of Etruria, and the chief benefactor of the Etruscan museum at the Vatican, cruelly imprisoned and exiled by the papal government in 1858, upon an accusation of having tampered with the revenues of Monte di Pietà.

Beyond the turn of the road leading to S. Stefano Rotondo (Ch. VII.), bas-reliefs of Our Saviour's Head (from the Acheirotopeton in the Sancta Sanctorum) between two candelabra—upon the different buildings, announce the property of the Lateran chapter.

The *Piazza di San Giovanni* is surrounded by a remarkable group of buildings. In front are the Baptistery and Basilica of the Lateran. On the right is a Hospital for women, capable of containing 600 patients; on the left, beyond the modern palace, are seen the buildings which enclose the Santa Scala, and some broken arches of the Aqua Marcia. In the centre of the piazza is the *Obelisk of the Lateran*, 150 feet high, the oldest object in Rome, being referred by translators of hieroglyphics to the year 1740 B.C., when it was raised in memory of the Pharaoh Thothmes IV. It was brought, from the temple of the Sun at Heliopolis, to Alexandria by Constantine, and removed thence by his son Constantius to Rome, where it was used, together with the obelisk now in the Piazza del Popolo, to ornament the Circus Maximus. Hence it was moved to its present site in 1588, by Fontana, for Sixtus V. The obelisk was then broken into three pieces, and in order to piece them together, some part had to be cut off, but it is still the tallest in the city. One of the inscriptions on the basement is false, as it narrates that Constantine received at the Lateran the baptism which he did not receive till he was dying at Nicomedia.

An octagon building of mean and miserable exterior is that of the *Baptistery of the Lateran*, sometimes called S. Giovanni in Fonte, built, not by Constantine, to whom it is falsely ascribed, but by Sixtus III. (430—40). Of his time are the two porphyry columns at the entrance on the side nearest the church, and the eight which form a colonnade round the interior, supporting a cornice from which rise the eight small columns of white marble, which sustain the dome. In the centre is the font of green basalt in which Rienzi bathed on the night of August 1, 1347, before his public appearance as a knight, when he summoned Clement VI. and other sovereigns of Europe to appear before him for judgment. The cupola is decorated with scenes from the life of John the Baptist by *Andrea Sacchi*. On the walls are frescoes pourtraying the life of Constantine by *Gimignano, Carlo Maratta,* and *Andrea Camassei.*

On the right is the *Chapel of St. John the Baptist*, built by Pope Hilary (461—67). Between two serpentine columns is a figure of St. John Baptist by *L. Valadier* after Donatello.

On the left is the *Chapel of St. John the Evangelist*, also built by Hilary, who presented its bronze doors (said to have

ORATORY OF S. VENANZIO.

once belonged to the Baths of Caracalla) in remembrance of his delivery from the fury of fanatical monks at the Second Council of Ephesus, where he appeared as the legate of Leo I.,—a fact commemorated by the inscription : " Liberatori suo B. Joanni Evangelistæ Hilarius Episcopus famulus Christi." The vault is covered with mosaics representing the Spotless Lamb in Paradise. Here is a statue of St. John by *Landini*.

Close by is the entrance to the *Oratory of S. Venanzio*,* built in 640 by John IV., and dedicated to St. Venantius, from a filial feeling to his father, who bore the same name. Nothing, however, remains of this time but the mosaics. Those in the apse represent the Saviour in the act of benediction with angels, and below him the Virgin (an aged woman) in adoration,† with St. Peter and St. John Baptist, St. Paul and St. John the Evangelist, St. Venantius and St. Domnus—and another figure unnamed, probably John IV., holding the model of a church. Outside the chancel arch are eight saints, with their names (Palmianus, Julius, Asterius, Anastasius, Maurus, Septimius, Antiochianus, Cajanus), the symbols of the evangelists, and the cities Bethlehem and Jerusalem ; also the verses :—

> " Martyribus Christi Domini pia vota Johannes
> Reddidit antistes sanctificante Deo.
> Ac sacri fontis simile fulgente metallo,
> Providus instanter hoc copulavit opus :
> Quo quisque gradiens et Christum pronus adorans,
> Effusasque preces impetrat ille suas."

* St. Venantius was a child martyred at Camerino, under Decius, in 250. Pope Clement X., who had been bishop of Camerino, had a peculiar veneration for this saint.
† This figure of the Virgin is of great interest, as introducing the Greek classical type under which she is so often afterwards represented in Latin art.

The next chapel, called the *Capella Borgia*, and used as the burial-place of that family, was once an open portico, but this character was destroyed by the building up of the intercolumniations. On its façade are a number of fragments of ancient friezes, &c. Over the inner door is a bas-relief of the Crucifixion, of 1494.

The piteous modernization of this ancient group of chapels is chiefly due to the folly of Urban VIII. The baptistery is used on Easter Eve for the ceremony of adult baptism, the recipients being called Jews.

The *Lateran* derives its name from a rich patrician family, whose estates were confiscated by Nero, when their head, Plautius Lateranus, was put to death for taking part in the conspiracy of Piso.* It afterwards became an imperial residence, and a portion of it being given by Maximianus to his daughter Fausta, second wife of Constantine, received the name of "Domus Faustæ." It was this which was given by Constantine to Pope Melchiades in 312,—a donation which was confirmed to St. Sylvester, in whose reign the first basilica was built here, and consecrated on November 9, 324, Constantine having laboured with his own hands at the work. This basilica was overthrown by an earthquake in 896, but was rebuilt by Sergius III. (904—11), being then dedicated to St. John the Baptist. This second basilica, whose glories are alluded to by Dante,—

———"Quando Laterano
Alle cose mortale andò di sopra."
Paradiso, xxxi.

---

* It was near the Lateran, on the site of the gardens of Plautius Lateranus, that the famous statues of the Niobedes, attributed to Scopus, now at Florence, were found. The fine tomb of the Plautii is a striking object on the road to Tivoli.

was of the greatest interest, but was almost entirely destroyed by fire in 1308. It was rebuilt, only to be again burnt down in 1360, when it remained for four years in utter ruin, in which state it was seen and mourned over by Petrarch. The fourth restoration of the basilica was due to Urban V. (1362—70), but it has since undergone a series of mutilations and modernizations, which have deplorably injured it. The west front still retains the inscription "Sacrosancta Lateranensis ecclesia, Omnium urbis et orbis Ecclesiarum Mater et Caput;" the Chapter of the Lateran still takes precedence even over that of St. Peter's; and every newly elected pope comes hither for his coronation.

"St. J. Lateran est regardé comme le siége du patriarchat romain. À St. Pierre le pape est souverain pontife. À St. J. Lateran il est évêque de Rome. Quand le pape est élu, il vient à St. J. Lateran prendre possession de son siége comme évêque de Rome."—*A. Du Pays.*

The west end of the basilica is in part a remnant of the building of the tenth century, and has two quaint towers (rebuilt by Sixtus IV.) at the end of the transept, and a rich frieze of terra-cotta. The church is entered from the transept by a portico, ending in a gloomy chapel which contains a statue of Henry IV., by *Niccolo Cordieri*. The *transept*—rich in colour from its basement of varied marbles, and its upper frescoes of the legendary history of Constantine—is by far the finest part of the basilica, which, as a whole, is infinitely inferior to Sta. Maria Maggiore. The nave, consisting of five aisles, is of grand proportions, but has been hideously modernized under *Borromini*, who has enclosed all its ancient columns, except two near the tribune, in tawdry plaster piers, in front of which are huge statues of the apostles; the roof is gilt and gaudy, the tabernacle ugly and ill-proportioned,—only the ancient pavement of opus-alexandrinum is fine. Confessionals for different languages are placed here as in St. Peter's. The *Tabernacle* was erected by Urban V. in the fourteenth century. Four granite columns support a gothic canopy, decorated at its angles with canopied statuettes. Between these, on either side, are three much restored frescoes by *Berni da Siena*, those in central panels representing the Annunciation, the Crucifixion, the Coronation of the Virgin, and the Saviour as a shepherd (very beautifully treated) feeding his flock with corn. The skulls of SS. Peter and Paul are said to be preserved here. The altar encloses the greater part of the famous wooden table, saved at great risk of life from the conflagration of 1308, upon which St. Peter is supposed to have celebrated mass in the house of Pudens.* The steps of the altar (at the top of which the pope is installed) have an allegorical enamelled border with emblems of an asp, a dragon, a lion, and basilisk, in allusion to Psalm xci.

In the confession, in front of the altar, is the bronze tomb of Martin V., Oddone Colonna (1417—24), the wise and just pope who was elected at the Council of Constance to put an end to the schism which had long divided the papacy, and which had almost reduced the capital of the Church to ruins. A bronze slab bears his figure, in low-relief, and is a fine work of *Antonio Filarete*, author of the bronze doors at St. Peter's. It bears the appropriate surname which was given to this justly-loved pope— "Temporum suorum felicitas."

The tribune is of the time of Nicholas IV. (1287—1292). Above the arch is a grand mosaic head of the Saviour,

---

* See Sta. Pudenziana, ch. x.

attributed to the time of Constantine, and evidently of the fourth century,—of great interest on this spot, as commemorating the vision of the Redeemer, who is said to have appeared here on the day of the consecration of the church by Sylvester and Constantine, looking down upon the people, and solemnly hallowing the work with his visible presence. The head, which is grand and sad in expression, is surrounded by six-winged seraphim. Below is an ornamented cross, above which hovers a dove—from whose beak, running down the cross, flow the waters which supply the four rivers of Paradise. The disciples, as harts (panting for the water-brooks) and sheep, flock to drink of the waters of life. In the distance is the New Jerusalem, within which the Phœnix, the bird of eternity, is seated upon the tree of Life, guarded by an angel with a two-edged sword. Beside the cross stand, on the left, the Virgin with her hand resting on the head of the kneeling pope, Nicholas IV. ; St. Peter with a scroll inscribed, " Tu es Christus filius Dei vivi ;" St. Paul with a scroll inscribed, "Salvatorem expectamus Dominum Jesum." On the right St. John the Baptist, St. John the Evangelist, St. Andrew (all with their names). Between the first and second of these figures are others, on a smaller scale, of St. Francis and St. Anthony of Padua. All these persons are represented as walking in a flowery Paradise, in which the souls of the blessed are besporting, and in front of which flows the Jordan. Below, between the windows, are figures of prophets, and (very small) of two Franciscans, who were the artists of the lower portion of the mosaic, as is shown by the inscriptions, " Jacobus Turriti, pictor, hoc opus fecit;" —" Fra Jacobus de Camerino socius magistri.".

Behind the tribune, is all that remains internally of the architecture of the tenth century, in the vaulted passage called "Portico Leonino," from its founder, Leo I. It is supported on low marble and granite columns with Ionic and Corinthian capitals. Here are collected a variety of relics of the ancient basilica. On either side of the entrance are mosaic tablets, which relate to the building of the church. Then, on the right, is a curious kneeling statue of Pope Nicholas IV., Masci (1287—92). On the left, in the centre, is an altar, above which is an ancient crucifix, and on either side tenth century statues of SS. Peter and Paul.

On the right is the entrance to the sacristy (whose inner bronze doors date from 1196), which contains an Annunciation by *Sebastian del Piombo*, and a sketch by *Raphael* for the Madonna, called "Della Casa d'Alba," now at St. Petersburg; also an ancient bas-relief, which represents the old and humble basilica of Pope Sergius. On the left, at the end of the passage, is a very handsome cinquecento ciborium, and near it the "Tabula Magna Lateranensis," containing the list of relics belonging to the church.

Near this, opening from the transept, is the *Capella del Coro*, with handsome wooden stallwork. It contains a portrait of Martin V., by *Scipione Gaetani*.

The altar of the Sacrament, which closes the transept, has four fluted bronze columns, said to have been brought from Jerusalem by Titus, and to be hollow and filled with earth from Palestine.* The last chapel in the left aisle is

* These columns are mentioned in the thirteenth century list of Lateran relics, which says that *all* the relics of the Temple at Jerusalem brought by Titus, were preserved at the Lateran.

the *Corsini Chapel*, erected in 1729 in honour of St. Andrea Corsini, from designs of Alessandro Galilei. It is in the form of a Greek cross, and ranks next to the Borghese Chapel in the richness of its marble decoration. The mosaic altar-piece, representing S. Andrea Corsini, is a copy from *Guido*. The founder of the chapel, Clement XII., Lorenzo Corsini (1730—40), is buried in a splendid porphyry sarcophagus which he plundered from the Pantheon. Above it is a bronze statue of the pope.* Opposite is the tomb of Cardinal Neri Corsini, with a number of statues of the Bernini school.

Beneath the chapel is a vault lined with sarcophagi of the Corsini. Its altar is surmounted by a magnificent Pietà— in whose beautiful and impressive figures it is difficult to recognise a work of the usually coarse and theatrical artist *Bernini*.

Of the many tombs of mediæval popes which formerly existed in this basilica,† none remain, except the memorial slab and epitaph of Sylvester II., Gerbert (999—1003). This pope is said (by the chronicler Martin Polonus de Corenza) to have been a kind of magician, who obtained first the archbishopric of Rheims, then that of Ravenna, and then the papacy, by the aid of the devil, to whom, in return, he promised to belong after death. When he ascended the throne, he asked the devil how long he could reign, and the devil, as is his custom, answered by a double-entendre, " If you never enter Jerusalem, you will reign a long time." He occupied the throne for four years, one month, and ten days, when, one day, as he was officiating in the basilica of Sta. Croce in Gerusalemme, he saw that he had passed the fatal threshold, and that his death was impending. Overwhelmed with repentance, he confessed

* There is a curious mosaic portrait of Clement XII. in the Palazzo Corsini.
† Sergius III. ob. 911; Agapetus II. ob. 956; John XII. ob. 964; Sylvester II. ob. 1003; John XVIII. ob. 1009; Alexander II. ob. 1073; Pascal II. ob. 1118; Calixtus II. ob. 1124; Honorius II. ob. 1140; Celestine II. ob. 1143; Lucius II. ob. 1145; Anastasius IV. ob. 1154; Alexander III. ob. 1159; Clement III. ob. 1191; Celestine III. ob. 1198; Innocent V. ob. 1276—were buried at St. John Lateran, besides those later popes whose tombs still exist.

his backslidings before the people, and exhorted them to lay aside pride, to resist the temptations of the devil, and to lead a good life. After this he begged of his attendants to cut his body in pieces after he was dead, as he deserved, and to place it on a common cart, and bury it wherever the horses stopped of their own accord. Then was manifested the will of the Divine Providence, that repentant sinners should learn that their God preserves for them a place of pardon even in this life,— for the horses went of their own accord to St. John Lateran, where he was buried. "Since then," says Platina, "the rattling of his bones, and the sweat, or rather the damp, with which his tomb becomes covered, has always been the infallible sign and forerunner of the death of a pope"!

Against the second pillar of the right aisle, counting from the west door, is a very interesting fresco of *Giotto*, originally one of many paintings executed by him for the loggia of the adjoining papal palace, whence the benediction and "plenary indulgence" were given in the jubilee year. It represents Boniface VIII. (Benedetto Gaetani, 1294—1303), the founder of the jubilee, between two priests.

"On y voit Boniface annonçant au peuple le jubilé. Le portrait du pape doit être ressemblant. J'ai reconnu dans cette physiognomie, où il y a plus de finesse que de force, la statue que j'avais vue couchée sur le tombeau de ce pape, dans les souterrains du Vatican."—*Ampère, Voyage Dantesque.*

Opening from this aisle are several chapels. The second is that of the newly established and rich family of Torlonia, which contains a marble Pietà, by Tenerani, and some handsome modern monuments. The third is that of the Massimi (designed by Giacomo della Porta), which has, as an altar-piece, the Crucifixion by *Sermoneta*. Beyond this, in the right aisle, are several remarkable tombs of cardinals, among which is the tomb of Cardinal Guissano, who died in 1287. The painters Cav. d'Arpino and Andrea Sacchi are buried in this church.

Entered from the last chapel in the left aisle (by a door which the sacristan will open) is the beautiful twelfth century *Cloister of the Monastery*, surrounded by low arches supported on exquisite inlaid and twisted columns, above which is a lovely frieze of coloured marbles. The court thus enclosed is a garden of roses; in the centre is a well (adorned with crosses) of the tenth century, called the "Well of the Woman of Samaria." In the cloister is a collection of architectural and traditional relics, including a beautiful old white marble throne, inlaid with mosaics, a candelabrum resting on a lion, and several other exquisitely wrought details from the old basilica; also a porphyry slab upon which the soldiers are said to have cast lots for the seamless robe; columns which were rent by the earthquake of the Crucifixion; a slab, resting on pillars, shown as a measure of the height of Our Saviour,* and a smaller slab, also on pillars, of which it is said that it was once an altar, at which the officiating priest doubted of the Real Presence, when the wafer fell from his hand through the stone, leaving a round hole which still remains.

Five General Councils have been held at the Lateran, viz. :—

 I.—March 19, 1123, under Calixtus II., with regard to the Investiture.
 II.—April 18, 1139, under Innocent II., to condemn the doctrines of Arnold of Brescia and Peter de Bruys, and to oppose the antipope Anacletus II.
 III.—March 5, 1179, under Alexander III., to condemn the doc-

---

* "Ces monuments, consacrés par la tradition, n'ont pas été jugés cependant assez authentiques pour être solennellement exposés à la vénération des fidèles."— *Gourneric*.

trines of Waldenses and Albigenses, and to end the schism caused by Frederick Barbarossa.

IV.—Nov. 11, 1215, at which 400 bishops assembled under Innocent III., to condemn the Albigenses, and the heresies of the Abbot Joachim.

V.—May 3, 1512, under Julius II. and Leo X., at which the Pragmatic Sanction was abolished, and a Concordat concluded between the Pope and Francis I. for the destruction of the liberties of the Gallican Church.

It is in the basilica of the Lateran that the Church places the first meeting between St. Francis and St. Dominic.

"Une nuit, pendant que Dominique dormait, il lui sembla voir Jésus-Christ se préparant à exterminer les superbes, les voluptueux, les avares, lorsque tout-à-coup la Vierge l'apaisa en lui présentant deux hommes: l'un d'eux lui-même ; quant à l'autre, il ne le connaissait pas ; mais le lendemain, la première personne qu'il aperçut, en entrant au Latran, fut l'inconnu qui lui était apparu en songe. Il était couvert de haillons et priait avec ferveur. Dominique se précipita dans ses bras, et l'embrassant avec effusion : 'Tu es mon compagnon,' lui dit-il ; 'nous courons la même carrière, demeurons ensemble, et aucun ennemi ne prévaudra contre nous.' Et, à partir de ce moment, dit la légende, ils n'eurent plus qu'un cœur et qu'une âme dans le Seigneur. Ce pauvre, ce mendiant, était saint François d'Assise."—*Gournerie, Rome Chrétienne*

Issuing from the west door of the basilica, we find ourselves in a wide portico, one of whose five doors is a Porta Santa. At the end, is appropriately placed an ancient marble statue of Constantine, who is in the dress of a Roman warrior, bearing the *labarum*, or standard of the cross, which is here represented as a lance surmounted by the monogram of Christ. From this portico we look down upon one of the most beautiful and characteristic views in Rome. On one side are the Alban Hills, blue in morning, or purple in evening light, sprinkled with white villages of historic interest—Albano, Rocca di Papa, Marino, Frescati, Colonna; on the other side are the

Sabine Mountains, tipped with snow; in the middle distance the long, golden-hued lines of aqueducts stretch away over the plain, till they are lost in the pink haze, and nearer still are the desolate basilica of Santa Croce, the fruit gardens of the Villa Wolkonski, interspersed with rugged fragments of massive brickwork, and the glorious old walls of the city itself. The road at our feet is the Via Appia Nuova, which leads to Naples, and which immediately passes through the modern gate of Rome, known as the Porta *San Giovanni* (built in the sixteenth century by Gregory XIII.). Nearer to us, on the right, is an ancient gateway, the finest on the Aurelian wall, bricked up by Ladislaus, king of Naples, in 1408. By this gate, known as the *Porta Asinaria*, from the family of the Asinarii, Belisarius entered Rome in 505, and Totila, through the treachery of the Isaurian Guard, in 546. Here also, in 1084, Henry IV. entered Rome against Hildebrand with his anti-pope Guibert; and, a few years after, the name of the gate itself was changed to Porta Perusta, in consequence of the injuries it received from Robert Guiscard, who came to the rescue of the lawful pontiff.

The broad open space which we see beneath the steps was the favourite walk of the mediæval popes.

"The splendid palace of the Lateran reflected the rays of the evening sun, as Francis of Assisi with two or three of his disciples approached it to obtain the papal sanction for the rules of his new Order. A group of churchmen in sumptuous apparel were traversing with slow and measured steps its lofty terrace, then called 'the Mirror,' as if afraid to overtake him who preceded them, in a dress studiously simple, and with a countenance wrapped in earnest meditation. Unruffled by passion, and yet elate with conscious power, that eagle eye, and those capacious brows, announced him the lord of a dominion which might have satisfied the pride of Diogenes, and the ambition of Alexander. Since the

Tugurium was built on the Capitoline, no greater monarch had ever called the seven hills his own. But, in his pontificate, no era had occurred more arduous than that in which Innocent III. saw the mendicants of Assisi prostrate at his feet. The interruption was as unwelcome as it was abrupt ; as he gazed at the squalid dress and faces of his suitors, and observed their bare and unwashed feet, his lip curled with disdain, and sternly commanding them to withdraw, he seemed again to retire from the outer world into some of the deep recesses of that capacious mind. Francis and his companions betook themselves to prayer ; Innocent to his couch. There (says the legend) he dreamed that a palm-tree sprouted up from the ground beneath his feet, and, swiftly shooting up into the heavens, cast her boughs on every side, a shelter from the heat, and a refreshment to the weary. The vision of the night dictated the policy of the morning, and assured Innocent that, under his fostering care, the Franciscan palm would strike deep her roots, and expand her foliage on every side, in the vineyard of the Church."—*Stephens' St. Francis of Assisi.*

The western façade of the basilica, built by Alessandro Galilei in 1734, has a fine effect at a distance, but the statues of Christ and the apostles which line its parapet are too large for its proportions.

The ancient Palace of the Lateran was the residence of the popes for nearly 1000 years. Almost all the events affecting the private lives of a vast line of ecclesiastical sovereigns happened within its walls. Plundered in each successive invasion, stricken with malaria during the autumn months, and often partially burnt, it was finally destroyed by the great enemy of Roman antiquities, Sixtus V. Among the scenes which occurred within its walls, perhaps the most terrible was that when John X., the completer of the Lateran basilica, was invaded here by Marozia, who was beginning to seize the chief power in Rome, and who carried the pope off prisoner to St. Angelo, after he had seen his brother Peter murdered before his eyes in the hall of the pontifical palace.

The only remnants preserved of this famous building are the private chapel of the popes, and the end wall of their dining-hall, known as the *Triclinium*, which contains a copy, erected by Benedict XIV., of the ancient mosaic of the time of Leo III. which formerly existed here, and the remains of which are preserved in the Vatican.

"In this mosaic, Hallam (Middle Ages) sees proof that the authority of the Greek Emperor was not entirely abrogated at Rome till long after the period of papal aggrandisement by Pepin and his son, but he is warranted by no probabilities in concluding that Constantine V., whose reign began A.D. 780, is intended by the emperor kneeling with St. Peter or Pope Sylvester."—*Hemans' Ancient Christian Art.*

Professor Bryce finds two paintings in which the theory of the mediæval empire is unmistakeably set forth; one of them in Rome, the other in Florence (a fresco in the chapter-house of S. M. Novella).

"The first of these is the famous mosaic of the Lateran triclinium, constructed by Pope Leo III., about A.D. 800, and an exact copy of which, made by the order of Sixtus V., may still be seen over against the façade of St. John Lateran. Originally meant to adorn the state banqueting-hall of the popes, it is now placed in the open air, in the finest situation in Rome, looking from the brow of a hill across the green ridges of the Campagna to the olive groves of Tivoli and the glistering crags and snow-capped summits of the Umbrian and Sabine Apennine. It represents in the centre Christ surrounded by the apostles, whom He is sending forth to preach the gospel; one hand is extended to bless, the other holds a book with the words 'Pax vobis.' Below and to the right Christ is depicted again, and this time sitting: on His right hand kneels Pope Sylvester, on His left the Emperor Constantine; to the one He gives the keys of heaven and hell, to the other a banner surmounted by a cross. In the group on the opposite, that is, on the left side of the arch, we see the Apostle Peter seated, before whom in like manner kneel Pope Leo III. and Charles the Emperor; the latter wearing, like Constantine, his crown. Peter, himself grasping the keys, gives to Leo the pallium of an archbishop, to Charles the banner of the Christian army. The inscription is 'Beatus Petrus dona vitam Leoni P. Pet victoriam Carulo regi dona ;' while round the arch is written, 'Gloria in excelsis Deo,' et in terra pax omnibus bonæ voluntatis.'

"The order and nature of the ideas here symbolized is sufficiently clear. First comes the revelation of the gospel, and the divine commission to gather all men into its fold. Next, the institution, at the memorable era of Constantine's conversion, of the two powers by which the Christian people is to be respectively taught and governed. Thirdly, we are shown the permanent Vicar of God, the apostle who keeps the keys of heaven and hell, re-establishing these same powers on a new and firmer basis. The badge of ecclesiastical supremacy he gives to Leo as the spiritual head of the faithful on earth, the banner of the Church militant to Charles, who is to maintain her cause against heretics and infidels."—*J. Bryce, Holy Roman Empire*, ch. vii. pp. 117, 118, 3rd ed., 1871.

In the building behind the Triclinium, attached to a convent of Passionist monks, and erected by Fontana for Sixtus V., is preserved *the Santa Scala*. This famous staircase, supposed to be that of the house of Pilate, ascended and descended by our Saviour, is said to have been brought from Jerusalem by Helena, mother of Constantine the Great, and has been regarded with especial reverence by the Roman Church for 1500 years. In 897 it was injured and partially thrown down by an earthquake, but was re-erected in the old Lateran palace, whence it was removed to its present site on the demolition of that venerable building. Clement XII. caused the steps to be covered by a wooden casing, which has since been repeatedly worn out by the knees of ascending pilgrims. Apertures are left, through which the marble steps can be seen; two of them are said to be stained with the blood of the Saviour!

At the foot of the stairs, within the atrium, are fine sculptures of *Giacometti*, representing the "Ecce Homo,"—and the "Kiss of Judas," purchased and placed here by Pius IX.

Between these statues the pilgrims kneel to commence the ascent of the Santa Scala. The effect of the staircase (especially on Fridays in Lent, and most of all on Good Friday), with the figures ascending on their knees in the dim light, and the dark vaulted ceiling covered with faded frescoes, is exceedingly picturesque.

"Reason may condemn, but feeling cannot resist the claim to reverential sympathy in the spectacle daily presented by the Santa Scala. Numerous indulgences have been granted by different popes to those who ascend it with prayer at each step. Whilst kneeling upon these stairs public penance used to be performed in the days of the Church's more rigorous discipline; as the saintly matron Fabiola there appeared a penitent before the public gaze, in sackcloth and ashes, A.D. 390. . . . . . There is no day on which worshippers may not be seen slowly ascending those stairs; but it is during Holy Week the concourse is at its height; and on Good Friday I have seen this structure completely covered by the multitude, like a swarm of bees settling on flowers!"—*Hemans' Ancient Sacred Art.*

"Brother Martin Luther went to accomplish the ascent of the Santa Scala—the Holy Staircase—which once, they say, formed part of Pilate's house. He slowly mounted step after step of the hard stone, worn into hollows by the knees of penitents and pilgrims. An indulgence for a thousand years—indulgence from penance—is attached to this act of devotion. Patiently he crept half-way up the staircase, when he suddenly stood erect, lifted his face heavenward, and, in another moment, turned and walked slowly down again.

"He said that, as he was toiling up, a voice as if from heaven, seemed to whisper to him the old, well-known words, which had been his battle-cry in so many a victorious combat,—'The just shall live by faith.'

"He seemed awakened, as if from a nightmare, and restored to himself. He dared not creep up another step; but, rising from his knees, he stood upright, like a man suddenly loosed from bonds and fetters, and with the firm step of a freeman, he descended the staircase, and walked from the place."—*Schönberg-Cotta Chronicles.*

"Did the feet of the Saviour actually tread these steps? Are these reliques really portions of his cross, crown of thorns, &c., or is all this fictitious? To me it is all one.

"'He is not here, he is risen!' said the angel at the tomb. The

worship of the bodily covering which the spirit has cast off belongs to the soul still in the larva condition; and the ascending of the Scala Santa on the knees is too convenient a mode for obtaining the forgiveness of sins, and at the same time a hindrance upon the only true way."
—*Frederika Bremer.*

Ascending one of the lateral staircases—no *foot* must touch the Santa Scala—we reach the outside of the *Sancta Sanctorum*, a chapel held so intensely sacred that none but the pope can officiate at its altar, and that it is *never* open to others, except on the morning before Palm Sunday, when the canons of the Lateran come hither to worship, in solemn procession, with torches and a veiled crucifix, and, even then, none but the clergy are allowed to pass its threshold. The origin of the sanctuary is lost in antiquity, but it was the private chapel of the mediæval popes in the old palace, and is known to have existed already, dedicated to St. Laurence, in the time of Pelagius I. (578—590), who deposited here some relics of St. Andrew and St. Luke. It was restored by Honorius III. in 1216, and almost rebuilt by Nicholas III. in 1277.

It is permitted to gaze through a grating upon the picturesque glories of the interior, which are chiefly of the thirteenth century. The altar is in a recess, supported by two porphyry columns. Above it a beautiful silver tabernacle, presented by Innocent III. (1198—1216), to contain the great relic, which invests the chapel with its peculiar sanctity,—a portrait of our Saviour (placed here by Stephen III. in 752), held by the Roman Church as authentic,—to have been begun by St. Luke and finished by an angel, whence the name by which it is known, "Acheirotopeton," or, the "picture made without hands."

"The different theories as to the acheirotopeton picture, and the manner in which it reached this city, are stated with naïveté by Maroni—. *i.e.*, that the apostles and the Madonna, meeting after the ascension, resolved to order a portrait of the Crucified, for satisfying the desire of the faithful, and commissioned St. Luke to execute the task ; that after three days' prayer and fasting, such a portrait was drawn in outline by that artist, but, before he had begun to colour, the tints were found to have been filled in by invisible hands; that this picture was brought from Jerusalem to Rome, either by St. Peter, or by Titus (together with the sacred spoils of the temple); or else expedited hither in a miraculous voyage of only twenty-four hours by S. Germanus, patriarch of Constantinople, who desired thus to save such a treasure from the outrages of the Iconoclasts ; and that, about A.D. 726, Pope Gregory II., apprised of its arrival at the mouth of the Tiber by revelation, proceeded to carry it thence, with due escort, to Rome ; since which advent it has remained in the Sancta Sanctorum."—*Hemans' Mediæval Christian Art.*

Above the altar is, in gilt letters, the inscription, " non est in tota sanctior urbe locus." Higher up, under gothic arches, and between twisted columns, are pictures of sainted popes and martyrs, but these have been so much retouched as to have lost their interest. The gratings here are those of the relic chamber, which contains the reputed sandals of Our Saviour, fragments of the true cross, &c. On the ceiling is a grand mosaic,—a head of Our Saviour within a nimbus, sustained by six-winged seraphim—ascribed to the eighth century. The sill in front of the screen is covered with money, thrown in as offerings by the pilgrims.

The chapel was once much larger. Its architect was probably Deodatus Cosmati. An inscription near the door tells us, " Magister Cosmatus fecit hoc opus."

Here, in the time when the Lateran palace was inhabited, the feet of twelve sub-deacons were annually washed by the pope on Holy Thursday. On the Feast of the Assumption the sacred picture used to be borne in triumph through the city, halting in the Forum, where the feet of the pope were washed in perfumed waters on the steps of Sta. Maria Nuova, and the "Kyrie Eleison" was chaunted a hundred times. This custom was abolished by Pius V. in 1566.

The *Modern Palace of the Lateran* was built from designs of Fontana by Sixtus V. In 1693 Innocent XII. turned it into a hospital,—in 1438 Gregory XVI. appropriated it as a museum. The entrance faces the obelisk in the Piazza di San Giovanni. The palace is always shown, but the terrible cold which pervades it makes it a dangerous place except in the late spring months, and a visit to it is often productive of fever.

The ground floor is the principal receptacle for antiquities, found at Rome within the last few years. It contains a number of very beautiful sarcophagi and bas-reliefs.

Entering under the corridor on the right, the most remarkable objects are :—

1*st Room.*—
LEFT WALL :
Relief of the Abduction of Helen.
RIGHT WALL :
High relief of two pugilists, 'Dares and Entellus.'
Grand relief of Trajan followed by senators, from the Forum of Trajan.
The sacred oak of Jupiter, with figures.
Bust of Marcus Aurelius.

2*nd Room.*—
Beautiful architectural fragments, chiefly from the Forum of Trajan.

3*rd Room.*—
ENTRANCE WALL :
Statue of Æsculapius.
RIGHT WALL :
Statue of Antinous, called the Braschi, found at Palestrina.

Bought from the Braschi family by Gregory XVI. for 12,000 scudi.

WALL OF EGRESS:
Sarcophagus of a child, with a relief representing pugilists.

4th Room.—

ENTRANCE WALL:
Greek relief of Medea and the daughters of Peleus.
Above (one of a number of busts), 762. Beautiful head of a Dryad.
Statue of Germanicus.

RIGHT WALL:
Statue of Mars.

WALL OF EGRESS:
Copy of the Faun of Praxiteles.

IN THE CENTRE:
A fine vase of Lumachella.

A passage is crossed to the

5th Room.—

IN THE CENTRE:
1. Sacrifice of Mithras.
2. A stag of basalt.
3. A cow.

RIGHT WALL:
Sepulchral urn, with a curious relief representing children and cock-fighting.

6th Room.—

An interesting collection of statues, from Cervetri (Cære), including those of Tiberius and Claudius; between them Agrippina, sixth wife of Claudius,—and others less certain.

BETWEEN THE WINDOWS:
Drusilla, sister of Claudius, and, on the wall, part of her epitaph.

7th Room.—

RIGHT WALL:
Faun dancing,—found near Sta. Lucia in Selce.

FACING THE ENTRANCE :
A grand statue of Sophocles (the gem of the collection), found at Terracina, 1838. Given by the Antonelli family.

"Sophocle, dans une pose aisée et fière, un pied en avant, un bras enveloppé dans son manteau qu'il serre contre son corps, contemple avec une majestueuse sérénité la nature humaine et la domine d'un regard sûr et tranquille."—*Ampère, Hist. Rom.* iii. 573.

8th *Room.*—
Statue of Neptune, from Porto—the legs and arms restored.

9th *Room.*—
Architectural fragments from the Via Appia and Forum.

10th *Room.*—
A series of interesting reliefs, found 1848, at the tomb of the Aterii at Centocelloe, representing the preparations for the funeral solemnities of a great Roman lady.

ENTRANCE WALL :
The building of the sepulchre. A curious machine for raising heavy stones is introduced.

RIGHT WALL :
The body of the dead surrounded by burning torches, the mourners tearing their hair and beating their breasts.

WALL OF EGRESS :
Showing several Roman buildings which the funeral procession would pass,—among them the Coliseum and the Arch of Titus—inscribed, "Arcus in sacra via summa."

Signor Rosa has considered this last relief of great importance, as indicating by the different monuments the route which a well-ordered funeral procession ought to pursue.

A second passage is crossed to the

11th *Room.*—
Containing several fine sarcophagi.

12th *Room.*—
ENTRANCE WALL :
Sarcophagus, with the story of Orestes.

RIGHT WALL :
Sarcophagus decorated with Cupids bearing garlands, and supporting a head of Augustus.

WALL OF EGRESS:
: Sarcophagus representing the destruction of the children of Niobe.

13*th Room.*—
ENTRANCE WALL:
: Statue of C. Lælius Saturninus.

IN THE CENTRE:
: Sarcophagus of P. Cæcilius Vallianus, representing a funeral banquet.

LEFT WALL:
: Unfinished statue of a captive barbarian, with sculptor's marks remaining, to guide the workman's chisel.

15*th Room.*—
This and the next room are devoted to objects recently found in the excavations at Ostia.

LEFT WALL:
: Mosaic in a niche.

16*th Room.*—
IN THE CENTRE:
: Reclining statue of Atys.

RIGHT WALL:
: Frescoes of the story of Orpheus and Eurydice, from a tomb at Ostia.

The *Christian Museum,* founded by Pius IX., and arranged by Padre Marchi and the Cavaliere Rossi, is of great interest. In the first hall is a statue of Christ by *Sosnowsky,* and in the wall behind it three mosaics,—two from the catacombs, that in the centre—of Christ with SS. Peter and Paul—from the old St. Peter's. Hence we ascend a staircase lined with Christian sarcophagi. At the foot are two statues of the Good Shepherd.

"Une des compositions de Calamis ne doit pas être oubliée à Rome, car ce sujet païen a été adopté par l'art chrétien des premiers temps. Les représentations du *Bon Pasteur rapportant la brebis,* expressions touchante de la miséricorde divine, ont leur origine dans le *Mercure porte-bélier* (Criophore). Quelquefois c'est un *berger* qui porte un bélier, une brebis ou un agneau ; l'on se rapproche ainsi a l'idée du *bon pasteur*. En général, le bon pasteur, dans les monuments chrétiens, porte une *brebis*, la brebis égarée de l'Évangile ; mais quelquefois aussi il porte *un bélier*, et alors le souvenir de l'original païen dans la composition chrétienne est manifeste."—*Ampère, Hist. Rom.* iii. 256.

The sarcophagus on the left, which tells the story of Jonah, is especially fine. The corridor above is also lined with sarcophagi. The best are on the left ; of these the most remarkable are, the 1st, the marriage at Cana ; 4th, the Good Shepherd repeated several times among vines, with cherubs gathering the grapes ; 7th, a sarcophagus with a canopy supported by two pavonazzetto columns, and on the wall behind, frescoes of the Good Shepherd, &c. At the raised end of the corridor is the seated statue of Hippolytus, Bishop of Porto in the third century (the upper part a restoration), found in the Catacomb of Sta. Cyriaca, and moved hither from the Vatican Library ; upon the chair is engraved the celebrated Paschal Calendar, which is supposed to settle the unorthodoxy of those early Christians who kept Easter at the same time as the Jews.

Hence, three rooms lined with drawings from the paintings in the different catacombs, lead to,—

THE PICTURE GALLERY.

1*st Room.*—

ENTRANCE WALL:
  Cartoon of stoning of Stephen : *Giulio Romano.*

Below this is the celebrated mosaic called *Asarotos*, representing an unswept floor after a banquet. It is inscribed with the name of its artist, *Heraclitus*, but is a copy from one of the two famous mosaics of Sosus of Pergamus (the other is " Pliny's Doves "). It was found on the Aventine in 1833 in the gardens of Servilius, and " probably adorned a dining-room where Cæsar may have supped with Servilia, the sister of

Cato, and mother of Brutus." A similar pavement is alluded to by Statius :—
> "Varias ubi picta per artes
> Gaudet humus superare novis asarota figuris."
> *Sylv.* i. 3, 55.

LEFT WALL:
    Christ and St. Thomas—a cartoon: *Camuccini.*

WINDOW WALL:
    The first sketch for the famous fresco of the Descent from the Cross at the Trinità de' Monti: *Daniele da Volterra.*

On the right is the entrance of the

2nd Room.—

ENTRANCE WALL:
    Annunciation: *Cav. d'Arpino.*

RIGHT WALL:
    George IV. of England (most strangely out of place): *Lawrence.*

WALL OF EGRESS:
    Assumption of the Virgin: *After Guercino.*

From the corner of this room, on the right, a staircase leads to a gallery, whence one may look down upon the huge and hideous mosaic pavement—with portraits of twenty-eight athletes—found in the Baths of Caracalla in 1822.

> "Les gladiateurs de la mosaïque de Saint Jean de Latran ont reçu la forte alimentation qu'on donnait à leurs pareils; ils ont bien cet air de résolution brutale que devaient avoir ceux qui prononçaient ce féroce serment que nous a conservé Pétrone: 'Nous jurons d'obéir à nôtre maître Eumolpe, qu'il nous ordonne de nous laisser brûler, enchainer, frapper, tuer par le fer ou autrement; et comme vrais gladiateurs, nous dévouons à notre maître nos corps et nos vies.'"—*Ampère, Hist. Rom.* iv. 33.

On the left of 1st room is the

3rd Room.—

ENTRANCE WALL:
    Madonna with SS. Peter, Dominic, and Anthony on the right,

and SS. John Baptist, Laurence, and Francis on the left: *Marco Palmezzano di Forli*, 1537.

IN THE LEFT CORNER:
Madonna and Saints: *Carlo Crivelli*, 1482.

LEFT WALL:
St. Thomas receiving the girdle of the Virgin (the Sacra Cintola of Prato)—with a predella: *Benozzo Gozzoli*.

WALL OF EGRESS:
Madonna with St. John Baptist and St. Jerome: *Palmezzano*.

4th Room.—

ENTRANCE WALL:
Sixtus V. as Cardinal: *Sassoferrato*.
Madonna: *Carlo Crivelli*, 1482—very highly finished.

LEFT WALL:
Sixtus V. as Pope: *Domenichino* (?).
Two Gobelins from pictures of Fra Bartolommeo at the Quirinal.

WALL OF EGRESS:
Christ with the Tribute Money: *Caravaggio*.

5th Room.—

ENTRANCE WALL:
Entombment: *Venetian School*.

LEFT WALL:
Greek Baptism: *Pietro Nocchi*, 1840.

WALL OF EGRESS:
Holy Family: *Andrea del Sarto*.

6th Room.—

ENTRANCE WALL:
Baptism of Christ: *Cesare da Sesto*.

LEFT WALL:
SS. Agnes and Emerentiana: *Luca Signorelli*; Annunciation: *F. Francia*; SS. Laurence and Benedict (very peculiar, as scarcely showing their faces at all, but magnificent in colour): *Luca Signorelli*.

WALL OF EGRESS:
Coronation of the Virgin, with wings, of saints, angels, and doves: *F. Filippo Lippi*.

BETWEEN THE WINDOWS: S. Jerome, in tempera: *Giovanni Sanzio, father of Raphael.*

7th Room.—
ENTRANCE WALL:
Pagan sacrifice: *Caravaggio* (?).
LEFT WALL:
Altar-piece by Antonio da Murano, 1464.
WALL OF EGRESS:
Christ at Emmaus: *Caravaggio.*

8th Room.—
An oil copy of the fresco of the Flagellation of St. Andrew by Domenichino, at S. Gregorio.

9th Room.—
A set of beautiful terracotta busts and reliefs by *Pettrich,* illustrative of North American Indian life. This room is called the Hall of Council, and is surrounded by fresco portraits of popes, and pictures allegorical of their arms, &c.

The walls of the open galleries on this floor of the palace have been covered with early Christian inscriptions from the catacombs, which have been thus arranged in arches:—

1—3. Epitaphs of martyrs and others of temp. Damasus I. (366 to 384).
4—7. Dated inscriptions from 238 to 557.
8—9. Inscriptions relating to doctrine.
10.—Inscriptions relating to popes, presbyters, and deacons.
11—12. Inscriptions relating to simple ecclesiastics.
13.—Inscriptions of affection to relations and friends.
14—16. Symbolical.
17.—Simple epitaphs from different catacombs.

On the third floor of the palace are casts from the bas-reliefs on the column of Trajan.

Before leaving the Lateran altogether, we must notice amongst its early institutions, the famous school of music which existed here throughout the middle ages.

"Gregory the Great, whose object it seems to have been to render religion a thing of the senses, was the founder of the music of the Church. He instituted the school for it in the Lateran, whence the Carlovingian monarchs obtained teachers of singing and organ-playing. The Frankish monks were sent thither for instruction."—*Dyer's Hist. of the City of Rome.*

Opposite the palace is the entrance of the *Villa Massimo Arsoli*, to which admission may be obtained by a permesso given at the Palazzo Massimo alle Colonne. There is little to see here, however, except a casino beautifully decorated with scenes taken from the great Italian poets by the modern German artists, Schnorr, Kock, Ph. Veit, Overbeck, and Führich.

"Les sujets sont tirés de Dante, de l'Arioste, et du Tasse. Dante a été confidé à Cornélius, l'Arioste à Schnorr, le Tasse à Overbeck, les trois plus célèbres noms de cette école qui croit pouvoir remonter par une imitation savante à la naïveté du xve. siècle."—*Ampère, Voyage Dantesque.*

Leading from the Piazza di San Giovanni to Sta. Maria Maggiore is the Via Immerulana, where, in the hollow, is the strange-looking *Church of SS. Pietro e Marcellino*, in which is preserved a miraculous painting of the Crucifixion; the figure upon the cross is supposed to move the eyes, when regarded by the faithful. This picture, a small replica of the magnificent Guido at S. Lorenzo in Lucina, is shown, behind a grille, by a nun of Sta. Theresa, veiled from head to foot in blue, like an immovable pillar of blue drapery.

"SS. Pietro e Marcellino stands in the valley behind the Esquiline, in the long, lonely road between Sta. Maria Maggiore and the Lateran. SS. Peter Exorcista and Marcellinus are always represented together in priestly habits, bearing their palms. Their legend relates, that in the persecution under Diocletian they were cast into prison. Artemius, keeper of the dungeon, had a daughter named Paulina, and she fell sick; and St. Peter offered to restore her to health, if her father would believe in the true God. And the jailer mocked him, saying, 'If I put thee into the deepest dungeon, and load thee with heavier chains, will thy God deliver thee? If he doth, I will believe in him.' And Peter answered, 'Be it so, not out of regard to thee; for it matters little to our God whether such an one as thou believe in him or not, but that the name of Christ may be glorified, and thyself confounded.'

"And in the middle of the night Peter and Marcellinus, in white shining garments, entered the chamber of Artemius as he lay asleep, who, being struck with awe, fell down and worshipped the name of Christ; and he, his wife, daughter, and three hundred others, were baptized. . After this the two holy men were condemned to die for the faith, and the executioner was ordered to lead them to a forest three miles from Rome, that the Christians might not discover their place of sepulture. And when he had brought them to a solitary thicket overgrown with brambles and thorns, he declared to them that they were to die, upon which they cheerfully fell to work and cleared away a space fit for the purpose, and dug the grave in which they were to be laid. Then they were beheaded (June 2), and died encouraging each other.

"The fame of SS. Pietro e Marcellino is not confined to Rome. In the reign of Charlemagne they were venerated as martyrs throughout Italy and Gaul; and Eginhard, the secretary of Charlemagne who married his daughter Emma, is said to have held them in particular honour. Every one, I believe, knows the beautiful story of Eginhard and Emma,—and the connection of these saints with them, as their chosen protectors, lends an interest to their solitary deserted church. In the Roma Sotterranea of Bosio, p. 126, there is an ancient fragment found in the catacombs, which represents St. Peter Exorcista, St. Marcellinus, and Paulina, standing together."—*Mrs. Jameson.*

Behind the Santa Scala, a narrow lane leads to the *Villa Wolkonski* (a "permesso" may be obtained through your banker), a most beautiful garden, running along the edge of the hill, intersected by the broken arches of the Aqua Claudia, and possessing exquisite views over the Campagna, with its lines of aqueducts to the Alban and Sabine mountains. *No one should omit to visit this villa.*

"Where the aqueducts, just about to enter the city, most nearly converge, and looking across the Campagna—which their arches only seem able to span—towards Albano and the hills, stands the Villa. Embosomed in olive and in ilex trees, it is rich in hoar cypresses, in urns, and in those pathetic fragments of old workmanship which an undergrowth of violets and acanthus half hides, and half reveals."—*Vera*.

About a mile beyond the Porta S. Giovanni, a road branches off on the left to the *Porta Furba*, an arch of the Aqua Felice, founded on the line of the Claudian and Marcian aqueducts. Artists may find a picturesque subject here in a pretty fountain, with a portion of the decaying aqueduct. Beyond the arch is the mound called *Monte del Grano*, which has been imagined to be the burial-place of Alexander Severus. Beyond this, the road (to Frescati) passes on the left the vast ruins, called *Sette Bassi*.

The direct road—which leads to Albano—reaches, about two miles from the gate, a queer building, called the Casa del Diavolo, on the outside of which some rude frescoes testify to the popular belief as to its owner. Just beyond this a field track on the left leads to the *Via Latina*, of which a certain portion, paved with huge polygonal blocks of lava, is now laid bare. Here are some exceedingly interesting and well-preserved tombs, richly ornamented with painting and stucco. The view, looking back upon Rome, or forward to the long line of broken arches of the Claudian aqueduct, seen between these ruined sepulchres, is most striking and beautiful.

Close by have been discovered remains of a villa of the Servilii, which afterwards belonged to the Asinarii. Here also, in 1858 (on the left of the Via Latina), Signor Fortunati discovered the long buried and forgotten *Basilica of S. Stefano*. It is recorded by Anastasius that this basilica was founded in the time of Leo I. (440—461) by Demetria, a lady who escaped from the siege by the Goths, with her mother, to Carthage, where she became a nun. It was restored by Leo III. at the end of the eighth century. The remains are interesting, though they do little more than show perfectly the substruction and plan of the ancient building. An inscription relating to the foundation of the church by Demetria has been found among the ruins.

Not far from this is the *Catacomb of the Santi-Quattro.*

Three and a half miles from Rome is the Osteria of *Tavolato*, near which is one of the most striking and picturesque portions of the Claudian Aqueduct. It is on the rising ground between this aqueduct and the road, that the *Temple of Fortuna Muliebris* is believed to have stood. This was the temple which Valeria, the sister of Publicola, and Volumnia, the mother of Coriolanus, claimed to erect at their own expense, when the senate asked them to choose their recompense for having preserved Rome by their entreaties.

"As Valeria, sister of Publicola, was sitting in the temple, as a suppliant before the image of Jupiter, Jupiter himself seemed to inspire her with a sudden thought, and she immediately rose, and called upon all the other noble ladies who were with her, to arise also, and she led them to the house of Volumnia, the mother of Caius (Coriolanus). There she found Virgilia, the wife of Caius, with his mother, and also his little children. Valeria then addressed Volumnia and Virgilia, and said, 'Our coming here to you is our own doing; neither the senate nor any mortal man have sent us; but the god in whose temple we were sitting as suppliants put it into our hearts, that we should come and ask you to join with us, women with women, without any aid of men, to win for our country a great deliverance, and for ourselves a name, glorious above all women, even above those Sabine wives in the old time, who stopped the battle between their husbands and their fathers. Come, then, with us to the camp of Caius, and let us pray to him to show us mercy.' Volumnia said, 'We will go with you:' and Virgilia took her young children with her, and they all went to the camp of the enemy.

"It was a sad and solemn sight to see this train of noble ladies, and the very Volscian soldiers stood in silence as they passed by, and pitied them and honoured them. They found Caius sitting on the general's seat, in the midst of the camp, and the Volscian chiefs were standing round him. When he first saw them he wondered what it could be; but presently he knew his mother, who was walking at the head of the train, and then he could not contain himself, but leapt down from his seat, and ran to meet her, and was going to kiss her. But she stopped him, and said, 'Ere thou kiss me, let me know whether I am speaking to an enemy or to my son; whether I stand in thy camp as thy prisoner or thy mother?' Caius could not answer her; and then she went on and said, 'Must it be, then, that had I never borne a son, Rome never would have seen the camp of an enemy; that had I remained childless, I should have died a free woman in a free city? But I am too old to bear much longer either thy shame or my misery. Rather look to thy wife and children, whom, if thou persistest, thou art dooming to an untimely death, or a long life of bondage.' Then Virgilia and his children came up to him and kissed him, and all the noble ladies wept, and bemoaned their own fate and the fate of their country. At last Caius cried out, 'O mother, what hast thou done to me?' and he wrung her hand vehemently, and said, 'Mother, thine is the victory; a happy victory for thee and for Rome, but shame and ruin to thy son.' Then he fell on her neck and embraced her, and he embraced his wife and his children, and sent them back to Rome; and led away the army of the Volscians, and never afterwards attacked Rome any more. The Romans, as was right, honoured Volumnia and Valeria for their deed, and a temple was built and dedicated to 'Woman's Fortune,' just on the spot where Caius had yielded to his mother's words; and the first priestess of the temple was Valeria, into whose heart Jupiter had first put the thought to go to Volumnia, and to call upon her to go out to the enemy's camp and entreat her son."—*Arnold's Hist. of Rome*, vol. i.

"Il y a peu de scènes dans l'histoire plus émouvantes que celle-là, et elle ne perd rien à la décoration du théâtre; en se plaçant sur un tertre à quatre milles de Rome, près de la voie Latine, dans un lieu où il n'y a aujourd'hui que des tombeaux et des ruines, on peut se figurer le camp des Volsques, dont les armes et les tentes étincellent au soleil. Les montagnes s'élèvent à l'horizon. A travers la plaine ardente et poudreuse défile une foule voilée dont les gémissements retentissent dans le silence de la campagne romaine. Bientôt Coriolan est entouré de cette multitude suppliante dont les plaintes, les cris, devaient avoir la vivacité des démonstrations passionnées des Romaines de nos jours. Coriolan eût résisté à tout ce bruit, il eût peut-être résisté aux larmes de sa femme et aux caresses de ses enfants ; il ne résista pas à la sévérité de sa mère.

"Le soir, par un glorieux coucher du soleil de Rome qui éclaire leur joie, la procession triomphante s'éloigne en adressant un chant de reconnaissance aux dieux, et lui se retire dans sa tente, étonné d'avoir pu céder."—*Ampère, Hist. Rom.* ii. 402.

The return drive to Rome may be varied by turning to the right about a mile beyond this, into a lane which leads past the so-called temple of Bacchus to the Via Appia Vecchia.

We may now follow the lines of white mulberry-trees across the open space in front of St. John Lateran, which is a continuation of the ancient papal promenade of "the Mirror," to Sta. Croce. The sister basilicas look at each other, and at Sta. Maria Maggiore, down avenues of trees. On the left are the walls of Rome, upon which run the arches of the Aqua Marcia.

"Few Roman churches are set within so impressive a picture as Santa Croce, approached on every side through these solitudes of vineyards and gardens, quiet roads, and long avenues of trees, that occupy such immense extent within the walls of Rome. The scene from the Lateran, looking towards this basilica across the level common, between lines of trees, with the distance of Campagna and mountains, the castellated walls, the arcades of the Claudian aqueduct, amid gardens and groves, is more than beautiful, full of memory and association. The other approach, by the unfrequented Via di Sta. Croce, presents the finest distances, seen through a foliage beyond the dusky towers of the Honorian walls, and a wide extent of slopes covered with vineyards, amid which stand at intervals some of those forlorn cottage farms, grey and dilapidated, that form characteristic features in Roman scenery. The majestic ruins of Minerva-Medica, the so-called temple of Venus and Cupid, the fragments of the Baths of St. Helena, the Castrense Amphitheatre, the arches of the aqueduct, half concealed in cypress and ivy, are objects which must increase the attractions of a walk to this sanctuary of the cross. But the exterior of the church is disappointing and inappropriate, retaining nothing antique except the square Lombardic tower of the twelfth century, in storeys of narrow-arched windows, its brickwork ornamented with disks of coloured marble, and a canopy, with columns, near the summit, for a statue no longer in its place."— *Hemans' Catholic Italy*, vol. i.

The site of the *Basilica of Sta. Croce in Gerusalemme* was once occupied by the garden of Heliogabalus, and afterwards by the palace of the Empress Helena, mother of Constantine, whose residence here was known as the Palatium Sessorianum, whence the name of Sessorian, sometimes given to the basilica.

The church was probably once a hall in the palace of Helena, to which an apse was added by Constantine, in whose reign it was consecrated by Pope Sylvester. It was repaired by Gregory II. early in the eighth century; the monastery was added by Benedict VII. about 975, and the whole was rebuilt by Lucius II. in 1144. The church was completely modernized by Benedict XIV. in the last century, and scarcely anything, except the tower, now remains externally, which is even as old as the twelfth century. The fine columns of granite and bigio-lumachellato, which now adorn the façade, were plundered from the neighbouring temple in 1744.

The interior of the church is devoid of beauty, owing to modernizations. Four out of twelve fine granite columns, which divided its nave and aisles, are boxed up in senseless plaster piers. The high altar is adorned with an urn of green basalt, sculptured with lions' heads, which contains the bodies of SS. Anastasius and Cæsarius. Two of the pillars of the baldacchino are of breccia-corallina. The fine frescoes of the tribune by *Pinturicchio* have been much retouched. They were executed under Alexander VI., on a commission from Cardinal Carvajal, who is himself represented as kneeling before the cross, which is held by the Empress Helena.

"The very important frescoes of the choir apsis of Sta. Croce (now much over-painted) are of Pinturicchio's better time. They represent the finding of the Cross, with a colossal Christ in a nimbus among angels above,—a figure full of wild grandeur."—*Kugler.*

"Near the entrance of the church is a valuable monument of the papal history of the tenth century, in a metrical epitaph to Benedict VII., recording his foundation of the adjoining monastery for monks, who were to sing day and night the praises of the Deity; his charities to the poor; and the deeds of the anti-pope Franco, called by Baronius (with play upon his assumed name Boniface) Malefacius, who usurped the Holy See, imprisoned and strangled the lawful pope, Benedict VI., and pillaged the treasury of St. Peter's, but in one month was turned out and excommunicated, when he fled to Constantinople. The chronology of this epitaph is by the ancient system of Indictions, the death of the pope dated XII. Indiction, corresponding to the year 984: and the Latin style of the tenth century is curiously exemplified in lines relating to the anti-pope:

'Hic primus repulit Franconis spurca superbi
Culmina qui invasit sedis apostolicæ
Qui dominumque suum captum in castro habebat
Carceris interea auctis constrictus in uno
Strangulatus ubi exuerat hominem.'"
Hemans' Catholic Italy.

The consecration of the Golden Rose, formerly sent to foreign princes, used to take place in this church. The principal observances here now are connected with the exhibition of the relics, of which the principal is the Title of the True Cross.

"In 1492, when some repairs were ordered by Cardinal Mendoza, a niche was discovered near the summit of the apse, enclosed by a brick front, inscribed 'Titulus Crucis.' In it was a leaden coffer, containing an imperfect plank of wood, 2 inches thick, 1½ palm long, 1 palm broad. On this, in letters more or less perfect, was the inscription in Hebrew, Greek, and Latin, *Jesus Nazarene King.* It was venerated by Innocent VIII., with the college of cardinals, and enclosed by Mendoza in the silver shrine, where it is exposed three times a year from the balcony. The relics are exposed on the 4th Sunday in Lent. On Good Friday the rites are more impressive here than in any other church, the procession of white-robed monks, and the deep toll of the bell announcing the display of the relics by the mitred abbot, are very solemn, and it is surprising, that while crowds of strangers submit to be crushed in the Sistine, scarcely one visits this ancient basilica on that day."—*Hemans' Catholic Italy.*

"The list of relics on the right of the apsis of Sta. Croce includes, the finger of St. Thomas Apostle, with which he touched the most holy side of our Lord Jesus Christ ; one of the pieces of money with which the Jews paid the treachery of Judas ; great part of the veil and of the hair of the most blessed Virgin ; a mass of cinders and charcoal, united in the form of a loaf, with the fat of St. Lawrence, martyr ; one bottle of the most precious blood of our Lord Jesus Christ ; another of the milk of the most blessed Virgin ; a little piece of the stone where Christ was born ; a little piece of the stone where our Lord sate when he pardoned Mary Magdalen ; of the stone where our Lord wrote the law, given to Moses on Mount Sinai ; of the stone where reposed SS. Peter and Paul ; of the cotton which collected the blood of Christ ; of the manna which fed the Israelites ; of the rod of Aaron, which flourished in the desert ; of the relics of the eleven prophets ! "—*Percy's Romanism.*

Two staircases near the tribune lead to the subterranean church, which has an altar with a pietà, and statues of SS. Peter and Paul of the twelfth century. Hence opens the chapel of Sta. Helena,* which women (by a perversion especially strange in this case) are never allowed to enter except on the festival of the saint, August 18. It is built upon a soil composed of earth brought by the empress from Palestine. Her statue is over the altar. The vault has mosaics (originally erected under Valentinian III., but restored by *Zucchi* in 1593) representing, in ovals, a half-length figure of

---

* Sta. Helena is claimed as an English saint, and all the best authorities allow that she was born in England,—according to Gibbon, at York—according to others, at Colchester, which town bears as its arms a cross between three crowns, in allusion to this claim. Some say that she was an innkeeper's daughter, others that her father was a powerful British prince, Coilus or Coel.

the Saviour; the Evangelists and their symbols; the Finding of the True Cross; SS. Peter and Paul; St. Sylvester, the conservator of the church; and Sta. Helena, with Cardinal Carvajal kneeling before her.

Here the feast of the "Invention of the True Cross" (May 3) is celebrated with great solemnity, when the hymns "Pange Lingua" and "Vexilla Regis" are sung, and the antiphon:—

"O Cross, more glorious than the stars, world famous, beauteous of aspect, holiest of things, which alone wast worthy to sustain the weight of the world: dear wood, dear nails, dear burden, bearing; save those present assembled in thy praise to-day. Alleluia."

And the collect:—

"O God, who by the glorious uplifting of the salvation-bearing cross, hast displayed the miracles of thy passion, grant that by the merit of that life-giving wood, we may attain the suffrages of eternal life, &c."

The adjoining *Monastery* belongs to the Cistercians. Only part of one wing is ancient. The library formerly contained many curious MSS., but most of these were lost to the basilica, when the collection was removed to the Vatican during the French occupation and the exile of Pius VII.

The garden of the monastery contains the ruin generally known as the *Temple of Venus and Cupid*, but considered by Dr Braun to be the Sessorian Basilica or law-court, where the causes of slaves (who were allowed to appeal to no other court) were wont to be heard. Behind the monastery is the *Amphitheatrum Castrense*, attributed to the time of Nero, when it is supposed to have been erected for the games of two cohorts of soldiers, quartered near here. It is ingrafted into the line of the Honorian walls, and is best seen from the outside of the city. Its arches and pillars, with Corinthian capitals, are all of brick.

(On the left of the Via Sta. Croce, which leads hence to Sta. Maria Maggiore, is the gate of the *Villa Altieri*, chiefly remarkable for its grand umbrella pine, the finest in the city. Further, on the right, is a tomb of unknown origin, now used as a farm-house and a wine-shop.)

Turning to the right from the basilica, we follow a lane which leads beneath some fine brick arches of an aqueduct of the time of Nero, cited by Ampère,* as exemplifying the perfection to which architecture attained in the reign of this emperor, " by the quality of the bricks, and the excellence and small quantity of the cement." These ruins are popularly called the Baths of Sta. Helena.

Passing these arches we find ourselves facing the *Porta Maggiore*, formed by two arches of the Claudian Aqueduct, formerly known as the Porta Labicana, and Porta Prenestina, of which the former was closed in the time of Honorius, and has never been re-opened. Three inscriptions remain, the first relating to the building of the aqueduct by the Emperor Tiberius Claudius;—the second and third to its restoration by Vespasian and Titus. Above the Aqua Claudia flowed a second stream, the Anio Novus.

Outside the gate, only lately disclosed, upon the removal of constructions of the time of Honorius (the fragments of those worth preserving are placed on the opposite wall), is the *Tomb of the Baker Eurysaces*, who was also one of the inspectors of aqueducts. The tomb is attributed to the early years of the Empire. Its first storey is surmounted by the inscription : " EST HOC MONUMENTUM MARCEI VERGILEI EVRYSACES PISTORIS REDEMPTORIS APPARET." Its second storey is composed of rows of the mortars used in baking,

---

* Emp. ii. 43.

placed sideways, and supporting a frieze with bas-reliefs telling the story of a baker's work, from the bringing of the corn into the mill to its distribution as bread. In the front of the tomb was formerly a relief of the baker and his wife, with a sarcophagus, and the inscription: "FUIT ATISTIA UXOR MIHEI—FEMINA OPTVMA VEIXSIT—QUOIVS CORPORIS RELIQUIÆ—QUOD SUPERANT SUNT IN—HOC PANARIO." This has been foolishly removed, and is now to be seen upon the opposite wall.

From this gate many pleasant excursions may be taken. The direct road leads to Palestrina by Zagarolo, and at 1½ mile from the gate passes, on the left, *Torre Pignatarra*, the tomb of Sta. Helena, whence the magnificent porphyry sarcophagus, now in the Vatican, was removed. The name is derived from the *pignatte*, or earthen pots, used in the building. Beneath it is a catacomb, now closed. The adjoining *Catacomb of SS. Pietro e Marcellino* contains some well preserved paintings; the most interesting is that of the Divine Lamb on a mound (from which four rivers flow as in the mosaics of the ancient basilicas), with figures of Petrus, Gorgonius, Marcellinus, and Tiburtius. At three miles from the gate the road reaches *Centocellæ*, whence, near the desolate tower called *Torre Pernice*, there is a most picturesque view of the aqueduct *Aqua Alexandrina*, built by Alexander Severus, with a double line of arches crossing the hollow. At five miles, on the right, is the Borghese farm of Torre Nuova, with a fine group of old stone pines.

The road which turns left from the gate leads by the *Aqua Bollicante*, where the Arvales sang their hymn, to the picturesque ruins of the *Torre dei Schiavi*, the palace of the

Emperors Gordian (A.D. 238), adjoining which are the remains of a round temple of Apollo. This is, perhaps, one of the most striking scenes in the Campagna and—backed by the violet mountains above Tivoli—is a favourite subject with artists.

"Les Gordiens, très-grands personnages, furent de très-petits empereurs. Ils montrent ce qu'était devenu l'aristocratie romaine dégénérée. Le premier, honnête et pusillanime, comme le prouvent son élection et sa mort, était un peu replet et avait dans l'air du visage quelque chose de solennel et de théâtral (*pompali vultu*). Il aimait et cultivait les lettres. Son fils également se fit quelque réputation en ce genre, grâce surtout à sa bibliothèque de soixante mille volumes; mais il avait d'autres goûts encore que celui des livres: on lui donne jusqu'à vingt-deux concubines en titre, et de chacune d'elles, il eut trois ou quatre enfants. Il menait une vie épicurienne dans ses jardins et sous des ombrages délicieux : c'étaient les jardins et les ombrages d'une villa magnifique que les Gordiens avaient sur la voie Prénestine, et dont Capitolin, au temps duquel elle existait encore, nous a laissé une description détaillée. Le péristyle était formé de deux cents colonnes des marbres les plus précieux, le cipollin, le pavonazetto, le jaune et le rouge antiques. La villa renfermait trois basiliques et les thermes que ceux de Rome surpassaient à peine. Telle était l'opulence d'une habitation privée vers le milieu du troisième siècle de l'empire."—*Ampère, Emp.* ii. 328.

The road which continues in a straight line from hence passes, on the left, the Torre Tre Teste. The eighth milestone is of historic interest, being described by Livy (v. 49) as the spot where the dictator Camillus overtook and exterminated the army of Gauls who were retreating from Rome with the spoils of the Capitol.

At the ninth mile is the *Ponte di Nono*, a magnificent old bridge with seven lofty arches of lapis-gabinus. This leads (twelve miles from Rome) to the dried-up lake and the ruins of Gabii (Castiglione), including that of the temple of Juno Gabina.

"Quique arva Gabinæ
Junonis, gelidumque Anienem, et roscida rivis
Hernica saxa colunt."
Virgil, Æn. vii. 682.

The road which branches off on the left leads (twelve miles from Rome) to *Lunghezza*, the fine old castle of the Strozzi family, situated on the little river Osa. Hence a beautiful walk through a wood leads to Castello del Osa, the ruins of the ancient *Collatia*, so celebrated from the tragedy of Lucretia. Two miles beyond the Torre dei Schiavi, on the left, is the fine castellated farm of *Cervaletto*, a property of the Borghese. A field road of a mile and half, passing in front of this (practicable for carriages), leads to another fine old castellated farm (five miles from Rome), close to which are the extraordinary *Grottoes of Cerbara*,—a succession of romantic caves of great size, in the tufa rocks, from which the material of the Coliseum was excavated. Here the "Festa degli Artisti" is held in May, which is well worth seeing,—the artists in costume riding in procession, and holding games, amid these miniature Petra-like ravines. Beyond Cerbara are remains of a villa of Lucius Verus, and, on the bank of the Anio, the romantically-situated castle of *Rustica*.

From the Porta Maggiore we may follow a lane along the inside of the wall, crossing the railway—whence there is a picturesque view of the temple of Minerva Medica—to *The Porta S. Lorenzo*, anciently called the Porta Tiburtina (the road to Tivoli passes through it), built in 402, by the Emperors Arcadius and Honorius, on the advice of Stilicho, as we learn from an inscription over the archway of the Marcian, Tepulan, and Julian Aqueducts, now half buried within the later brick gateway.

The road just beyond the gate is connected with the story of the favourite saint of the Roman people.

"When Sta. Francesca Romana had no resource but to beg for the sick under her care, she went to the basilica of S. Lorenzo fuori Mura, where was the station of the day, and seated herself amongst the crowd of beggars, who, according to custom, were there assembled. From the rising of the sun to the ringing of the vesper-bell, she sate there, side by side with the lame, the deformed, and the blind. She held out her hand as they did, gladly enduring, not the semblance, but the reality, of that deep humiliation. When she had received enough wherewith to feed the poor at home, she rose, and entering the old basilica, adored the Blessed Sacrament, and then walked back the long and weary way, blessing God all the while."—*Lady G. Fullerton.*

A quarter of a mile beyond the gate we come in sight of the church and monastery, but the effect is much spoilt by the hideous modern cemetery, formed since the following description was written :—

"S. Lorenzo is as perfect a picture of a basilica externally, as S. Clemente is internally. Viewing it from a little distance, the whole pile—in its grey reverend dignity—the row of stones indicating the atrium, with an ancient cross in the centre—the portico overshadowing faded frescoes—the shelving roof, the body-wall bulging out and lapping over, like an Egyptian temple—the detached Lombard steeple—with the magic of sun and shadow, and the background of the Campagna, bounded by the blue mountains of Tivoli—together with the stillness, the repose, interrupted only by the chirp of the grasshopper, and the distant intermitted song of the Contadino—it forms altogether such a scene as painters love to sketch, and poets to re-people with the shadows of past ages; and I open a wider heaven for either fraternity to fly their fancies in, when I add that it was there the ill-fated Peter de Courtenay was crowned Emperor of the East."—*Lord Lindsay, Christian Art.*

"To St. Laurence was given a crown of glory in heaven, and upon earth eternal and universal praise and fame; for there is scarcely a city or town in all Christendom which does not contain a church or altar dedicated to his honour. The first of these was built by Constantine outside the gates of Rome, on the spot where he was buried; and another was built on the summit of the hill, where he was martyred; besides these, there are at Rome four others; and in Spain the Escurial, and at Genoa the Cathedral."—*Mrs. Jameson.*

We have already followed St. Laurence to the various spots in Rome connected with his story,—to the green space at the Navicella, where he distributed his alms before the house of St. Cyriaca (in whose catacomb he was first buried); to the basilica in the Palace of the Cæsars, where he was tried and condemned; to S. Lorenzo in Fonte, where he was imprisoned; to S. Lorenzo Pane e Perna, where he died; to S. Lorenzo in Lucina, where his supposed gridiron is preserved; and now we come to his grave, where a grand basilica has arisen around the little oratory, erected by Constantine, which marked his first burial-place in the Catacombs.

The first basilica erected here was built in the end of the sixth century, by Pope Pelagius II., but this was repeatedly enlarged and beautified by succeeding popes, and at length was so much altered in 1216, by Honorius III., that the old basilica became merely the choir or tribune of a larger and more important church. So many other changes have since taken place, that Bunsen remarks upon S. Lorenzo as more difficult of explanation than any other of the Roman churches.

In front of the basilica stands a bronze statue of St. Laurence, upon a tall granite pillar.

The portico is supported by six Ionic columns, four of them spiral. Above these is a mosaic frieze of the thirteenth century. In the centre is the Spotless Lamb, having, on the right, St. Laurence, Honorius III., and another figure; and on the left three heads, two of whom are supposed to be the virgin martyr Sta. Cyriaca, and her mother Tryphœna, buried in the adjoining cemetery. Above this is a very richly decorated marble frieze, boldly relieved with lions' heads. The gable of the church is faced with modern mosaics of saints. Within the portico are four splendid sarcophagi; that on the left of the entrance is adorned with reliefs representing a vintage, with cupids as the vine-gatherers, and contains the remains of Pope Damasus II., who died in 1049, after a reign of only twenty-three days. At the sides of the door are two marble lions. The walls of the portico are covered with a very curious series of frescoes, lately repainted. They represent four consecutive stories.

On the right :—

A holy hermit, living a life of solitude and prayer, heard a rushing noise, and, looking out of his window, saw a troop of demons, who told him that the Emperor Henry II. had just expired, and that they were hurrying to lay claim to his soul. The hermit trembled, and besought them to let him know as they returned how they had succeeded. Some days after, they came back and narrated that when the Archangel was weighing the good and evil deeds of the emperor in his balance, the weight was falling in their favour—when suddenly the roasted St. Laurence appeared, bearing a golden chalice, which the emperor, shortly before his death, had bestowed upon the Church, and cast it into the scale of good deeds, and so turned the balance the other way, but that in revenge they had broken off one of the golden handles of the chalice. And when the hermit heard these things he rejoiced greatly; and the soul of the emperor was saved and he became a canonized saint,—and the devils departed blaspheming.

The order of the frescoes representing this legend is :—

    1, 2. Scenes in the life of Henry II.
    3. The Emperor offers the golden chalice.
    4. A banquet scene.
    5. The hermit discourses with the devils.
    6. The death of Henry II.—1024.

7. The dispute for the soul of the Emperor.
8. It is saved by St. Laurence.

The second series represents the whole story of the acts, trial, martyrdom, and burial of St. Laurence; one or two frescoes in this were entirely effaced, and have been added by the restorer. Of the old series were :—

1. The investiture of St. Laurence as deacon.
2. St. Laurence washes the feet of poor Christians.
3. He heals Sta. Cyriaca.
4. He distributes alms on the Cœlian.
5. He meets St. Sixtus led to death, and receives his blessing.
6. He is led before the prefect.
7. He restores sight to Lucillus.
8. He is scourged.
9. He baptizes St. Hippolytus.
11. He refuses to give up the treasures of the Church.
13, 14, 15. His burial by St. Hippolytus.

The third series represents the story of St. Stephen, followed by that of the translation of his relics to this basilica.

The relics of St. Stephen were preserved at Constantinople, whither they had been transported from Jerusalem by the Empress Eudoxia, wife of Theodosius II. Hearing that her daughter Eudoxia, wife of Valentinian II., Emperor of the West, was afflicted with a devil, she begged her to come to Constantinople that her demon might be driven out by the touch of the relics. The younger Eudoxia wished to comply, —but the devil refused to leave her, unless St. Stephen was brought to Rome. An agreement was therefore made that the relics of St. Stephen should be exchanged for those of St. Laurence. St. Stephen arrived, and the empress was immediately relieved of her devil, but when the persons who had brought the relics of St. Stephen from Constantinople were about to take those of St. Laurence back with them, they all fell down dead ! Pope Pelagius prayed for their restoration to life, which was granted for a short time, to prove the efficacy of prayer, but they all died again ten days after! Thus the Romans knew that it would be criminal to fulfil their promise, and part with the relics of St. Laurence, and the bodies of the two martyrs were laid in the same sarcophagus.

The frescoes in the left wall represent a separate story :—

A holy sacristan arose before the dawn to enjoy solitary prayers before the altars of this church. Once when he was thus employed, he found that he was not alone, and beheld three persons, a priest, a deacon, and sub-deacon, officiating at the altar, and the church around him filled with worshippers, whose faces bore no mortal impress. Tremblingly he drew near to him whom he dreaded the least, and inquired of the deacon, who this company might be. 'The priest whom thou seest is the blessed apostle Peter,' answered the spirit, 'and I am Laurence who suffered cruel torments for the love of my master Christ, upon a Wednesday, which was the day of his betrayal ; and in remembrance of my martyrdom we are come to-day to celebrate here the mysteries of the Church ; and the sub-deacon who is with us is the first martyr, St. Stephen,—and the worshippers are the apostles, the martyrs, and virgins who have passed with me into Paradise, and have come back hither to do me honour ; and of this solemn service thou art chosen as the witness. When it is day, therefore, go to the pope and tell what thou hast seen, and bid him, in my name, to come hither and to celebrate a solemn mass with all his clergy, and to grant indulgences to the faithful.' But the sacristan trembled and said, 'If I go to the pope he will not believe me : give me some visible sign, then, which will show what I have seen.' And St. Laurence ungirt his robe, and giving his girdle to the sacristan, bade him show it in proof of what he told. In the morning the old man related what he had seen to the abbot of the monastery, who bore the girdle to the then pope, Alexander II. The pope accompanied him back to the basilica,— and on their way they were met by a funeral procession, when, to test the powers of the girdle, the pope laid it on the bier, and at once the dead arose and walked. Then all men knew that the sacristan had told what was true, and the pope celebrated mass as he had been bidden, and promised an indulgence of forty years to all who should visit on a Wednesday any church dedicated to St. Laurence.

This story is told in eight pictures :—

1. The sacristan sees the holy ones.
2. The Phantom Mass.
3. The sacristan tells the abbot.
4. The abbot tells the pope.
5. The pope consults his cardinals.
6. The dead is raised by the girdle.

7. Mass is celebrated at St. Lorenzo, and souls are freed from purgatory by the intercession of the saint.
8. Prayer is made at the shrine of St. Laurence.

The nave—which is the basilica of Honorius III.—is divided from its side aisles by twenty-two Ionic columns of granite and cipollino. The sixth column on the right has a lizard and a frog amongst the decorations of its capital, which led Winckelmann to the supposition that these columns were brought hither from the Portico of Octavia, because Pliny describes that the architects of the Portico of Metellus, which formerly occupied that site, were two Spartans, named Sauros and Batrachus, who implored permission to carve their names upon their work; and that when leave was refused, they introduced them under this form,—Batrachus signifying a frog, and Sauros a lizard.

Above the architrave are frescoes by *Fracassini*, of the lives and martyrdoms of SS. Stephen and Laurence. Higher up are saints connected with the history of the basilica. The roof is painted in patterns. The splendid opus-alexandrinum pavement is of the tenth century. On the left of the entrance is a baptismal font, above which are more frescoes relating to the story of St. Laurence. On the right, beneath a mediæval canopy, is a very fine sarcophagus, sculptured with a wedding scene,—adapted as the tomb of Cardinal Fieschi, nephew of Innocent IV., who died in 1256. Inside the canopy, is a fresco of Christ throned, to whom St. Laurence presents the cardinal, and St. Stephen Innocent IV. Behind stand St. Eustace and St. Hippolytus. The west end of the church is closed by the inscription, " Hi sunt qui venerunt de tribulatione magna, et laverunt stolas suas in sanguine agni."

The splendid ambones in the nave, inlaid with serpentine and porphyry, are of the twelfth century. That on the right, with a candelabrum for the Easter candle, was for the gospel ; that on the left for the epistle.

At the end of the left aisle, a passage leads down to a subterranean chapel, used for prayer for the souls in purgatory. Here is the entrance to the *Catacombs of Sta. Ciriaca*, which are said to extend as far as Sant' Agnese, but which have been much and wantonly injured in the works for the new cemetery. Here the body of St. Laurence is related to have been found. Over the entrance is inscribed :—

"Hæc est tumba illa toto orbe terrarum celeberrima ex cimeterio S. Cyriacæ Matronæ ubi sacrum si quis fecerit pro defunctis eorum animas e purgatorii pœnis divi Laurentii meritis evocabit." *

Passing the triumphal arch, we enter the early basilica of Pope Pelagius II. (572—590), which is on a lower level than that of the nave. Here are twelve splendid columns of pavonazzetto, of which the two first bear trophies carved above the acanthus leaves of their capitals. These support an entablature formed from various antique fragments, put together without uniformity,—and a triforium, divided by twelve small columns.

On the inside, which was formerly the outside, of the triumphal arch, is a restored mosaic of the time of Pelagius, representing the Saviour seated upon the world, having on the right St. Peter, St. Laurence, and St. Pelagius, and on the left St. Paul and St. Stephen, and with them, in a warrior's dress, St. Hippolytus, the soldier who was appointed to guard St. Laurence in prison, and who, being converted by

---

* The existence of this inscription makes the destruction of this catacomb under Pius IX. the more extraordinary.

him, was dragged to death by wild horses, after seeing nineteen of his family suffer before his eyes. He is the patron saint of horses. Here also are the mystic cities, Bethlehem and Jerusalem.

A long poetical inscription is known to have once existed here; only two lines remain round the arch :—

> "Martyrium flaminis olim Levita subisti
> Jure tuis templis lux veneranda redit."

The high altar, with a baldacchino, supported by four porphyry columns, covers the remains of SS. Laurence and Stephen, enclosed in a silver shrine by Pelagius II., a pope so munificent that he had given up his own house as a hospital for aged poor. St. Justin is also buried here.

"No one knew what had become of the body of St. Stephen for 400 years, when Lucian, a priest of Carsamagala, in Palestine, was visited in a dream by Gamaliel, the doctor of the law at whose feet Paul was brought up in all the learning of the Jews; and Gamaliel revealed to him that after the death of Stephen he had carried away the body of the saint, and had buried it in his own sepulchre, and had also deposited near it the body of Nicodemus and other saints; and this dream having been repeated three times, Lucian went with others deputed by the bishop, and dug with mattocks and spades in the spot which had been indicated,—a sepulchre in a garden,—and found what they supposed to be the remains of St. Stephen, their peculiar sanctity being proved by many miracles. These relics were first deposited in Jerusalem, in the church of Sion, and afterwards by the younger Theodosius carried to Constantinople, whence they were taken to Rome, and placed by Pope Pelagius in the same tomb with St. Laurence. It is related that when they opened the sarcophagus, and lowered into it the body of St. Stephen, St. Laurence moved on one side, giving the place of honour on the right hand to St. Stephen: hence the common people of Rome have conferred on St. Laurence the title of 'Il cortese Spagnuolo'—the courteous Spaniard."—*Jameson's Sacred and Legendary Art.*

Behind the altar is a mosaic screen, with panels of porphyry and serpentine, and an ancient episcopal throne.

The lower church was filled up with soil till 1864, when restorations were ordered here. These were entrusted to Count Vespignani, and have been better carried out than most church alterations in Rome ; but an interesting portico, with mosaics by one of the famous Cosmati family, has been destroyed to make room for some miserable arrangements connected with the modern cemetery.

It was in this basilica that Peter Courtenay, Count of Auxerre, with Yolande his wife, received the imperial crown of Constantinople from Honorius III. in 1217.

Adjoining the church is the very picturesque *Cloister of the Monastery*, built in 1190, for Cistercian monks, but assigned as a residence for any Patriarchs of Jerusalem who might visit Rome. Here are preserved many ancient inscriptions, and other fragments from the neighbouring catacombs.

The basilica is now almost engulfed in the Cemetery of S. Lorenzo, the great modern burial-ground of Rome. It was opened in 1837, but has been much enlarged in the last ten years. Hither wend the numerous funerals which are seen passing through the streets after Ave-Maria, with a procession of monks bearing candles. A frightful gate, with a laudatory inscription to Pius IX., and a hideous modern chapel, have been erected. There are very few fine monuments. The best are those in imitation of the cinquecento tombs of which there are so many in the Roman churches. That by Podesti, the painter, to his wife, in the right corridor of the cloister, is touching. The 'higher ground to the left, behind the church, is occupied by the tombs of the rich. Those of the poor are indiscriminately scattered over a wide plain. A range of cliffs on the left were perforated by the catacombs of Sta. Cyriaca, which, with the bad taste so constantly displayed in Rome, have been wantonly and shamefully broken up. Those who do not wish to descend into a catacomb, may here see (from without) all their arrangements—in the passages lined with sepulchres, and even some small chapels, lined with rude frescoes, laid open to the air, where the cliff has been cut away.

A Roman funeral is a most sad sight, and strikes one with an unutterable sense of desolation.

"After a death the body is entirely abandoned to the priests, who take possession of it, watch over it, and prepare it for burial; while the family, if they can find refuge anywhere else, abandon the house and remain away a week. .... The body is not ordinarily allowed to remain in the house more than twelve hours, except on condition that it is sealed up in lead or zinc. At nightfall a sad procession of *becchini* and *frati* may be seen coming down the street, and stopping before the house of the dead. The *becchini* are taken from the lowest classes of the people, and hired to carry the corpse on the bier and to accompany it to the church and cemetery. They are dressed in shabby black *cappe*, covering their head and face as well as their body, and having two large holes cut in front of the eyes to enable them to see. These *cappe* are girdled round the waist, and the dirty trousers and worn-out shoes are miserably manifest under the skirts of their dress— showing plainly that their duty is occasional. All the *frati* and *becchini*, except the four who carry the bier, are furnished with wax candles, for no one is buried in Rome without a candle. You may know the rank of the person to be buried by the lateness of the hour and the number of the *frati*. If it be the funeral of a person of wealth or a noble, it takes place at a late hour, the procession of *frati* is long, and the bier elegant. If it be a state-funeral, as of a prince, carriages accompany it in mourning, the coachman and lackeys are bedizened in their richest liveries, and the state hammer-cloths are spread on the boxes, with the family arms embossed on them in gold. But if it be a pauper's funeral, there are only *becchini* enough to carry the bier to the grave, and two *frati*, each with a little candle ; and the sunshine is yet on the streets when they come to take away the corpse.

"You will see this procession stop before the house where the corpse is lying. Some of the *becchini* go up-stairs, and some keep guard below.

Scores of shabby men and boys are gathered round the *frati* ; some attracted simply by curiosity, and some for the purpose of catching the wax, which gutters down from the candles as they are blown by the wind. The latter may be known by the great horns of paper which they carry in their hands. While this crowd waits for the corpse, the *frati* light their candles, and talk, laugh, and take snuff together. Finally comes the body, borne down by four of the *becchini*. It is in a common rough deal coffin, more like an ill-made packing-case than anything else. No care or expense has been laid out upon it to make it elegant, for it is only to be seen for a moment. Then it is slid upon the bier, and over it is drawn the black velvet pall with golden trimmings, on which a cross, death's head, and bones are embroidered. Four of the *becchini* hoist it on their shoulders, the *frati* break forth into their hoarse chaunt, and the procession sets out for the church. Little and big boys and shabby men follow along, holding up their paper horns against the sloping candles to catch the dripping wax. Every one takes off his hat, or makes the sign of the cross, or mutters a prayer, as the body passes ; and with a dull, sad, monotonous chaunt, the candles gleaming and flaring, and casting around them a yellow flickering glow, the funeral winds along through the narrow streets, and under the sombre palaces and buildings, where the shadows of night are deepening every moment. The spectacle seen from a distance, and especially when looked down upon from a window, is very effective ; but it loses much of its solemnity as you approach it; for the *frati* are so vulgar, dirty, and stupid, and seem so utterly indifferent and heartless, as they mechanically croak out their psalms, that all other emotions yield to a feeling of disgust."—*Story's Roba di Roma.*

"Ces rapprochements soudains de l'antiquité et des temps modernes, provoqués par la vue d'un monument dont la destinée se lie à l'une et aux autres, sont très-fréquents à Rome. L'histoire poétique d'Énée aurait pu m'en fournir plusieurs. Ainsi dans l'Énéide, aux funérailles de Pallas, une longue procession s'avance, portant des flambeaux funèbres, suivant l'usage antique, dit Virgile. En effet, on se souvient que l'usage des cierges remontait à l'abolition des sacrifices humains, accompli dans les temps héroïques par le dieu pélasgique Hercule. La description que fait Virgile des funérailles de Pallas pourrait convenir à un de ces enterrements romains où l'on voit de longues files de capucins marchant processionnellement en portant des cierges.

    . . . 'Lucet via longo
    Ordine flammarum.'"

               Æn. xi. 143.
—*Ampère*, i. 217.

On the other side of the road from S. Lorenzo is the *Catacomb of St. Hippolytus*, interesting as described by the Christian poet Prudentius, who wrote at the end of the fourth century.

"Not far from the city walls, among the well-trimmed orchards, there lies a crypt buried in darksome pits. Into its secret recesses a steep path in the winding stairs directs one, even though the turnings shut out the light. The light of day, indeed, comes in through the doorway, as far as the surface of the opening, and illuminates the threshold of the portico; and when, as you advance further, the darkness as of night seems to get more and more obscure throughout the mazes of the cavern, there occur at intervals apertures cut in the roof which convey the bright rays of the sun upon the cave. Although the recesses, twisting at random this way and that, form narrow chambers with darksome galleries, yet a considerable quantity of light finds its way through the pierced vaulting down into the hollow bowels of the mountain. And thus throughout the subterranean crypt it is possible to perceive the brightness and enjoy the light of the absent sun. To such secret places is the body of Hippolytus conveyed, near to the spot where now stands the altar dedicated to God. That same altar-slab (mensa) gives the sacrament, and is the faithful guardian of its martyrs' bones, which it keeps laid up there in expectation of the Eternal Judge, while it feeds the dwellers by the Tiber with holy food. Wondrous is the sanctity of the place! The altar is at hand for those who pray, and it assists the hopes of men by mercifully granting what they need. Here have I, when sick with ills both of soul and body, oftentimes prostrated myself in prayer and found relief. . . . . Early in the morning men come to salute (Hippolytus): all the youth of the place worship here: they come and go until the setting of the sun. Love of religion collects together into one dense crowd both Latins and foreigners; they imprint their kisses on the shining silver; they pour out their sweet balsams; they bedew their faces with tears."—See *Roma Sotterranea*, p. 98.

CHAPTER XIV.

IN THE CAMPUS MARTIUS.

S. Antonio dei Portoguesi—Torre della Scimia—S. Agostino—S. Apollinare—Palazzo Altemps—Sta. Maria dell' Anima—Sta. Maria della Pace—Palazzo del Governo Vecchio—Monte Giordano and Palazzo Gabrielli—Sta. Maria Nuova—Sta. Maria di Monserrato—S. Girolamo della Carità—Sta. Brigitta—S. Tommaso degl' Inglese—Palazzo Farnese—Sta. Maria della Morte—Palazzo Falconieri—Campo di Fiore—Palazzo Cancelleria—SS. Lorenzo e Damaso—Palazzo Linote—Palazzo Spada—Trinità dei Pellegrini—Sta. Maria in Monticelli—Palazzo Santa Croce—S. Carlo a Catinari—Theatre of Pompey—S. Andrea della Valle—Palazzo Vidoni—Palazzo Massimo alle Colonne—S. Pantaleone—Palazzo Braschi—Statue of Pasquin—Sant' Agnese—Piazza Navona—Palazzo Pamfili—S. Giacomo degli Spagnuoli—Palazzo Madama—S. Luigi dei Francesi—The Sapienza—S. Eustachio—Pantheon—Sta. Maria sopra Minerva—Il Piè die Marmo.

THE Campus Martius, now an intricate labyrinth of streets, occupying the wide space between the Corso and the Tiber, was not included within the walls of ancient Rome, but even to late imperial times continued to be covered with gardens and pleasure-grounds, interspersed with open spaces, which were used for the public exercises and amusements of the Roman youth.

"Tunc ego me memini ludos in gramine Campi
Aspicere, et didici, lubrice Tibri, tuos."
Ovid, Fast. vi. 237.

"Tot jam abiere dies, cum me, nec cura theatri,
Nec tetigit Campi, nec mea musa juvat."
Propert. ii. *El.* 13.

The vicinity of the Tiber afforded opportunities for practice in swimming.

"Quamvis non alius flectere equum sciens
Æque conspicitur gramine Martio."
Hor. iii. *Od.* 7.

"Altera gramineo spectabis Equiria campo,
Quem Tiberis curvis in latus urget aquis."
Ovid, Fast. iii. 519.

"Once, upon a raw and gusty day,
The troubled Tiber chafing with her shores,
Cæsar said to me, 'Dar'st thou, Cassius, now
Leap in with me into this angry flood,
And swim to yonder point?' Upon the word,
Accoutred as I was, I plunged in,
And bade him follow,—so, indeed, he did:
The torrent roared; and we did buffet it
With lusty sinews; throwing it aside,
And stemming it with hearts of controversy."
Shakspeare, Julius Cæsar.

It was only near the foot of the Capitol that any buildings were erected under the republic, and these only public offices; under the empire a few magnificent edifices were scattered here and there over the plain. In the time of Cicero, the Campus was quite uninhabited; it is supposed that the population were first attracted here when the aqueducts were cut during the Lombard invasion, which drove the inhabitants from the hills, and obliged them to seek a site where they could avail themselves of the Tiber.

The hills, which were crowded by a dense population in ancient Rome, are now for the most part deserted; the plain, which was deserted in ancient Rome, is now thickly covered with inhabitants.

The plain was bounded on two sides by the Quirinal and Capitoline hills, which were both in the hands of the Sabines, but it had no connection with the Latin hill of the Palatine. Thus it was dedicated to the Sabine god, Mamers or Mars, either before the time of Servius Tullius, as is implied by Dionysius, or after the time of the Tarquins, as stated by Livy.

Tarquinius Superbus had appropriated the Campus Martius to his own use, and planted it with corn. After he was expelled, and his crops cut down and thrown into the Tiber, the land was restored to the people. Here the tribunes used to hold the assemblies of the plebs in the Prata Flaminia at the foot of the Capitol, before any buildings were erected as their meeting-place.

The earliest building in the Campus Martius of which there is any record, is the Temple of Apollo, built by the consul C. Julius, in B.C. 430. Under the censor C. Flaminius, in B.C. 220, a group of important edifices arose on a site which is ascertained to be nearly that occupied by the Palazzo Caetani, Palazzo Mattei, and Sta. Caterina dei Funari. The most important was the Circus Flaminius, where the plebeian games were celebrated under the care of the plebeian ædiles, and which in later times was flooded by Augustus, when thirty-six crocodiles were killed there for the amusement of the people.*

Close to this Circus was the *Villa Publica*, erected B.C. 438, for taking the census, levying troops, and such other public business as could not be transacted within the city.

* Dyer's Rome, 70.

Here, also, foreign ambassadors were received before their entrance into the city, as afterwards at the Villa Papa Giulio, and here victorious generals awaited the decree which allowed them a triumph.* It was in the Villa Publica that Sylla cruelly massacred three thousand partisans of Marius, after he had promised them their lives.

> "Tunc flos Hesperiæ, Latii jam sola juventus,
> Concidit, et miseræ maculavit ovilia Romæ."
> *Lucan*, ii. 196.

The cries of these dying men were heard by the senate who were assembled at the time in the *Temple of Bellona* (restored by Appius Claudius Cæcus in the Samnite War), which stood hard by, and in front of which at the extremity of the Circus Flaminius, where the Piazza Paganica now is, stood the *Columna Bellica*, where the Ferialis, when war was declared, flung a lance into a piece of ground, supposed to represent the enemy's country, when it was not possible to do it at the hostile frontier itself. Julius Cæsar flung the spear here when war was declared against Cleopatra.†

> "Prospicit a templo summum brevis area Circum.
> Est ibi non parvæ parva columna notæ.
> Hinc solet hasta manu, belli prænuncia, mitti;
> In regem et gentes, cum placet arma capi."
> *Ovid, Fast.* vi. 205.

Almost adjoining the Villa Publica was the Septa, where the Comitia Centuriata of the plebs assembled for the election of their tribunes.• The other name of this place of assembly, Ovilia, or the sheepfolds, bears witness to its primitive construction, when it was surrounded by a wooden barrier. In later times the Ovilia was more

* Ampère, Hist. ii. 10. † Ampère, Emp. i. 184.

richly adorned ; Pliny describes it as containing two groups of sculpture—Pan and the young Olympus, and Chiron and the young Achilles—for which the keepers were responsible with their lives ;* and under the empire it was enclosed in magnificent buildings.

In B.C. 189 the *Temple of Hercules Musagetes* was built by the censor Fulvius Nobilior. It occupied a site on the north-west of the portico of Octavia.† Sylla restored it :—

> "Altera pars Circi custode sub Hercule tuta est;
> Quod Deus Euboico carmine munus habet.
> Muneris est tempus, qui Nonas Lucifer ante est:
> Si titulos quaeris; Sulla probavit opus."
> *Ovid, Fast.* vi. 209.

This temple was rebuilt by L. Marcius Philippus, stepfather of Augustus, and surrounded by a portico called after him Porticus Philippi.‡

> "Vites censeo porticum Philippi,
> Si te viderit Hercules, peristi."
> *Martial*, v. *Ep.* 50. §

The *Portico of Octavia* itself was originally built by the prætor, Cn. Octavius, in B.C. 167, and rebuilt by Augustus, who re-dedicated it in memory of his sister. Close adjoining was the *Porticus Metelli*, built B.C. 146, by Cæcilius Metellus.|| It contained two *Temples of Juno and Jupiter.*¶ Another *Temple of Juno* stood between this and the theatre of Pompey, having been erected by M. Æmilius Lepidus in

---

* Pliny, H. N. xxxv. 37, 2 ; and 49, 4.
† Dyer, 111. ‡ Dyer, 211.
§ It was close to this temple of Hercules that the bodies of Sta. Symphorosa and her seven sons, martyred under Hadrian (" the seven Biothanati "), were buried by order of the emperor. Sta. Symphorosa herself had been hung up here by her hair, before being drowned in the Tiber.
|| Dyer, 113. 115. ¶ Ampère, Hist. Rom. iii. 198.

BUILDINGS OF THE CAMPUS MARTIUS. 153

B.C. 170, together with a *Temple of Diana*.* Near the same spot was a *Temple of Fortuna Equestris*, erected in consequence of a vow of Q. Fulvius Flaccus when fighting against the Celtiberians in B.C. 176; a *Temple of Isis and Serapis;* and a *Temple of Mars*, erected by D. Junius Brutus, for his victories over the Gallicians in B.C. 136; † at this last-named temple the people, assembled in their centuries, voted the war against Philip of Macedon. In the same neighbourhood was the *Theatre of Balbus*, a general under Julius Cæsar, occupying the site of the Piazza della Scuola.

The munificence of Pompey extended the public buildings much further into the Campus. He built, after his triumph, a *Temple of Minerva* on the site now occupied by the Church of Sta. Maria sopra Minerva, on which the beautiful statue called "the Giustiniani Minerva" was found, and the *Theatre of Pompey*, surrounded by pillared porticoes and walks shaded with plane-trees.

"Scilicet umbrosis sordet Pompeia columnis
  Porticus aulæis nobilis Attalicis :
Et creber pariter platanis surgentibus ordo,
  Flumina sopito quæque Marone cadunt."
                        Propertius, ii. *El.* 32.

"Tu modo Pompeia lentus spatiare sub umbra,
  Cum Sol Herculei terga leonis adit."
                        Ovid, de Art. Am. i. 67.

"Inde petit centum pendentia tecta columnis,
  Illinc Pompeii dona, nemusque duplex."
                        Martial, ii. *Ep.* 14.

Under the empire important buildings began to rise up further from the city. The *Amphitheatre of Statilius Taurus*, whose ruins are supposed to be the foundation of the

* Dyer, 115.   † Dyer, 115, 116.

Monte-Citorio, was built by a general under Augustus; the magnificent *Pantheon*, the *Baths of Agrippa*, and the *Diribitorium*—where the soldiers received their pay—whose huge and unsupported roof was one of the wonders of the city,* were due to his son-in-law. Agrippa also brought the *Aqua Virgo* into the city to supply his baths, conveying it on pillars across the Flaminian Way, the future Corso.

"Qua vicina pluit Vipsanis porta columnis,
Et madet assiduo lubricus imbre lapis,
In jugulum pueri, qui roscida templa subibat,
Decidit hiberno prægravis unda gelu."
Martial, iv. *Ep.* 18.

Near this aqueduct was a temple of Juturna;

"Te quoque lux eadem, Turni soror, æde recepit;
Hic ubi Virginea campus obitur aqua."
Ovid, Fast. i. 463.

and another of Isis.

"A Meroë portabit aquas, ut spargat in æde
Isidis, antiquo quæ proxima surgit ovili."
Juvenal, Sat. vi. 528.

These were followed by the erection of the *Temple of Neptune*—by some ascribed to Agrippa, who is said to have built it in honour of his naval victories, by others to the time of the Antonines; by the great *Imperial Mausoleum*, then far out in the country; and by the *Baths of Nero*, on the site now occupied by S. Luigi and the neighbouring buildings.

" . . . Quid Nerone pejus?
Quid thermis melius Neronianis?"
Martial, vii. *Ep.* 33.

* Pliny, H. N. xxxvi. 15, 24.

"... Fas sit componere magnis
Parva, Neronea nec qui modo totus in unda
Hic iterum sudare negat."
Statius, Silv. i. 5.

Besides these were an *Arch of Tiberius*, erected by Claudius; a *Temple of Hadrian* and *Basilica of Matidia*, built by Antoninus Pius, in honour of his predecessors; the *Temple and Arch of Marcus Aurelius*, near the site of the present Palazzo Chigi; and an *Arch of Gratian, Valentinian II., and Theodosius.*

Of all these various buildings nothing remains except the Pantheon, a single arch of the Baths of Agrippa, some disfigured fragments of the Mausoleum, a range of columns belonging to the temple of Neptune, and a portion of the Portico of Octavia. The interest of the Campus Martius is almost entirely mediæval or modern, and the objects worth visiting are scattered amid such a maze of dirty and intricate streets, that they are seldom sought out except by those who make a long stay in Rome, and care for everything connected with its history and architecture.

Following the line of streets which leads from the Piazza di Spagna to St. Peter's (Via Condotti, Via Fontanella Borghese), beyond the Borghese Palace, let us turn to the left by the Via della Scrofa,* at the entrance of which is the *Palazzo Galitzin* on the right, and the *Palazzo Cardelli* on the left.

Passing, on the right, *St. Ivo of Brittany*, the national church of the Bretons, the second turn on the right, Via S.

* So called from a fountain adorned with the figure of a sow, which once existed here.

Antonio dei Portoguesi, shows a church dedicated to St. Anthony of Padua, and the fine mediæval tower called *Torre della Scimia*.

In this tower once lived a man who had a favourite ape. One day this creature seized upon a baby, and rushing to the summit, was seen from below, by the agonized parents, perched upon the battlements, and balancing their child to and fro over the abyss. They made a vow in their terror that if the baby were restored in safety, they would make provision that a lamp should burn nightly for ever before an image of the Virgin on the summit. The monkey, without relaxing its hold of the infant, slid down the wall, and bounding and grimacing, laid the child at its mother's feet. Thus a lamp always burns upon the battlements before an image of the Madonna.

This building is better known, however, as " Hilda's Tower," a fictitious name which it has received from Hawthorne's mysterious novel.

"Taking her way through some of the intricacies of the city, Miriam entered what might be called either a widening of a street or a small piazza. The neighbourhood comprised a baker's oven, emitting the usual fragrance of sour bread ; a shoe shop ; a linendraper's shop ; a pipe and cigar shop ; a lottery office ; a station for French soldiers, with a sentinel pacing in front ; and a fruit stand, at which a Roman matron was selling the dried kernels of chesnuts, wretched little figs, and some bouquets of yesterday. A church, of course, was near at hand, the façade of which ascended into lofty pinnacles, whereon were perched two or three winged figures of stone, either angelic or allegorical, blowing stone trumpets in close vicinity to the upper windows of an old and shabby palace. This palace was distinguished by a feature not very common in the architecture of Roman edifices ; that is to say, a mediæval tower, square, massive, lofty, and battlemented and machicolated at the summit.

" At one of the angles of the battlements stood a shrine of the Virgin, such as we see everywhere at the street-corners of Rome, but seldom or never, except in this solitary instance, at a height above the ordinary level of men's views and aspirations. Connected with this old tower and its lofty shrine, there is a legend ; and for centuries a lamp has been burning before the Virgin's image at noon, at midnight, at all hours of the twenty-four, and must be kept burning for ever, as long as the tower shall stand ; or else the tower itself, the palace, and whatever estate belongs to it, shall pass from its hereditary possessor, in accordance with an ancient vow, and become the property of the Church.

" As Miriam approached, she looked upward, and saw—not, indeed, the flame of the never-dying lamp, which was swallowed up in the broad sunlight that brightened the shrine—but a flock of white doves, shining, fluttering, and wheeling above the topmost height of the tower, their silver wings flashing in the pure transparency of the air. Several of them sat on the ledge of the upper window, pushing one another off by their eager struggle for this favourite station, and all tapping their beaks and flapping their wings tumultuously against the panes ; some had alighted in the street, far below, but flew hastily upward, at the sound of the window being thrust ajar, and opening in the middle, on rusty hinges, as Roman windows do."—*Transformation*.

The next street, on the right, leads to the Church *of S. Agostino*, built originally by Bacio Pintelli, in 1483, for Cardinal d'Estouteville, archbishop of Rouen and Legate in France (the vindicator of Joan of Arc), but altered in 1740 by Vanvitelli. The delicate work of the front, built of travertine robbed from the Coliseum, is much admired by those who do not seek for strength of light and shadow. This church—dedicated to her son—contains the remains of Sta. Monica, brought hither from Ostia, where she died. The chapel of St. Augustin, in the right transept, contains a gloomy picture by *Guercino* of St. Augustin between St. John Baptist and St. Paul the Hermit. The high altar, by Bernini, has an image of the Madonna brought from Sta. Sophia at Constantinople, and attributed to St. Luke. The second chapel in the left aisle has a group of the

Virgin and Child with St. Anna, by *Andrea Sansovino*, 1512. On the third pilaster, to the left of the nave, is a fresco of Isaiah by *Raphael*, painted in 1512, but retouched by Daniele de Volterra in the reign of Paul IV. The prophet holds a scroll with words from Isaiah xxvi. 2. Few will agree with the stricture of Kugler :—

> "In a fresco, representing the prophet Isaiah and two angels, who hold a tablet, the comparison is unfavourable to Raphael. An effort to rival the powerful style of Michael-Angelo is very visible in this picture ; an effort which, notwithstanding the excellence of the execution in parts, has produced only an exaggerated and affected figure."—*Kugler*, ii. 371.

The church overflows with silver hearts and other votive offerings, which are all addressed to the Madonna and Child of *Andrea Sansovino*, close to the west entrance, which is really a fine piece of sculpture—for an object of Roman Catholic idolatry.

> "On the pedestal of the image is inscribed—'N. S. Pio VII. concede in perpetuo 100 giorni d'indulgenza da lucrarsi una volta al giorno da tutte quelle che divotamente toccheranno il piede di questa S. Immagine recitando un Ave Maria per il bisogno di S. Chiesa. 7 Giug. MD.CCCXXII."

Around this statue are, or were a short time ago, a whole array of assassins' daggers hung up, strange instances of trespass-offering.

> "The Church of S. Agostino is the Methodist meeting-house, so to speak, of Rome, where the extravagance of the enthusiasm of the lower orders is allowed the freest scope. Its Virgin and Child are covered, smothered, with jewels, votive offerings of those whose prayers the image had heard and answered. All round the image the walls are covered with votive offerings likewise ; some of a similar kind—jewels, watches, valuables of different descriptions. Some offerings again consist of

pictures, representing, generally in the rudest way, some sickness or accident, cured or averted by the appearance in the clouds of the Madonna, as seen in the image. Almost the whole side of the church is covered, from pavement to roof, with these curious productions."— *Alford's Letters from Abroad.*

"It is not long since the report was spread, that one day when a poor woman called upon this image of the Madonna for help, it began to speak, and replied, 'If I had only something, then I could help thee, but I myself am so poor!'

"This story was circulated, and very soon throngs of credulous people hastened hither to kiss the foot of the Madonna, and to present her with all kinds of gifts. The image of the Virgin, a beautiful figure in brown marble, now sits shining with ornaments of gold and precious stones. Candles and lamps burn around, and people pour in, rich and poor, great and small, to kiss, some of them two or three times—the Madonna's foot, a gilt foot, to which the forehead also is devotionally pressed. The marble foot is already worn away with kissing, the Madonna is now rich. . . Below the altar it is inscribed in golden letters that Pius VII. promised two hundred days' absolution to all such as should kiss the Madonna's foot, and pray with the whole heart *Ave Maria.*"—*Frederika Bremer.*

Passing the arch, just beyond this, is the *Church of S. Apollinare*, built originally by Adrian I. (772—795), but modernized under Benedict XIV. by Fuga. It contains a number of relics of saints brought from the East by Basilian monks. Over the altar, on the left, in the inner vestibule, is a Madonna by *Perugino*. The church now belongs to the German college.

S. Apollinare is said to have accompanied St. Peter from Antioch to Rome, and to have remained here as his companion and assistant (whence the church dedicated to him here). He was afterwards sent to preach the faith in Ravenna, where he became the first Christian bishop, and suffered martyrdom outside the Rimini gate, July 23, A.D. 79.

Adjoining this church is the *Seminario Romano*, founded by Pius IV., on a system drawn up by his nephew, S. Carlo

Borromeo. Eight hundred young boys are annually educated here. In order to gain admittance, it is necessary to be of Roman birth, to be acquainted with grammar, and to wish to take orders. Pupils are held to their first intention of entering the priesthood, by being compelled to refund all the expenses of their education, if they renounce it.

Nearly opposite the church is the *Palazzo Altemps*, built 1580, by Martino Lunghi. Its courtyard, due, like all the best palace work in Rome, to Baldassare Peruzzi, is exceedingly graceful and picturesque. Ancient statues and flowering shrubs occupy the spaces between the arches of the ground-floor, and on the first-floor is a loggia, richly decorated with delicate arabesques in the style of Giovanni da Udine. Near this loggia is a chapel of exceedingly beautiful proportions, and delicately worked detail. It has several good frescoes, especially the Flight into Egypt, and Sta. Cecilia singing to the Virgin and the Child. At the west end is a small gracefully proportioned music-gallery, in various coloured marbles; in an inner chapel is a fine bronze crucifix. The palace, of which the most interesting parts are shown on request, is now the property of the Duke of Gallese, to whom it came by the marriage of Jules Hardouin, Duke of Gallese, with Donna Lucrezia d'Altemps.

Following the Via S. Agostino by the mediæval *Torre Sanguinea*, whose name bears witness to the mediæval frays of popes and anti-popes, we reach the German national church of *Sta. Maria dell' Anima*, which derives its name from a marble group of the Madonna invoked by two souls in purgatory, found among the foundations, and now inserted in the tympanum of the portal. It was originally built c. 1440, with funds bequeathed by "un certo Giovanni Pietro," but enlarged in 1514; the façade is by Giuliano da Sangallo. The door-frames, of delicate workmanship, are by Antonio Giamberti.

The front entrance is generally closed, but one can always gain admittance from behind, through the courtyard of the German hospital.

The interior is peculiar, from its great height and width in comparison with its length. It is divided into three almost equal aisles. Over the high altar is a damaged picture of the Holy Family with saints, by *Giulio Romano*. On the right is the fine tomb of Pope Adrian VI., Adrian Florent (1522—23), designed by Baldassare Peruzzi, and carried out by Michelangelo Sanese and Niccolo Tribolo. This pope, the son of a ship-builder at Utrecht, was professor at the university of Louvain, and tutor of Charles V. After the witty, brilliant age of Julius II. and Leo X., he ushered in a period of penitence and devotion. He drove from the papal court the throng of artists and philosophers who had hitherto surrounded it, and he put a stop to the various great buildings which were in progress, saying, " I do not wish to adorn priests with churches, but churches with priests." Still he found the times so much too frivolous for him, that he only survived a year. In his epitaph we read :—

"Hadrianus hic situs est, qui nihil sibi infelicius in vita quam quod imperaret, duxit."*

and—

"Proh dolor! quantum refert in quæ tempora vel optimi.
. . . . . Cujusque virtus incidat!"

* "Here rests Hadrian, who found his greatest misfortune in being obliged to command."

The tomb was erected at the expense of Cardinal William of Enkenfort, the only prelate to whom he had time to give a hat.

"It is an irony, that Adrian, who despised all the arts on principle, and looked upon Greek statues as idolatrous, had a more artistic monument than Leo X. of the house of Medici. Baldassare Peruzzi made the design, its sculptures were carried out by Michelangelo Sanese and Tribolo, and they merit the highest acknowledgment. Here, as is so often the case, the architecture is, as it were, a frontispiece ; but the way in which the pope is represented, resembles, in conformity with his character, the type of the middle ages. He is stretched upon a simple marble sarcophagus, and slumbers with his head supported by his hand. His countenance (Adrian was very handsome) is deeply marked and sorrowful. In the lunette above, following the ancient type, appears Mary with the Child between St. Peter and St. Paul. Below, in the niches, stand the figures of the four cardinal virtues: Temperance holds a chain ; Courage a branch of a tree, while a lion stands by her side ; Justice has an ostrich by her side ; Wisdom carries a mirror and a serpent. These figures are executed with great care. Lastly, under the sarcophagus is a large bas-relief representing the entry of the pope to Rome. He sits on horseback in the dress of a cardinal ; behind him follow cardinals and monks ; the senator of Rome renders homage on his knees, while from the gate the eternal Rome comes forth to meet him. This Cypria, so well adorned by his predecessors, seems ill-pleased to do homage to this cross old man. With secret pleasure one sees a pagan idea carried out in the corner: the Tiber is represented as a river god with his horn of abundance ; and thus the devout pope could not defend himself against the heathen spirit of the time, which has at least attached itself to his tomb."—*Gregorovius, Grabmäler der Päpste.*

Opposite the pope, on the left of the choir, is the fine tomb of a Duke of Cleves, who died 1575, by Egidius of Riviere and Nicolaus of Arras.

The body of the church has several good pictures. In the 1st chapel of the right aisle is St. Bruno receiving the keys of the cathedral of Miessen in Saxony from a fisherman, who had found them in the inside of a fish, by *Carlo Sara-*

STA. MARIA DELLA PACE. 163

ceni; in the 2nd chapel, the monument of Cardinal Slusius; in the 3rd chapel, an indifferent copy of the Pietà of Michael Angelo, by *Nanni di Bacio Bigio.* In the 1st chapel of the left aisle is the martyrdom of St. Lambert, *C. Saraceni.*

<small>The two pictures in this church are cited by Lanzi as the best works of this comparatively rare artist, sometimes called Carlo Veneziano, 1585—1625. He sought to follow in the steps of Caravaggio; many will think that he surpassed him, when they look upon the richness of colour and grand effect of light and shadow which is displayed here.</small>

In the 3rd chapel (del Christo Morto), frescoes from the life of Sta. Barbara, *Mich. Coxcie,* altar-piece (the entombment) and frescoes by *Salviati.*

On the left of the west door is the tomb of Cardinal Andrea of Austria, nephew of Ferdinand II., who died 1650; on the right that of Cardinal Enckenovirt, died 1500. In the passage towards the sacristy is a fine bas-relief, representing Gregory XIII. giving a sword to the Duke of Cleves.

Close to this church is that of *Sta. Maria della Pace,* built in 1487, by Baccio Pintelli, to fulfil a curious *ex-voto* made by Sixtus IV. Formerly there stood here a little chapel dedicated to St. Andrew, in whose portico was an image of the Virgin. One day a drunken soldier pierced the bosom of this Madonna with his sword, when blood miraculously spirted forth. Sixtus IV. (Francesco della Rovere, 1471—84) visited the spot with his cardinals, and vowed to compensate the Virgin by building her a church, if she would grant peace to Europe and the Church, then afflicted by a cruel war with the Turks. Peace was restored, and the Church of "St. Mary of Peace" was erected by the grateful pope. Pietro da Cortona added the peculiar semicircular portico under Alexander VII. The interior has only a short nave ending under an octagonal cupola.

Above the 1st chapel on the right (that of the Chigi family) are the *Four Sibyls of Raphael*.

"This is one of Raphael's most perfect works: great mastery is shown in the mode of filling and taking advantage of the apparently unfavourable space. The angels who hold the tablets to be written on, or read by the Sibyls, create a spirited variety in the severe symmetrical arrangement of the whole. Grace in the attitudes and movements, with a peculiar harmony of form and colour, pervade the whole picture; but important restorations have unfortunately become necessary in several parts. An interesting comparison may be instituted between this work and the Sibyls of Michael Angelo. In each we find the peculiar excellence of the great masters; for while Michael Angelo's figures are grand, sublime, profound, the fresco of the Pace bears the impress of Raphael's severe and ingenious grace. The four Prophets, on the wall over the Sibyls, were executed by Timoteo della Vite, after drawings by Raphael."—*Kugler*.

"The Sibyls have suffered much from time, and more, it is said, from restoration; yet the forms of Raphael, in all their loveliness, all their sweetness, are still before us; they breathe all the soul, the sentiment, the chaste expression, and purity of design that characterize his works. The dictating angels hover over the heads of the gifted maids, one of whom writes with rapid pen the irreversible decrees of Fate. The countenances and musing attitudes of her sister Sibyls express those feelings of habitual thoughtfulness and pensive sadness natural to those who are cursed with the knowledge of futurity, and all its coming evils."—*Eaton's Rome*.

"The Sibyls are simply beautiful women of antique form, to whom, with the aid of books, scrolls, and inscriptions, the Sibyllic idea has been given, but who would equally pass for the abstract personifications of virtues or cities. They are four in number,—the Cumana, Phrygia, Persica, and Tiburtina; all, with the exception of the last, in the fulness of youth and beauty, and occupied, apparently, with no higher aim than that of displaying both. Indeed, the Tiburtina matches ill with the rest, either in character or action. She is aged, has an open book on her lap, but turns with a strange and rigid action as if suddenly called. The very comparison with her tends to divest the others of the Sibylline character. In this, the angels who float above, and obviously inspire them, also help, for while adding to the charm of the composition, which is one of the most exquisite as to mere art, they interfere with that inwardly inspired expression which all other art has given to these women.

"The inscription on the scroll of the Cumæan Sibyl gives in Greek the words, 'The Resurrection of the Dead.' The Persica is writing on the scroll held by the angel, 'He will have the lot of Death.' The beautiful Phrygia is presented with a scroll, 'The heavens surround the sphere of the earth ;' and the Tiburtina has under her the inscription, 'I will open and arise.' The fourth angel floats above, holding the seventh line of Virgil's Eclogue, 'Jam nova progenies.'"—*Lady Eastlake's 'History of Our Lord.'*

The 1st chapel on the left has monuments of the Ponzetti family. The 2nd chapel on the left has an altar-piece of the Virgin between St. Bridget and St. Catherine, by *Baldassare Peruzzi;* in the front of the picture kneels the donor, Cardinal Ponzetti. The 1st altar on the right has the Adoration of the Shepherds by *Sermoneta*. The 2nd chapel, the burial-place of the Santa Croce family, has rich carved work of the sixteenth century. The high altar, designed by Carlo Maderno, has an ancient (miracle-working) Madonna. Of the four paintings of the cupola, the Nativity of the Virgin is by *Francesco Vanni;* the Visitation, *Carlo Maratta;* the Presentation in the Temple, *Baldassare Peruzzi;* the Death of the Virgin, *Morandi*.

Newly-married couples have the touching custom of attending their first mass here, and invoking "St. Mary of Peace" to rule the course of their new life.

The *Cloister of the Convent*, entered on the left under the dome, was designed by *Bramante* for Cardinal Caraffa in 1504.

From the portico of the church the Via in Parione leads to the *Via del Governo Vecchio*. Here, on the right, is the *Palazzo del Governo Vecchio*, with a richly-sculptured doorway, and ancient cloistered court.

Proceeding as far as the Piazza del Orologio, we see on the right an eminence known as *Monte Giordano*, supposed to be artificial, and to have arisen from the ruins of ancient buildings.

> Its name is derived from Giordano Orsini, a noble of one of the oldest Roman families, who built the palace there, which is now known as the *Palazzo Gabrielli*, and which has rather a handsome fountain. It was probably in consequence of the name Jordan, that this hillock was chosen in mediæval times as the place where the Jews in Rome received the newly-elected pope on his way to the Lateran, and where their elders, covered with veils, presented him, on their knees, with a copy of the Pentateuch bound in gold. Then the Jews spoke in Hebrew, saying, "Most holy Father, we Hebrew men beseech your Holiness, in the name of our synagogue, to vouchsafe to us that the Mosaic Law, given on Mount Sinai by the Almighty God to Moses our priest, may be confirmed and approved, as also other eminent popes, the predecessors of your Holiness, have approved and confirmed it." And the pope replied, "We confirm the Law, but we condemn your faith and interpretation thereof, because He who you say is to come, the Lord Jesus Christ, is come already, as our Church teaches and preaches."

Turning to the left, we enter a piazza, one side of which is occupied by the convent of the Oratorians, and the vast *Church of Santa Maria in Valicella, or the Chiesa Nuova*, built by Martino Lunghi for Gregory XIII. and S. Filippo Neri. The façade is by Rughesi. The decorations of the magnificently-ugly interior are partly due to Pietro da Cortona, who painted the roof and cupola.

On the left of the tribune is the gorgeous *Chapel of S. Filippo Neri*, containing the shrine of the saint, rich in lapis-lazuli and gold, surmounted by a mosaic copy of the picture by *Guido* in the adjoining convent.

On the right, in the 1st chapel, is the Crucifixion, by *Scipione Gaetani;* in the 3rd chapel, the Ascension, *Maziano*. On the left, in the 2nd chapel, is the Adoration of the Magi,

Cesare Nebbia; in the 3rd chapel, the Nativity, *Durante Alberti;* in the 4th chapel, the Visitation, *Baroccio.* In the left transept are statues of SS. Peter and Paul, by *Valsoldo,* and the Presentation in the Temple, by *Baroccio.* When S. Filippo Neri saw this picture, he said to the painter "Ma come avete ben fatto!—Che vera somiglianza!—E così che mi ha apparato tante volte la Santa Vergine."

The high altar has four columns of porta-santa. Its pictures are by *Rubens* in his youth;—that in the centre represents the Virgin in a glory of angels; on the right are St. Gregory, S. Mauro, and St. Papias; on the left St. Domitilla, St. Nereus, and St. Achilleus.

The Sacristy, entered from the left transept, is by Marucelli. It has a grand statue of S. Filippo Neri, by *Algardi.* The ceiling is painted by *Pietro da Cortona*—the subject is an angel bearing the instruments of the passion to heaven.

The *Monastery,* built by Borromini, contains the magnificent library founded by S. Filippo. The cell of the saint is accessible, even to ladies. It retains his confessional, chair, shoes, rope-girdle,—and also a cast taken from his face after death, and some pictures which belonged to him, including one of Sta. Francesca Romana, and the portrait of an archbishop of Florence. In the private chapel adjoining, is the altar at which he daily said mass, over which is a picture of his time. Here also are the crucifix which was in his hands when he died, his candlesticks, and some sacred pictures on tablets which he carried to the sick. The door of the cell is the same, and the little bell by which he summoned his attendant. In a room below is the carved coffin in which he lay in state, a picture of him lying dead, and the portrait by *Guercino* from which the mosaic in the church is taken. A curious picture in this chamber represents an earthquake at Beneventum, in which Pope Gregory XIV. believed that his life was saved by an image of S. Filippo. When S. Filippo Nero died,—as in the case of S. Antonio,—the Catholic world exclaimed intuitively, "Il Santo è morto!"

> " Let the world flaunt her glories! each glittering prize,
> Though tempting to others, is naught in my eyes.
> A child of St. Philip, my master and guide,
> I would live as he lived, and would die as he died.
>
> "If scanty my fare, yet how was he fed?
> On olives and herbs and a small roll of bread.
> Are my joints and bones sore with aches and with pains?
> Philip scourged his young flesh with fine iron chains.
>
> "A closet his home, where he, year after year,
> Bore heat or cold greater than heat or cold here;
> A rope stretch'd across it, and o'er it he spread
> His small stock of clothes; and the floor was his bed.
>
> "One lodging besides; God's temple he chose,
> And he slept in its porch his few hours of repose;
> Or studied by light which the altar-lamp gave,
> Or knelt at the martyr's victorious grave."
>
> *J. H. Newman*, 1857.

The church of the Chiesa Nuova belongs exclusively to the Oratorian Fathers. Pope Leo XII. wished to turn it into a parish church.

"It was said that the superior of the house took, and showed, to the Holy Father, an autograph memorial of the founder St. Philip Neri to the pope of his day, petitioning that his church should never be a parish. And below it was written that pope's promise, also in his own hand, that it never should. This pope was St. Pius V. Leo bowed to such authorities, said that he could not contend against two saints, and altered his plans."—*Wiseman's Life of Leo XII.*

"S. Filippo Neri was good-humoured, witty, strict in essentials, indulgent in trifles. He never commanded; he advised, or perhaps requested: he did not discourse, he conversed: and he possessed, in a remarkable degree, the acuteness necessary to distinguish the peculiar merit of every character."—*Ranke.*

"S. Filippo Neri laid the foundation of the Congregation of Oratorians in 1551. Several priests and young ecclesiastics associating themselves with him, began to assist him in his conferences, and in reading prayers and meditations to the people in the Church of the Holy Trinity. They were called Oratorians, because at certain hours every morning and afternoon, by ringing a bell, they called the people to the church to prayers and meditations. In 1564, when the saint had formed his congregation into a regular community, he preferred several of his young ecclesiastics to holy orders; one of whom was the eminent Cæsar Baronius, whom, for his sanctity, Benedict XIV., by a decree dated on the 12th of January, 1745, honoured with the title of 'Venerable Servant of God.' At the same time he formed his disciples into a community, using one common purse and table, and he gave them rules and statutes. He forbade any of them to bind themselves to this state by vow or oath, that all might live together joined only by the bands of fervour and holy charity; labouring with all their strength to establish the kingdom of Christ in themselves by the most perfect sanctification of their own souls, and to propagate the same in the souls of others, by preaching, instructing the ignorant, and teaching the Christian doctrine."—*Alban Butler.*

"S. Filippo Neri exacted from his scholars and associates various undignified outward acts. He required from a young Roman prince, who wished to enjoy the distinction of being a member of his Order, that he should walk through Rome with a fox's tail fastened on behind: and when the prince declined to submit to this, he was declined admission to the Order. Another was made to go through the city without a coat; and another, with torn and tattered sleeves. A nobleman took compassion on the last, and offered him a new pair of sleeves: the youth declined, but afterwards, by command of the master, was obliged gratefully to fetch and wear them. During the building of the new church, he compelled his disciples to bring up the materials like day labourers, and to lay their hands to the work."—*Goethe, Romische Briefe.*

It was in the piazza in front of this church that (during the reign of Clement XIV.) a beautiful boy was wont to improvise wonderful verses to the admiration of the crowds who surrounded him. This boy was named Trapassi, and was the son of a grocer in the neighbourhood. The Arcadian Academy changed his name into Greek, and called him " Metastasio."

From the corner of the piazza in front of the Chiesa Nuova, the Via Calabraga leads into the Via Monserrato, which it enters between Sta. Lucia del Gonfalone on the right, and S. Stefano in Piscinula on the left ;—then, passing on the right S. Giacomo in Aino—behind which, and the Palazzo Ricci, is Santo Spirito dei Napolitani, a much frequented and popular little church—we reach *Sta. Maria di Monserrato*, built by Sangallo, in 1495, where St. Ignatius Loyola was wont to preach and catechise.

Here, behind the altar, under a stone unmarked by any epitaph, repose at last the remains of Pope Alexander VI., Rodrigo Borgia (1492—1503),—the infamous father of the beautiful and wicked Cæsar and Lucretia Borgia, who is believed to have died from accidentally drinking in a vineyard-banquet the poison which he had prepared for one of his own cardinals. When exhumed and turned out of the pontifical vaults of St. Peter's by Julius II., he found a refuge here in his national church. The bones of his uncle Calixtus III., Alfonso Borgia (1455—58), rest in the same grave.

A little further, on the left, is the *Church of S. Tommaso degli Inglesi*, rebuilt 1870, on the site of a church founded by Offa, king of the East Saxons in 775, but destroyed by fire in 817. It was rebuilt, and was dedicated by Alexander III. (1159) to St. Thomas à Becket, who had lodged in the adjoining hospital when he was in Rome. Gregory XIII., in 1575, united the hospital which existed here with one for English sailors on the Ripa Grande, dedicated to St. Edmund the Martyr, and converted them into a college for English missionaries.

"Nothing like a hospice for English pilgrims existed till the first great Jubilee, when John Shepherd and his wife Alice, seeing this want, settled in Rome, and devoted their substance to the support of poor palmers from their own country. This small beginning grew into sufficient importance for it to become a royal charity; the King of England became its patron, and named its rector, often a person of high consideration. Among the fragments of old monuments scattered about the house by the revolution, and now collected and arranged in a corridor of the college, is a shield surmounted by a crown, and carved with the ancient arms of England, lions or lionceaux, and fleur-de-lis, quarterly. This used formerly to be outside the house, and under it was inscribed:

'Hæc conjuncta duo,
Successus debita legi,
Anglia dant, regi
Francia signa suo.
Laurentius Chance me fecit M.CCC.XIJ.'"

Cardinal Wiseman.

In the hall of the college are preserved portraits of Roman Catholics who suffered for their faith in England under Henry VIII. and Elizabeth.

The small cloister has a beautiful tomb of Christopher Bainbrigg, archbishop of York, British envoy to Julius II., who died at Rome 1514, and a monument of Sir Thomas Dereham, ob. 1739. Against the wall is the monument of Martha Swinburne, a prodigy of nine years old, inscribed:

"Memoriæ Marthæ, Henrici et Marthæ Swinburne . Nat . Angliæ . ex . Antiqua . et . Nobili . Familia . Caphæton . Northumbriæ . Parentes . Mœstiss . Filiæ . Carissimæ . Pr . Quæ . Ingenio . Excellenti . Forma . Eximia . Incredibili . Doctrina . Moribus . Suavissimis . Vix . Ann . viii . Men . xi. Tantum . Præreptaæ . Romæ . v . ID . SEPT . AN . MDCCLXVIII.

"Martha Swinburne, born Oct. X. MDCCLVIII. Died Sept. VIII. MDCCLXVII. Her years were few, but her life was long and full. She spoke English, French, and Italian, and had made some progress in the Latin tongue; knew the English and Roman histories, arithmetic, and geography; sang the most difficult music at sight with one of the finest voices in the world, was a great proficient on the harpsichord, wrote well, and danced many sorts of dances with strength and elegance. Her face was beautiful and majestic, her body a perfect model, and all her motions graceful. Her docility in doing everything to make her parents happy, could only be equalled by her sense and aptitude. With so many perfections, amidst the praises of all persons, from the sovereign down to the beggar in the street, her heart was incapable of vanity; affectation and arrogance were unknown to her. Her beauty and accomplishments made her the admiration of all beholders, the love of all that enjoyed her company. Think, then, what the pangs of her wretched parents must be on so cruel a separation. Their only comfort is in the certitude of her being completely happy beyond the reach of pain, and for ever freed from the miseries of this life. She can never feel the torments they endure for the loss of a beloved child. Blame them not for indulging an innocent pride in transmitting her memory to posterity as an honour to her family and to her native country England. Let this plain character, penned by her disconsolate father, draw a tear of pity from every eye that peruses it."

The arm of St. Thomas à Becket is the chief "relic" preserved here.

At the end of the street are two exceedingly ugly little churches—very interesting from their associations. On the right is *St. Girolamo della Carità*, founded on the site of the house of Sta. Paula, where she received St. Jerome upon his being called to Rome from the Thebaid by Pope Damasus in 392. Here he remained for three years, till, embittered by the scandal excited by his residence in the house of the widow, he returned to his solitude.

In 1519 S. Filippo Neri founded here a *Confraternity* for the distribution of dowries to poor girls, for the assistance of debtors, and for the maintenance of fourteen priests for the visitation and confession of the sick.

"Lorsque St. Philippe de Neri fut prêtre, il alla se loger à Saint-Jérôme *della Carità*, où il demeura trente-cinq ans, dans la société des pieux ecclésiastiques qui administraient les sacrements dans cette paroisse. Chaque soir, Philippe ouvrait, dans sa chambre qui existe encore, des conférences sur tous les points du dogme catholique; les jeunes gens affluaient à ces saintes réunions : on y voyait Baronius ; Bordini, qui fut archevêque; Salviati, frère du cardinal ; Tarugia, neveu du pape Jules III. Un désir ardent d'exercer ensemble le ministère de la prédication et les devoirs de la charité porta ces pieux jeunes gens à vivre en commun, sous la discipline du vertueux prêtre, dont le parole était si puissante sur leurs cœurs."—*Gournerie.*

The masterpiece of Domenichino, the Last Communion of St. Jerome, in which Sta. Paula is introduced kissing the hand of the dying saint, hung in this church till carried off to Paris by the French.

Opposite this is the *Church of Sta. Brigitta*, on the site of the dwelling of the saint, a daughter of the house of Brahé, and wife of Walfon, duke of Nericia, who came hither in her widowhood, to pass her declining years near the Tomb of the Apostles. With her, lived her daughter St. Catherine of Sweden, who was so excessively beautiful, and met with so many importunities in that wild time (1350), that she made a vow never to leave her own roof except to visit the churches. The crucifix, prayer-book, and black mantle of St. Bridget are preserved here.*

"St. Bridget exercised a reformatory influence as well upon the higher class of the priesthood in Rome as in Naples. For she did not alone satisfy herself with praying at the graves of the martyrs, she earnestly exhorted bishops and cardinals, nay, even the pope himself, to a life of the true worship of God and of good works, from which they had almost universally fallen, to devote themselves to worldly ambition. She awoke the consciences of many, as well by her prayers and remonstrances, as by her example. For she herself, of a rich and noble race, that of a Brahé, one of the nobles in Sweden, yet lived here in Rome, and laboured like a truly humble servant of Christ. 'We must walk

---

* There is a chapel dedicated to St. Bridget in S. Paolo fuori Mura. Sion House, in England, was a famous convent of the Brigittines.

barefoot over pride, if we would overcome it,' said she, and Brigitta Brahé did so ; and, in so doing, overcame those proud hearts, and won them to God."—*Frederika Bremer.*

We now reach the *Palazzo Farnese*,—the most magnificent of all the Roman palaces,—begun by Paul III., Alessandro Farnese (1534—50), and finished by his nephew, Cardinal Alessandro Farnese. Its architects were Antonio di Sangallo, Michael Angelo, and Giacomo della Porta, who finished the façade towards the Tiber. The materials were plundered partly from the Coliseum and partly from the theatre of Marcellus ; the granite basons of the fountains in front are from the baths of Caracalla. The immense size of the blocks of travertine used in the building give it a solid grandeur.

This palace was inherited by the Bourbon kings of Naples by descent from Elizabetta Farnese, who was the last of her line, and it has for the last few years been the residence of the Neapolitan Court, who have lived here in the utmost seclusion since their exile. For this reason the palace is now very seldom shown. Its vast halls are painted with the masterpieces of Annibale Caracci—huge mythological subjects,—and a few frescoes by Guido, Domenichino, Daniele da Volterra, Taddeo Zucchero, and others; but there has not been much to see since the dispersion of the Farnese gallery of sculpture, of which the best pieces (the Bull, Hercules, Flora, &c.) are in the museum at Naples. In the courtyard is the sarcophagus which is said once to have held the remains of Cecilia Metella.

"The painting the gallery at the Farnese Palace is supposed to have partly caused the death of Caracci. Without fixing any price he set about it, and employed both himself and all his best pupils nearly seven years in perfecting the work, never doubting that the Farnese family, who had employed him, would settle a pension upon him, or keep him in their service. When his work was finished they paid him as you would pay a house-painter, and this ill-usage so deeply affected him, that he took to drinking, and never painted anything great afterwards."—*Miss Berry's Journals.*

Behind the Palazzo Farnese runs the *Via Giulia*, which contains the ugly fountain of the Mascherone. Close to the arch which leads to the Farnese gardens is the church of *Sta. Maria della Morte*, or *Dell' Orazione*, built by Fuga. It is in the hands of a pious confraternity who devote themselves to the burial of the dead.

"L'église de la *Bonne-Mort* a son caveau, décoré dans le style funèbre comme le couvent des Capucins. On y conserve aussi élégamment que possible les os des noyés, asphyxiés et autres victimes des accidents. La confrérie de la *Bonne-Mort* va chercher les cadavres ; un sacristain assez adroit les dessèche et les dispose en ornements. J'ai causé quelque temps avec cet artiste : 'Monsieur,' me disait-il, 'je ne suis heureux qu'ici, au milieu de mon œuvre. Ce n'est pas pour les quelques écus que je gagne tous les jours en montrant la chapelle aux étrangers ; non ; mais ce monument que j'entretiens, que j'embellie, que j'égaye par mon talent, est devenu l'orgueil et la joie de ma vie.' Il me montra ses matériaux, c'est-à-dire quelques poignées d'ossements jetés en tas dans un coin, fit l'éloge de la pouzzolane, et témoigna de son mépris pour la chaux. 'La chaux brûle les os,' me dit-il, 'elle les fait tomber en poussière. On ne peut faire rien de bon avec les os qui ont été dans la chaux. C'est de la drogue (*robbaccia*).'"—*About.*

Beyond the arch is the *Palazzo Falconieri* (with falcons at the corners), built by Borromini about 1650. There is something rather handsome in its tall three-arched loggia, as seen from the back of the courtyard, which overhangs the Tiber opposite the Farnesina. Cardinal Fesch (uncle of Napoleon I.) lived here, and here formed his fine gallery of pictures.

"The whole of Cardinal Fesch's collection was dispersed at his death, having been vainly offered by him, during the last years of his life, for sale to the English Government, for an annuity of 4000*l*. per annum."—*Eaton's Rome.*

Further on are the *Carceri Nuove*, prisons established by Innocent X. (appropriately reached by the Via del Malpasso), and then the *Palazzo Sacchetti*, built by Antonio da Sangallo for his own residence, and adorned by him with the arms of his patron, Paul III., and the grateful inscription, "Tu mihi quodcumque hoc rerum est." The collection of statues which was formed here by Cardinal Ricci, was removed to the Capitol by Benedict XIV., and became the foundation of the present Capitoline collection.

In front of the Palazzo Farnese, beyond its own piazza, is that known as the *Campo di Fiore*, a centre of commerce among the working classes. Here the most terrible of the Autos da Fé were held by the Dominicans, in which many Jews and other heretics were burnt alive.

One of the most remarkable sufferers here was Giordano Bruno, who was born at Nola, A.D. 1550. His chief heresy was ardent advocacy of the Copernican system,—the author of which had died ten years before his birth. He was also strongly opposed to the philosophy of Aristotle, and gave great offence by setting forth views of his own, which strongly tended to pantheism. He visited Paris, England, and Germany, and everywhere excited hostility by the uncompromising expression of his opinions. It was at Venice that he first came into the power of his ecclesiastical enemies. After six years of imprisonment in that city, he was brought to Rome to be put to death. His execution took place in the Campo di Fiore on the 17th of February, 1600, in the presence of an immense concourse. It was noted that when the monks offered him the crucifix as he was led to the stake, he turned away and refused to kiss it. This put the finishing touch to his career, in the estimation of all beholders. Scioppus, the Latinist, who was present at the execution, with a sarcastic allusion to one of Bruno's heresies, the infinity of worlds, wrote, "The flames carried him to those worlds which he had imagined."*

* See Penny Cyclopædia, and Lewes's Hist. of Philosophy.

On the left of this piazza is the gigantic *Palace of the Cancelleria*, begun by Cardinal Mezzarota, and finished in 1494 by Cardinal Riario, from designs of Bramante. The huge blocks of travertine of which it is built were taken from the Coliseum. The colonnades have forty-four granite pillars, said to have belonged to the theatre of Pompey. The roses with which their (added) capitals are adorned are in reference to the arms of Cardinal Riario, nephew of Sixtus IV.

This palace was the seat of the Tribunal of the Cancelleria Apostolica. In June, 1848, the Roman Parliament, summoned by Pius IX., was held here. In July, while the deputies were seated here, the mob burst into the council-chamber, and demanded the instant declaration of war against Austria. On the 16th of November, its staircase was the scene of the murder of Count Rossi.

"C'était le 16 Novembre, 1848, le ministre de Pie IX., voué dès longtemps à la mort, dont la presse séditieuse disait : 'Si la victime condamnée parvient à s'échapper, elle sera poursuivie sans relâche, en tout lieu, le coupable sera frappé par une main invisible, se fût-il réfugié sur le sein de sa mère ou dans le tabernacle du Christ.'

"Dans la nuit du 14 au 15 Novembre, de jeunes étudiants, réunis dans cette pensée, s'exercent sans frémir sur un cadavre apporté à prix d'or au théâtre Capranica, et quand leurs mains infâmes furent devenues assez sûres pour le crime, quand ils sont certains d'atteindre au premier coup la veine jugulaire, chacun se rend à son poste—'Gardez-vous d'aller au Palais Législatif, la mort vous y attend,' fait dire au ministre une Française alors à Rome, Madame la Comtesse de Menon : 'Ne sortez pas, ou vous serez assassiné !' lui écrit de son côté la Duchesse de Rignano Mais l'intrépide Rossi, n'écoutant que sa conscience, arrive au Quirinal. A son tour le pape le conjure d'être prudent, de ne point s'exposer, afin, lui dit-il, 'd'éviter à nos ennemis un grand crime, et à moi une immense douleur.'—'Ils sont trop lâches, ils n'oseront pas.' Pie IX. le bénit et il continue de se diriger vers la chancellerie . . . .

". . . . Sa voiture s'arrête, il descend au milieu d'hommes sinistres, leur lance un regard de dédain, et continuant sans crainte ni peur, il commence à monter ; la foule le presse en sifflant, l'un le frappe sur l'épaule gauche, d'un mouvement instinctif, il retourne la tête, découvrant la veine fatale, il tombe, se relève, monte quelques marches, et retombe inondé de sang."—*M. de Bellevue.*

Entered from the courtyard of the palace is the Church *of SS. Lorenzo e Damaso*, removed by Cardinal Riario in 1495, from another site, where it had been founded in 560 by the sainted pope Damasus. It consists of a short nave and aisles, and is almost square, with an apse and chapels. The doors are by Vignola. At the end of the left aisle is a curious black virgin, much revered. Opening from the right aisle is the chapel of the Massimi, with several tombs ; a good modern monument of Princess Gabrielli, &c. Against the last pilaster is a seated statue of S. Hippolytus, Bishop of Porto, taken from that at the Lateran. His relics are preserved here, with those of S. Giovanni Calabita, and many other saints. The tomb of Count Rossi is also here, inscribed " Optimam mihi causam tuendam assumpsi, miserebitur Deus." The story of his death is told in the words: " Impiorum consilio meditata cæde occubuit." He was embalmed and buried on the very night of his murder, for fear of further outrage. St. Francis Xavier used to preach in this church in the sixteenth century.

Standing a little back from the street, in the Via de' Baullari, is a pretty little palace, carefully finished in all its details, and attributed to Baldassare Peruzzi. It is sometimes called *Palazzetto Farnese*, sometimes *Palazzo Linote*, and is now almost in a state of ruin.

Turning to the left, in front of the Palazzo Farnese, we reach the Piazza Capo di Ferro, one side of which is occupied by the *Palazzo Spada alla Regola*, built in 1564, by Cardinal Capodifero, but afterwards altered and adorned by

Borromini. The courtyard is very rich in sculptured ornament. The palace is always visible, but has a rude and extortionate porter.

In a picturesque and dimly-lighted hall on the first-floor, partially hung with faded tapestries, is the famous statue believed to be that of Pompey, at the foot of which Julius Cæsar fell. Suetonius narrates that it was removed by Augustus from the Curia, and placed upon a marble Janus in front of the basilica. Exactly on that spot was the existing statue found, lying under the partition-wall of two houses, whose proprietors intended to evade disputes by dividing it, when Cardinal Capodifero interfered, and in return received it as a gift from Pope Julius III., who bought it for 500 gold crowns.

> " And thou, dread statue ! yet existent in
> The austerest form of naked majesty,—
> Thou who beheldest, 'mid the assassins' din,
> At thy bathed base the bloody Cæsar lie,
> Folding his robe in dying dignity,
> An offering to thine altar from the queen
> Of gods and men, great Nemesis ! did he die,
> And thou, too, perish, Pompey ? have ye been
> Victors of countless kings, or puppets of a scene ? "
> *Byron, Childe Harold.*

" I saw in the Palazzo Spada, the statue of Pompey : the statue at whose base Cæsar fell. A stern, tremendous figure ! I imagined one of greater finish : of the last refinement : full of delicate touches : losing its distinctness in the giddy eyes of one whose blood was ebbing before it, and settling into some such rigid majesty as this, as Death came creeping over the upturned face."—*Dickens.*

" Cæsar was persuaded at first by the entreaties of his wife Calpurnia, who had received secret warning of the plot, to send an excuse to the senate ; but afterwards, being ridiculed by Brutus for not going, was carried thither in a litter. . . . . At the moment when Cæsar descended from his litter at the door of the hall, Popilius Læna approached him, and was observed to enter into earnest conversation with him. The conspirators regarded one another, and mutually revealed their despair with a glance. Cassius and others were grasping their daggers beneath their robes ; the last resource was to despatch themselves. But Brutus, observing that the manner of Popilius was that of one supplicating rather than warning, restored his companions' confidence with a smile. Cæsar entered ; his enemies closed in a dense mass around him, and while they led him to his chair kept off all intruders. Trebonius was specially charged to detain Antonius in conversation at the door. Scarcely was the victim seated, when Tillius Cimber approached with a petition for his brother's pardon. The others, as was concerted, joined in the supplication, grasping his hands, and embracing his neck. Cæsar at first put them gently aside, but, as they became more importunate, repelled them with main force. Tillius seized his toga with both hands, and pulled it violently over his arms. Then P. Casca, who was behind, drew a weapon, and grazed his shoulder with an ill-directed stroke. Cæsar disengaged one hand, and snatched at the hilt, shouting, 'Cursed Casca, what means this?'—'Help,' cried Casca to his brother Lucius, and at the same moment the others aimed each his dagger at the devoted object. Cæsar for an instant defended himself, and even wounded one of his assailants with his stylus; but when he distinguished Brutus in the press, and saw the steel flashing in his hand also, 'What, thou too, Brutus!' he exclaimed, let go his hold of Casca, and drawing his robe over his face, made no further resistance. The assassins stabbed him through and through, for they had pledged themselves, one and all, to bathe their daggers in his blood. Brutus himself received a wound in their eagerness and trepidation. The victim reeled a few paces, propped by the blows he received on every side, till he fell dead at the foot of Pompeius' statue."—*Merivale*, ch. xxi.

The collection of pictures in this palace is little worth seeing. Among its other sculptures are eight grand reliefs, which, till 1620, were turned upside down, and used as a pavement in Sant' Agnese fuori Mura ; and a fine statue of Aristotle.

"Aristote est à Rome, vous pouvons l'aller voir au palais Spada, tel que le peignent ses biographes et des vers de Christodore sur une statue qui était à Constantinople, les jambes grêles, les joues maigres, le bras hors du manteau, *exserto brachio*, comme dit Sidoine Apollinaire d'une autre statue qui était à Rome. Le philosophe est ici sans barbe aussi bien que sur plusieurs pierres gravées; on attribuait à Aristote l'habitude de se raser, rare parmi les philosophes et convenable à un sage qui vivait à la cour. Du reste, c'est bien là *le maître de ceux qui savent*, selon l'expression de Dante, corps usé par l'étude, tête petite mais qui enferme et comprend tout."—*Ampère, Hist. Rom.* iii. 547.

A little further, on the right, is the *Church of the Trinità dei Pellegrini*, built in 1614; the façade designed by Francesco de' Sanctis. It contains a picture of the Trinity by *Guido*.

The hospital attached to this church was founded by S. Filippo Neri for receiving and nourishing pilgrims of pious intention, who had come from more than sixty miles' distance, for a space of from three to seven days. It is divided into two parts, for males and females. Here, during the Holy Week, the feet of the pilgrims are publicly washed, those of the men by princes, cardinals, &c., those of the women by queens, princesses, and other ladies of rank. In this case the washing is a reality, the feet not having been "prepared beforehand," as for the Lavanda at St. Peter's.

An authentic portrait of S. Filippo Neri is preserved here, said to have been painted surreptitiously by an artist who happened to be one of the inmates of the hospital. When S. Filippo saw it, he said, "You should not have stolen me unawares."

The building in front of this church is the *Monte di Pietà*, founded by the Padre Calvo, in the fifteenth century, to preserve the people from suffering under the usury of the Jews. It is a government establishment, where money is lent at the rate of five per cent. to every class of person. Poor people, especially "Donne di facenda," who have no work in the summer, thankfully avail themselves of this and pawn their necklaces and earrings, which they are able to redeem when the means of subsistence come back with the return of the forestieri. Many Roman servants go through this process annually, and though the Monte di Pietà is often a scene of great suffering when unredeemed goods are sold for the benefit of the establishment, it probably in the main serves to avert much evil from the poorer classes.

A short distance further, following the Via dei Specchi, surrounded by miserable houses (in one of which is a beautiful double gothic window, divided by a twisted column), is the small *Church of Sta. Maria in Monticelli*, which has a fine low campanile of 1110. Admission may always be obtained through the sacristy to visit the famous "miracle-working" picture called "Gesù Nazareno," a modern half-length of Our Saviour, with the eyelids drooping and half-closed. By an illusion of the painting, the eyes, if watched steadily, appear to open and then slowly to close again as if falling asleep,—in the same way that many English family portraits appear to follow the living bystanders with their eyes; but the effect is very curious. In the case of this picture, the pope turned Protestant, and disapproving of the attention it excited, caused its secret removal. Remonstrance was made, that the picture had been a "regalo" to the church, and ought not to be taken away, and when it was believed to be sufficiently forgotten, it was sent back by night. The mosaics in the apse of this obscure church are for the most part quite modern, but enclose a very grand and expressive head of the Saviour of the World, which dates from 1099, when it was ordered by Pope Paschal II.

A little to the left of this church is the *Palazzo Santa*

Croce. This palace will bring to mind the murder of the Marchesa Costanza Santa Croce, by her two sons (because she would not name them her heirs), on the day when the fate of Beatrice Cenci was trembling in the balance, which brought about her condemnation—the then pope, Clement VIII., determining to make her terrible punishment "an example to all parricides."

Prince Santa Croce claims to be a direct descendant of Valerius Publicola, the "friend of the people," who is commemorated in the name of a neighbouring church, "Sancta Maria de Publicolis."

This is one of the few haunted houses in Rome : it is said that by night two statues of Santa Croce cardinals descend from their pedestals, and rattle their marble trains about its long galleries.

Hence a narrow street leads to the *Church of S. Carlo a Catinari*, built in the seventeenth century, from designs of Rosati and Soria. It is in the form of a Greek cross. The very lofty cupola is adorned with frescoes of the cardinal virtues by *Domenichino*, and a fresco of S. Carlo, by *Guido*, once on the façade of the church, is now preserved in the choir. Over the high altar is a large picture by *Pietro da Cortona*, of S. Carlo in a procession during the plague at Milan. In the first chapel on the right, is the Annunciation, by *Lanfranco;* in the second chapel, on the left, the Death of St. Anna, by *Andrea Sacchi*. On the pilaster of the last chapel on the right is a good modern tomb, with delicate detail. The cord which S. Carlo Borromeo wore round his neck in the penitential procession during the plague at Milan, is preserved as a relic here. The Catinari, from whom this church is named, were makers of wooden dishes, who had stalls in the adjoining piazza, or sold their wares on its steps. The street opening from hence (Via de Giubbonari) contains on its right the Palazzo Pio; at the back of which are the principal remains of *The Theatre of Pompey*, which was once of great magnificence. In the portico (of a hundred columns) attached to this theatre, Brutus sate as prætor, on the morning of the murder of Julius Cæsar, and close by was the Curia, or senate-house, where :

——" In his mantle muffling up his face,
Even at the base of Pompey's statue,
Which all the while ran blood, great Cæsar fell." *

Behind the remains of the theatre, perhaps on the very site of the Curia, rises the fine modern *Church of S. Andrea della Valle*,† begun in 1591, by Olivieri, and finished by Carlo Maderno. The façade is by Carlo Rainaldi. The cupola is covered with frescoes by *Lanfranco*, those of the four Evangelists at the angles being by *Domenichino*, who also painted the flagellation and glorification of St. Andrew in the tribune. Beneath the latter are frescoes of events in the life of St. Andrew by *Calabrese*.

"In the fresco of the Flagellation, the apostle is bound by his hands and feet to four short posts set firmly in the ground; one of the executioners, in tightening a cord, breaks it, and falls back; three men prepare to scourge him with thongs: in the foreground we have the usual group of the mother and her frightened children. This is a composition full of dramatic life and movement, but unpleasing."— *Jameson's Sacred Art*, p. 229.

In the second chapel on the left is the tomb of Giovanni della Casa, archbishop of Beneventum, 1556.

* Shakespeare, Julius Cæsar, act iii. sc. 2.
† So called from a slight hollow, scarcely now perceptible, left by a reservoir made by Agrippa for the public benefit, and used by Nero in his fêtes.

The last piers of the nave are occupied by the tombs of Pius II., Eneas Sylvius Piccolomini (1458—64), and Pius III., Todeschini (1503), removed from the old basilica of St. Peter's. The tombs are hideous erections in four stages, by Niccolo della Guardia and Pietro da Todi. The epitaph of the famous Eneas Sylvius is as good as a biography.

"Pius II., sovereign pontiff, a Tuscan by nation, by birth a native of Siena, of the family of the Piccolomini, reigned for six years. His pontificate was short, but his glory was great. He reunited a Christian Council (Basle) in the interests of the faith. He resisted the enemies of the holy Roman see, both in Italy and abroad. He placed Catherine of Siena amongst the saints of Christ. He abolished the Pragmatic Sanction in France. He re-established Ferdinand of Arragon in the kingdom of Sicily. He increased the power of the Church. He established the alum mines which were discovered near Talpha. Zealous for religion and justice, he was also remarkable for his eloquence. As he was setting out for the war which he had declared against the Turks, he died at Ancona. There he had already his fleet prepared, and the doge of Venice, with his senate, as companions in arms for Christ. Brought to Rome by a decree of the fathers, he was laid in this spot, where he had ordered the head of St. Andrew, which had been brought him from the Peloponnese, to be placed. He lived fifty-eight years, nine months, and twenty-seven days. Francis, cardinal of Siena, raised this to the memory of his revered uncle. MCDLXIV."

Pius III., who was the son of a sister of Eneas Sylvius, only reigned for twenty-six days. His tomb was the last to be placed in the old St. Peter's, which was pulled down by his successor.

To the right, from S. Andrea della Valle runs the Via della Valle, on the right of which is the *Palazzo Vidoni* (formerly called Caffarelli, and Stoppani), the lower portion of which was designed by Raphael, in 1513, the upper floor being a later addition. There are a few antiquities preserved here, among them the "Calendarium Prænestinum" of Verrius Flaccus, being five months of a Roman calendar found by Cardinal Stoppani at Palestrina. At the foot of the stairs is a statue of Marcus Aurelius. At one corner of the palace on the exterior is the mutilated statue familiarly known as the *Abbate Luigi*, which was made to carry on witty conversation with the Madama Lucrezia near S. Marco, as Pasquin did with Marforio.

To the left from St. Andrea della Valle runs the *Via S. Pantaleone*, on the right of which, cleverly fitting into an angle of the street, is the gloomy but handsome *Palazzo Massimo alle Colonne*, built c. 1526 by Baldassare Peruzzi. The semi-circular portico has six Doric columns. The staircase and fountain are peculiar and picturesque. In the loggia is a fine antique lion.

The palace is not often shown, but is a good specimen of one of the smaller Roman princely houses. In the drawing-room, well placed, is the famous *Statue of the Discobolus*, a copy of the bronze statue of Myron, found in 1761, upon the Esquiline, near the ruined nymphæum known as the Trophies of Marius. This is more beautiful and better preserved than the Discobolus of the Vatican, of which the head is modern.

"Le tête du discobole Massimi se retourne vers le bras qui lance le disque, ἀπεστραμμένον εἰς τὴν δισκοφόρον. Cette tête est admirable, ce qui est encore une resemblance avec Myron, qui excellait dans les têtes comme Polyclète dans les poitrines et Praxitèle dans les bras."— *Ampère*, iii. 271.

The entrance-hall has its distinctive dais and canopy adorned with the motto of the family "Cunctando Restituit," in allusion to the descent which they claim from the great dictator Fabius Maximus, who is described by Ennius as having "saved the republic by delaying."

"Napoléon interpella un Massimo avec cette brusquerie qui intimidait tant de gens: 'Est il vrai,' lui dit-il, 'que vous descendiez de Fabius-Maximus?'

"'—Je ne saurais le prouver,' répondit le noble romain, 'mais c'est un bruit qui court depuis plus de mille ans dans notre famille.'"—*About*.

On the second floor is a chapel in memory of the temporary resuscitation to life by S. Filippo Neri of Paul Massimo, a youth of fourteen, who had died of a fever, March 16th, 1584.

"S. Filippo Neri was the spiritual director of the Massimo family; it is in his honour that the Palazzo Massimo is dressed up in festal guise every 16th of March. The annals of the family narrate, that the son and heir of Prince Fabrizio Massimo died of a fever at the age of fourteen, and that St. Philip, coming into the room amid the lamentations of the father, mother, and sisters, laid his hand upon the brow of the youth, and called him by his name, on which he revived, opened his eyes, and sate up—'Art thou unwilling to die?' asked the saint. 'No,' sighed the youth. 'Art thou resigned to yield thy soul to God?' 'I am.' 'Then go,' said Philip. 'Va, che sii benedetto, e prega Dio per noi.' —The boy sank back on his pillow with a heavenly smile on his face and expired."—*Jameson's Monastic Orders*.

The back of the palace towards the Piazza Navona is covered with curious frescoes in distemper by *Daniele di Volterra*.

In buildings belonging to this palace, Pannartz and Schweinheim established the first printing office in Rome in 1455. The rare editions of this time bear in addition to the name of the printers, the inscription, " In ædibus Petri de Maximis."

"Conrad Sweynheim et Arnold Pannartz s'établirent près de Subiaco, au monastère de Sainte-Scholastique, qui était occupé par les Bénédictins de leur nation, et publièrent successivement, avec le concours des moines, les *Œuvres de Lactance*, la *Cité de Dieu* de saint Augustin, et le traité *de Oratore* de Cicéron. En 1467, ils se transportèrent à Rome, au palais Massimi, où ils s'associèrent Jean André de Bussi, évêque d'Aleria, qui avait étudié sous Victorin de Feltre, et dont la science leur fut d'une haute utilité pour la correction de leurs textes. Le savant évêque leur donnait son temps, ses veilles :—'Malheureux métier,' disait-il, 'qui consiste non pas à chercher des perles dans le fumier, mais du fumier parmi les perles !'—Et cependant il s'y adonnait avec passion, sans même y trouver l'aisance. Les livres, en effet, se vendirent d'abord si mal que Jean-André de Bussi n'avait pas toujours de quoi se faire faire la barbe. Les premiers livres qu'il publia chez Conrad et Arnold furent la *Grammaire de Donatus*, à trois cents exemplaires, et les *Épitres familières de Cicéron*, à cinq cent cinquante."—*Gournerie, Rome Chrétienne*, ii. 79, 1.

Further, on the right, is the modernized *Church of S. Pantaleone*, built originally in 1216 by Honorius III., and given by Gregory XV., in 1641, to S. Giuseppe Calasanza, founder of the Order of the Scolopians, and of the institution of the Scuola Pia. He died in 1648, and is buried here in a porphyry sarcophagus.

Adjoining this, is the very handsome *Palazzo Braschi*, the last result of papal nepotism in Rome,—built at the end of the last century by Morelli, for the Duke Braschi, nephew of Pius VI. The staircase, which is, perhaps, the finest in Rome, is adorned with sixteen columns of red oriental granite. Annual subscription balls for charities are held in this palace.

At the further corner of the Braschi palace stands the mutilated but famous statue called Pasquino, from a witty tailor, who once kept a shop opposite, and who used to entertain his customers with all the clever scandal of the day. After the tailor's death his name was transferred to the statue, on whose pedestal were appended witty criticisms on passing events, sometimes in the form of dialogues which Pasquino was supposed to hold with his friend Marforio, another statue at the foot of the Capitol. From the repartees appended to this statue the term Pasquinade is derived.

Pasquin has naturally been regarded as a mortal enemy by the popes, who, on several occasions, have made vain attempts to silence him. The bigoted Adrian VI. wished to have the statue burnt and then thrown into the Tiber, but it was saved by the suggestion of Ludovico Suessano, that his ashes would turn into frogs, who would croak louder than he had done. When Marforio, in the hope of stopping the dialogues, was shut up in the Capitoline museum, the pope attempted to incarcerate Pasquino also, but he was defended by his proprietor, Duke Braschi. Among offensive Pasquinades which have been placed here are:

"Venditur hic Christus, venduntur dogmata Petri,
Descendam infernum ne quoque vendar ego."

Among the earliest Pasquinades were those against the venality and evil life of Alexander VI. (Rodrigo Borgia, 1492—1503):

"Vendit Alexander claves, altaria, Christum:
Emerat ille prius, vendere jure potest."

and,

"Sextus Tarquinius, Sextus Nero—Sextus et iste;
Semper sub Sextis perdita Roma fuit."

and, upon the body of his son Giovanni, murdered by his brother Cæsar Borgia, being fished up on the following day from the Tiber:

"Piscatorem hominum re te non, Sexte, putemus,
Piscaris natum retibus ecce tuum."

In the reign of the warlike Julius II. (1503—13), of whom it is said that he threw the keys of Peter into the Tiber, while marching his army out of Rome, declaring that the sword of Paul was more useful to him:

"Cum Petri nihil efficiant ad prælia claves,
Auxilio Pauli forsitan ensis erit."

and, in allusion to his warlike beard :

"Huc barbam Pauli, gladium Pauli, omnia Pauli :
Claviger ille nihil ad mea vota Petrus."

At a moment of great unpopularity :

"Julius est Romæ, quid abest ? Date, numina, Brutum.
Nam quoties Romæ est Julius, illa perit."

In reference to the sale of indulgences and benefices by Leo X. :

"Dona date, astantes ; versus ne reddite ; sola
Imperat æthereis alma Moneta deis."

and to his love of buffoons :

"Cur non te fingi scurram, Pasquille, rogasti ?
Cum Romæ scurris omnia jam licent."

and with reference to the death of Leo, suddenly, under suspicion of poison, and without the sacrament :

"Sacra sub extrema, si forte requiritis, horâ
Cur Leo non potuit sumere : vendiderat."

On the death of Clement VII. (1534), attributed to the mismanagement of his physician, Matteo Curzio :

"Curtius occidit Clementem—Curtius auro
Donandus, per quem publica parta salus."

To Paul III. (1534—50) who attempted to silence him, Pasquin replied :

"Ut canerent data multa olim sunt vatibus æra ;
Ut taceam, quantum tu mihi, Paule, dabis."

Upon the spoliation of ancient Rome by Urban VIII. :

"Quod non fecerunt barbari, fecerunt Barberini."

Upon the passion of Innocent X. (1644—55) for his sister-in-law, Olympia Maldacchini:

"Magis amat Olympiam quam Olympum."

Upon Christina of Sweden, who died at Rome, in 1689:

"Regina senza Regno,
Christiana senza Fede,
E Donna senza Vergogna."

In reference to the severities of the Inquisition during the reign of Innocent XI. (1676—89):

"Se parliamo, in galera; se scriviamo, impiccati; se stiamo in quiete, al santo uffizio. Eh!—che bisogna fare?"

To Francis of Austria, on his visit to Rome:

"Gaudium urbis,—fletus provinciarum,—risus mundi.

After an awful storm, and the plunder of the works of art by Napoleon occurring together:

"L'Altissimo in sù, ci manda la tempesta,
L'Altissimo qua giù, ci toglia quel che resta,
E fra le Due Altissimi,
Stiamo noi malissimi."

During the stay of the French in Rome:

"I Francesi son tutti ladri."

. . . .

"Non tutti—ma Buona parte."

Against the vain-glorious follies of Pius VI., Pasquin was especially bitter. Pius finished the sacristry of St. Peter's, and inscribed over its entrance, " Quod ad Templi Vaticani ornamentum publico vota flagitabant, Pius VI. fecit." The next day Pasquin retorted:

"Publica! mentiris! Non publica vota fuere,
Sed tumidi ingenii vota fuere tui."

Upon his nepotism, when building the Braschi palace:

"Tres habuit fauces, et terno Cerberus ore
Latratus intra Tartara nigra dabat.
Et tibi plena fame tria sunt vel quatuor ora
Quæ nulli latrant, quemque sed illa vocant."

And in allusion to the self-laudatory inscriptions of this pope upon all his buildings, at a time when the two-baiocchi loaf of the common people was greatly reduced in size; one of these tiny loaves was exhibited here, with the satirical notice, " Munificentia Pii Sexti."

But perhaps the most remarkable of all Pasquin's productions is his famous Antithesis Christi:

"Christus regna fugit—Sed vi Papa subjugat urbem.
Spinosam Christus—Triplicem gerit ille coronam.
Abluit ille pedes—Reges his oscula præbent.
Vectigal solvit—Sed clerum hic eximit omnem.
Pavit oves Christus—Luxum hic sectatur inertem.
Pauper erat Christus—Regna hic petit omnia mundi.
Bajulat ille crucem—Hic servis portatur avaris.
Spernit opes Christus—Auri hic ardore tabescit.
Vendentes pepulit templo—Quos suscipit iste.
Pace venit Christus—Venit hic radiantibus armis.
Christus mansuetus venit—Venit ille superbus.
Quas leges dedit hic—Præsul dissolvit iniquus.
Ascendit Christus—Descendit ad infera Præsul."

The statue called Pasquin is said to represent Menelaus with the body of Patroclus, and to be the same as two groups which still exist at Florence, but so little remains of either of these heroes, that it could only have been when overpowered by "L'esprit de contradiction," that Bernini protested that this was "the finest piece of ancient sculpture in Rome."

" A l'angle que forment deux rues de Rome se voit encore il Pasquino, nom donné par le peuple à un des plus beaux restes de la sculpture antique. Bernin, qui exagérait, disait le plus beau ; cette assertion fut sur le point d'attirer un duel à celui qui se l'était permise. Tout homme qui s'avise d'avoir une opinion sur les monuments de Rome s'applaudira pour son compte, en le regrettant peut-être, qu'on ne prenne plus si à cœur les questions archéologiques."—*Ampère, Hist. Rome,* iii. 440.

"Jan. 16, 1870. The public opinion of Rome has only one traditional organ. It is that mutilated block of marble called Pasquin's statue. . . . . . on which are mysteriously affixed by unknown hands the frequent squibs of Roman mother-wit on the events of the day. That organ has now uttered its cutting joke on the Fathers in Council. Some mornings ago there was found pasted in big letters on this defaced and truncated stump of a once choice statue the inscription, 'Libero come il Concilio.' The sarcasm is admirably to the point."—*Times.*

Following the Via dell' Anima from hence, on the right, opposite the mediæval *Torre Mellina*, is the *Church of Sant' Agnese*. It was built in 1642 by Girolamo Rainaldi, in the form of a Greek cross, upon the site of the scaffold where St. Agnes, in her fourteenth year, was compelled to be burnt alive.* When

"The blessed Agnes, with her hands extended in the midst of the flames, prayed thus: 'It is to thee that I appeal, to thee, the all-powerful, adorable, perfect, terrible God. O my Father, it is through thy most blessed Son that I have escaped from the menaces of a sacrilegious tyrant, and have passed unblemished through shameful abominations. And thus I come to thee, to thee whom I have loved, to thee whom I have sought, and whom I have always chosen."—*Roman Breviary.*

Then the flames, miraculously changed into a heavenly shower, refreshed instead of burning her, and dividing in two, and leaving her uninjured, consumed her executioners, and the virgin saint cried :—

"I bless Thee, O Father of my God and Saviour Jesus Christ, who, by the power of this thy well-beloved Son, commanded the fire to respect me.".

* The story of St. Agnes is told by St. Jerome.

"At this age, a young girl trembles at an angry look from her mother ; the prick of a needle draws tears as easily as a wound. Yet fearless under the bloody hands of her executioners, Agnes is immoveable under the heavy chains which weigh her down ; ignorant of death, but ready to die, she presents her body to the point of the sword of a savage soldier. Dragged against her will to the altar, she holds forth her arms to Christ through the fires of the sacrifice; and her hand forms even in those blasphemous flames the sign which is the trophy of a victorious Saviour. She presents her neck and her two hands to the fetters which they bring for her, but it is impossible to find any small enough to encircle her delicate limbs."—*St. Ambrose.*

The statue of St. Sebastian in this church is an antique, altered by *Maini*, that of St. Agnes is by *Ercole Ferrata;* the bas-relief of St. Cecilia is by *Antonio Raggi.* Over the entrance is the half-length figure and tomb of Innocent X. (Gio. Battista Pamfili, 1644—55), an amiable but feeble pope, who was entirely governed by his strong-minded and avaricious sister-in-law, Olympia Maldacchini, who deserted him on his death-bed, making off with the accumulated spoils of his ten years' papacy, which enabled her son, Don Camillo, to build the Palazzo Doria Pamfili, in the Corso, and the beautiful Villa Doria Pamfili.*

"After the three days during which the body of Innocent remained exposed at St. Peter's, say the memoirs of the time, no one could be found who would undertake his burial. They sent to tell Donna Olympia to prepare for him a coffin, and an escutcheon, but she answered that she was a poor widow. Of all his other relations and nephews, not one gave any sign of life ; so that at length the body was carried away into a chamber where the masons kept their tools. Some one, out of pity, placed a lighted tallow-candle near the head ; and some one else having mentioned that the room was full of rats, and that they might eat the corpse, a person was found who was willing to pay for a watcher. And after another day had elapsed, Monsignor Scotti, the majordomo, had pity upon him, and prepared him a coffin of poplarwood, and Monsignor Segni, Canon of St. Peter's, who had been his majordomo, and whom he had dismissed, returned him good for evil, and expended five crowns for his burial."—*Gregorovius.*

* Donna Olympia soon after died of the plague at her villa near Viterbo.

Beneath the church are vaulted chambers, said to be part of the house of infamy where St. Agnes was publicly exposed * before her execution.

"As neither temptation nor the fear of death could prevail with Agnes, Sempronius thought of other means to vanquish her resistance; he ordered her to be carried by force to a place of infamy, and exposed to the most degrading outrages. The soldiers, who dragged her thither, stripped her of her garments; and when she saw herself thus exposed, she bent down her head in meek shame and prayed; and immediately her hair, which was already long and abundant, became like a veil, covering her whole person from head to foot; and those who looked upon her were seized with awe and fear as of something sacred, and dared not lift their eyes. So they shut her up in a chamber, and she prayed that the limbs which had been consecrated to Jesus Christ should not be dishonoured, and suddenly she saw before her a white and shining garment, with which she clothed herself joyfully, praising God, and saying, 'I thank thee, O Lord, that I am found worthy to put on the garment of thine elect!' and the whole place was filled with miraculous light, brighter than the sun at noon-day.

* * * * * *

"The chamber, which, for her preservation, was filled with heavenly light, has become, from the change of level all over Rome, as well as from the position of the church, a subterranean cell, and is now a chapel of peculiar sanctity, into which you descend by torchlight. The floor retains the old mosaic, and over the altar is a bas-relief, representing St. Agnes, with clasped hands, and covered only by her long tresses, while two ferocious soldiers drive her before them. The upper church, as a piece of architecture, is beautiful, and rich in precious marbles and antique columns. The works of art are all mediocre, and of the 17th century, but the statue over her altar has considerable elegance. Often have I seen the steps of this church, and the church itself, so crowded with kneeling worshippers at matins and vespers, that I could not make my way among them;—principally the women of the lower orders, with their distaffs and market baskets, who had come thither to pray, through the intercession of the patron saint, for the gifts of meekness and chastity,—gifts not abounding in these regions."—*Jameson's Sacred Art.*

Yorkshire maidens, anxious to know who their future

---

* "Les maisons de la Place Navone sont assises sur la base des anciens gradins du cirque de Domitien. Sous ces gradins étaient les voûtes habitées par des femmes perdues."—*Ampère, Emp.* ii. 137.

spouse is to be, still consult St. Agnes on St. Agnes' Eve, after 24 hours' abstinence from everything but pure spring water, in the distich :

> "St. Agnes, be a friend to me,
> In the boon I ask of thee;
> Let me this night my husband see."

Here, on the festival of St. Agnes, the papal choir sing the antiphons of the virgin saint, and the hymn "Jesu Corona Virginum."

The front of Sant' Agnese opens upon the *Piazza Navona*, a vast oblong square on the site of the ancient Circus Agonalis, decorated with three fountains. That in the centre, by Bernini, supports an obelisk brought from the Circus of Maxentius, where it was erected in honour of Domitian. Around the mass of rock which supports the obelisk are figures of the gods of the four largest rivers (Danube, Nile, Ganges, Rio de la Plata). That of the Nile veiled his face, said Bernini, that he might not be shocked by the façade which was added by Borromini to the Church of St. Agnes.

"Bernin s'ingéra de creuser un des fameux piliers de St. Pierre pour y pratiquer un petit escalier montant à la tribune ; aussitôt le dôme prit coup et se fendit. On fut obligé de le relier tout entier avec un cercle de fer. Ce n'est point raillerie, le cercle y est encore ; le mal n'a pas augmenté depuis. Par malheur pour le pauvre cavalier, on trouva dans les Mémoires de Michel-Ange qu'il avait recommandé, *sub pœnâ capitis*, de ne jamais toucher aux quatre piliers massifs faits pour supporter le dôme, sachant de quelle masse épouvantable il allait les charger ; le pape voulait faire pendre Bernin, qui, pour se rédimer, inventa la fontaine Navone."—*De Brosses*.

The lower fountain, also by Bernini, is adorned with tritons and the figure of a Moor. The great palace to the right of the church is the *Palazzo Pamfili*, built by Rainaldi for Innocent X. in 1650. It possesses a ceiling painted by *Pietro di Cortona* with the adventures of Eneas. Its music-hall is still occasionally used for public concerts. It was in this palace that the notorious Olympia Maldacchini, foundress of the Pamfili fortunes, besported herself during the reign of her brother-in-law, Innocent X.

"The great object of Donna Olympia was to keep at a distance from Innocent every person and every influence that could either lessen her own, or go shares in the profits to be extracted from it. For this, after all, was the great and ultimate scope of her exertions. To secure the profits of the papacy in hard cash; this was the problem. No appointment to office of any kind was made, except in consideration of a proportionable sum paid down into her own coffers. This often amounted to three or four years' revenue of the place to be granted. Bishoprics and benefices were sold as fast as they became vacant. One story is told of an unlucky disciple of Simon, who on treating with the popess, for a very valuable see, just fallen vacant, and hearing from her a price, at which it might be his, far exceeding all he could command, persuaded the members of his family to sell all they had for the purpose of making this profitable investment. The price was paid, and the bishopric was given to him, but with a fearful resemblance to the case of Ananias, he died within the year; and his ruined family saw the see a second time sold by the insatiable and incorrigible Olympia. . . . During the last year of Innocent's life, Olympia literally hardly ever quitted him. Once a week, we read, she left the Vatican, secretly by night, accompanied by several porters carrying sacks of coin, the proceeds of the week's extortions and sales, to her own palace. And, during these short absences, she used to lock the pope into his chamber, and take the key with her!'—*Trollope's Life of Olympia Pamfili*.

On the opposite side of the piazza, some architectural fragments denote the half-ruined *Church of S. Giacomo degli Spagnuoli* of the fifteenth century. It possesses a gothic rose window, which is almost unique in Rome. There is a handsome door on the other side towards the Via della Sediola. The lower end of the square near this is occupied by the *Palazzo Lancellotti*, built by Pirro Ligorio, behind which is the frescoed front of Palazzo Massimo, mentioned above. The Piazza Navona has been used as a market ever since 1447. In the hot months, the singular custom prevails of occasionally stopping the escape of water from the fountains, and so turning the square into a lake, through which the rich splash about in carriages, and eat ices and drink coffee in the water, while the poor look on from raised galleries. It is supposed that this practice is a remnant of the pleasures of the Naumachia, once annually exhibited almost on this very spot, formerly the Circus Agonalis.

Vitale Mascardi gives an extraordinary account of the magnificent tournament held here in 1634 in honour of the visit of Prince Alexander of Poland, when the piazza was hung with draperies of gold and silver, and Donna Anna Colonna and Donna Costanza Barberini awarded gorgeous prizes of diamonds to noble and princely competitors.

Nearly opposite Sant' Agnese, a short street leads (passing on the left, Arvotti's, the famous Roman-scarf shop) to the front of the *Palazzo Madama,* which is sometimes said to derive its name from Margaret of Parma, daughter of Charles V., who once occupied it, and sometimes from Catherine de' Medici, who also lived here, and under whom it was altered in its present form by Paolo Marucelli. The balcony towards the piazza is the scene every Saturday at noon of the drawing of the Roman lottery.

"In the middle of the balcony, on the rail, is fixed a glass barrel, with a handle to turn it round. Behind it stand three or four officials, who have been just now ushered in with a blast from two trumpeters, also stationed in the balcony. Immediately behind the glass barrel itself stands a boy of some twelve or thirteen years, dressed in the white uniform of one of the orphan establishments, with a huge white shovel hat. Some time is occupied by the folding, and putting into the barrel, pieces of paper, inscribed with the numbers, from one onwards. Each of these is proclaimed, as folded and put in, by one of the officials who acts as spokesman or crier. At last, after eighty-seven, eighty-eight, and eighty-nine have been given out, he raises his voice to a chant, and sings forth, *Numero novanta,* 'number ninety,' this completing the number put in.

'And now, or before this, appears on the balcony another character —no less a person than a Monsignore, who appears, not in his ordinary, but in his more solemn official costume; and this connects the ceremonial directly with the spiritual authority of the realm. And now commences the drawing. The barrel having been for some time turned rapidly round to shuffle the numbers, the orphan takes off his hat, makes the sign of the cross, and having waved his open hand in the air to show that it is empty, inserts it into the barrel, and draws out a number, giving it to the Monsignore, who opens it and hands it to the crier. This latter then proclaims it—'*Prima-estratta, numero venti cinque.*' Then the trumpets blow their blast, and the same is repeated four times more: the proclamation varying each time, *Seconda estratta, Terza, Quatra, Quinta,* etc., five numbers being thus the whole drawn, out of ninety put in. This done, with various expressions of surprise, delight, or disappointment from the crowd below, the officials disappear, the square empties itself, and all is as usual till the next Saturday at the same time. . . . .

"In almost every street in Rome are shops devoted to the purchase of lottery tickets. Two numbers purchased with the double chance of these two numbers turning up are called an *ambo,* and three purchased with the treble chance of those three turning up, are called a *terno,* and, of course, the higher and more perilous the stake, the richer the prize, if obtained."—*Alford's Letters from Abroad.*

"Les étrangers qui viennent à Rome commencent par blâmer sévèrement la loterie. Au bout de quelque temps, l'esprit de tolérance qui est dans l'air pénètre peu-à-peu jusqu'au fond de leur cerveau ; ils excusent un jeu philanthropique qui fournit au pauvre peuple six jours d'espérances pour cinq sous. Bientôt, pour se rendre compte du mécanisme de la loterie, ils entrent euxmêmes dans un bureau, en évitant de se laisser voir. Trois mois après, ils poursuivent ouvertement une combinaison savante ; ils ont une théorie mathématique qu'ils signeraient volontiers de leur nom ; ils donnent des leçons aux nouveaux arrivés ; ils érigent le jeu en principe et jurent qu'un homme est impardonnable s'il ne laisse pas une porte ouverte à la Fortune."—*About, Rome Contemporaine.*

The court at the back of the palazzo is now occupied by the General Post Office.

Close by is the *Church of S. Luigi dei Francesi*, rebuilt 1589, with a façade by Giacomo della Porta. It contains a number of tombs of eminent Frenchmen who have died in Rome, and some good pictures.

Following the right aisle, the second chapel has frescoes from the life of Sta. Cecilia, by *Domenichino* (she gives clothes to the poor,—is crowned by an angel with her husband Valerian,—refuses to sacrifice to idols,—suffers martyrdom,—enters into heaven).

"Domenichino is often cold and studied in the principal subject, while the subordinate persons have much grace, and a noble character of beauty. Of this the two frescoes in S. Luigi at Rome, from the life of Sta. Cecilia, are striking examples. It is not the saint herself, bestowing her goods from a balcony, who contributes the chief subject, but the masterly group of poor people struggling for them below. The same may be said of the death of the saint, where the admiration and grief of the bystanders are inimitable."—*Kugler*.

"Reclining on a couch, in the centre of the picture, her hand pressed on her bosom, her dying eyes raised to heaven, the saint is breathing her last; while female forms, of exquisite beauty and innocence, are kneeling around, or bending over her. The noble figure of an old man, whose clasped hands and bent brow seem to bespeak a father's affection, appears on one side; and lovely children, in all the playful graces of unconscious infancy, as usual in Domenichino's paintings, by contrast heighten, yet relieve, the deep pathos of the scene. From above, an angel—such an angel as Domenichino alone knew how to paint, a cherub form of light and loveliness—is descending on rapid wing, bearing to the expiring saint the crown and palm of glory."—*Eaton's Rome*.

The copy of Raphael's Sta. Cecilia over the altar is by *Guido*. The fourth chapel has on the right frescoes by *Girolamo Sicciolante*, on the left by *Pellegrino da Bologna*, the altar-piece is by *Giacomo del Conte*. The fifth chapel has on the right the monument of Agincourt (ob. 1814), the famous archæologist, on the left that of Guerin the painter.

S. LUIGI DEI FRANCESI.

The high altar has an Assumption by *Bassano*.
The first chapel in the left aisle has a St. Sebastian by *Massei*. In the fifth chapel, of St. Matthew, three pictures by *Caravaggio* represent the vocation and martyrdom of that saint.

"The paintings of Caravaggio at S. Luigi belong to his most comprehensive works. The Martyrdom of St. Matthew, with the angel with a palm branch squatting upon a cloud, and a boy running away, screaming, though highly animated, is an offensive production. On the other hand, the Calling of the Apostle may be considered as a *genre* picture of grand characteristic figures ; for instance, those of the money-changers and publican at the table ; some of them counting money, others looking up astonished at the entrance of the Saviour."—*Kugler*.

"Over the altar is St. Matthew writing his Gospel ; he looks up at the attendant angel, who is behind with outspread wings, and in the act of dictating. On the left is the Calling of St. Matthew : the saint, who has been counting money, rises with one hand on his breast, and turns to follow the Saviour : an old man, with spectacles on his nose, examines with curiosity the personage whose summons has had such a miraculous effect : a boy is slyly appropriating the money which the apostle has thrown down. The third picture is the martyrdom of the saint, who, in the sacerdotal habit, lies extended on a block ; while a half-naked executioner raises the sword, and several spectators shrink back with horror. There is nothing dignified or poetical in these representations ; and though painted with all that power of effect which characterized Caravaggio, then at the height of his reputation, they have also his coarseness of feeling and execution : the priests were (not without reason) dissatisfied ; and it required all the influence of his patron, Cardinal Giustiniani, to induce them to retain the pictures in the church where we now see them."—*Jameson's Sacred Art*, p. 146.

Amongst the monuments scattered over this church are those of Cardinal d'Ossat, ambassador of Henry IV. ; Cardinal de la Grange d' Arquien, father-in-law of Sobieski, who died at the age of 105 ; Cardinal de la Trémouille, ambassador of Louis XIV. ; Madame de Montmorin, with an epitaph by Chateaubriand ; and Claude Lorraine, who is buried at the Trinità di Monti.

The pillars which separate the nave and aisles are of splendid Sicilian jasper. They were intended for S. Ignazio, but when the Order of the Jesuits was dissolved by Clement XIV., he presented them to S. Luigi.

The site of this church, the Palazzo Madama, and their adjoining buildings, was once occupied by the baths of Nero. They are commemorated by the name of the small church " S. Salvatore in Thermis."

In front of S. Luigi are the *Palaces Patrizi and Giustiniani*, and, following—to the right—the Via della Sediola, on the left is the entrance to the *University of the Sapienza*, founded by Innocent IV. in 1244 as a law school. Its buildings were begun by Pius III. and Julius II., and extended by Leo X. on plans of Michael Angelo. The portico was built under Gregory XIII. by Giacomo della Porta. The northern façade was erected by Borromini, with the ridiculous church (S. Ivo), built in the form of a bee to flatter Urban VIII., that insect being his device. The building is called the Sapienza, from the motto, " Initium Sapientiæ timor Domini," engraved over the window above the principal entrance. Forty professors teach here all the different branches of law, medicine, theology, philosophy, and philology.

Behind the Sapienza is the small *Piazza di S. Eustachio*, containing on three sides the Giustiniani, Lante, and Maccarini palaces, and celebrated for the festival of the Befana,* which takes place here.

" The Piazza and all the adjacent streets are lined with booths covered with every kind of plaything for children. These booths are gaily illuminated with rows of candles and the three-wick'd brass *lucerne* of Rome ; and at intervals, painted posts are set into the pavement, crowned

* A corruption of " Epiphania "—Epiphany.

with pans of grease, with a wisp of tow for wick, from which flames blaze and flare about. Besides these, numbers of torches carried about by hand lend a wavering and picturesque light to the scene. By eight o'clock in the evening crowds begin to fill the piazza and the adjacent streets. Long before one arrives the squeak of penny-trumpets is heard at intervals; but in the piazza itself the mirth is wild and furious, and the din that salutes one's ears on entering is almost deafening. The object of every one is to make as much noise as possible, and every kind of instrument for this purpose is sold at the booths. There are drums beating, *tamburelli* thumping and jingling, pipes squeaking, watchman's rattles clacking, penny-trumpets and tin-horns shrilling, the sharpest whistles shrieking,—and mingling with these is heard the din of voices, screams of laughter, and the confused burr and buzz of a great crowd. On all sides you are saluted by the strangest noises. Instead of being spoken to, you are whistled at. Companies of people are marching together in platoons, or piercing through the crowd in long files, and dancing and blowing like mad on their instruments. It is a perfect witches' Sabbath. Here, huge dolls dressed as Polichinello or Pantaloon are borne about for sale,—or over the heads of the crowd great black-faced jumping-jacks, lifted on a stick, twitch themselves in fantastic fits,—or, what is more Roman than all, long poles are carried about strung with rings of hundreds of *Giambelli* (a light cake, called jumble in English), which are screamed for sale at a *mezzo baiocco* each. There is no alternative but to get a drum, whistle, or trumpet, and join in the racket,—and to fill one's pocket with toys for the children, and absurd presents for one's older friends. The moment you are once in for it, and making as much noise as you can, you begin to relish the jest. The toys are very odd, particularly the Roman whistles; some of these are made of pewter, with a little wheel that whirls as you blow; others are of terra-cotta, very rudely modelled into every shape of bird, beast, or human deformity, each with a whistle in its head, breast, or tail, which it is no joke to hear, when blown close to your ears by a stout pair of lungs. The scene is extremely picturesque. Above, the dark vault of night, with its far stars, the blazing and flaring of lights below, and the great, dark walls of the Sapienza and church looking down grimly upon the mirth."—*Story's Roba di Roma.*

The *Church of S. Eustachio* commemorates one, who, first a brave soldier of the army of Titus in Palestine, became master of the horse under Trajan, and general under Hadrian, and who suffered martyrdom for refusing to sacrifice to idols, by being roasted alive in a brazen bull before the Coliseum, with his wife Theophista, and his sons, Agapetus and Theophistus. The relics of these saints repose in a porphyry sarcophagus under the high altar. The stags' heads on the portico and on the apex of the gable refer to the legend of the conversion of St. Eustace.

"One day, while hunting in the forest, he saw before him a white stag, of marvellous beauty, and he pursued it eagerly, and the stag fled before him, and ascended a high rock. Then Placidus (Eustace was called Placidus before his conversion), looking up, beheld, between the horns of the stag, a cross of radiant light, and on it the image of the crucified Redeemer; and being astonished and dazzled by this vision, he fell on his knees, and a voice which seemed to come from the crucifix cried to him, and said, 'Placidus! why dost thou pursue me? I am Christ, whom thou hast hitherto served without knowing me. Dost thou now believe?' And Placidus fell with his face to the earth, and said, 'Lord, I believe!' And the voice answered, saying, 'Thou shalt suffer many tribulations for my sake, and shalt be tried by many temptations; but be strong and of good courage, and I will not forsake thee.' To which Placidus replied, 'Lord, I am content. Do thou give me patience to suffer!' And when he looked up again the glorious vision had departed."—*Jameson's Sacred Art*, p. 792.

A similar story is told of St. Hubert, St. Julian, and St. Felix.

A fresco of St. Peter, by *Pierino del Vaga*, in this church, was much admired by Vasari, who dilates upon the boldness of its design, the simple folds of its drapery, its careful drawing and judicious treatment.

Two streets lead from the Piazza S. Eustachio to—

The Pantheon, the most perfect pagan building in the city, built B.C. 27, by Marcus Agrippa, the bosom friend of Augustus Cæsar, and the second husband of his daughter Julia. The inscription in huge letters, perfectly legible from beneath, "M. AGRIPPA. L. F. COS. TERTIUM FECIT," records its construction. Another inscription on the architrave, now almost illegible, records its restoration under Septimius Severus and his son Caracalla, c. 202, who, " Pantheum vetustate corruptum cum omni cultu restitverunt." Some authorities have maintained that the Pantheon was originally only a vast hall in the baths of Agrippa, acknowledged remains of which exist at no great distance ; but the name " Pantheum " was in use as early as A.D. 59.

In A.D. 399 the Pantheon was closed as a temple in obedience to a decree of the Emperor Honorius, and in 608 was consecrated as a Christian church by Pope Boniface IV., with the permission of the Emperor Phocas, under the title of *Sta. Maria ad Martyres*. To this dedication we owe the preservation of the main features of the building, though it had been terribly maltreated. In 663 the Emperor Constans, who had come to Rome with great pretence of devotion to its shrines and relics, and who only staid there twelve days, did not scruple, in spite of its religious dedication, to strip off the tiles of gilt bronze with which the roof was covered, and carry them off with him to Syracuse, where, upon his murder, a few years after, they fell into the hands of the Saracens. In 1087 it was used by the anti-pope Guibert as a fortress, whence he made incursions upon the lawful pope, Victor III., and his protector, the Countess Matilda. In 1101, another anti-pope, Sylvester IV., was elected here. Pope Martin V., after the return from Avignon, attempted the restoration of the Pantheon by clearing away the mass of miserable buildings in which it was encrusted, and his efforts were continued by Eugenius IV., but Urban VIII. (1623—44), though he spent 15,000 scudi upon the Pantheon, and added the two ugly campaniles, called in derision "the asses' ears," of their architect, Bernini, did not hesitate to plunder the gilt bronze ceiling of the portico, 450,250 lbs. in weight, to make the baldacchino of St. Peter's, and cannons for the Castle of S. Angelo. Benedict XIV. (1740—58) further despoiled the building by tearing away all the precious marbles which lined the attic, to ornament other buildings.

The Pantheon was not originally, as now, below the level of the piazza, but was approached by a flight of five steps. The portico, which is 110 feet long and 44 feet deep, is supported by sixteen grand Corinthian columns of oriental granite, 36 feet in height. The ancient bronze doors remain. On either side are niches, once occupied by colossal statues of Augustus and Agrippa.

"Agrippa wished to dedicate the Pantheon to Augustus, but he refused, and only allowed his statue to occupy a niche on the right of the peristyle, while that of Agrippa occupied the niche on the left."— *Merivale.*

The *Interior* is a rotunda, 143 feet in diameter, covered by a dome. It is only lighted by an aperture in the centre, 28 feet in diameter. Seven great niches around the walls once contained statues of different gods and goddesses, that of Jupiter being the central figure. All the surrounding columns are of giallo-antico, except four, which are of pavonazzetto, painted yellow. It is a proof of the great value and rarity of giallo-antico, that it was always impossible to obtain more to complete the set.

"L'intérieur du Panthéon, comme l'extérieur, est parfaitement conservé, et les édicules, placés dans le pourtour du temple forment les chapelles de l'église. Jamais la simplicité ne fut alliée à la grandeur dans une plus heureuse harmonie. Le jour, tombant d'en haut et glissant le long des colonnes et des parois de marbre, porte dans l'âme un sentiment de tranquillité sublime, et donne à tous les objets, dit Serlio, un air de beauté. Vue du dehors, la coupole de plomb qui a remplacé l'ancienne coupole de bronze couverte de tuiles dorées, fait bien comprendre l'expression de Virgile, lequel l'avait sous les yeux et peut-être en vue, quand il écrivait :

. . . . 'Media testudine templi.'

En effet, cette coupole surbaissée ressemble tout à fait à la carapace d'une tortue."—*Ampère, Emp.* i. 342.

"Being deep in talk, it so happened that they found themselves near the majestic, pillared portico and huge black rotundity of the Pantheon. It stands almost at the central point of the labyrinthine intricacies of the modern city, and often presents itself before the bewildered stranger when he is in search of other objects. Hilda, looking up, proposed that they should enter.

"They went in, accordingly, and stood in the free space of that great circle, around which are ranged the arched recesses and stately altars, formerly dedicated to heathen gods, but Christianized through twelve centuries gone by. The world has nothing else like the Pantheon. So grand it is, that the pasteboard statues over the lofty cornice do not disturb the effect, any more than the tin crowns and hearts, the dusty artificial flowers, and all manner of trumpery gewgaws, hanging at the saintly shrines. The rust and dinginess that have dimmed the precious marble on the walls; the pavement, with its great squares and rounds of porphyry and granite, cracked crosswise and in a hundred directions, showing how roughly the troublesome ages have trampled here; the grey dome above, with its opening to the sky, as if heaven were looking down into the interior of this place of worship, left unimpeded for prayers to ascend the more freely: all these things make an impression of solemnity, which St. Peter's itself fails to produce.

"'I think,' said Kenyon, 'it is to the aperture in the dome—that great eye, gazing heavenward—that the Pantheon owes the peculiarity of its effect. It is so heathenish, as it were—so unlike all the snugness of our modern civilization! Look, too, at the pavement directly beneath the open space ! So much rain has fallen there, in the last two thousand years, that it is green with small, fine moss, such as grows over tombstones in damp English churchyards.'

"'I like better,' replied Hilda, 'to look at the bright, blue sky, roofing the edifice where the builders left it open. It is very delightful, in a breezy day, to see the masses of white cloud float over the opening, and then the sunshine fall through it again, fitfully, as it does now. Would it be any wonder if we were to see angels hovering there, partly in and

partly out, with genial, heavenly faces, not intercepting the light, but transmuting it into beautiful colours? Look at that broad, golden beam—a sloping cataract of sunlight—which comes down from the aperture, and rests upon the shrine, at the right hand of the entrance.'"
—*Hawthorne.*

. . . . "'Entrons dans le temple,' dit Corinne: 'vous le voyez, il reste découvert presque comme il l'était autrefois. On dit que cette lumière qui venait d'en haut était l'emblème de la divinité supérieure à toutes les divinités. Les païens ont toujours aimé les images symboliques. Il semble en effet que ce langage convient mieux à la religion que la parole. La pluie tombe souvent sur ces parvis de marbre; mais aussi les rayons du soleil viennent éclairer les prières. Quelle sérénité; quel air de fête on remarque dans cet édifice! Les païens ont divinisé la vie, et les chrétiens ont divinisé la mort: tel est l'esprit des deux cultes.'"—*Mad. de Staël.*

"In the ancient Pantheon, when the music of Christian chaunts rises among the shadowy forms of the old vanished gods painted on the walls, and the light streams down, not from painted windows in the walls, but from the glowing heavens above, every note of the service echoes like a peal of triumph, and fills my heart with thankfulness."—*Mrs. Charles.*

"'Where,' asked Redschid Pasha, on his visit to the Pantheon, 'are the statues of the heathen gods?' 'Of course they were removed when the temple was Christianized,' was the natural answer. 'No,' he replied, 'I would have left them standing to show how the true God had triumphed over them in their own house.'"—*Cardinal Wiseman.*

"No, great Dome of Agrippa, thou art not Christian! canst not,
Strip and replaster and daub and do what they will with thee, be so!
Here underneath the great porch of colossal Corinthian columns,
Here as I walk, do I dream of the Christian belfries above them;
Or, on a bench as I sit and abide for long hours, till thy whole vast
Round grows dim as in dreams to my eyes, I repeople thy niches,
Not with the martyrs, and saints, and confessors, and virgins, and children,
But with the mightier forms of an older, austerer worship;
And I recite to myself, how
      'eager for battle here
  Stood Vulcan, here matronal Juno,
    And, with the bow to his shoulder faithful,
  He who with pure dew laveth of Castaly
  His flowing locks, who holdeth of Lycia

> The oak forest and the wood that bore him,
> Delos' and Patara's own Apollo.' "
>
> A. H. Clough.

Some antiquarians have supposed that the aperture at the top of the Pantheon was originally closed by a huge " Pigna," or pine-cone of bronze, like that which crowned the summit of the mausoleum of Hadrian, and this belief has been encouraged by the name of a neighbouring church being S. Giovanni della Pigna.

The Pantheon has become the burial-place of painters. Raphael, Annibale Caracci, Taddeo Zucchero, Baldassare Peruzzi, Pierino del Vaga, and Giovanni da Udine, are all buried here.

The third chapel on the left contains the *tomb of Raphael* (born April 6, 1483; died April 6, 1520). From the pen of Cardinal Bembo is the epigram:

> "Ille hic est Raphael, timuit quo sospite vinci
> Rerum magna parens, et moriente mori."*

"Raphael mourut à l'age de 37 ans. Son corps resta exposé pendant trois jours. Au moment où l'on s'apprêtait à le descendre dans sa dernière demeure, on vit arriver le pape (Leon X.) qui se prosterna, pria quelques instants, bénit Raphael, et lui prit pour la dernière fois la main, qu'il arrosa de ses larmes (si prostrò innanzi l'estinto Rafaello et baciogli quella mano, tra le lagrime). On lui fit de magnifiques funérailles, auxquelles assistèrent les cardinaux, les artistes, &c."—*A. Du Pays.*

> "When Raphael went,
> His heavenly face the mirror of his mind,
> His mind a temple for all lovely things
> To flock to and inhabit—when He went,
> Wrapt in his sable cloak, the cloak he wore,
> To sleep beneath the venerable Dome,

---

* "Living, great nature feared he might outvie
  Her works; and, dying, fears herself to die."
  Pope's Translation (without acknowledgment in his Epitaph on Sir Godfrey Kneller.

> By those attended, who in life had loved,
> Had worshipped, following in his steps to Fame,
> ('Twas on an April-day, when Nature smiles,)
> All Rome was there. But, ere the march began,
> Ere to receive their charge the bearers came,
> Who had not sought him? And when all beheld
> Him, where he lay, how changed from yesterday,
> Him in that hour cut off, and at his head
> His last great work;* when, entering in, they looked
> Now on the dead, then on that masterpiece,
> Now on his face, lifeless and colourless,
> Then on those forms divine that lived and breathed,
> And would live on for ages—all were moved;
> And sighs burst forth, and loudest lamentations."
>
> *Rogers.*

Taddeo Zucchero and Annibale Caracci are buried on either side of Raphael. Near the high altar is a monument to Cardinal Gonsalvi (1757—1824), the faithful secretary and minister of Pius VII., by *Thorwaldsen*. This, however, is only a cenotaph, marking the spot where his heart is preserved. His body rests with that of his beloved brother Andrew in the church of S. Marcello.

During the middle ages the pope always officiated here on the day of Pentecost, when, in honour of the descent of the Holy Spirit, showers of white rose-leaves were continually sent down through the aperture during service.

"Though plundered of all its brass, except the ring which was necessary to preserve the aperture above; though exposed to repeated fire; though sometimes flooded by the river, and always open to the rain, no monument of equal antiquity is so well preserved as this rotunda. It passed with little alteration from the pagan into the present worship; and so convenient were its niches for the Christian altar, that Michael Angelo, ever studious of ancient beauty, introduced their design as a model in the Catholic church."—*Forsyth.*

* Raphael lay in state beneath his last great work, the **Transfiguration**.

"Simple, erect, severe, austere, sublime—
Shrine of all saints and temple of all gods,
From Jove to Jesus—spared and bless'd by time,
Looking tranquillity, while falls or nods
Arch, empire, each thing round thee, and man plods
His way through thorns to ashes—glorious dome!
Shalt thou not last? Time's scythe and tyrant's rods
Shiver upon thee—sanctuary and home
Of art and piety—Pantheon! pride of Rome!"
Byron, Childe Harold.

In the Piazza della Rotonda is a small *Obelisk* found in the Campus Martius.

"At a few paces from the streets where meat is sold, you will find gathered round the fountain in the Piazza della Rotonda, a number of bird-fanciers, surrounded by cages in which are multitudes of living birds for sale. Here are Java sparrows, parrots and parroquets, grey thrushes and nightingales, red-breasts (*petti rossi*), yellow canary-birds, beautiful sweet-singing little *cardellini*, and gentle ringdoves, all chattering, singing, and cooing together, to the constant splashing of the fountain. Among them, perched on stands, and glaring wisely out of their great yellow eyes, may be seen all sorts of owls, from the great solemn *barbigiani*, and white-tufted owl, to the curious little *civetta*, which gives its name to all sharp-witted heartless flirts, and the *aziola*, which Shelley has celebrated in one of his minor poems."—*Story's Roba di Roma.*

(Following the Via della Rotonda from hence, in the third street on the left is the small semicircular ruin called, from a fancied resemblance to the favourite cake of the people, *Arco di Ciambella*. This is the only remaining fragment of the baths of Agrippa, unless the Pantheon itself was connected with them.)

Behind the Pantheon, is the *Piazza della Minerva*, where a small *Obelisk* was erected 1667 by Bernini, on the back of an elephant. It is exactly similar to the obelisk in front of the Pantheon, and they were both found near this site, where they formed part of the decorations of the Campus Martius.

The hieroglyphics show that it dates from Hophres, a king of the 25th dynasty. On the pedestal is the inscription:

> "Sapientis Ægypti insculptas obelisco figuras
> Ab elephanto belluarum fortissimo gestari
> Quisquis hic vides, documentum intellige
> Robustæ mentis esse solidam sapientiam sustinere."

One side of the piazza is occupied by the mean ugly front of the *Church of Sta. Maria sopra Minerva*, built in 1370 upon the ruins of a temple of Minerva founded by Pompey. It is the only gothic church in Rome of importance. In 1848—55 it was redecorated with tawdry imitation marbles, which have only a good effect when there is not sufficient light to see them. In spite of this, the interior is very interesting, and its chapels are a perfect museum of relics of art or history. The services, too, in this church were, under the papal government, exceedingly imposing, especially the procession on the night before Christmas, the mass of St. Thomas Aquinas, and that of "the white mule day." Some celebrated divine generally preaches here at 11 A.M. every morning in Lent.

Hither, on the feast of the Annunciation, comes the famous "Procession of the White Mule," when the host is borne by the grand almoner riding on the papal mule, followed by the pope in his glass coach, and a long train of cardinals and other dignitaries. Up to the time of Pius VI., it was the pope himself who rode upon the white mule, but Pius VII. was too infirm, and since his time they have given it up. But this procession has continued to be one of the finest *spectacles* of the kind, and has been an opportunity for a loyal demonstration, balconies being hung with scarlet draperies, and flowers showered down upon the papal coach, while the pope, on arriving and departing, has usually been received with tumultuous " evivas."

On the right of the entrance is the tomb of Diotisalvi, a Florentine knight, ob. 1482. Beginning the circuit of the church by the right aisle, the first chapel has a picture of S. Ludovico Bertrando, by *Baciccio*, the paintings on the pilasters being by *Muziano*. In the second, the Colonna Chapel, is the tomb of the late Princess Colonna (Donna Isabella Alvaria of Toledo) and her child, who both died at Albano in the cholera of 1867. The third chapel is that of the Gabrielli family. The fourth is that of the Annunciation. Over its altar is a most interesting picture, shown as a work of Fra Angelico, but more probably that of *Benozzo Gozzoli*. It represents Monsignore Torquemada attended by an angel, presenting three young girls to the Virgin, who gives them dowries: the Almighty is seen in the clouds. Torquemada was a Dominican Cardinal, who founded the association of the Santissima-Annunziata, which holds its meetings in this chapel, and which annually gives dowries to a number of poor girls, who receive them from the pope when he comes here in state on the 25th of March. On this occasion, the girls who are to receive the dowries are drawn up in two lines in front of the church. Some are distinguished by white wreaths. They are those who are going to " enter into religion," and who consequently receive double the dowry of the others, on the plea that " money placed in the hands of religion bears interest for the poor."

Torquemada is himself buried in this chapel, opposite the tomb, by Ambrogio Buonvicino, of his friend Urban VII., Giov. Battista Castagna, 1590,—who was pope only for eleven days.

The fifth chapel is the burial-place of the Aldobrandini family. It contains a faded Last Supper, by *Baroccio*.

"The Cenacolo of Baroccio, painted by order of Clement VIII. (1594), is remarkable for an anecdote relating to it. Baroccio, who was not eminent for a correct taste, had in his first sketch reverted to the ancient fashion of placing Satan close behind Judas, whispering in his ear, and tempting him to betray his master. The pope expressed his dissatisfaction,—'che non gli piaceva il demonio se dimesticasse tanto con Gesù Christo,'—and ordered him to remove the offensive figure."—*Jameson's Sacred Art*, p. 277.

Here are the fine tombs erected by Clement VIII. (Ippolito Aldobrandini) as soon as he obtained the papacy, to his father and mother. Their architecture is by *Giacomo della Porta*, but the figures are by *Cordieri*, the sculptor of Sta. Silvia's statue. At the sides of the mother's tomb are figures emblematical of Charity, by that of the father, figures of Humility and Vanity. Beyond his mother's tomb is a fine statue of Clement VIII. himself (who is buried at Sta. Maria Maggiore), by *Ippolito Buzi*.

"Hippolyte Aldobrandini, qui prit le nom de Clément VIII., était le cinquième fils du célèbre jurisconsulte Silvestro Aldobrandini, qui, après avoir professé à Pise et joui d'une haute autorité à Florence, avait été condamné à l'exil par le retour au pouvoir des Médicis ses ennemis. La vie de Silvestre devint alors pénible et calamiteuse. Dépouillé de ses biens, il fut, du moins, toujours ennoblir son malheur par la dignité de son caractère. Sa famille présentait un rare assemblage de douces vertus et de jeunes talents qu'une forte éducation développait chaque jour avec puissance. Appelé à Rome par Paul III., qui le nomma avocat consistorial, Silvester s'y transporta avec son épouse, la pieuse Leta Deti, qui, pendant trente-sept ans, fut pour lui comme son bon ange, et avec tous ses enfants, Jean, qui devait être un jour cardinal ; Bernard, qui devint un vaillant guerrier ; Thomas, qui préparait déjà peut-être sa traduction de Diogène-Laërce ; Pierre, qui voulut être jurisconsulte comme son père ; et le jeune Hippolyte, un enfant alors, dont les saillies inquiétaient le vieillard, car il ne savait comment pourvoir à son éducation et utiliser cette vivacité de génie qui déjà brillait

dans son regard. Hippolyte fut élevé aux frais du cardinal Farnèse; puis, tous les emplois, toutes les dignités vinrent successivement au-devant de lui, sans qu'il les cherchât autrement qu'en s'en rendant digne."
—*Gourneric, Rome Chrétienne*, ii. 238.

The sixth chapel contains two fine cinque-cento tombs; on the left, Benedetto Superanzio, bishop of Nicosa, ob. 1495; on the right, a Spanish bishop, Giovanni da Coca, with frescoes. Close to the former tomb, on the floor, is the grave of (archdeacon) Robert Wilberforce, who died at Albano in 1857.

Here we enter the right transept. On the right is a small dark chapel containing a fine Crucifix, attributed to Giotto. The central, or Caraffa Chapel, is dedicated to St. Thomas Aquinas, and is covered with well-preserved frescoes. On the right, St. Thomas Aquinas is represented surrounded by allegorical figures, by *Filippino Lippi*. Over the altar is a beautiful Annunciation, in which a portrait of the donor, Cardinal Olivieri Caraffa, is introduced. Above is the Assumption of the Virgin. On the ceiling are the four Sibyls, by *Raffaelino del Garbo*.

Against the left wall is the tomb of Paul IV., Gio. Pietro Caraffa (1555—59), the great supporter of the Inquisition, the patron of the Jesuits, the persecutor of the Jews (whom he shut up with walls in the Ghetto),—a pope so terrible to look upon, that even Alva, who feared no man, trembled at his awful aspect. Such he is represented upon his tomb, with deeply-sunken eyes and strongly-marked features, with one hand raised in blessing—or cursing, and the keys of St. Peter in the other. The tomb was designed by Pirro Ligorio; the statue is the work of Giacomo and Tommaso Casignuola, and being made in marble of different pieces and colours, is cited by Vasari as an instance of a sculptor's ingenuity in imitating painting with his materials. The epitaph runs:

"To Jesus Christ, the hope and the life of the faithful; to Paul IV. Caraffa, sovereign pontiff, distinguished amongst all by his eloquence, his learning, and his wisdom; illustrious by his innocence, by his liberality, and by his greatness of soul; to the most ardent champion of the catholic faith, Pius V., sovereign pontiff, has raised this monument of his gratitude and of his piety. He lived eighty-three years, one month, and twenty days, and died the 14th August, 1559, the fifth year of his pontificate." *

On the transept wall, just outside this chapel, is the beautiful gothic tomb of Guillaume Durandus, bishop of Mende,† with a recumbent figure guarded by two angels, the background being occupied by a mosaic of the Virgin and Child, by *Giovanni Cosmati*.

The first chapel on a line with the choir—the burial-place of the Altieri family—has an altar-piece, by *Carlo Maratta*, representing five saints canonized by Clement X., presented to the Virgin by St. Peter. On the floor is the incised monument of a bishop of Sutri.

The second chapel—which contains a fine cinque-cento tomb—is that of the Rosary. Its ceiling, representing the Mysteries of the Rosary, is by *Marcello Venusti;* the history of St. Catherine of Siena is by *Giovanni de' Vecchi;* the large and beautiful Madonna with the Child over the altar is attributed to *Fra Angelico*. Here is the tomb of Cardinal Capranica of 1470.

Beneath the high altar, with lamps always burning before it, is a marble sarcophagus with a beautiful figure, enclosing

---

* See Gregorovius, Grabmäler der Päpste.

† Author of the "Rationale Divinorum Officiorum"—"A treasure of information on all points connected with the decorations and services of the mediæval church. Durandus was born in Provence about 1220, and died in 1290 at Rome."—*Lord Lindsay*.

the body of St. Catherine of Siena. In it her relics were deposited in 1461, by Antoninus, archbishop of Florence. On the last pillar to the right is an inscription stating that, " all the indulgences and privileges in every church, of all the religious orders, mendicant or not mendicant, in every part of the world, are granted especially to this church, where is the body of St. Catherine of Siena."

" St. Catherine was one of twenty-five children born in wedlock to Jacopo and Lupa Benincasa, citizens of Siena. Her father exercised the trade of dyer and fuller. In the year of her birth, 1347, Siena reached the climax of its power and splendour. It was then that the plague of Bocaccio began to rage, which swept off 80,000 citizens, and interrupted the building of the great Duomo. In the midst of so large a family and during these troubled times, Catherine grew almost unnoticed, but it was not long before she manifested her peculiar disposition. At six years old she already saw visions and longed for a monastic life: about the same time she used to collect her childish companions together and preach to them. As she grew her wishes became stronger ; she refused the proposals which her parents made that she should marry, and so vexed them by her obstinacy that they imposed on her the most servile duties in their household. These she patiently fulfilled, at the same time pursuing her own vocation with unwearied ardour. She scarcely slept at all, and ate no food but vegetables and a little bread, scourged herself, wore sackcloth, and became emaciated, weak, and half delirious. At length the firmness of her character and the force of her hallucination won the day. Her parents consented to her assuming the Dominican robe, and at the age of thirteen she entered the monastic life. From this moment till her death we see in her the ecstatic, the philanthropist, and the politician combined to a remarkable degree. For three whole years she never left her cell except to go to church, maintaining an almost unbroken silence. Yet, when she returned to the world, convinced at length of having won by prayer and pain the favour of her Lord, it was to preach to infuriated mobs, to toil among men dying of the plague, to execute diplomatic negotiations, to harangue the republic of Florence, to correspond with queens, and to interpose between kings and popes. In the midst of this varied and distracting career she continued to see visions, and to fast and scourge herself. The domestic virtues and the personal wants and wishes of a woman were annihilated in her ; she lived for the

Church, for the poor, and for Christ, whom she imagined to be constantly supporting her. At length she died (at Rome, on the 29th of April, 1380, in her 33rd year) worn out by inward conflicts, by the tension of a half-delirious ecstasy, by want of food and sleep, and by the excitement of political life."—*Cornhill Mag.* Sept. 1866.

On the right of the high altar is a statue of St. John, by *Obicci*,—on the left is the famous statue of Christ, by *Michael Angelo*. This is one of the sculptures which Francis I. tried hard to obtain for Paris. Its effect is marred by the bronze drapery.

Behind, in the choir, are the tombs of two Medici popes. On the left is Leo X., Giovanni de Medici (1513—21). This great pope, son of Lorenzo the Magnificent, was destined to the papacy from his cradle. He was ordained at seven years old, was made a cardinal at seventeen, and pope at thirty-eight, and at the installation procession to the Lateran, rode upon the same white horse, upon which he had fought and had been taken prisoner at the battle of Ravenna. His reign was one of fêtes and pleasures. He was the great patron of artists and poets, and Raphael and Ariosto rose into eminence under his protection. His tomb is from a design of Antonio di Sangallo, but the figure of the pope is by Raffaello da Montelupo.

Near the foot of Leo X.'s tomb is the flat monumental stone of Cardinal Bembo, his friend, and the friend of Raphael, who died 1547. His epitaph has been changed. The original inscription, half-pagan, half-Christian, ran :

"Hic Bembus jacet Aonidum laus maxima Phœbi
   Cum sole, et luna vix periturus honos.
Hic et fama jacet, spes, et suprema galeri
   Quam non ulla queat restituisse dies.
Hic jacet exemplar vitæ omni fraude carentis,
   Summa jacet, summa hic cum pietate fides."

On the right of the choir is the tomb, by Sangallo, of Clement VII., Giulio de Medici (1523—34), son of the Giulio who fell in the conspiracy of the Pazzi,—who in his unhappy reign saw the sack of Rome (1527) under the Constable de Bourbon, and the beginning of the separation from England under Henry VIII. The figure of the pope is by *Baccio Bandinelli*. Among other graves here is that of the English Cardinal Howard, ob. 1694. Just beyond the choir is a passage leading to a door into the Via S. Ignazio. Immediately on the left is the slab tomb of Fra Angelico da Fiesole. It is inscribed :

> " Hic jacet Vene Pictor Fl. Jo. de Florentia Ordinis
>   prædicatorum, 1404.
> " Non mihi sit laudi quod eram velut alter Apelles,
>   Sed quod lucra tuis omnia, Christe, dabam.
> Altera nam terris opera exstant, altera cœlo.
>   Urbs me Johannem flos tulit Etruriæ." *

"Fra Angelico was simple and most holy in his manners,—and let this serve for a token of his simplicity, that Pope Nicholas one morning offering him refreshment, he scrupled to eat flesh without the licence of his superior, forgetful for the moment of the dispensing authority of the pontiff. He shunned altogether the commerce of the world, and living in holiness and in purity, was as loving towards the poor on earth as I think his soul must be now in heaven. He worked incessantly at his art, nor would he ever paint other than sacred subjects. He might have been rich, but cared not to be so, saying that true riches consisted rather in being content with little. He might have ruled over many, but willed it not, saying there was less trouble and hazard of sin in obeying others. Dignity and authority were within his grasp, but he disregarded them, affirming that he sought no other advancement than to escape hell and draw nigh to Paradise. He was most meek and temperate, and by a chaste life loosened himself from the snares of the world, ofttimes saying that the student of painting hath need of quiet and to live without anxiety, and that the dealers in the things of Christ

---

* It is no honour to me to be like another Apelles, but rather, O Christ, that I gave all my gains to thy poor. One was a work for earth, the other for heaven- a city, the flower of Etruria, bare me, John.

ought to live habitually with Christ. Never was he seen in anger with the brethren, which appears to me a thing most marvellous, and all but incredible; his admonitions to his friends were simple and always softened by a smile. Whoever sought to employ him, he answered with the utmost courtesy, that he would do his part willingly so the prior were content.—In sum, this never sufficiently to be lauded father was most humble and modest in all his words and deeds, and in his paintings graceful and devout; and the saints which he painted have more of the air and aspect of saints than those of any other artist. He was wont never to retouch or amend any of his paintings, but left them always as they had come from his hand at first, believing, as he said, that such was the will of God. Some say that he never took up his pencil without previous prayer. He never painted a crucifix without tears bathing his cheeks; and throughout his works, in the countenance and attitude of all his figures, the correspondent impress of his sincere and exalted appreciation of the Christian religion is recognisable. Such was this verily Angelic father, who spent the whole time of his life in the service of God and in doing good to the world and to his neighbour. And truly a gift like his could not descend on any but a man of most saintly life, for a painter must be holy himself before he can depict holiness."—*Lord Lindsay, from Vasari.*

In the same passage are tombs of Cardinal Alessandrino, by Giacomo della Porta; of Cardinal Pimentel, by Bernini; and of Cardinal Bonelli, by Carlo Rainaldi.

Beyond this, in the left transept, is the 'Chapel of S. Domenico, with eight black columns, appropriate to the colour of the Order, and an interesting picture of the saint. Here is the tomb of Benedict XIII., Vincenzo-Maria Orsini (1724—30), by Pietro Bracci. This pope, who had been a Dominican monk, laboured hard in his short reign for the reformation of the Church, and the morals of the clergy.

Over a door leading to the Sacristy are frescoes representing the election of Eugenius IV. in 1431, and of Nicholas V. in 1447, which both took place in this church. The altar of the sacristy has a Crucifixion, by Andrea Sacchi.

Returning down the left aisle, the second chapel, counting

from this end, is that of the Lante family, which contains the fine tomb of the Duchess Lante, ob. 1840, by *Tenerani*, with the Angel of the Resurrection, a sublime upward-gazing figure seated upon the sarcophagus. Here is a picture of St. James, by *Baroccio*.

The third chapel is that of S. Vincenzo Ferreri, apostle of the Order of Preachers, with a miracle-working picture, by *Bernardo Castelli*. The fourth chapel—of the Grazioli family—has on the right a statue of St. Sebastian, by *Mino da Fiesole*, and over the altar a lovely head of our Saviour, by *Perugino*. This chapel was purchased by the Grazioli from the old family of Maffei, of which there are some fine tombs. The fifth chapel—of the Patrizi family—contains the famous miraculous picture called "La Madonna Consolatrice degli afflitti," in honour of which Pope Gregory XVI. conceded so many indulgences, as we read by the inscription.

"La santità di N. S. Gregorio Papa XVI. con breve in data 17 Sept. 1836. Ho accordato l'indulgenzia plenaria a chiunque confessato e communicato visiterà divotamente questa santa imagine della B. Vergine sotto il titolo di consolatrice degli afflitti nella seconda dominica di Luglio e suo ottavo di ciascun anno: concede altresì la parziale indulgenza di 200 giorni in qualunque giorno dell' anno a chiunque almeno contrito visiterà la detta S. Immagine: le dette indulgenze poi sono pure applicabili alle benedette anime del purgatorio."

The last chapel, belonging to a Spanish nobleman, contains the picture of the Crucifixion, which is said to have conversed with Sta. Rosa di Lima.

Near the entrance is the tomb of Cardinal Giacomo Tebaldi, ob. 1466, and beneath it that of Francesco Tornabuoni, by *Mino da Fiesole*. It was for the tomb of the wife of this Tornabuoni, who died in childbirth, that the wonderful relief of Verocchio, now in the Uffizi at Florence, was executed. In the pavement is the gravestone of Paulus

Manutius, the printer, son of the famous Aldus Manutius of Venice, with the inscription, " Paulo Manutio Aldi Filio. Obiit CIƆIƆLXXIV."

The great *Dominican Convent of the Minerva*, lately suppressed, was the residence of the General of the Order. It contains the *Bibliotheca Casanatensis* (so called from its founder, Cardinal Casanata), the largest library in Rome after that of the Vatican, comprising 120,000 printed volumes and 4500 MSS. It is open from 8 to 11 A.M., and $1\frac{1}{2}$ to $3\frac{1}{2}$ P.M. This convent has always been connected with the history of the Inquisition. Here, on June 22, 1633, Galileo was tried before its tribunal for the " heresy " of saying that the earth went round the sun, instead of the sun round the earth, and was forced to recant upon his knees, this " accursed, heretical, and detestable doctrine." As he rose from his humiliation, he is said to have consoled himself by adding, in an undertone, " E pur si muove." When the " Palace of the Holy Office " was stormed by the mob in the revolution of 1848, it was feared that the Dominican convent would have been burnt down.

The very beautiful cloister of the convent, which has a vaulted roof richly painted in arabesques, contains grand fifteenth century tombs,—of Cardinal Tiraso, ob. 1502, and of Cardinal Astorgius, ob. 1503. S. Antonino, archbishop of Florence, who lived in the reigns of Eugenius IV. and Nicholas V., was prior of this convent.

From the Minerva, the *Via del Piè di Marmo*, so called from a gigantic marble foot which stands on one side of it, leads to the Corso.*

* That part of the ancient Campus Martius which contains the Theatre of Marcellus and Portico of Octavia, is described in Chapter V.; that which belongs to the Via Flaminia in Chapter II.

CHAPTER XV.

THE BORGO AND ST. PETER'S.

Via Tordinona—S. Salvatore in Lauro—House of Raphael—S. Giovanni de' Fiorentini—Bridge and Castle of S. Angelo—Sta. Maria Traspontina—Palazzo Giraud—Piazza Scossa-Cavalli—Hospital of Santo Spirito—Piazza and Obelisk of the Vatican—S. Peter's; its portico, tombs, crypts, dome, and sacristy—Churches of S. Stefano and Sta. Marta—Il Cimeterio dei Tedeschi—Palazzo del Santo-Uffizio—S. Salvatore in Torrione—S. Michaele in Sassia.

CONTINUING in a direct course from the Piazza Borghese, we pass through a series of narrow dirty streets quite devoid of interest, but bordering on one side upon the Tiber, of which—with its bridge, S. Angelo and St. Peter's—beautiful views may be obtained from little courts and narrow strips of shore, at the back of the houses.

A short distance after passing (on left) the Locanda dell' Orso, where Montaigne used to stay when he was in Rome, and beneath which are some curious vaulted chambers of c. A.D. 1500, the street, which repeatedly changes its name, is called *Via Tordinona*, from the Tor di Nona, which once stood here, but was destroyed in 1690. It was used as a prison, as is shown by the verse of Regnier :

"Qu'un barisel vous mit dedans la tour de Nonne."

(One of the narrow streets on the left of the Via Tordinona debouches into the Via dei Coronari, close to the

Church of S. Salvatore in Lauro, built on the site of a laurel-grove, which flourished near the portico of Europa. It contains a picture of the Nativity, by *Pietro da Cortona*, and a modern work of *Gagliardi*, representing S. Emidio, S. Nicolo da Tolentino, and S. Giacomo della Marina, the three protectors of Ancona. In a side chapel, opening out of the cloisters, is the rich tomb of Pope Eugenius IV. (Gabriele Condolmieri, ob. 1439), with his recumbent figure by Isaia da Pisa. Francesco Salviati painted a portrait of this pope for the adjoining convent, to which he had belonged, as well as a fine fresco of the Marriage of Cana.*

(There are several other fine monuments in the same chapel with the tomb, which in 1867 was given up as a barrack to the Flemish zouaves, at the great risk of injury to its delicate carvings.)

Passing the *Apollo Theatre*, the Via Tordinona emerges upon the quay of the Tiber, opposite S. Angelo. Hence several streets diverge into the heart of the city.

(At the corner of the Via di Banchi is a house with a frieze, richly sculptured with lions' heads, &c. On the left is the *Church of San Celso in Banchi*, in front of which Lorenzo Colonna, the protonotary, was murdered by the Orsini and Santa Croce, immediately after the death of Sixtus IV. (1484); and where his mother, finding his head cut off, and seizing it by the hair, shrieked forth her curses upon his enemies. On the right, further down the street, is the *Church of Sta. Caterina da Siena*, which contains an interesting altar-piece by *Girolamo Genga*, representing the return of Gregory XI. from Avignon, which was due to her influence.)

* Vasari, v.

The house joining the Ponte S. Angelo is said to have been that of the "Violinista," the friend of Raphael, who is familiar to us from his portrait in the Sciarra Palace. Some say that Raphael died while he was on a visit to him. But the best authorities maintain that he died in a house built for him by Bramante, in the Piazza Rusticucci, which was pulled down to enlarge the Piazza of St. Peter's. No. 124, Via Coronari, not far from the Ponte S. Angelo, is shown as the house in which the great painter lived previously to this, and is that which he bequeathed to the chapel in the Pantheon in which he is buried. It was partly rebuilt in 1705, when Carlo Maderno painted on its façade a portrait of Raphael in *chiaro-scuro*, now almost obliterated. The house at present belongs to the canons of Sta. Maria Maggiore.

(The Via *S. Giovanni de' Fiorentini* leads to the *Church* of that name, abutting picturesquely into the angle of the Tiber. This is the national church of the Tuscans, and was built at the expense of the city of Florence. In the tribune are tombs of the Falconieri family. Here are several fine pictures; a St. Jerome writing, by *Cigoli*, who is buried in this church; St. Jerome praying before a crucifix, *Tito Santi** (1538—1603); St. Francis, *Tito Santi;* SS. Cosmo and Damian condemned to martyrdom by fire,—a grand work of *Salvator Rosa*.

"Some of the altar-pieces of Salvator-Rosa (1615—1673), are well conceived and full of effect, especially when they represent a horrible subject, like the martyrdom in S. Giovanni de' Fiorentini."—*Lanzi*, ii. 165.

The Chapel of the Crucifix is painted by *Lanfranco:*

* A scholar of Bronzino.

the third chapel on the right has frescoes by *Tempesta* on the roof, relating to the history of S. Lorenzo.

The building of this church was begun in the reign of Leo X. by Sansovino, who, for want of space, laid its foundations, at enormous expense, in the bed of the Tiber. While overlooking this, he fell from a scaffold, and being dangerously hurt, was obliged to give up his place to Antonio da Sangallo.* Soon after Pope Leo died, and the work, with many others, was suspended during the reign of Adrian VI. Under Clement VII. Sansovino returned, but was driven away, robbed of all his possessions in the sack of Rome, under the Constable de Bourbon. The church was finished by Giacomo della Porta in 1588, but Alessandro Galileo added the façade in 1725.

"En 1488, une affreuse épidémie décimait les malheureux habitants des environs de Rome; les mourants étaient abandonnés, les cadavres restaient sans sépulture. Aussitôt quelques Florentins forment une confrérie sous le titre de *la Pitié*, pour rendre aux pestiférés les derniers devoirs de la charité chrétienne: c'est à cette confrérie qu'on doit la belle église de Saint-Jean des Florentins, à Strada Giulia."—*Gournerie, Rome Chrétienne.*

The *Ponte S. Angelo* is the Pons Elius of Hadrian, built as an approach to his mausoleum, and only intended for this, as another public bridge existed close by, at the time of its construction. It is almost entirely ancient, except the parapets. The statues of St. Peter and St. Paul, at the extremity, were erected by Clement VII., in the place of two chapels, in 1530, and the angels, by Clement IX., in 1688. The pedestal of the third angel on the right is a relic of the siege of Rome in 1849, and bears the impress of a cannon-ball.

* See Vasari, vol. vii.

These angels, which have been called the "breezy maniacs" of Bernini, are only from his designs. The two angels which he executed himself, and intended for this bridge, are now at S. Andrea delle Fratte. The idea of Clement IX. was a fine one, that "an avenue of the heavenly host should be assembled to welcome the pilgrim to the shrine of the great apostle."

Dante saw the bridge of S. Angelo divided lengthways by barriers to facilitate the movement of the crowds going to and from St. Peter's on the occasion of the first jubilee, 1300.

"Come i Romani per l'esercito molto,
L'anno del giubbileo, su per lo ponte
Hanno a passar la gente modo tolto ;
 Che dall' un lato tutti hanno la fronte
Verso 'l castello, e vanno a Santo Pietro,
Dall' altra sponda vanno verso 'l monte."
Inferno, xviii. 29.

From the Ponte S. Angelo, when the Tiber is low, are visible the remains of the bridge by which the ancient *Via Triumphalis* crossed the river. Close by, where Santo Spirito now stands, was the Porta Triumphalis, by which victors entered the city in triumph.

Facing the bridge, is the famous *Castle of S. Angelo*, built by the Emperor Hadrian as his family tomb, because the last niche in the imperial mausoleum of Augustus was filled when the ashes of Nerva were laid there. The first funeral here was that of Elius Verus, the first adopted son of Hadrian, who died before him. The emperor himself died at Baiæ, but his remains were transported hither from a temporary tomb at Pozzuoli by his successor Antoninus Pius, by whom the mausoleum was completed in A.D. 140.

Here, also, were buried, Antoninus Pius, A.D. 161 ; Marcus Aurelius, 180 ; Commodus, 192 ; and Septimius Severus, in an urn of gold, enclosed in one of alabaster, A.D. 211; Caracalla, in 217, was the last emperor interred here. The well-known lines of Byron :

> " Turn to the mole which Hadrian rear'd on high,
> Imperial mimic of old Egypt's piles,
> Colossal copyist of deformity,
> Whose travell'd phantasy from the far Nile's
> Enormous model, doom'd the artist's toils
> To build for giants, and for his vain earth,
> His shrunken ashes, raise this dome ! How smiles
> The gazer's eye with philosophic mirth,
> To view the huge design which sprung from such a birth."

seem rather applicable to the *Pyramid* of Caius Cestius than to this mausoleum.

The castle, as it now appears, is but the skeleton of the magnificent tomb of the emperors. Procopius, writing in the sixth century, describes its appearance in his time. "It is built," he says, "of Parian marble; the square blocks fit closely to each other without any cement. It has four equal sides, each a stone's throw in length. In height it rises above the walls of the city. On the summit are statues of men and horses, of admirable workmanship, in Parian marble." Canina, in his "Architectura Romana," gives a restoration of the mausoleum, which shows how it consisted of three storeys : 1, a quadrangular basement, the upper part intersected with Doric pillars, between which were spaces for epitaphs of the dead within, and surmounted at the corners by marble equestrian statues ; 2, a circular storey, with fluted Ionic colonnades : 3, a circular storey, surrounded by Corinthian columns, between which were statues. The whole was surmounted by a pyramidal roof, ending in a bronze fir-cone.

"The mausoleum which Hadrian erected for himself on the further bank of the Tiber far outshone the tomb of Augustus, which it nearly confronted. Of the size and dignity which characterized this work of Egyptian massiveness, we may gain a conception from the existing remains; but it requires an effort of imagination to transform the scarred and shapeless bulk before us, into the graceful pile which rose column upon column, surmounted by a gilded dome of span almost unrivalled." *Merivale*, ch. lxvi.

The history of the Mausoleum, in the middle ages, is almost the history of Rome. It was probably first turned into a fortress by Honorius, A.D. 423. From Theodoric it derives the name of "Carcer Theodorici." In 537, it was besieged by Vitiges, when the defending garrison, reduced to the last extremity, hurled down all the magnificent statues which decorated the cornice, upon the besiegers. In A.D. 498 Pope Symmachus removed the bronze fir-cone at the apex of the roof to the court of St. Peter's, whence it was afterwards transferred to the Vatican garden, where it is still to be seen between two bronze peacocks, which probably stood on either side of the entrance.

Belisarius defended the castle against Totila, whose Gothic troops captured and held it for three years, after which it was taken by Narses.

It was in 530 that the event occurred which gave the building its present name. Pope Gregory the Great was leading a penitential procession to St. Peter's, in order to offer up prayers for the staying of the great pestilence which followed the inundation of 589; when, as he was crossing the bridge, even while the people were falling dead around him, he looked up at the mausoleum, and saw an angel on its summit, sheathing a bloody sword,* while a choir of angels around chaunted with celestial voices, the anthem, since adopted by the Church in her vesper service—" *Regina cœli, lætare—quia quem meruisti portare—resurrexit, sicut dixit, Alleluja* "—To which the earthly voice of the pope solemnly responded, " *Ora pro nobis Deum, Alleluja.*"†

In the tenth century the fortress was occupied by the infamous Marozia, who, in turn, brought her three husbands (Alberic, Count of Tusculum; Guido, Marquis of Tuscany; and Hugo, King of Italy) thither, to tyrannise with her over Rome. It was within the walls of this building that Alberic, her son by her first husband, waiting upon his royal stepfather at table, threw a bowl of water over him, when Hugo retorted by a blow, which was the signal for an insurrection, the people taking part with Alberic, putting the king to flight, and imprisoning Marozia. Shut up within these walls, Pope John XI. (931—936), son of Marozia by her first husband, ruled under the guidance of his stronger-minded brother Alberic; here, also, Octavian, son of Alberic, and grandson of Marozia, succeeded in forcing his election as John XII.

* It is interesting to observe that the same vision was seen under the same circumstances in other periods of history.

"So the Lord sent pestilence upon Israel, and there fell of Israel seventy thousand men. And God sent an angel to Jerusalem to destroy it . . . . and David lifted up his eyes, and saw the angel of the Lord stand between the earth and the heaven, having a drawn sword in his hand stretched out over Jerusalem."—1 Chron. xxi. 14—16.

" Before the plague of London had begun (otherwise than in St. Giles's), seeing a crowd of people in the street, I joined them to satisfy my curiosity, and found them all staring up into the air, to see what a woman told them appeared plain to her. This was an angel clothed in white, with a fiery sword in his hand, waving it, or brandishing it over his head : she described every part of the figure to the life, and showed them the motion and the form."—*Defoe, Hist. of the Plague.*

† The pictures at Ara Cœli and Sta. Maria Maggiore both claim to be that carried by St. Gregory in this procession. The song of the angels is annually commemorated on St. Mark's Day, when the clergy pass by in procession to St. Peter's, and the Franciscans of Ara Cœli and the canons of Sta. Maria Maggiore, halting here, chaunt the antiphon, *Regina cœli, lætare.*

(being the first pope who took a new name), and scandalised Christendom by a life of murder, robbery, adultery, and incest.

In 974 the castle was seized by Cencio (Crescenzio Nomentano), the consul, who raised up an anti-pope (Boniface VII.) here, with the determination of destroying the temporal power of the popes, and imprisoned and murdered two popes, Benedict VI. (972), and John XIV. (984), within these walls. In 996 another lawful pope, Gregory V., calling in the emperor Otho to his assistance, took the castle, and beheaded Cencio, though he had promised him life if he would surrender. From this governor the fortress long held the name of Castello de Crescenzio, or Turris Crescentii, by which it is described in mediæval writings. A second Cencio supported another anti-pope, Cadolaus, here in 1063, against Pope Alexander II. A third Cencio imprisoned Gregory VII. here in 1084. From this time the possession of the castle was a constant point of contest between popes and anti-popes. In 1313 Arlotto degli Stefaneschi, having demolished most of the other towers in the city, arranged the same fate for S. Angelo, but it was saved by cession to the Orsini. It was from hence, on December 15, 1347, that Rienzi fled to Bohemia, at the end of his first period of power, his wife having previously made her escape disguised as a friar.

"The cause of final ruin to this monument" is described by Nibby to have been the resentment of the citizens against a French governor who espoused the cause of the anti-pope (Clement VII.) against Urban VI. in 1378. It was then that the marble casings were all torn from the walls and used as street pavements.

A drawing of Sangallo of 1465 shows the "upper part of the fortress crowned with high square towers and turreted buildings; a cincture of bastions and massive square towers girding the whole; two square-built bulwarks flanking the extremity of the bridge, which was then so connected with these outworks that passengers would have immediately found themselves inside the fortress after crossing the river. Marlianus, 1588, describes its double cincture of fortifications—a large round tower at the inner extremity of the bridge; two towers with high pinnacles, and the cross on their summits, the river flowing all around." *

The castle began to assume its present aspect under Boniface IX. in 1395. John XXIII., 1411, commenced the covered way to the Vatican, which was finished by Alexander VI.; and roofed by Urban VIII., in 1630. By the last-named pope the great outworks of the fortress were built under Bernini, and furnished with cannon made from the bronze roof of the Pantheon. Under Paul III. the interior was decorated with frescoes, and a colossal marble angel erected on the summit, in the place of a chapel (S. Angelo inter Nubes), built by Boniface IV. The marble angel was exchanged by Benedict XIV. for the existing angel of bronze, by a Dutch artist, Verschaffelt.

"Paul III. voulant justifier le nom donné à cette forteresse, fit placer au sommet de l'édifice une statue de marbre, représentant un ange tenant à la main une épée nue. Cet ouvrage de Raphaël de Montelupo a été remplacé, du temps de Benoît XIV., par une statue de bronze qui fournit cette belle réponse à un officier français assiégé dans le fort. 'Je me rendrai quand l'ange remettra son épée dans le fourreau.'

" . . . . Cet ange a l'air naïf d'une jeune fille de dix-huit ans, et ne cherche qu'à bien remettre son épée dans le fourreau."—*Stendhal*, i. 33.

* Hemans' Story of Monuments in Rome.

CASTLE OF S. ANGELO.

"I suppose no one ever looked at this statue critically—at least, for myself, I never could ; nor can I remember now whether, as a work of art, it is above or below criticism ; perhaps both. With its vast wings, poised in air, as seen against the deep blue skies of Rome, or lighted up by the golden sunset, to me it was ever like what it was intended to represent—like a vision."—*Jameson's Sacred Art*, p. 98.

Of the castle, as we now see it externally, only the quadrangular basement is of the time of Hadrian ; the round tower is of that of Urban VIII., its top added by Paul III. The four round towers of the outworks, called after the four Evangelists, are of Nicholas V., 1447.

The *interior* of the fortress can be visited by an order. Excavations made in 1825 have laid open the sepulchral chamber in the midst of the basement. Here stood, in the centre, the porphyry sarcophagus of Hadrian, which was stolen by Pope Innocent II. to be used as his own tomb in the Lateran, where it was destroyed by the fire of 1360, the cover alone escaping, which was used for the tomb of Otho II., in the atrium of St. Peter's, and which, after filling this office for seven centuries, is now the baptismal font of that basilica. A spiral passage, thirty feet high, and eleven wide, up which a chariot could be driven, gradually ascends through the solid mass of masonry. There is wonderfully little to be seen. A saloon of the time of Paul III. is adorned with frescoes of the life of Alexander the Great, by *Pierino del Vaga*. This room would be used by the pope in case of his having to take refuge in S. Angelo. An adjoining room, adorned with a stucco frieze of Tritons and Nereids, is that in which Cardinal Caraffa was strangled (1561) under Pius IV., for alleged abuses of authority under his uncle, Paul IV.—his brother, the Marquis Caraffa, being beheaded in the castle the same night. The reputed prison of Beatrice Cenci is shown, but it is very uncertain that she was ever confined here,—also the prison of Cagliostro, and that of Benvenuto Cellini, who escaped, and broke his leg in trying to let himself down by a rope from the ramparts. The statue of the angel by *Montelupo* is to be seen stowed away in a dark corner. Several horrible *trabocchette* (oubliettes) are shown.

On the roof, from which there is a beautiful view, are many modern prisons, where prisoners suffer terribly from the summer sun beating upon their flat roofs.

Among the sculptures found here were the Barberini Faun, now at Munich, the Dancing Faun, at Florence, and the Bust of Hadrian at the Vatican. The sepulchral inscriptions of the Antonines existed till 1572, when they were cut up by Gregory XIII. (Buoncompagni), and the marble used to decorate a chapel in St. Peter's! The magnificent Easter display of fireworks (from an idea of Michael Angelo, carried out by Bernini), called the girandola, used to be exhibited here, but now takes place at S. Pietro in Montorio, or from the Pincio. From 1849 to 1870, the castle was occupied by French troops, and their banner floated here, except on great festivals, when it was exchanged for that of the pope.

Running behind, and crossing the back streets of the Borgo, is the covered passage intended for the escape of the popes to the castle. It was used by Alexander VI. when invaded by Charles VIII. in 1494, and twice by Clement VII. (Giulio di Medici), who fled, in 1527, from Moncada, viceroy of Naples, and in May, 1527, during the terrible sack of Rome by the troops of the Constable de Bourbon.

"Pendant que l'on se battait, Clement VII. était en prières devant l'autel de sa chapelle au Vatican, détail singulier chez un homme qui avait commencé sa carrière par être militaire. Lorsque les cris des mourants lui annoncèrent la prise de la ville, il s'enfuit du Vatican au château St. Ange par le long corridor qui s'élève au-dessus des plus hautes maisons. L'historien Paul-Jove, qui suivait Clement VII., relevait sa longue robe pour qu'il pût marcher plus vîte, et lorsque le pape fut arrivé au pont qui le laissait à découvert pour un instant, Paul-Jove le couvrit de son manteau et de son chapeau violet, de peur qu'il ne fût reconnu à son rochet blanc et ajusté par quelque soldat bon tireur.

"Pendant cette longue fuite le long du corridor, Clement VII. apercevait au-dessous de lui, par les petites fenêtres, ses sujets poursuivis par les soldats vainqueurs qui déjà se répandaient dans les rues. Ils ne faisaient aucun quartier à personne, et tuaient à coups de pique tout ce qu'ils pouvaient atteindre."—*Stendhal*, i. 388.

"The Escape" consists of two passages; the upper open like a loggia, the lower covered, and only lighted by loop-holes. The keys of both are kept by the pope himself.

S. Angelo is at the entrance of *the Borgo*, promised at the Italian invasion of September, 1870, as the sanctuary of the papacy, the tiny sovereignty where the temporal sway of the popes should remain undisturbed,—the sole relic left to them of all their ancient dominions. The Borgo, or *Leonine City*, is surrounded by walls of its own, which were begun in A.D. 846, by Pope Leo IV., for the better defence of St. Peter's from the Saracens, who had been carrying their devastations up to the very walls of Rome. These walls, 10,800 feet in circumference, were completed in four years by labourers summoned from every town and monastery of the Roman states. Pope Leo himself daily encouraged their exertions by his presence. In 852 the walls were solemnly consecrated by a vast procession of the whole Roman clergy barefooted, their heads strewn with ashes, who sprinkled them with holy water, while the pope offered a prayer composed by himself,* at each of the three gates.

The adjoining Piazza Pia is decorated with a fountain erected by Pius IX. The principal of the streets which meet here is the Via del Borgo Nuovo, the main artery to St. Peter's. On its left is the *Church of Sta. Maria Traspontina*, built 1566, containing two columns which bear inscriptions, stating that they were those to which St. Peter and St. Paul were respectively attached, when they suffered flagellation by order of Nero !

This church occupies the site of a Pyramid supposed to have been erected to Scipio Africanus, who died at Liternum, B.C. 183, and which was regarded in the middle ages as the tomb of Romulus. Its sides were once coated with marble, which was stripped off by Donus I. This pyramid is represented on the bronze doors of St. Peter's.

A little further is the *Palazzo Giraud*, belonging to Prince Torlonia. It was built, 1506, by Bramante, for Cardinal Adriano da Corneto,† who gave it to Henry VIII., by whom it was given to Cardinal Campeggio. Thus it was for a short time the residence of the English ambassador before the Reformation. Innocent XII. converted it into a college for priests, by whom it was sold to the Marquis Giraud.

Facing this palace is the *Piazza Scossa Cavalli*, with a pretty fountain. Its name bears witness to a curious legend, which tells how when St. Helena returned from

---

* " Deus, qui apostolo tuo Petro collatis clavibus regni celestis ligandi et solvendi pontificium tradidisti ; concede ut intercessionis ejus auxilio, a peccatorum nostrorum legibus liberemur : et hanc civitatem, quam te adjuvante fundavimus, fac ab ira tua in perpetuum permanere securam, et de hostibus, quorum causa constructa est, novos et multiplicatos habere triumphos, per Dominum nostrum," &c.

† The same whom Alexander VI. had intended to poison, when he poisoned himself instead.

HOSPITAL OF SANTO SPIRITO.

Palestine, bringing with her the stone on which Abraham was about to sacrifice Isaac, and that on which the Virgin Mary sate down at the time of the presentation of the Saviour in the Temple, the horses drawing these precious relics stood still at this spot, and refused every effort to make them move. Then Christian people, "recognising the finger of God," erected a church on this spot (S. Giacomo Scossa Cavalli), where the stones are still to be seen.

The Strada del Borgo Sto. Spirito contains the immense *Hospital of Santo Spirito*, running along the bank of the Tiber. This establishment was founded in 1198 by Innocent III. Sixtus IV., in 1471, ordered it to be rebuilt by Bacio Pintelli, who added a hall 376 feet long by 44 high and 37 wide. Under Benedict XIV., Ferdinando Fuga built another great hall. The altar in the midst of the great hall is the only work of Andrea Palladio in Rome. The church was designed by Bacio Pintelli, but built by Antonio di San Gallo under Paul III. Under Gregory XIII., Ottaviano Mascherino built the palace of the governor, which unites the hospital with the church.

The institution comprises a hospital for every kind of disease, containing in ordinary times 1620 beds, a number which can be almost doubled in time of necessity; a lunatic asylum containing an average of 450 inmates; and a foundling hospital, where children are received from all parts of the papal states, and even from the Neapolitan towns. Upwards of 3000 foundlings pass through the hospital annually, but the mortality is very great,—in the return of 1846, as much as fifty-seven per cent. The person who wishes to deposit an infant rings a bell, when a little bed is turned towards the grille near the door, in which the baby is deposited. Close to this is another grille, without any apparent use. "What is that for?" you ask. "Because, when nurses come in from the country, they might be tempted to take the children for money, and yet not feel any natural tenderness towards them, but by looking through the second grille, they can see the child, and discover if it is *simpatico*, and if not, they can go away and leave it."

At the end of the street one enters the Piazza Rusticucci (where Raphael died), from which open the magnificent colonnades of Bernini, which lead the eye up to the façade of St. Peter's, while the middle distance is broken by the silvery spray of its glittering fountains.

The *Colonnades* have 284 columns, are sixty-one feet wide, and sixty-four high; they enclose an area of 777 English feet; they were built by Bernini for Alexander VII., 1657—67. In the centre is the famous red granite *Obelisk of the Vatican*, brought to Rome from Heliopolis by Caligula, in a ship which Pliny describes as being "nearly as long as the left side of the port of Ostia." It was used to adorn the circus of Nero, and was brought from a position near the present sacristy of St Peter's by Sixtus V. in 1586. Here it was elevated by Domenico Fontana, who estimated its weight at 963,537 Roman pounds; and employed 800 men, 150 horses, and 46 cranes in its removal.

The obelisk was first exorcised as a pagan idol, and then dedicated to the Cross. Its removal was preceded by high mass in St. Peter's, after which Pope Sixtus bestowed a solemn benediction upon Fontana and his workmen, and ordained that none should speak, upon pain of death, during the raising of the obelisk. The immense mass was slowly rising upon its base, when suddenly it ceased to move, and it was evident that the ropes were giving way. An awful moment of suspense ensued, when the breathless silence was broken by a cry of "Acqua alle funi!"— *throw water on the ropes*, and the workmen, acting on the advice so unexpectedly received, again saw the monster move, and gradually settle on its base. The man who saved the obelisk was Bresca, a sailor of Bordighiera, a village of the Riviera di Ponente, and Sixtus V., in his gratitude, promised him that his native village should ever henceforth have the privilege of furnishing the Easter palms to St. Peter's. A vessel laden with palm-branches, which abound in Bordighiera, is still annually sent to the Tiber in the week before Palm Sunday, and the palms, after being prepared and plaited by the nuns of S. Antonio Abbate, are used in the ceremonial in St. Peter's.

The height of the whole obelisk is 132 feet, that of the shaft, eighty-three feet. Upon the shaft is the inscription to Augustus and Tiberius: "DIVO. CÆS. DIVI. JULII. F. AUGUSTO.—TI. CÆSARI. DIVI. AUG. F.—AUGUSTA. SACRUM." The inscriptions on the base show its modern dedication to the Cross *—" Ecce Crux Domini—Fugite partes adversæ— Vicit Leo de tribu Juda."

"Sixte-quint s'applaudissait du succès, comme de l'œuvre la plus gigantesque des temps modernes; des médailles furent frappées; Fontana fut créé noble romain, chevalier de l'Éperon d'or, et reçut une gratification de 5,000 écus, indépendamment des matériaux qui avaient servi à l'entreprise, et dont la valeur s'élevait à 20,000 écus (108,000 fr.); enfin des poëmes, dans toutes les langues, sur ce nouveau triomphe

* At the time of its erection Sixtus V. conceded an indulgence of ten years to all who, passing beneath the obelisk, should adore the cross on its summit, repeating a pater-noster.

de la croix, furent adressés aux différents souverains de l'Europe."—*Gournerie, Rome Chrétienne*, ii. 232.

"In summer the great square basks in unalluring magnificence in the midday sun. Its tall obelisk sends but a slim shadow to travel round the oval plane, like the gnomon of a huge dial; its fountains murmur with a delicious dreaminess, sending up massive jets like blocks of crystal into the hot sunshine, and receiving back a broken spray, on which sits serene an unbroken iris, but present no 'cool grot,' where one may enjoy their freshness; and in spite of the shorter path, the pilgrim looks with dismay at the dazzling pavement and long flight of unsheltered steps between him and the church, and prudently plunges into the forest of columns at either side of the piazza, and threads his way through their uniting shadows, intended, as an inscription* tells him, for this express purpose."—*Cardinal Wiseman*.

"Un jour Pie V. traversait, avec l'ambassadeur de Pologne, cette place du Vatican. Pris d'enthousiasme au souvenir du courage des martyrs qui l'ont arrosée de leurs larmes, et fertilisée par leur sang, il se baisse, et saisissant dans sa main une poignée de poussière : 'Tenez,' dit-il au représentant de cette noble nation, 'prenez cette poussière formée de la cendre des saints, et imprégnée du sang des martyrs.'

"L'ambassadeur ne portait pas dans son cœur la foi d'un pape, ni dans son âme les illuminations d'un saint ; il reçut pourtant avec respect cette rélique étrange à ses yeux : mais revenu en son palais, retirant, d'une main indifférente peut-être, le linge qui la contenait, il le trouva ensanglanté.

"La poussière avait disparu. La foi du pontife avait évoqué le sang des martyrs, et ce sang généreux reparaissait à cet appel pour attester, en face de l'hérésie, que l'Église romaine, au xvie siècle, était toujours celle pour laquelle ces héros avaient donné leur vie sous Néron."—*Une Chrétienne à Rome*.

No one can look upon the Piazza of St. Peter's without associating it with the great religious ceremonies with which it is connected, especially that of the Easter Benediction.

"Out over the great balcony stretches a white awning, where priests and attendants are collected, and where the pope will soon be seen. Below, the piazza is alive with moving masses. In the centre are drawn

* The inscription is from Isaiah iv. 6, "A tabernacle for a shadow in the daytime from the heat, and for a place of refuge, and for a covert from storm and from rain."

up long lines of soldiery, with yellow and red pompons, and glittering helmets and bayonets. These are surrounded by crowds on foot, and at the outer rim are packed carriages filled and overrun with people, mounted on the seats and boxes. What a sight it is!—above us the great dome of St. Peter's, and below, the grand embracing colonnade, and the vast space, in the centre of which rises the solemn obelisk thronged with masses of living beings. Peasants from the Campagna and the mountains are moving about everywhere. Pilgrims in oil-cloth cape and with iron staff demand charity. On the steps are rows of purple, blue, and brown umbrellas, for there the sun blazes fiercely. Everywhere crop forth the white hoods of Sisters of Charity, collected in groups, and showing, among the parti-coloured dresses, like beds of chrysanthemums in a garden. One side of the massive colonnade casts a grateful shadow over the crowd beneath, that fill up the intervals of its columns; but elsewhere the sun burns down and flashes everywhere. Mounted on the colonnade are crowds of people leaning over, beside the colossal statues. Through all the heat is heard the constant plash of the sun-lit fountains, that wave to and fro their veils of white spray. At last the clock strikes. In the far balcony are seen the two great showy peacock fans, and between them a figure clad in white, that rises from a golden chair, and spreads his great sleeves like wings as he raises his arms in benediction. That is the pope, Pius the Ninth. All is dead silence, and a musical voice, sweet and penetrating, is heard chanting from the balcony;—the people bend and kneel; with a cold gray flash, all the bayonets gleam as the soldiers drop to their knees, and rise to salute as the voice dies away, and the two white wings are again waved; —then thunder the cannon,—the bells clash and peal,—a few white papers, like huge snow-flakes, drop wavering from the balcony;—these are Indulgences, and there is an eager struggle for them below;—then the pope again rises, again gives his benediction,* waving to and fro his right hand, three fingers open, and making the sign of the cross,—

---

* It may not be uninteresting to give the actual words of the benediction:—

"May the holy apostles Peter and Paul, in whose power and dominion we trust, pray for us to the Lord! Amen.

"Through the prayers and merits of the blessed, eternal Virgin Mary, of the blessed archangel Michael, the blessed John the Baptist, the holy apostles Peter and Paul, and all saints—may the Almighty God have mercy upon you, may your sins be forgiven you, and may Jesus Christ lead you to eternal life. Amen.

"Indulgence, absolution, and forgiveness of all sins—time for true repentance, a continual penitent heart and amendment of life,—may the Almighty and merciful God grant you these! Amen.

"And may the blessing of Almighty God, Father, Son, and Holy Spirit, descend upon you, and remain with you for ever. Amen."

and the peacock fans retire, and he between them is borne away,—and Lent is over."—*Story's Roba di Roma.*

The first church which existed on or near the site of the present building, was the oratory founded in A.D. 90, by Anacletus, bishop of Rome, who is said to have been ordained by St. Peter himself, and who thus marked the spot where many Christian martyrs had suffered in the circus of Nero, and where St. Peter was buried after his crucifixion.

In 306 Constantine the Great yielded to the request of Pope Sylvester, and began the erection of a basilica on this spot, labouring with his own hands at the work, and himself carrying away twelve loads of earth, in honour of the twelve apostles.* Anastasius describes how the body of the great apostle was exhumed at this time, and re-interred in a shrine of silver, enclosed in a sarcophagus of gilt bronze. The early basilica measured 395 feet in length by 212 in width. Its nave and aisles were divided by eighty-six marble pillars of different sizes, in great part brought from the Septizonium of Severus, and it had an atrium, and a *paradisus*, or quadrangular portico, along its front.† Though only half the size of the present cathedral, still it covered a greater space than any mediæval cathedral except those of Milan and Seville, with which it ranked in size.‡

The old basilica suffered severely in the Saracenic inva-

---

* "Exuens se chlamyde, et accipiens bidentem, ipse primus terram aperuit ad fundamenta basilicæ Sancti Petri continendam ; deinde in numero duodecim apostolorum duodecim cophinos plenos in humeris superimpositos bajulans, de eo loco ubi fundamenta Basilicæ Apostoli erant jacenda."—*Cod. Vat. 7. Sancta Cœcil.* 2.

† The façade of the old basilica is seen in Raphael's fresco of the Incendio del Borgo, and its interior in that of the Coronation of Charlemagne.

‡ See Fergusson's Handbook of Architecture, vol. ii.

sion of 846, when some authorities maintain that even the tomb of the great apostle was rifled of its contents, but it was restored by Leo IV., who raised the fortifications of the Borgo for its defence.

Among the most remarkable of its early *pilgrims* were, Theodosius, who came to pray for a victory over Eugenius; Valentinian, emperor of the East, with his wife Eudoxia, and his mother Galla-Placidia; Belisarius, the great general under Justinian; Totila; Cedwalla, king of the West Saxons, who came for baptism; Concred, king of the Mercians, who came to remain as a monk, having cut off and consecrated his long hair at the tomb of St. Peter; Luitprand, king of the Lombards; Ina of Wessex, who founded a church here in honour of the Virgin, that Anglo-Saxons might have a place of prayer, and those who died, a grave; Carloman of France, who came for absolution and remained as a monk, first at S. Oreste (Soracte), then at Monte Casino; Richard of England; Bertrade, wife of Pepin, and mother of Charlemagne; Offa, the Saxon, who made his kingdom tributary to St. Peter; Charlemagne (four times), who was crowned here by Leo III.; Lothaire, crowned by Paschal I.; and, in the last year of the reign of Leo IV., Ethelwolf, king of the Anglo-Saxons, who was crowned here, remained a year, and who brought with him his boy of six years old, afterwards the great Alfred.

Of the old basilica, the crypt is now the only remnant, and there are collected the few relics preserved of the endless works of art with which it was filled, and which for the most part were lost or wilfully destroyed, when it was pulled down. Its destruction was first planned by Nicholas V.

(1450), but was not carried out till the time of Julius II., who in 1506 began the new St. Peter's from designs of Bramante. The four great piers and their arches above were completed, before the deaths of both Bramante and Pope Julius interrupted the work. The next pope, Leo X., obtained a design for a church in the form of a Latin cross from Raphael, which was changed, after his death (on account of expense) to a Greek cross, by Baldassare Peruzzi, who only lived to complete the tribune. Paul III. (1534) employed Antonio di Sangallo as an architect, who returned to the design of a Latin cross, but died before he could carry out any of his intentions. Giulio Romano succeeded him and died also. Then the pope, "being inspired by God," says Vasari, sent for Michael Angelo, then in his seventy-second year, who continued the work under Julius III., returning to the plan of a Greek cross, enlarging the tribune and transepts, and beginning the dome on a new plan, which he said would "raise the Pantheon in the air." The dome designed by Michael Angelo, however, was very different to that which we now admire, being much lower, flatter, and heavier. The present dome is due to Giacomo della Porta, who brought the great work to a conclusion in 1590, under Sixtus V., who devoted 100,000 gold crowns annually to the building. In 1605 Paul V. destroyed all that remained of the old basilica, and employed Carlo Maderno as his architect, who once more returned to the plan of the Latin cross, and completed the present ugly façade in 1614. The church was dedicated by Urban VIII., November 18th, 1626; the colonnade added by Alexander VII., 1667, the sacristy by Pius VI., in 1780. The building of the present St. Peter's extended altogether over 176 years, and its expenses were so great that Julius II. and Leo X. were obliged to meet them by the sale of indulgences, which led to the Reformation. The expense of the main building alone has been estimated at 10,000,000*l*. The annual expense of repairs is 6300*l*.

"St. Pierre est une sorte de ville à part dans Rome, ayant son climat, sa température propre, sa lumière trop vive pour être religieuse, tantôt deserte, tantôt traversée par des sociétés de voyageurs, ou remplie d'une foule attirée par les cérémonies religieuses (à l'époque des jubilés le nombre des pèlerins s'est parfois élevé à Rome, jusqu'a 400,000). Elle a ses reservoirs d'eau ; sa fontaine coulant perpetuellement au pied de la grande coupole, dans un bassin de plomb, pour la commodité des travaux ; ses rampes, par lesquelles les bêtes de somme peuvent monter ; sa population fixe, habitant ses terrasses. Les San Pietriné, ouvriers chargés de tous les travaux qu'exige la conservation d'un aussi précieux edifice, s'y succèdent de père en fils, et forment une corporation qui a ses lois et sa police."—*A. Du Pays.*

The façade of St. Peter's is 357 feet long and 144 feet high. It is surmounted by a balustrade six feet in height, bearing statues of the Saviour and the Twelve Apostles. Over the central entrance is the loggia where the pope is crowned, and whence he gives the Easter benediction. The huge inscription runs—"In . Honorem . Principis . Apost . Paulus V . Burghesius . Romanus . Pont . Max . A. MDCXII . Pont. VII."

"I don't like to say the façade of the church is ugly and obtrusive. As long as the dome overawes, that façade is supportable. You advance towards it—through, O such a noble court ! with fountains flashing up to meet the sunbeams ; and right and left of you two sweeping half-crescents of great columns ; but you pass by the courtiers and up to the steps of the throne, and the dome seems to disappear behind it. It is as if the throne was upset, and the king had toppled over."—*Thackeray, The Newcomes.*

A wide flight of steps, at the foot of which are statues of

St Peter by *De Fabris*, and St. Paul by *Tadolini*, lead by fine entrances to the *Vestibule*, which is 468 feet long, 66 feet high, and 50 feet wide. Closing it on the right is a statue of Constantine by *Bernini*—on the left that of Charlemagne by *Cornacchini*. Over the principal entrance (facing the door of the church) is the celebrated *Mosaic of the Navicella*, executed 1298, by *Giotto*, and his pupil, *Pietro Cavallini*.

"For the ancient basilica of St. Peter, Giotto executed his celebrated mosaic of the Navicella, which has an allegorical foundation. It represents a ship, with the disciples, on an agitated sea; the winds, personified as demons, storm against it; above appear the Fathers of the Old Testament speaking comfort to the sufferers. According to the early Christian symbolization, the ship denoted the Church. Nearer, and on the right, in a firm attitude, stands Christ, the Rock of the Church, raising Peter from the waves. Opposite sits a fisherman in tranquil expectation, denoting the hope of the believer. The mosaic has frequently changed its place, and has undergone so many restorations, that the composition alone can be attributed to Giotto. The fisherman and the figures hovering in the air are, in their present form, the work of Marcello Provenzale."—*Kugler*, i. 127.

"This mosaic is ill placed and ill seen for an especial reason. Early converts from paganism retained the heathen custom of turning round to venerate the sun before entering a church, so that in the old basilica, as here, the mosaic was thus placed to give a fitting object of worship. The learned Cardinal Baronius never, for a single day, during the space of thirty years, failed to bow before this symbol of the primitive Church, tossed on the stormy sea of persecution and of sin, saying, 'Lord, save me from the waves of sin as thou didst Peter from the waves of the sea.'"
—*Mrs. Elliot's Historical Pictures*.

The magnificent central door of bronze is a remnant from the old basilica, and was made in the time of Eugenius IV., 1431—39, by Antonio Filarete, and Simone, brother of Donatello. The bas-reliefs of the compartments represent the martyrdoms of SS. Peter and Paul, and the principal events in the reign of Eugenius,—the Council of Florence, the Coronation of Sigismund, emperor of Germany, &c. The bas-reliefs of the framework are entirely mythological; Ganymede, Leda and her Swan, &c., are to be distinguished.

"Corinne fit remarquer à Lord Nelvil que sur les portes étaient représentées en bas-relief les métamorphoses d'Ovide. On ne se scandalise point à Rome, lui dit-elle, des images du paganisme, quand les beaux-arts les ont consacrées. Les merveilles du génie portent toujours à l'âme une impression religieuse, et nous faisons hommage au culte chrétien de tous les chefs-d'œuvre que les autres cultes ont inspirés."—*Mad. de Staël.*

Let into the wall between the doors are three remarkable inscriptions: 1. Commemorating the donation made to the church by Gregory II., of certain olive-grounds to provide oil for the lamps; 2. The bull of Boniface VIII., 1300, granting the indulgence proclaimed at every jubilee; 3. In the centre, the Latin epitaph of Adrian I. (Colonna, 772—95), by Charlemagne,* one of the most ancient memorials of the papacy:

"The father of the Church, the ornament of Rome, the famous writer
  Adrian, the blessed pope, rests in peace:
God was his life, love was his law, Christ was his glory;
He was the apostolic shepherd, always ready to do that which was
  right.
Of noble birth, and descended from an ancient race,
He received a still greater nobility from his virtues.
The pious soul of this good shepherd was always bent
Upon ornamenting the temples consecrated to God.
He gave gifts to the churches, and sacred dogmas to the people;
And showed us all the way to heaven.
Liberal to the poor, his charity was second to none,
And he always watched over his people in prayer.
By his teachings, his treasures, and his buildings, he raised,
O illustrious Rome, thy monuments, to be the honour of the town
  and of the world.

* As in the portico of the temple of Mars were preserved the verses of the poet Attius upon Junius Brutus.

Death could not injure him, for its sting was taken away by the death
  of Christ;
    It opened for him the gate of the better life.
I, Charles, have written these verses, while weeping for my father;
    O my father, my beloved one, how lasting is my grief for thee.
Dost thou think upon me, as I follow thee constantly in spirit;
Now reign blessed with Christ in the heavenly kingdom.
The clergy and people have loved you with a heart-love,
Thou wert truly the love of the world, O excellent priest.
O most illustrious, I unite our two names and titles,
Adrian and Charles, the king and the father.
O thou who readest these verses, say with pious heart the prayer;
O merciful God, have pity upon them both.
Sweetly slumbering, O friend, may thy earthly body rest in the
  grave,
And thy spirit wander in bliss with the saints of the Lord
Till the last trumpet sounds in thine ears,
Then arise with Peter to the contemplation of God.
Yes, I know that thou wilt hear the voice of the merciful judge
Bid thee to enter the paradise of thy Saviour.
Then, O great father, think upon thy son,
And ask, that with the father the son may enter into joy.
Go, blessed father, enter into the kingdom of Christ,
And thence, as an intercessor, help thy people with thy prayers.
Even so long as the sun rolls upon its fiery axis,
Shall thy glory, O heavenly father, remain in the world.

Adrian the pope, of blessed memory, reigned for three-and-twenty years, ten months, and seventeen days, and died on the 25th of December."

The walled-up door on the right is the *Porta Santa*, only opened for the jubilee, which has taken place every twenty-fifth year (except 1850) since the time of Sixtus IV. The pope himself gives the signal for the destruction of the wall on the Christmas-eve before the sacred year.

"After preliminary prayers from Scripture singularly apt, the pope goes down from his throne, and, armed with a silver hammer, strikes the wall in the doorway, which, having been cut round from its jambs and lintel, falls at once inwards, and is cleared away in a moment by the

San Pietrini. The pope, then, bare-headed and torch in hand, first enters the door, and is followed by his cardinals and his other attendants to the high altar, where the first vespers of Christmas Day are chaunted as usual. The other doors of the church are then flung open, and the great queen of churches is filled."—*Cardinal Wiseman.*

" Arrêtez-vous un moment ici, dit Corinne à Lord Nelvil, comme il était déjà sous le portique de l'église ; arrêtez-vous, avant de soulever le rideau qui couvre la porte du temple ; votre cœur ne bat-il pas à l'approche de ce sanctuaire ? et ne ressentez-vous pas, au moment d'entrer, tout ce que ferait éprouver l'attente d'un évènement solennel ? "—*Mad. de Staël.*

We now push aside the heavy double curtain and enter the Basilica.

" Hilda had not always been adequately impressed by the grandeur of this mighty cathedral. When she first lifted the heavy leathern curtains, at one of the doors, a shadowy edifice in her imagination had been dazzled out of sight by the reality."—*Hawthorne.*

" The interior burst upon our astonished gaze, resplendent in light, magnificence, and beauty, beyond all that imagination can conceive. Its apparent smallness of size, however, mingled some degree of surprise, and even disappointment, with my admiration ; but as I walked slowly up its long nave, empanelled with the rarest and richest marbles, and adorned with every art of sculpture and taste, and caught through the lofty arches opening views of chapels, and tombs, and altars of surpassing splendour, I felt that it was, indeed, unparalleled in beauty, in magnitude, and magnificence, and one of the noblest and most wonderful of the works of man."—*Eaton's Rome.*

" St. Peter's, that glorious temple—the largest and most beautiful, it is said, in the world, produced upon me the impression rather of a Christian pantheon, than of a Christian church. The æsthetic intellect is edified more than the God-loving or God-seeking soul. The exterior and interior of the building appear to me more like an apotheosis of the popedom than a glorification of Christianity and its doctrine. Monuments to the popes occupy too much space. One sees all round the walls angels flying upwards with papal portraits, sometimes merely with papal tiaras."—*Frederika Bremer.*

" L'Architecture de St. Pierre est une musique fixée."—*Madame de Staël.*

" The building of St. Peter's surpasses all powers of description. It appears to me like some great work of nature, a forest, a mass of rocks, or something similar; for I never can realise the idea that it is the work of man. You strive to distinguish the ceiling as little as the canopy of heaven. You lose your way in St. Peter's, you take a walk in it, and ramble till you are quite tired; when divine service is performed and chaunted there, you are not aware of it till you come quite close. The angels in the Baptistery are enormous giants; the doves, colossal birds of prey; you lose all sense of measurement with the eye, or proportion; and yet who does not feel his heart expand, when standing under the dome, and gazing up at it." — *Mendelssohn's Letters.*

"But thou, of temples old, or altars new,
Standest alone—with nothing like to thee—
Worthiest of God, the holy and the true.
Since Zion's desolation, when that He
Forsook His former city, what could be
Of earthly structures, in His honour piled,
Of a sublimer aspect? Majesty,
Power, Glory, Strength, and Beauty,—all are aisled
In this eternal ark of worship undefiled.

"Enter: its grandeur overwhelms thee not;
And why? it is not lessen'd; but thy mind,
Expanded by the genius of the spot,
Has grown colossal, and can only find
A fit abode wherein appear enshrined
Thy hopes of immortality; and thou
Shalt one day, if found worthy, so defined,
See thy God face to face, as thou dost now
His Holy of Holies, nor be blasted by His brow."
                                    Byron, Childe Harold.

"On pousse avec peine une grosse portière de cuir, et nous voici dans Saint-Pierre. On ne peut qu'adorer la religion qui produit de telles choses. Rien du monde ne peut être comparé à l'intérieur de Saint Pierre. Après un an de séjour à Rome, j'y allais encore passer des heures entières avec plaisir."—*Fontana, Tempio Vaticano Illustrato.*

"Tandis que, dans les églises gothiques, l'impression est de s'agenouiller, de joindre les mains avec un sentiment d'humble prière et de profond regret; dans Saint-Pierre au contraire, le mouvement involontaire serait d'ouvrir les bras en signe de joie, de relever la tête avec bonheur et épanouissement. Il semble, que là, le péché n'accable plus; le sentiment vif du pardon par le triomphe de la résurrection remplit seul le cœur."—*Eugénie de la Ferronays.*

"The temperature of St. Peter's seems, like the happy islands, to experience no change. In the coldest weather it is like summer to your feelings, and in the most oppressive heats it strikes you with a delightful sensation of cold—a luxury not to be estimated but in a climate such as this."—*Eaton's Rome.*

On each side of the nave are four pillars with Corinthian pilasters, and a rich entablature supporting the arches. The roof is vaulted, coffered, and gilded. The pavement is of coloured marble, inlaid from designs of Giacomo della Porta and Bernini. In the centre of the floor, immediately within the chief entrance, is a round slab of porphyry, upon which the emperors were crowned.

The enormous size of the statues and ornaments in St. Peter's do away with the impression of its vast size, and it is only by observing the living, moving figures, that one can form any idea of its colossal proportions. A line in the pavement is marked with the comparative size of the other great Christian churches. According to this the length of St. Peter's is $613\frac{1}{2}$ feet; of St. Paul's, London, $520\frac{1}{2}$ feet; Milan Cathedral, 443 feet; St. Sophia, Constantinople, $360\frac{1}{2}$ feet. The height of the dome in the interior is 405 feet; on the exterior, 448 feet. The height of the baldacchino is $94\frac{1}{2}$ feet.

The first impulse will be to go up to the shrine, around which a circle of eighty-six gold lamps is always burning, and to look down into the Confessional, where there is a beautiful kneeling statue of Pope Pius VI. (Braschi, 1785—1800) by *Canova*. Hence one can gaze up into the dome, with its huge letters in purple-blue mosaic upon a gold ground (each six feet long).* "Tu es Petrus, et super

---

* These letters are in real mosaic. Those in the nave and transepts are in paper—to complete them in mosaic would have been too expensive.

hanc petram ædificabo ecclesiam meam, et tibi dabo claves regni cœlorum." Above this are four colossal mosaics of the Evangelists from designs of the Cav. d'Arpino ; the pen of St. Luke is seven feet in length.

"The cupola is glorious, viewed in its design, its altitude, or even its decorations ; viewed either as a whole or as a part, it enchants the eye, it satisfies the taste, it expands the soul. The very air seems to eat up all that is harsh or colossal, and leaves us nothing but the sublime to feast on :—a sublime peculiar as the genius of the immortal architect, and comprehensible only on the spot."—*Forsyth.*

"Ce dôme, en le considérant même d'en bas, fait éprouver une sorte de terreur ; on croit voir des abîmes suspendus sur sa tête."—*Madame de Staël.*

The Baldacchino, designed by Bernini in 1633, is of bronze, with gilt ornaments, and was made chiefly with bronze taken from the roof of the Pantheon. It covers the high altar, which is only used on the most solemn occasions. Only the pope can celebrate mass there, or a cardinal who is authorised by a papal brief.

"Without a sovereign priest officiating before and for his people, St. Peter's is but a grand aggregation of splendid churches, chapels, tombs, and works of art. With him, it becomes a whole, a single, peerless temple, such as the world never saw before. That central pile, with its canopy of bronze as lofty as the Farnese Palace, with its deep-diving stairs leading to a court walled and paved with precious stones, that yet seems only a vestibule to some cavern or catacomb, with its simple altar that disdains ornament in the presence of what is beyond the reach of human price,—that which in truth forms the heart of the great body, placed just where the heart should be, is then animated, and surrounded by living and moving sumptuousness. The immense cupola above it, ceases to be a dome over a sepulchre, and becomes a canopy over an altar ; the quiet tomb beneath is changed into the shrine of relics below the place of sacrifice—the saints under the altar ;—the quiet spot at which a few devout worshippers at most times may be found, bowing under the hundred lamps, is crowded by rising groups, beginning from the lowest step, increasing in dignity and in richness of sacred robes, till, at the summit and in the centre, stands supreme the pontiff himself, on the very spot which becomes him, the one living link in a chain, the first ring of which is rivetted to the shrine of the Apostles below . . . . St. Peter's is only itself when the pope is at the high altar, and hence only by, or for, him it is used."—*Cardinal Wiseman.*

The four huge piers which support the dome are used as shrines for the four great relics of the church, viz., 1. The lance of S. Longinus, the soldier who pierced the side of our Saviour, presented to Innocent VIII., by Pierre d'Aubusson, grandmaster of the Knights of Rhodes, who had received it from the Sultan Bajazet;* 2. The head of St. Andrew, said to have been brought from Achaia in 1460, when its arrival was celebrated by Pius II. ; 3. A portion of the true cross, brought by Sta. Helena ; 4. The napkin of Sta. Veronica, said, doubtless from the affinity of names, to bear the impression—vera-icon—of our Saviour's face.

" The 'Volto-Santo,' said to be the impress of the countenance of our Saviour on the handkerchief of Sta. Veronica, or Berenice, which wiped his brow on the way to Calvary, was placed in the Vatican by John VII., in 707, and afterwards transferred to the Church of Santo Spirito, where six Roman noblemen had the care of it, each taking charge of one of the keys with which it was locked up. Among the privileges enjoyed for this office, was that of receiving, every year, from the hospital of Santo Spirito at the feast of Pentecost, two cows, whose flesh, an ancient chronicle says, 'si mangiavano li, con gran festa.' In 1440, this picture was carried back to St. Peter's, whence it has not since been moved. When I examined the head on the Veronica handkerchief, it struck me as undoubtedly a work of early Byzantine art, perhaps of the seventh or eighth century, painted on linen. It is with implicit acceptance of its claims that Petrarch alludes to it—'verendam populis Salvatoris Imaginem.' Ep. ix., lib. 2. During the republican domination in 1849, it was rumoured that about Easter, the canons of St. Peter saw the Volto-Santo turn pale, and ominously change colour while they gazed upon it."—*Hemans' Catholic Italy*, vol. i.

* Innocent sent two bishops to receive it at Ancona, two cardinals to receive it at Narni, and went himself, with all his court, to meet it at the Porto del Popolo.

The ceremony of exhibiting the relics from the balcony above the statue of Sta. Veronica takes place on Holy Thursday, Good Friday, and Easter Day, but the height is so great that nothing can really be distinguished.

"To-day we gazed on the Veronica—the holy impression left by our Saviour's face on the cloth Sta. Veronica presented to him to wipe his brow, bowed under the weight of the Cross. We had looked forward to this sight for days, for seven thousand years of indulgence from penance are attached to it.

"But when the moment came we could see nothing but a black board hung with a cloth, before which another white cloth was held. In a few minutes this was withdrawn, and the great moment was over, the glimpse of the sacred thing on which hung the fate of seven thousand years."—*Schönberg-Cotta Chronicles.*

The niches in the piers are occupied by four statues, of Longinus, St. Andrew, Sta. Helena, and Sta. Veronica, holding the napkin or "sudarium," "flourishing a marble pocket-handkerchief." *

"Malheureusement toutes ces statues pêchent par le gout. Le rococo, mis à la mode par le Bernin, est surtout exécrable dans le genre colossale. Mais la présence du génie de Bramante et de Michel-Ange se fait tellement sentir, que les choses ridicules ne le sont plus ici; elles ne sont qu' insignifiantes. Les statues colossales des piliers représentent : St. André, par François Quesnoy (Fiamningo), elle excita la jalousie du Bernin ; St. Veronique par M. Mochi, dont il blamait les draperies volantes (dans un endroit clos). Un plaisant lui répondait que leur agitation provenait du vent qui soufflait par les crevasses de la coupole, depuis qu'il avait affaibli les piliers par des niches et tribunes : St. Hélène par A. Bolgi, St. Longin par Bernin."—*A. Du Pays.*

Not very far from the confessional, against the last pier on the right of the nave, stands the statue of St. Peter, said to have been cast by Leo the Great, from the old statue of Jupiter Capitolinus. It is of very rude workmanship. Its extended foot is eagerly kissed by Roman Catholic de-

* Eaton's Rome.

votees, who then rub their foreheads against its toes. Protestants wonder at the feeling which this figure excites. Gregory II. wrote of it to Leo the Isaurian : " Christ is my witness, that when I enter the temple of the prince of the Apostles, and contemplate his image, I am filled with such emotion, that tears roll down my cheeks like the rain from heaven." On high festivals the statue is dressed up in full pontificals. On the day of the jubilee of Pius IX. (June 16, 1871), it was attired in a lace alb, stole, and gold-embroidered cope, fastened at the breast by a clasp of diamonds; and its foot was kissed by upwards of 20,000 persons during the day.

"La coutume antique chez les Grecs d'habiller et de parer les statues sacrées s'était conservée à Rome et s'y conserve encore. Tout le monde a vu la statue de saint Pierre revêtir dans les grandes solennités ses magnifiques habits de pape. On lavait les statues des dieux, on les frottait, on les frisait comme des poupées. Les divinités du Capitole avaient un nombreux domestique attaché à leur personne et qui était chargé de ce soin. L'usage romain a subsisté chez les populations latines de l'Espagne et elles l'ont porté jusqu'au Mexique où j'ai vu, à Puebla, la veille d'une fête, une femme de chambre faire une toilette en règle à une statue de la Vierge."—*Ampère, Hist. Rom.* iv. 91.

Along the piers of the nave and transepts are ranged statues of the different Founders, male and female, of religious Orders.

Returning to the main entrance, we will now make the tour of the basilica. Those who expect to find monuments of great historical interest will, however, be totally disappointed. Scarcely anything remains above-ground which is earlier than the sixteenth century. Of the tombs of the eighty-seven popes who were buried in the old basilica, the greater part were totally lost at its destruction;—a few were removed to other churches (those of the Piccolomini to S. Andrea della Valle, &c.), and some fragments are still to be seen in the crypt. Only two monuments were replaced in the new basilica, those of the two popes who lived in the time and excited the indignation of Savonarola—"Sixtus IV., with whose cordial concurrence the assassination of Lorenzo di Medici was attempted—and Innocent VIII., the main object of whose policy was to secure place and power for his illegitimate children."

"The side-chapels are splendid, and so large that they might serve for independent churches. The monuments and statues are numerous, but all are subordinate, or unite harmoniously with the large and beautiful proportions of the chief temple. Everything there is harmony, light, beauty—an image of the church-triumphant, but a very worldly, earthly image; and whilst the mind enjoys its splendour, the soul cannot, in the higher sense, be edified by its symbolism."—*Frederika Bremer.*

The first chapel on the right derives its name from the *Pietà of Michael Angelo,* representing the dead Saviour upon the knees of the Madonna, a work of the great artist in his twenty-fourth year, upon an order from the French ambassador, Cardinal Jean de Villiers, abbot of St. Denis. The sculptor has inscribed his name (the only instance in which he has done so) upon the girdle of the Virgin. Francis I. attempted to obtain this group from Michael Angelo in 1507, together with the statue of Christ at the Minerva, "comme de choses que l'on m'a assuré estre des plus exquises et excellentes en votre art." Opening from this chapel are two smaller ones. That on the right has a Crucifix by *Pietro Cavallini;* the mosaic, representing St. Nicholas of Bari, is by *Christofari.* That on the left is called *Cappella della Colonna Santa,* from a column, said to have been brought from Jerusalem, and to have been that against which our

Saviour leant, when he prayed and taught in the temple. It is inscribed:

"Hæc est illa columna in qua DNS N' Jesus XPS appodiatus dum populo prædicabat et Deo pño preces iu templo effundebat adhærendo, stabatque una cum aliis undeci hic circumstantibus de Salomonis templo in triumphum. Hujus Basilicæ hic locata fuit demones expellit et immundis spiritibus vexatos liberos reddit et multa miracula cotidie facit. P. reverendissimum prem̄ et Dominum Dominus. Card. de Ursinis. A.D. MDCCCXXXVIII."

A more interesting object in this chapel is the sarcophagus (once used as a font) of Anicius Probus, a prefect of Rome in the fourth century, of the great family of the Anicii, to which St. Gregory the Great belonged. Its five compartments have bas-reliefs, representing Christ and the Apostles.

Returning to the aisle, on the right, is the tomb of Leo XII., Annibale della Genga (1823—29) by *Fabris;* on the left is the tomb of Christina of Sweden, daughter of Gustavus Adolphus, who died at Rome, 1689, by *Carlo Fontana,* with a bas-relief by Teudon, representing her abjuration of Protestantism in 1655, in the cathedral of Innspruck.

On the right is the altar of St. Sebastian, with a mosaic copy of Domenichino's picture at Sta. Maria degli Angeli; beyond which is the tomb of Innocent XII., Antonio Pignatelli (1691—1700). This was the last pope who wore the martial beard and moustache, which we see represented in his statue. Pignatella is Italian for a little cream-jug; in allusion to this we may see three little cream-jugs in the upper decorations of this monument, which is by *Filippo Valle.* On the left is the tomb, by *Bernini,* of the Countess Matilda, foundress of the temporal power of the popes, who died in 1115, was buried in a monastery near Mantua, and transported hither by Urban VIII. in 1635. The bas-relief represents the absolution of Henry IV. of Germany, by Hildebrand, which took place at her intercession and in her presence.

We now reach, on the right, the large *Chapel of the Santissimo Sacramento*, decorated with a fresco altar-piece, representing the Trinity, by *Pietro da Cortona*, and a tabernacle of lapis-lazuli and gilt bronze, copied from Bramante's little temple at S. Pietro in Montorio. Here is the magnificent tomb of Sixtus IV., Francesco della Rovere (1471—81), removed from the choir of the old St. Peter's, where it was erected by his nephew, Cardinal Giulio della Rovere, afterwards Pope Julius II. This pope's reign was entirely occupied with politics, and he was secretly involved in the conspiracy of the Pazzi at Florence; he was the first pope who carried nepotism to such an extent as to found a principality (Imola and Forli) for his nephew Girolamo Riario. The tomb is a beautiful work of the Florentine artist, *Antonio Pollajuola*, in 1493. The figure of the pope reposes upon a bronze couch, surrounded, in memory of his having taught successively in the six great universities of Italy, with allegorical bas-reliefs of Arithmetic, Astrology, Philology, Rhetoric, Grammar, Perspective, Music, Geography, Philosophy, and Theology, which last is represented like a pagan Diana, with a quiver of arrows on her shoulders. Close to this monument of his uncle, a flat stone in the pavement marks the grave of Julius II., for whom the grand tomb at S. Pietro in Vincoli was intended.

Returning to the aisle, we see on the right the tomb of Gregory XIII., Ugo Buoncompagni (1572—85), during whose reign the new calendar was invented, an event commemorated in a bas-relief upon the monument, which was not erected till 1723, and is by *Camillo Rusconi*. The figure of the pope (he died aged eighty-four) is in the attitude of benediction: beneath are Wisdom, represented as Minerva, and Faith, holding a tablet inscribed, " Novi opera hujus et fidem." Opposite this is the paltry tomb of Gregory XIV., Nicolo Sfrondati (1590—91).

"Le tombeau de Gregoire XIII., que le massacre de Saint Barthélemy réjouit si fort, est de marbre. Le tombeau de stuc ou d'abord il avait été placé, a été accordé, après son départ, au cendres de Grégoire XIV."—*Stendhal.*

On the left, against the great pier, is a mosaic copy of Domenichino's Communion of St. Jerome. On the right is the chapel of the Madonna, founded by Gregory XIII., and built by Giacomo della Porta. The cupola has mosaics by Girolamo Muziano. Beneath the altar is buried St. Gregory Nazianzen, removed hither from the convent of Sta. Maria in the Campo Marzo by Gregory XIII.

St. Gregory Nazianzen (or St. Gregory Theologos) was son of St. Gregory and St. Nonna, and brother of St. Gorgonia and St. Cesarea. He was born *c*. A.D. 328. In his childhood he was influenced by a vision of the two virgins, Temperance and Chastity, summoning him to pursue them to the joys of Paradise. Being educated at Athens (together with Julian the Apostate), he formed there a great friendship with St. Basil. He became first the coadjutor, afterwards the successor, of his father, in the bishopric of Nazianzen, but removed thence to Constantinople, where he preached against the Arians. By the influence of Theodosius, he was ordained Bishop of Constantinople, but was so worn out by the cabals and schisms in the Church, that he resigned his office, and retired to his paternal estate, where he passed the remainder of his life in the composition of Greek hymns and poems. He died May 9, A.D. 390.

On the right is the tomb of Benedict XIV., Prospero Lambertini (1740—58), by *Pietro Bracci*, a huge and ugly monument. On the left is the tomb of Gregory XVI., Mauro-Cappellari (1831—46), by *Amici*, erected in 1855 by the cardinals he had created.

Turning into the right transept, used as a council-chamber (for which purpose it proved thoroughly unsatisfactory), 1869—70, we find several fine mosaics from pictures, viz. : The Martyrdom of SS. Processus and Martinianus from the Valentin at the Vatican ; the Martyrdom of St. Erasmus from Poussin ; St. Wenceslaus, king of Bohemia, from Caroselli ; Our Saviour walking on the sea to the boat of St. Peter, from Lanfranco.

Opposite to the last-named mosaic is the famous monument of Clement XIII., Carlo Rezzonico (1758—69), in whose reign the Order of Jesuits was attacked by all the sovereigns of the house of Bourbon, and expelled from Portugal, France, Spain, Naples, and Parma. The pope, who had long defended them, was about to yield to the pressure put upon him and had called a consistory for their suppression, but died suddenly on the evening before its assembling. This tomb, the greatest work of Canova, was uncovered April 4, 1795, in the presence of an immense crowd, with whom the sculptor mingled, disguised as an abbé, to hear their opinion. The pope (aged 75) is represented in prayer, upon a pedestal, beneath which is the entrance to a vault, guarded by two grand marble lions. On the right is Religion, standing erect with a cross ; on the left the Genius of Death, holding a torch reversed. The beauty of this work of Canova is only felt when it is compared with the monuments of the seventeenth century in St. Peter's ; " then it seems as if they were separated by an abyss of centuries." *

* Gregorovius, Grabmüller der Päpste.

Beyond this are mosaics from the St. Michael of Guido at the Cappuccini, and from the Martyrdom of St. Petronilla, of Guercino, at the Capitol. Each of these large mosaics has cost about 150,000 francs.

Now, on the right, is the tomb of Clement X., Gio. Baptista Altieri (1670—76), by *Rossi*, the statue by *Ercole Ferrata;* and on the left, is a mosaic of St. Peter raising Tabitha from the dead, by Costanzi.

Ascending into the tribune, we see at the end of the church, beneath the very ugly window of yellow glass, the "Cathedra Petri" of *Bernini*, supported by figures of the four Fathers of the Church, Augustine, Ambrose, Chrysostom, and Athanasius. Enclosed in this, is a very ancient wooden senatorial chair, encrusted with ivory, which is believed to have been the episcopal throne of St. Peter and his immediate successors. Late Roman Catholic authorities (Mgr. Gerbet, &c.) consider that it may perhaps have been originally the chair of the senator Pudens, with whom the apostle lodged. A magnificent festival in honour of St. Peter's chair (Natale Petri de Cathedra) has been annually celebrated here from the earliest times, and is mentioned in a calendar of Pope Liberius of A.D. 354. It was said that if any pope were to reign longer than the traditional years of the government of St. Peter (Pius IX. is the first pope who has done so), St. Peter's chair would be again brought into use.

On the right of the chair is the tomb of Urban VIII., Matteo Barberini (1623—44), who was chiefly remarkable from his passion for building, and who is perpetually brought to mind through the immense number of his erections which still exist. The tomb is by *Bernini*, the architect of his endless fountains and public buildings, and has the usual fault of this sculptor in overloading his figures (except in that of Urban himself, which is very fine,*) with meaningless drapery. Figures of Charity and Justice stand by the black marble sarcophagus of the pope, and a gilt skeleton is occupied in inscribing the name of Urban on the list of Death. The whole monument is alive with the bees of the Barberini. The pendant tomb on the left is that of Paul III., Alessandro Farnese (1534—50), in whose reign the Order of the Jesuits was founded. This pope (the first Roman who had occupied the throne for 103 years—since Martin V.) was learned, brilliant, and witty. He was adored by his people, in spite of his intense nepotism, which induced him to form Parma into a duchy for his natural son Pierluigi, to build the Farnese Palace, and to marry his grandson Ottavio to Marguerite, natural daughter of Charles V., to whom he gave the Palazzo Madama and the Villa Madama as a dowry. His tomb, by *Guglielmo della Porta*, perhaps the finest in St. Peter's, cost 24,000 Roman crowns; it was erected in the old basilica just before its destruction in 1562,—and in 1574 was transferred to this church, where its position was the source of a quarrel between the sculptor and Michael Angelo, by whose interest he had obtained his commission.† It was first placed on the site where the Veronica now stands, whence it was moved to its present position in 1629. The figure of the pope is in bronze. In its former place four marble statues adorned the pedestal ; two are now removed to the Farnese Palace ; those which remain, of Prudence and Justice, were once entirely nude, but were draped by Bernini. The statue

* There is a fine portrait of Urban VIII. by Pietro da Cortona, in the Capitol gallery.
† See Vasari, vi. 265.

of Prudence is said to represent Giovanna Gaetani da Sermoneta, the mother of the pope, and that of Justice his famous sister-in-law, Giulia.

"On a dit de ces figures que c'était le Rubens en sculpture."—*A. Du Pays*.

Near the steps of the tribune are two marble slabs, on which Pius IX. has immortalised the names of the cardinals and bishops who, on December 8, 1854, accepted, on this spot, his dogma of the Immaculate Conception.

Turning towards the left transept;—on the left is a mosaic of St. Peter healing the lame man, from *Mancini*. On the right is the tomb of Alexander VIII., Pietro Ottobuoni (1689—91), by *Giuseppe Verlosi* and *Angelo Rossi*, gorgeous in its richness of bronze, marbles, and alabasters. Beyond this is the altar of Leo the Great, over which is a huge bas-relief, by *Algardi*, representing S. Leo calling down the assistance of SS. Peter and Paul against the invasion of Attila.

"The king of the Huns, terrified by the apparition of the two apostles in the air, turns his back and flies. We have here a picture in marble, with all the faults of taste and style which prevailed at that time, but the workmanship is excellent; it is, perhaps, the largest bas-relief in existence, excepting the rock sculpture of the Indians and Egyptians—at least fifteen feet in height."—*Jameson's Sacred Art*, p. 685.

Next to this is the Cappella della Colonna, possessing a much revered Madonna from a pillar of the old basilica, and beneath it an ancient Christian sarcophagus containing the remains of Leo II. (ob. 683), Leo III. (ob. 816), and Leo IV. (ob. 855). In the pavement near these two altars is the slab tomb of Leo XII. (ob. 1828), with an epitaph illustrating Invocation of Saints, but touching in its humility.

"Commending myself, a suppliant, to my great celestial patron Leo,

I, Leo XII., his humble client, unworthy of so great a name, have chosen a place of sepulture, near his holy ashes."

Over the door known as the Porta Sta. Marta (from the church in the square behind St. Peter's, to which it leads), is the tomb of Alexander VII., Fabio Chigi (1655—67), the last work of *Bernini*, who had built for this pope the Scala-Regia and the Colonnade of St. Peter's. This is, perhaps, the worst of all the papal monuments—a hideous figure of Death is pushing aside an alabaster curtain and exhibiting his hour-glass to the kneeling pope.

Opposite to this tomb is an oil painting on slate, by *Francesco Vanni*, of the Fall of Simon Magus. The south transept has a series of mosaic pictures ; The Incredulity of St. Thomas from Camuccini, the Crucifixion of St. Peter' and a St. Francis from Guido, and, on the pier of the Cupola, Ananias and Sapphira from the Roncalli at Sta. Maria degli Angeli, and the Transfiguration from Raphael.*

Opposite the mosaic of Ananias and Sapphira is the last tomb erected in St. Peter's, that of Pius VIII., Francesco Castiglione (1829—31), by *Tenerani*. It represents the pope kneeling, and above him the Saviour in benediction, with SS. Peter and Paul. It is of no great merit.

The Cappella Clementina has the Miracle of St. Gregory the Great from the Andrea Sacchi at the Vatican. Close to this is the fine tomb of Pius VII., Gregorio Chiaramonte (1800—23), who crowned Napoleon,—who suffered exile for seven years for refusing to abdicate the temporal power,— and who returned in triumph to die at the Quirinal, after having re-established the Order of the Jesuits. His monument is the work of *Thorwaldsen*, graceful and simple, though

* This mosaic occupied ten men constantly for nine years, and cost 60,000 francs.

perhaps too small to be in proportion to the neighbouring tombs. The figure of the pope, a gentle old man (he died at the age of eighty-one, having reigned twenty-three years), is seated in a chair; figures of Courage and Faith adorn the pedestal. The tomb was erected by Cardinal Gonsalvi, the faithful friend and minister of this pope (who died very poor, having spent all his wealth in charity), at an expense of 27,000 scudi.

Turning into the left aisle,—on the right is the tomb of Leo XI., Alessandro de Medici (1605), to which one is inclined to grudge so much space, considering that the pope it commemorates only reigned twenty-six days. The tomb, in allusion to this short life, is sculptured with flowers, and bears the motto, *Sic Florui*. It is the work of *Algardi*. The figures of Wisdom and Abundance, which adorn the pedestal, are fine specimens of this allegorical type.

Opposite, is the tomb of Innocent XI., Benedetto Odescalchi (1676—89), by *Etienne Monot*, with a bas-relief representing the raising of the siege of Vienna by King John Sobieski.

Near this, is the entrance to the Cappella del Coro, the very inconvenient chapel (decorated with gilding and stucco by Giacomo della Porta), in which the vesper services are held. The altar-piece is a mosaic copy of the Conception by Pietro Bianchi at the Angeli. In the pavement is the gravestone of Clement XI., Giov. Francesco Albani (1700—21).

Under the next arch of the aisle, on the left, is the interesting tomb of Innocent VIII., Gio. Battista Cibò (1484—92), by Pietro and Antonio Pollajuolo. The pope is represented asleep upon his sarcophagus, and a second time above, seated on a throne, his right hand extended in benediction, and his left holding the sacred lance of Longinus (said to have been that which pierced the side of our Saviour), sent to him by the sultan Bajazet. It is supposed that it was owing to the representation of this relic, that this tomb alone (except that of Sixtus IV., uncle of the destroyer), was replaced after the destruction of the old basilica. Upon the sarcophagus of the pope is inscribed, in allusion to the name of Innocent, the 11th verse of the 26th Psalm, "In innocentiâ meâ ingressus sum, redime me Domine et miserere mei." Opposite, is a tomb which is a kind of Memento Mori to the living pope, which always bears the name of his predecessor, and in which his corpse will be deposited, till his real tomb is prepared. "This tomb is now empty, and awaits its prey, Pius IX." *

Passing the Cappella della Presentazione, which contains a mosaic from the "Presentation of the Virgin," by *Romanelli*, we reach the last arch, which contains the tombs of the Stuarts. On the right is the monument, by *Filippo Barigioni*, of Maria Clementina Sobieski, wife of James III., called in the inscription "Queen of Great Britain, France, and Ireland"; on the left is that by Canova to the three Stuart princes, James III. and his sons, Charles Edward, and Henry—Cardinal York. It bears this inscription :

"JACOBO III.
JACOBI II., MAGNÆ BRIT . REGIS FILIO
KAROLO EDOARDO
ET HENRICO, DECANO PATRUM
CARDINALIUM,
JACOBI III. FILIIS,
REGIÆ STIRPIS STVARDIÆ POSTREMIS
ANNO MDCCCXIX
BEATI MORTUI QUI IN DOMINO MORIUNTUR."

* Gregorovius.

"George IV., fidèle à sa réputation du *gentleman* le plus accompli des trois royaumes, a voulu honorer la cendre des princes malheureux que de leur vivant il eût envoyés à l'échafaud s'ils fussent tombés en son pouvoir."—*Stendhal.*

"Beneath the unrivalled dome of St. Peter's, lie mouldering the remains of what was once a brave and gallant heart; and a stately monument from the chisel of Canova, and at the charge, as I believe, of the house of Hanover, has since arisen to the memory of *James the Third, Charles the Third, and Henry the Ninth, Kings of England,*— names which an Englishman can scarcely read without a smile or a sigh! Often at the present day does the British traveller turn from the sunny crest of the Pincian, or the carnival throng of the Corso, to gaze, in thoughtful silence, on that mockery of human greatness, and that last record of ruined hopes! The tomb before him is of a race justly expelled; the magnificent temple that enshrines it is of a faith wisely reformed; yet who at such a moment would harshly remember the errors of either, and might not join in the prayer even of that erring Church for the departed, 'Requiescant in pace.'"—*Lord Mahon.*

The last chapel is the Baptistery, and contains, as a font, the ancient porphyry cover of the sarcophagus of Hadrian, which was afterwards used for the tomb of the Emperor Otho II. The mosaic of the Baptism of our Saviour is from Carlo Maratta.

Distributed around the whole basilica are confessionals for every Christian tongue.

"Au milieu de toutes les créations hardies et splendides de l'art dans le basilique de St. Pierre, il est une impression morale qui saisit l'esprit, à la vue des confessionaux des diverses langues. Il y a là encore une autre espèce de grandeur."—*A. Du Pays.*

The Crypt of St. Peter's can always be visited by gentlemen, on application in the sacristy; but by ladies only with a special permission. The entrance is near the statue of Sta. Veronica. The visitor is terribly hurried in his inspection of this, the most historically interesting part of the basilica, and the works of art it contains are so ill-arranged, as to be difficult to investigate or remember. The crypt is divided into two portions, the *Grotte Nuove*, occupying the area beneath the dome, and opening into some ancient lateral chapels,—and the *Grotte Vecchie*, which extended under the whole nave of the old basilica, and reaches as far as the Cappella del Coro of the present edifice.

The first portion entered is a corridor in the Grotte Nuove. Hence open, on the right, two ancient chapels. The first, *Sta. Maria in Portico*, derives its name from a picture of the Virgin, attributed to *Simone Memmi*, which stood in the portico of the old basilica; it contains, besides several statues from the magnificent monument of Nicholas V., which perished with the old church, a statue of St. Peter which stood in the portico, and the cross which crowned its summit. The second chapel, *Sta. Maria delle Partorienti*, has a mosaic of our Saviour in benediction, from the tomb of Otho II.; a mosaic of the Virgin, of the eighth century; several ancient inscriptions; and, at the entrance, statues of the two apostles James, from the tomb of Nicholas V. Behind this chapel were preserved the remains of Leo II., III., and IX., till they were removed to the upper church by Leo XII.

Entering the *Grotte Vecchie*, we find a nave and aisles separated by pilasters with low arches. Following the south aisle we are first arrested by the marble inscription relating to the donation of lands made by the Countess Matilda to the church in 1102. Near this is the small *Cappella del Salvatore*, containing a bas-relief of the Virgin and Child by *Arnolfo*, which once decorated the tomb of Boniface VIII., —and the grave of Charlotte, Queen of Cyprus, who died in 1487. Near this are the sepulchral urns of the three Stuart princes, commemorated in the upper church. At the end of this aisle is the tomb of the Emperor Otho II., who died at Rome in A.D. 983; this formerly stood in the portico of the basilica.

Here is the empty tomb of Alexander VI., Rodrigo Borgia (1492—1503), the wicked and avaricious father of Cæsar and Lucretia, who is believed to have died of the poison which he intended for one of his cardinals. The body of this pope was not allowed to rest in peace. Julius II., the bitter enemy of the Borgias, turned it out of its tomb, and had it carried to S. Giacomo degli Spagnuoli, whence, when that church was pulled down, it was taken to Sta. Maria di Monserrato. The empty sarcophagus is surmounted by the figure of Alexander, who was himself a handsome old man, and in whose features may be traced the lineaments of the splendid Cæsar Borgia, known to us from the picture in the Borghese Palace.

At the end of the central nave is the sarcophagus of Christina of Sweden, who has a monument in the upper church.

The first tomb in the south aisle, beginning from the west, is that of Boniface VIII., Benedetto Gaetani (1294—1303).

"The last prince of the Church, who understood the papacy in the sense of universal dominion, in the spirit of Gregory VII., of Alexander and Innocent III. Two kings held the bridle of his palfrey as he rode from St. Peter's to the Lateran after his election. He received Dante as the ambassador of Florence; in 1300 he instituted the jubilee; and his reign—filled with contests with Philip le Bel of France and the Colonnas—ended in his being taken prisoner in his palace at Anagni by Sciarra Colonna and William of Nogaret, and subjected to the most cruel indignities. He was rescued by his fellow-citizens and conducted to Rome by the Orsini, but he died thirty seven days after of grief and mortification. The Ghibelline story relates that he sate alone silently gnawing the top of his staff, and at length dashed out his brains against the wall, or smothered himself with his own pillows. But the contemporary verse of the Cardinal St. George describes him as dying quietly in the midst of his cardinals, at peace with the world, and having received all the consolations of the Church."—*See Milman's Latin Christianity*, vol. v.

The character of Boniface has ever been one of the battlefields of history. He was scarcely dead when the epitaph, " He came in like a fox, he ruled like a lion, he died like a dog," was proclaimed to Christendom. He was consigned by Dante to the lowest circle of Hell; yet even Dante expressed the universal shock with which Christendom beheld "the Fleur de lis enter Anagni, and Christ again captive in his Vicar,—the mockery, the gall and vinegar, the crucifixion between living robbers, the cruelty of the second Pilate." In later times, Tosti, Drumann, and lastly, Cardinal Wiseman, have engaged in his defence.

Boniface VIII. was buried with the utmost magnificence in a splendid chapel, which he had built himself, and adorned with mosaics, and where a grand tomb was erected to him. Of this nothing remains now, but the sarcophagus, which bears a majestic figure of the pope by *Arnolfo del Cambio*.

"The head is unusually beautiful, severe and noble in its form, and corresponds perfectly with the portrait which we have (at the Lateran) from the hand of Giotto, which represents his face as beardless and of the most perfect oval. His head is covered by a long, pointed mitre, like a sugar-loaf, decked with two crowns. This proud man was indeed the first who wore the double crown,—all his predecessors having been content with a simple crowned mitre. This new custom existed till the time of Urban V., by whom the third crown was added."—*Gregorovius, Grabmäler der Päpste.*

Close to that of Boniface are the sarcophagi of Pius II.,

Æneas Sylvius Piccolomini (1458—64) and Pius III., Antonio Todeschini Piccolomini (1503), whose monuments are removed to S. Andrea della Valle.

Next beyond Boniface is the tomb of Adrian IV. (Nicholas Breakspeare, 1154—59), the only Englishman who ever occupied the papal throne.* He is buried in a pagan sarcophagus of red granite, adorned with Medusa heads in relief, and without any inscription.

Opposite this, is a sarcophagus bearing the figure of Nicholas V., Tomaso di Sarzana (1447—55), being nearly all that has been preserved of the glorious tomb of that pope, who founded the Vatican library, collected around him a court of savants and poets, and "with whom opened the age of papacy to which belonged the times of Julius II. and Leo X." His epitaph, attributed to Pius II., is by his secretary Mafeo Vegio.

"The bones of Nicholas V. rest in this grave,
Who gave to thee, O Rome! thy golden age.
Famous in council, more famous in shining virtue,
He honoured wise men, who was himself the wisest of all.
He gave healing to the world, long wounded with schism,
And renewed at once its manners and customs, and the buildings and temples of the city.
He gave an altar to St. Bernardino of Siena
When he celebrated the holy year of jubilee.
He crowned with gold the forehead of Frederick and his wife,
And gave order to the affairs of Italy by the treaty which he made.
He translated many Greek writings into the Latin tongue ;—
Then offer incense to-day at his holy grave."

Next comes a remnant of the tomb of Paul II., Pietro Barbo (1464—71), chiefly remarkable for his personal

---

* He had been bishop of St. Alban's, and a missionary for the conversion of Norway.

beauty, of which he was so vain, that when he issued from the conclave as pope, he wished to take the name of Formosus. This pontiff built the Palazzo S. Marco, and gave a name to the Corso, by establishing the races there. He also prepared for himself one of the most splendid tombs in the old basilica, for which he obtained Mino da Fiesole as an architect. It was his wish to lie in the porphyry sarcophagus of Sta. Costanza, which he stole from her church for this purpose; hence the simplicity of the existing sarcophagus, which bears his effigy. Beyond this, are sarcophagi of Julius III., Gio. Maria Ciocchi del Monte (1550—55), builder of the Villa Papa Giulio; and Nicholas III., Orsini (1277—81), who made a treaty with Rudolph of Hapsburg, and obtained from him a ratification of the donation of the Countess Matilda. Then comes the sarcophagus of Urban VI., Bartolomeo Prignani (1378—87), the sole relic of a most magnificent tomb of this cruel pope, who is believed to have died of poison. It bears his figure, and in the front, a bas-relief of him receiving the keys from St. Peter. His epitaph runs:

> "Here rests the just, wise, and noble prince,
> Urban VI., a native of Naples.
> He, full of zeal, gave a safe refuge to the teachers of the faith.
> That gained for him, noble one, a fatal poison cup at the close of the repast.
> Great was the schism, but great was his courage in opposing it,
> And in the presence of this mighty pope Simony sate dumb.
> But it is needless to reiterate his praises upon earth,
> While heaven is shining with his immortal glory.

> "Sepelitur in beati Petri Basilica, paucis admodum ejus mortem, utpote hominis rustici et inexorabilis, flentibus. Hujus autem sepulchrum adhuc visitur cum epitaphio satis rustico et inepto."—*Platina*.

Next come the sarcophagi of Innocent VII., Cosmato de Miliorati (1404—6), bearing his figure; of Marcellus II., Marcello Cervini (1555), who only reigned twenty-five days; and of Innocent IX., Giov. Antonio Facchinetti (1591—92), who reigned only sixty.

Near these is the urn of Agnese Gaetani Colonna, the only lady not of royal birth buried in the basilica.

Hence we return to the corridor of the Grotte Nuove, containing a number of mosaics and statues detached from different papal tombs, the best being those from that of Nicholas V. and that of Paul II., by *Mino da Fiesole* (a figure of Charity is especially beautiful), and a bas-relief of the Virgin and Child, by *Arnolfo*, from the tomb of Benedict VIII.

Here also are a half-length statue of Boniface VIII., ascribed to *Andrea Pisano;* a half-length of Benedict XII., by *Paolo di Siena;* and a figure of St. Peter seated on a gothic throne which once supported a statue of Benedict XII.

The *Chapel of St. Longinus* has a mosaic from a picture by Andrea Sacchi. Near the entrance of the shrine are marble reliefs of the martyrdoms of St. Peter and St. Paul. Opposite to the entrance of the shrine is the magnificent sarcophagus of Junius Bassus, Christian prefect of Rome, who died A.D. 359. It was discovered near its present site in 1595. It is adorned with admirable sculptures from the Old and New Testament.

Opening from the centre of the circular passage is the *Confession or Shrine of SS. Peter and Paul*, which contains the sarcophagus brought from the Catacomb near S. Sebastiano in 257, and which the Roman Catholic Church has always revered as that of St. Peter. On the altar, consecrated in 1122, are two ancient pictures of St. Peter and St. Paul. Only half the bodies of the saints are held to be preserved here, the other portion of that of St. Peter being at the Lateran, and of St. Paul at S. Paolo fuori Mura.

To the Roman Catholic mind this is naturally one of the most sacred spots in the world, since it holds literally the words of St. Ambrose, that: "Where Peter is, there is the Church,—and where the Church is, there is no death, but life eternal." *

"From this place Peter, from this place Paul, shall be caught up in the resurrection. Oh consider with trembling that which Rome will behold, when Paul suddenly rises with Peter from this sepulchre, and is carried up into the air to meet the Lord."—*St. John Chrysostom, Homily on the Ep. to the Romans.*

"Among the cemeteries ascribed by tradition to apostolic times, the crypts of the Vatican would have the first claim on our attention, had they not been almost destroyed by the foundations of the vast basilica which guards the tomb of St. Peter. . . . The *Liber Pontificalis* says that Anacletus, the successor of Clement in the Apostolic See, '*built* and adorned the sepulchral monument (*construxit memoriam*) of blessed Peter, since he had been ordained priest by St. Peter, and other burial-places where the bishops might be laid.' It is added that he himself was buried there ; and the same is recorded of Linus and Cletus, and of Evaristus, Sixtus I., Telesphorus, Hyginus, Pius I., Eleutherius, and Victor, the last of whom was buried A.D. 203 ; and after St. Victor, no other pontiff is recorded to have been buried at the Vatican until Leo the Great was laid in St. Peter's, A.D. 461. The idea conveyed by the words *construxit memoriam* is that of a monument above-ground according to the usual Roman custom ; and we have seen that such a monument, even though it covered the tomb of Christian bishops, would not be likely to be disturbed at any time during the first or second century. For the reason we have already stated, it is impossible to confront these ancient notices with any existing monuments. It is worth mentioning, however, that De Rossi believes that the sepulchre

* The principal authorities for the fact of St. Peter's being at Rome—so often denied by ultra-protestants—are : St. Jerome, Catalogus scriptorum ecclesiasticorum, in Petro ; Tertullian, de Prescriptionibus, c. xxxvi. ; and Eusebius, Historia Ecclesiastica, lib. ii. cap. xxiv.

of St. Linus was discovered in this very place early in the seventeenth century, bearing simply the name of *Linus.*"—*Northcote and Brownlow, Roma Sotterranea.*

To ascend the *Dome of St. Peter's* requires a special order. The entrance is from the first door in the left aisle, near the tomb of Maria-Clementina Sobieski. The ascent is by an easy staircase *à cordoni*, the walls of which bear memorial tablets of all the royal personages who have ascended it. The aspect of the roof is exceedingly curious from the number of small domes and houses of workmen with which it is studded,—quite a little village in themselves. A chamber in one of the pillars which support the dome contains a model of the ancient throne of St. Peter, and a model of the church, by Michael Angelo and his predecessor, Antonio di Sangallo. The dome is 300 feet above the roof, and 613½ feet in circumference. An iron staircase leads thence to the ball, which is capable of containing sixteen persons.

"Cette hauteur fait frémir," dit Beyle, "quand on songe aux tremblements de terre qui agitent fréquemment l'Italie, et qu'un instant peut vous priver du plus beau monument qui existe. Certainement jamais il ne serait relevé: nous sommes trop *raisonnables.*"

"De Brosse raconte que deux moines espagnoles, qui se trouvaient dans la boule de St. Pierre lors de la secousse de 1730, eurent une telle peur, que l'un d'eux mourut sur la place."—*A. Du Pays.*

The *Sacristy of St. Peter's,* which is entered by a grey marble door on the left, before turning into the south transept, was built by Pius VI., in 1755, from designs of *Carlo Marchione.* It consists of three halls, with a corridor adorned with columns and inscriptions from the old church, and with statues of SS. Peter and Paul, which stood in front of it. The central hall, *Sagrestia Commune,* is adorned with eight fluted pillars of grey marble (bigio) from Hadrian's

Villa. On the left is the *Sagrestia dei Canonici*, with the Cappella dei Canonici, which has two pictures, the Madonna and Saints (Anna, Peter, and Paul), by *Francesco Penni*, and the Madonna and Child, *Giulio Romano*. Hence opens the *Stanza Capitolare*, containing an interesting remnant of the many works of Giotto in the old basilica under Boniface VIII. (for which he received 3020 gold florins), in three panel pictures belonging to the ciborium for the high altar ordered by Cardinal Stefaneschi, and representing,— Christ with that Cardinal,—the Crucifixion of St. Peter,— the Execution of St. Peter,—and on the back of the same panel, another picture, in which Cardinal Stefaneschi is offering his ciborium to St. Peter.

"The fragments which are preserved of the painting which Giotto executed for the Church of St. Peter cannot fail to make us regret its loss. The fragments are treated with a grandeur of style which has led Rumohr to suspect that the susceptible imagination of Giotto was unable to resist the impression which the ancient mosaics of the Christian basilicas must have produced upon him." — *Rio. Poetry of Christian Art.*

Here also are several fragments of the frescoes (of angels and apostles), by *Melozzo da Forlì*, which existed in the former dome of the SS. Apostoli, and of which the finest portion is now at the Quirinal Palace. On the right is the *Sagrestia dei Beneficiati*, which contains a picture of the Saviour giving the keys to St. Peter, by *Muziano*, and an image called La Madonna della Febbre, which stood in the old Sacristy. Opening hence is the *Treasury of St. Peter's*, containing some ancient jewels, crucifixes, and candelabra, by Benvenuto Cellini and Michael Angelo, and, among other relics, the famous sacerdotal robe called the *Dalmatica di Papa San Leone*, "said to have been embroidered at

Constantinople for the coronation of Charlemagne as Emperor of the West, but fixed by German criticism as a production of the twelfth, or the early part of the thirteenth century. The emperors, at least, have worn it ever since, while serving as deacons at the pope's altar during their coronation-mass."

"It is a large robe of stiff brocade, falling in broad and unbroken folds in front and behind,—broad and deep enough for the Goliath-like stature and the Herculean chest of Charlemagne himself. On the breast the Saviour is represented in glory, on the back the Transfiguration, and on the two shoulders Christ administering the Eucharist to the Apostles. In each of these last compositions, our Saviour, a stiff but majestic figure, stands behind the altar, on which are deposited a chalice and a paten or basket containing crossed wafers. He gives, in the one case, the cup to St. Paul, in the other the bread to St. Peter,—they do not kneel, but bend reverently to receive it; five other disciples await their turn in each instance,—all are standing.

"I do not apprehend your being disappointed with the Dalmatica di San Leone, or your dissenting from my conclusion, that a master, a Michael-Angelo I would almost say, then flourished at Byzantium.

"It was in this Dalmatica—then *semée* all over with pearls and glittering in freshness—that Cola di Rienzi robed himself over his armour in the sacristy of St. Peter's and thence ascended to the Palace of the Popes, after the manner of the Cæsars, with sounding trumpets and his horsemen following him—his truncheon in his hand and his crown on his head—'terribile e fantastico,' as his biographer describes him— to wait upon the Legate."—*Lord Lindsay's Christian Art*, i. 137.

Above the Sacristy are the *Archives of St. Peter's*, containing, among many other ancient MSS., a life of St. George, with miniatures, by *Giotto*. The entrance to the Archivio, at the end of the corridor, is adorned with fragments of the chains of the ports of Smyrna and Tunis. Here, also, is a statue of Pius VI., by *Agostino Penna*.

It is quite worth while to leave St. Peter's by the Porta

Sta. Marta beneath the tomb of Alexander VII., in order to examine the exterior of the church from behind, where it completely dwarfs all the surrounding buildings. Among these are the *Church of S. Stefano*, with a fine door composed of antique fragments, and the dismal *Church of Sta. Marta*, which contains several of the Roman weights known as "Pietra di Paragone," said to have been used in the martyrdoms. Beyond the Sacristy is the pretty little *Cimeterio dei Tedeschi*, the oldest of Christian burial-grounds, said to have been set apart by Constantine, and filled with earth from Calvary. It was granted to the Germans in 1779, by Pius VI. Close by is the *Church of Sta. Maria della Pietà in Campo Santo.*

Not far from hence (in a street behind the nearest colonnade) is the *Palazzo del Santo Uffizio—or of the Inquisition.* This body, for some time past, suppressed everywhere except in the States of the Pope, was established here in 1536 by Paul III., acting on the advice of Cardinal Caraffa, afterwards Paul IV., for inquiry into cases of heresy, and the punishment of ecclesiastical offences. It was by the authority of the "Holy Office" that the "Index" of prohibited books was first drawn up. Paul IV., on his deathbed, summoned the cardinals to his side, and recommended to them this "Santissimo Tribunale," as he called it, and succeeding popes have protected and encouraged it. The character of the Inquisition has been much changed from that which it bore three hundred years ago; but even in late years, many cases of extreme severity have been reported,—especially one of a French bishop cruelly imprisoned for sixteen years in one of its dungeons (merely because he had received his consecration from a French constitutional prelate), and who was only released when its doors were opened in the revolution of 1848.

"Within these walls has been confined for many years a very extraordinary person—the archbishop of Memphis . . . Pope Leo XII. received a letter from the Pacha of Egypt informing his Holiness, that he and a large portion of his subjects desired to be received into the bosom of the Church of Rome ; and announcing that he and they were willing to conform, provided the pope would send out an archbishop, with a suitable train of ecclesiastics, and requesting that his Holiness would do him the favour of appointing a certain young student whom he named, the first archbishop of Memphis, and despatch him to Egypt. No doubt was entertained as to the truth of this communication, but an objection presented itself in the youth of the ecclesiastical student whom the Pacha wished to have as his archbishop. The pope consulted his cardinals, who advised him not to make the dangerous precedent of raising a novice to so high a rank in the Church, but his Holiness, tempted by the desire of converting a kingdom to Christianity, resolved to conform to the wishes of the Pacha, and did consecrate the youth archbishop of Memphis. The archbishop was sent out attended by a train of priests to Egypt. When the ship arrived, the authorities in Egypt declared the affair was an imposition. His Grace confessed the fraud, was arrested, and reconducted to Rome. He was the author of the letter which imposed on the pope—his original intention having been to confess to the pope as a priest, after his consecration, the imposition he had practised ; and as the pope could not betray a secret imparted to him at the confessional, the offender might have obtained absolution, and escaped punishment. Whether this would have been practicable I know not ; but it was not accomplished, and as the youth had the rank of archbishop indelibly imprinted on him, nothing remained but to confine his Grace for the remainder of his life ; and accordingly he was confined to this prison near the Vatican, whence he may find it difficult to escape."—*Whiteside's Italy*, 1860.

The tribunal of the Inquisition was formally abolished by the Roman Assembly in February, 1849, but was re-established by Pius IX. in the following June. Its meetings, however, now take place in the Vatican, and the old palace of the Holy Office was long used as a barrack for French soldiers.

In the interior of the building is a lofty hall, with gloomy frescoes of Dominican saints,—and many terrible dungeons and cells in which the victim is unable to stand upright, having their vaulted ceilings lined with reeds, to deaden sound,—but all this is seldom seen. When the people rushed into the Inquisition at the revolution, a number of human bones were found in these vaults, which so excited the popular fury, that an attack on the Dominican convent at the Minerva was anticipated. Ardent defenders of the papacy maintain that these bones had been previously transported to the Inquisition from a cemetery, to get up a sensation.*

Built up into the back of this palace is the tribune of the *Church of S. Salvatore in Torrione or in Macello*, whose foundation is ascribed to Charlemagne (797). Senerano (Sette Chiese) supposes that the French had here their schola or special centre for worship and assemblage. The windows of this building are among the few examples of gothic in Rome, and there are good terrra-cotta mouldings. It may best be seen from the *Porta Cavalleggieri*, which was designed by Sangallo, and derives its name from the cavalry barracks close by.

A short distance from the lower end of the Colonnade is the *Church of S. Michaele in Sassia*, whose handsome tower is a relic of the church founded by Leo IV., who built the walls of the Borgo, especially for funeral masses for the souls of those who fell in its defence against the Saracens. Raphael Mengs is buried in the modern church.

The name of this church commemorates the Saxon settlement "called Burgus Saxonum, Vicus Saxonum, Schola

* See Hemans' Catholic Italy, vol. i.

Saxonum, and simply Saxia or Sassia," * founded c. 727 by Ina, king of Wessex, and enlarged in 794 by Offa, king of Mercia, when he made a pilgrimage to Rome in penance for the murder of Ethelbert, king of East-Anglia. Ina founded here a church, " Sta. Maria quæ vocatur Schola Saxorum," which is mentioned as late as 854. Dyer (Hist. of the City of Rome) says that " when Leo IV. enclosed this part of the city, it obtained the name of Borgo, from the Burgus Saxonum, and one of the gates was called Saxonum Posterula. The 'Schola Francorum' was also in the Borgo."

* See Dyer's Hist. of the City of Rome, p. 358.

CHAPTER XVI.

THE VATICAN.

History of the Vatican Quarter and of the Palace—Scala Regia—Pauline Chapel—Sistine Chapel—Sala Ducale—Court of St. Damasus—Galleria Lapidaria—Braccio Nuovo—Museo Chiaramonti—The Belvedere—Gallery of Statues—Hall of Busts—Sala delle Muse—Sala Rotonda—Sala a Croce Greca—Galleria dei Candelabri—Galleria degli Arazzi—Library—Appartamenti Borgia—Etruscan Museum — Egyptian Museum — Gardens—Villa Pia — Loggie—Stanze—Chapel of S. Lorenzo—Gallery of Pictures.

THE hollow of the Janiculum between S. Onofrio and the Monte Mario is believed to have been a site of Etruscan divination.

"Fauni vatesque canebant."
Ennius.

Hence the name, which is now only used in regard to the papal palace and the basilica of St. Peter, but which was once applied to the whole district between the foot of the hill and the Tiber near S. Angelo.

". . . ut paterni
Fluminis ripæ, simul et jocosa
Redderet laudes tibi Vaticani
Montis imago."
Horace, i. Od. 20.

Tacitus speaks of the unwholesome air of this quarter. In this district was the Circus of Caligula, adjoining the gardens of his mother Agrippina, decorated by the obelisk which now stands in the front of St. Peter's.* Here Seneca describes that while Caligula was walking by torchlight, he amused himself by the slaughter of a number of distinguished persons—senators and Roman ladies. Afterwards it became the Circus of Nero, who from his adjoining gardens used to watch the martyrdom of the Christians †—mentioned by Suetonius as "a race given up to a new and evil superstition"—and who used their living bodies, covered with pitch and set on fire, as torches for his nocturnal promenades.

The first residence of the popes at the Vatican was erected by St. Symmachus (A.D. 498—514) near the forecourt of the old St. Peter's, and here Charlemagne is believed to have resided on the occasion of his several visits to Rome during the reigns of Adrian I. (772—795) and Leo III. (795—816). This ancient palace having fallen into decay during the twelfth century, it was rebuilt in the thirteenth by Innocent III. It was greatly enlarged by Nicholas III. (1277—1281), but the Lateran continued to be the papal residence, and the Vatican palace was only used on state occasions, and for the reception of any foreign sovereigns visiting Rome. After the return of the popes from Avignon, the Lateran palace had fallen into decay, and for the sake of the greater security afforded by the vicinity of S. Angelo, it was determined to make the pontifical residence at the Vatican, and the first conclave was held there in 1378. In order to increase its security, John XXIII. constructed the covered passage to

* Pliny, xxxv. 15. † Tac. Ann. xv. 44.

S. Angelo in 1410. Nicholas V. (1447—1455) had the idea of making it the most magnificent palace in the world, and of uniting in it all the government offices and dwellings of the cardinals, but died before he could do more than begin the work. The building which he commenced was finished by Alexander VI., and still exists under the name of Tor di Borgia. In 1473 Sixtus IV. built the Sistine Chapel, and in 1490 "the Belvedere" was erected as a separate garden-house by Innocent VIII. from designs of Antonio da Pollajuolo. Julius II., with the aid of Bramante, united this villa to the palace by means of one vast courtyard, and erected the Loggie around the Court of St. Damasus; he also laid the foundation of the Vatican Museum in the gardens of the Belvedere. The Loggie were completed by Leo X.; the Sala Regia and the Pauline Chapel were built by Paul III. Sixtus V. divided the great court of Bramante into two by the erection of the library, and began the present residence of the popes, which was finished by Clement VIII. (1592—1605). Urban VIII. built the Scala Regia; Clement XIV. and Pius VII., the Museo Pio-Clementino; Pius VII., the Braccio Nuovo; Leo XII., the picture-gallery; Gregory XVI., the Etruscan Museum; and Pius IX., the handsome staircase leading to the court of Bramante.

The length of the Vatican palace is 1151 English feet; its breadth, 767. It has eight grand staircases, twenty courts, and is said to contain 11,000 chambers of different sizes.

(The collections in the Vatican may be visited daily with an order and at fixed hours, except on Sundays and high festivals. Permission to make drawings must be obtained from the maggior-domo.)

The principal entrance of the Vatican is at the end of the right colonnade of St. Peter's. Hence a door on the right opens upon the staircase leading to the Cortile di S. Damaso, and is the nearest way to the collections of statues and pictures.

Following the great corridor, and passing on the left the entrance to the portico of St. Peter's, we reach the *Scala Regia*, a magnificent work of Bernini, formerly guarded by the picturesque Swiss soldiers. Hence we enter the *Sala Regia*, built in the reign of Paul III. by Antonio di Sangallo, and used as a hall of audience for ambassadors. It is decorated with frescoes illustrative of the history of the popes.

ENTRANCE WALL :
    Alliance of the Venetians with Paul V. against the Turks, and Battle of Lepanto, 1571 : *Vasari*.

RIGHT WALL :
    Absolution of the Emperor Henry IV., by Gregory VII. : *Federigo* and *Taddeo Zucchero*.

LEFT WALL :
    Massacre of St. Bartholomew : *Vasari*.

OPPOSITE WALL, towards the Sala Regia :
    Return of Gregory XI. from Avignon.
    Benediction of Frederick Barbarossa by Alexander III., in the Piazza of S. Marco : *Giuseppe Porta*.

On the right is the entrance of the *Pauline Chapel* (Cappella Paolina), also built (1540) by Antonio di Sangallo for Paul III. Its decorations are chiefly the work of *Sabbatini* and *F. Zucchero*, but it contains two frescoes by *Michael Angelo*.

[1] "Two excellent frescoes, executed by Michael Angelo on the side walls of the Pauline Chapel, are little cared for, and are so much blackened by the smoke of lamps that they are seldom mentioned. The Crucifixion of St. Peter, under the large window, is in a most unfavourable light, but is distinguished for its grand, severe composition. That on the opposite wall—the Conversion of St. Paul—is still tolerably distinct. The long train of his soldiers is seen ascending in the background. Christ, surrounded by a host of angels, bursts upon his sight from the storm-flash. Paul lies stretched on the ground—a noble and finely-developed form. His followers fly on all sides, or are struck motionless by the thunder. The arrangement of the groups is excellent, and some of the single figures are very dignified; the composition has, moreover, a principle of order and repose, which, in comparison with the Last Judgment, places this picture in a very favourable light. If there are any traces of old age to be found in these works, they are at most discoverable in the execution of details."—*Kugler*, p. 308.

On the left of the approach from the Scala Regia is the *Sistine Chapel* (Cappella Sistina), built by Bacio Pintelli in 1473 for Sixtus IV. The lower part of the walls of this wonderful chapel was formerly hung on festivals with the tapestries executed from the cartoons of Raphael; the upper portion is decorated in fresco by the great Florentine masters of the fifteenth century.

"It was intended to represent scenes from the life of Moses on one side of the chapel, and from the life of Christ on the other, so that the old law might be confronted by the new,—the type by the typified."—*Lanzi*.

The following is the order of the frescoes, type and antitype together:

Over the altar—now destroyed to make way for the Last Judgment:

| 1. Moses in the Bulrushes: *Perugino*. | 1. Christ in the Manger: *Perugino*. |

(Between these was the Assumption of the Virgin, in which Pope Sixtus IV. was introduced, kneeling: *Perugino*.)

On the left wall, still existing:

2. Moses and Zipporah on the way to Egypt, and the circumcision of their son: *Luca Signorelli.*

3. Moses killing the Egyptian, and driving away the shepherds from the well: *Sandro Botticelli.*

4. Moses and the Israelites, after the passage of the Red Sea: *Cosimo Rosselli.*

5. Moses giving the Law from the Mount: *Cosimo Rosselli.*

6. The punishment of Korah, Dathan, and Abiram, who aspired uncalled to the priesthood: *Sandro Botticelli.*

7. The last interview of Moses and Joshua: *Luca Signorelli.*

On the right wall, still existing:

2. The Baptism of Christ: *Perugino.*

3. The Temptation of Christ: *Sandro Botticelli.*

4. The calling of the Apostles on the Lake of Gennesareth: *Domenico Ghirlandajo.*

5. Christ's Sermon on the Mount: *Cosimo Rosselli.*

6. The institution of the Christian Priesthood. Christ giving the keys to Peter: *Perugino.*

7. The Last Supper: *Cosimo Rosselli.*

On the entrance wall:

8. Michael bears away the body of Moses (Jude 9): *Cecchino Salviati.*

8. The Resurrection: *Domenico Ghirlandajo,* restored by *Arrigo Fiamingo.*

On the pillars between the windows are the figures of twenty-eight popes, by *Sandro Botticelli.*

"Vasari says that the two works of Luca Signorelli surpass in beauty all those which surround them,—an assertion which is at least questionable as far as regards the frescoes of Perugino ; but with respect to all the rest, the superiority of Signorelli is evident, even to the most inexperienced eye. The subject of the first picture is the journey of Moses and Zipporah into Egypt : the landscape is charming, although evidently ideal ; there is great depth in the aërial perspective ; and in the various groups scattered over the different parts of the picture there are female forms of such beauty, that they may have afforded models to Raphael. The same graceful treatment is also perceptible in the representation of the death of Moses, the mournful details of which have given scope to the poetical imagination of the artist. The varied group to whom Moses has just read the Law for the last time, the sorrow of Joshua, who is kneeling before the man of God, the charming landscape, with the river Jordan threading its way between the mountains, which are made singularly beautiful, as if to explain the regrets of Moses when the angel announces to him that he will not enter into the promised land—all form a series of melancholy scenes perfectly in harmony with one another, the only defect being that the whole is crowded into too small a space."— *Rio. Poetry of Christian Art.*

The avenue of pictures is a preparation for the surpassing grandeur of the ceiling :

"The *ceiling* of the Sistine Chapel contains the most perfect works done by *Michael Angelo* in his long and active life. Here his great spirit appears in its noblest dignity, in its highest purity ; here the attention is not disturbed by that arbitrary display to which his great power not unfrequently seduced him in other works. The ceiling forms a flattened arch in its section ; the central portion, which is a plain surface, contains a series of large and small pictures, representing the most important events recorded in the book of Genesis—the Creation and Fall of Man, with its immediate consequences. In the large triangular compartments at the springing of the vault, are sitting figures of the prophets and sibyls, as the foretellers of the coming of the Saviour. In the soffits of the recesses between these compartments, and in the arches underneath, immediately above the windows, are the ancestors of the Virgin, the series leading the mind directly to the Saviour. The external connection of these numerous representations is formed by an architectural framework of peculiar composition, which encloses the single subjects, tends to make the principal masses conspicuous, and gives to the whole an appearance of that solidity and support so necessary, but so seldom attended to, in soffit decorations, which may be considered as if suspended. A great number of figures are also connected with the framework ; those in unimportant situations are executed in the colour of stone or bronze ; in the more important, in natural colours. These serve to support the architectural forms, to fill up and to connect the whole. They may be best described as the living and embodied *genii* of architecture. It required the unlimited power of an architect, sculptor, and painter, to conceive a structural whole of so much grandeur, to design the decorative figures with the significant repose required by the sculpturesque character, and yet to preserve their subordination to the principal subjects, and to keep the latter in the proportions and relations best adapted to the space to be filled."—*Kugler*, p. 301.

The pictures from the Old Testament, beginning from the altar, are :

1. The Separation of Light and Darkness.
2. The Creation of the Sun and Moon.
3. The Creation of Trees and Plants.
4. The Creation of Adam.
5. The Creation of Eve.
6. The Fall and the Expulsion from Paradise.
7. The Sacrifice of Noah.
8. The Deluge.
9. The Intoxication of Noah.

"The scenes from Genesis are the most sublime representations of these subjects;—the Creating Spirit is unveiled before us. The peculiar type which the painter has here given of the form of the Almighty Father has been frequently imitated by his followers, and even by Raphael, but has been surpassed by none. Michael Angelo has represented him in majestic flight, sweeping through the air, surrounded by *genii*, partly supporting, partly borne along with him, covered by his floating drapery; they are the distinct syllables, the separate virtues of his creating word. In the first (large) compartment we see him with extended hands, assigning to the sun and moon their respective paths. In the second, he awakens the first man to life. Adam lies stretched on the verge of the earth, in the act of raising himself; the Creator touches him with the point of his finger, and appears thus to endow him with feeling and life. This picture displays a wonderful depth of thought in the composition, and the utmost elevation and majesty in the general treatment and execution. The third subject is not less important, representing the Fall of Man and his Expulsion from Paradise. The tree of knowledge stands in the midst, the serpent (the upper part of the body being that of a woman) is twined around the stem; she bends down towards the guilty pair, who are in the act of plucking the forbidden fruit. The figures are nobly graceful, particularly that of Eve. Close to the serpent hovers the angel with the sword, ready to drive the fallen beings out of Paradise. In this double action, this union of two separate moments, there is something peculiarly poetic and significant : it is guilt and punishment in one picture. The sudden and lightning-like appearance of the avenging angel behind the demon of darkness has a most impressive effect."—*Kugler*, p. 304.

"It was the seed of Eve that was to bruise the serpent's head. Hence it is that Michael Angelo made the Creation of Eve the central subject on the ceiling of the Sistine Chapel. He had the good taste to suggest, and yet to avoid, that literal rendering of the biblical story which in the ruder representations borders on the grotesque, and which Milton, with all his pomp of words, could scarcely idealise."—*Mrs. Jameson, Hist. of Our Lord.*

The lower portion of the ceiling is divided into triangles occupied by the Prophets and Sibyls in solemn contemplation, accompanied by angels and genii. Beginning from the left of the entrance, their order is,—

	1. Jonah.	
2. Jeremiah.		7. Sibylla Libyca.
3. Sibylla Persica.		8. Daniel.
4. Ezekiel.		9. Sibylla Cumæa.
5. Sibylla Erythræa.		10. Isaiah.
6. Joel.		11. Sibylla Delphica.
	12. Zachariah.	

"The prophets and sibyls in the triangular compartments of the curved portion of the ceiling are the largest figures in the whole work; these, too, are among the most wonderful forms that modern art has called into life. They are all represented seated, employed with books or rolled manuscripts; genii stand near or behind them. These mighty beings sit before us pensive, meditative, inquiring, or looking upwards with inspired countenances. Their forms and movements, indicated by the grand lines and masses of the drapery, are majestic and dignified. We see in them beings, who, while they feel and bear the sorrows of a corrupt and sinful world, have power to look for consolation into the secrets of the future. Yet the greatest variety prevails in the attitudes and expression—each figure is full of individuality. Zacharias is an aged man, busied in calm and circumspect investigation; Jeremiah is bowed down absorbed in thought—the thought of deep and bitter grief; Ezekiel turns with hasty movement to the genius next to him, who points upwards, with joyful expectation, &c. The sibyls are equally characteristic: the Persian—a lofty, majestic woman, very aged; the Erythræan—full of power, like the warrior goddess of wisdom; the Delphic—like Cassandra, youthfully soft and graceful, but with strength to bear the awful seriousness of revelation."—*Kugler*, p. 304.

"The belief of the Roman Catholic Church in the testimony of the Sibyl is shown by the well-known hymn, said to have been composed by Pope Innocent III. at the close of the thirteenth century, beginning with the verse :—

> 'Dies iræ, dies illa,
> Solvet sæclum in favilla,
> Teste David cum Sibylla.

It may be inferred that this hymn, admitted into the liturgy of the Roman Church, gave sanction to the adoption of the Sibyls into Christian art. They are seen from this time accompanying the prophets and apostles in the cyclical decorations of the church. . . . . . But the highest honour that art has rendered to the Sibyls has been by the hand of Michael Angelo, on the ceiling of the Sistine Chapel. Here, in the conception of a mysterious order of women, placed above and without all considerations of the graceful or the individual, the great master was peculiarly in his element. They exactly fitted his standard of art, not always sympathetic, nor comprehensible to the average human mind, of which the grand in form and the abstract in expression, were the first and last conditions. In this respect, the Sibyls on the Sistine Chapel ceiling are more Michael Angelesque than their companions the Prophets. For these, while types of the highest monumental treatment, are yet men, while the Sibyls belong to a distinct class of beings, who convey the impression of the very obscurity in which their history is wrapt—creatures who have lived far from the abodes of men, who are alike devoid of the expression of feminine sweetness, human sympathy, or sacramental beauty ; who are neither Christians nor Jewesses, Witches nor Graces, yet living, grand, beautiful, and true, according to laws revealed to the great Florentine genius only. Thus their figures may be said to be unique, as the offspring of a peculiar sympathy between the master's mind and his subject. To this sympathy may be ascribed the prominence and size given them—both Prophets and Sibyls—as compared to their usual relation to the subjects they environ. They sit here in twelve throne-like niches, more like presiding deities, each wrapt in self-contemplation, than as tributary witnesses to the truth and omnipotence of Him they are intended to announce. Thus they form a gigantic framework round the subjects of the Creation, of which the birth of Eve, as the type of the Nativity, is the intentional centre. For some reason, the twelve figures are not Prophets and Sibyls alternately—there being only five Sibyls to seven

Prophets—so that the Prophets come together at one angle. Books and scrolls are given indiscriminately to them.

"The Sibylla Persica, supposed to be the oldest of the sisterhood, holds the book close to her eyes, as if from dimness of sight, which fact, contradicted as it is by a frame of obviously Herculean strength, gives a mysterious intentness to the action.

"The Sibylla Libyca, of equally powerful proportions, but less closely draped, is grandly wringing herself to lift a massive volume from a height above her head on to her knees.

"The Sibylla Cumana, also aged, and with her head covered, is reading with her volume at a distance from her eyes.

"The Sibylla Delphica, with waving hair escaping from her turban, is a beautiful young being—the most human of all—gazing into vacancy or futurity. She holds a scroll.

"The Sibylla Erythræa, grand bare-headed creature, sits reading intently with crossed legs, about to turn over her book.

"The Prophets are equally grand in structure, and though, as we have said, not more than men, yet they are the only men that could well bear the juxtaposition with their stupendous female colleagues. Ezekiel, between Erythræa and Persica, has a scroll in his hand that hangs by his side, just cast down, as he turns eagerly to listen to some voice.

"Jeremiah, a magnificent figure, sits with elbow on knee, and head on hand, wrapt in the meditation appropriate to one called to utter lamentation and woe. He has neither book nor scroll.

"Jonah is also without either. His position is strained and ungraceful—looking upwards, and apparently remonstrating with the Almighty upon the destruction of the gourd, a few leaves of which are seen above him. His hands are placed together with a strange and trivial action, supposed to denote the counting on his fingers the number of days he was in the fish's belly. A formless marine monster is seen at his side.

"Daniel has a book on his lap, with one hand on it. He is young, and a piece of lion's skin seems to allude to his history."—*Lady Eastlake, Hist. of Our Lord*, i. 248.

In the recesses between the prophets and sibyls are a series of lovely family groups representing the Genealogy of the Virgin, and expressive of calm expectation of the future. The four corners of the ceiling contain groups illustrative of the power of the Lord displayed in the especial deliverances of his chosen people.

Near the altar are :
Right.—The deliverance of the Israelites by the brazen serpent.
Left.—The execution of Haman
Near the entrance are :
Right.—Judith and Holofernes.
Left.—David and Goliath.

It was when Michael Angelo was already in his sixtieth year that Clement VII. formed the idea of effacing the three pictures of Perugino at the end of the chapel, and employing him to paint the vast fresco of *The Last Judgment* in their place. It occupied the artist for seven years, and was finished in 1541 when Paul III. was on the throne. To induce him to pursue his work with application, Paul III. went himself to his house attended by ten cardinals; "an honour," says Lanzi, "unique in the annals of art." The pope wished that the picture should be painted in oil, to which he was persuaded by Sebastian del Piombo, but Michael Angelo refused to employ anything but fresco, saying that oil-painting was work for women and for idle and lazy persons.

"In the upper half of the picture we see the Judge of the world, surrounded by the apostles and patriarchs; beyond these, on one side, are the martyrs; on the other, the saints, and a numerous host of the blessed. Above, under the two arches of the vault, two groups of angels bear the instruments of the passion. Below the Saviour another group of angels holding the book of life sound the trumpets to awaken the dead. On the right is represented the resurrection; and higher, the ascension of the blessed. On the left, hell, and the fall of the condemned, who audaciously strive to press to heaven.

"The day of wrath (' dies iræ ') is before us—the day, of which the old hymn says,—

' Quantus tremor est futurus,
Quando judex est venturus
Cuncta stricte discussurus.'

The Judge turns in wrath towards the condemned and raises his right hand, with an expression of rejection and condemnation; beside him the Virgin veils herself with her drapery, and turns, with a countenance full of anguish, toward the blessed. The martyrs, on the left, hold up the instruments and proofs of their martyrdom, in accusation of those who had occasioned their temporal death: these the avenging angels drive from the gates of heaven, and fulfil the sentence pronounced against them. Trembling and anxious, the dead rise slowly, as if still fettered by the weight of an earthly nature; the pardoned ascend to the blessed; a mysterious horror pervades even their hosts—no joy, nor peace, nor blessedness, are to be found here.

"It must be admitted that the artist has laid a stress on this view of his subject, and this has produced an unfavourable effect upon the upper half of his picture. We look in vain for the glory of heaven, for beings who bear the stamp of divine holiness, and renunciation of human weakness; everywhere we meet with the expression of human passion, of human efforts. We see no choir of solemn, tranquil forms, no harmonious unity of clear, grand lines, produced by ideal draperies; instead of these, we find a confused crowd of the most varied movements, naked bodies in violent attitudes, unaccompanied by any of the characteristics made sacred by holy tradition. Christ, the principal figure of the whole, wants every attribute but that of the Judge: no expression of divine majesty reminds us that it is the Saviour who exercises this office. The upper part of the composition is in many parts heavy, notwithstanding the masterly boldness of the drawing; confused, in spite of the separation of the principal and accessory groups; capricious, notwithstanding a grand arrangement of the whole. But, granting for a moment that these defects exist, still this upper portion, as a whole, has a very impressive effect, and, at the great distance from which it is seen, some of the defects alluded to are less offensive to the eye. The lower half deserves the highest praise. In these groups, from the languid resuscitation and upraising of the pardoned, to the despair of the condemned, every variety of expression, anxiety, anguish, rage, and despair, is powerfully delineated. In the convulsive struggles of the condemned with the evil demons, the most passionate energy displays itself, and the extraordinary skill of the artist here finds its most appropriate exercise. A peculiar tragic grandeur pervades alike the beings who are given up to despair and their hellish tormentors. The representation of all that is fearful, far from being repulsive, is thus invested with that true moral dignity which is so essential a condition in the higher aims of art."—*Kugler*, p. 308.

"The Last Judgment is now more valuable as a school of design than as a fine painting, and it will be sought more for the study of the artist, than the delight of the amateur. Beautiful it is not—but it is sublime ;—sublime in conception, and astonishing in execution. Still, I believe, there are few who do not feel that it is a labour rather than a pleasure to look at it. Its blackened surface—its dark and dingy sameness of colouring—the obscurity which hangs over it—the confusion and multitude of naked figures which compose it—their unnatural position, suspended in the air, and the sameness of form and attitude, confound and bewilder the senses. These were, perhaps, defects inseparable from the subject, although it was one admirably calculated to call forth the powers of Michael Angelo. To merit in colouring it has confessedly no pretensions, and I think it is also deficient in expression—that in the conflicting passions, hopes, fears, remorse, despair, and transport, that must agitate the breasts of so many thousands in that awful moment, there was room for powerful expression which we do not see here. But it is faded and defaced ; the touches of immortal genius are lost for ever ; and from what it is, we can form but a faint idea of what it was. Its defects daily become more glaring—its beauties vanish ; and, could the spirit of its great author behold the mighty work upon which he spent the unremitting labour of seven years, with what grief and mortification would he gaze upon it now.

"It may be fanciful, but it seems to me that in this, and in every other of Michael Angelo's works, you may see that the ideas, beauties, and peculiar excellences of statuary, were ever present to his mind ; that they are the conceptions of a sculptor embodied in painting.

. . . . St. Catharine, in a green gown, and somebody else in a blue one, are supremely hideous. Paul IV., in an unfortunate fit of prudery, was seized with the resolution of whitewashing over the whole of the Last Judgment, in order to cover the scandal of a few naked female figures. With difficulty was he prevented from utterly destroying the grandest painting in the world, but he could not be dissuaded from ordering these poor women to be clothed in this unbecoming drapery. Daniele da Volterra, whom he employed in this office (in the lifetime of Michael Angelo), received, in consequence, the name of Il Braghettone (the breeches-maker)."—*Eaton's Rome.*

Michael Angelo avenged himself upon Messer Biagio da Cesena, master of the ceremonies, who first suggested the indelicacy of the naked figures to the pope, by introducing him in hell, as Midas, with ass's ears. When Cesena begged

Paul IV. to cause this figure to be obliterated, the pope sarcastically replied, "I might have released you from purgatory, but over hell I have no power."

"Michel-Ange est extraordinaire, tandis qu'Orcagna * est religieux. Leurs compositions se résument dans les deux Christs qui jugent. L'un est un bourreau qui foudroie, l'autre est un monarque qui condamne en montrant la plaie sacrée de son côté pour justifier sa sentence."—*Cartier, Vie du Père Angelico.*

"The Apostles in Michael Angelo's Last Judgment stand on each side of the Saviour, who is not, here, Saviour and Redeemer, but inexorable Judge. They are grandly and artificially grouped, all without any drapery whatever, with forms and attitudes which recall an assemblage of Titans holding a council of war, rather than the glorified companions of Christ."—*Jameson's Sacred and Legendary Art*, i. 179.

The Sistine Chapel is associated in the minds of all Roman sojourners with the great ceremonies of the Church, but especially with the Miserere of Passion Week.

"On Wednesday afternoon began the Miserere in the Sistine Chapel. . . . The old cardinals entered in their magnificent violet-coloured velvet cloaks, with their white ermine capes; and seated themselves side by side, in a great half-circle, within the barrier, whilst the priests who had carried their trains seated themselves at their feet. By the little side door of the altar the holy father now entered in his purple mantle and silver tiara. He ascended his throne. Bishops swung the vessels of incense around him, whilst young priests, in scarlet vestments, knelt, with lighted torches in their hands, before him and the high altar.

"The reading of the lessons began.† But it was impossible to keep the eyes fixed on the lifeless letters of the missal—they raised themselves, with the thoughts, to the vast universe which Michael Angelo had breathed forth in colours upon the ceiling and the walls. I contemplated his mighty sibyls and wondrously glorious prophets, every one of them a subject for a painting. My eyes drank in the magnificent processions, the beautiful groups of angels; they were not to me painted pictures, all stood living before me. The rich tree of know-

---
* In the Campo-Santo of Pisa.
† Fifteen Psalms are sung before the Miserere begins, and one light is extinguished for each—the Psalms being represented by fifteen candles.

ledge, from which Eve gave the fruit to Adam: the Almighty God, who floated over the waters, not borne up by angels, as the older masters had represented him—no, the company of angels rested upon him and his fluttering garments. It is true I had seen these pictures before, but never as now had they seized upon me. My excited state of mind, the crowd of people, perhaps even the lyric of my thoughts, made me wonderfully alive to poetical impressions; and many a poet's heart has felt as mine did!

"The bold foreshortenings, the determinate force with which every figure steps forward, is amazing, and carries one quite away! It is a spiritual Sermon on the Mount in colour and form. Like Raphael, we stand in astonishment before the power of Michael Angelo. Every prophet is a Moses like that which he formed in marble. What giant forms are those which seize upon our eye and our thoughts as we enter! But, when intoxicated with this view, let us turn our eyes to the background of the chapel, whose whole wall is a high altar of art and thought. The great chaotic picture, from the floor to the roof, shows itself there like a jewel, of which all the rest is only the setting. We see there the Last Judgment.

"Christ stands in judgment upon the clouds, and the apostles and his mother stretch forth their hands beseeching for the poor human race. The dead raise the gravestones under which they have lain; blessed spirits float upwards, adoring, to God, whilst the abyss seizes its victims. Here one of the ascending spirits seeks to save his condemned brother, whom the abyss already embraces in its snaky folds. The children of despair strike their clenched fists upon their brows and sink into the depths! In bold foreshortening, float and tumble whole legions between heaven and earth. The sympathy of the angels; the expression of lovers who meet; the child that, at the sound of the trumpet, clings to the mother's breast, is so natural and beautiful, that one believes oneself to be among those who are waiting for judgment. Michael Angelo has expressed in colours what Dante saw and has sung to the generations of the earth.

"The descending sun, at that moment, threw his last beams in through the uppermost windows. Christ, and the blessed around him, were strongly lighted up; whilst the lower part, where the dead arose, and the demons thrust their boat, laden with damned, from shore, were almost in darkness.

"Just as the sun went down the last Psalm was ended, and the last light which now remained was extinguished, and the whole picture-world vanished in the gloom from before me; but, in that same moment, burst forth music and singing. That which colour had bodily revealed arose now in sound: the day of judgment, with its despair and its exultation, resounded above us.

"The father of the Church, stripped of his papal pomp, stood before the altar, and prayed to the holy cross; and upon the wings of the trumpet resounded the trembling quire, 'Populus meus, quid feci tibi?' Soft angel notes rose above the deep song, tones which ascended not from a human breast: it was not a man's nor a woman's: it belonged to the world of spirits: it was like the weeping of angels dissolved in melody."—*Anderson's Improvisatore.*

"Le *Miserere*, c'est-à-dire, *ayez pitié de nous*, est un psaume composé de versets qui se chantent alternativement d'une manière très-différente. Tour-à-tour une musique céleste se fait entendre, et le verset suivant, dit en récitatif, et murmuré d'un ton sourd et presque rauque, on dirait que c'est la réponse des caractères durs aux cœurs sensibles, que c'est le réel de la vie qui vient flétrir et repousser les vœux des âmes généreuses; et quand le chœur si doux reprend, on renaît à l'espérance; mais lorsque le verset récité recommence, une sensation de froid saisit de nouveau; ce n'est pas la terreur qui la cause, mais le découragement de l'enthousiasme. Enfin le dernier morceau, plus noble et plus touchant encore que tous les autres, laisse au fond de l'âme une impression douce et pure: Dieu nous accorde cette même impression avant de mourir.

"On éteint les flambeaux; la nuit s'avance; les figures des prophètes et des sibylles apparaissent comme des fantômes enveloppés du crépuscule. Le silence est profond, la parole ferait un mal insupportable dans cet état de l'âme, où tout est intime et intérieur; et quand le dernier son s'éteint, chacun s'en va lentement et sans bruit; chacun semble craindre de rentrer dans les intérêts vulgaires de ce monde."—*Mad. de Staël.*

Opposite the Sistine Chapel is the entrance of the *Sala Ducale*, in which the popes formerly gave audience to foreign princes, and which is now used for the consistories for the admission of cardinals to the sacred college. Its decorations were chiefly executed by Bernini for Alexander VII. The landscapes are by *Brill*. This hall is used as a passage to the Loggie of Bramante.

The small portion of the Vatican inhabited by the pope is never seen except by those who are admitted to a special audience. The rooms of the aged pontiff are furnished with a simplicity which would be inconceivable in the abode of any other sovereign prince. It is a lonely life, as the dread of an accusation of nepotism has prevented any of the later popes from having any of their family with them, and etiquette always obliges them to dine, &c., alone. No one, whatever the difference of creed, can look upon this building inhabited by the venerable old men who have borne so important a part in the history of Christianity and of Europe, without the deepest interest.

> "Je la vois cette Rome, où d'augustes vieillards,
> Héritiers d'un apôtre et vainqueurs des Césars,
> Souverains sans armée et conquérants sans guerre,
> A leur triple couronne ont asservi la terre."
> *Racine.*

Two hundred and fifty-five popes are reckoned from St. Peter to Pio IX. inclusive. A famous prophecy of S. Malachi, first printed in 1595, is contained in a series of mottoes, one for each of the whole line of pontiffs until the end of time. Following this it will be seen that only eleven more popes are needed to exhaust the mottoes, and to close the destinies of Rome, and of the world. The later ones run thus :—

"Pius VII. Aquila Rapax.
Leo XII. Canis et coluber.
Pius VIII. Vir religiosus.
Gregory XVI. de Balneis Etruriæ.
Pius IX. Crux de cruce.
. . . Lumen in cœlo.
. . . Ignis ardens.
. . . Religio depopulata.
. . . Fides intrepida.
. . . Pastor angelicus.
. . . Pastor et nauta.
. . . Flos florum.
. . . De medietate lunæ.
. . . De labore solis.
. . . Gloria olivæ.

In persecutione extrema sacra Romanæ Ecclesiæ sedebit PETRUS Romanus, qui pascet oves in multis tribulationibus: quibus transactis, civitas septicollis diruetur, et JUDEX tremendus judicabit populum."

The Cardinal Secretary of State has rooms above the pontifical apartments. His collection of antique gems is of European celebrity.

"Antonelli loge au Vatican, sur la tête du pape. Les Romains demandent, en manière du calembour, lequel est le plus haut, du pape ou d'Antonelli."—*About, Question Romaine.*

The entrance to the Museum of Statues (for those who do not come from the Sala Regia) is by the central door on the left of the Cortile S. Damaso, whence you ascend a staircase and follow the loggia on the first floor, covered with stuccoes and arabesques by *Giovanni da Udine*, to the door of

The *Galleria Lapidaria*, a corridor 2131 feet in length. Its sides are covered on the right with Pagan, on the left with Early Christian inscriptions. Ranged along the walls are a series of sarcophagi, cippi, and funeral altars, some of them very fine. The last door on the left of this gallery is the entrance to the Library.

Separated from this by an iron gate, which is locked, except on Mondays, but opened by a custode (fee 50 c.), is the Museo Chiaramonti; but the visitors should first enter, on the left,

The *Braccio-Nuovo*, built under Pius VII. in 1817, by Raphael Stern, a fine hall, 250 feet long, filled with gems of sculpture. Perhaps most worth attention are (the *chefs d'œuvre* being marked with an asterisk):

Right.—
    5. *Caryatide.

This statue was admirably restored by Thorwaldsen. Its Greek origin is undoubted, and it is supposed to be the missing figure from the Erechtheum at Athens.

"Quand une fille des premières familles n'avait pour vêtement, comme celle-ci, qu'une chemise et par-dessus une demi-chemise ; quand elle avait l'habitude de porter des vases sur sa tête, et par suite de se tenir droite ; quand pour toute toilette elle retroussait ses cheveux ou les laissait tomber en boucles ; quand le visage n'était pas plissé par les mille petites grâces et les mille petites préoccupations bourgeoises, une femme pouvait avoir la tranquille attitude de cette statue. Aujourd'hui il en reste un débris dans les paysannes des environs qui portent leurs corbeilles sur la tête, mais elles sont gâtées par le travail et les haillons. Le sein paraît sous la chemise ; la tunique colle et visiblement n'est qu'un linge ; on voit la forme de la jambe qui casse l'étoffe au genou ; les pieds apparaissent nus dans les sandales. Rien ne peut rendre le sérieux naturel du visage. Certainement, si on pouvait revoir la personne réelle avec ses bras blancs, ses cheveux noirs, sous la lumière du soleil, les genoux plieraient, comme devant une déesse, de respect et de plaisir."—*Taine, Voyage en Italie.*

8. Commodus.

"La statue de Commode est tres curieuse par le costume. Il tient à la main une lance, il a des espèces de bottes : tout cela est du chasseur, enfin il porte la tunique à manches dont parle Dion Cassius, et qui était son costume d'amphithéâtre."—*Ampère, Emp.* ii. 246.

9. Colossal head of a Dacian, from the Forum of Trajan.

11. Silenus and the infant Bacchus.

This is a copy from the Greek, of which there were several replicas. One, formerly in the Villa Borghese, is now at Paris. The original group is described by Pliny, who says that the name of the sculptor was lost even in his time. The greater portion of the child, the left arm and hand of Silenus, and the ivy-leaves, are restorations.

' Je pense que ce chef-d'œuvre est une imitation modifiée du *Mercure nourricier de Bacchus*, par Céphisodote, fils de Praxitèle."—*Ampère, Hist. Rom.* iii. 332.

14. *Augustus, found 1863, in the villa of Livia at Prima-Porta.

"This is, without exception, the finest portrait statue of this class in the whole collection. . . . . The cuirass is covered with small figures, in basso-relievo, which, as works of art, are even finer than the statue itself, and merit the most careful examination. These small figures are, in their way, marvels of art, for the wonderful boldness of execution and minuteness of detail shown in them. They are almost like cameos, and yet, with all the delicacy of finish displayed, there is no mere smoothness of surface. The central group is supposed to represent the restoration to Augustus by King Phraates of the eagles taken from

Crassus and Antony. Considerable traces of colour were found on this statue and are still discernible. Close examination will also show that the face and eyes were coloured."—*Shakspere Wood.*

17. Æsculapius.
20. Nerva ? Head modern.
23. *Pudicitia. From the Villa Mattei. Head modern.

"The portrait of a noble Roman lady, much disfigured by restorations. This statue shows the neglect, by a sculptor of great ability, of that thoroughness of execution which was such a characteristic of Greek art. Compare the great beauty of the lower portion of the drapery, seen from the front, with the poverty of execution at the back."—*Shakspere Wood.*

"Qu'on regarde une statue toute voilée, par exemple celle de la Pudicité : il est evident que le vêtement antique n'altère pas la forme du corps, que les plis collants ou mouvants reçoivent du corps leurs formes et leurs changements, qu'on suit sans peine à travers les plis l'équilibre de toute la charpente, la rondeur de l'épaule ou de la hanche, le creux du dos."—*Taine.*

26. Titus. Found 1828, near the Lateran (with his daughter Julia).
27, 40, 92. Colossal busts of Medusa, from the temple of Venus at Rome.
32, 33. Fauns, sitting, from the villa of Quintilius at Tivoli.
38. Ganymede, found at Ostia ; on the tree against which he leans is engraved the name of Phædimus.
29. Vase of black basalt, found on the Quirinal. It stands on a mosaic, from the Tor Marancia.
41. Faun playing on a flute, from the villa of Lucullus
44. Wounded Amazon (both arms and legs are restorations).

"Les trois Amazones blessées de Rome ne peuvent être que des copies de la célèbre Amazone de Crésilas . . . . Ce Crésilas fut l'auteur du guerrier grec mourant qui selon toute apparence a inspiré le prétendu Gladiateur mourant auquel s'applique merveilleusement bien ce que dit Pline du premier."—*Ampère, Hist. Rom.* iii. 263.

47. Caryatide.
48. Bust of Trajan.
50. *Diana contemplating the sleeping Endymion.
53. Euripides.

"Le plus remarquable portrait d'Euripide est une belle statue au Vatican. Cette statue donne une haute idée de la sublimité de l'art tragique en Grèce . . . . . Regardez ce poëte, combien toute sa personne a de gravité et de grandeur, rien n'avertit qu'on a devant les yeux celui qui aux yeux des juges sévères, affaiblissait l'art et le corrompait ; l'attitude est simple, la visage sérieux, comme il convient à un poëte philosophe. Ce serait la plus belle statue de poëte tragique si la statue de Sophocle n'existait pas."—*Ampère*, iii. 572.

62. *Demosthenes, found near Frescati.

"Both hands were wanting, and the restorer has replaced them holding a roll . . . . They were originally placed with the fingers clasped together, and the proofs are these. An anecdote is related of an Athenian soldier, who had hidden some stolen money in the clasped hands of a statue of Demosthenes ; and if you observe the lines formed by the fore-arms, from the elbows to half-way down the wrists, where the restoration commences, you will find that, continued on, they would bring the wrists very much nearer to each other than they now are in the restoration. It is possible that this is the identical statue spoken of."—*Shakspere Wood*.

67. *Apoxyomenos. An Athlete scraping his arm with a strigil ; found 1849 in the Vicolo delle Palure in the Trastevere.

This is a replica of the celebrated bronze statue of Lysippus, and is described by Pliny, who narrates that it was brought from Greece by Agrippa to adorn the baths which he built for the people, and that Tiberius so admired it, that he carried it off to his palace, but was forced to restore it by the outcries of the populace, the next time he appeared in public.

Left.—

71. Amazon. (Arms and feet restorations by Thorwaldsen.)
77. Antonia, from Tusculum.
81. Bust of Hadrian.
83. Juno ? (head, a restoration) from Hadrian's villa.
86. Fortune with a cornucopia, from Ostia.
92. Venus Anadyomena.

" La gracieuse Vénus Anadyomène, que chacun connaît, a le mérite de nous rendre une peinture perdue d'Apelles ; elle en a un autre encore, c'est de nous conserver dans ce portrait—qui n'est point en buste—quelques traits de la beauté de Campaspe, d'après laquelle Apelles, dit-on, peignit sa Venus Anadyomène."—*Ampère*, iii. 324.

96. Bust of Marc Antony, from the Tor Sapienza.
109. *Colossal group of the Nile, found, temp. Leo X., near Sta. Maria sopra Minerva.

A Greek statue. The sixteen children clambering over it are restorations, and allude to the sixteen cubits' depth with which the river annually irrigates the country. On the plinth, the accompaniments of the river,—the ibis, crocodile, hippopotamus, &c., are represented.

111. Julia, daughter of Titus, found near the Lateran.

"Cette princesse, de la nouvelle et bourgeoise race des Flaviens, n'offre rien du noble profil et de la fière beauté des Agrippines: elle a un nez écrasé et l'air commun. La coiffure de Julie achève de la rendre disgracieuse: c'est une manière de pouf assez semblable à une éponge. Comparé aux coiffures du siècle d'Auguste, le tour de cheveux ridicule de Julie montre la décadence du goût, plus rapide dans la toilette que dans l'art."—*Ampère, Emp.* ii. 120.

112. Bust of Juno, called the Juno Pentini.

114. *Minerva Medica, found in the temple so called; formerly in the Giustiniani collection.

A most beautiful Greek statue, much injured by restoration.

"In the Giustiniani palace is a statue of Minerva which fills me with admiration. Winckelmann scarcely thinks anything of it, or at any rate does not give it its proper position; but I cannot praise it sufficiently. While we were gazing upon the statue, and standing a long time beside it, the wife of the custode told us that it was once a sacred image, and that the English, who are of that religion, still held it in veneration, being in the habit of kissing one of its hands, which was certainly quite white, while the rest of the statue was of a brownish colour. She added, that a lady of this religion had been there a short time before, had thrown herself on her knees, and worshipped the statue. Such a wonderful action she, as a Christian, could not behold without laughter, and fled from the room, for fear of exploding."—*Goethe.*

117. Claudius.

120. A replica of the Faun of Praxiteles, inferior to that at the Capitol.

"Le jeune Satyre qui tient une flûte est trop semblable à celui du Capitole pour n'être pas de même une reproduction de l'un des deux Satyres isolés de Praxitèle, son Satyre d'Athènes ou son Satyre de Mégare; on pourrait croire aussi que le Satyre à la flûte a eu pour original le Satyre de Protogène qui, bien que peint dans Rhodes assiégée, exprimait le calme le plus profond et qu'on appelait *celui qui se repose* (*anapauomenos*); on pourrait le croire, car la statue a toujours une jambe croisée sur l'autre, attitude qui, dans le langage de la sculpture antique, désigne le repos. Il ne serait pas impossible non plus que Protogène se fût inspiré de Praxitèle; mais en ce cas il n'en avait pas reproduit complétement le charme, car Apelles, tout en admirant une autre figure de Protogène, lui reprochait de manquer de grâce. Or, le Satyre à la flûte est très-gracieux; ce qui me porte à croire qu'il vient directement de Praxitèle plutôt que de Praxitèle par Protogène."—*Ampère, Hist. Rom.* iii. 308.

 123. L. Verus. Naked statue.
 126. Athlete; the discus a restoration.
 129. Domitian, from the Giustiniani collection.
 132. Mercury (the head a restoration by Canova), from the Villa Negroni.

Here we re-enter the *Museo Chiaramonti*, lined with sculptures, chiefly of inferior interest. They are arranged in thirty compartments. We may notice:

 1. 6, 13. Autumn and Winter, two sarcophagi from Ostia, the latter bearing the name of Publius Elius Verus.
 VIII. r. 176. A beautiful mutilated fragment, supposed to be one of the daughters of Niobe.
 r. 197. Head of Roma, from Laurentum.
 XIV. r. 352. Venus Anadyomena.
 XVI. r. 400. Tiberius, seated, found at Veii in 1811.
 r. 401. Augustus, from Veii.
 XVII. r. 417. *Bust of the young Augustus, found at Ostia, 1808.
 XX. r. 494. Seated statue of Tiberius, from Piperno.
 r. 495. Cupid bending his bow, a copy of a statue by Lysippus.
 XXI. r. 550, 512. Two busts of Cato.
 XXIV. r. 589. Mercury, found near the Monte di Pietà.
 XXV. r. 606. Head of Neptune, from Ostia.
 XXX. r. 732. Recumbent Hercules, from Hadrian's Villa.

At the end of this gallery is the entrance to the Giardino della Pigna (described under the Vatican Gardens). Admittance may probably be obtained from hence for a fee of 50 c. At the top of the short staircase, on the left, is the entrance of the Egyptian Museum. Here we enter the *Museo Pio-Clementino*, founded under Clement XIV., but chiefly due to the liberality and taste of Pius VI., in whose reign, however, most of the best statues were carried off to Paris, though they were restored to Pius VII.

In the centre of 1st *Vestibule* is the *Torso Belvidere, found in the baths of Caracalla, and sculptured, as is told by a Greek inscription on its base, by Apollonius, son of Nestor of Athens. It was to this statue that Michael-Angelo declared that he owed his power of representing the human form, and in his blind old age he used to be led up to it, that he might pass his hands over it, and still enjoy, through touch, the grandeur of its lines.

> "And dost thou still, thou mass of breathing stone
> (Thy giant limbs to night and chaos hurled),
> Still sit as on the fragment of a world,
> Surviving all, majestic and alone?
> What tho' the Spirits of the North, that swept
> Rome from the earth when in her pomp she slept,
> Smote thee with fury, and thy headless trunk
> Deep in the dust 'mid tower and temple sunk;
> Soon to subdue mankind 'twas thine to rise,
> Still, still unquelled thy glorious energies!
> Aspiring minds, with thee conversing, caught
> Bright revelations of the good they sought;
> By thee that long-lost spell in secret given,
> To draw down gods, and lift the soul to Heaven."
> *Rogers.*

"Quelle a été l'original du torse d'Hercule, ce chef-d'œuvre que palpait de ses mains intelligentes Michel-Ange aveugle et réduit à ne plus voir que par elles ? Heyne a pensé que ce pouvait être une copie en grand de l'Hercule *Epitrapezios* de Lysippe, mais par le style cette statue me semble antérieure à Lysippe. Cependant on lit sur le torse le nom d'Apollonios d'Athènes, fils de Nestor, et la forme des lettres ne permet pas de placer cette inscription plus haut que le dernier siècle de la République.

"Comment admettre que cette statue, aussi admirée par Winckelmann que par Michel-Ange, ce débris auquel on revient après l'éblouissement de l'Apollon du Belvidère, pour retrouver une sculpture plus mâle et plus simple, un style plus fort et plus grand ; comment admettre qu'une

telle statue soit l'œuvre d'un sculpteur inconnu dont Pline ne parle point, ni personne autre dans l'antiquité, et qu'elle date d'un temps si éloigné de la grande époque de Phidias, quand elle semble y tenir de si près ?
" . . . . Pourquoi le torse du Vatican ne serait-il pas d'Alcamène, ou, si l'on veut, d'après Alcamène, par Apollonios ?"—*Ampère, Hist. Rome*, iii. p. 360, 363.

Close by, in a niche, is the celebrated peperino *Tomb of L. Cornelius Scipio Barbatus, consul B.C. 297. It supports a bust, supposed, upon slight foundation, to be that of the poet Ennius. Inscriptions from other tombs of the Scipios are inserted in the neighbouring wall.†

"L'épitaphe de Scipion le Barbu semble le résumé d'une oraison funèbre ; elle s'adresse aux spectateurs : 'Cornélius Scipion Barbatus, né d'un père vaillant, homme courageux et prudent, dont la beauté égalait la vertu. Il a été parmi vous consul, censeur, édile ; il a pris Taurasia, Cisauna, le Samnium. Ayant soumis toute la Lucanie, il en a emmené des ôtages.'

"Y a-t-il rien de plus grand ? Il a pris le Samnium et la Lucanie. Voilà tout.

"Ce sarcophage est un des plus curieux monuments de Rome. Par la matière, par la forme des lettres et le style de l'inscription, il vous représente la rudesse des Romains au sixième siècle. Le goût très-pur de l'architecture et des ornements vous montre l'avénement de l'art grec tombant, pour ainsi dire, en pleine sauvagerie romaine. Le tombeau de Scipion le Barbu est en pépérin, ce tuf rugueux, grisâtre, semé de taches noires. Les caractères sont irréguliers, les lignes sont loin d'être droites, le latin est antique et barbare, mais la forme et les ornements du tombeau sont grecs. Il y a là des volutes, des triglyphes, des denticules ; on ne saurait rien imaginer qui fasse mieux voir la culture grecque venant surprendre et saisir la rudesse latine."—*Ampère, Hist. Rom.* iii. 132.

The *Round Vestibule* contains a fine vase of pavonazzetto. The adjoining balcony contains a curious Wind Indicator, found (1779) near the Coliseum. Hence there is a lovely view over the city. In the garden beneath is a fountain

† See the account of the "Tombs of the Scipios" in Chapter IX.

with a curious bronze ship floating in its bason (see Vatican Gardens).

At the end of the 3rd *Vestibule* stands the *Statue of Meleager, with a boar's head and a dog, supposed to have been begun in Greece by some famous sculptor, and finished in Rome (the dog, &c.) by an inferior workman.

"Meleager is represented in a position of repose, leaning on his spear, the mark of the junction of which, with the plinth, is still to be seen. The want of the spear gives the statue the appearance of leaning too much to one side, but if you can imagine it replaced, you will see that the pose is perfectly and truthfully rendered. This statue was found at the commencement of the sixteenth century, outside the Porta Portese, in a vineyard close to the Tiber."—*Shakspere Wood*.

"Ce Méléagre du Vatican respire une grâce tranquille, et, placé entre le sublime *Torse* et les merveilles du Belvédère, semble être là pour attendre et pour accueillir de son air aimable et un peu mélancolique, où l'on a cru voir le signe d'une destinée qui devait être courte, l'enthousiasme du voyageur."—*Ampère, Hist. Rom.* iii. 515.

From the central vestibule we enter the *Cortile del Belvidere*, an octagonal court built by *Bramante*, having a fountain in the centre, and decorated with fine sarcophagi and vases, &c. From this opens, beginning from the right; the—

First Cabinet, containing the Perseus, and the two Boxers —Kreugas and Damoxenus, by *Canova*.

The Second Cabinet, containing *the Antinous (now called Mercury), perhaps the most beautiful statue in the world. It was found on the Esquiline near S. Martino al Monte. It has never been injured by restoration, but was broken across the ankles when found, and has been unskilfully put together.

"Je suis bien tenté de rapporter à un original de Polyclète, qui aimait les formes carrées, le Mercure du Belvédère, qui n'est pas très-svelte pour un Mercure. On a cru reconnaître que les proportions de cette statue se rapprochaient beaucoup des proportions préscrites par Polyclète. Poussin, comme Polyclète, ami des formes carrées, déclarait le Mercure, qu'on appelait alors sans motif un Antinoüs, le modèle le plus parfait des proportions du corps humain ; il pourrait à ce titre remplacer jusqu'à un certain point la statue de Polyclète, appelée *la règle*, parcequ'elle passait pour offrir ce modèle parfait, et *faisait règle* à cet égard. De plus, on sait qu'un Mercure de Polyclète avait été apporté à Rome."—*Ampère, Hist. Rom.* iii. 267.

Third Cabinet, of *the Laocoon. This wonderful group was discovered near the Sette Sale on the Esquiline in 1506, while Michael-Angelo was at Rome. The right arm of the father is a terra-cotta restoration, and is said by Winckelmann to be the work of Bernini ; the arms of the sons are additions by Agostino Cornacchini of Pistoia. There is now no doubt that the Laocoon is the group described by Pliny.

"The fame of many sculptors is less diffused, because the number employed upon great works prevented their celebrity; for there is no one artist to receive the honour of the work, and where there are more than one they cannot all obtain an equal fame. Of this the Laocoon is an example, which stands in the palace of the emperor Titus,—a work which may be considered superior to all others both in painting and statuary. The whole group,—the father, the boys, and the awful folds of the serpents,—were formed out of a single block, in accordance with a vote of the senate, by Agesander, Polydorus, and Athenodorus, Rhodian sculptors of the highest merit."—*Pliny*, lib. xxxvi. c. 4. '

"Les trois sculpteurs rhodiens qui travaillèrent ensemble au Laocoon étaient probablement un père et ses deux fils, qui exécutèrent l'un la statue du père, et les autres celles des deux fils, touchante analogie entre les auteurs et l'ouvrage.

"Les auteurs du Laocoon étaient Rhodiens, ce peuple auquel, dit Pindare, Minerve a donné de l'emporter sur tous les mortels par le travail habile de leurs mains, et dont les rues étaient garnies de figures vivantes qui semblaient marcher. Or, le grand éclat, la grande puissance de Rhodes, appartiennent surtout à l'époque qui suivit la mort d'Alexandre. Après qu'elle se fût délivrée du joug macédonien, presque toujours alliée de Rome, Rhodes fut florissante par le commerce, les armes et la liberté, jusqu'au jour où elle eut embrassé le parti de César ; Cassius prit d'assaut la capitale de l'île et dépouilla ses temples de tous leurs ornements. Le coup fut mortel à la république de Rhodes, qui depuis ne s'en releva plus.

"C'est avant cette fatale époque, dans l'époque de la prospérité rhodienne, entre Alexandre et César, que se place le grand développement de l'art comme de la puissance des Rhodiens, et qu'on est conduit naturellement à placer la création d'un chef-d'œuvre tel que le Laocoon.

"Pline dit que les trois statues dont se compose le groupe étaient d'un seul morceau, et ce groupe est formé de plusieurs, on en a compté jusqu'à six. Ceci semblerait faire croire que nous n'avons qu'une copie, mais j'avoue ne pas attacher une grande importance à cette indication de Pline, compilateur plus érudit qu'observateur attentif. Michel-Ange, dit-on, remarqua le premier que le Laocoon n'était pas d'un seul morceau; Pline a très-bien pu ne pas s'en apercevoir plus que nous et répéter de confiance une assertion inexacte."—*Ampère, Hist. Rom.* iii. 382, 385, 387.

. . . "Turning to the Vatican, go see
Laocoon's torture dignifying pain—
A father's love and mortal's agony
With an immortal's patience blending, vain
The struggle; vain against the coiling strain
And gripe, and deepening of the dragon's grasp,
The old man's clench ; the long envenom'd chain
Rivets the living links,—the enormous asp
Enforces pang on pang, and stifles gasp on gasp."
Childe Harold.

"The circumstance of the two sons being so much smaller than the father, has been criticised by some, but this seems to have been necessary to the harmony of the composition. The same apparent disproportion exists between Niobe and her children, in the celebrated group at Florence, supposed to be by Scopas. The raised arms of the three figures are all restorations, as are some portions of the serpents. Originally, the raised hands of the old man rested on his head, and the traces of the junction are clearly discernible. For this we have also the evidence of an antique gem, on which it is thus engraved. This work was found in the baths (?) of Titus, in the reign of Julius II., by a certain Felix de Fredis, who received half the revenue of the gabella of the Porta San Giovanni as a reward, and whose epitaph, in the church of Ara Cœli, records the fact."—*Shakspere Wood.*

"Il y avait dans la vie, au seizième siècle, je ne sais qu'elle excitation fébrile, quelle aspiration vers le beau, vers l'inconnu, qui disposait les esprits à l'enthousiasme. . . . . Félix de Frédis fut gratifié d'une part dans les revenus de la porte de Saint Jean de Latran, pour avoir trouvé le groupe du Laocoon, et, lorsque l'ordre fut donné de transporter au Belvédère le Laocoon, l'Apollon, la Vénus, Rome entière s'émut, on jetait des fleurs au marbre, on battait des mains ; dépuis les thermes de Titus jusqu'au Vatican, le Laocoon fut porté en triomphe ; et Sadolet chantait sur le mode virgilien que durent reconnaître les échos de l'Esquilin et du palais d'Auguste."—*Gournerie, Rome Chrétienne.*

"I felt the Laocoon very powerfully, though very quietly ; an immortal agony, with a strange calmness diffused through it, so that it resembles the vast rage of the sea, calm on account of its immensity; or the tumult of Niagara, which does not seem to be tumult, because it keeps pouring on for ever and ever."

"It is a type of human beings, struggling with an inexplicable trouble, and entangled in a complication which they cannot free themselves from by their own efforts, and out of which Heaven alone can help them."—*Hawthorne, Notes on Italy.*

The Fourth Cabinet contains *the Apollo Belvedere, found in the sixteenth century at Porto d'Anzio (Antium), and purchased by Julius II. for the Belvedere Palace, which was at that time a garden pavilion separated from the rest of the Vatican, and used as a museum of sculpture. It is now decided that this statue, beautiful as it is, is not the original work of a Greek sculptor, but a copy, probably from the bronze of Calamides, which represented Apollo, as the defender of the city, and which was erected at Athens after the cessation of a great plague. Four famous statues of Apollo are mentioned by Pliny as existing at Rome in his time, but this is not one of them.

"Or view the Lord of the unerring bow,
The God of life, and poesy, and light—
The Sun in human limbs array'd, and brow
All radiant from his triumph in the fight ;
The shaft hath just been shot—the arrow bright

> With an immortal's vengeance ; in his eye
> And nostril beautiful disdain, and might,
> And majesty flash their full lightnings by,
> Developing in that one glance the Deity."
>
> *Childe Harold.*

> " Bright kindling with a conqueror's stern delight,
> His keen eye tracks the arrow's fateful flight:
> Burns his indignant cheek with vengeful fire,
> And his lip quivers with insulting ire :
> Firm fix'd his tread, yet light, as when on high
> He walks th' impalpable and pathless sky :
> The rich luxuriance of his hair, confined
> In graceful ringlets, wantons on the wind,
> That lifts in sport his mantle's drooping fold,
> Proud to display that form of faultless mould.
> Mighty Ephesian ! with an eagle's flight
> Thy proud soul mounted through the fields of light,
> View'd the bright conclave of Heaven's blest abode,
> And the cold marble leapt to life a god :
> Contagious awe through breathless myriads ran,
> And nations bow'd before the work of man.
> For mild he seem'd, as in Elysian bowers,
> Wasting in careless ease the joyous hours ;
> Haughty, as bards have sung, with princely sway
> Curbing the fierce flame-breathing steeds of day ;
> Beauteous as vision seen in dreamy sleep
> By holy maid on Delphi's haunted steep,
> Mid the dim twilight of the laurel grove,
> Too fair to worship, too divine to love."
>
> *Henry Hart Milman.*

In the second portico, between Canova's statues and the Antinous, is (No. 43) a Venus and Cupid,—interesting because the Venus is a portrait of Sallustia Barbia Orbiana, wife of Alexander Severus. It was discovered in the fifteenth century, in the ruin near Sta. Croce in Gerusalemme, to which it has given a name. In the third portico, between the Antinous and the Laocoon, are two beautiful dogs. Between these we enter :

The *Sala degli Animali*, containing a number of representations of animals in marble and alabaster. Perhaps the best is No. 116—two greyhounds playing. The statue of Commodus on horseback (No. 139) served as a model to Bernini for his figure of Constantine in the portico of St. Peter's.

"La Salle des Animaux au Vatican est comme un musée de l'école de Myron ; le naturel parfait qu'il donna à ses représentations d'animaux y éclate partout. C'est une sorte de ménagerie de l'art, et elle mérite de s'appeler, comme celle du Jardin des Plantes, une ménagerie *d'animaux vivants*.

"Ces animaux sont pourtant d'un mérite inégal : parmi les meilleurs morceaux on compte des chiens qui jouent ensemble avec beaucoup de vérité, un cygne dont le duvet, un mouton tué dont la toison sont très-bien rendus, une tête d'âne très-vraie et portant une couronne de lierre, allusion au rôle de l'âne de Silène dans les mystères bacchiques."— *Ampère, Hist. Rom.* iii. 276.

On the right we enter :

The *Galleria delle Statue*, once a summer-house of Innocent VIII., but arranged as a statue-gallery under Pius VI. In its lunettes are remains of frescoes by *Pinturicchio*. Beginning on the right, are :

> 248. An armed statue of Claudius Albinus standing on a cippus which marked the spot where the body of Caius Cæsar was burnt, inscribed C. CÆSAR GERMANICI CÆSARIS HIC CREMATUS EST.
> 250. The *Statue called "The Genius of the Vatican," supposed to be a copy from a Cupid of Praxiteles which existed in the Portico of Octavia in the time of Pliny. On the back are the holes for the metal pins which supported the wings.
> 251. Athlete.
> 253. Triton, from Tivoli.
> 255. Paris.

Le Vatican possède une statue de Pâris jugeant les déesses. Cette statue est-elle, comme on le pense généralement, une copie du Pâris d'Euphranor ?

"Euphranor avait-il choisi le moment où Pâris juge les déesses ? Les expressions de Pline pourraient en faire douter: il ne l'affirme point; il dit que dans la statue d'Euphranor on eût pu reconnaître le juge des trois déesses, l'amant d'Hélène et le vainqueur d'Achille.

* * * * * *

"La statue du Vatican est de beaucoup la plus remarquable des statues de Pâris. On y sent, malgré ses imperfections, la présence d'un original fameux; de plus, son attitude est celle de Pâris sur plusieurs vases peints et sur plusieurs bas-reliefs, et nous verrons que les bas-reliefs reproduisaient très-souvent une statue célèbre. Il m'est impossible, il est vrai, de voir dans le Pâris du Vatican tout ce que Pline dit du Pâris d'Euphranor. Je ne puis y voir que le juge des déesses. L'expression de son visage montre qu'il a contemplé la beauté de Vénus, et que le prix va être donné. Rien n'annonce l'amant d'Hélène, ni surtout le vainqueur d'Achille ; mais ce qui était dans l'original aurait pu disparaître de la copie."—*Ampère, Hist. Rom.* iii. 300.

256. Young Hercules.
259. Figure probably intended for Apollo, restored as Minerva.
260. A Greek relief, from a tomb.
261. Penelope, on a pedestal, with a relief of Bacchus and Ariadne.

"L'attente de Pénélope nous est présente, et, pour ainsi dire, dure encore pour nous dans cette expressive Pénélope, dont le torse nous a montré un spécimen de l'art grec sous la forme la plus ancienne."— *Ampère, Hist. Rome,* iii. p. 452.

264. *Apollo Sauroctonos (killing a lizard), found on the Palatine in 1777—a copy of a work of Praxiteles. Several other copies are in existence, one in bronze, in the Villa Albani, inferior to this. The right arm and the legs above the knees are restorations, well executed.

"Apollon presque enfant épie un lézard qui se glisse le long d'un arbre. On sait, à n'en pouvoir douter, d'après la description de Pline et de Martial, que cet Apollon, souvent répété, est une imitation de celui de Praxitèle, et quand on ne le saurait pas, on l'eût deviné."— *Ampère,* iii. 313.

265. Amazon, found in the Villa Mattei, the finest of the three Amazons in the Vatican, which are all supposed to be copies from the fifty statues of Amazons, which decorated the temple of Diana at Ephesus.
267. Drunken Satyr.

268. Juno, from Otricoli.
271, 390. Posidippus and Menander, very fine statues, perfectly preserved, owing to their having been kept through the middle ages in the church of S. Lorenzo Pane e Perna, where they were worshipped under the belief that they were statues of saints, a belief which arose from their having metal discs over their heads, a practice which prevailed with many Greek statues intended for the open air. The marks of the metal pins for these discs may still be seen, as well as those for a bronze protection for the feet, to prevent their being worn away by the kisses of the faithful,—as on the statue of St. Peter at St. Peter's.

Between these statues we enter :

The *Hall of Busts.* Perhaps the best are :

278. Augustus, with a wreath of corn.
289. Julia Mammæa, mother of Alexander Severus.
299. Jupiter-Serapis, in basalt.
325. Jupiter.
357. Antinous.
388. *Roman Senator and his wife, from a tomb. (These busts, having been much admired by the great historian, were copied for the monument of Niebuhr at Bonn, erected, by his former pupil the King of Prussia, to his memory—with that of his loving wife Gretchen, who only survived him nine days.)

"Les têtes de deux époux, représentés au devant de leur tombeau d'où ils semblent sortir à mi-corps et se tenant par le main, sont surtout d'une simplicité et d'une vérité inexprimable. La femme est assez jeune et assez belle, l'époux est vieux et très-laid ; mais ce groupe a un air honnête et digne qui répond pour tous deux d'une vie de sérénité et de vertu. Nul récit ne pourrait aussi bien que ces deux figures transporter au sein des mœurs domestiques de Rome ; en. leur présence on se sent pénétré soi-même d'honnêteté, de pudeur et de respect, comme si on était assis au chaste foyer de Lucrèce."—*Ampère, Hist. Rom.* iv. 103.

Re-entering the Gallery of Statues, and following the left wall, are :

392. Septimius Severus
393. Girl at a spring ?

394. Neptune.
395. Apollo Citharœdus.
396. Wounded Adonis.
397. Bacchus, from Hadrian's Villa.
398. Macrinus (Imp. 217).
399. Æsculapius and Hygeia, from Palestrina.
400. Euterpe.
401. Mutilated group from the Niobides, found near Porta San Paolo.
405. Danaide.
406. Copy of the Faun of Praxiteles, very beautiful, but inferior to that at the Capitol.
422. Head of a fountain, with Bacchanalian Procession.

(Here is the entrance of the *Gabinetto delle Maschere*, which contains works of small importance. It is named from the mosaic upon the floor, of masks from Hadrian's Villa. It is seldom shown, probably because it contains a chair of rosso-antico, called "Sedia forata," found near the Lateran, and supposed to be the famous "Sella Stercoraria" used at the installation of the mediæval popes, and associated with the legend of Pope Joan.

"Le Pape élu (Célestine III. 1191) se prosterne devant l'autel pendant que l'on chante le Te Deum : puis les Cardinaux Evêques le conduisent à son siége derrière l'autel : là ils viennent à ses pieds, et il leur donne le baiser de paix. On le mène ensuite à une chaise posée devant la portique de la Basilique du Sauveur de Latran. Cette chaise était nommée dès lors '*Stercoraria*,' parceque elle est percée au fond : mais l'ouverture est petite, et les antiquaires jugent que c'étoit pour égouter l'eau, et que cette chaise servait à quelque bain."—*Fleury, Histoire Ecclésiastique*, xv. p. 525.),

462. Cinerary Urn of Alabaster.
414.*Sleeping Ariadne, found *c*. 1503—formerly supposed to represent Cleopatra.

"The effect of sleep, so remarkable in this statue, and which could not have been rendered by merely closing the lids over the eyes, is produced by giving positive form to the eyelashes ; a distinct ridge, being raised at right angles to the surface of the lids, with a slight indented line along the edge to show the division."—*Shakspere Wood.*

"La figure est certainement idéale et n'est point un portrait ; mais ce qui ne laisse aucun doute sur le nom à lui donner, c'est un bas-relief, un peu refait, il est vrai, qu'on a eu la très-heureuse idée de placer auprès d'elle.

" On y voit une femme endormie dont l'attidude est tout à fait pareille à celle de la statue, Thésée qui va s'embarquer pendant le sommeil d'Ariane, et Bacchus qui arrive pour la consoler. C'est exactement ce que l'on voyait peint dans le temple de Bacchus à Athènes.

"Cette statue, belle sans doute, mais peut-être trop vantée, doit être postérieure à l'époque d'Alexandre. Sa pose gracieuse est presque maniérée : on dirait qu'elle se regarde dormir. La disposition de la draperie est compliquée et un peu embrouillée, à tel point que les uns prennent pour une couverture ce que d'autres regardent comme un manteau."—*Ampère, Hist. Rom.* iii. 534.

Beneath this figure is a fine sarcophagus, representing the Battle of the Giants.

412, 413. "The Barberini Candelabra" from Hadrian's Villa.
416. Ariadne.
417. Mercury.
420. Lucius Verus—on a pedestal which supported the ashes of Drusus in the Mausoleum of Augustus.

From the centre of the Sala degli Animali we now enter : The *Sala delle Muse*, adorned with sixteen Corinthian columns from Hadrian's Villa. It is chiefly filled with statues and busts from the villa of Cassius at Tivoli. The statues of the Muses and that called Apollo Musagetes (No. 516) are generally attributed to the time of the Antonines.

"Nous savons que l'Apollon Citharède de Scopas était dans le temple d'Apollon Palatin, élevé par Auguste ; les médailles, Properce et Tibulle, nous apprennent que le dieu s'y voyait revêtu d'une longue robe.

' Ima videbatur talis illudere palla.'

Tib. iii. 4, 35.

' Pythius in longa carmina veste sonat.'

Prop. ii. 31, 16.

"Nous ne pouvons donc hésiter à admettre que l'Apollon de la salle des Muses au Vatican a eu pour premier original l'Apollon de Scopas.

"Nous savons aussi qu'un Apollon de Philiscus et un Apollon de Timarchide (celui-ci tenant la lyre), sculpteurs grecs moins anciens que Scopas, étaient dans un autre temple d'Apollon, près du portique d'Octavie, en compagnie des Muses, comme l'Apollon Citharède du Vatican a été trouvé avec celles qui l'entourent aujourd'hui dans la salle des Muses. Il est donc vraisemblable que cet Apollon est d'après Philiscus ou Timarchide, qui eux-mêmes avaient sans doute copié l'Apollon *à la lyre* de Scopas et l'avaient placé au milieu des Muses.

"Apollon est là, ainsi que plus anciennement il avait été représenté sur le coffre de Cypsélus, avec cette inscription qui conviendrait à la statue du Vatican : 'Alentour est le chœur gracieux des Muses, auquel il préside ;' et, comme dit Pindare, 'au milieu du beau chœur des Muses, Apollon frappe du plectrum d'or la lyre aux sept voix.'"— *Ampère, Hist. Rom.* iii. 292.

Here we reach the *Sala Rotonda*, built by Pius VI., paved with a mosaic found in 1780 in the baths of Otricoli, and containing in its centre a grand porphyry vase from the baths of Titus. On either side of the entrance are colossal heads of Tragedy and Comedy, from Hadrian's Villa. Beginning from the right are :

539. *Bust of Jupiter from Otricoli—the finest extant.
540. Antinous, from Hadrian's Villa. All the drapery (probably once of bronze) is a restoration.

"Antinous was drowned in the Nile, A.D. 131. Some accounts assert that he drowned himself in obedience to an oracle, which demanded for the life of the emperor Hadrian the sacrifice of the object dearest to him. However this may be, Hadrian lamented his death with extravagant weakness, proclaimed his divinity to the jeering Egyptians, and consecrated a temple in his honour. He gave the name of Besantinopolis to a city in which he was worshipped in conjunction with an obscure divinity named Besa."—*Merivale,* lxvi.

541. Faustina the elder, wife of Antoninus Pius.
542. Augustus, veiled.
543. *Hadrian, found in his mausoleum.
544. *Colossal Hercules, in gilt bronze, found (1864) near the

Theatre of Pompey. The feet and ankles are restorations by Tenerani.

546. *Bust of Antinous.
547. Sea-god, from Pozzuoli.
548. *Nerva.

"Among the treasures of antiquity preserved in modern Rome, none surpasses,—none perhaps equals,—in force and dignity, the sitting statue of Nerva, which draws all eyes in the rotonda of the Vatican, embodying the highest ideal of the Roman magnate, the finished warrior, statesman, and gentleman of an age of varied training and wide practical experience."—*Merivale*, ch. xliii.

549. Jupiter Serapis.
550. *The Barberini Juno.
551. Claudius.
552. Juno Sospita, from Lanuvium. This is the only statue in the Vatican of which we can be certain that it was a worshipped idol ; the sandals of the Tyrrhenian Juno turn up at the end,—no other Juno wears these sandals.
553. Plotina, wife of Trajan.
554. Julia Domna, wife of Septimius Severus.
556. Pertinax.

The *Sala a Croce Greca* contains :

On the right.—The porphyry sarcophagus of Sta. Constantia, daughter of Constantine the Great, adorned with sculptures of a vintage, brought hither most inappropriately, from her church near St' Agnese.

On the left.—The porphyry sarcophagus of Sta. Helena, mother of Constantine the Great, carried off from her tomb (now called Torre Pignatarra) by Anastasius IV., and placed in the Lateran, whence it was brought hither by Pius VI. The restoration of its reliefs, representing battle scenes of the time of Constantine, cost £20,000.

At the end of the hall on the right is a recumbent river-god, said to have been restored by Michael Angelo. The stairs, adorned with twenty ancient columns from Palestrina, lead to :

The *Sala della Biga*, so called from a white marble chariot, drawn by two horses. Only the body of the chariot (which long served as an episcopal throne in the church of S. Marco) and part of the horse on the right, are ancient; the remainder is restoration. Among the sculptures here, are :

608. Bearded Bacchus.
609. An interesting sarcophagus representing a chariot-race. The chariots are driven by Amorini, who are not attending to what they are about, and drive over one another. The eggs and dolphins on the winning-posts indicated the number of times they had gone round ; each time they passed another egg and dolphin were put up.
610. Bacchus, as a woman.
611. Alcibiades?
612. Veiled priest, from the Giustiniani collection.
614. Apollo Citharœdus.
615. Discobolus, copy of a bronze statue by Naubides.
616. *Phocion, very remarkable and beautiful from the extreme simplicity of the drapery.
618. Discobolus, copy of the bronze statue of Myron—inferior to that at the Palazzo Massimo.

"Il n'y a pas une statue dont l'original soit connu avec plus de certitude que le Discobole. Cet original fut l'athlète lançant le disque de Myron.

" C'est bien la statue se contournant avec effort dont parle Quintilien ; en effet, la statue, penchée en avant et dans l'attitude du jet, porte le corps sur une jambe, tandis que l'autre est traînante derrière lui. Ce n'est pas la main, c'est la personne tout entière qui va lancer le disque."
—*Ampère, Hist. Rom.* iii. 270.

619. Charioteer.

Proceeding in a straight line from the top of the stairs, we enter :

The *Galleria dei Candelabri*, 300 feet long, filled with small pieces of sculpture. Among these we may notice in the centre, on the right, Bacchus and Silenus, found near the Sancta-Sanctorum, also :

194. Boy with a goose.
224. Nemesis.

'Une petite statue du Vatican rappelle une curieuse anecdote dont le héros est Agoracrite. Alcamène et lui avaient fait chacun une statue de Vénus. Celle d'Alcamène fut jugée la meilleure par les Athéniens. Agoracrite, indigné de ce qui lui semblait une injustice, transforma la sienne en Némésis, déesse vengeresse de l'équité violée, et le rendit aux habitants du bourg de Rhamnus, à condition qu'elle ne serait jamais exposée à Athènes. Ceci montre combien sa Vénus avait gardé la sévérité du type primitif. Ce n'est pas de la Vénus du Capitole ou de la Vénus de Médicis, qu'on aurait pu faire une Némésis. Némésis avait pour emblème la coudée, signe de la *mesure* que Némésis ne permet point de dépasser, et l'avant-bras était la figure de la *coudée*, par suite, de la mesure. C'est pourquoi quand on représentait Némésis on plaçait toujours l'avant-bras de manière d'attirer sur lui l'attention. Dans la Némésis du Vatican la donnée sévère est devenue un motif aimable. Cet avant-bras, qu'il fallait montrer pour rappeler une loi terrible, Némésis le montre en effet, mais elle s'en sert avec grâce pour rattacher son vêtement."—*Ampère, Hist. Rom.* iii. 260.

253. Statuette of Ceres, the head from some other statue.

Hence we enter :

The *Galleria degli Arazzi* (open gratis on Mondays), hung with tapestries from the New Testament History, executed for the lower walls of the Sistine Chapel, in 1515—16, for Leo X., from the cartoons of *Raphael*, of which seven were purchased in Flanders by Charles I., and are now at Hampton Court. The tapestries are ill arranged. According to their present order, beginning on the left wall, they are :

1. St. Peter receiving the keys. (On the border, the flight of Cardinal de' Medici from Florence in 1494, disguised as a Franciscan Monk.)
2. The Miraculous draught of Fishes.
3. The Sacrifice at Lystra.
4. St. Paul preaching at Athens.
5. The Saviour and Mary Magdalene.
6. The Supper at Emmaus.
7. The Presentation in the Temple.
8. The Adoration of the Shepherds.

9. The Ascension.
10. The Adoration of the Magi.
11. The Resurrection.
12. The Day of Pentecost.

Returning, on the right wall, are :

1. An Allegorical Composition of the Triumph of Religion (by *Van Orley* and other pupils of Raphael).
2. The Stoning of Stephen (on the border the return of the Cardinal de' Medici to Florence as Legate).
3. Elymas the Sorcerer (?—removed 1869-70).
4, 5, 6. Massacre of the Innocents.
7. (Smaller than the others.) Christ falling under the Cross.
8. Christ appearing to his disciples on the shore of the Lake of Galilee.
9. Peter and John healing the lame man.
10. The Conversion of St. Paul.

The Arazzi were long used as church decorations on high festivals.

"On Corpus-Christi Day I learnt the true destination of the Tapestries, when they transformed colonnades and open spaces into handsome halls and corridors : and while they placed before us the power of the most gifted of men, they gave us at the same time the happiest example of art and handicraft, each in its highest perfection, meeting for mutual completion."—*Goethe*.

The *Library of the Vatican* is shown from 12 to 3, except on Sundays and festivals, but the visitor is hurried through in a crowd by a custode, and there is no time for examination of the individual objects. The entrance is by a door on the left at the end of the Galleria Lapidaria, which leads to the museum of statues. The Papal Library was founded by the early popes at the Lateran. The Public Library was begun by Nicholas V., and greatly increased under Sixtus IV. (1475) and Sixtus V. (1588), who built the present halls for the collection. In 1623 the library was increased by the gift of the "Bibliotheca Palatina" of Heidelberg, captured by Tilly from Maximilian of Bavaria; in 1657 by the "Bibliotheca Urbinas," founded by Federigo da Montefeltro; in 1690 by the "Bibliotheca Reginensis," or "Alexandrina," which belonged to Christina of Sweden; in 1746 by the Bibliotheca Ottoboniana, purchased by the Ottobuoni pope, Alexander VIII. The number of Greek, Latin, and Oriental MSS. in the collection has been reckoned at 23,580.

The ante-chambers are hung with portraits of the Librarians;—among them, in the first room, is that of Cardinal Mezzofanti. In this room are facsimiles of the columns found in the Triopium of Herodes Atticus (see the account of the Valle Caffarelli), of which the originals are at Naples. From the second ante-chamber we enter the *Great Hall*, 220 feet long, decorated with frescoes by *Scipione Gaetani*, *Cesare Nebbia*, and others,—unimportant in themselves, but producing a rich general effect of colour. No books or MSS. are visible; they are all enclosed in painted cupboards, so that of a *library* there is no appearance whatever, and it is only disappointing to be told that in one cupboard are the MSS. of the Greek Testament of the fifth century, Virgil of the fifth, and Terence of the fourth centuries, and that another contains a Dante, with miniatures by *Giulio Clovio*,* &c. Ranged along the middle of the hall are some of the handsome presents made to Pius IX. by different foreign potentates, including the Sèvres font, in which the Prince Imperial was baptized, presented by Napoleon III., and some candelabra given by Napoleon I. to Pius VII. At the end of the hall, long corridors open

* Who is buried by the altar of S. Pietro in Vincoli.

out on either side. Turning to the left, the second room has two interesting frescoes—one representing St. Peter's as designed by Michael Angelo, the other the erection of the obelisk in the Piazza S. Pietro under Fontana. At the end of the third room are two ancient statues, said to represent Aristides, and Hippolytus Bishop of Porto. The fourth room is a museum of Christian antiquities, and contains, on the left, a collection of lamps and other small objects from the Catacombs; on the right, some fine ivories by *Guido da Spoleto*, and a Deposition from the Cross attributed to *Michael Angelo*. The room beyond this, painted by *Raphael Mengs*, is called the Stanza dei Papiri, and is adorned with papyri of the fifth, sixth, and seventh centuries. The next room has an interesting collection of pictures, by early masters of the schools of *Giotto*, *Giottino*, *Cimabue*, and *Fra Angelico*. Here is a Prie Dieu, of carved oak and ivory, presented to Pius IX. by the four bishops of the province of Tours.

At the end of this room, not generally shown, is the *Chapel of St. Pius V.*

The *Appartamenti Borgia*, which are reached from hence, are only shown by a special permission, difficult to obtain. They consist of four rooms, which were built by Alexander VI., though their beautiful decorations were chiefly added by Leo X. The *first room* is painted by *Giovanni da Udine* and *Pierino del Vaga*, and represents the course of the planets,—Jupiter drawn by eagles, Venus by doves, Diana (the moon) by nymphs, Mars by wolves, Mercury by cocks, Apollo (the sun) by horses, Saturn by dragons. These frescoes, executed at the time Michael Angelo was painting the Last Judgment, are interesting as the last revival under Clement VII. of the pagan art so popular in the papal palace under Leo X.

The second room, painted by *Pinturicchio*, has beautiful lunettes of the Annunciation, Adoration of the Magi, Resurrection, Ascension, Descent of the Holy Ghost, and Assumption of the Virgin. The ceiling of the *third room* has paintings by *Pinturicchio* of the Martyrdom of St. Sebastian; the Visitation of St. Elizabeth; the Meeting of St. Anthony with St. Paul, the first hermit; St. Catherine before Maximian; the Flight of St. Barbara; St. Julian of Nicomedia; and, over the door, the Virgin and Child. This last picture is of curious historical interest, as a relic of the libertinism of the court of Alexander VI. (Rodrigo Borgia), the "figure of the Virgin being a faithful representation of Giulia Farnese, the too celebrated Vanozza," mistress of the pope, and mother of his children, Cæsar and Lucrezia. "She held upon her knees the infant Jesus, and Alexander knelt at her feet."

The fourth room, also painted by *Pinturicchio*, is adorned with allegorical figures of the Arts and Sciences, and of the Cardinal Virtues.

"On the accession of the infamous Alexander VI., Pinturicchio was employed by him to paint the Appartamento Borgia, and a great number of rooms, both in the castle of S. Angelo and in the pontifical palace. The patronage of this pope was still more fatal to the arts than that of the Medici at Florence. The subjects represented in the castle of S. Angelo were drawn from the life of Alexander himself, and the portraits of his relations and friends were introduced there,—amongst others, those of his brothers, sisters, and that of the infamous Cæsar Borgia. To all acquainted with the scandalous history of this family, this representation appeared a commemoration of their various crimes, and it was impossible to regard it in any other light, when, in addition to the publicity they affected to give to these scandalous excesses, they appeared desirous of making art itself their accomplice; and by an excess of profanation hitherto unexampled in the Catholic world, Alexander VI. caused himself to be represented, in a room in the Vatican, in the costume of one of the Magi, kneeling before the holy Virgin, whose head was no other than the portrait of the beautiful Giulia Farnese ('Vanozza'), whose adventures are unfortunately too well known. We may indeed say that the walls have in this case made up for the silence of the courtiers: for on them was traced, for the benefit of contemporaries and posterity, an undeniable proof of the depravity of the age.

"At the sight of that Appartamento Borgia, which is entirely painted by Pinturicchio, we shall experience a sort of satisfaction in discovering the inferiority of this purely mercenary work, as compared with the other productions of the same artist, and we cannot but rejoice that it is so unworthy of him. Such an ignoble task was not adapted to an artist of the Umbrian school, and there is good reason to believe that, after this act of servility, Pinturicchio became disgusted with Rome, and returned to the mountains of Umbria, in search of nobler inspirations."— *Rio. Poetry of Christian Art.*

A door on the right of the room with the old pictures opens into a room containing a very interesting collection of ancient frescoes. On the right wall is the celebrated "*Nozze Aldobrandini*," found in 1606 * in some ruins belonging to the baths of Titus near the arch of Gallienus on the Esquiline, and considered to be the finest specimen of ancient pictorial art in Rome. It was purchased at first by the Aldobrandini family, whence its name. It represents an ancient Greek ceremony, possibly the nuptials of Peleus and Thetis. There is a fine copy by Nicholas Poussin in the Doria Palace.

"S'il fait allusion à un sujet mythologique, le réel y est à côté de l'idéal, et la mythologie y est appliquée à la représentation d'un mariage ordinaire. Tout porte à y voir une peinture romaine, mais l'auteur s'était inspiré des Grecs, comme on s'en inspirait presque toujours à Rome. La nouvelle mariée, assise sur le lit nuptial et attendant son époux, a cette expression de pudeur virginale, d'embarras modeste, qui

* Gourneric, Rome Chrétienne, ii. 62.

avait rendu célèbre un tableau dont le sujet était le mariage de Roxane et l'auteur Ætion, peintre grec."—*Ampère, Hist. Rom.* iv. 127.

Opposite to this is a Race of the Cupids, from Ostia. The other frescoes in this room were found in the ruins on the Esquiline and at the Torre di Marancia.

The *Etruscan Museum* can be visited on application to the custode, every day except Monday, from 10 to 2. It is reached by the staircase which passes the entrance to the Gallery of Candelabra: after which one must ring at a closed door on the right.

"This magnificent collection is principally the fruit of the excavating partnership established, some twelve or fifteen years since, between the Papal government and the Campanari of Toscanella; and will render the memory of Gregory XVI., who forwarded its formation with more zeal than he ordinarily displayed, ever honoured by all interested in antiquarian science. As the excavations were made in the neighbourhood of Vulci, most of the articles are from that necropolis; yet the collection has been considerably enlarged by the addition of others previously in the possession of the government, and still more by recent acquisitions from the Etruscan cemeteries of Cervetri, Corneto, Bomarzo, Orte, Toscanella, and other sites within the Papal dominions."—*Dennis.*

The 1st Room—

Contains three sarcophagi of terra-cotta from Toscanella, with three life-size figures reposing upon them. Their extreme length is remarkable. The figure on the left wears a fillet, indicating priesthood. The head of the family was almost always priest or priestess. Most of the objects in terra-cotta, which have been discovered, come from Toscanella. The two horses' heads in this room, in nenfro, *i.e.* volcanic tufa, were found at the entrance of a tomb at Vulci.

The 2nd Room—

Is a corridor filled with cinerary urns, chiefly from Volterra, bearing recumbent figures, ludicrously stunted. The large sarcophagus on the left supports the bearded figure of a man, and is adorned with reliefs of a figure in a chariot and musicians painted red. The urns in this room are of alabaster, which is the characteristic of Volterra.

The 3rd Room—

Has in the centre a large sarcophagus of nenfro, found at Tarquinii, in 1834, supporting a reclining figure of a Lucumo, with a scroll in his hand, "recalling the monuments of the middle ages." At the sides are reliefs representing the story of Clytemnestra and Ægisthus,—the Theban brothers,—the sacrifice of Clytemnestra,—and Pyrrhus slaying the infant Astyanax. In this room is a slab with a bilingual inscription, in Latin and Umbrian, from Todi. In the corners are some curious cinerary urns shaped like houses.

The 4th Room—

Is the Chamber of Terra-cottas. In the centre is a most beautiful statue of Mercury found at Tivoli. At the sides are fragments of female figures from Vulci,—and an interesting terra-cotta urn from Toscanella, with a youth lying on a couch. "From the gash in his thigh, and the hound at his bed-side, he is usually called Adonis; but it may be merely the effigy of some young Etruscan, who met his death in the wild-boar chase."

The 5th Room.—

This and the three following rooms are occupied by Vases. The vases in the 5th room are mostly small amphoræ, in the second or Archaic style, with black figures on the ground of the clay. On a column, near the window, is a *Crater*, or mixing-vase, from Vulci, with parti-coloured figures on a very pale ground, and in the most beautiful style of Greek art. It represents Mercury presenting the infant Bacchus to Silenus. To the left of the window is a humorous representation of the visit of Jupiter and Mercury to Alcmena, who is looking at them out of a window. In the cabinets are objects in crystal from Palestrina.

The 6th Room.—

In the centre of this room are five magnificent vases. The central, from Cervetri, "is of the rare form called *Holmos*—a large globe-shaped bowl on a tall stand, like an enormous cup and ball;" its paintings are of wild animals. Nearest the entrance is, with three handles, "a *Calpis*, of the third or perfect style," from Vulci, with paintings of Apollo and six Muses. Behind this, from Vulci, is "a large *Amphora* of the second or Archaic style," in which hardness and severity of design are combined with most conscientious execution of detail. It represents Achilles ("Achilleos") and Ajax ("Aiantos") playing at dice, or *astralagi*. Achilles cries " Four ! " and Ajax " Three ! "—the said words, in choice Attic, issuing from their mouths. The maker's name, " Echsekias," is recorded, as well as that of " the brave Onetorides " to whom it was presented. On the other side of the vase is a family scene of " Kastor " with his horse, and " Poludeukes " playing with his dog, " Tyndareos " and " Leda " standing by. 4th, is an *Amphora* from Cære, representing the body of Achilles borne to Peleus and Thetis. 5th, is a *Calpis* from Vulci, representing the death of Hector in the arms of Minerva.

The 6th vase on the shelf of the entrance wall is the kind of amphora called a *Pelice*, from Cære. " Two men are represented sitting under an olive-tree, each with an amphora at his feet," and one who is measuring the oil exclaims, " O father Jupiter, would that I were rich ! " On the reverse of the vase is the same pair, at a subsequent period, when the prayer has been heard, and the oil-dealer cries, " Verily, yea, verily, it hath been filled to overflowing." By the window is a *Calpis*, representing a boy with a hoop in one hand, and a stolen cock in the other, for which his tutor is reproving him.

The 7th Room—

Is an arched corridor. In the second niche, is a *Hydria* with Minerva and Hercules, from Vulci. Sixth on the line, is an *Amphora* from Vulci; " ' Ekabe ' (Hecuba) presents a goblet to her son, ' the brave Hector,' —and regards him with such intense interest, that she spills the wine as she pours it out to him. ' Priamos ' stands by, leaning on his staff, looking mournfully at his son, as if presaging his fate." Many other vases in this room are of great beauty.

The 8th Room—

" Contains *Cylices* or *Pateræ*, which are more rare than the upright vases, and not inferior in beauty."

The 9th Room—

Entered from the 6th room, is the jewel room. Among the bronzes on the right, is a warrior in armour found at Todi in 1835 and a bronze couch with a raised place for the head, found in the Regulini Galassi tomb at Cervetri, where it bore the corpse of a high priest. A boy with a bulla, sitting, from Tarquinii, is " supposed to represent Tages, the mysterious boy-god, who sprung from the furrows of that site."

At the opposite end of the room is a biga or war-chariot, not Etruscan, but Roman, found in the villa of the Quintilii, near the Via

Appia. Near this are some colossal fragments of bronze statues, found near Civita Vecchia. A beautiful oval *Cista*, with a handle formed by two swans bearing a boy and a girl, is from Vulci; and so are the braziers or censers retaining the tongs, shovel, and rake, found with them:—"the tongs are on wheels, and terminate in serpents' heads; the shovel handle ends in a swan's neck; and the rake in a human hand." Among the smaller relics are a curious bottle from Cære, with an Etruscan alphabet and spelling lesson (!) scratched upon it, and a pair of Etruscan clogs found in a tomb at Vulci.

In the centre of the room is the jewel-case of glass. The whole of the upper division and one compartment of the lower are devoted to Cervetri (Cære). All these objects are from the Regulini Galassi tomb, for all the other tombs had been rifled at an early period, except one, whence the objects were taken by Campana. The magnificent oak-wreath with the small ornaments and the large ear-rings were worn by a lady, over whom was written in Etruscan characters, "Me Larthia," —I, the Great Lady,—evidently because at the time of her death, 3000 years ago, it was supposed that she was so very great that the memory of her name could never by any possibility perish, and that therefore it was quite unnecessary to record it. The tomb was divided, and she was walled up with precious spices (showing what the commerce of Etruria must have been) in one half of it. It was several hundred years before any one was found of sufficient dignity to occupy the other half of the great lady's tomb. Then the high priest of Etruria died, and was buried there with all his ornaments. His were the large bracelets, the fillets for the head, with the plate of gold covering the head, and a second plate of gold which covered the forehead—worn only on the most solemn occasions. This may be considered to have been the headdress of Aaron. His also was the broad plate of gold, covering the breast, reminding of the Urim and Thummim. The bronze bed on which he lay (and on which the ornaments were found lying where the body had mouldered) is preserved in another part of the room, and the great incense burner filled with precious spices which was found by his side. The three large bollas on his breast were filled with incense, whose perfume was still so strong when the tomb was opened, that those who burnt it could not remain in the room.

The ivy leaves on the ornaments denote the worship of Bacchus, a late period in Etruria: laurel denotes a victor in battle or the games.

The 10*th Room*—

(Entrance on right of the jewel-room), is a passage containing a number of Roman water-pipes of lead, and the bronze figure of a boy with a bird and an Etruscan inscription on his leg, from Perugia.

The 11th Room—
Is hung with paintings on canvas copied from the principal tombs of Vulci and Tarquinii. Beginning from the right, on entering, they take the following order :

From the Camera del Morto : Tarquinii.
From the Grotta delle Bighe, or Grotta Stackelberg : Tarquinii.
From the Grotta Querciola : Tarquinii
From the Grotta della Iscrizioni : Tarquinii.
From the Grotta del Triclinio, or Grotta Marzi : Tarquinii.
From the Grotta del Barone, or Grotta del Ministro : Tarquinii.
From the painted tomb at Vulci.

"All the paintings from Tarquinii are still to be seen on that site, though not in so perfect a state as they are here represented. But the tomb at Vulci is utterly destroyed."

Each of the paintings is most interesting. That of the death-bed scene proves that the Etruscans believed in the immortality of the soul. In the upper division a daughter is mounting on a stool to reach the high bed and give a last kiss to her dying father, while the son is wailing and lamenting in the background. Below, is the rejoicing spirit, freed from the trammels of the flesh.

In the scenes representing the games, the horses are painted bright red and bright blue, or black and red. These may be considered to have been the different colours of the rival parties. A number of jars for oil and wine are arranged in this room. All the black pottery is from Northern Etruria.

The 12th Room (entered from the left of the jewel room) is a very meagre and most inefficient facsimile of an ordinary Etruscan tomb. It is guarded by two lions in nenfro, found at Vulci.*

The Egyptian Museum is entered by a door on the left of the entrance of the Museo Pio-Clementino. It is open

---

* For a detailed account of this collection, see Dennis' "Cities and Cemeteries of Etruria," whence many of the quotations above are taken ; also Mrs. Hamilton Gray's "Sepulchres of Etruria."

gratis on Mondays from 12 to 3. The collection is chiefly due to Pius VII. and Gregory XVI. The greater part is of no especial importance.

The 6th Room contains eight statues of the goddess Pasht from Carnac.

The 8th Room is occupied by Roman imitations of Egyptian statues, from the Villa Adriana.

"Ces statues sont toutes des traductions de l'art égyptien en art grec. L'alliance, la fusion de la sculpture égyptienne et de la sculpture gréco-romaine est un des traits les plus saillantes de cosmopolitisme si étranger à d'anciennes traditions nationales, et dont Adrien, par ses voyages, ses goûts, ces monuments, fut la plus éclatante manifestation.

"Sauf l'Antinoüs, les produits de cette sculpture d'imitation bien que datant d'une époque encore brillante de l'art romain, ne sauraient le disputer à leurs modèles. Pour s'en convaincre, il suffit de les comparer aux statues vraiment égyptiennes qui remplissent une salle voisine. Dans celles-ci, la réalité du détail est méprisée et sacrifiée; mais les traits fondamentaux, les linéaments essentiels de la forme sont rendus admirablement. De là un grand style, car employer l'expression la plus générale, c'est le secret de la grandeur du style, comme a dit Buffon. Cette élévation, cette sobriété du génie égyptien ne se retrouvent plus dans les imitations bâtardes du temps d'Adrien."—*Ampère, Emp.* ii. 197, 202.

On the right is the Nile in black marble; opposite the entrance is a colossal statue of Antinous, the favourite of Hadrian, in white marble.

"Il est naturel qu'Antinoüs, qui s'était, disait-on, précipité dans le Nil, ait été représenté sous les traits d'un dieu égyptien .... La physiognomie triste d'Antinoüs sied bien à un dieu d'Égypte, et le style grec emprunte au reflet du style égyptien une grandeur sombre."— *Ampère, Emp.* ii. 196.

The 9th *Room* contains colossal Egyptian statues. On the right is the figure of the mother of Rhamses II. (Sesostris) between two lions of basalt, which were found in the Baths of Agrippa, and which long decorated the Fontana dei Termini. Upon the base of these lions is inscribed the name of the Egyptian king Nectanebo.

"Dans cette sculpture bien égyptienne, on sent déjà le souffle de l'art grec. La pose de ces lions est la pose roide et monumentale des lions à tête humaine de Louqsor; la crinière est encore de convention, mais la vie est exprimée, les muscles sont accusés avec un soin et un relief que la sculpture purement égyptienne n'a pas connus."—*Ampère, Emp.* ii. 198.

"Ces lions ont une expression remarquable de force et de repos; il y a quelque chose dans leur physiognomie qui n'appartient ni à l'animal ni à l'homme: ils semblent une puissance de la nature, et l'on conçoit, en les voyant, comment les dieux du paganisme pouvaient être représentés sous cet emblème."—*Mad. de Staël.*

In the centre of the entrance-wall are, Ptolemy-Philadelphus, and, on his left, his queen Arsinoë, of red granite. These were found in the gardens of Sallust, and were formerly preserved in the Senator's Palace.

"There is a fine collection of Egyptian antiquities in the Vatican; and the ceilings of the rooms in which they are arranged, are painted to represent a starlight sky in the desert. It may seem an odd idea, but it is very effective. The grim, half-human monsters from the temples, look more grim and monstrous underneath the deep dark blue; it sheds a strange uncertain gloomy air on everything—a mystery adapted to the objects; and you leave them, as you find them, shrouded in a solemn night."—*Dickens.*

The Egyptian Gallery has an egress into the Sala a Croce Greca.

The windows of the Egyptian Museum look upon the inner *Garden of the Vatican*, which may be reached by a door at the end of the long gallery of the Museo Chiaramonti, before ascending to the Torso. The garden which is thus entered, called *Giardino della Pigna*, is in fact merely the second great quadrangle of the Vatican, planted with shrubs and flowers. Several interesting relics are preserved here.

In the centre is the *Pedestal of the Column of Antoninus Pius*, found in 1709 on the Monte Citorio. The column was a simple memorial pillar of granite, erected by the two adopted sons of the emperor, Marcus Aurelius and Lucius Verus. It was broken up to mend the obelisk of Psammeticus I. at the Monte Citorio. Among the reliefs of the pedestal is one of a winged genius guiding Antoninus and Faustina to Olympus. In the great semicircular niche of Bramante, at the end of the court-garden, is the famous *Pigna*, a gigantic fir-cone, which once crowned the summit of the Mausoleum of Hadrian. Thence it was first removed to the front of the old basilica of St. Peter's. In the fresco of the old St. Peter's at S. Martino al Monte, the pigna is introduced, but it is there placed in the centre of the nave, a position it never occupied. Dante saw it at St. Peter's, and compares it to a giant's head (it is eleven feet high) which he saw through the mist in the last circle of hell.

"La faccia mi parea lunga e grossa
Come la pina di S. Pietro in Roma."

On either side of the pigna are two bronze peacocks, which are said to have stood on either side the entrance of Hadrian's Mausoleum.

"Je pense qu'ils y avaient été placés en l'honneur des impératrices dont les cendres devaient s'y trouver. La paon consacré à Junon était le symbole de l'apothéose des impératrices, comme l'oiseau dédié à Jupiter celui de l'apothéose des empereurs, car le mausolée d'Adrien n'était pas pour lui seul, mais, comme avaient été le mausolée d'Auguste et le temple des Flaviens, pour toute la famille impériale."—*Ampère, Emp.* ii. 212.

A flight of steps leads from this court to the narrow *Terrace of the Navicella*, in front of the palace, so called from a bronze ship with which its fountain is decorated. The visitor should beware of the tricksome water-works upon this terrace.

Beyond the courtyard is the entrance to the larger garden, which may be reached in a carriage by those who do not wish to visit the palace on the way, by driving round through the courts at the back of St. Peter's. Formerly it was always open till 2 P.M., after which hour the pope went there to walk, or to ride upon his white mule. It is a most delightful retreat for the hot days of May and June, and before that time its woods are carpeted with wild violets and anemones. No one who has not visited them can form any idea of the beauty of these ancient groves, interspersed with fountains and statues, but otherwise left to nature, and forming a fragment of sylvan scenery quite unassociated with the English idea of a garden. They are backed by the walls of the Borgo, and a fine old tower of the time of Leo IV. The *Casino del Papa*, or Villa Pia,* built by Pius IV. in the lower and more cultivated portion of the ground, is the chef-d'œuvre of the architect, Pirro Ligorio, and is decorated with paintings by *Baroccio*, *Zucchero*, and *Santi di Tito*, and a set of terra-cotta reliefs collected by Agincourt and Canova. The shell decorations are pretty and curious.

During the hours which he spent daily in this villa, its founder Pius IV. enjoyed that easy and simple life for which he was far better fitted by nature than for the affairs of government; but here also he received the counsels of his nephew S. Carlo Borromeo, who, summoned to Rome in 1560, became for several succeeding years the real ruler of the state. Here he assembled around him all those who were distinguished by their virtue or talents, and held many

---

* Vasari calls it Palazzo nel Bosco del Belvedere.

of the meetings which received the name of *Notte Vaticane*—at first employed in the pursuit of philosophy and poetry, but—after the necessity of Church reform became apparent both to the pope and to S. Carlo—entirely devoted to the discussion of sacred subjects. In this villa the late popes, Pius VIII. and Gregory XVI., used frequently to give their audiences.

The sixteenth century was the golden age for the Vatican. Then the splendid court of Leo X. was the centre of artistic and literary life, and the witty and pleasure-loving pope made these gardens the scene of his banquets and concerts ; and, in a circle to which ladies were admitted, as in a secular court, listened to the recitations of the poets who sprang up under his protection, beneath the shadow of its woods.

"Le Vatican était encombré, sous Leon X., d'historiens, de savants, de poëtes surtout. ' La tourbe importune des poëtes,' s'écrie Valérianus, ' le poursuit de porte en porte, tantôt sous les portiques, tantôt à la promenade, tantôt au palais, tantôt à la chambre, *penetralibus in imis ;* elle ne respecte ni son repos, ni les graves affaires qui l'occupent aujourd'hui que l'incendie ravage le monde.' On remarquait dans cette foule : Berni, le poëte burlesque ; Flaminio, le poëte élégiaque ; Molza, l'enfant de Pétrarque, et Postumo, Maroni, Carteromachus, Fedra Inghirami, le savant bibliothécaire, et *la grande lumière d'Arezzo,* comme dit l'Arioste, *l'unique Accolti.* Accolti jouit pendant toute la durée du seizième siècle d'une réputation que la postérité n'a pas confirmée. On l'appelait le *céleste.* Lorsqu'il devait réciter ses vers, les magasins étaient fermés comme en un jour de fête, et chacun accourait pour l'entendre. Il était entouré de prélats de la première distinction ; un corps de troupes suisses l'accompagnait, et l'auditoire était éclairé par des flambeaux. Un jour qu'Accolti entrait chez le pape :—Ouvrez toutes les portes, s'écria Léon, et laissez entrer la foule. Accolti récita un *ternale* à la Vierge, et, quand il eut fini, mille acclamations retentirent : *Vive le poète divin, vive l'incomparable Accolti !* Léon était le premier à applaudir, et le duché de Nessi devenait la récompense du poëte.

"Une autre fois, c'était Paul Jove, l'homme aux *oui-dires*, comme l'appelle Rabelais, qui venait lire des fragments de son histoire, et que Léon X. saluait du titre de Tite-Live italien. Il y avait dans ces éloges, dans ces encouragements donnés avec entraînement, mais avec tact, je ne sais quel souffle de vie pour l'intelligence, qui l'activait et qui lui faisait rendre au centuple les dons qu'elle avait reçus du ciel. Rome entière était devenue un musée, une académie ; partout des chants, partout la science, la poésie, les beaux-arts, une sorte de volupté dans l'étude. Ici, c'est Calcagnini, qui a déjà déviné la rotation de la terre ; là, Ambrogio de Pise, qui parle chaldéen et arabe; plus loin, Valérianus, que la philologie, l'archéologie, la jurisprudence revendiquent à la fois, et qui se distrait de ses doctes travaux par des poésies dignes d'Horace."
—*Gournerie, Rome Chrétienne,* ii. 114.

The *Loggie of Raphael* are reached, except on Mondays, by the staircase on the left of the fountain in the Cortile S. Damaso. Two sides of the corridors on the second floor (formerly open) are decorated in stucco by *Marco da Faenza* and *Paul Schnorr* and painted by *Sicciolante da Sermoneta, Tempesta, Sabbatini,* and others. The third corridor, entered on the right (opened by a custode), contains the celebrated frescoes, executed by Raphael, or from the designs of Raphael, by Giulio Romano, Pierino del Vaga, Pellegrino da Modena, Francesco Penni, and Raffaello da Colle. Of the fifty-two subjects represented, forty-eight are from the Old Testament, only the four last being from the Gospel History, as an appropriate introduction to the pictures which celebrate the foundation and triumphs of the Church, in the adjoining stanze. The stucco decorations of the gallery are of exquisite beauty ; especially remarkable, perhaps, are those of the windows in the first arcade, where Raphael is represented drawing,—his pupils working from his designs,—and Fame celebrating his work. The frescoes are arranged in the following order :

1st Arcade.
1. Creation of Light.*
2. Creation of Dry Land.
3. Creation of the Sun and Moon.
4. Creation of Animals.
} *Raphael.*

2nd Arcade.
1. Creation of Eve. *Raphael.*
2. The Fall.
3. The Exile from Eden.
4. The Consequence of the Fall.
} *Giulio Romano.*

3rd Arcade.
1. Noah builds the Ark.
2. The Deluge.
3. The Coming forth from the Ark.
4. The Sacrifice of Noah.
} *Giulio Romano.*

4th Arcade.
1. Abraham and Melchizedek.
2. The Covenant of God with Abraham.
3. Abraham and the three Angels.
4. Lot's flight from Sodom.
} *Francesco Penni.*

5th Arcade.
1. God appears to Isaac.
2. Abimelech sees Isaac with Rebecca.
3. Isaac gives Jacob the blessing.
4. Isaac blesses Esau also.
} *Francesco Penni.*

6th Arcade.
1. Jacob's Ladder.
2. Jacob meets Rachel.
3. Jacob upbraids Laban.
4. The journey of Jacob.
} *Pellegrino da Modena.*

7th Arcade.
1. Joseph tells his dream.
2. Joseph sold into Egypt.
3. Joseph and Potiphar's wife.
4. Joseph interprets Pharaoh's dream.
} *Giulio Romano.*

* "This is perhaps the grandest of the whole series. Here the Almighty is seen rending like a thunderbolt the thick shroud of fiery clouds, letting in that light under which his works were to spring into life."—*Lady Eastlake.*

THE STANZE.

8th Arcade.
1. The Finding of Moses.
2. Moses and the Burning Bush.
3. The Destruction of Pharaoh.
4. Moses striking the rock.
} *Giulio Romano.*

9th Arcade.
1. Moses receives the Tables of the Law.
2. The Worship of the Golden Calf.
3. Moses breaks the Tables.
4. Moses kneels before the Pillar of Cloud.
} *Raffaello da Colle.*

10th Arcade.
1. The Israelites cross the Jordan.
2. The Fall of Jericho.
3. Joshua stays the course of the Sun.
4. Joshua and Eleazer divide the Promised Land.
} *Pierino del Vaga.*

11th Arcade.
1. Samuel anoints David.
2. David and Goliath.
3. The Triumph of David.
4. David sees Bathsheba.
} *Pierino del Vaga.*

12th Arcade.
1. Zadok anoints Solomon.
2. The Judgment of Solomon.
3. The Coming of the Queen of Sheba.
4. The Building of the Temple.
} *Pellegrino da Modena.*

13th Arcade.
1. The Adoration of the Shepherds.
2. The Coming of the Magi.
3. The Baptism of Christ.
4. The Last Supper.
} *Giulio Romano.*

"From the Sistine Chapel we went to Raphael's Loggie, and I hardly venture to say that we could scarcely bear to look at them. The eye was so educated and so enlarged by those grand forms and the glorious completeness of all their parts, that it could take no pleasure in the imaginative play of arabesques, and the scenes from Scripture, beautiful as they are, had lost their charm. To see these works *often* alternately and to compare them at leisure and without prejudice, must be a great pleasure, but all sympathy is at first one-sided."—*Goethe, Römische Briefe.*

Close to the entrance of the Loggie is that of *The Stanze*, three rooms decorated under Julius II. and Leo X. with frescoes by Raphael, for each of which he received 1200 ducats. These rooms are approached through,—

The *Sala di Constantino*, decorated under Clement VII. (Giulio di Medici) in 1523—34, after the death of Raphael, who however had prepared drawings for the frescoes, and had already executed in oil the two figures of Justice and Urbanity. The rest of the compositions, completed by his pupils, are in fresco.

"Raphaël se multiplie, il se prodigue, avec une fécondité de toutes les heures. De jeunes disciples, admirateurs de son beau génie, le servent avec amour, et sont déjà admis à l'honneur d'attacher leurs noms à quelques parties de ses magnifiques travaux. Le maître leur distribue leur tâche : à Jules Romain, le brillant coloris des vêtements et peut-être même le dessin de quelques figures ; au Fattore, à Jean d'Udine, les arabesques ; à frère Jean de Vérone les clairs-obscurs des portes et des lambris qui doivent compléter la décoration de ces spendides appartements. Et lui, que se réserve-t-il?—la pensée qui anime tout, le génie qui enfante et qui dirige."—*Gournerie, Rome Chrétienne.*

Entrance Wall.—The Address of Constantine to his troops and the vision of the Fiery Cross: *Giulio Romano.* On the left, St. Peter between the Church and Eternity,—on the right, Clement I. (the martyr) between Moderation and Gentleness.

Right Wall.—The Battle of the Ponte Molle and the Defeat of Maxentius by Constantine, designed by Raphael, and executed by *Giulio Romano.* On the left is Sylvester I. between Faith and Religion, on the right Urban I. (the friend of Cecilia) between Justice and Charity.

Left Wall.—The donation of Rome by Constantine to Sylvester I. (A.D. 325), *Raffaello da Colle.* (The head of Sylvester was a portrait of Clement VII., the reigning pope ; Count Castiglione the friend of Raphael, and Giulio Romano, are introduced amongst the attendants.) On the left, Sylvester I. with Fortitude ; on the right, Gregory VII. with Strength.

Wall of Egress.—The supposititious Baptism of Constantine, interesting as pourtraying the interior of the Lateran baptistery in the 15th century, by *Francesco Penni*, who has introduced his own portrait in a black dress and velvet cap. On left, is Damasus I. (A.D. 366—384), between Prudence and Peace; on right, Leo I. (A.D. 440-462), between Innocence and Truth. The paintings on the socles represent scenes in the life of Constantine by *Giulio Romano*.

The *Stanza d'Eliodoro*, painted in 1511—1514, shows the Church triumphant over her enemies, and the miracles by which its power has been attested. On the roof are four subjects from the Old Testament,—the Covenant with Abraham; the Sacrifice of Isaac; Jacob's dream; Moses at the burning bush.

Entrance Wall.—Heliodorus driven out of the Temple (Maccabees iii.). In the background Onias the priest is represented praying for divine interposition;—in the foreground Heliodorus, pursued by two avenging angels, is endeavouring to bear away the treasures of the Temple. Amid the group on the left is seen Julius II. in his chair of state, attended by his secretaries. One of the bearers in front is Marc-Antonio Raimondi, the engraver of Raphael's designs. The man with the inscription, 'Jo. Petro de Folicariis Cremonen,' was secretary of briefs to Pope Julius.

"Here you may almost fancy you hear the thundering approach of the heavenly warrior and the neighing of his steed; while in the different groups who are plundering the treasures of the Temple, and in those who gaze intently on the sudden consternation of Heliodorus, without being able to divine its cause, we see the expression of terror, amazement, joy, humility, and every passion to which human nature is exposed."—*Lanzi*.

Left Wall.—The Miracle of Bolsena. A priest at Bolsena, who refused to believe in the doctrine of transubstantiation, is convinced by the bleeding of the host. On the right kneels Julius II., with Cardinal Riario, founder of the Cancelleria. This was the last fresco executed by Raphael under Julius II.

Right Wall.—Peter delivered from prison. A fresco by Pietro della Francesca was destroyed to make room for this picture, which is said to have allusion to the liberation of Leo X., while Legate in Spain, after his capture at the battle of Ravenna. This fresco is considered especially remarkable for its four lights, those from the double representation of the angel, from the torch of the soldier, and from the moon.

Wall of Egress.—The Flight of Attila. Leo I. (with the features of Leo X.) is represented on his white mule, with his cardinals, calling upon SS. Peter and Paul, who appear in the clouds, for aid against Attila. The Coliseum is seen in the background.

The *Stanza della Segnatura* is so called from a judicial assembly once held here. The frescoes in this chamber are illustrative of the Virtues of Theology, Philosophy, Poetry, and Jurisprudence, who are represented on the ceiling by *Raphael*, in the midst of arabesques by *Sodoma*. The square pictures by Raphael refer:—the Fall of Man to Theology; the Study of the Globe to Philosophy; the Flaying of Marsyas to Poetry; and the Judgment of Solomon to Jurisprudence.

Entrance Wall.—"The School of Athens." Raphael consulted Ariosto as to the arrangement of its 52 figures. In the centre, on the steps of a portico, are seen Plato and Aristotle, Plato pointing to heaven, and Aristotle to earth. On the left is Socrates conversing with his pupils, amongst whom is a young warrior, probably Alcibiades. Lying upon the steps in front is Diogenes. To his left Pythagoras is writing on his knee, and near him, with ink and pen, is Empedocles. The youth in the white mantle is Francesco Maria della Rovere, nephew of Julius II. On the right, is Archimedes, drawing a geometrical problem upon the floor. The young man near him with uplifted hands is Federigo II., Duke of Mantua. Behind these are Zoroaster and Ptolemy, one with a terrestrial, the other with a celestial globe, addressing two figures which represent Raphael and his master Perugino. The drawing in brown upon the socle beneath this fresco, is by *Pierino del Vaga*, and represents the death of Archimedes.

Right Wall.—" Parnassus," Apollo surrounded by the Muses, on his right Homer, Virgil, and Dante. Below, on the right, Sappho, supposed to be addressing Corinna, Petrarch, Propertius, and Anacreon; on the left, Pindar and Horace, Sannazzaro, Boccaccio, and others. Beneath this, in grisaille, are,—Alexander placing the poems of Homer in the tomb of Achilles,—and Augustus preventing the burning of Virgil's Eneid.

Left Wall.—Above the window are Prudence, Fortitude, and Temperance. On the left, Justinian delivers the Pandects to Tribonian. On the right, Gregory IX. (with the features of Julius II.) delivers the Decretals to a jurist;—Cardinal de' Medici, afterwards Leo X., Cardinal Farnese, afterwards Paul III., and Cardinal del Monte, are represented near the pope. In the socle beneath is Solon addressing the people of Athens.

Wall of Egress.—" The Disputa," so called from an impression that it represents a Dispute upon the Sacrament. In the upper part of the composition the heavenly host are present;—Christ between the Virgin and St. John Baptist;—On the left, St. Peter, Adam, St. John, David, St. Stephen, and another;—On the right, St. Paul, Abraham, St. James, Moses, St. Laurence, and St. George. Below is an altar surrounded by the Latin fathers, Gregory, Jerome, Ambrose, and Augustine. Near St. Augustine stand St. Thomas Aquinas, St. Anacletus with the palm of a martyr, and Cardinal Buonaventura reading. Those in front are Innocent III., and in the background Dante, near whom a monk in a black hood is pointed out as Savonarola. The Dominican on the extreme left is supposed to be Fra Angelico. The other figures are uncertain.

" Raphaël a bien jugé Dante en plaçant parmi les Théologiens, dans la *Dispute du Saint Sacrement*, celui pour la tombe duquel a été écrit ce vers, aussi vrai qu'il est plat :

' Theologus Dantes, nullius dogmatis expers.' "

Ampère, Voyage Dantesque.

The chiaro-scuros on the socle beneath this fresco are by *Pierino del Vaga* (added under Paul III.) and represent, 1, A heathen sacrifice ; 2, St. Augustine finding a child attempting to drain the sea ; 3, The Cumæan Sibyl and Augustus.

"Raphael commenced his work in the Vatican by painting the ceiling and the four walls of the room called *della Segnatura*, on the surface of which he had to represent four great compositions, which embraced the principal divisions of the encyclopædia of that period ; namely, Theology, Philosophy, Poetry, and Jurisprudence.

" It will be conceived, that to an artist imbued with the traditions of the Umbrian school, the first of these subjects was an unparalleled piece of good fortune ; and Raphael, long familiar with the allegorical treatment of religious compositions, turned it here to the most admirable account ; and, not content with the suggestions of his own genius, he availed himself of all the instruction he could derive from the intelligence of others. From these combined inspirations resulted, to the eternal glory of the Catholic faith and of Christian art, a composition without a rival in the history of painting, and we may also add without a name ; for to call it lyric or epic is not enough, unless, indeed, we mean, by using these expressions, to compare it with the allegorical epic of

Dante, alone worthy to be ranked with this marvellous production of the pencil of Raphael.

"And let no one consider this praise as idle and groundless, for it is Raphael himself who forces the comparison upon us, by placing the figure of Dante among the favourite sons of the Muses; and, what is still more striking, by draping the allegorical figure of Theology in the very colours in which Dante has represented Beatrice; namely, the white veil, the red tunic, and the green mantle, while on her head he has placed the olive crown.

"Of the four allegorical figures which occupy the compartments of the ceiling, and which were all painted immediately after Raphael's arrival in Rome, Theology and Poetry are incontestably the most remarkable. The latter would be easily distinguished by the calm inspiration of her glance, even were she without her wings, her starry crown, and her azure robe, all having allusion to the elevated region towards which it is her privilege to soar. The figure of Theology is quite as admirably suited to the subject she personifies; she points to the upper part of the grand composition, which takes its name from her, and in which the artist has provided inexhaustible food for the sagacity and enthusiasm of the spectator.

"This work consists of two grand divisions,—Heaven and Earth,—which are united to one another by that mystical bond, the Sacrament of the Eucharist. The personages whom the Church has most honoured for learning and holiness are ranged in picturesque and animated groups on either side of the altar, on which the consecrated wafer is exposed. St. Augustine dictates his thoughts to one of his disciples; St. Gregory, in his pontifical robes, seems absorbed in the contemplation of celestial glory; St. Ambrose, in a slightly different attitude, appears to be chaunting the Te Deum; while St. Jerome, seated, rests his hands on a large book, which he holds on his knees. Pietro Lombardo, Duns Scotus, St. Thomas Aquinas, Pope Anacletus, St. Buonaventura, and Innocent III. are no less happily characterised; while, behind all these illustrious men, whom the Church and succeeding generations have agreed to honour, Raphael has ventured to introduce Dante with his laurel crown, and, with still greater boldness, the monk Savonarola, publicly burnt ten years before as a heretic.

"In the glory, which forms the upper part of the picture, the Three Persons of the Trinity are represented, surrounded by patriarchs, apostles, and saints: it may, in fact, be considered in some sort as a *résumé* of all the favourite compositions produced during the last hundred years by the Umbrian school. A great number of the types, and particularly those of Christ and the Virgin, are to be found in the earlier works of Raphael himself. The Umbrian artists, from having so long exclusively employed themselves on mystical subjects, had certainly attained to a marvellous perfection in the representation of celestial beatitude, and of those ineffable things of which it has been said that the heart of man cannot conceive them, far less, therefore, the pencil of man pourtray; and Raphael, surpassing them in all, and even in this instance while surpassing himself, appears to have fixed the limits, beyond which Christian art, properly so called, has never since been able to advance."—*Rio. Poetry of Christian Art.*

The *Stanza of the Incendio del Borgo* is decorated with frescoes illustrative of the triumphs of the Church from events in the reigns of Leo III. and Leo IV. The roof has four frescoes by *Perugino* illustrative of the Saviour in glory.

Entrance Wall.—The Victory of Leo IV. over the Saracens at Ostia, by *Giovanni da Udine*, from designs of Raphael. The pope is represented with the features of Leo X.; behind him are Cardinal Giulio de' Medici (Clement VII.), Cardinal Bibbiena, and others. The castle of Ostia is seen in the background. Beneath are Ferdinand the Catholic and the Emperor Lothaire, by *Polidoro da Caravaggio*.

Left Wall.—The "Incendio del Borgo," a fire in the Leonine City in 847. In the background Leo IV. is seen in the portico of the old St. Peter's arresting with a cross the progress of the flames, on their approach to the basilica. In the foreground is a group of fugitives, by *Giulio Romano*, resembling Æneas escaping from Troy with Anchises, followed by Ascanius and Creusa. Beneath are Godfrey de Bouillon and Astulf (Ethelwolf), the latter with the inscription: "Astulphus Rex sub Leone IV. Pont. Britanniam Beato Petro vectigalem fecit."

Right Wall.—The Justification of Leo III. before Charlemagne, by *Pierino del Vaga*. The pope is a portrait of Leo X., the emperor of Francis I.

Wall of Egress.—The Coronation of Charlemagne in the old St. Peter's. Leo X. is again represented as Leo III., and Francis I. as Charlemagne. This fresco is partly by *Raphael*, partly by *Pierino del Vaga*. On the socle is Charlemagne, by *Polidoro da Caravaggio*.

A Fifth Chamber has been decorated under Pius IX. with frescoes by *Fracassini*, in honour of the recent dogma of the Immaculate Conception. The Proclamation of the Dogma;

the Adoration of the image of the Virgin; and the Reception of the news by the Virgin in heaven, from an angelic messenger, are duly represented!

From the corner of the Sala del Constantino, a custode, if requested, will give access to the

Cappella di San Lorenzo, a tiny chapel 'covered with frescoes executed by Fra Angelico for Nicholas V. in 1447. The upper series represents events in the life of St. Stephen.

1. His Ordination by St. Peter.
2. His Almsgiving.
3. His Preaching.
4. He is brought before the Council at Jerusalem ("his accuser has the dress and shaven crown of a monk").
5. He is dragged to Execution.
6. He is Stoned. Saul is among the spectators.

"Angelico has represented St. Stephen as a young man, beardless, and with a most mild and candid expression. His dress is the deacon's habit, of a vivid blue."—*Mrs. Jameson.*

The lower series represents the life of St. Laurence.

1. He is ordained by Sixtus II. (with the features of Nicholas V.).
2. Sixtus II. delivers the treasures of the Church to him for distribution among the poor.
3. He Distributes them in Alms.
4. He is carried before Decius the Prefect.
5. He suffers Martyrdom A.D. 253.

Introduced in the side arches, are the figures of St. Jerome, St. Ambrose, St. Augustine, St. Gregory, St. John Chrysostom, St. Athanasius, St. Leo—as the protector of Rome, and St. Thomas Aquinas—as painted by the Dominican Angelico, and for a Dominican pope Nicholas V.

"The Consecration of St. Stephen, the Distribution of Alms, and, above all, his Preaching, are three pictures as perfect of their kind as any that have been produced by the greatest masters, and it would be difficult to imagine a group more happily conceived as to arrangement, or more graceful in form and attitude, than that of the seated females listening to the holy preacher; and if the furious fanaticism of the executioners, who stone him to death, is not expressed with all the energy we could desire, this may be attributed to a glorious incapacity in this angelic imagination, too exclusively occupied with love and ecstasy to be ever able to familiarise itself with those dramatic scenes in which hateful and violent passions were to be represented."—*Rio. Poetry of Christian Art.*

"The soul of Angelico lives in perpetual peace. Not seclusion from the world. No shutting out of the world is needful for him. There is nothing to shut out. Envy, lust, contention, discourtesy, are to him as though they were not; and the cloister walls of Fiesole no penitential solitude, barred from the stir and joy of life, but a possessed land of tender blessing, guarded from the entrance of all but holiest sorrow. The little cell was as one of the houses of heaven prepared for him by his Master. What need had it to be elsewhere? Was not the Val d'Arno, with its olive woods in white blossom, paradise enough for a poor monk? Or could Christ be indeed in heaven more than here? Was He not always with him? Could he breathe or see, but that Christ breathed beside him, or looked into his eyes? Under every cypress avenue the angels walked; he had seen their white robes,—whiter than the dawn,—at his bedside, as he woke in early summer. They had sung with him, one on each side, when his voice failed for joy at sweet vesper and matin time; his eyes were blinded by their wings in the sunset, when it sank behind the hills of Luni."—*Ruskin's Modern Painters.*

The same staircase which is usually ascended to reach the Stanze (that on the left of the fountain in the Cortile S. Damaso) will also lead, by turning to the left in the loggia of the third floor, to:

The Gallery of Pictures, founded by Pius VII., who acted on the advice of Cardinal Gonsalvi and of Canova, and formed the present collection from the pictures which had been carried off by the French from the Roman churches, upon their restoration. The pictures have, to a great extent, been recently rearranged and are not all numbered. Each picture is worthy of separate examination. They are contained in four rooms, and according to their present position are:

1st *Room.*—

ENTRANCE WALL:
1. St. Jerome: *Leonardo da Vinci,* painted in bistre.
16. St. John Baptist: *Guercino.*
4. The Annunciation, Adoration of the Magi, and Presentation in the Temple: *Raphael ;*—formerly a predella to the Coronation of the Virgin in the third room.
5. The dead Christ and Mary Magdalen: *Andrea Mantegna,*—from the Aldrovandi gallery at Bologna.
7. Madonna with the Child and St. John: *Fr. Francia.*

RIGHT WALL:
    The Story of St. Nicolo of Bari: *Fra Angelico da Fiesole,*—two out of the three predella pictures once in the sacristy of S. Domenico at Florence, whence they were carried off to Paris, where the third remains.
    (Above,) The Adoration of the Shepherds: *Murillo.*
    The Virgin surrounded by Angels: *Fra Angelico.*
3. The Story of St. Hyacinth: *Benozzo Gozzoli.*
    (Above,) The Marriage of St. Catherine: *Murillo.*
2. "I Tre Santi:" *Perugino.*

Part of a large predella in the church of S. Pietro Casinensi at Perugia. Several saints from this predella still remain in the sacristy of S. Pietro; two are at Lyons.

"In the centre is St. Benedict, with his black cowl over his head and long parted beard, the book in one hand, and the asperge in the other. On one side, St. Placidus, young, and with a mild, candid expression, black habit and shaven crown. On the other side is St. Flavia (or St. Catherine?), crowned as a martyr, holding her palm, and gazing upward with a divine expression."—*Mrs. Jameson.*

(Above this) The Holy Family and Saints: *Bonifazio.*

Left Wall.—The Dead Christ, with the Virgin, St. John, and the Magdalen lamenting: *Carlo Crivelli.*

Wall of Egress.—Faith, Hope, and Charity, *Raphael :*—circular medallions in bistre, which once formed a predella for "the Entombment" in the Borghese gallery.

2nd Room.—

Entrance Wall.—The Communion of St. Jerome: *Domenichino*. This is the master-piece of the master, and perhaps second only to the Transfiguration. It was painted for the monks of Ara Cœli, who quarrelled with the artist, and shut up the picture. Afterwards they commissioned Poussin to paint an altar-piece for their church, and, instead of supplying him with fresh canvas, produced the picture of Domenichino, and desired him to paint over it. Poussin indignantly threw up his engagement, and made known the existence of the picture, which was afterwards preserved in the church of S. Girolamo della Carità, whence it was carried off by the French. St. Jerome, dying at Bethlehem, is represented receiving the Last Sacraments from St. Ephraim of Syria, while St. Paula kneels by his side.

"The Last Communion of St. Jerome is the subject of one of the most celebrated pictures in the world,—the St. Jerome of Domenichino, which has been thought worthy of being placed opposite to the Transfiguration of Raphael, in the Vatican. The aged saint,—feeble, emaciated, dying,—is borne in the arms of his disciples to the chapel of his monastery, and placed within the porch.* A young priest sustains him; St. Paula, kneeling, kisses one of his thin bony hands; the saint fixes his eager eyes on the countenance of the priest, who is about to administer the Sacrament,—a noble, dignified figure in a rich ecclesiastical dress; a deacon holds the cup, and an attendant priest the book; the lion droops his head with an expression of grief;† the eyes and attention of all are on the dying saint, while four angels, hovering above, look down upon the scene."—*Jameson's Sacred Art.*

"And Jerome's death (A.D. 420) drawing near, he commanded that he should be laid on the bare ground and covered with sackcloth, and calling the brethren around him, he spake sweetly to them, and exhorted them in many holy words, and appointed Eusebius to be their abbot in his room. And then, with tears, he received the blessed Eucharist, and sinking backwards again on the earth, his hands crossed on his heart, he sung the 'Nunc Dimittis,' which being finished, it being the

---

* The candle is ingeniously made crooked in the socket, not to interfere with the lines of the architecture, while the flame is straight.

† "According to the 'Spiritual Meadow' of John Moschus, who died A.D. 620, the lion is said to have pined away after Jerome's death, and to have died at last on his grave."

hour of compline, suddenly a great light, as of the noonday sun, shone round about him, within which light angels innumerable were seen by the bystanders, in shifting motion, like sparks among the dry reeds. And the voice of the Saviour was heard, inviting him to heaven, and the holy Doctor answered that he was ready. And after an hour, that light departed, and Jerome's spirit with it."—*Lord Lindsay, from Peter de Natalibus.*

Right Wall.—"The Madonna di Foligno," *Raphael*, ordered in 1511 by Sigismondo Conti for the church of Ara Cœli (where he is buried), and removed in 1565 to Foligno, when his great-niece, Anna Conti, took the veil there at the convent of St' Anna. The angel in the foreground bears a tablet, with the names of the painter and donor, and the date 1512. The city of Foligno is seen in the background, with a falling bomb, from which one may believe that the picture was a votive offering from Sigismondo for an escape during a siege. The picture was originally on panel, and was transferred to canvas at Paris.

"The Madonna di Foligno, however beautiful in the whole arrangement, however excellent in the execution of separate parts, appears to belong to a transition state of development. There is something of the ecstatic enthusiasm which has produced such peculiar conceptions and treatment of religious subjects in other artists—Correggio, for example—and which, so far from harmonizing with the unaffected serene grace of Raphael, has in this instance led to some serious defects. This remark is particularly applicable to the figures of St. John and St. Francis: the former looks out of the picture with a fantastic action, and the drawing of his arm is even considerably mannered. St. Francis has an expression of fanatical ecstasy, and his countenance is strikingly weak in the painting (composed of reddish, yellowish, and grey tones, which cannot be wholly ascribed to their restorer). Again, St. Jerome looks up with a sort of fretful expression, in which it is difficult to recognise, as some do, a mournful resignation; there is also an exaggerated style of drawing in the eyes, which sometimes gives a sharpness to the expression of Raphael's figures, and appears very marked in some of his other pictures. Lastly, the Madonna and the Child, who turn to the donor, are in attitudes which, however graceful, are not perhaps sufficiently tranquil for the majesty of the queen of heaven. The expression of the Madonna's countenance is extremely sweet, but with more of the character of a mere woman than of a glorified being. The figure of the donor, on the other hand, is excellent, with an expression of sincerity and truth; the angel with the tablet is of unspeakable intensity and exquisite beauty —one of the most marvellous figures that Raphael has created."—*Kugler.*

"In the upper part of the composition sits the Virgin in heavenly glory ; by her side is the Infant Christ, partly sustained by his mother's veil, which is drawn round his body : both look down benignly on the votary, Sigismund Conti, who, kneeling below, gazes up with an expression of the most intense gratitude and devotion. It is a portrait from the life, and certainly one of the finest and most life-like that exist in painting. Behind him stands St. Jerome, who, placing his hand upon the head of the votary, seems to present him to his celestial protectress. On the other side, John the Baptist, the meagre wild-looking prophet of the desert, points upward to the Redeemer. More in front kneels St. Francis, who, while he looks up to heaven with trusting and imploring love, extends his right hand towards the worshippers supposed to be assembled in the church, recommending them also to the protecting grace of the Virgin. In the centre of the picture, dividing these two groups, stands a lovely angel-boy, holding in his hand a tablet, one of the most charming figures of this kind Raphael ever painted ; the head, looking up, has that sublime, yet perfectly childish grace, which strikes one in those awful angel-boys in the 'Madonna di San Sisto.' The background is a landscape, in which appears the city of Foligno at a distance ; it is overshadowed by a storm-cloud, and a meteor is seen falling ; but above these bends a rainbow, pledge of peace and safety. The whole picture glows throughout with life and beauty, hallowed by that profound religious sentiment which suggested the offering, and which the sympathetic artist seems to have caught from the grateful donor. It was dedicated in the church of the Ara Cœli at Rome, which belongs to the Franciscans, hence St. Francis is one of the principal figures. When I was asked, at Rome, why St. Jerome had been introduced into the picture, I thought it might be thus accounted for :—The patron saint of the donor, St. Sigismund, was a king and warrior, and Conti might possibly think it did not accord with his profession, as a humble ecclesiastic, to introduce him here. The most celebrated convent of the Jeronymites in Italy is that of St. Sigismund, near Cremona, placed under the special protection of St. Jerome, who is also in a general sense the patron of all ecclesiastics ; hence, perhaps, he figures here as the protector of Sigismund Conti."—*Jameson's Legends of the Madonna*, p. 103.

Wall of Egress.—"The Transfiguration:" *Raphael.* The grandest picture in the world. It was originally painted by order of Cardinal Giulio de' Medici (afterwards Clement VII.) Archbishop of Narbonne, for that provincial cathedral. But it was scarcely finished when Raphael died, and it hung over his death-bed as he lay in state, and was carried in his funeral procession.

"And when all beheld
Him where he lay, how changed from yesterday—
Him in that hour cut off, and at his head
His last great work ; when, entering in, they look'd,
Now on the dead, then on that masterpiece—
Now on his face, lifeless and colourless,
Then on those forms divine that lived and breathed,
And would live on for ages—all were moved,
And sighs burst forth and loudest lamentations."
Rogers.

The three following quotations may perhaps represent the practical, æsthetical, and spiritual aspects of the picture.

" It is somewhat strange to see the whole picture of the Transfiguration —including the three apostles, prostrate on the mount, shading their dazzled senses from the insufferable brightness—occupying only a small part of the top of the canvas, and the principal field filled with a totally distinct and certainly unequalled picture—that of the demoniac boy, whom our Saviour cured on coming down from the mount, after his transfiguration. This was done in compliance with the *orders* of the monks of S. Pietro in Montorio, for which church it was painted. It was the universal custom of the age—the yet unbanished taste of Gothic days—to have two pictures, a celestial and a terrestrial one, wholly unconnected with each other ; accordingly, we see few, even of the finest paintings, in which there is not a heavenly subject above and an earthly below—for the great masters of that day, like our own Shakspeare, were compelled to suit their works to the taste of their employers."
—*Eaton's Rome.*

" It must ever be matter of wonder that any one can have doubted of the grand unity of such a conception as this. In the absence of the Lord, the disconsolate parents bring a possessed boy to the disciples of the Holy One. They seem to have been making attempts to cast out the Evil Spirit ; one has opened a book, to see whether by chance any spell were contained in it which might be successful against this plague, but in vain. At this moment appears He who alone has the power, and appears transfigured in glory. They remember His former mighty deeds ; they instantly point aloft to the vision as the only source of healing. How can the upper and lower parts be separated ? Both are one ; beneath is Suffering craving for Aid ; above is active Power and helpful Grace. Both refer to one another ; both work in one another. Those who, in our dispute over the picture, thought with me, confirmed their view by this consideration : Raffaelle, they said, was ever distinguished by the exquisite propriety of his conceptions. And is it likely that this painter, thus gifted by God, and everywhere recognisable by the excellence of this His gift, would in the full ripeness of his powers have thought and painted wrongly? Not so; he is, as nature is, ever right, and then most deeply and truly right when we least suspect it."—*Goethe's Werke*, iii. p. 33.

"In looking at the Transfiguration we must bear in mind that it is not an historical but a devotional picture,—that the intention of the painter was not to represent a scene, but to excite religious feelings by expressing, so far as painting might do it, a very sublime idea.

"If we remove to a certain distance from the picture, so that the forms shall become vague, indistinct, and only the masses of colour and the light and shade perfectly distinguishable, we shall see that the picture is indeed divided as if horizontally, the upper half being all light, and the lower half comparatively all dark. As we approach nearer, step by step, we behold above, the radiant figure of the Saviour floating in mid-air, with arms outspread, garments of transparent light, glorified visage upturned as if in rapture, and the hair lifted and scattered as I have seen it in persons under the influence of electricity. On the right, Moses; on the left, Elijah; representing respectively the old Law and the old Prophecies, which both testified of Him. The three disciples lie on the ground, terror-struck, dazzled. There is a sort of eminence or platform, but no perspective, no attempt at real locality, for the scene is revealed as in a vision, and the same soft transparent light envelopes the whole. This is the spiritual life, raised far above the earth, but not yet in heaven. Below is seen the earthly light, poor humanity struggling helplessly with pain, infirmity, and death. The father brings his son, the possessed, or as we should now say, the epileptic boy, who oftentimes falls into the water, or into the fire, or lies grovelling on the earth, foaming and gnashing his teeth; the boy struggles in his arms,—the rolling eyes, the distorted features, the spasmodic limbs, are at once terrible and pitiful to look on.

"Such is the profound, the heart-moving significance of this wonderful picture. It is, in truth, a fearful approximation of the most opposite things; the mournful helplessness, suffering, and degradation of human nature, the unavailing pity, are placed in immediate contrast with spiritual light, life, hope,—nay, the very fruition of heavenly rapture.

"It has been asked, who are the two figures, the two saintly deacons, who stand on each side of the upper group, and what have they to do with the mystery above, or the sorrow below? Their presence shows that the whole was conceived as a vision, or a poem. The two saints are St. Laurence and St. Julian, placed there at the request of the Cardinal de' Medici, for whom the picture was painted, to be offered by him as an act of devotion as well as munificence to his new bishopric; and these two figures commemorate in a poetical way, not unusual at the time, his father, Lorenzo, and his uncle, Giuliano de' Medici. They would be better away; but Raphael, in consenting to the wish of his patron that they should be introduced, left no doubt of the significance of the whole composition, that it is placed before worshippers as a revelation of the double life of earthly suffering and spiritual faith, as an excitement to religious contemplation and religious hope.

"In the Gospel, the Transfiguration of Our Lord is first described, then the gathering of the people and the appeal of the father in behalf of his afflicted son. They appear to have been simultaneous; but painting only could have placed them before our eyes, at the same moment, in all their suggestive contrast. It will be said that in the brief record of the Evangelist, this contrast is nowhere indicated, but the painter found it there and was right to use it,—just the same as if a man should choose a text from which to preach a sermon, and, in doing so, should evolve from the inspired words many teachings, many deep reasonings, besides those most obvious and apparent.

"But, after we have prepared ourselves to understand and to take into our heads all that this wonderful picture can suggest, considered as an emanation of the mind, we find that it has other interests for us, considered merely as a work of art. It was the last picture which came from Raphael's hand; he was painting on it when he was seized with his last illness. He had completed all the upper part of the composition, all the ethereal vision, but the lower part of it was still unfinished, and in this state the picture was hung over his bier; when, after his death, he was laid out in his painting-room, and all his pupils and friends, and the people of Rome, came to look upon him for the last time; and when those who stood round raised their eyes to the Transfiguration, and then bent them on the lifeless form extended beneath it, 'every heart was like to burst with grief' (*faceva scoppiare l'anima di dolore a ognuno che quivi guardava*), as, indeed, well it might.

"Two-thirds of the price of the picture, 655 'ducati di camera,' had already been paid by the Cardinal de' Medici, and, in the following year, that part of the picture which Raphael had left unfinished was completed by his pupil Giulio Romano, a powerful and gifted, but not a refined or elevated, genius. He supplied what was wanting in the colours and chiaroscuro according to Raphael's design, but not certainly as Raphael himself would have done it. The sum which Giulio received he bestowed as a dowry on his sister, when he gave her in marriage to Lorenzetto the sculptor, who had been a friend and pupil of Raphael.

The cardinal did not send the picture to Narbonne, but, unwilling to deprive Rome of such a masterpiece, he presented it to the church of San Pietro in Montorio, and sent in its stead the Raising of Lazarus, by Sebastian del Piombo, now in our National Gallery. The French carried off the Transfiguration to Paris in 1797, and when restored, it was placed in the Vatican, where it now is."—*Mrs. Jameson's History of Our Lord*, vol. i.

3rd Room.—

Entrance Wall.—Madonna and Saints : *Titian*.

" Titian's altar-piece is a specimen of his pictures of this class. St. Nicholas, in full episcopal costume, is gazing upwards with an air of inspiration. St. Peter is looking over his shoulder at a book, and a beautiful St. Catherine is on the other side. Farther behind, are St. Francis and St. Anthony of Padua ; on the left St. Sebastian, whose figure recurs in almost all of these pictures. Above, in the clouds, with angels, is the Madonna, who looks cheerfully on, while the lovely Child holds a wreath, as if ready to crown a votary."—*Kugler.*

" In this picture there are three stages, or whatever they are called, the same as in the Transfiguration. Below, saints and martyrs are represented in suffering and abasement ; on every face is depicted sadness, nay, almost impatience ; one figure in rich episcopal robes looks upwards, with the most eager and agonized longing, as if weeping, but he cannot see all that is floating above his head, but which *we* see, standing in front of the picture. Above, Mary and her Child are in a cloud, radiant with joy, and surrounded by angels, who have woven many garlands ; the Holy Child holds one of these, and seems as if about to crown the saints beneath, but his Mother withholds his hand for the moment (?). The contrast between the pain and suffering below, whence St. Sebastian looks forth out of the picture with gloom and almost apathy, and the lofty unalloyed exultation in the clouds above, where crowns and palms are already awaiting him, is truly admirable. High above the group of Mary hovers the Holy Spirit, from whom emanates a bright streaming light, thus forming the apex of the whole composition. I have just remembered that Goethe, at the beginning of his first visit to Rome, describes and admires this picture ; and he speaks of it in considerable detail. It was at that time in the Quirinal."— *Mendelssohn's Letters.*

Sta. Margherita da Cortona : *Guercino.* She is represented kneeling,—angels hovering above,—in the background is the Convent of Cortona.

RIGHT WALL:

Martyrdom of St. Laurence: *Spagnoletto*.
22. The Magdalen, with angels bearing the instruments of the Passion: *Guercino*.
23. The Coronation of the Virgin: *Pinturicchio*.
24. The Resurrection: *Perugino*. The figures are sharply relieved against a bright green landscape and a perfectly green sky. The figure of the risen Saviour is in a raised gold nimbus surrounded by cherubs' heads, as in the fresco of Pinturicchio at the Ara Cœli. The escaping soldier is said to be a portrait of Perugino, introduced by Raphael,—the sleeping soldier that of Raphael, by Perugino.
25. "La Madonna di Monte Luco," designed by Raphael: the upper part painted by *Giulio Romano*, the lower by *Francesco Penni* (Il Fattore). The apostles looking into the tomb of the Virgin, find it blooming with heartsease and ixias. Above, the Virgin is crowned amid the angels. There is a lovely landscape seen through a dark cave, which ends awkwardly in the black clouds. This picture was painted for the convent of Monte Luco near Spoleto.

The Nativity: *Giovanni Spagna*.

27. The Coronation of the Virgin: *Raphael*. The predella in the first room belonged to this picture, which was painted for the Benedictines of Perugia.
28. The Virgin and Child enthroned under an arcade—with S. Lorenzo, St. Louis, S. Ercolano, and S. Costanzo, standing: On the step of the throne is inscribed 'Hoc Petrus de Chastro Plebis Pinxit.'
29. Virgin and Child: *Sassoferrato*. A fat mundane Infant and a coarse Virgin seated on a crescent moon. The Child holds a rosary.

END WALL:

The Entombment: *Caravaggio*.

"Caravaggio's entombment of Christ is a picture wanting in all the characteristics of holy sublimity; but is nevertheless full of solemnity, only perhaps too like the funeral solemnity of a gipsy chief. A figure of such natural sorrow as the Virgin, who is represented as exhausted with weeping, with her trembling outstretched hands, has seldom been painted. Even as mother of a gipsy chief, she is dignified and touching."—*Kugler*.

LEFT WALL (RETURNING):

31. Doge A. Gritti (*Titian*), half-length, in a yellow robe.
Two very large pictures in many compartments, by *Niccolo Alunno*, of the Crucifixion and Saints. (Between them.)

Sixtus IV. and his Court : *Melozzo da Forlì*. A fresco, removed from the Vatican library by Leo XII., which is a most interesting memorial of an important historical family. Near the figure of the pope, Sixtus IV., who is known to Roman travellers from his magnificent bronze tomb in the Chapel of the Sacrament at St. Peter's, stand two of his nephews, of whom one is Giuliano della Rovere, afterwards Julius II., and the other Pietro Riario, who, from the position of a humble Franciscan monk, was raised, in a few months, by his uncle, to be Bishop of Treviso, Cardinal-Archbishop of Seville, Patriarch of Constantinople, Archbishop of Valentia, and Archbishop of Florence, when his life changed, and he lived with such extravagance, and gave banquets so magnificent, that "never had pagan antiquity seen anything like it ;" * but within two years "he died (not without suspicion of poison), to the great grief of Pope Sixtus, and to the infinite joy of the whole college of cardinals."† The kneeling figure represents Platina, the historian of the popes and prefect of the Vatican library. In the background stand two other nephews of the pope, Cardinal Giovanni della Rovere, and Girolamo Riario, who was married by his uncle (or father ?), the pope, to the famous Caterina Sforza,—was suspected of being the originator of the conspiracy of the Pazzi,—was created Count of Forlì, and to whose aggrandisement Sixtus IV. sacrificed every principle of morality and justice : he was murdered at Forli, April 14th, 1488. Beneath is inscribed:

> "Templa domum expositis fora moenia pontes :
> Virgineam Trivii quod repararis aquam
> Prisca licet nautis statuas dare commoda portus :
> Et Vaticanum cingere Sixte jugum :
> Plus tamen urbs debet : nam quæ squalore latebat.
> Gemitur in celebri bibliotheca loco."

4th Room.—

ENTRANCE WALL :

32. The Martyrdom of SS. Processus and Martinianus, the gaolers of St. Peter : *Valentin*. It is stigmatised by Kugler as "an unimportant and bad picture," but, perhaps from the con-

---

* See Stefano Infessura, Rev. Ital. Script. tom. iii.
† Corio, 1st mil. p. 876.

nection of the subject with the story of St. Peter, has been thought worthy of being copied in mosaic in the basilica, whence this picture was brought.

"This picture is terrible for dark and effective expression ; it is just one of those subjects in which the Caravaggio school delighted."— *Jameson's Sacred Art.*

33. Martyrdom of St. Peter : *Guido Reni.*

" This has the heavy powerful forms of Caravaggio, but wants the passionate feeling which sustains such subjects,—it is a martyrdom and nothing more,—it might pass for an enormous and horrible genre picture."—*Kugler.*

34. Martyrdom of St. Erasmus : *N. Poussin.* A most horrible picture of the disembowelment of the saint upon a wheel. It was copied in mosaic in St. Peter's when the picture was removed from thence.

LEFT WALL :

35. The Annunciation : *Baroccio.* From Sta. Maria di Loreto, detained in the Vatican in exchange for a mosaic, after it was sent back by the French.

36. St. Gregory the Great—the miracle of the Brandeum : *Andrea Sacchi.*

" The Empress Constantia sent to St. Gregory requesting some of the relics of St. Peter and St. Paul. He excused himself, saying that he dared not disturb their sacred remains for such a purpose,—but he sent her part of a consecrated cloth (Brandeum) which had enfolded the body of St. John the Evangelist. The empress rejected this gift with contempt: whereupon Gregory, to show that such things are hallowed not so much in themselves as by the faith of believers, laid the Brandeum on the altar, and after praying he took up a knife and pierced it, and blood flowed as from a living body."—*Jameson's Sacred Art,* p. 321.

37. The Ecstasy of Sta. Michelina: *Baroccio.* This picture is mentioned by Lanzi as " Sta. Michelina estatica *sul Calvario.*" The story appears to be lost.

BETWEEN THE WINDOWS :

The Madonna and Child with St. Jerome and St. Bartholomew : *Moretto da Brescia (Buonvicino).*

38. The Dream of Sta. Helena (of the finding of the true Cross) : *Paolo Veronese.* Once in the Capitol collection.

RIGHT WALL (RETURNING):
39. Madonna with St. Thomas and St. Jerome: *Guido.* The St. Thomas is very grand.
40. Madonna della Cintola with St. John and St. Augustin. Signed 1521: *Cesare da Sesto.*
41. Salvator Mundi. Christ seated on the rainbow: *Correggio ?*
42. St. Romualdo: *Andrea Sacchi.* The saint sees the vision of a ladder by which the friars of his Order ascend to heaven. The monks in white drapery are grand and noble figures.

" It is recorded in the legend of St. Romualdo, that, a short time before his death, he fell asleep beside a fountain near his cell; and he dreamed, and in his dream he saw a ladder like that which the patriarch Jacob beheld in his vision, resting on the earth, and the top of it reaching to heaven; and he saw the brethren of his Order ascending by twos and by threes, all clothed in white. When Romualdo awoke from his dream, he changed the habit of his monks from black to white, which they have ever since worn in remembrance of this vision."—*Jameson's Monastic Orders*, p. 117.

A door on the ground-floor of the Cortile di S. Damaso will admit visitors (with an order) to visit the *Papal Manufactory of Mosaics,* whence so many beautiful works have issued, and where others are always in progress.

" Ghirlandajo, who felt the utmost enthusiasm for the august remains of Roman grandeur, was still more deeply impressed by the sight of the ancient mosaics of the Christian basilicas, the image of which was still present to his mind when he said, at a more advanced age, that ' mosaic was the true painting for eternity.' "—*Rio.*

CHAPTER XVII.

THE ISLAND AND THE TRASTEVERE.

Ponte Quattro Capi — Gaetani Tower — S. Bartolomeo in Isola — Temple of Æsculapius—Hospital of the Benfratelli—Mills on the Tiber—Ponte Cestio—Fornarina's House—S. Benedetto a Piscinuola—Castle of the Alberteschi—S. Crispino—Palazzo Ponziani—Sta. Maria in Cappella—Sta. Cecilia—Hospital of S. Michele—Porta Portese—Sta. Maria del Orto—S. Francesco a Ripa—Castle of the Anquillara—S. Chrisogono—Hospital of S. Gallicano—Sta. Maria in Trastevere—S. Calisto—Convent of Sta. Anna—S. Cosimato—Porta Settimiana—Sta. Dorotea—Ponte Sisto.

FOLLOWING the road which leads to the Temple of Vesta, &c., as far as the Via Savelli, and then turning down past the gateway of the Orsini palace, with its two bears,—we reach the *Ponte Quattro Capi*.

This was the ancient Pons Fabricius, built of stone in the place of a wooden bridge, A.U.C. 733, by Fabricius, the Curator Viarum. It has two arches, with a small ornamental one in the central pier. In the twelfth century the greater part was faced with brickwork. An inscription, only partly legible, remains. L . FABRICIUS . C . T . CUR . VIAR . FACIUNDUM . CURAVIT . EIDEMQ . PROBAVIT .—Q . LEPIDUS . M . F . M . LOLLIUS . M . F . COS . EX . S . C . PROBAVERUNT. From this inscription the inference has been drawn that the senate always allowed forty years to elapse between the completion of a public work, and the grant to it of their public approval. This bridge, according to Horace, was a favourite spot with those who wished to drown themselves ; hence Damasippus would have leaped into the Tiber, if it were not for the precepts of the stoic Stertinius :

> " Unde ego mira
> Descripsi docilis præcepta hæc, tempore quo me
> Solatus jussit sapientem pascere barbam,
> Atque a Fabricio non tristem ponte reverti."
> *Horace, Sat.* ii. 3.

The name of the bridge changed with time to " Pons Tarpeius " and " Pons Judæorum," from the neighbouring Ghetto. It is now called Ponte Quattro Capi, from two busts of the four-headed Janus, which adorn its parapet, and are supposed to have come from the temple of " Janus Geminus," which stood in this neighbourhood.

On crossing this bridge, we are on the Island in the Tiber, the formation of which is ascribed by tradition to the produce of the corn-fields of the Tarquins (cast contemptuously upon the waters after their expulsion), which accumulated here, till soil gathered around them, and a solid piece of land was formed. Of this, Ampère says :

> "L'effet du courant rapide du fleuve est plutôt de détruire les îles que d'en former. C'est ainsi qu'une petite île a été entraînée par la violence des eaux en 1718."—*Histoire Romaine à Rome.*

On this island, anciently known as the *Isola Tiberina*, were three temples,—those, namely, of Æsculapius :

> " Unde Coroniden circumflua Tibridis alveo
> Insula Romuleæ sacris adsciverit urbis."
> *Ovid, Metam.* xv. 624.
>
> " Accepit Phœbo Nymphaque Coronide natum
> Insula, dividua quam premit amnis aqua."
> *Ovid, Fast.* i. 291.

of Jupiter :

> "Jupiter in parte est, cepit locus unus utrumque :
> Junctaque sunt magno templa nepotis avo."
> *Ovid, Fast.* i. 293.

and of Faunus :

> "Idibus agrestis fumant altaria Fauni,
> Ilic ubi discretas insula rumpit aquas."
> *Ovid, Fast.* ii. 193.

Here also was an altar to the Sabine god Semo-Sancus, whose inscription, legible in the early centuries of Christianity, led various ecclesiastical authors into the error that the words "Semoni Sanco" referred to Simon Magus.*

In imperial times the island was used as a prison : among remarkable prisoners immured here was Arvandus, Prefect of Gaul, A.D. 468. In the reign of Claudius sick slaves were exposed and left to die here,—that emperor—by a strange contradiction in one who caused fallen gladiators to be butchered "for the pleasure of seeing them die"—making a law that any slave so exposed should receive his liberty if he recovered. In the middle ages the island was under the jurisdiction of the Cardinal Bishop of Porto, who lived in the Franciscan convent. Under Leo X. a fête was held here in which Camillo Querno, the papal poet, was crowned with ivy, laurel, and cabbage (!). In 1656 the whole island was appropriated as a hospital for those stricken with the plague,—a singular coincidence for the site of the temple of Æsculapius.

The first building on the left, after passing the bridge, is a fine brick tower, of great historic interest, as the only relic of a castle, built by the family of the Anicii, of which St.

---

* Ampère, i. 436.

Gregory the Great was a member, and two of whom were consuls together under Honorius:

> "Est in Romuleo procumbens insula Tibri,
> Qua medius geminas interfluit alveus urbes,
> Discretas subeunte freto, pariterque minantes
> Ardua turrigeræ surgunt in culmina ripæ.
> Hic stetit et subitum prospexit ab aggere votum.
> Unanimes fratres junctos stipante senatu
> Ire forum, strictasque procul radiare secures,
> Atque uno bijuges tolli de limine fasces."
> *Claudius, Paneg. in Prob. et Olyb. Cons.* 226.

From the Anicii the castle passed to the Gaetani. It was occupied as a fortress by the Countess Matilda, after she had driven the faction of the anti-pope Guibert out of the island, and was the refuge where two successive popes, Victor III. and Urban II., lived under her protection.*

The centre of the island is now occupied by the *Church and Convent of S. Bartolomeo*, which gives it its present name.

The piazza in front of the church is occupied by a pillar, erected at the private expense of Pius IX., to commemorate the opening of the Vatican Council of 1869—70,—adorned with statues of St. Bartholomew, St. Paulinus of Nola, St. Francis, and S. Giovanni di Dio. Here formerly stood an ancient obelisk (the only one of unknown origin). A fragment of it was long preserved at the Villa Albani, whence it is said to have been removed to Urbino. The church, a basilica, was founded by Otho III. *c.* 1000; its campanile dates from 1118. The nave and aisles are divided by red granite columns, said to be relics of the ancient temple,—as is a marble well-head under the stairs leading to the tribune. This was restored in 1798, and dedicated to St. Adalbert

---

* See Hemans' Monuments in Rome

of Gnesen, who bestowed upon the church its great relic, the body of St. Bartholomew, which he asserted to have brought from Beneventum, though the inhabitants of that town profess that they still possess the *real* body of the apostle, and sent that of St. Paulinus of Nola to Rome instead. The dispute about the possession of this relic ran so high as to lead to a siege of Beneventum in the middle ages. The convent belongs to the Franciscans (Frati-Minori), who will admit male visitors into their pretty little garden at the end of the island, to see the remains of

The Temple of Æsculapius, built after the great plague in Rome, in B.C. 291, when, in accordance with the advice of the Sibylline books, ambassadors were sent to Epidaurus to bring Æsculapius to Rome;—they returned with a statue of the god, but as their vessel sailed up the Tiber, a serpent, which had lain concealed during the voyage, glided from it, and landed on this spot, hailed by the people under the belief that Æsculapius himself had thus come to them. In consequence of this story the form of a ship was given to this end of the island, and its bow may still be seen at the end of the convent garden, with the famous serpent of Æsculapius sculptured upon it in high relief.* The curious remains still existing are not of sufficient size to bear out the assertion often made that the whole island was enclosed in the travertine form of a ship, of which the temple of Jupiter at the other end afterwards formed the prow, and the obelisk the mast.

"Pendant les guerres Samnites, Rome fut de nouveau frappée par une de ces maladies auxquelles elle était souvent en proie ; celle-ci dura

* Piranesi's engraving shows that a hundred years ago there existed, in addition, a colossal bust, and a hand holding the serpent-twined rod of Æsculapius.

trois années. On eut recours aux livres Sibyllins. En cas pareil ils avaient prescrit de consacrer un temple à Apollon ; cette fois ils prescrivirent d'aller à Epidaure chercher le fils d'Apollon, Esculape, et de l'amener à Rome. Esculape, sous la forme d'un serpent, fut transporté d'Epidaure dans l'île Tibérine, où on lui éleva un temple, et où ont été trouvés des *ex-voto*, représentant des bras, des jambes, diverses autres parties du corps humain, *ex-votos* qu'on eût pu croire provenir d'une église de Rome, car le catholicisme romain a adopté cet usage païen sans y rien changer.

"Pourquoi place-t-on le temple d'Esculape en cet endroit ? On a vu que l'île Tibérine avait été très-anciennement consacrée au culte d'un dieu des Latins primitifs, Faunus ; or ce dieu rendait ses oracles près des sources thermales ; its devaient avoir souvent pour l'objet la guérison des malades qui venaient demander la santé à ces sources. De plus, les malades consultaient Esculape dans les songes par incubation, comme dans l'Ovide, Numa va consulter Faunus sur l'Aventin. Il n'est donc pas surprenant qu'on ait institué le culte du dieu grec de la santé, là où le dieu latin Faunus rendait ses oracles dans des songes, et où étaient probablement des sources d'eau chaude qui ont disparu comme les *lautulæ* près du Forum romain.

"On donna à l'île la forme d'un vaisseau, plus tard un obélisque figura le mât ; en la regardant du Ponte Rotto, on reconnaît encore très bien cette forme, de ce côté, on voit sculpté sur le mur qui figure le vaisseau d'Esculape une image du dieu avec un serpent entortillé autour de son sceptre. La belle statue d'Esculape, venue des jardins Farnèse, passe pour avoir été celle de l'île Tibérine. Un temple de Jupiter touchait à ce temple d'Esculape.

"Un jour que je visitais ce lieu, le sacristain de l'église de St. Barthélemy me dit, '*Al tempo d'Esculapio quando Giove regnava*.' Phrase singulière, et qui montre encore vivante une sorte de foi au paganisme chez les Romains."—*Ampère*, iii. 42.

Opposite S. Bartolomeo, on the site of the temple of Faunus, is the *Hospital of S. Giovanni Calabita*, also called *Benfratelli*, entirely under the care of the brethren of S. Giovanni di Dio, who cook, nurse, wash, and otherwise do all the work of those who pass under their care, often to the number of 1200 in the course of the year, though the hospital is very small.

"C'est à Pie V. que les frères de l'ordre de la *Charité*, institué par saint Jean de Dieu, durent leur premier établissement à Rome.

"Au milieu du cortége triomphal qui accompagnait don Juan d'Autriche (1571), lors de son retour de Lépante, on remarquait un pauvre homme misérablement vêtu et à l'attitude modeste. Il se nommait Sébastien Arias *des frères de Jean de Dieu*. Jean de Dieu était mort sans laisser d'autre règle à ses disciples que ces touchantes paroles qu'il répétait sans cesse, *faites le bien, mes frères;* et Sébastien d'Arias venait à Rome pour demander au pape l'autorisation de former des couvents et d'avoir des hospices où ils pussent suivre les exemples de dévouement que leur avait laissés Jean de Dieu. Or, Sébastien rencontra don Juan à Naples, et le vainqueur de Lépante le prit avec lui. Il se chargea même d'appuyer sa requête, et Pie V. s'empressa d'accorder aux frères non-seulement la bulle qu'ils désiraient, mais encore un monastère dans l'île du Tibre."—*Gournerie, Rome Chrétienne*, ii. 206.

A narrow lane near this leads to the other end of the island, where the temple of Jupiter stood. It is worth while to go thither for the sake of the view of the river and its bridges, which is to be obtained from a little quay leading to one of the numerous water-mills which exist near this. These floating *Mills* (which bear sacred monograms upon their gables) are interesting as having been invented by Belisarius in order to supply the people and garrison with bread, during the siege of Rome by Vitiges, when the Goths had cut the aqueducts, and thus rendered the mills on the Janiculan useless.

The bridge, of one large and two smaller arches, which connects the island with the Trastevere, is now called the *Ponte S. Bartolomeo*, but was anciently the Pons Cestius, or Gratianus, built A.U.C. 708, by the Prætor Lucius Cestius, who was probably father to the Caius Cestius buried near the Porta S. Paolo. It was restored A.D. 370 by the emperors Valentinian, Valens, and Gratian, as is seen from the fragments of a red letter inscription on the inside of the parapet, in which the title "Pontifex Maximus" is ascribed to each—"a title accepted without hesitation," says Gibbon, "by seven Christian emperors, who were invested with more absolute authority over the religion they had deserted, than over that which they professed."

We now enter *the Trastevere*, the city "across the Tiber," —the portion of Rome which is most unaltered from mediæval times, and whose narrow streets are still overlooked by many ancient towers, gothic windows, and curious fragments of sculpture. The inhabitants on this side differ in many respects from those on the other side of the Tiber. They pride themselves upon being born "Trasteverini," profess to be the direct descendants of the ancient Romans, seldom intermarry with their neighbours, and speak a dialect peculiarly their own. It is said that in their dispositions also they differ from the other Romans, that they are a far more hasty, passionate, and revengeful, as they are a stronger and more vigorous race. The proportion of murders (a crime far less common in Rome than in England) is larger in this than in any other part of the city. This, it is believed, is partly due to the extreme excitement which the Trasteverini display in the pursuit of their national games, especially that of Morrà :—

"Morrà is played by the men, and merely consists in holding up, in rapid succession, any number of fingers they please, calling out at the same time the number their antagonist shows. Nothing, seemingly, can be more simple or less interesting. Yet, to see them play, so violent are their gestures, that you would imagine them possessed by some diabolical passion. The eagerness and rapidity with which they carry it on render it very liable to mistake and altercation ; then frenzy fires them, and too often furious disputes arise at this trivial play that end in murder. Morrà seems to differ in no respect from the *Micare Digitis* of the ancient Romans."—*Eaton's Rome*.

A house with gothic windows on the right, soon after passing the bridge, is pointed out as that once inhabited by the *Fornarina*, beloved of Raphael, and so well known to us from his portrait of her in the Tribune at Florence.

Crossing the Via Longarina, we find ourselves in the little piazza of *S. Benedetto a Piscinuola*, where there is a tiny church, with a good brick campanile intersected by terra-cotta mouldings, which occupies the site of the house inhabited by St. Benedict before his retreat to Subiaco. The exterior is uninviting, but the interior very curious; an atrium with antique columns opens to a vaulted chapel (of the same design as the Orto del Paradiso at Sta. Prassede), in which is a picture of the Virgin and Child, revered as that before which St. Benedict was wont to pray. Hence is entered the cell of the saint, of rough-hewn stones. His stone pillow is shown.

The church has ancient pillars, and a rich opus-alexandrinum pavement.

"Over the high altar is a picture—full-length—of St. Benedict, which Mabillon ('Iter Italicum') considers a genuine contemporary portrait—though Nibby and other critics suppose it less ancient. The figure on gold background is seated in a chair with gothic carvings, such as were in mediæval use; the black cowl is drawn over the head, the hair and beard are white; the aspect is serious and thoughtful, in one hand a crozier, in the other the book of rules drawn up by the Saint, displaying the words with which they begin: 'Ausculta fili precepta magistri."—*Hemans' Ancient Sacred Art*.

Turning down the Via Longarina towards the river, we pass, on the left, considerable remains of the old mediæval *Castle of the Alberteschi Family*, consisting of a block of palatial buildings of handsome masonry, with numerous antique fragments built into them, and a very rich porch sculptured with egg and billet mouldings of *c.* A.D. 1150, and beyond these, separated from them by a modern street, a high brick tower of *c.* A.D. 1100. Above one of the windows of this tower, a head of Jupiter is engrafted in the wall.

We now reach the entrance of the Ponte Rotto (described Chap. V.). Close to this bridge is the Church of *S. Crispino al Ponte* (the saint is buried at S. Lorenzo Pane e Perna). The front is modernized, but the east end displays rich terra-cotta cornices, and is very picturesque. On the river bank below this are the colossal lions' heads mentioned in Chap. V.

Turning up the Via dei Vascellari, we pass on the right, the ancient *Palace of the Ponziani Family*, once magnificent, but now of humble and rude exterior, and scarcely to be distinguished, except in March, during the festa of Sta. Francesca Romana, when old tapestries are hung out upon its white-washed walls, and the street in front is thickly strewn with box-leaves.

"The modern building that has been raised on the foundation of the old palace is the Casa dei Esercizii Pii, for the young men of the city. There the repentant sinner who longs to break the chain of sin, the youth beset by some strong temptation, one who has heard the inward voice summoning him to higher paths of virtue, another who is in doubt as to the particular line of life to which he is called, may come, and leave behind him for three, or five, or ten days, as it may be, the busy world, with all its distractions and its agitations, and, free for the time being from temporal cares, the wants of the body being provided for, and the mind at rest, may commune with God and their own souls.

"Over the Casa dei Esercizii Pii the sweet spirit of Francesca seems still to preside. On the day of her festival its rooms are thrown open, every memorial of the gentle saint is exhibited, lights burn on numerous altars, flowers deck the passages, leaves are strewn in the chapel, on the stairs, in the entrance-court ; gay carpets, figured tapestry, and crimson silks hang over the door, and crowds of people go in and out, and kneel before the relics or the pictures of the dear saint of Rome. It is a touching festival, which carries back the mind to the day when the young bride of Lorenzo Ponziano entered these walls for the first time, in all the sacred beauty of holiness and youth."—*Lady G. Fullerton.*

In this house, also, Sta. Francesca Romana died, having come hither from her convent to nurse her son who was ill, and having been then seized with mortal illness herself.

" Touching were the last words of the dying mother to her spiritual children : ' Love, love,' was the burden of her teaching, as it had been that of the beloved disciple. ' Love one another,' she said, ' and be faithful unto death. Satan will assault you, as he has assaulted me, but be not afraid. You will overcome him through patience and obedience ; and no trial will be too grievous, if you are united to Jesus ; if you walk in His ways, He will be with you.' On the seventh day of her illness, as she had herself announced, her life came to a close. A sublime expression animated her face, a more ethereal beauty clothed her earthly form. Her confessor for the last time inquired what it was her enraptured eyes beheld, and she answered, ' The heavens open! the angels descend! the angel has finished his task. He stands before me. He beckons me to follow him.' These were the last words Francesca uttered."—*Lady G. Fullerton's Life of Sta. F. Romana.*

Almost opposite the Ponziani Palace, an alley leads to the small chapel of *Sta. Maria in Cappella*, which has a good brick campanile, dating from 1090. This building is attached to a hospital for poor women ill of incurable diseases, attended by sisters of charity, and entirely under the patronage of the Doria family.

We now reach the front of the *Convent and Church of Sta. Cecilia* (facing which is a picturesque mediæval house), in many ways one of the most interesting buildings in the city.

Cecilia was a noble and rich Roman lady, who lived in the reign of Alexander Severus. She was married at sixteen to Valerian, a heathen, with whom she lived in perpetual virginity, telling him that her guardian angel watched over her by day and night.

> "I have an angel which thus loveth me—
> That with great love, whether I wake or sleep,
> Is ready aye my body for to keep."
>
> *Chaucer.*

At length Valerian and his brother Tiburtius were converted to Christianity by her prayers, and the exhortations of Pope Urban I. The husband and brother were beheaded for refusing to sacrifice to idols, and Cecilia was shortly afterwards condemned by Almachius, prefect of Rome, who was covetous of the great wealth she had inherited by their deaths. She was first shut up in the *Sudatorium* of her own baths, and a blazing fire was lighted, that she might be destroyed by the hot vapours. But when the bath was opened, she was found still living, "for God," says the legend, "had sent a cooling shower, which had tempered the heat of the fire, and preserved the life of the saint." Almachius, then, who dreaded the consequences of bringing so noble and courageous a victim to public execution, sent a lictor to behead her in her own palace, but he executed his office so ill, that she still lived after the third blow of his axe, after which the Roman law forbade that a victim should be stricken again. "The Christians found her bathed in her blood, and during three days she still preached and taught, like a doctor of the Church, with such sweetness and eloquence, that four hundred pagans were converted. On the third day she was visited by Pope Urban, to whose care she tenderly committed the poor whom she nourished, and to him she bequeathed the palace in which she had lived, that it might be consecrated as a temple to the Saviour. Then, "thanking God that he considered her, a humble woman, worthy to share the glory of his heroes, and with her eyes apparently fixed upon the heavens opening before her, she departed to her heavenly bridegroom, upon the 22nd November, A.D. 280."

The foundation of the church dates from its consecration by Pope Urban I., after the death of St. Cecilia, but it was rebuilt by Paschal I. in 821, and miserably modernized by Cardinal Doria in 1725. The exterior retains its ancient campanile of 1120, and its atrium of marble pillars, evidently collected from pagan edifices and surmounted by a frieze of mosaic, in which medallion heads of Cecilia, Valerian, Tiburtius, Urban I., and others are introduced. In the courtyard of the convent, which belongs to Benedictine nuns, is a fine specimen of the Roman vase called Cantharus, perhaps coeval with St. Cecilia's own residence here.

Right of the door, on entering, is the tomb of Adam of Hertford, Bishop of London, who died 1398, the only one spared from a cruel death, of the cardinals who conspired against Urban VI., and were taken prisoners at Lucera—from fear of King John who was his friend. His sarcophagus is adorned with the arms of England, then three leopards and fleurs-de-lis quartered. On the opposite side of the entrance is the tomb of Cardinal Fortiguerra, conspicuous in the contests of Pius II. and Paul II. with the Malatestas and

Savellis in the fifteenth century. The drapery is a beautiful specimen of the delicate carving of detail during that period.

The altar canopy, which bears the name of its artist, Arnolphus, and the date 1286, is a fine specimen of gothic work, and has statuettes of Cecilia, Valerian, Tiburtius, and Urban. Beneath the altar is the famous statue of St. Cecilia.

In the archives of the Vatican remains an account written by Pope Paschal I. (A.D. 817—24) himself, describing how, "yielding to the infirmity of the flesh," he fell asleep in his chair during the early morning service at St. Peter's, with his mind pre-occupied with a longing to find the burial-place of Cecilia, and discover her relics. Then in a glorified vision the virgin-saint appeared before him, and revealed the spot where she lay, with her husband and brother-in-law, in the catacomb of Calixtus, and there they were found, and transported to her church on the following day.

In the sixteenth century, Sfondrato, titular cardinal of the church, opened the tomb of the martyr, when the embalmed body of Cecilia was found, as it had been previously found by Paschal, robed in gold tissue, with linen clothes steeped in blood at her feet, "not lying upon the back, like a body in a tomb, but upon its right side, like a virgin in her bed, with her knees modestly drawn together, and offering the appearance of sleep." Pope Clement VIII. and all the people of Rome rushed to look upon the saint, who was afterwards enclosed as she was found, in a shrine of cypress wood cased in silver. But before she was again hidden from sight, the greatest artist of the day, Stefano

Maderno, was called in by Sfondrato, to sculpture the marble portrait which we now see lying upon her grave. Sfondrato (whose tomb is in this church) also enriched her shrine with the ninety-six silver lamps which burn constantly before it. In regarding this statue it will be remembered that Cecilia was not beheaded, but wounded in the throat,—a gold circlet conceals the wound.

> In the statue " the body lies on its side, the limbs a little drawn up ; the hands are delicate and fine,—they are not locked, but crossed at the wrists : the arms are stretched out. The drapery is beautifully modelled, and modestly covers the limbs. . . . . It is the statue of a lady, perfect in form, and affecting from the resemblance to reality in the drapery of white marble, and the unspotted appearance of the statue altogether. It lies as no living body could lie, and yet correctly, as the dead when left to expire,—I mean in the gravitation of the limbs."—*Sir C. Bell.*
>
> The inscription says : "Behold the body of the most holy virgin Cecilia, whom I myself saw lying incorrupt in her tomb. I have in this marble expressed for thee the same saint in the very same posture of body."

The tribune is adorned with mosaics of the ninth century, erected in the lifetime of Paschal I. (see his *square nimbus*). The Saviour is seen in the act of benediction, robed in gold : at his side are SS. Peter and Paul, St. Cecilia and St. Valerian, St. Paschal I. carrying the model of his church, and St. Agatha, whom he joined with Cecilia in its dedication. The mystic palm-trees and the phœnix, the emblem of eternity, are also represented, and, beneath, the four rivers, and the twelve sheep, emblematical of the apostles, issuing from the gates of Bethlehem and Jerusalem, to the adoration of the spotless Lamb. The picture of St. Cecilia behind the altar is attributed to *Guido.*

At the end of the right aisle is an ancient fresco representing the dream of Pope Paschal,—the (mitred) pope asleep upon his throne, and the saint appearing before him in a rich robe adorned with gems. This is the last of a series of frescoes which once existed in the portico of the church. The rest were destroyed in the seventeenth century. There are copies of them in the Barberini Library, viz.

    1. The marriage feast of Valerian and Cecilia.
    2. Cecilia persuades Valerian to seek for St. Urban.
    3. Valerian rides forth to seek for Urban.
    4. Valerian is baptized.
    5. An Angel crowns Cecilia and Valerian.
    6. Cecilia converts her executioners.
    7. Cecilia suffers in the bath.
    8. The Martyrdom of Cecilia.
    9. The Burial of Cecilia.
   10. The dream of Paschal.

Opening out of the same aisle are two chambers in the house of St. Cecilia, one the sudatorium of her baths, in which she was immured, actually retaining the pipes and calorifers of an ancient Roman bath.

The Festa of St. Cecilia is observed in this church on November 22nd, when—

—" rapt Cecilia, seraph-haunted queen of harmony "—*

is honoured in beautiful music from the papal choir assembled here. Visitors to Bologna will recollect the glorious figure of St. Cecilia by Raphael, rapt in ecstasy, and surrounded by instruments of music. This association with Cecilia probably arises from the tradition of the church, which tells how Valerian, returning from baptism by Pope Urban, found her singing hymns of triumph for his conversion, of which he had supposed her to be ignorant, and that

* Wordsworth.

when the bath was opened after her three days' imprisonment, she was again found singing the praises of her Saviour.

It is said that "she sang with such ravishing sweetness, that even the angels descended from heaven to listen to her, or to join their voices with hers."

The antiphons sung upon her festival are.

"And Cecilia, thy servant, serves thee, O Lord, even as the bee that is never idle.

"I bless thee, O Father of my Lord Jesus Christ, for through thy Son the fire hath been quenched round about me.

"I asked of the Lord a respite of three days, that I might consecrate my house as a church.

"O Valerian, I have a secret to tell thee; I have for my lover an angel of God, who, with great jealousy, watches over my body.

"The glorious virgin ever bore the Gospel of Christ in her bosom, and neither by day nor night ceased from conversing with God in prayer."

And the anthem:

"While the instruments of music were playing, Cecilia sang unto the Lord, and said, Let my heart be undefiled, that I may never be confounded.

"And Valerianus found Cecilia praying in her chamber with an angel."

It will be remembered that Cecilia is one of the chosen saints *daily* commemorated in the canon of the mass.

"Nobis quoque peccatoribus famulis tuis, de multitudine miserationum tuarum sperantibus, partem aliquam et societatem donare digneris cum tuis sanctis Apostolis et Martyribus: cum Joanne, Stephano, Matthia, Barnaba, Ignatio, Alexandro, Marcellino, Petro, Felicitate, Perpetua, Agata, Lucia, Agnete, *Cæcilia*, Anastasia, et omnibus sanctis."

Just beyond St. Cecilia is the immense *Hospital of S. Michele*, founded by Cardinal Odescalchi, nephew of Innocent XI., in 1693, as a refuge for vagabond children, where they might be properly brought up and taught a trade. Innocent XII. (Pignatelli) added to this foundation a hospital for sick persons of both sexes, and each succeeding pope has increased the buildings and their endowment. The establishment is now divided into an asylum for old men and women, a school with ateliers for boys and girls, and a penitentiary (" Casa delle Donne cattive "). A large church was attached to the hospital by Leo XII. No old men are admitted who have not inhabited Rome for five years; if they are still able to work a small daily task is given to them. The old women, as long as they can work, are obliged to mend and wash the linen of the establishment. The boys, for the most part orphans, are received at the age of eleven. The girls receive a dowry of 300 francs if they marry, but double that sum if they consent to enter a convent. A printing press is attached to the hospital.

S. Michele occupies the site of the sacred grove of the goddess Furina (not of the Furies), where Caius Gracchus was killed, B.C. 123. Protected by his friends, he escaped from the Aventine, where he had first taken refuge, and crossed the Pons Sublicius. A single slave reached the grove of Furina with him, who having in vain sought for a horse to continue their flight, first slew his master and then himself. One Septimuleius then cut off the head of Gracchus, and—a proclamation having been issued that any one who brought the head of Caius Gracchus should receive its weight in gold—first filled it with lead, and then carried it on a spear to the consul Opimius, who paid him his blood-money.

At the end of this street is the *Porta Portese*, built by

Urban VIII., through which runs the road to Porto and Fiumicino.

Outside this gate was the site of the camp of Tarquin,—afterwards given by the senate to Mutius-Scævola, for his bravery in the camp of Lars Porsenna. The vineyards here have an interest to Roman Catholics as the scene of one of the miracles attributed to Sta. Francesca Romana.

"One fine sunny January day, Francesca and her companions had worked since dawn in the vineyards of the Porta Portese. They had worked hard for several hours, and then suddenly remembered that they had brought no provisions with them. They soon became faint and hungry, and, above all, very thirsty. Perna, the youngest of all the oblates, was particularly heated and tired, and asked permission of the Mother Superior to go to drink water at a fountain some way off on the public road.

"'Be patient, my child,' Francesca answered, and they went on with their work; but Francesca withdrawing aside, knelt down, and said, 'Lord Jesus, I have been thoughtless in forgetting to provide food for my sisters,—help us in our need.'

"Perna, who had kept near the Mother Superior, said to herself, with some impatience, 'It would be more to the purpose to take us home at once.' Then Francesca, turning to her, said, 'My child, you do not trust in God; look up and see.' And Perna saw a vine entwined around a tree, whose dead and leafless branches were loaded with grapes. In speechless astonishment the oblates assembled around the tree, for they had all seen its bare and withered branches. Twenty times at least they had passed before it, and the season for grapes was gone by. There were exactly as many bunches as persons present.'—*See Lady G. Fullerton's Life of Sta. F. Romana.*

From the back of S. Michele a cross street leads to the *Church of Sta. Maria dell' Orto*, designed by Giulio Romano, *c.* 1530, except the façade, which is by Martino Lunghi. The high altar is by Giacomo della Porta. The church contains an Annunciation by *Taddeo Zucchero*.

"Cette église appartient à plusieurs corporations; chacune a sa tombe devant sa propre chapelle, et sur le couvercle sont gravées ses armes particulières ; un coq sur la tombe des marchands de volaille, une pantoufle sur celle des savetiers, des artichauts sur celle des jardiniers, &c."
—*Robello.*

Close to this, at the end of the street which runs parallel with S. Michele, is the *Church of S. Francesco a Ripa*, the noviciate of the Franciscans—" Frati Minori." The convent contains the room (approached through the church) in which St. Francis lived, during his visits at Rome, with many relics of him. His stone pillow and his crucifix are shown, and a picture of him by G. de' Lettesoli. An altar in his chamber supports a reliquary in which 18,000 relics are displayed!

The church was rebuilt soon after the death of St. Francis by the knight Pandolfo d' Anquillara (his castle is in the Via Lungaretta), whose tomb is in the church, with his figure, in the dress of a Franciscan monk, which he assumed in the latter part of his life. It was again rebuilt by Cardinal Pallavicini, from designs of Matteo Rossi. Among its pictures are the Virgin and St. Anne by *Baciccio*, the Nativity by *Simon Vouet*, and a dead Christ by *Annibale Caracci*. On the left of the altar is the Altieri chapel, in which is a recumbent statue of the blessed Luigi Albertoni, by *Bernini*. In the third chapel on the right is a mummy, said to be that of the virgin martyr Sta. Semplicia. The convent garden has some beautiful palm-trees.

Following the Via Morticelli we regain the Via Lungaretta near S. Benedetto. This street, more than any other in Rome, retains remnants of mediæval architecture. On the right (opposite the opening to the west end of S. Chrisogono) is the entrance to the old *Castle of the Anguil-*

lara *Family*, of whom were Count Pandolfo d' Anguillara already mentioned, and Everso, his grandson, celebrated for his highway robberies between Rome and Viterbo in the fifteenth century; also Orso d' Anguillara, senator of Rome, who crowned Petrarch at the Capitol on Easter Day, 1341. "The family device, two crossed eels, surmounted by a helmet, and a wild boar holding a serpent in his mouth, is believed to refer to the story of the founder of their house, Malagrotta, a second St. George, who slew a terrible serpent, which had devastated the district round his abode, and received in recompense from the pope the gift of as much land as he could walk round in one day."*

The existing remains consist of an arch, called " L' Arco dell' Annunziata," and a brick tower, which is now in the possession of a Signor Forti, who exhibits here, during Epiphany, a remarkably pretty *Presepio*, in which the Holy Family and the Shepherds are seen backed by the real landscape. For those who witness this sight it will be interesting to turn to the origin of a Presepio.

"St. Francis asked [of Pope Honorius III. 1223], with his usual simplicity, to be allowed to celebrate Christmas with certain unusual ceremonies which had suggested themselves to him—ceremonies which he must have thought likely to seize upon the popular imagination and impress the unlearned folk. He would not do it on his own authority, we are told, lest he should be accused of levity. When he made this petition, he was bound for the village of Grecia, a little place not far from Assisi, where he was to remain during that sacred season. In this village, when the eve of the nativity approached, Francis instructed a certain grave and worthy man, called Giovanni, to prepare an ox and an ass, along with a manger and all the common fittings of a stable, for his use, in the church. When the solemn night arrived, Francis and his brethren arranged all these things into a visible representation of the occurrences of the night at Bethlehem. The manger was filled with hay,

* Hemans' Monuments in Rome.

the animals were led into their places; the scene was prepared as we see it now through all the churches of Southern Italy—a reproduction, so far as the people know how, in startling realistic detail of the surroundings of the first Christmas. . . . . We are told that Francis stood by this, his simple theatrical (for such, indeed, it was—no shame to him) representation, all the night long, sighing for joy, and filled with an unspeakable sweetness."—*Mrs. Oliphant, St. Francis.*

On the left, is the fine *Church of S. Chrisogono*, founded by Pope Sylvester, but rebuilt in 731, and again by Cardinal Scipio Borghese (who modernized so many of the old churches), in 1623. The tower is mediæval (rebuilt?), but spoilt by whitewash; the portico has four ancient granite columns. The interior is a basilica, the nave being separated from the aisles by twenty-two granite columns, and the tribune from the nave by two magnificent columns of porphyry. The baldacchino, of graceful proportions, rests on pillars of yellow alabaster. Over the tabernacle is a picture of the Virgin and Child by the *Cav. d'Arpino*. The mosaic in the tribune, probably only the fragment of a larger design, represents the Madonna and Child enthroned, between St. James the Great and St. Chrisogonus. The stalls are good specimens of modern wood-carving. Near the end of the right aisle is the modern tomb of Anna Maria Taigi, lately beatified and likely to be canonized, though readers of her life will find it difficult to imagine why,—the great point of her character being that she was a good wife to her husband, though he was "ruvido di maniere, e grossolano." Stephen Langton, Archbishop of Canterbury, was titular cardinal of this church.

S. Chrisogono, represented in the mosaic as a young knight, stood by Sta. Anastasia during her martyrdom, exhorting her to patient endurance. He was afterwards himself beheaded under Diocletian, and his body thrown into the sea.

In 1866 an *Excubitorium* of the viith cohort of Vigiles (a station of Roman firemen) was discovered near this church. Several chambers were tolerably perfect.

On the left, we pass the *Hospital of S. Gallicano*, founded by Benedict XIII. (Orsini), in 1725, as is told by the inscription over the entrance, for the "neglectis rejectisque ab omnibus." The interior contains two long halls opening into one another, the first containing 120 beds for men, the second 88 for women. Patients affected with maladies of the skin are received here to the number of 100. The principal treatment is by means of baths, which gives the negative, within these walls, to the Italian saying that "an ancient Roman took as many baths in a week as a modern Roman in all his life." The establishment is at present under the management of the Benfratelli ("Fate bene fratelli"). S. Gallicano, to whom the hospital is dedicated, was a Benfratello of the time of Constantine, who devoted his time and his fortune to the poor.

At the upper end of the Via Lungaretta is a piazza with a very handsome fountain, on one side of which is the *Church of Sta. Maria in Trastevere*, supposed to be the first church in Rome dedicated to the Virgin. It was founded by St. Calixtus in A.D. 224, on the site of the Taberna-Meritoria, an asylum for old soldiers; where, according to Don Cassius, a fountain of pure oil sprang up at the time of our Saviour's birth, and flowed away in one day to the Tiber, a story which gave the name of "Fons Olei" to the church in early times. It is said that wine-sellers and tavern-keepers (popinarii) disputed with the early Christian inhabitants for this site, upon which the latter had raised some kind of humble oratory, and that they carried their complaint before Alexander Severus, when the emperor awarded the site to the Christians, saying, " I prefer that it should belong to those who honour God, whatever be their form of worship."

"Ce souvenir augmente encore l'intérêt qui s'attache à l'église de Santa Maria in Trastevere. Les colonnes antiques de granit égyptien de cette basilique et les belles mosaïques qui la décorent me touchent moins que la tradition d'après laquelle elle fut élevée là où de pauvres chrétiens se rassemblaient dans un cabaret purifié par leur piété, pour y célébrer le culte qui devait un jour étaler ses magnificences sous le dôme resplendissant de Saint-Pierre."—*Ampère, Emp.* ii. 318.

The church was rebuilt in 340 by Julius I., and after a series of alterations was again almost entirely reconstructed in 1139 by Innocent II., as a thanksgiving offering for the submission of the anti-pope. Eugenius III. (1145—50) finished what was left uncompleted, but the new basilica was not consecrated till the time of Innocent III. (1198—1216). The tower, apse, tribune, and mosaics belong to the early restoration ; the rest is due to alterations made by Bernardino Rossellini for Nicholas V.

The west façade is covered with mosaics ; the upper part —representing the Saviour throned between angels—and the lower—of palms, the twelve sheep, and the mystic cities—are additions by Pius IX. in 1869. The central frieze was begun in the twelfth century under Eugenius III., and completed in the fourteenth by Pietro Cavallini. It represents the Virgin and Child enthroned in the midst, and ten female figures, generally described as the Ten Virgins,—but Hemans remarks :

"It is evident that such subject cannot have been in the artist's thoughts, as each stately figure advances towards the throne with the same devout aspect and graceful serenity, the same faith and confidence; the sole observable distinctions being that the two with unlit lamps are somewhat more matronly, their costumes simpler, than is the case with the rest; and that instead of being crowned, as are the others, these two wear veils. Explanation of such attributes may be found in the mystic meaning—the light being appropriate to virgin saints, the oil taken to signify benevolence or almsgiving; and we may conclude that those without light represent wives or widows, the others virgin saints, in this group. Two other diminutive figures (the scale indicating humility), who kneel at the feet of Mary, are Innocent II. and Eugenius III., both vested in the pontifical mantle, but bareheaded. Originally the Mother and Child *alone* had the nimbus around the head, as we see in a water-colour drawing from this original (now in the Barberini Library) dated 1640, made *before* a renovation by which that halo has been given alike to all the female figures. Another much faded mosaic, the Madonna and Child, under an arched canopy, high up on the campanile, may perhaps be as ancient as those on the façade."—*Mediæval Christian Art.*

The portico contains two frescoes of the Annunciation, one of them ascribed to *Cavallini*. Its walls are occupied by early Christian and pagan inscriptions. One, of the time of Trajan, is regarded with peculiar interest : " MARCUS COCCEUS LIB . AUG . AMBROSIUS PRÆPOSITUS, VESTIS ALBÆ, TRIUMPHALIS, FECIT, NICE CONJUGI SUÆ CUM QUA VIXIT ANNOS XXXXV., DIEBUS XI., SINE ULLA QUERELA." Between the doors is preserved a curious relic—the stone said to have been attached to St. Calixtus when he was thrown into the well. The interior is that of a basilica. The nave, paved with opus-alexandrinum, is divided from the aisles by twenty-two ancient granite columns, whose Ionic capitals are in several instances decorated with heads of pagan gods. They support a richly-decorated architrave. The roof, in the centre of which is a picture of the Assumption of the Virgin, is painted by *Domenichino*. On the right of the entrance is a ciborium by Mino da Fiesole. The high altar covers a confessional, beneath which are the remains of five early popes, removed from the catacombs. Among the tombs are those of the painters, Lanfranco and Ciro Ferri, and of Bastari, librarian of the Vatican, editor of the dictionary of the Della Cruscan Academy, and canon of this church, ob. 1775. Pope Innocent II. is buried here without a tomb.

In the left transept is a beautiful gothic tabernacle over an altar, erected by Cardinal d'Alençon, nephew of Charles de Valois, and brother of Philippe le Bel. On one side is the tomb of that cardinal (the fresco represents the martyrdom of his patron St. Philip, who is pourtrayed as crucified with his head downwards like St. Peter); on the other is the monument of Cardinal Stefaneschi, by *Paolo*, one of the first sculptors of the fourteenth century. Opening from hence is a chapel, which has a curious picture of the Council of Trent by *Taddeo Zucchero*. At the end of the right aisle are several more fine tombs of the sixteenth century, and the chapel of the Madonna di Strada Cupa, designed by *Domenichino*, from whose hand is the figure of a child scattering flowers, sketched out in one corner of the vaulting.

The upper part of the tribune is adorned with magnificent mosaics, (restored in modern times by Camuccini,) of the time of Innocent II.

"In the centre of the principal group on the vault is the Saviour, seated, with his Mother, crowned and robed like an Eastern Queen, beside him, both sharing the same gorgeous throne and footstool; while a hand extends from a fan-like glory with a jewelled crown held over his head; *she* (a singular detail here) giving benediction with the usual action; He embracing her with the left arm, and in the right hand holding a tablet that displays the words 'Veni, electa mea, et ponam in thronum meum;' to which corresponds the text, from the song of Solomon, on a tablet in her left hand, 'Læva ejus sub capite meo et dextera illius amplexabitur me.' Below the heavenly throne stand, each with name inscribed in gold letters, Innocent II., holding a model of this church; St. Laurence, in deacon's vestments, with the Gospels and the jewelled cross; the sainted popes, Calixtus I., Cornelius, and Julius I.; St. Peter (in classic white vestments), and Calepodius, a martyr of the third century, here introduced because his body, together with those of the other saints in the same group, was brought from the catacombs to this church.

"As to ecclesiastical costume, this work affords decisive evidence of its ancient splendour and varieties. We do not see the keys in the hands of St. Peter, but the large tonsure on his head; that ecclesiastical badge which he is said to have invented, and which is sometimes the sole peculiarity (besides the ever-recognisable type) given to this Apostle in art.

"Above the archivolt we see a cross between the Alpha and Omega, and the winged emblems of the Evangelists; laterally, Jeremiah and Isaiah, each with a prophetic text on a scroll; along a frieze below, twelve sheep advancing from the holy cities, Jerusalem and Bethlehem, towards the Divine Lamb, who stands on a mount whence issue the four rivers of Paradise—or, according to perhaps juster interpretation, the four streams of gospel truth. Palms and a phœnix are seen beside the two prophets; also a less common symbol—caged birds, that signify the righteous soul incarcerated in the body, or (with highest reference) the Saviour in his assumed humanity; such accessory reminding of the ancient usage, in some countries, of releasing birds at funerals, and of that still kept up amidst the magnificent canonization-rites, of offering various kinds of birds, in cages, at the papal throne.

"Remembering the date of the composition before us, about a century and a half before the time of Cimabue and Giotto, we may hail in it, if not an actual Renaissance, the dawn, at least, that heralds a brighter day for art, compared with the deep gloom previous."—*Hemans' Mediæval Christian Art.*

Below these are another series of mosaics representing six scenes in the life of the Virgin, the work of Pietro Cavallini, of the thirteenth century, when they were ordered by Bertoldo Stefaneschi, who is himself introduced in one of the subjects. In the centre of the tribune is an ancient marble episcopal throne, raised by a flight of steps.

In the *Sacristy* is a picture of the Virgin with S. Rocco and S. Sebastiano, by *Perugino*. Here are preserved some beautiful fragments of mosaics of birds, &c., from the catacombs.

Outside the right transept of Sta. Maria is a picturesque shrine, and there are many points about this ancient church which are interesting to the artist. The palace, which forms one side of the piazza at the west end of the church, formerly *Palazzo Moroni*, is now used as the summer residence of the Benedictine monks of S. Paolo, who are driven from their convent by the malaria during the hot months. During the revolutionary government of 1848—49, a number of priests suffered death here, which has led to the monastery being regarded as "the Carmes of Rome." The modern *Church of S. Calisto* contains the well in which he suffered martyrdom, A.D. 222. This well, now seen through a door near the altar, was then in the open air, and the pope was thrown into it from the window of a house in which he had been imprisoned and scourged, and where he had converted the soldier who was appointed to guard him. His festival is celebrated here with great splendour by the monks.

Opposite S. Calisto is the *Monastery of St. Anna*, in which were passed the last days of the beautiful and learned Vittoria Colonna. As her death approached she was removed to the neighbouring house of her kinsman Giuliano Cesarini, and there she expired (February, 1547) in the presence of her devoted friend, Michael Angelo, who always regretted that he had not in that solemn moment ventured to press his lips for the first and last time to her beautiful countenance. She was buried, by her own desire, in the convent chapel, without any monument.

Hence a lane leads to the *Church of S. Cosimato*, in an open space facing the hill of S. Pietro in Montorio (where stands of seats are placed during the Girandola). A courtyard is entered through a low arch supported by two ancient columns, having a high roof with rich terra-cotta mouldings, —beautiful in colour. The court contains an antique fountain, and is exceedingly picturesque. The church has carefully sculptured details of cornice and moulding; the door is a good specimen of mediæval wood-carving. The wall on the left of the altar is occupied by a most beautiful fresco of *Pinturicchio*, representing St. Francis and St. Clare standing on either side of the Virgin and Child. Opening from the end of the left aisle is a very interesting chapel, decorated with frescoes, and containing a most beautiful altar of the fifteenth century, in honour of the saints Severa and Fortunata, with statuettes of Faith, Justice, Charity, and Hope. Attached to the church is a very large convent of Poor Clares, which produced two saints, Theodora and Seraphina, in the fifteenth century.

Following the Via della Scala, on the south side of Sta. Maria in Trastevere, we reach the *Porta Settimiana*, built by Alexander VI. on the site of a gateway raised by Honorius, which marked the position of an arch of Septimius Severus. This is the entrance of the Via Lungara, containing the Corsini and Farnesina Palaces (see Chapter XX.). The gateway has forked battlements, but is much spoilt by recent plasterings. Near this is *Sta. Dorotea*, an ugly church, but important in church history from its connection with the foundation of the Order of the Theatins, which arose out of a revulsion from the sensuous age of Leo X.; and as containing the tomb of their founder, Don Gaëtano di Teatino, the friend of Paul IV.

"Dès le règne de Léon X., quelques symptômes d'une réaction

religieuse se manifestèrent dans les hautes classes de la société romaine. On vit un certain nombre d'hommes éminents s'affilier les uns aux autres, afin de trouver dans de saintes pratiques assez de force pour résister à l'atmosphère énervante qui les entourait. Ils prirent pour leur association le titre et les emblèmes de l'amour divin, et ils s'assemblèrent, à des jours déterminés, dans l'église de Sainte-Dorothée, près de la porte Settimiana. Parmi ces hommes de foi et d'avenir, on citait un archevêque, Caraffa ; un protonotaire apostolique, Gaëtan de Thiène ; un noble Vénitien aussi distingué par son caractère que par ses talents, Contarini ; et cinquante autres dont les noms rappellaient tons, ou une illustration ou une haute position sociale, tels que Lippomano, Sadolet, Ghiberti.

"Mais bientôt ces premiers essais de rupture avec la tendance générale des esprits enflammèrent le zèle de plusieurs des membres de la Congrégation de *l'Amour divin*. Caraffa surtout, dont l'âme ardente n'avait trouvé qu'anxiétés et fatigue dans les grandeurs, aspirait à une vie d'action qui lui permît de s'employer, de tous ses moyens, à la réforme du monde. Il trouva dans Gaëtan de Thiène des dispositions conformes à ce qu'il désirait. Gaëtan avait cependant un caractère très-différent du sien : doué d'une angélique douceur, craignant de se faire entendre, recherchant la méditation et la retraite, il eût voulu, lui aussi, réformer le monde, mais il n'eût pas voulu en être connu. Les qualités diverses de ces deux hommes rares se combinèrent heureusement dans l'exécution du projet qu'ils avaient conçu, c'était de former des ecclésiastiques voués, tout ensemble à la contemplation et à une vie austère, à la prédication et au soin des malades ; des ecclésiastiques qui donnassent partout au clergé l'exemple de l'accomplissement des devoirs de sa sainte mission."— *Gournerie, Rome Chrétienne*, ii. 157.

"When Dorothea, the maiden of Cæsarea, was condemned to death by Sapritius, she replied, 'Be it so, then I shall the sooner stand in the presence of Christ, my spouse, in whose garden are the fruits of paradise, and roses that never fade.' As she was being led to execution, the young Theophilus mocking said, 'O maiden, goest thou to join thy bridegroom ? send me then, I pray thee, of the fruits and flowers which grow in his garden.' And the maiden bowed her head and smiled, saying, 'Thy request is granted, O Theophilus,' whereat he laughed, and she went forward to death.

"And behold, at the place of execution, a beautiful child, with hair like the sunbeam, stood beside her, and in his hand was a basket containing three fresh roses and three apples. And she said, 'Take these to Theophilus, and tell him that Dorothea waits for him in the garden from whence they came.'

"And the child sought Theophilus, and gave him the flowers and the fruits, saying, 'Dorothea sends thee these,' and vanished. And the heart of Theophilus melted, and he ate of the fruit from heaven, and was converted and professed himself one of Christ's servants, so that he also was martyred, and was translated into the heavenly garden."—*Legend*.

This story is told in nearly all the pictures of Sta. Dorotea.

Hence we reach the *Ponte Sisto*, built 1473—75 by Sixtus IV. in the place of the Pons Janiculensis, (or, according to Ampère, the Pons Antoninus,) which Caracalla had erected to reach the garden in the Trastevere, formerly belonging to his brother Geta,—but which was known as the Pons Fractus after a flood had destroyed part of it in 792. The Acts of Eusebius describe the many Christian martyrdoms which took place from this bridge. S. Symphorosa under Hadrian, S. Sabas under Aurelian, S. Calepodius under Alexander, and S. Anthimius under Diocletian, were thrown into the Tiber from hence, with many others, whose bodies, usually drifting to the island then called Lycaonia, were recovered there by their faithful disciples.* An inscription upon the bridge begs the prayers of the passengers for its papal founder.

Beautiful views may be obtained from this bridge,—on the one side, of the island, of the temple of Vesta, and the Alban hills; on the other, of St. Peter's, rising behind the Farnesina Gardens, and the grand mass of the Farnese Palace, towering above the less important buildings.

"They had reached the bridge and stopped to look at the view, perhaps the most beautiful of all those seen from the Roman bridges.

* See the Acts of the Martyrs St. Hippolytus and St. Adrian, and the Acts of St. Calepodius, quoted by Canina, R. Aut. p. 584.

Looking towards the hills, the Tiber was spanned by Ponte Rotto, under which the old black mills were turning ceaselessly, almost level with the tawny water; the sunshine fell full on the ruins of the Palatine, about the base of which had gathered a crowd of modern buildings; a brick campanile, of the middle ages, rose high above them against the blue sky, which was seen through its open arches; beyond were the Latin Hills; on the other hand, St. Peter's stood pre-eminent in the distance; nearer, a stack of picturesque old houses were half hidden by orange-trees, where golden fruit clustered thickly; women leant from the windows, long lines of flapping clothes hung out to dry; below, the ferry-boat was crossing the river, impelled by the current. Modern and ancient Rome all mingled together—everywhere were thrilling names connected with all that was most glorious in the past. The moderns are richer than their ancestors, the past is theirs as well as the present."—*Mademoiselle Mori.*

Close to the further entrance of the bridge, opposite the Via Giulia, is the *Fountain of the Ponte Sisto*, built by Paul V. from a design of Fontana. The water, which falls in one body from a niche in the wall of a palace, is discharged a second time from the mouths of two monsters below.

CHAPTER XVIII.

THE TRE FONTANE AND S. PAOLO.

The Marmorata—Arco di S. Lazzaro—Protestant Cemetery—Pyramid of Caius Cestius—Monte-Testaccio—Porta S. Paolo—Chapel of the Farewell—The Tre Fontane (SS. Vincenzo ed Anastasio—Sta. Maria Scala Cœli—S. Paolo alle Tre Fontane)—Basilica and Monastery of S. Paolo.

BEYOND the Piazza Bocca della Verità, the *Via della Marmorata* is spanned by an arch which nearly marks the site of the *Porta Trigemina*, by which Marius fled to Ostia before Sylla in B.C. 88. Near this stood the statue erected by public subscription to Minucius, whose jealousy brought about the execution of the patriot Mælius, B.C. 440. Here also was the temple of Jupiter Inventor, whose dedication was attributed to the gratitude of Hercules for the restoration of his cattle, carried off by Cacus to his cave on the neighbouring Aventine.

It was at the Porta Trigemina that Camillus (B.C. 391), sent into exile to Ardea by the accusations of the plebs, stayed, and, stretching forth his hands to the Capitol, prayed to the gods who reigned there that if he was unjustly expelled, Rome might "one day have need of Camillus."

Passing the arch, the road skirts the wooded escarpment

of the Aventine, crowned by its three churches—Sta. Sabina, S. Alessio, and the Priorato.

"De ce côté, entre l'Aventin et le Tibre, hors de la porte Trigemina, étaient divers marchés, notamment le marché aux bois, le marché à la farine et au pain, les *horrea*, magasins de blés. Le voisinage de ces marchés, de ces magasins et de l'emporium, produisait un grand mouvement de transport et fournissait de l'occupation à beaucoup de portefaix. Plaute* fait allusion à ces porteurs de sacs de la porte Trigemina. On peut en voir encore tous les jours remplir le même office au même lieu."
— *Ampère, Hist. Rom.* iv. 75.

From the landing-place for modern Carrara marble, a new road on the right, planted with trees, leads along the river to the ancient *Marmorata*, discovered 1867—68, when many magnificent blocks of ancient marble were found buried in the mud of the Tiber. Recent excavations have laid bare the inclined planes by which the marbles were landed, and the projecting bars of stone with rings for mooring the marble vessels.

In the neighbouring vineyard are the massive ruins of the *Emporium*, or magazine for merchandise, founded by M. Æmilius Lepidus and L. Æmilius Paulus, the ædiles in B.C. 186. Upon the ancient walls of this time is engrafted a small and picturesque winepress of the fifteenth century. The neighbouring vineyard is much frequented by marble collectors.

A short distance beyond the turn to the Marmorata the main road is crossed by an ancient brick arch, called *Arco di S. Lazzaro*, or Arco della Salara, by the side of which is a hermitage.

About half a mile beyond this we reach the *Porta S.*

* Plautus, Capt. i. 1, 22.

Paolo, built by Belisarius on the site of the Ancient Porta Ostiensis.

It was here, just within the Ostian Gate, that the Emperor Claudius, returning from Ostia to take vengeance upon Messalina, was met by their two children, Octavia and Britannicus, accompanied by a vestal, who insisted upon the rights of her Order, and imperiously demanded that the empress should not be condemned undefended.

"Totila entra par la porte Asinaria et une autre fois par la porte Ostiensis, aujourd'hui porte Saint-Paul ; par la même porte, Genséric, que la mer apportait, et qui, en s'embarquant, avait dit à son pilote : ' Conduis-moi vers le rivage que menace la colère divine.' "—*Ampère, Emp.* ii. 325.

Close to this, is the famous *Pyramid of Caius Cestius*. It is built of brick, coated with marble, and is 125 feet high, and 100 feet wide at its square basement. In the midst is a small sepulchral chamber, painted with arabesques. Two inscriptions on the exterior show that the Caius Cestius buried here was a prætor, a tribune of the people, and one of the "Epulones" appointed to provide the sacrificial feasts of the gods. He died about 30 B.C., leaving Agrippa as his executor, and desiring by his will that his body might be buried, wrapped up in precious stuffs. Agrippa, however, applied to him the law which forbade luxurious burial, and spent the money, partly upon the pyramid and partly upon erecting two colossal statues in honour of the deceased, of which the pedestals have been found near the tomb. In the middle ages this was supposed to be the sepulchre of Remus.

"Cette pyramide, sauf les dimensions, est absolument semblable aux pyramides d'Égypte. Si l'on pouvait encore douter que celles-ci

PYRAMID OF CAIUS CESTIUS. 395

é aient des tombeaux, l'imitation des pyramides égyptiennes dans un tombeau romain serait un argument de plus pour prouver qu'elles avaient une destination funéraire. La chambre qu'on a trouvée dans le monument de Cestius était décorée de peintures dont quelques unes ne sont pas encore effacées. C'était la coutume des peuples anciens, notamment des Egyptiens et des Etrusques, de peindre l'intérieur des tombeaux, que l'on fermait ensuite soigneusement. Ces peintures, souvent très-considérables, n'étaient que pour le mort, et ne devaient jamais être vues par l'œil d'un vivant. Il en était certainement ainsi de celles qui décoraient la chambre sépulchrale de la pyramide de Cestius, car cette chambre n'avait aucune entrée. L'ouverture par laquelle on y pénètre aujourd'hui est moderne. On avait déposé le corps ou les cendres avant de terminer le monument, on acheva ensuite de la bâtir jusqu'au sommet."—*Ampère, Emp.* i. 347.

"St. Paul was led to execution beyond the city walls, upon the road to Ostia. As he issued forth from the gate, his eyes must have rested for a moment on that sepulchral pyramid which stood beside the road, and still stands unshattered, amid the wreck of so many centuries, upon the same spot. That spot was then only the burial-place of a single Roman ; it is now the burial-place of many Britons. The mausoleum of Caius Cestius rises conspicuously amongst humbler graves, and marks the site where Papal Rome suffers her Protestant sojourners to bury their dead. In England and in Germany, in Scandinavia and in America, there are hearts which turn to that lofty cenotaph as the sacred point of their whole horizon ; even as the English villager turns to the grey church tower, which overlooks the grave-stones of his kindred. Among the works of man, that pyramid is the only surviving witness of the martyrdom of St. Paul; and we may thus regard it with yet deeper interest, as a monument unconsciously erected by a pagan to the memory of a martyr. Nor let us think they who lie beneath its shadow are indeed resting (as degenerate Italians fancy) in unconsecrated ground. Rather let us say, that a spot where the disciples of Paul's faith now sleep in Christ, so near the soil once watered by his blood, is doubly hallowed ; and that their resting-place is most fitly identified with the last earthly journey, and the dying glance of their own patron saint, the apostle of the Gentiles."—*Conybeare and Howson.*

At the foot of the Pyramid is the *Old Protestant Cemetery*, a lovely spot, now closed. Here is the grave of Keats, with the inscription :

"This grave contains all that was mortal of a young English poet, who, on his death-bed, in the bitterness of his heart at the malicious power of his enemies, desired these words to be engraven on his tombstone: 'Here lies one whose name was writ in water.' February 24, 1821."

> "Go thou to Rome—at once the paradise,
> The grave, the city, and the wilderness;
> And where its wrecks like shattered mountains rise,
> And flowering weeds, and fragrant copses dress
> The bones of desolation's nakedness,
> Pass, till the spirit of the spot shall lead
> Thy footsteps to a slope of green access,
> Where, like an infant's smile, over the dead,
> A light of laughing flowers along the grass is spread,
>
> "And grey walls moulder round, on which dull Time
> Feeds, like slow fire upon a hoary brand;
> And one keen pyramid, with wedge sublime,
> Pavilioning the dust of him who planned
> This refuge for his memory, doth stand
> Like flame transformed to marble; and beneath
> A field is spread, on which a newer band
> Have pitched in Heaven's smile their camp of death,
> Welcoming him we lose with scarce extinguished breath."
>
> *Shelley's Adonais.*

Very near the grave of Keats is that of Augustus William Hare, the elder of the two brothers who wrote the "Guesses at Truth," ob. 1834.

"When I am inclined to be serious, I love to wander up and down before the tomb of Caius Cestius. The Protestant burial-ground is there, and most of the little monuments are erected to the young—young men of promise, cut off when on their travels full of enthusiasm, full of enjoyment; brides, in the bloom of their beauty, on their first journey; or children borne from home in search of health. This stone was placed by his fellow-travellers, young as himself, who will return to the house of his parents without him; that, by a husband or a father, now in his native country. His heart is buried in that grave.

"It is a quiet and sheltered nook, covered in the winter with violets; and the pyramid, that overshadows it, gives it a classic and singularly solemn air. You feel an interest there, a sympathy you were not prepared for. You are yourself in a foreign land ; and they are for the most part your countrymen. They call upon you in your mother tongue - in English—in words unknown to a native, known only to yourself : and the tomb of Cestius, that old majestic pile, has this also in common with them. It is itself a stranger among strangers. It has stood there till the language spoken round about it has changed ; and the shepherd, born at the foot, can read the inscription no longer."— *Rogers.*

The *New Burial Ground* was opened in 1825. It extends for some distance along the slope of the hill under the old Aurelian Wall, and is beautifully shaded by cypresses, and carpeted with violets. Amid the forest of tombs we may notice that which contains the heart of Shelley (his body having been burnt upon the shore at Lerici, where it was thrown up by the sea), inscribed :

"Percy Bysshe Shelley, Cor Cordium. Natus IV. Aug. MDCCXCII. Obiit VIII. Jul. MDCCCXXII.
'Nothing of him that doth fade,
But doth suffer a sea change
Into something rich and strange.'"

Another noticeable tomb is that of Gibson the sculptor, who died 1868.

From the fields in front of the cemetery (*Prati del Popolo Romano*) rises the *Monte Testaccio*, only 160 feet in height, but worth ascending for the sake of the splendid view it affords. The extraordinary formation of this hill, which is entirely composed of broken pieces of pottery, has long been an unexplained bewilderment.

"Le Monte-Testaccio est pour moi des nombreux problèmes qu'offrent les antiquités romaines le plus difficile à résoudre. On ne peut s'arrêter à discuter sérieusement la tradition d'après laquelle il aurait été formé avec les débris des vases contenant les tributs qu'apportaient à Rome les peuples soumis par elle. C'est là évidemment une légende du moyen âge née du souvenir de la grandeur romaine et imaginée pour exprimer la haute idée qu'on s'en faisait, comme on avait imaginé ces statues de provinces placées au Capitole, et dont chacune portait au cou une cloche qui sonnait tout-à-coup d'elle-même, quand une province se soulevait, comme on a prétendu que le lit du Tibre était pavé en airain par les tributs apportés aux empereurs romains. Il faut donc chercher une autre explication."—*Ampère, Emp.* ii. 386.

Just outside the Porta S. Paolo is (on the right) a vineyard which belonged to Sta. Francesca Romana (born 1384, canonized 1608 by Paul V.).

"Instead of entering into the pleasures to which her birth and riches entitled her, Sta. Francesca went every day, disguised in a coarse woollen garment, to her vineyard, and collected faggots, which she brought into the city on her head, and distributed to the poor. If the weight exceeded her womanly strength, she loaded therewith an ass, following after on foot in great humility."—*Mrs. Jameson's Monastic Orders.*

A straight road a mile and a half long leads from the gate to the basilica. Half way (on the left) is the humble chapel which commemorates the farewell of St. Peter and St. Paul on their way to martyrdom, inscribed :

"In this place SS. Peter and Paul separated on their way to martyrdom.
"And Paul said to Peter, 'Peace be with thee, Foundation of the Church, Shepherd of the flock of Christ.'
"And Peter said to Paul, 'Go in peace, Preacher of good tidings, and Guide of the salvation of the just.'" *

Passing the basilica, which looks outside like a very ugly railway station, let us visit the scene of the martyrdom, before entering the grand church which arose in consequence.

The road we now traverse is the scene of the legend of Plautilla.

* See the Epistle of St. Denis, the Areopagite, to Timothy.

"St. Paul was beheaded by the sword outside the Ostian gate, about two miles from Rome, at a place called the Aqua Salvias, now the 'Tre Fontane.' The legend of his death relates that a certain Roman matron named Plautilla, one of the converts of St. Peter, placed herself on the road by which St. Paul passed to his martyrdom, to behold him for the last time; and when she saw him she wept greatly, and besought his blessing. The apostle then, seeing her faith, turned to her, and begged that she would give him her veil to blind his eyes when he should be beheaded, promising to return it to her after his death. The attendants mocked at such a promise, but Plautilla, with a woman's faith and charity, taking off her veil, presented it to him. After his martyrdom, St. Paul appeared to her, and restored the veil stained with his blood.

"In the ancient representations of the martyrdom of St. Paul, the legend of Plautilla is seldom omitted. In the picture by Giotto in the sacristy of St. Peter's, Plautilla is seen on an eminence in the background, receiving the veil from the hands of St. Paul, who appears in the clouds above; the same representation, but little varied, is executed in bas-relief on the bronze doors of St. Peter's."—*Jameson's Sacred Art.*

The lane which leads to the Tre Fontane turns off to the left a little beyond S. Paolo.

"In all the melancholy vicinity of Rome, there is not a more melancholy spot than the Tre Fontane. A splendid monastery, rich with all the offerings of Christendom, once existed there: the ravages of that mysterious scourge of the Campagna, the malaria, have rendered it a desert; three ancient churches and some ruins still exist, and a few pale monks wander about the swampy dismal confines of the hollow in which they stand. In winter you approach them through a quagmire; in summer, you dare not breathe in their pestilential vicinity; and yet there is a sort of dead beauty about the place, something hallowed as well as sad, which seizes on the fancy."—*Jameson's Sacred Art.*

The convent was bestowed in 1867 by Pius IX. upon the French Trappists, and twelve brethren of the Order went to reside there. Entering the little enclosure, the first church on the right is *Sta. Maria Scala Cœli,* supposed to occupy the site of the cemetery of S. Zeno, in which the 12,000 Christians employed in building the Baths of Diocletian were buried. The present edifice was the work of Vignola and

Giacomo della Porta in 1582. The name is derived from the legend that here St. Bernard had a vision of a ladder which led to heaven, its foot resting on this church, and of angels on the ladder leading upwards the souls whom his prayers had redeemed from purgatory. The mosaics in the apse were the work of *F. Zucchero*, in the sixteenth century, and are perhaps the best of modern mosaics. They represent the saints Zeno, Bernard, Vincenzo, and Anastasio, adored by Pope Clement VIII. and Cardinal Aldobrandini, under whom the remodelling of the church took place.

The second church is the basilica of *SS. Vincenzo ed Anastasio*, founded by Honorius I. (625), and restored by Honorius III. (1221), when it was consecrated afresh. It is approached by an atrium with a penthouse roof, supported by low columns, and adorned with decaying frescoes, among which the figure of Honorius III. may be made out. The interior, which reeks with damp, is almost entirely of the twelfth century. The pillars are adorned with coarse frescoes of the apostles.

"S. Vincenzo alle Tre Fontane so far deviates from the usual basilican arrangement as almost to deserve the appellation of gothic. It has the same defect as all the rest—its pier arches being too low, for which there is no excuse here; but both internally and externally it shows a uniformity of design, and a desire to make every part ornamental, that produces a very pleasing effect, although the whole is merely of brick, and ornament is so sparingly applied as only just to prevent the building sinking to the class of mere utilitarian erections."—*Fergusson's Handbook of Architecture*, vol. ii.

The two saints whose relics are said to repose here were in no wise connected in their lifetime. S. Vincenzo, who suffered A.D. 304, was a native of Saragossa, cruelly tortured to death at Valencia, under Dacian, by being racked on a slow fire over a gridiron, "of which the bars were framed like scythes." His story is told with horrible detail by Prudentius. Anastasius, who died A.D. 628, was a native of Persia, who had become a Christian and taken the monastic habit at a convent near

Jerusalem. He was tortured and finally strangled, under Chosroes, at Barsaloe, in Assyria. He is not known to be represented anywhere in art, save in the almost obliterated frescoes in the atrium of this church.

The third church, *S. Paolo alle Tre Fontane*, was built by Giacomo della Porta for Cardinal Aldobrandini in 1590. It contains the pillars to which St. Paul is said to have been bound, the block of marble upon which he is supposed to have been beheaded, and the three fountains which sprang forth, wherever the severed head struck the earth during three bounds which it made after decapitation. In proof of this story, it is asserted that the water of the first of these fountains is still warm, of the second tepid, of the third cold. Three modern altars above the fountains are each decorated with a head of the apostle in bas-relief.

"A la première, l'âme vient à l'instant même de s'échapper du corps. Ce chef glorieux est plein de vie! A la seconde, les ombres de la mort couvrent déjà ses admirables traits; à la troisième, le sommeil éternel les a envahis, et, quoique demeurés tout rayonnants de beauté, ils disent, sans parler, que dans ce monde ces lèvres ne s'entr'ouvriront plus, et que ce regard d'aigle s'est voilé pour toujours."—*Une Chrétienne à Rome.**

The pavement is an ancient mosaic representing the Four Seasons, brought from the excavations at Ostia. The interior of this church has been beautified at the expense of a French nobleman, and the whole enclosure of the Tre Fontane has been improved by Mgr. de Merode.

* The accounts of the apostle's death vary greatly: "St. Prudentius says that both St. Peter and St. Paul suffered together in the same field, near a swampy ground, on the banks of the Tiber. Some say St. Peter suffered on the same day of the month, but a year before St. Paul. But Eusebius, St. Epiphanius, and most others, affirm that they suffered the same year, and on the 29th of June."—*Alban Butler.*

"As the martyr and his executioners passed on (from the Ostian gate), their way was crowded with a motley multitude of goers and comers between the metropolis and its harbour—merchants hastening to superintend the unlading of their cargoes—sailors eager to squander the profits of their last voyage in the dissipations of the capital—officials of the government charged with the administration of the provinces, or the command of the legions on the Euphrates or the Rhine—Chaldean astrologers—Phrygian eunuchs—dancing-girls from Syria, with their painted turbans—mendicant priests from Egypt, howling for Osiris—Greek adventurers, eager to coin their national cunning into Roman gold—representatives of the avarice and ambition, the fraud and lust, the superstition and intelligence, of the Imperial world. Through the dust and tumult of that busy throng, the small troop of soldiers threaded their way silently, under the bright sky of an Italian midsummer. They were marching, though they knew it not, in a procession more really triumphal than any they had ever followed, in the train of general or emperor, along the Sacred Way. Their prisoner, now at last and for ever delivered from captivity, rejoiced to follow his Lord 'without the gate.' The place of execution was not far distant, and there the sword of the headsman ended his long course of sufferings, and released that heroic soul from that feeble body. Weeping friends took up his corpse, and carried it for burial to those subterranean labyrinths, where, through many ages of oppression, the persecuted Church found refuge for the living, and sepulchres for the dead.

"Thus died the apostle, the prophet, and the martyr, bequeathing to the Church, in her government, and her discipline, the legacy of his apostolic labours; leaving his prophetic words to be her living oracles; pouring forth his blood to be the seed of a thousand martyrdoms. Thenceforth, among the glorious company of the apostles, among the goodly fellowship of the prophets, among the noble army of martyrs, his name has stood pre-eminent. And wheresoever the holy Church throughout all the world doth acknowledge God, there Paul of Tarsus is revered, as the great teacher of a universal redemption and a catholic religion—the herald of glad tidings to all mankind."—*Conybeare and Howson.*

Let us now return to the grand Basilica which arose to commemorate the martyrdom on this desolate site, and which is now itself standing alone on the edge of the Campagna, entirely deserted except by a few monks who linger in its monastery through the winter months, but take flight to St. Calisto before the pestilential malaria of the summer,—though in the middle ages it was not so, when S. Paolo was surrounded by the flourishing fortified suburb of Joanopolis (so called from its founder, John VIII.), whose possession was sharply contested in the wars between the popes and anti-popes.*

The first church on this site was built in the time of Constantine, on the site of the vineyard of the Roman matron Lucina, where she first gave a burial-place to the apostle. This primal oratory was enlarged into a basilica in 386 by the emperors Valentinian II. and Theodosius. The church was restored by Leo III. (795—816), and every succeeding century increased its beauty and magnificence. The sovereigns of England, before the Reformation, were protectors of this basilica—as those of France are of St. John Lateran, and of Spain of Sta. Maria Maggiore—and the emblem of the Order of the Garter may still be seen amongst its decorations.

"The very abandonment of this huge pile, standing in solitary grandeur on the banks of the Tiber, was one source of its value. While it had been kept in perfect repair, little or nothing had been done to modernize it, and alter its primitive form and ornaments, excepting the later addition of some modern chapels above the transept; it stood naked and almost rude, but unencumbered with the lumpish and tasteless plaster encasement of the old basilica in a modern Berninesque church, which had disfigured the Lateran cathedral under pretence of supporting it. It remained genuine, though bare, as S. Apollinare in Classe, at Ravenna, the city eminently of unspoiled basilicas. No chapels, altars, or mural monuments softened the severity of its outlines; only the series of papal portraits, running round the upper line of the walls, redeemed this sternness. But the unbroken files of columns

* It is under the shadow of S. Paolo that Cervantes ("Wanderings of Persiles and Sigismunda") places the scene of the death of Periander.

along each side, carried the eye forward to the great central object, the altar and its 'Confession ;' while the secondary row of pillars, running behind the principal ones, gave depth and shadow, mass and solidity, to back up the noble avenue along which one glanced."—*Cardinal Wiseman.*

On the 15th of July, 1823, this magnificent basilica was almost totally destroyed by fire, on the night which preceded the death of Pope Pius VII.

" Quelque-chose de mystérieux s'est lié dans l'esprit des Romains à l'incendie de St. Paul, et les gens à l'imagination de ce peuple parlent avec ce sombre plaisir qui tient à la mélancolie, ce sentiment si rare en Italie, et si fréquent en Allemagne. Dans le grand nef, sur le mur, au dessus des colonnes, se trouvait la longue suite des portraits de tous les papes, et le peuple de Rome voyait avec inquiétude qu'il n'y avait plus de place pour le portrait du successeur de Pie VII. De là les fruits de la suppression du saint-siége. Le vénérable pontife, qui était presqu' un martyre aux yeux de ses sujets, touchait à ses derniers moments lorsqu'arriva l'incendie de Saint-Paul. Il eut lieu dans la nuit du 15 au 16 Juillet. 1823 ; cette même nuit, le pape, presque mourant, fut agité par un songe, qui lui présentait sans cesse un grand malheur arrivé à l'église de Rome. Il s'éveilla en sursaut plusieurs fois, et demanda s'il n'était rien arrivé de nouveau. Le lendemain, pour ne pas aggraver son état, on lui cacha l'incendie, et il est mort après sans l'avoir jamais su."—*Stendhal,* ii. 94.

" Not a word was said to the dying Pius VII. of the destruction of St. Paul. For at St. Paul's he had lived as a quiet monk, engaged in study and in teaching, and he loved the place with the force of an early attachment. It would have added a mental pang to his bodily sufferings to learn the total destruction of that venerable sanctuary, in which he had drawn down by prayer the blessings of heaven on his youthful labour."—*Wiseman, Life of Pius VII.*

The restoration of the basilica was immediately begun, and a large contribution levied for the purpose from all Roman Catholic countries. In 1854 it was re-opened in its present form by Pius IX. Its exterior is below contempt: its interior, supported by eighty granite columns, is most striking and magnificent, but it is cold and uninteresting when compared with the ancient structure, "rich with inestimable remains of ancient art, and venerable from a thousand associations." *

If we approach the basilica by the door on the side of the monastery, we enter, first, a portico, containing a fine statue of Gregory XVI., and many fragments of the ancient mosaics, collected after the fire;—then, a series of small chapels which were not burnt, from the last of which ladies can look into the beautiful *cloister* of the twelfth century, which they are not permitted to enter, but which men may visit (through the sacristy), and inspect its various architectural remains, and a fine sarcophagus, adorned with reliefs of the story of Apollo and Marsyas.

The church is entered by the south end of the transept. Hence we look down upon the nave (306 feet long and 222 wide) with its four ranges of granite columns (quarried near the Lago Maggiore), surmounted by a mosaic series of portraits of the popes, each five feet in diameter,—most of them of course being imaginary. The grand triumphal arch which separates the transept from the nave is a relic of the old basilica, and was built by Galla-Placidia, sister of Honorius, in 440. On the side towards the nave it is adorned with a mosaic of Christ adored by the twenty-four elders, and the four beasts of the Revelation;—on that towards the transept by the figure of the Saviour, between St. Peter and St. Paul.

It bears two inscriptions, the first:

"Theodosius cœpit,—perfecit Honorius aulam
Doctoris mundi sacratam corpore Pauli."

The other, especially interesting as the only inscription

* Mrs. Jameson.

commemorating the great pope who defended Rome against Attila :

"Placidiæ pia mens operis decus homne (*sic*) paterni
Gaudet pontificis studio splendere Leonis."

The mosaics of the tribune, also preserved from the fire, were designed by *Cavallini*, a pupil of Giotto, in the thirteenth century, and were erected by Honorius III. They represent the Saviour with St. Peter and St. Andrew on the right, and St. Paul and St. Luke on the left,—and beneath these twelve apostles and two angels. The Holy Innocents (supposed to be buried in this church!) are represented lying at the feet of our Saviour.

"In the mosaics of the old basilica of S. Paolo the Holy Innocents were represented by a group of small figures holding palms, and placed immediately beneath the altar or throne, sustaining the gospel, the cross, and the instruments of the passion of our Lord. Over these figures was the inscription, H. I. S. INNOCENTES."—*Jameson's Sacred Art.*

Beneath the triumphal arch stands the ugly modern baldacchino, which encloses the ancient altar canopy, erected, as its inscription tells us, by Arnolphus and his pupil Petrus, in 1285. In front is the "Confession," where the Apostle of the Gentiles is believed to repose. The baldacchino is inscribed :

"Tu es vas electionis,
Sancte Paule Apostole,
Prædicator veritatis
In universo mundo."

It is supported by four pillars of Oriental alabaster, presented by Mehemet Ali, pasha of Egypt. The altars of malachite, at the ends of the transepts, were given by the Emperor Nicholas of Russia.

"Les schismatiques et les mussulmans eux-mêmes sont venus rendre hommage à ce souverain de la parole, qui entraînait les peuples au martyre et subjuguait toutes les nations."—*Une Chrétienne à Rome.*

In a building so entirely modern, there are naturally few individual objects of interest. Among those saved * from the old basilica, is the magnificent paschal candlestick, covered with sculpture in high-relief. The altar at the south end of the transept has an altar-piece representing the Assumption, by *Agricola*, and statues of St. Benedict, *Baini*, and Sta. Scholastica, by *Tenerani*. Of the two chapels between this and the tribune, the first has a statue of St. Benedict by *Tenerani;* the second, the Cappella del Coro, was saved from the fire, and is by *Carlo Maderno*.

The altar at the north end of the transept is dedicated to St. Paul, and has a picture of his conversion, by *Camuccini*. At the sides are statues of St. Gregory by *Laboureur* and of S. Romualdo by *Stocchi*. Of the chapels between this and the tribune, the first, dedicated to St. Stephen, has a statue of the saint, by *Rinaldi;* the second is dedicated to St. Bridget (Brigitta Brahe), and contains the famous crucifix of Pietro Cavallini, which is said to have spoken to her in 1370.

"Not far from the chancel is a beautiful chapel, dedicated to St. Bridget, and ornamented with her statue in marble. During her residence in Rome, she frequently came to pray in this church; and here is preserved, as a holy relic, the cross from which, during her ecstatic devotion, she seemed to hear a voice proceeding."—*Frederika Bremer.*

The upper walls of the nave are decorated with frescoes by *Galiardi, Podesti*, and other modern artists.

* Among the most interesting of the objects lost in the fire were the bronze gates ordered by Hildebrand (afterwards Gregory VII.) when legate at Constantinople, for Pantaleone Castelli, in 1070, and adorned with fifty-four scriptural compositions, wrought in silver thread.

The two great festivals of St. Paul are solemnly observed in this basilica upon January 25 and June 30, and that of the Holy Innocents upon December 28.

Very near S. Paolo, the main branch of the little river Almo, the "cursuque brevissimus Almo" of Ovid, falls into the Tiber. This is the spot where the priests of Cybele used to wash her statue and the sacred vessels of her temple, and to raise their loud annual lamentation for the death of her lover, the shepherd Atys:

> "Est locus, in Tiberim quo lubricus influit Almo,
> Et nomen magno perdit ab amne minor,
> Illic purpurea canus cum veste sacerdos,
> Almonis dominam sacraque lavit aquis."
> *Ovid, Fast.* iv. 337.

> "Phrygiæque matris Almo quà levat ferrum."
> *Martial, Ep.* iii. 472.

"Un vieux prêtre de Cybèle, vêtu de pourpre, y lavait chaque année la pierre sacrée de Pessinunte, tandis que d'autres prêtres poussaient des hurlements, frappaient sur le tambour de basque qu'on place aux mains de Cybèle, soufflaient avec fureur dans les flûtes phrygiennes, et que l'on se donnait la discipline,—ni plus ni moins qu'on le fait encore dans l'église des *Caravite*,—avec des fouets garnis de petits cailloux ou d'osselets."—*Ampère, Hist. Rom.* iii. 145.

The Campagna on this side of Rome is perhaps more stricken by malaria than any other part, and is in consequence more utterly deserted. That this terrible scourge has followed upon the destruction of the villas and gardens which once filled the suburbs of Rome, and that it did not always exist here, is evident from the account of Pliny, who says:

"Such is the happy and beautiful amenity of the Campagna that it seems to be the work of a rejoicing nature. For truly so it appears in the vital and perennial salubrity of its atmosphere (*vitalis ac perennis salubritatis cæli temperies*), in its fertile plains, sunny hills, healthy woods, thick groves, rich varieties of trees, breezy mountains, fertility in fruits, vines, and olives, its noble flocks of sheep, abundant herds of cattle, numerous lakes, and wealth of rivers and streams pouring in upon its many seaports, in whose lap the commerce of the world lies, and which run largely into the sea as it were to help mortals."

Under the emperors, the town of Ostia (founded by Ancus Martius) reached such a degree of prosperity, that its suburbs are described as joining those of Rome, so that one magnificent street almost united the two. There is now, beyond S. Paolo, a road through a desert, only one human habitation breaking the utter solitude.

CHAPTER XIX.

THE VILLAS BORGHESE, MADAMA, AND MELLINI.

Protestant Churches—Villa Borghese—Raphael's Villa—Casino and Villa of Papa Giulio—(Claude's Villa—Arco-Oscuro—Acqua-Acetosa)—Chapel of St. Andrew—Ponte-Molle (Castle of Crescenza—Prima Porta—The Crimera—The Allia)—(The Via Cassia)—Villa Madama—Monte Mario—Villa Mellini—Porta Angelica.

IMMEDIATELY outside the Porta del Popolo, on the left, are the English and American churches.

"As to the position selected for these buildings, it is to be observed that, although restricted by the regulations of the Roman Catholic hierarchy to a locality outside the walls, the greatest possible attention has been paid to the convenience of the English, the great majority of whose dwelling-houses are in this immediate quarter. The English church in Rome, therefore, though nominally outside the walls, is really, as regards centrality, in the very heart of the city. The greatest possible facilities are afforded by the authorities to our countrymen in all matters relating to the establishment; and though the general behaviour of the Roman inhabitants is such as to render the precaution almost unnecessary, the protection of the police and military is invariably afforded during the hours of divine service. . . . . Whatever be the disagreements on points of religious faith between Protestant and Catholic, there is at least one point of feeling in common between both in this respect; for the streets are tranquil, the shops are shut, the demeanour of the people is decent and orderly, and, notwithstanding the distance from England, Sunday feels more like a Sunday at Rome than in any other town in Europe."—*Sir G. Head's* "*Tour in Rome.*"

The papal government of Rome had more tolerance for a religion which was not its own than that of the early emperors. Augustus refused to allow the performance of Egyptian rites within a mile of the city walls.

On the right of the Gate is the handsome entrance of the beautiful *Villa Borghese*, most liberally thrown open to the public on every day except Monday, when the Villa Doria is open.

"The entrance to the Villa Borghese is just outside the Porta del Popolo. Passing beneath that not very impressive specimen of Michael Angelo's architecture, a minute's walk will transport the visitor from the small uneasy lava stones of the Roman pavement, into broad, gravelled carriage drives, whence a little further stroll brings him to the soft turf of a beautiful seclusion. A seclusion, but seldom a solitude; for priest, noble, and populace, stranger and native, all who breathe the Roman air, find free admission, and come hither to taste the languid enjoyment of the day-dream which they call life.

"The scenery is such as arrays itself to the imagination when we read the beautiful old myths, and fancy a brighter sky, a softer turf, a more picturesque arrangement of venerable trees, than we find in the rude and untrained landscapes of the western world. The ilex-trees, so ancient and time-honoured are they, seem to have lived for ages undisturbed, and to feel no dread of profanation by the axe any more than overthrow by the thunder-stroke. It has already passed out of their dreamy old memories that only a few years ago they were grievously imperilled by the Gauls' last assault upon the walls of Rome. As if confident in the long peace of their lifetime, they assume attitudes of evident repose. They lean over the green turf in ponderous grace, throwing abroad their great branches without danger of interfering with other trees, though other majestic trees grow near enough for dignified society, but too distant for constraint. Never was there a more venerable quietude than that which sleeps among their sheltering boughs; never a sweeter sunshine than that which gladdens the gentle bloom which these leafy patriarchs strive to diffuse over the swelling and subsiding lawns.

"In other portions of the grounds the stone pines lift their dense clumps of branches upon a slender length of stem, so high that they look like green islands in the air, flinging down a shadow upon the turf so far off that you scarcely know which tree has made it.

"Again, there are avenues of cypress, resembling dark flames of huge funeral candles, which spread dusk and twilight round about them instead of cheerful radiance. The more open spots are all a-bloom, early in the season, with anemones of wondrous size, both white and rose-coloured, and violets that betray themselves by their rich fragrance, even if their blue eyes fail to meet your own. Daisies, too, are abundant, but larger than the modest little English flower, and therefore of small account.

"These wooded and flowery lawns are more beautiful than the finest English park scenery, more touching, more impressive, through the neglect that leaves nature so much to her own ways and methods. Since man seldom interferes with her, she sets to work in her quiet way and makes herself at home. There is enough of human care, it is true, bestowed long ago, and still bestowed, to prevent wildness from growing into deformity; and the result is an ideal landscape, a woodland scene that seems to have been projected out of the poet's mind. If the ancient Faun were other than a mere creation of old poetry, and could reappear anywhere, it must be in such a scene as this.

"In the openings of the wood there are fountains plashing into marble basons, the depths of which are shaggy with water-weeds; or they tumble like natural cascades from rock to rock, sending their murmur afar, to make the quiet and silence more appreciable. Scattered here and there with careless artifice, stand old altars, bearing Roman inscriptions. Statues, grey with the long corrosion of even that soft atmosphere, half hide and half reveal themselves, high on pedestals, or perhaps fallen and broken on the turf. Terminal figures, columns of marble or granite porticoes and arches, are seen in the vistas of the wood-paths, either veritable relics of antiquity, or with so exquisite a touch of artful ruin on them that they are better than if really antique. At all events, grass grows on the tops of the shattered pillars, and weeds and flowers root themselves in the chinks of the massive arches and fronts of temples, as if this were the thousandth summer since their winged seeds alighted there.

"What a strange idea—what a needless labour—to construct artificial ruins in Rome, the native soil of ruin! But even these sportive imitations, wrought by man in emulation of what time has done to temples and palaces, are perhaps centuries old, and, beginning as illusions, have grown to be venerable in sober earnest. The result of all is a scene, such as is to be found nowhere save in these princely villa-residences in the neighbourhood of Rome; a scene that must have required generations and ages, during which growth, decay, and man's intelligence wrought kindly together, to render it so gently wild as we behold it now.

"The final charm is bestowed by the malaria. There is a piercing, thrilling, delicious kind of regret in the idea of so much beauty being thrown away, or only enjoyable at its half-development, in winter and early spring, and never to be dwelt amongst, as the home scenery of any human being. For if you come hither in summer, and stray through these glades in the golden sunset, fever walks arm-in-arm with you, and death awaits you at the end of the dim vista. Thus the scene is like Eden in its loveliness; like Eden, too, in the fatal spell that removes it beyond the scope of man's actual possessions."—*Transformation.*

"Oswald et Corinne terminèrent leur voyage de Rome par la Villa-Borghèse, celui de tous les jardins et de tous les palais romains où les splendeurs de la nature et des arts sont rassemblées avec le plus de goût et d'éclat. On y voit des arbres de toutes les espèces et des eaux magnifiques. Une réunion incroyable de statues, de vases, de sarcophages antiques, se mêlent avec la fraîcheur de la jeune nature du sud. La mythologie des anciens y semble ranimée. Les naïades sont placées sur le bord des ondes, les nymphes dans les bois dignes d'elles, les tombeaux sous les ombrages élyséens; la statue d'Esculape est au milieu d'une île; celle de Vénus semble sortir des ondes; Ovide et Virgile pourraient se promener dans ce beau lieu; et se croire encore au siècle d'Auguste. Les chefs-d'œuvre de sculpture que renferme le palais, lui donnent une magnificence à jamais nouvelle. On aperçoit de loin à travers les arbres, la ville de Rome et Saint-Pierre, et la campagne, et les longues arcades, débris des aqueducs qui transportaient les sources des montagnes dans l'ancienne Rome. Tout est là pour la pensée, pour l'imagination, pour la rêverie.

"Les sensations les plus pures se confondent avec les plaisirs de l'âme, et donnent l'idée d'un bonheur parfait; mais quand on demande, pourquoi ce séjour ravissant n'est-il pas habité? l'on vous répond que le mauvais air (*la cattiva aria*) ne permet pas d'y vivre pendant l'été."— *Madame de Staël.*

The *Casino*, at the further end of the villa, built by Cardinal Scipio Borghese, the favourite nephew of Paul V., contains a collection of sculpture. The first room entered is a great hall, with a ceiling painted by *Mario Rossi*, and a floor paved with an ancient mosaic discovered at the Torre Nuova (one of the principal Borghese farms) in 1835.

"Cette mosaïque fort curieuse nous offre et les combats des gladiateurs entre eux et leurs luttes avec les animaux féroces. Cette mosaïque est d'un dessin aussi barbare que les scènes représentées ; tout est en harmonie, le sujet et le tableau. Le sentiment de répulsion qu'inspire la cruauté romaine n'en est que plus complet ; celle-ci n'est point adoucie par l'art et paraît dans toute sa laideur.

"On voit les gladiateurs poursuivre, s'attaquer, se massacrer, couverts d'armures qui ressemblent à celle des chevaliers : vous diriez une odieuse parodie du moyen âge. Dans le corps de l'un des combattants un glaive est enfoncé. Des cadavres sont gisant parmi les flaques de sang ; à côté d'eux est le Θ fatal, initiale du mot grec Θάνατος—à laquelle leur juge impitoyable, le peuple, les a condamnés ; du grec partout. Le maître excite ses élèves on leur montrant le fouet et la palme ; les vainqueurs élèvent leurs épées, et sans doute la foule applaudit. Ils ont un air de triomphe. Ce sont des acteurs renommés. Auprès de chacun son nom est écrit ; ces noms barbares ou étranges : l'un s'appelle Buccibus, un autre Cupidor, un autre Licentiosus, avis effronté aux dames romaines."—*Ampère*, iv. 31.

The collection in this villa contains no exceedingly important statues. In the vestibule are some reliefs from the arch of Claudius in the Corso, destroyed in 1527. Leaving the great hall to the left we may notice :

1*st Room.*—
IN THE CENTRE:
Juno Pronuba, from Monte Calvi.

2*nd Room.*—
IN THE CENTRE:
A Fighting Amazon, on horseback.

3*rd Room.*—
4. Daphne changed into a Laurel.
13. Anacreon, seated.

"La statue d'Anacréon est très-remarquable, elle ressemble à la figure du poëte sur une médaille de Téos. Le style est simple et grandiose, l'expression énergique plutôt que gracieuse, la draperie est rude, la statue respire l'enthousiasme ; ce n'est pas le faux Anacréon que nous connaissons et dont les poésies sont postérieures au moins en grande partie à la date du véritable ; c'est le vieil et primitif Anacréon ; cet Anacréon-là ne vit plus que dans cet énergique portrait, seule image de son inspiration véritable, dont les produits authentiques ont presque entièrement disparu."—*Ampère, Hist. Rom.* iii. 567.

4th Room.—
> A handsome gallery with paintings by *Marchetti* and *De Angelis*, adorned with porphyry busts of the twelve Cæsars.
> 32. Bronze statue of a boy.

6th Room.—
> IN THE CENTRE:
> A Greek poet, probably Alcæus.
> 7. The Hermaphrodite ; found near Sta. Maria Vittoria.

7th Room.—
> IN THE CENTRE:
> Boy on a Dolphin.

" D'autres statues peuvent dériver de la grande composition maritime de Scopas. Tel est la Palémon, assis sur un dauphin, de la villa Borghese, d'après lequel a été évidemment conçu le Jonas de l'église de Sainte-Marie du Peuple, qu'on attribue à Raphaël."—*Ampère, Hist. Rom.* iii. 284.

8th Room.—
> 1. Dancing Satyr.

The *Upper Story*, reached by a winding staircase from the Galleria, contains :

1st Room.—Three fine works by *Bernini*.
> David with the sling : executed in his 18th year.
> Apollo and Daphne.
> Æneas carrying off Anchises : executed when the sculptor was only 15 years old.

2nd Room.—
> Filled with a collection of portraits, for the most part unknown. Worthy of attention are the portraits of Paul V. by *Caravaggio*, and of his father Marc-Antonio Borghese, attributed to *Guido ;* also

the busts of Paul V. and of Cardinal Scipio Borghese, who built the villa, by *Bernini*.

5th Room.—

Statue of Princess Pauline Borghese, sister of Napoleon I., by *Canova*, as Venus-Victrix.

"Canova esteemed his statue of the Princess Borghese as one of his best works. No one else could have an opportunity of judging of it, for the prince, who certainly was not jealous of his wife's person, was so jealous of her statue, that he kept it locked up in a room in the Borghese Palace, of which he kept the key, and not a human being, not even Canova himself, could get access to it."—*Eaton's Rome*.

Canova took Chantrey to see this statue by night, wishing, as was his wont, to show it by the light of a single taper. Chantrey, wishing to do honour to the artist, insisted upon holding the taper for the best light himself, which gave rise to Moore's lines:

"When he, thy peer in art and fame,
Hung o'er the marble with delight;
And while his ling'ring hand would steal
O'er every grace the taper's rays,
Gave thee, with all the generous zeal
Such master-spirits only feel,
The best of fame—a rival's praise!"

In the upper part of the grounds, not far from the walls of Rome, stood the Villa Olgiati, once the *Villa of Raphael*. It contained three rooms ornamented with frescoes from the hand of the great master. The best of these are now preserved in a room at the end of the gallery in the Borghese Palace. The villa was destroyed during the siege of Rome in 1849, when many of the fine old trees were cut down on this side of the grounds.

"The Casino of Raphael was unfurnished, except with casks of wine, and uninhabited, except by a *contadina*. The chamber which was the bedroom of Raphael was entirely adorned with the work of his own hands. It was a small pleasant apartment, looking out on a little green lawn, fenced in with trees irregularly planted. The walls were covered with arabesques, in various whimsical and beautiful designs—such as the sports of children; Loves balancing themselves on poles, or mounted on horseback, full of glee and mirth; Fauns and Satyrs; Mercury and Minerva; flowers and curling tendrils, and every beautiful composition that could suggest itself to a classic imagination in its most sportive mood. The cornice was supported by painted Caryatides. The coved roof was adorned with four medallions, containing portraits of his mistress, the Fornarina—it seemed as if he took pleasure in multiplying that beloved object, so that wherever his eyes turned her image might meet them. There were three other paintings, one representing a Terminus with a target before it, and a troop of men shooting at it with bows and arrows which they had stolen from unsuspecting Cupid, lying asleep on the ground. The second represented a figure, apparently a god, seated at the foot of a couch, with an altar before him, in a temple or rotunda, and from the gardens which appeared in perspective through its open intercolumniations, were seen advancing a troop of gay young nymphs, bearing vases full of roses upon their heads.* .... The last and best of these paintings represented the nuptials of Alexander the Great and Roxana."—*Eaton's Rome.*

Just outside the Porta del Popolo, a small gate on the left of the Villa Borghese leads to the *Villa Esmeade*,—the property of an Englishman,—of considerable extent, and possessing beautiful views of Rome and the Sabine mountains from its heights, which are adorned with a few ancient statues and vases.

Unpleasantly situated near the gate of the Villa Borghese is the Pig-market. Fortunately the manner of pig-killing at Rome is not so noisy as that in northern countries. The throats of the animals are not cut, but they are pierced under the left shoulder with a long pointed bodkin, which kills them almost instantly—no blood flowing. In a very few minutes a whole pen-full of pigs can be stilettoed in this manner—indeed, for any one interested in farming matters, the slaughter of the Roman pigs is a sight worth seeing.

We now enter upon the ugly dusty road which leads in a straight line to the Milvian Bridge. By this road the last

* This picture is now called the Nuptials of Vertumnus and Pomona.

triumphal procession entered Rome—that of the Emperor Honorius and Stilicho (described by the poet Claudian) in A.D. 403—a whole century having then elapsed since the Romans had beheld their last triumph—that of Diocletian.

Under the line of hills (Monte Parioli) on the right of the road are the *Catacombs of St. Valentine*. On the other side, the same hills are undermined by the *Catacombs of SS. Gianutus and Basilla*.

Half a mile from the gate, rises conspicuously on the right of the road the *Casino of Papa Giulio*, with picturesque overhanging cornices and sculptured fountain. The courtyard has a quaint cloister. This is the "Villino," and, far behind, but formerly connected with it by a long corridor, is the *Villa of Papa Giulio*, containing several rooms with very richly decorated ceilings, painted by *Taddeo Zucchero*. Michael Angelo was consulted by the pope as to the building of this villa, and Vasari made drawings for it, but "the actual architect was Vignola, a modest genius, who had to suffer severely, together with all his fellow-workmen, from the tracasseries of the pope's favourite, the bishop Aliotti, whom the less-enduring Michael Angelo was wont to nickname Monsignor Tante Cose."

" The villa of Papa Giulio is still visited by the stranger. Restored to the presence of those times, he ascends the spacious steps to the gallery, whence he overlooks the whole extent of Rome, from Monte Mario, with all the windings of the Tiber. The building of this palace, the laying out of its gardens, were the daily occupation of Pope Julius III. The place was designed by himself, but was never completed ; every day brought with it some new suggestion or caprice, which the architects must at once set themselves to realize. This pontiff desired to forward the interests of his family ; but he was not inclined to involve himself in dangerous perplexities on their account. The pleasant blameless life of his villa was that which was best suited to him. He gave entertainments, which he enlivened with proverbial and other modes of expression, that sometimes mingled blushes with the smiles of his guests. In the important affairs of the Church and State, he took no other share than was absolutely inevitable. This Pope Julius died March 23, 1555."—*Ranke's Hist. of the Popes.*

"C'est uniquement comme protecteur des arts et comme prince magnifique que nous pouvons envisager Jules III. Sa mauvaise santé lui faisait rechercher le repos et les douceurs d'une vie grande et libre. Aussi avait-il fait édifier avec une sorte de tendresse paternelle cette belle *villa*, qui est célèbre, dans l'histoire de l'art, sous le nom de Vigne de pape Jules. Michel-Ange, Vasari, Vignole en avaient dessiné les profils ; les nymphées et les fontaines étaient d'Ammanati ; les peintures de Taddeo Zuccari. Du haut d'une galerie élégante on découvrait les sept collines, et d'ombreuses allées, tracées par Jules III., égaraient les pas du vieillard dans ce dédale de tertres et de vallées qui sépare le pont où périt Maxence de la ville éternelle."—*Gournerie, Rome Chrétienne,* ii. 172.

Pope Julius used to come hither, with all his court, from the Vatican by water. The richly-decorated barge, filled with venerable ecclesiastics, gliding between the osier-fringed banks of the yellow Tiber, with its distant line of churches and palaces, would make a fine subject for a picture.

Nearly opposite the Casino Papa Giulio, on the further bank of the Tiber, is the picturesque classic *Villa of Claude Lorraine*, whither he was wont to retire during the summer months, residing in the winter in the Tempietto at the head of the Trinità steps. This villa is best seen from the walk by the river-side, which is reached by turning at once to the left on coming out of the Porta del Popolo. Hence it makes a good foreground to the view of the city and distant heights of the Janiculan.

"This road is called 'Poussin's Walk,' because the great painter used to go along it from Rome to his villa near Ponte Molle. One sees here an horizon such as one often finds in Poussin's pictures."—*Frederika Bremer.*

Close to the Villa Papa Giulio is the tunnel called *Arco Oscuro*, passing which, a steep lane with a beautiful view towards St. Peter's, ascends between the hillsides of the Monte Parione, and descends on the other side (following the turn to the right) to the Tiber bank, about two miles from Rome, where is situated the *Acqua Acetosa*, a refreshing mineral spring like seltzer water, enclosed in a fountain erected by Bernini for Alexander VII. There is a lovely view from hence across the Campagna in the direction of Fidenæ (Castel Giubeleo) and the Tor di Quinto.

"A green hill, one of those bare table-lands so common in the Campagna, rises on the right. Ascend it to where a broad furrow in the slope seems to mark the site of an ancient road. You are on a plateau, almost quadrangular in form, rising steeply to the height of nearly two hundred feet above the Tiber, and isolated, save at one angle, where it is united to other high ground by a narrow isthmus. Not a tree—not a shrub on its turf-grown surface—not a house—not a ruin—not one stone upon another, to tell you that the site had been inhabited. Yet here once stood Antemnæ, the city of many towers,[*] one of the most ancient of Italy ![†] Not a trace remains above ground. Even the broken pottery, that infallible indicator of bygone civilisation, which marks the site and determines the limits of habitation on many a now desolate spot of classic ground, is here so overgrown with herbage that the eye of an antiquary would alone detect it. It is a site strong by nature, and well adapted for a city, as cities then were; for it is scarcely larger than the Palatine Hill, which, though at first it embraced the whole of Rome, was afterwards too small for a single palace. It has a peculiar interest as one of the three cities of Sabina,[‡] whose daughters, ravished by the followers of Romulus, became the mothers of the Roman race. Antemnæ was the nearest city to Rome—only three miles distant—and therefore must have suffered most from the inhospitable violence of the Romans."—*Dennis' Cities of Etruria*, ch. iii.

[*] Turrigeræ Antemnæ.—*Virg. Æn.* vii. 631.
[†] ——Antemnæque prisco
    Crustumio prior.
[‡] The other two were Cæcina and Crustumium.

There is a walk—rather dangerous for carriages—by the river, from hence, to the Ponte Molle. Here Miss Bathurst was drowned by being thrown from her horse into the Tiber.

The river bank presents a series of picturesque views, though the yellow Tiber in no way reminds us of Virgil's description :

"Cæruleus Tybris cœlo gratissimus amnis."
Æn. viii. 64.

Continuing to follow the main road, on the left is the round *Church of St. Andrew*, with a Doric portico, built by Vignola, in 1527, to commemorate the deliverance of Clement VII. from the Germans.

Further, on the right, is another *Chapel in honour of St. Andrew's Head*.

"One of the most curious instances of relique worship occurred here in the reign of Æneas Sylvius, Pope Pius II. The head of St. Andrew was brought in stately procession from the fortress of Narni, whither, as the Turks invaded the Morea, it had been brought for safety from Patras. It was intended that the most glorious heads of St. Peter and St. Paul should go forth to meet that of their brother apostle. But the mass of gold which enshrined, the cumbrous iron which protected these reliques, was too heavy to be moved ; so, without them, the pope, the cardinals, the whole population of Rome, thronged forth to the meadows near the Milvian Bridge. The pope made an eloquent address to the head, a hymn was sung entreating the saint's aid in the discomfiture of the Turks. It rested that day on the altar of Santa Maria del Popolo, and was then conveyed through the city, decorated with all splendour, to St. Peter's. Cardinal Bessarion preached a sermon, and the head was deposited with those of his brother apostles under the high-altar."—*Milman's Latin Christianity.*

A mile and a half from the gate, the Tiber is crossed by the *Ponte Molle*, built by Pius VII. in 1815, on the site and foundations of the Pons Milvius, which was erected B.C. 109 by the Censor M. Æmilius Scaurus. It was here that, on the night of December 3, B.C. 63, Cicero captured the emissaries of the Allobrogi, who were engaged in the conspiracy of Catiline. Hence, on October 27, A.D. 312, Maxentius was thrown into the river and drowned after his defeat by Constantine at the Saxa Rubra. It was on this occasion that the seven-branched candlestick of Jerusalem was dropped into the river, where it has probably ever since been embedded. The statues of Our Saviour and John the Baptist, at the further entrance of the bridge, are by *Mochi*.

Here are a number of taverns and *Trattorie*, much frequented by the lower ranks of the Roman people, and for which especial open omnibuses run from the Porta del Popolo. Similar places of public amusement seem to have existed here from imperial times. Ovid describes the people coming out hither in troops by the Via Flaminia to celebrate the fête of Anna Perenna, an old woman who supplied the plebs with cakes during the retreat to the Mons Sacer, but who afterwards, from a similitude of names, was confounded with Anna, sister of Dido.

> "Idibus est Annæ festum geniale Perennæ,
>   Haud procul a ripis, advena Tibri, tuis.
> Plebs venit, ac virides passim disjecta per herbas
>   Potat; et accumbit cum pare quisque sua.
> Sub Jove pars durat; pauci tentoria ponunt:
>   Sunt, quibus e ramo frondea facta casa est:
> Pars, ubi pro rigidis calamos statuere columnis,
>   Desuper extentas imposuere togas.
> Sole tamen vinoque calent; annosque precantur,
>   Quot sumant cyathos, ad numerumque bibunt.
> Invenies illic, qui Nestoris ebibat annos:
>   Quæ sit per calices facta Sibylla suos.

> Illic et cantant, quidquid didicere theatris,
> Et jactant faciles ad sua verba manus:
> Et ducunt posito duras cratere choreas,
> Multaque diffusis saltat amica comis.
> Quum redeunt, titubant, et sunt spectacula vulgo,
> Et fortunatos obvia turba vocat.
> Occurri nuper. Visa est mihi digna relatu
> Pompa: senem potum pota trahebat anus."
>
> *Fast.* iii. 523.

Here three roads meet. That on the right is the old Via Flaminia, begun B.C. 220 by C. Flaminius the censor. This was the great northern road of Italy, which, issuing from the city by the Porta Ratumena, which was close to the tomb of Bibulus, followed a line a little east of the modern Corso, and passed the Aurelian wall by the Porta Flaminia, near the present Porta del Popolo. It extended to Ariminum (Rimini), a distance of 210 miles.*

(Following this road for about $1\frac{1}{2}$ mile, on the left are the ruins called *Tor di Quinto*. A little further on the right of the road are some tufa-rocks, with an injured tomb of the Nasones. Following the valley under these rocks to the left we reach ($1\frac{1}{2}$ mile) the fine *Castle of Crescenza*, now a farmhouse, picturesquely situated on a rocky knoll,—once inhabited by Poussin, and reproduced in the background of many of his pictures. In the interior are some remains of ancient frescoes.

On this road, seven miles from Rome, is Prima Porta, where are the ruins of the *Villa of Livia*, wife of Augustus, and mother of Tiberius. When first opened, several small rooms in the villa, supposed to be baths, were covered with frescoes and arabesques in a state of the most marvellous beauty and

---

* See Dyer's Hist. of the City of Rome.

preservation, but they are now greatly injured by damp and exposure. From the character of the paintings, a trelliswork of fruit and flowers, amid which birds and insects are sporting, it is supposed that they are the work of Ludius, described in Pliny, who "divi Augusti ætate primus instituit amœnissimam parietum picturam, villas et porticus ac topiaria opera, lucos, nemora. . . . . blandissimo aspectu minimoque impendio." It was here that the magnificent statue of Augustus, now in the Braccio Nuovo of the Vatican, was discovered in 1863.

"What Augustus's affection for Livia was, is well known. 'Preserve the remembrance of a husband who has loved you very tenderly,' were the last words of the emperor, as he lay on his death-bed. And when asked how she contrived to retain his affection, Dion Cassius tells us that she replied, 'My secret is very simple: I have made it the study of my life to please him, and I have never manifested any indiscreet curiosity with regard to his public or private affairs.'" — *Weld.*

Just beyond this, the Tiber receives the little river *Valca*, considered to be identical with the Crimera. Hither the devoted clan of the Fabii, 4000 in number, retired from Rome, having offered to sustain, at their own cost and risk, the war which Rome was then carrying on against Veii. Here, because they felt a position within the city untenable on account of the animosity of their fellow-patricians, which had been excited by their advocacy of the agrarian law, and their popularity with the plebeians, they established themselves on a hillock overhanging the river, which they fortified, and where they dwelt for three years. At the end of that time the Veiientines, by letting loose herds of cattle like the *Vaccine*, which one still sees wandering in that part of the Campagna, drew them into an ambuscade, and they were all cut off to a man. According to Dionysius, a portion of the little army remained to guard the fort, and the rest fled to another hill, perhaps that now known as Vaccareccia. These were the last to be exterminated.

> "They fought from dawn to sunset. The enemy slain by their hand formed heaps of corpses which barred their passage."—They were summoned to surrender, but they preferred to die.—"The people of Veii showered arrows and stones upon them from a distance, not daring to approach them again. The arrows fell like thick snow. The Fabii, with swords blunted by force of striking, with bucklers broken, continued to fight, snatching fresh swords from the hands of the enemy, and rushing upon them with the ferocity of wild beasts."—*Dionysius*, ix. 21.

A little beyond this, ten miles from Rome, is the stream *Scannabecchi*, which descends from the Crustuminian Hills, and is identical with the Allia, "infaustum Allia nomen," where the Romans were (B.C. 390) entirely defeated with great slaughter by the Gauls, before the capture of the city, in which the aged senators were massacred at the doors of their houses.

It was in the lands lying between the villa of Livia and the Tiber that *Saxa Rubra* * was situated, where Constantine (A.D. 312) gained his decisive victory over Maxentius, who, while attempting to escape over the Milvian Bridge, was pushed by the throng of fugitives into the Tiber, and perished, engulfed in the mud. The scene is depicted in the famous fresco of Giulio Romano, in the stanze of the Vatican.

On the opposite side of the river, Castel Giubeleo, on the site of the Etruscan Fidenæ, is a conspicuous object.)

---

* Masses of reddish rock of volcanic tufa are still to be seen here, breaking through the soil of the Campagna.

(The direct road from the Ponte Molle is the ancient *Via Cassia*, which must be followed for some distance by those who make the interesting excursions to Veii, Galera, and Bracciano, each easily within the compass of a day's expedition. On the left of this road, three miles from Rome, is the fine sarcophagus of Publius Vibius Maximus and his wife Regina Maxima, popularly known as "Nero's Tomb.")

Following the road to the left of the Ponte Molle, we turn up a steep incline to the deserted *Villa Madama*, built by Giulio Romano, from designs of Raphael for Cardinal Giulio de' Medici, afterwards Clement VII. It derives its name from Margaret of Austria, daughter of Charles V., and wife, first of Alessandro de' Medici, and then of Ottavio Farnese, duke of Parma; from this second marriage, it descended through Elisabetta Farnese, to the Bourbon kings of Naples. The neglected halls contain some fresco decorations by *Giulio Romano* and *Giovanni da Udine*.

"They consist of a series of beautiful little pictures, representing the sports of Satyrs and Loves ; Juno, attended by her peacocks ; Jupiter and Ganymede ; and various subjects of mythology and fable. The paintings in the portico have been of first-rate excellence ; and I cannot but regret, that designs so beautiful should not be engraved before their last traces disappear for ever. A deep fringe on one of the deserted chambers, representing angels, flowers, Caryatides, &c., by Giulio Romano ; and also a fine fresco on a ceiling, by Giovanni da Udine, of Phœbus driving his heavenly steeds, are in somewhat better preservation.

"It was in the groves that surrounded Villa Madama, that the Pastor Fido of Guarini was represented for the first time before a brilliant circle of princes and nobles, such as these scenes will see no more, and Italy itself could not now produce."—*Eaton's Rome*.

The frescoes and arabesques executed here by Giovanni

da Udine were considered at the time as among the most successful of his works. Vasari says that in these he "wished to be supreme, and to excel himself." Cardinal de' Medici was so delighted with them that he not only heaped benefits on all the relations of the painter, but rewarded him with a rich canonry, which he was allowed to transfer to his brother.

One can scarcely doubt from the description of Martial that this villa occupies the site of that in which the poet came to visit his friend and namesake.

> "Juli jugera pauca Martialis,
> Hortis Hesperidum beatiora,
> Longo Janiculi jugo recumbunt.
> Lati collibus imminent recessus;
> Et planus modico tumore vertex
> Cœlo perfruitur sereniore:
> Et, curvas nebula tegente valles,
> Solus luce nitet peculiari:
> Puris leniter admoventur astris
> Celsæ culmina delicata villæ.
> Hinc septem dominos videre montes,
> Et totam licet æstimare Romam."

The Villa Madama is situated on one of the slopes of *Monte Mario*, which is ascended by a winding carriage-road from near the Porta Angelica. This hill, in ancient times called Clivus Cinnæ, was in the middle ages Monte Malo, and is thus spoken of by Dante (Paradiso, xv. 109). Its name changed to Mario, through Mario Mellini, its possessor in the time of Sixtus V. Passing the two churches of Sta. Maria del Rosario and Sta. Croce di Monte Mario,* we reach a gate with an old pine-tree. This is the *Villa Mellini* (for which an order is supposed to

---

* Built by Mario Mellini in the fifteenth century.

be necessary, though a franc will usually cause the gates to fly open), which possesses a magnificent view over Rome, from its terraces, lined with ilexes and cypresses.

"The Monte Mario, like Cooper's Hill, is the highest, boldest, and most prominent part of the line ; it is about the height and steepness too of Cooper's Hill, and has the Tiber at the foot of it, like the Thames at Anchorwick. To keep up the resemblance, there is a sort of terrace at the top of the Monte Mario, planted with cypresses, and a villa, though dilapidated, crowns the summit, as well as at our old friend above Egham. Here we stood, on a most delicious evening, the ilex and the gum-cistus in great profusion about us, the slope below full of vines and olives, the cypresses above our heads, and before our eyes all that one has read of in Roman History—the course of the Tiber between the hills that bound it, coming down from Fidenæ and receiving the Allia and the Anio ; beyond, the Apennines, the distant and higher summits still quite white with snow ; in front, the Alban Hills ; on the right, the Campagna to the sea ; and just beneath us the whole length of Rome, ancient and modern—St. Peter's and the Coliseum, rising as the representatives of each—the Pantheon, the Aventine, the Quirinal, all the well-known objects distinctly laid before us. One may safely say that the world cannot contain many views of such mingled beauty and interest as this."—*Dr. Arnold.*

"Les maisons de campagne des grands seigneurs donnent l'idée de cette solitude, de cette indifférence des possesseurs au milieu des plus admirables séjours du monde. On se promène dans ces immenses jardins, sans se douter qu'ils aient un maître. L'herbe croît au milieu des allées ; et, dans ces mêmes allées abandonnées, les arbres sont taillés artistement, selon l'ancien goût qui régnait en France ; singulière bizarrerie que cette négligence du nécessaire, et cette affectation de l'inutile !"—*Mad. de Staël.*

(Behind the Monte Mario, about four miles from Rome, is the church of *S. Onofrio in Campagna*, with a curious ossuary.)

Just outside the Porta Angelica was the vineyard in which Alexander VI. died.

"This is the manner in which Pope Alexander VI. came to his death.

"The cardinal datary, Arian de Corneto, having received a gracious intimation that the pontiff, together with the Duke Valentinos, designed to come and sup with him at his vineyard, and that his Holiness would bring the supper with him, the cardinal suspected that this determination had been taken for the purpose of destroying his life by poison, to the end that the duke might have his riches and appointments, the rather as he knew that the pope had resolved to put him to death by some means, with a view to seizing his property as I have said,—which was very great. Considering of the means by which he might save himself, he could see but one hope of safety—he sent in good time to the pope's carver, with whom he had a certain intimacy, desiring that he would come to speak with him; who, when he had come to the said cardinal, was taken by him into a secret place, where, they two being retired, the cardinal showed the carver a sum, prepared beforehand, of 10,000 ducats, in gold, which the said cardinal persuaded the carver to accept as a gift and to keep for love of him. and after many words, they were at length accepted, the cardinal offering, moreover, all the rest of his wealth at his command—for he was a very rich cardinal, for he said that he could not keep the said riches by any other means than through the said carver's aid, and declared to him, 'You know of a certainty what the nature of the pope is, and I know that he has resolved, with the Duke Valentinos, to procure my life by poison, through your hand,'—wherefore he besought the carver to take pity on him, and to give him his life. And having said this, the carver declared to him the manner in which it was ordered that the poison should be given to him at the supper, but being moved to compassion he promised to preserve his life. Now the orders were that the carver should present three boxes of sweetmeats, in tablets or lozenges, after the supper, one to the pope, one to the said cardinal, and another to the duke, and in that for the cardinal there was poison: and thus being told, the said cardinal gave directions to the aforesaid carver in what manner he should serve them, so as to cause that the box of poisoned confect which was to be for the cardinal, should be placed before the pope, so that he might eat thereof, and so poison himself, and die. And the pope being come accordingly with the duke to supper on the day appointed, the cardinal threw himself at his feet, kissing them and embracing them closely; then he entreated his Holiness with most affectionate words, saying, he would never rise from those feet until his Holiness had granted him a favour. Being questioned by the pontiff what this favour was, and requested to rise up, he would first have the grace he demanded, and the promise of his Holiness to grant it. Now after much persuasion, the pope remained sufficiently astonished, seeing the perseverance of the cardinal, and that he would not rise, and promised to grant the favour. Then the cardinal rose up and said, 'Holy Father, it is not fitting that when the master comes to the house of his servant, the servant should eat with his master like an equal (confrezer parimente),' and therefore the grace he demanded was the just and honest one, that he, the servant, should wait at the table of his master; and this favour the pope granted him. Then having come to supper, and the time for serving the confectionery having arrived, the carver put the poisoned sweetmeats into the box, according to the first order given to him by the pope, and the cardinal being well informed as to which box had no poison, tasted of that one, and put the poisoned confect before the pope. Then his Holiness, trusting to his carver, and seeing the cardinal tasting, judged that no poison was there, and ate of it heartily; while of the other, which the pope thought was poisoned, but which was not, the cardinal ate. Now at the hour accustomed, according to the quality of that poison, his Holiness began to feel its effect, and so died thereof; but the cardinal, who was yet much afraid, having physicked himself and vomited, took no harm and escaped, though not without difficulty."—*Sanuto*, iv., *Translation in Ranke's Hist. of the Popes.*

The wine of the Vatican hill has had a bad reputation even from classical times. "If you like vinegar," wrote Martial, " drink the wine of the Vatican!"* and again, "To drink the wine of the Vatican is to drink poison." †

(Here, also, is the entrance of the *Val d' Inferno*, a pleasant winter walk, where, near the beginning of the Cork Woods, are some picturesque remains of an ancient nymphæum.)

The *Porta Angelica*, built by Pius IV. (1559—1566), leads into the Borgo, beneath the walls of the Vatican.

Those who return from hence to the English quarter in the evening, will realize the vividness of Miss Thackeray's description :—

* Martial, Ep. x. 45, 5.   † Martial, Ep. vi. 92, 3.

",They passed groups standing round their doorways ; a blacksmith hammering with great straight blows at a copper pot, shouting to a friend, a young baker, naked almost, except for a great sheet flung over his shoulders, and leaning against the door of his shop. The horses tramp on. Listen to the flow of fountains gleaming white against the dark marbles,—to the murmur of voices. An old lady, who has apparently hung all her wardrobe out of window, in petticoats and silk hankerchiefs, is looking out from beneath these banners at the passers in the streets. Little babies, tied up tight in swaddling-clothes, are being poised against their mother's hips ; a child is trying to raise the great knocker of some feudal-looking arch, hidden in the corner of the street. Then they cross the bridge, and see the last sun's rays flaming from the angel's sacred sword. Driving on through the tranquil streets, populous and thronged with citizens, they see brown-faced, bronze-headed Torsos in balconies and window-frames ; citizens sitting tranquilly, resting on the kerb-stones, with their feet in the gutters ; grand-looking women resting against their doorways. Sibyls out of the Sistine were sitting on the steps of the churches. In one stone archway sat the Fates spinning their web. There was a holy family by a lemonade-shop, and a whole heaven of little Coreggio angels perching dark-eyed along the road. Then comes a fountain falling into a marble basin, at either end of which two little girls are clinging and climbing. Here is a little lighted May-altar to the Virgin, which the children have put up under the shrine by the street-corner. They don't beg clamorously, but stand leaning against the wall, waiting for a chance miraculous baioch ?"—*Bluebeard's Keys.*

CHAPTER XX.

THE JANICULAN.

Gate of Sto. Spirito—Church, Convent, and Garden of S. Onofrio—The Lungara—Palazzo Salviati and the Botanic-Garden—S. Giovanni alla Lungara—Palazzo Corsini—The Farnesina—Porta Settimiana—S. Pietro in Montorio—Fontana Paolina—Villa Lante—Porta and Church of S. Pancrazio—Villa Doria-Pamfili—Chapel of St. Andrew's Head.

THE Janiculan is a steep crest of hill which rises abruptly on the west bank of the Tiber, and breaks imperceptibly away on the other side into the Campagna towards Civita Vecchia. Its lower formation is a marine clay abounding in fossils, but its upper surface is formed of the yellow sand which gave it the ancient name of Mons Aureus,—still commemorated in Montorio—S. Pietro in Montorio.

A tradition universally received in ancient times, and adopted by Virgil, derives the name of Janiculum from Janus, who was the sun-god, as Jana, or Diana, was the moon-goddess. On this hill Janus is believed to have founded a city, which is mentioned by Pliny under the name of Antinopolis. Ovid makes Janus speak for himself as to his property:

"Arx mea collis erat, quem cultrix nomine nostro
Nuncupat hæc ætas, Janiculumque vocat." *

Fons, the supposed son of Janus, is known to have had an altar here in very early times.† Janus Quirinus was a

---

* Fast. i. 246. † Ampère, Hist. Rom. i. 227.

war-god, "the sun armed with a lance." Thus, in time of peace, the gates of this temple were closed, both because his worship was then unnecessary, and from an idea of preventing war from going forth. It was probably in this character that he was honoured on a site which the Romans looked upon as "the key of Etruria," while other nations naturally regarded it as "the key of Rome."

Janus was represented as having a key in his hand.

"Ille tenens dextra baculum, clavemque sinistra."

"Par un hasard singulier, Janus, qu'on représentait une clef à la main, était le dieu du Janicule, voisin du Vatican, où est le tombeau de Saint Pierre, que l'on représente aussi tenant une clef. Janus, comme Saint Pierre, son futur voisin, était le portier céleste."—*Ampère, Hist. Rom.* i. 229.

When the first Sabine king of Rome, Numa Pompilius, "like the darlings of the gods in the golden age, fell asleep, full of days,"* he was buried upon the sacred hill of his own people, and the books of his sacred laws and ordinances were buried near him in a separate tomb.† In the sixth century of the republic, a monument was discovered on the Janiculan, which was believed to be that of Numa, and certain books were dug up near it which were destroyed by the senate in the fear that they might give a too freethinking explanation of the Roman mythology.‡

Ancus Martius, the fourth king of Rome, connected the Janiculan with the rest of the city by building the Pons Sublicius, the first bridge over the Tiber; and erected a citadel on the crest of the hill as a bulwark against Etruria, with which he was constantly at war.§ Some escarpments, supposed to belong to the fortifications of Ancus, have

* Niebuhr, i. 240.   † Arnold, Hist. vol. i.
‡ Ampère, Hist. Rom. i. 389.   § Niebuhr, i. 353.

lately been found behind the Fontana Paolina. It was from this same ridge that his Etruscan successor, Tarquinius Priscus, coming from Tarquinii (Corneto), had his first view of the city over which he came to reign, and here the eagle, henceforth to be the emblem of Roman power, replaced upon his head the cap which it had snatched away as he was riding in his chariot. Hence, also, Lars Porsena, king of Etruria, looked upon Rome, when he came to the assistance of Tarquinius Superbus, and retired in fear of his life after he had seen specimens of Roman endurance, in Horatius Cocles, who kept the falling bridge; in Mutius, who burnt his hand in the charcoal; and in the hostage, Clœlia, who swam home across the Tiber,—all anecdotes connected with the Janiculan.

After the time of the kings this hill appears less frequently in history. But it was here that the consul Octavius, the friend of Sylla, was murdered by the partisans of Marius, while seated in his curule chair,—near the foot of the hill Julius Cæsar had his famous gardens, and on its summit the Emperor Galba was buried. The Christian associations of the hill will be noticed at the different points to which they belong.

From the Borgo (Chap. XV.) the unfinished gate called *Porta Sto. Spirito*, built by Antonio da San Gallo, leads into the Via Lungara, a street three-quarters of a mile long, formed by Sixtus V., and occupying the whole length of the valley between the Tiber and the Janiculan.

Immediately on the right, the steep "Salita di S. Onofrio" leads up the hillside to the *Church of S. Onofrio*, built in 1439 by Nicolo da Forca Palena, in honour of the Egyptian hermit, Honophrius.

S. ONOFRIO.

"St. Onofrius was a monk of Thebes, who retired to the desert, far from the sight of men, and dwelt there in a cave for sixty years, and during all that time never beheld one human being, or uttered one word of his mother-tongue except in prayer. He was unclothed, except by some leaves twisted round his body, and his beard and hair had become like the face of a wild beast. In this state he was discovered by a holy man whose name was Paphnutius, who, seeing him crawling on the ground, knew not at first what live thing it might be."—*Jameson's Sacred Art.*

From the little platform in front of the convent is one of the loveliest views over the city. The church is approached by a portico, decorated with glazed frescoes by *Domenichino*. Those on either side of the door represent the saints of the Hieronomyte Order (the adjoining convent belongs to Hieronomytes), viz.: S. Jerome, Sta. Paula, St. Eustochium, S. Pietro Gambacorta of Pisa, St. Augustine the hermit, S. Nicolo di Forca Palena, S. Onofrio and the Blessed Benedict of Sicily, Philip of St. Agatha, Paul of Venice, Bartholomew of Cesarea, Mark of Manuta, Philip of Fulgaria, and John of Catalonia. Over the door is a Madonna and Child. In the side arcade are three scenes in the life of St. Jerome. 1. Represents his baptism as a young man at Rome. 2. Refers to his vision of the Judgment (described in his letter to Eustochium), in which he heard the Judge of the World ask what he was, and he answered, "I am a Christian." But the Judge replied, "No, you lie, for you are a Ciceronian," and he was condemned to be scourged, but continued to protest that he was a Christian between every lash. 3. Is a scene alluded to in another letter to Eustochium, in which Jerome says, "O how often when alone in the desert with the wild beasts and scorpions, half dead with fasting and penance, have I fancied myself a spectator of the sins of Rome, and of the dances of its young women."

The church has a solemn and picturesque interior. It ends in a tribune richly adorned with frescoes, those of the upper part (the Coronation of the Virgin, and eight groups of saints and angels) being by *Pinturicchio*, those of the lower (the Virgin and Saints, Nativity, and Flight into Egypt) by *Baldassare Peruzzi*.

On the left of the entrance is the original monument of Tasso (with a portrait), erected after his death by Cardinal Bevilacqua. Greatly inferior in interest is a monument recently placed to his memory in the adjoining chapel, by subscription, the work of *De Fabris*. Near this is the grave of the poet, Alessandro Guidi, ob. 1712. In the third chapel on the left is the grave of the learned Cardinal Mezzofanti, born at Bologna, 1774, died at Rome, 1849.

The first chapel on the right, which is low and vaulted, with stumpy pillars, is covered with frescoes relating to S. Onofrio.

The second chapel on the right, which is very richly decorated, contains a Madonna crowned by Angels, by *Annibale Caracci*. Beyond this is the fine tomb of Archbishop Sacchi, ob. 1502. The beautiful lunette, of the Madonna teaching the Holy Child to read, is by *Pinturicchio*. The tomb is inscribed:

"Labor et gloria vita fuit,
Mors requies."

Ladies are never admitted to visit the convent, except on April 25th, the anniversary of the death of Tasso. It is approached by a cloister, decorated with frescoes from the life of S. Onofrio.

"S. Onofrio is represented as a meagre old man, with long hair and beard, grey and matted, a leafy branch twisted round his loins, a stick in his hand. The artist generally tries to make him look as haggard and inhuman as possible."—*Mrs. Jameson*.

In a passage on the first floor is a beautiful fresco of the Virgin and Child with the donor, by *Leonardo da Vinci*.

"To 1513 belongs a Madonna, painted on the wall of the upper corridor of the convent of S. Onofrio. It is on a gold ground: the action of the Madonna is beautiful, displaying the noblest form, and the expression of the countenance is peculiarly sweet; but the Child, notwithstanding his graceful action, is somewhat hard and heavy, so as almost to warrant the conclusion that this picture belongs to an earlier period, which would suppose a previous visit to Rome."—*Kugler*.

Torquato Tasso came to Rome in 1594, on the invitation of Clement VIII., that he might be crowned on the Capitol, but as he arrived in the month of November, and the weather was then very bad, it was decided to postpone the ceremony till late in the following spring. This delay was a source of trouble to Tasso, who was in feeble health, and had a presentiment that his death was near. Before the time for his crowning arrived he had removed to S. Onofrio, saying to the monks who received him at the entrance, "My fathers, I have come to die amongst you!" and he wrote to one of his friends, "I am come to begin my conversation in heaven in this elevated place, and in the society of these holy fathers." During the fourteen days of his illness, he became perfectly absorbed in the contemplation of divine subjects, and upon the last day of his life, when he received the papal absolution, exclaimed, "I believe that the crown which I looked for upon the Capitol is to be changed for a better crown in heaven." Throughout the last night a monk prayed by his side till the morning, when Tasso was heard to murmur, "In manus tuas, Domine," and then he died. The room in which he expired, April 25, 1595, contains his bust, crucifix, inkstand, autograph, a mask taken from his face after death, and other relics. The archives of S. Onofrio have this entry:

"Torquato Tasso, illustrious from his genius, died thus in our monastery of S. Onofrio. In April, 1595, he caused himself to be brought here that he might prepare for death with greater devotion and security, as he felt his end approaching. He was received courteously by our fathers, and conducted to chambers in the loggia, where everything was ready for him. Soon afterwards he became dangerously ill, and desired to confess and receive the most Holy Sacrament from the prior. Being asked to write his will, he said that he wished to be buried at S. Onofrio, and he left to the convent his crucifix and fifty scudi for alms, that so many masses might be said for his soul, in the manner that is read in the book of legacies in our archives. Pope Clement VIII. was requested for his benediction, which he gave amply for the remission of sins. In his last days he received extreme unction, and then, with the crucifix in his hand, contemplating and kissing the sacred image, with Christian contrition and devotion, being surrounded by our fathers, he gave up his spirit to the Creator, on April 25, 1595, between the eleventh and twelfth hours (*i.e.*, between 7 and 8 A.M.), in the fiftieth year of his age. In the evening his body was interred with universal concourse in our church, near the steps of the high altar, the Cardinal Giulio, Aldobrandini, under whose protection he had lived during the last years, being minded to erect to him, as soon as possible, a sumptuous sepulchre, which, however, was never carried into effect; but after the death of the latter, the Signor Cardinal Bevilacqua raised to his memory the monument which is seen on entering the church on the left side."

Ladies are admitted to the beautiful garden of the convent on ringing at the first large gate on the left below the church.

This lovely plot of ground, fresh with running streams, possesses a glorious view over the city, and the Campagna beyond S. Paolo. At the further extremity, near a picturesque group of cypresses, are remains of the oak planted by Tasso, the greater part of which was blown down in 1842. A young sapling is shooting up beside it. Beyond this is the little amphitheatre, overgrown with grass and flowers, where S. Filippo Neri used to teach children, and assemble them "for the half-dramatic musical performances which were an original form of his oratorios. Here every 25th of April a musical entertainment of the Accademia is held in memory of Tasso,—his bust, crowned with laurel wreaths, and taken from the cast after death, being placed in the centre of the amphitheatre." *

Returning to the Lungara, on the left is a Lunatic Asylum, founded by Pius IX., with a pompous inscription, and beyond it, a chain bridge to S. Giovanni dei Fiorentini. On the right is the handsome *Palazzo Salviati*, which formerly contained a fine collection of pictures, removed to the Borghese Palace, when, upon the property falling into the hands of Prince Borghese, he sold the palace to the government, who now use it as a repository for the civil archives. The adjoining garden now belongs to the Sapienza, and has been turned into a *Botanic Garden*. The modernized church of S. *Giovanni alla Lungara* dates from the time of Leo IV. (845—857), and is now attached to a reformatory. On the right is a large *Convent of the Buon Pastore*.

We now reach, on the right, the magnificent *Palazzo Corsini*, built originally by the Riario family, from whom it was bought by Clement XII. in 1729, for his nephew Cardinal Neri Corsini, for whom it was altered to its present form by *Fuga*.

This palace was in turn the resort of Caterina Sforza, the brave duchess of Imola; of the learned Poet Cardinal di S. Giorgio; of Michael Angelo, who remained here more than a year on a visit to the cardinal, "who," says Vasari, "being of small understanding in art, gave him no commission"; and of Erasmus, who always remembered the pleasant conversations (confabulationes melliflua) of the "Riario Palace," as it was then called. In the seventeenth century

* Hemans.

the palace became the residence of Queen Christina of
Sweden, who died here on April 19, 1689, in a room which
is distinguished by two columns of painted wood.

"With her residence in Rome, the habits of Christina became more
tranquil and better regulated. She obtained some mastery over herself, suffered certain considerations of what was due to others to prevail,
and consented to acknowledge the necessities incident to the peculiarities of her chosen residence. She took a constantly increasing part in
the splendour, the life, and the business of the Curia, becoming indeed
eventually altogether identified with its interests. The collections she
had brought with her from Sweden, she now enlarged by so liberal an
expenditure, and with so much taste, judgment, and success, that she
surpassed even the native families, and elevated the pursuit from a mere
gratification of curiosity, to a higher and more significant importance
both for learning and art. Men such as Spanheim and Havercamp
thought the illustration of her coins and medals an object not unworthy
of their labours, and Sante Bartolo devoted his practised hand to her
cameos. The Coreggios of Christina's collection have always been the
richest ornament of every gallery into which the changes of time have
carried them. The MSS. of her choice have contributed in no small
degree to maintain the reputation of the Vatican library, into which they
were subsequently incorporated. Acquisitions and possessions of this
kind filled up the hours of her daily life, with an enjoyment that was at
least harmless. She also took interest and an active part in scientific
pursuits ; and it is much to her credit that she received the poor exiled
Borelli, who was compelled to resort in his old age to teaching as a
means of subsistence. The queen supported him with her utmost power,
and caused his renowned and still unsurpassed work, on the mechanics
of animal motion, by which physiological science has been so import-
antly influenced and advanced, to be printed at her own cost. Nay, I
think we may even venture to affirm, that she herself, when her character and intellect had been improved and matured, exerted a powerfully efficient and enduring influence on the period, more particularly
on Italian literature. In the year 1680, she founded an academy in her
own residence for the discussion of literary and political subjects ; and
the first rule of this institution was, that its members should carefully
abstain from the turgid style, overloaded with false ornament, which
prevailed at the time, and be guided only by sound sense and the models
of the Augustan and Medicean ages. From the queen's academy proceeded such men as Alessandro Guidi, who had previously been addicted

to the style then used, but after some time passed in the society of Christina, he not only resolved to abandon it, but even formed a league with some of his friends for the purpose of labouring to abolish it altogether. The Arcadia, an academy to which the merit of completing this good work is attributed, arose out of the society which assembled around the Swedish queen. On the whole, it must needs be admitted, that in the midst of the various influences pressing around her, Christina preserved a noble independence of mind. To the necessity for evincing that ostentatious piety usually expected from converts, or which they impose on themselves, she would by no means subject herself. Entirely Catholic as she was, and though continually repeating her conviction of the pope's infallibility, and of the necessity for believing all doctrines enjoined either by himself or the Church, she had nevertheless an extreme detestation of bigots, and utterly abhorred the direction of father confessors, who were at that time the exclusive rulers of all social and domestic life. She would not be prevented from enjoying the amusements of the carnival, concerts, dramatic entertainments, or whatever else might be offered by the habits of life at Rome; above all, she refused to be withheld from the internal movement of an intellectual and animated society. She acknowledged a love of satires, and took pleasure in Pasquin. We find her constantly mingled in the intrigues of the court, the dissensions of the papal houses, and the factions of the cardinals. . . . She attached herself to the mode of life presented to her with a passionate love, and even thought it impossible to live if she did not breathe the atmosphere of Rome."—*Ranke's Hist. of the Popes.*

In 1797 this palace was used as the French embassy, and on the 28th of December was the scene of a terrible skirmish, when Joseph Buonaparte, then ambassador, attempted to interfere between the French democratic party and the papal dragoons, and when young General Duphot, who was about to be married to Buonaparte's sister-in-law, was shot by his side in a balcony. These events, after which Joseph Buonaparte immediately demanded his passports and departed, were among the chief causes which led to the invasion of Rome by Berthier, and the imprisonment of Pius VII.*

The collections now in the palace have all been formed

---

* See Thiers' History of the French Revolution.

since the death of Queen Christina. The *Picture Gallery* is open to the public from nine to twelve, every day except Sundays and holidays.

The following criticism, applicable to all the private galleries in Rome, is perhaps especially so to this:

"You may generally form a tolerably correct conjecture of what a gallery will contain, as to subject, before you enter it,—a certain quantity of Landscapes, a great many Holy Families, a few Crucifixions, two or three Pietàs, a reasonable proportion of St. Jeromes, a mixture of other Saints and Martyrdoms, and a large assortment of Madonnas and Magdalenes, make up the principal part of all the collections in Rome; which are generally comprised of quite as many bad as good paintings."
—*Eaton's Rome.*

The 1st room is chiefly occupied by pretty but unimportant landscapes by *Orizzonti* and *Vanvitelli*, and figure pieces by Locatelli. We may notice (the best pictures being marked with an asterisk):

1st Room.—
24, 26. *Canaletti.*

2nd Room.—
12. Madonna and Child in glory: *Eliz. Sirani.*
11, 27. Fruit: *Mario di Fiori.*
15. Landscape: *G. Poussin.*
17, 19. Landscapes with Cattle: *Berghem.*
20. Pietà: *Lod. Caracci.*
41. S. Andrea Corsini: *Fr. Gessi.*

3rd Room.—
1. Ecce Homo: *Guercino.**
9. Madonna and Child: *A. del Sarto.*
13. Holy Family: *Barocci.*
16, 20. Rock Scenes: *Salvator Rosa.*
17. Madonna and Child: *Caravaggio.*
23. Sunset: *Both.**
26. Holy Family: *Fra Bartolomeo.*
43. Two Martyrdoms: *Carlo Saraceni.*
44. Julius II.: *after Raphael.*

The portrait of Julius II. (della Rovere) is a replica or copy of that at the Pitti Palace. There are other duplicates in

PALAZZO CORSINI.

the Borghese Gallery, at the National Gallery in England, and at Leigh Court in Somersetshire. Julius II. ob. 1513.
49. St. Appollonia : *Carlo Dolce.*
50. Philip II. of Spain : *Titian.*
52. Vanity : *Carlo Saraceni.**
88. Ecce Homo : *Carlo Dolce.*

4th Room.—
1. Clement XII. (Lorenzo Corsini, 1730—40) : *Benedetto Luti.*
4. Cupid asleep : *Guido Reni.*
11. Daughter of Herodias : *Guido Reni* *
16. Madonna : *Guido Reni.*
22. Christ and the Magdalen : *Barocci.*
27. Two Heads : *Lod. Caracci.*
28. St. Jerome : *Titian.*
40. Faustina Maratta—his daughter : *Carlo Maratta.*
41. Fornarina : *Giulio Romano, after Raphael,*—replica of the picture at Florence.
42. Old Man : *Guido.*
44. A Hare : *Albert Durer.**
55. Death of Adonis : *Spagnoletto.*

In this room is an ancient marble chair, found near the Lateran—and on a table " the Corsini Vase," in silver, with reliefs representing the judgment of Areopagus upon the matricide of Orestes.

5th Room.—(In which Christina died, with a ceiling by the *Zuccari.*)

2. Holy Family : *Pierino del Vaga.*
12. St. Agnes : *Carlo Dolce.* *
14. Madonna reading : *Sassoferrato.*
20. Ulysses and Polyphemus : *Lanfranco.*
23. Madonna and Child : *Albani.*
26. Madonna and Child : *Sassoferrato.*
37. Addolorata : *Guido Reni.*
38. Ecce Homo : *Guido Reni.*
39. St. John : *Guido Reni.*

6th Room.—
19. Portrait : *Holbein.*
20. Mgr. Ghiberti : *Titian.*
21. Children of Charles V. : *Titian.* *

22. Old Woman : *Rembrandt.**
23. Male Portrait : *Giorgione.*
31. Caterina Bora, Wife of Luther : *Holbein.**
32. Male Portrait : *Vandyke.*
34. Nativity of the Virgin. Miniature from *Durer.*
40. Cardinal Divitius de Bibbiena : *Bronzino.*
47. Portrait of Himself : *Rubens.**
48. A Doge of Venice : *Tintoret.*
54. Cardinal Alessandro Farnese : *Titian.**
68. Cardinal Neri Corsini : *Baciccio.*

7th Room.—
1. Madonna and Child : *Murillo.**
13. Landscape : *G. Poussin.*
15. St. Sebastian : *Rubens.*
18. Christ bearing the Cross : *Garofalo.*
21. Christ among the Doctors : *Luca Giordano.*
22. Descent of the Holy Spirit : *Fra Angelico.*
23. Last Judgment : *Fra Angelico.*
24. Ascension : *Fra Angelico.*

"A Last Judgment by Angelico da Fiesole, with wings containing the Ascension and the Descent of the Holy Ghost, is in the Corsini Gallery. Here we perceive a great richness of expression and beauty of drapery ; the rapture of the blessed is told, chiefly by their embraces and by their attitudes of prayer and praise. It is a remarkable feature, and one indicative of the master, that the ranks of the condemned are entirely filled by monks."—*Kugler.*

26. Martyrdom of St. Bartholomew : *Lod. Caracci.*
30. Woman taken in Adultery : *Titian.**
35. Gonfaloniere of the Church : *Domenichino.*

8th Room.—
8. Christ before Pilate : *Vandyke.*
12. St. George : *Ercole Grandi.*
13. Contemplation : *Guido Reni.*
15. Landscape : *G. Poussin.*
17. Judith and Head of Holofernes : *Gérard de la Nuit.*
24. St. Jerome : *Guercino.*
25. St. Jerome : *Spagnoletto.*
43. Mosaic portrait of Clement XII. and his nephew Cardinal Neri Corsini.

In this room are two modern family busts with touching inscriptions.

CABINET :
26. Madonna and Child : *Spagna.**

9*th Room.*—
2. Village Interior : *Teniers.*
9. Innocent X. : *Velasquez* (a replica of the Doria portrait).
26. Female Portrait : *Bronzino.*
28, 29. Battle-pieces: *Salvator Rosa.*
30. Two Heads : *Giorgione.*
40. Madonna Addolorata : *Cignani.*
49. Madonna and Child : *Gherardesco da Siena.*

One of the gems of the collection, a highly finished Madonna and Child of Carlo Dolce, is usually shown in a glass case in the first room.

The Corsini Library (open every day except Wednesdays) contains a magnificent collection of MSS. and engravings, founded by Cardinal Neri Corsini. It has also some beautiful original drawings by the old masters. Behind the palace, on the slope of the Janiculan, are large and beautiful *Gardens* adorned with fountains, cypresses, and some grand old plane-trees. There is a fine view from the Casino on the summit of the hill.

"A magnificent porter in cocked hat and grand livery conducted the visitors across the quadrangle, unlocked the ponderous iron gates of the gardens, and let them through, leaving them to their own devices, and closing and locking the gates with a crash. They now stood in a wide avenue of ilex, whose gloomy boughs, interlacing overhead, effectually excluded the sunlight ; nearly a quarter of a mile further on, the ilexes were replaced by box and bay trees, beneath which the sun and shade divided the path between them, trembling and flickering on the ground and invading each other's dominions with every breath of wind. The strangers heard the splash of fountains as they walked onwards by banks precipitous as a hill-side, and covered with wild rank herbage and tall trees. Stooping to gather a flower, they almost started, as looking up, they saw, rising against a sky fabulously blue, the unfamiliar green ilex and dark cypress spire."—*Mademoiselle Mori.*

Opposite the Corsini Palace is the beautiful villa of *the*

Farnesina (open on Sundays from 10 to 3), built in 1506 by Baldâssare Peruzzi for the famous banker Agostino Chigi, who here gave his sumptuous and extravagant entertainments to Leo X. and his court—banquets at which three fish cost as much as 230 crowns, and after which the plate that had been used, was all thrown into the Tiber.* This same Agostino Chigi was one of the greatest of art patrons, and has handed down to us not only the decorations of the Farnesina, but the Sibyls of Sta. Maria della Pace, which he also ordered from Raphael.

"Le jour où Leon X. alla prendre possession de la basilique de Latran, l'opulent Chigi se distingua. Le théâtre qui s'élevait devant son palais était rempli des envoyés de tous les peuples, blancs, cuivrés, et noirs ; au milieu d'eux on distinguait les images de Vénus, de Mars, de Minerve, allusion singulière aux trois pontificats d'Alexander VI., de Jules II., et de Leon X. *Vénus a eu son temps:* disait l'inscription ; *Mars a eu le sien; c'est aujourd'hui le règne de Minerve.* Antoine de San-Marino, qui demeurait près de Chigi, répondit aussitôt en plaçant sur sa boutique la statue isolée de Vénus, avec ce peu de mots : Mars a régné, Minerve règne, Vénus régnera toujours."—*Gournerie, Rome Chrétienne,* ii. 109.

The Farnesina contains some of the most beautiful existing frescoes of Raphael and his school. The principal hall was once open, but has now been closed in to preserve the paintings. Its ceiling was designed by *Raphael* (1518—20), and painted by *Giulio Romano* and *Francesco Penni*, with twelve scenes from the story of Psyche as narrated by Apuleius :

A king had three daughters. The youngest was named Psyche, and was more lovely than the sunshine. Venus, the queen of beauty, was herself jealous of her, and bade her son Cupid to destroy her charms by inspiring her with an unworthy love (1). But Cupid, when he beheld

* It has been supposed that the beautiful silver vase which is shown in the Corsini Palace, and which was picked up in the Tiber, belonged to this plate.

Psyche, loved her himself, showed her to the Graces (2), and carried her off. He only visited her in the darkness of night, and bade her always to repress her curiosity as to his appearance. But while Cupid was sleeping, Psyche lighted a lamp, and looked upon him,—and a drop of the hot oil fell upon him and he awoke. Then he left her alone in grief and solitude. Venus in the mean time learnt that Cupid was faithless to her, and imprisoned him, and sought assistance from Juno and Ceres that she might find Psyche, but they refused to aid her (3). Then she drove to seek Jupiter in her chariot drawn by doves (4), and implored him to send Mercury to her assistance (5). Jupiter listened to her prayer, and Mercury was sent forth to seek for Psyche (6). Venus then showed her spite against Psyche, and imposed harsh tasks upon her which she was nevertheless enabled to perform. At length she was ordered to bring a casket from the infernal regions (7), and even this, to the amazement of Venus, she succeeded in effecting (8). Cupid, escaped from captivity, then implored Jupiter to restore Psyche to him. Jupiter embraced him (9), and bade Mercury summon the gods to a council on the subject (see the ceiling on the right). Psyche was then brought to Olympus (10), and became immortal, and the gods celebrated her nuptial banquet (ceiling painting on left).

"On the flat of the ceiling are two large compositions, with numerous figures,—the Judgment of the Gods, who decide the dispute between Venus and Cupid, and the Marriage of Cupid and Psyche in the festal assembly of the gods. In the lunettes of the ceiling are *amorini*, with the attributes of those gods who have done homage to the power of Love. In the triangular compartments between the lunettes are different groups, illustrative of the incidents in the fable. They are of great beauty, and are examples of the most tasteful disposition in a given space. The picture of the three Graces, that in which Cupid stands in an imploring attitude before Jupiter ; a third, where Psyche is borne away by Loves, are extremely graceful. Peevish critics have designated these representations as common and sensual, but the noble spirit visible in all Raphael's works prevails also in these : religious feeling could naturally find no place in them; but they are conceived in a spirit of the purest artlessness, always a proof of true moral feeling, and to which a narrow taste alone could object. In the execution, indeed, we recognise little of Raphael's fine feeling ; the greatest part is by his scholars, after his cartoons, especially by G. Romano. The nearest of the three Graces, in the group before alluded to, appears to be by Raphael's own hand."—*Kugler.*

The paintings were injuriously retouched by *Carlo Ma-*

ratta. The garlands round them are by *Giovanni da Udine.* The second room contains the beautiful fresco of Galatea floating in a shell drawn by dolphins, by *Raphael* himself.

"Raphael not only designed, but executed this fresco; and faded as is its colouring, the mind must be dead to the highest beauties of painting, that can contemplate it without admiration. The spirit and beauty of the composition, the pure and perfect design, the flowing outline, the soft and graceful contours, and the sentiment and sweetness of the expression, all remain unchanged; for time, till it totally obliterates, has no power to injure them. . . The figures of the attendant Nereid, and of the triumphant Triton who embraces her, are beautiful beyond description."—*Eaton's Rome.*

"The fresco of Galatea was painted in 1514. The greater part of this is Raphael's own work, and the execution is consequently much superior to that of the others. It represents the goddess of the sea borne over the waves in her shell; tritons and sea-nymphs sport joyously around her; *amorini*, discharging their arrows, appear in the air like an angel-glory. The utmost sweetness, the most ardent sense of pleasure, breathe from this work; everything lives, feels, vibrates with enjoyment."—*Kugler.*

The frescoes of the ceiling, representing Diana in her Car, and the story of Medusa, are by *Baldassare Peruzzi;* the lunettes are by *Sebastian del Piombo* and *Daniele da Volterra.* Michael Angelo came one day to visit the latter, and not finding him at his work, left the colossal head, which remains in a lunette of the left wall, as a sign of his visit.

In the upper story are two rooms; the first, adorned with a frieze of subjects from Ovid's Metamorphoses, contains large architectural paintings by *Baldassare Peruzzi;* the second has the Marriage of Alexander and Roxana, and the family of Darius in the presence of Alexander, by *Sodoma.*

The *Porta Settimiana* at the end of the Lungara preserves in its name a recollection of the gardens of Septimius Severus, which existed in this quarter. From hence the Via delle Fornaci ascends the hill, and leads to the broad

S. PIETRO IN MONTORIO.

new carriage-road, formed in 1867 under the superintendence of the Cav. Trochi. A Via-Crucis with a staircase will conduct the pedestrian by a shorter way to the platform on the hill-top.

The succession of beggars who infest this hill and stretch out their maimed limbs or kiss their hands to the passers-by will call to mind the lines of Juvenal :

"Cæcus adulator, dirusque a ponte satelles,
Dignus Aricinos qui mendicaret ad axes,
Blandaque devexæ jactaret basia rhedæ."
                                                  Sat. iv. 116.

The Church of S. Pietro in Montorio was built by Ferdinand and Isabella of Spain, from designs of Baccio Pintelli, on the site of an oratory founded by Constantine upon the supposed spot of St. Peter's crucifixion.

The first chapel on the right belongs to the Barberini, and contains pictures by *Sebastian del Piombo*, (painted in oil upon stone, a process which has caused them to be much blackened by time,) from drawings of *Michael Angelo*. The central picture represents the Scourging of Christ, a subject of which Sebastian was especially fond, as it gave the opportunity of displaying his great anatomical power. On the left is St. Peter, on the right St. Francis,—on the ceiling is the Transfiguration,—outside the arch are a Prophet and a Sibyl. The second chapel on the right has paintings by pupils of Perugino ; the fifth contains St. Paul healed by Ananias, by *Vasari*.

The fourth chapel on the right is of some interest in the history of art. Julius III. had it greatly at heart to build and beautify this chapel as a memorial to his family, to contain the tombs of his uncle Cardinal Antonio di Monti, and of Fabiano, who first founded the splendours of his house.

The work was entrusted to Michael Angelo and Vasari, who were at that time on terms of intimate friendship. They disputed about their subordinates. Vasari wished to employ Simone Mosca for the ornaments, and Raffaello da Montalupo for the statues; Michael Angelo objected to having any ornamental work at all, saying that where there were to be marble figures, there ought to be nothing else, and he would have nothing to do with Montalupo because his figures for the tomb of Julius II. had turned out so ill. When the chapel was finished Michael Angelo confessed himself in the wrong for not having allowed more ornament. The statues were entrusted to Bartolomeo Ammanati.

The first chapel on the left has St. Francis receiving the stigmata attributed to *Giovanni de Vecchi.*

"A barber of the Cardinal S. Giorgio was an artist, who painted very well in tempera, but had no idea of design. He made friends with Michael-Angelo, who made him a cartoon of a St. Francis receiving the stigmata, which the barber carefully carried out in colour, and his picture is now placed in the first chapel on the left of the entrance of S. Pietro in Montorio."—*Vasari,* vi.

The third chapel on the left contains a Virgin and Child with St. Anne, of the school of Perugino; the fourth, a fine Entombment, by an unknown hand; the fifth, the Baptism of Christ, said to be by *Daniele da Volterra.*

The Transfiguration of Raphael was painted for this church, and remained here till the French invasion. When it was returned from the Louvre it was kept at the Vatican. Had it been restored to this church, it would have been destroyed in the siege of 1849, when the tribune and bell-tower were thrown down. Here, in front of the high altar, the unhappy Beatrice Cenci was buried without any monument.

Irish travellers may be interested in the gravestones in

the nave, of Hugh O'Neil of Tyrone, Baron Dungannon, and O'Donnell of Tyrconnell (1608). Near the door is the fine tomb, with the beautiful sleeping figure of Julian, Archbishop of Ragusa, ob. 1510, inscribed "Bonis et Mors et Vita dulcis est." An inscription below the steps in front of the church commemorates the translation of a miraculous image of the Virgin hither in 1714.

In the cloister is the *Tempietto*, a small domed building resting on sixteen Doric columns, built by Bramante in 1502, on the spot where St. Peter's cross is said to have stood. A few grains of the sacred sand from the hole in the centre of the chapel are given to visitors by the monks as a relic.

"St. Peter, when he was come to the place of execution, requested of the officers that he might be crucified with his head downwards, alleging that he was not worthy to suffer in the same manner his divine Master had died before him. He had preached the cross of Christ, had borne it in his heart, and its marks in his body, by sufferings and mortification, and he had the happiness to end his life on the cross. The Lord was pleased not only that he should die for his love, but in the same manner himself had died for us, by expiring on the cross, which was the throne of his love. Only the apostle's humility made a difference, in desiring to be crucified with his head downward. His Master looked toward heaven, which by his death he opened to men; but he judged that a sinner formed from dust, and going to return to dust, ought rather in confusion to look on the earth, as unworthy to raise his eyes to heaven. St. Ambrose, St. Austin, and St. Prudentius ascribe this his petition partly to his humility, and partly to his desire of suffering more for Christ. Seneca mentions that the Romans sometimes crucified men with their heads downward; and Eusebius testifies that several martyrs were put to that cruel death. Accordingly, the executioners easily granted the apostle his extraordinary request. St. Chrysostom, St. Austin, and St. Austerius say that he was nailed to the cross; Tertullian mentions that he was tied with cords. He was probably both nailed and bound with ropes."—*Alban Butler.*

The view from the front of the church is almost unrivalled. Behind it is the famous *Fontana Paolina*, whose name, by a curious coincidence, combines those of its architect, Fontana, and its originator, Paul V. It was erected in 1611, and is supplied with water from the Lake of Bracciano, by the aqueduct of the Aqua Trajana, thirty-five miles in length. The red granite columns, which divide the fountain, were brought from the temple of Minerva in the Forum Transitorium.

"The pleasant, natural sound of falling water, not unlike that of a distant cascade in the forest, may be heard in many of the Roman streets and piazzas, when the tumult of the city is hushed ; for consuls, emperors, and popes, the great men of every age, have found no better way of immortalising their memories, than by the shifting, indestructible, ever new, yet unchanging, up-gush and down-fall of water. They have written their names in that unstable element, and proved it a more durable record than brass or marble."—*Hawthorne.*

"Il n'y a rien encore, dans quelque état que ce soit, à opposer aux magnifiques fontaines qu'on voit à Rome dans les places et les carrefours, ni à l'abondance des eaux qui ne cessent jamais de couler; magnificence d'autant plus louable que l'utilité publique y est jointe."—*Duclos.*

A little beyond this fountain is the modern *Porta S. Pancrazio*, near the site of the ancient Porta Aurelia, built by Pius IX. in 1857, to replace a gate destroyed by the French under Oudinot in 1849. Many buildings outside the gate, injured at the same time, still remain in ruins.

The lane on the right, inside the gate, leads to the *Villa Lante*, built in 1524 by Giulio Romano, for Bartolomeo da Pescia, secretary of Clement VII. It still contains some frescoes of Giulio Romano, though they are only lately uncovered, as the house was used, until the last two years, as a succursale to the Convent of the Sacré Cœur at the Trinità de' Monti.

Not far outside the gate are the *Church and Convent of S. Pancrazio*, founded in the sixth century by Pope Symmachus, but modernized in 1609 by Cardinal Torres. Here Crescenzio Nomentano, the famous consul of Rome in the tenth century, is buried ; here Narses, after the defeat of Totila, was met by the pope and cardinals, and conducted in triumph to St. Peter's to return thanks for his victory ; here, also, Peter II. of Arragon was crowned by Innocent III., and Louis of Naples was received by John XII.

A flight of steps leads from the church to the *Catacomb of Calepodius*, where many of the early popes and martyrs were buried. It has no especial characteristic to make it worth visiting. Another flight of steps leads to the spot where S. Pancrazio was martyred. His body rests with that of St. Victor beneath the altar. A parish church in London is dedicated to St. Pancras, in whose name kings of France used to confirm their treaties.

"In the persecution under Diocletian, this young saint, who was only fourteen years of age, offered himself voluntarily as a martyr, defending boldly before the emperor the cause of the Christians. He was therefore beheaded by the sword, and his body was honourably buried by Christian women. His church, near the gate of S. Pancrazio, has existed since the year 500. St. Pancras was in the middle ages regarded as the protector against false oaths, and the avenger of perjury. It was believed that those who swore falsely by St. Pancras were immediately and visibly punished ; hence his popularity."—*Jameson's Sacred Art.*

(Turning to the left from the gate, on the side of the hill between this and the Porta Portese, is the *Catacomb of S. Ponziano*.

" Here is the only perfect specimen still extant of a primitive subterranean baptistery. A small stream of water runs through this cemetery, and at this one place the channel has been deepened so as to form a kind of reservoir, in which a certain quantity of water is retained. We descend into it by a flight of steps, and the depth of water it contains varies with the height of the Tiber. When that river is swollen so as to block up the exit by which this stream usually empties itself, the waters are sometimes so dammed back as to inundate the adjacent galleries of the catacomb ; at other times there are not above three or four feet of water. At the back of the font, and springing out of the water, is painted a beautiful Latin cross, from whose sides leaves and flowers are budding forth, and on the two arms rest ten candlesticks, with the letters Alpha and Omega suspended by a little chain below them. On the front of the arch over the font is the Baptism of our Lord in the river Jordan by St. John, whilst St. Abdon, St. Sennen, St. Miles, and other saints of the Oriental Church occupy the sides. These paintings are all of late date, perhaps of the seventh or eighth century: but there is no reason to doubt but that the baptistery had been so used from the earliest times. We have distinct evidence in the Acts of the Martyrs that the sacrament was not unfrequently administered in the cemeteries."—*The Roman Catacombs—Northcote.*

In this catacomb is an early *Portrait of Christ*, much resembling that at SS. Nereo ed Achilleo.

"The figure is, however, draped, and the whole work has certain peculiarities which appear to mark a later period of art. Both these portraits agree, if not strictly, yet in general features, with the description in Lentulus's letter (to the Roman senate), and portraits and descriptions together serve to prove that the earliest Christian delineators of the person of the Saviour followed no arbitrary conception of their own, but were guided rather by a particular traditional type, differing materially from the Grecian ideal, and which they transmitted in a great measure to future ages."—*Kugler*, i. 16.

In this vicinity are the Catacombs of SS. Abdon and Sennen, of St. Julius, and of Sta. Generosa.)

Opposite the Porta S. Pancrazio is the entrance of the beautiful *Villa Pamfili Doria* (open to pedestrians and to *two-horse* carriages after 12 o'clock on Mondays and Fridays), called by the Italians "Belrespiro." The *Casino* contains a few (not first-rate) ancient statues, and some views of Venice in the seventeenth century by *Heintius*. The garden, for which especial permission must be obtained, is full of beautiful azaleas and camellias.

From the ilex-fringed terrace in front of the casino is one of the best views of St. Peter's, which is here seen without the town,—backed by the Campagna, the Sabine Mountains, and the blue peak of Soracte. The road to the left leads through pine-shaded lawns and woods, and by some modern ruins, to the lake, above which is a graceful fountain. A small temple raised in 1851 commemorates the French who fell here during the siege of Rome in 1849. The word "Mary" in large letters of clipped box on the other side of the grounds is a memorial of the late beloved Princess Doria (Lady Mary Talbot). Not far from this is a columbarium.

The site of the Villa Doria was once occupied by the gardens of Galba, and here the murdered emperor is believed to have been buried.

"Un certain Argius, autrefois esclave de Galba, ramassa son corps, qui avait subi mille outrages, et alla lui creuser une humble sépulture dans les jardins de son ancien maître; mais il fallut retrouver la tête : elle avait été mutilée et promenée par les goujats de l'armée. Enfin Argius la trouva le lendemain, et la réunit au corps déjà brûlé. Les jardins de Galba étaient sur le Janicule, près de la voie Aurélienne, et on croit que le lieu qui vit le dernier dénouement de cette affreuse tragédie est celui qu'occupe aujourd'hui la plus charmante promenade de Rome, là où inclinent avec tant de grâce sur les pentes semées d'anémones et où dessinent si délicatement sur l'azur du ciel et des montagnes leurs parasols élégants les pins de la villa Pamphili."—*Ampère, Emp.* ii. 80.

The foundation of the Villa Pamfili Doria is due to the wealth extorted by Olympia Maldacchini during the reign of her brother-in-law, Innocent X.

"Innocent X. fut, pour ainsi dire, contraint de fonder la maison Pamphili. Les casuistes et les jurisconsultes levèrent ses scrupules, car il en avait. Ils lui prouvèrent que le pape était en droit d'économiser sur les revenus du saint-siége pour assurer l'avenir de sa famille. Ils fixèrent, avec une modération qui nous fait dresser les cheveux sur la tête, le chiffre des libéralités permises à chaque pape. Suivant eux, le souverain pontife pouvait, sans abuser, établir un majorat de quatre mille francs de rente nette, fonder une seconde géniture en faveur de quelque parent moins avantagé, et donner neuf cent mille francs de dot à chacune de ses nièces. Le général des jésuites, R. P. Vitelleschi, approuva cette décision. Là-dessus, Innocent X. se mit à fonder la maison Pamphili, à construire le palais Pamphili, a créer la villa Pamphili, et a pamphiliser, tant qu'il put, les finances de l'église et de l'état."—*About, Rome Contemporaine.*

There are two ways of returning to Rome from the Villa Doria—one, which descends straight into the valley to the Porta Cavalleggieri, passing on the left the Church of Sta. Maria delle Fornaci; the other, skirting the walls of the city beneath the Villa Lante, which passes a *Chapel*, where St. Andrew's head, lost one day by the canons of St. Peter's, was miraculously re-discovered!

" On ne voit pas que de nouveaux monuments religieux se rapportent aux deux apparitions de Pyrrhus en Italie; seulement les augures firent rétablir le temple du dieu des foudres nocturnes, le dieu étrusco-sabin Summanus, en expiation sans doute de ce que la tête de la statue de Summanus, placée sur le temple de Jupiter Capitolin, avait été détachée par la foudre, et, après qu'on l'eut cherchée en vain, retrouvée dans le Tibre.

" Je ne compare pas, mais j'ai vu le long des murs de Rome, entre la porte Cavalleggieri et la porte Saint Pancrace, une petite chapelle élevée au lieu où l'on a retrouvé la tête de Saint André apportée solennellement de Constantinople à Rome au quinzième siècle, et qui s'était perdue.'
—*Ampère, Hist. Rom.* iii. 55.

"Therefore farewell, ye hills, and ye, ye envineyarded ruins!
  Therefore farewell, ye walls, palaces, pillars, and domes!
Therefore farewell, far seen, ye peaks of the mythic Albano,
  Seen from Montorio's height, Tibur and Æsula's hills!
Ah, could we once ere we go, could we stand, while, to ocean descending,
  Sinks o'er the yellow dark plain slowly the yellow broad sun,
Stand from the forest emerging at sunset, at once in the champaign,
  Open, but studded with trees, chestnuts umbrageous and old,
E'en in those fair open fields that incurve to thy beautiful hollow,
  Nemi imbedded in wood, Nemi inurn'd in the hill!—
Therefore farewell, ye plains, and ye hills, and the City Eternal!
  Therefore farewell! we depart, but to behold you again!"
A. H. Clough, Amours de Voyage.

THE END.

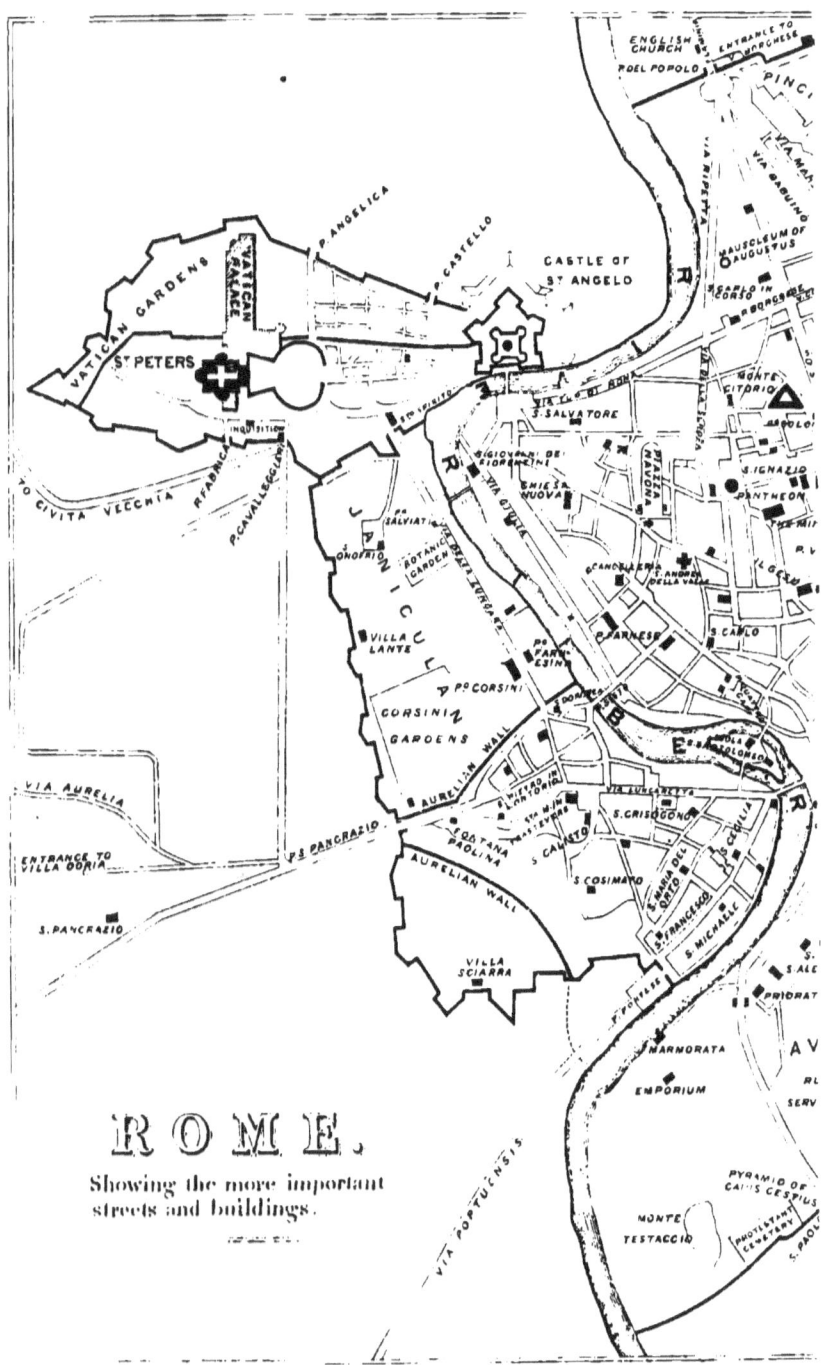

ROME.
Showing the more important streets and buildings.

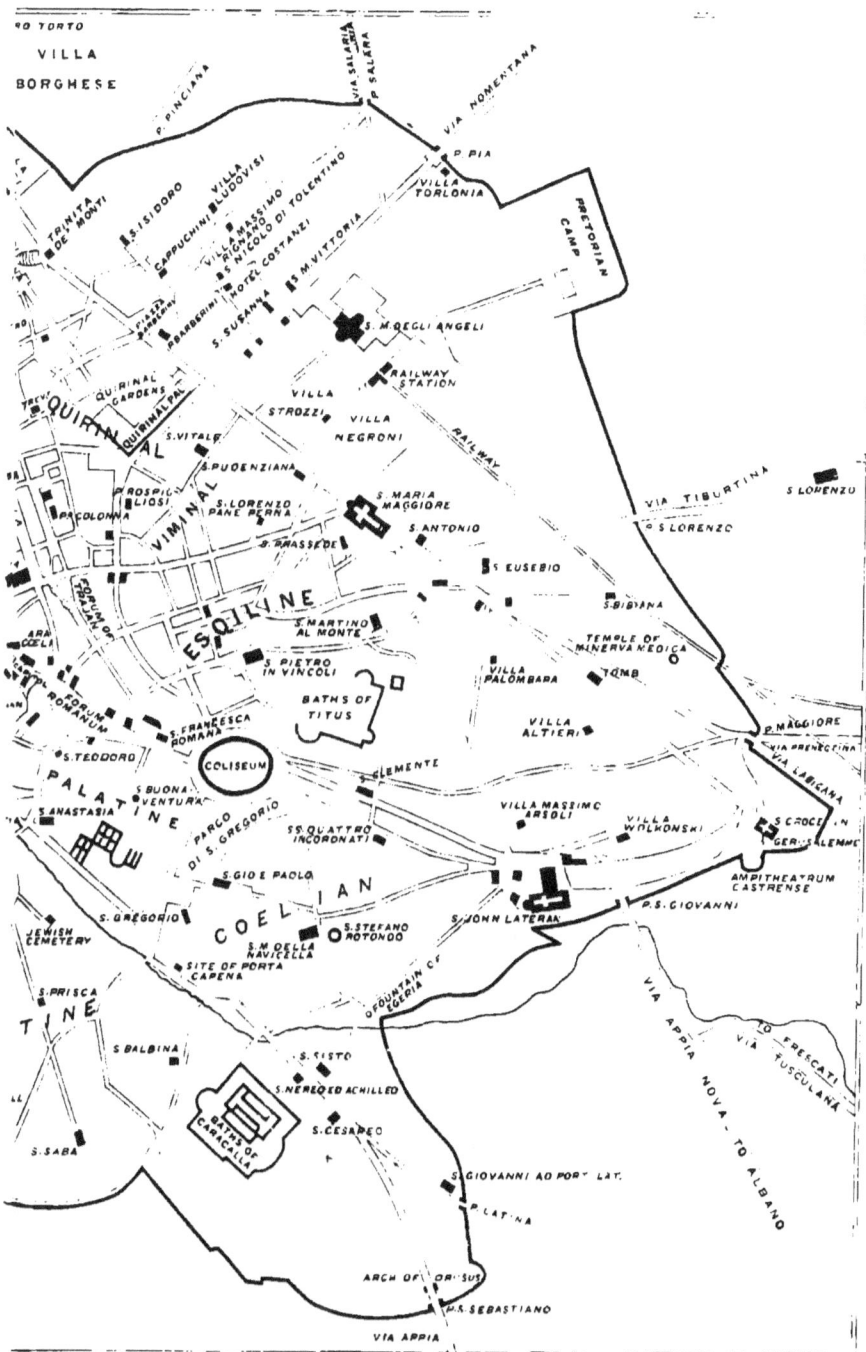

INDEX.

A.

Academy for French Art-students, i. 49; costume described, 55; of St. Luke, 59, 167
Accademia, annual entertainment in honour of Tasso at, ii. 437
Æsculapius, temple of, ii. 364
Agger of Servius Tullius, remains of, ii. 38
Agnese, St., martyrdom of, ii. 193, 195
Agrippa, baths of, ii. 211
Alban Hills, i. 368, 373
Albani, Fra, i. 69, 141, 267, 268, 455; ii. 443
Alberteschi family, Castle of the, ii. 368
Albertinelli, Mariotto, i. 459
Aldobrandini family, burial-place of, ii. 214
Alexis, St., legend of, i. 362
Algardi, ii. 167, 265
Allegrani, i. 461
Almo, the, i. 373, 375, 413; ii. 408
Altieri family, burial-place of, ii. 216
Alunno, Niccolo, ii. 357
Amici, ii. 260
Ammanati, i. 72; ii. 450
Amphitheatrum Castrense, ii. 131
Angelico, Fra, ii. 216, 324, 348, 444
Angelo, St., Castle of, i. 37; view of, 43; its original use, 227; its architecture, 228; its history, as a fortress, 229—232; alterations in it, caused by popes, 232; intérior, 233; prisons, 234; sculptures, 234; passage intended for the escape of popes to the Castle, 234; Ponte, ii. 225, 226

Anicii, Castle built by the family of the, ii. 362
Anio, river, ii. 31; Castle of Rustica on banks of, 135
Antemnæ, site of, ii. 420
Antinous, the most beautiful statue in the world, ii. 308
Antiquities, shops at which to buy, i. 29; in Kircherian Museum, 88; in Palazzo Torlonia, 104; in Museum of Guidi, 379; principal receptacle in Rome for, ii. 114; in Palazzo Vidoni, 185; collection of, in the Vatican, 300; chair used at the installation of mediæval popes, 316; in the Vatican library, 324; in the Egyptian Museum, 333
Apollo, Temple of, i. 296; ii. 134 Belvedere, ii. 311
Appia, Via, i. 372; beginning of beauty of, 424
Aqua Acetosa, ii. 420
 Alexandrina, ii. 133
 Argentina, used by Castor and Pollux, i. 229
 Bollicante, ii. 133
 Claudia, ii. 113
 Felice, ii. 124
 Marcia, remains of, ii. 95
Aqueduct, Claudian, ii. 125.
Arches—
 of Ancient Basilica, ii. 405
 of Aqua Claudia, ii. 123
 l'Arco dell' Annunziata, ii. 380
 Arco di S. Lazzaro, ii. 393
 Arco Oscuro, ii. 420
 Arco dei Pantani, i. 165
 of Cloaca Maxima, i. 229
 of Constantine, i. 206, 319, 375
 of Dolabella, i. 330

458   INDEX.

Arches—*continued.*
  of Drusus, i. 376, 387
  of Gallienus, ii. 71
  of Janus, i. 229
  of Septimius Severus, i. 170, 173;
    miniature, 232
  three gigantic, i. 184
  of Tiberius, i. 173
  in Palace of Tiberius, i. 291
  of Titus, i. 200
Architecture, Museum of antiquities of, i. 122, 170, 311; decadence of, 232; primitive ecclesiastical, 343; specimens of pagan, 405; of street, ii. 63; of tenth century, remains of, in the Lateran, 102; relics of, 104; of St. Peter's, 244; of the interior of Sistine Chapel, 288; remnants of mediæval, 379; remains of ancient, in cloister of Basilica, 405
Arnolphus, ii. 373
Arpino, Cav. d', i. 267, 459; ii. 43, 88; tomb of, 105; works of, 119, 252, 381
Art, Museum of, i. 39; specimen of, of the Middle Ages, 193; decadence of, 232; influence of Byzantine upon Roman, 341; earliest instance of the Transfiguration treated in, 380; catacomb, 402; encouragement of, by Herodes, 414; criticisms, showing the difference of French and English taste in, ii. 43; remains of ancient pictorial, 53; relics of, 212; finest specimen in Rome of ancient pictorial, 326
Artists, studios of, i. 30; lists of subjects for, 34; frescoes by modern German, 54; models for, 56; view familiar to, ii. 62; casino decorated by modern German, 122; picturesque subjects for, 124, 134; Festa degli Artiste, 135; points in Sta. Maria in Trastevere interesting to, 387
Arx, i. 115
Atticus, Herodes, romantic story of, i. 414, 415
Augustine, St., place of departure from Rome of, i. 319
Augustus, Palace of, i. 279; Crypto-Porticus, 281; Tablinum, 285; Lararium, 285; Peristyle, 285; Triclinium, 286; Nymphæum,

287; Bibliotheca, Theatre, Sacrificial Altar, 288
Aurelian, Wall of, i. 385; Temple of the Sun, 436; favourite residence of, ii. 12
Ave-Maria bell, i. 44, 57
Aventine, the, i. 348; origin of name, and story of, 349; temples on, 351—353; reason of decline of its popularity, 354; best approach to, 355; Jewish burial-ground, 355; Convent and Church of Sta. Sabina, 356; Church and Convent of S. Alessio, 362; view of St. Peter's from, 365; legend of Cacus, 366; Church of S. Sabba, 369

B.

Babuino, the, i. 36
Baciccio, i. 444; ii. 213, 379, 443
Badalocchi, i. 323
Baglioni, ii. 41
Balconies, in Corso, i. 61; of house of Lucrezia Borgia, ii. 62; in vestibule of the Torso, 307
Bambino, Il Santissimo, story of, i. 151
Bandinelli, Baccio, ii. 219
Baptistery of the Lateran, ii. 96
Barberini, Piazza, i. 436; Palazzo, 436; library, 437; bees of the, 438, ii. 262; collection of pictures, i. 439; pine, celebrated, 443; Cardinal, ii. 9; casino of the, 12; castle, 34; garden, 45; tomb of Urban VIII., 261
Barcaccia, the, i. 57
Barigione, Filippo, ii. 266
Baroccio [Barocci], i. 70, 97, 454, 455; ii. 167, 214, 221, 335, 358, 442, 443
Bartolomeo, Fra, i. 68, 82, 140, 455; ii. 442
Basaiti, i. 94
Basilicas (*pagan*)—
  of Æmilius Paulus, i. 181
  Constantine, remains of, i. 184; ii. 80
  Julia, i. 175
  Palace of the Cæsars, in the, i. 282
  Porcia, i. 182
  Sessorian, ii. 131
Basilicas (*Christian*)
  St' Agnese fuori le Mura, ii. 26

INDEX. 459

Basilicas (*Christian*)—*continued.*
S. Alessandro, ii. 32
Sta. Croce, ii. 128
Eudoxian, ii. 54
St. John Lateran, ii. 98
S. Lorenzo, ii. 136
Sta. Maria Maggiore, ii. 81
Original building on site of St. Peter's, story of the, ii. 242
S. Paolo fuori le Mura, ii. 402
S. Sebastiano, i. 416
S. Stefano, ii. 124
Bassano, Giac., i. 70; ii. 201
Baths—
of Agrippa, only remaining fragment, ii. 211
of Caracalla, i. 376
of Constantine, i. 436
of Diocletian, ii. 36, 38
discoveries amongst ruins of, i. 377
enervating influence of, i. 377
of Nero, ii. 202
of Titus, ii. 52
Battoni, i, 456; ii. 41
Befana, festival of the, ii. 202
Bellini, Giov., i. 71, 94, 140, 141, 439
Belvidere, view from, i. 50
Benedict, St., house inhabited by, ii. 368
Benvenuti, Gio. Batt., i. 96
Benzoni, i. 225
Berghem, ii. 72; ii. 442
Bernini, i. 41, 57, 76, 78, 98, 137, 139; ii. 14, 43, 69, 75, 89, 103, 157, 196, 206, 211, 238, 246, 251, 252, 257, 261, 264, 283, 298, 379, 420
Bianchi, P., ii. 41
Bivium, i. 390
Bocca della Verita, in Sta. Maria in Cosmedin, i. 233
Bologna, Pellegrino da, ii. 200
Bonifazio, i. 71, 99; ii. 348
Borghese, Camillo, tomb of, ii. 87
Cervaletto, property of the, ii. 87
Chapel, legend commemorated in, ii. 81; picture attributed to St. Luke in, 85
Inscriptions, in possession of the family, i. 414
Palazzo, i. 65
Piazza, i. 66
Picture Gallery, i. 66
Princess, funeral of, ii. 88
Villa, unhealthiness of, i. 21;

Borghese—*continued.*
entrance and gardens of, ii. 411, 412; casino in, 413
Borgia, burial-place of family, ii. 98
Cæsar, ii. 325
Lucrezia, ii. 62
Rodrigo, Pope Alexander VI., grave of, ii. 170; empty tomb of, 269; representations of the life of, 325
Borgo, the, or *Leonine City*, ii. 235
Borgognone, i. 444
Borromeo, S. Carlo, ii. 63
Borromini, ii. 99, 175, 178
Boschetto, the, i. 50
Both, ii. 442
Botticelli Sandro, i. 67, 99, 140, 440; ii. 287
Bracci, Pietro, ii. 259
Bramante, ii. 244, 284, 298, 308
Brandini, i. 444
Brescia, Moretto da, ii. 358
Bresciano, Prospero, ii. 42
Breughel, i. 96
Brill, Paul, i. 457; ii. 41, 298
Bronzes, i. 29; in Kircherian Museum, 88
Bronzino, i. 67, 69, 83, 96, 97, 99, 439; ii. 444, 445
Burial-ground, New, Prati del Popolo Romano, ii. 397
Burial-place of Sta. Domitilla, i. 411

C.

Cæsars, Palace of the, i. 250; foundation of, 274; its ruins, 275; excavations and discoveries in, 276, 305
Caffè, Nuovo, i. 72
Cagnacci, Guido, i. 167
Caius Gracchus, spot where he was killed, ii. 377
Calendar, Paschal, ii. 118; New, invented in reign of Gregory XIII., 258
Caligula, Palace of, i. 292; bridge of, 299; obelisk brought to Rome by, ii. 238; circus of, 283
Camassei, ii. 96
Cambiaso, Luc., i. 71
Cameos, i. 29
Camosci, Pietra, ii. 62
Campagna, i. 43, 51; view of, 378; ruins of tombs in, 424; infection by malaria of, 403, 408

460 INDEX.

Campaniles of—
　Sta. Cecilia, ii. 372
　S. Giovanni a Porta Latina, i. 384
　S. Lorenzo in Lucina, i. 73
　S. Lorenzo Pane e Perna, i. 468
　Sta. Maria in Cosmedin, i. 234
　Sta. Maria in Monticelli, ii. 182
　S. Sisto, i. 382
Campo, Militare, ii. 34 ; di Fiore, the scene of Autos da Fé, 176
Campus Esquilinus, ii. 36
Campus Martius, situation, extent, and origin of, ii. 148—150 ; earliest buildings of, 150—155 ; remains of buildings of, 155 ; its interest and condition, 155
Camuccini, ii. 119, 407
Canaletti, ii. 442
Canova, i. 101 ; ii. 251, 266, 308, 347, 415
Cantharus, specimen of a Roman vase, ii. 372
Capena, Porta, site of, i. 373 ; historical interest of, 432
Capitol, the, i. 36 ; story of the Hill, 109 ; temples on, 111—115 ; Piazza del Campidoglio, 119 ; Tower of, 121 ; Tabularium, 122 ; Museo Capitolino, 122 ; Gallery of Sculpture, 125 ; Picture-Gallery, 140 ; Tarpeian Rock, 143 ; Church of Ara-Cœli, 144—152 ; Mamertine Prisons, 153
Cappuccini, Piazza, ii. 7; Cemetery,10
Caravaggio, i. 83, 140, 141, 439, 459; ii. 120, 121, 201, 345, 356, 442
Carinæ, ii. 47
Caritas Romana, i. 241
Carracci, Agostino, i. 83, 100
Carracci, Ann., i. 41, 69, 95—97, 99, 139, 324, 325 ; ii. 174 ; tomb of, in the Pantheon, 210 ; paintings by, 379, 436
Carracci, Lud., i. 141, 458 ; ii. 442—444
Casale dei Pazzi, ii. 32
Casino—
　in Villa Albani, ii. 17
　in Villa Borghese, ii. 413
　del Papa, ii. 335
　of Papa Giulio, ii. 418
　in Quirinal Palace, i. 456
　in Palazzo Rospigliosi, i. 456
　of Sculpture, ii. 14
Castel Giubeleo, ii. 425
Castelli, Bernardo, ii. 221

Castles of—
　St. Angelo, i. 37, 43 ; ii. 227—234
　the Alberteschi family, ii. 368
　the Anicii family, ii. 368
　the Anquillara, ii. 379
　Crescenza, ii. 423
　Rustica, ii. 135
Catacombs—
　ad Nymphas, ii. 33
　of St' Agnese, ii. 29
　of Calepodius, ii. 453
　of St. Calixtus, origin and character of, i. 390—399 ; paintings in, 401—405
　of Sta. Ciriaca, destruction of, ii. 142, 145
　of S. Felicitas, ii. 20
　of SS. Gianutus and Basilla, ii. 418
　of St. Hippolytus, ii. 147
　Jewish, i. 407
　of SS. Nereo ed Achilleo, i. 408
　of SS. Pietro e Marcellino, ii. 133
　of St. Pretextatus, i. 405
　of S. Ponziano, ii. 453
　of Sta. Priscilla, graves of martyrs in, ii. 20—24
　of the Santi Quattro, ii. 125
　of S. Sebastiano, i. 417
　of St. Valentin, ii. 418
Cathedra Petri, in St. Peter's, ii. 261
Catherine, St., of Siena, life of, ii. 217
Cavallini, Pietro, ii. 246, 256, 384, 386, 406
Cavaluccio, ii. 63
Cecilia, Sta., account of, ii. 371 ; relics and tomb of, 373 ; house of, 375 ; Festa of, 375
Ceiling of Sistine Chapel, painting of, ii. 288—292
Cemeteries—
　oldest Christian, i. 409
　ruins of early Christian, ii. 29
　of S. Lorenzo, ii. 144
　old Protestant, graves of Keats and Hare in, ii. 395, 396
　of S. Zeno, site of, ii. 399
Cenci, tragedies in the family of the, i. 260—267 ; portraits of Lucrezia and Beatrice, 440 ; grave of Beatrice, ii. 450
Centocellæ, ii. 133
Chapels—
　of Sant' Agnese, ii. 195
　of St. Andrew, i. 325 ; in honour of St. Andrew's head, ii. 421

Chapels—*continued.*
  in Ara-Cœli, i. 148
  of St. Barbara, i. 326
  in Baths of Titus, ii. 53
  Borghese, ii. 85
  of Caetani family, i. 470
  Cappella Borgia, ii. 98
  of S. Carlo Borromeo, ii. 69
  in Catacomb of S. Agnese, ii. 30
  Corsini, ii. 103
  of S. Cosimato, ii. 388
  of Santa Croce, i. 444 ; ii. 89
  of S. Filippo Neri, ii. 166
  of Sta. Francesca Romana, i. 196
  of S. Giovanni in Oleo, i. 384
  of Sta. Helena, ii. 130
  of the Holy Sacrament, ii. 89
  of St. John the Baptist, ii. 96
  of St. John the Evangelist, ii. 96
  of San Luigi Gonzaga, i. 86
  in which St. Luke wrote, i. 89
  of the Madonna di Strada Cupa, ii. 385
  of Sta. Maria degli Angeli, ii. 41
  of Sta. Maria in Campitelli, i. 269
  of Sta. Maria in Cappella, ii. 370
  of Sta. Maria sopra Minerva, ii. 213—221
  in Sta. Maria del Popolo, i. 39—42
  of Sta. Martina, i. 189
  Orto del Paradiso, ii. 66
  in Palazzo Altemps, ii. 160
  of the Passion, i. 343
  commemorating the parting of St. Peter and St. Paul, ii. 398
  of the Patrizi family, ii. 88
  containing St. Peter's chains, ii. 61
  of S. Pietro in Montorio, ii. 449
  of the Popes, i. 395
  of the Presepio, i. 149
  Private, of the Pope, i. 455
  Protestant, i. 37
  of the Rosary, i. 358
  Salviati, i. 324
  series of small, remains of ancient basilica, ii. 405 ; in modern basilica, 407
  Sistine, i. 58
  of S. Stanislas Kostka, i. 445
  Subterranean, i. 188
  of S. Sylvestro, i. 341
  of the Virgin, i. 445
  In St. Peter's—
    Baptistery, ii. 267
    dei Canonici, ii. 276
    Cappella Clementine, ii. 264

Chapels—*continued.*
  Cappella della Colonna, ii. 263
  Capella della Colonna Santa, ii. 256
  del Coro, ii. 265
  of the Madonna, ii. 259
  Sta. Maria in Portico, Sta. Maria delle Partoriente, and Cappella del Salvatore, ii. 268
  Pietà of Michael Angelo, ii. 256
  della Presentazione, ii. 266
  of the Santissimo Sacramento, ii. 258
  In the Vatican—
    Cappella di San Lorenzo, ii. 346
    Pauline, ii. 285
    of St. Pius V., ii. 324
    Sistine, ii. 286
Chapter House, of Convent of S. Sisto, i. 382 ; of Lateran, ii. 99
Chigi, Agostini, great art patron in the reign of Leo X., ii. 446
Churches of—
  S. Adriano, i. 190
  Sta. Agata dei Goti, i. 461
  St' Agnese, ii. 193
  St' Agnese fuori le Mura, ii. 26
  S. Agostino, ii. 157
  S. Alessio, i. 362
  Sta. Anastasia, i. 224
  S. Andrea a Monte Cavallo, i. 444
  S. Andrea delle Fratte, i. 75
  S. Andrea della Valle, ii. 184
  St. Andrew, i. 421
  S. Angelo in Pescheria, i. 248
  S. Antonio Abbate, ii. 78
  S. Apollinare, ii. 159
  SS. Apostoli, i. 100
  Ara-Cœli, i. 117, 144
  Sta. Balbina, i. 370
  S. Bartolomeo, ii. 363
  S. Benedetto a Piscinuola, ii. 368
  S. Bernardo, ii. 39, 45
  Sta. Bibiana, ii. 74
  Sta. Brigitta, ii. 173
  S. Buonaventura, i. 204
  S. Caio, i. 443 ; ii. 45
  S. Calisto, ii. 387
  S. Cappuccini, ii. 7
  La Caravita, i. 85
  S. Carlo a Catinari, ii. 183
  S. Carlo in Corso, National Church of the Lombards, i. 64
  S. Carlo a Quattro Fontane, i. 43
  Sta. Caterina de' Funari, i. 268
  Sta. Caterina di Siena, i. 459 ; ii. 224

Churches of—*continued.*
Sta. Cecilia, ii. 370
San Celso in Banchi, ii. 224
S. Cesareo, i. 382
S. Claudio, i. 76
S. Clemente, i. 342 ; ii. 95
S. Cosimato, ii. 388
SS. Cosmo e Damiano, i. 183, 191
Sta. Costanza, ii. 28
S. Crisogono, ii. 381
S. Crispino al Ponte, ii. 369
Sta. Croce in Gerusalemme, i. 54 ; ii. 127
I Crociferi, i. 81
SS. Domenico e Sisto, i. 461
S. Dionisio, i. 474
Domine Quo Vadis, i. 389
Sta. Dorotea, ii. 388
English and American, ii. 410
S. Eusebio, ii. 77
S. Eustachio, ii. 203
S. Francesco di Paola, ii. 62
    a Ripa, ii. 379
Sta. Francesca Romana, i. 195
Gesù e Maria, i. 61
S. Giacomo degli Incurabili, i. 61
S. Giacomo Scossa Cavalli, ii. 237
S. Giorgio in Velabro, i. 231
S. Giovanni Decollato, i. 239
S. Giovanni de' Fiorentini, National Church of the Tuscans, ii. 225
S. Giovanni alla Lungara, ii. 439
SS. Giovanni e Paolo, i. 321, 327
S. Giovanni della Pigna, ii. 209
S. Giovanni a Porta Latina, i. 384
S. Girolamo della Carità, ii. 172
S. Girolamo degli Schiavoni, i. 60
S. Giuseppe dei Falegnami, i. 157
Gothic, of the Caëtani, i. 424
Greek, i. 54
S. Gregorio, i. 319, 322
important to sight-seers, i. 32
S. Ignazio, i. 85
Il Gesù, i. 106
S. Isidoro, ii. 11
S. Ivo of Brittany, ii. 155
SS. Lorenzo e Damaso, ii. 178
S. Lorenzo in Fonte, i. 468
    in Lucina, i. 73
    fuori le Mura, ii. 136
    Pane e Perna, i. 466
S. Luigi dei Francesi, ii. 200
S. Marcello, i. 87

Churches of—*continued.*
S. Marco, i. 105
Sta. Maria degli Angeli, ii. 40
    dell' Anima, ii. 160
    in Aquiro, i. 79
    Aventina, i. 365
    in Campitelli, i. 269
    in Cappella, ii. 370
    della Concezione, ii. 7
    in Cosmedin, i. 232
    in Domenico, i. 332
    delle Fornaci, ii. 456
    Liberatrice, i. 190
    di Loreto, i. 162
    Maggiore, i. 54
    sopra Minerva, ii. 212
    di Monserrato, ii. 170
    in Montecelli, ii. 182
    in Monti, i. 464
    del Orto, ii. 378
    della Pace, ii. 163
    della Pietà in Campo Santo, ii. 278
    del Popolo, i. 39
    Scala Cœli, ii. 399
    Traspontina, ii. 236
    in Trastevere, ii. 382
    in Trivia, i. 81
    in Valicella, ii. 166
    in Via Lata, i. 89
    di Vienna, i. 162
    della Vittoria, ii. 43
Sta. Marta, ii. 278
Sta. Martina, i. 188
S. Martino al Monte, ii. 63
S. Michaele in Sassia, ii. 280
SS. Nereo ed Achilleo, i. 379
S. Nicolo in Carcere, i. 240
    in Tolentino, ii. 12
S. Onofrio, ii. 434
S. Onofrio in Campagna, ii. 428
dell' Orazione, ii. 175
S. Pancrazio, ii. 452
S. Pantaleone, ii. 188
S. Paolo fuori le Mura, ii. 403
    Primo Eremita, i. 473
    alle Tre Fontane, ii. 401
the Perpetua Adoratrice del Divin Sacramento del Altare, i. 446
S. Pietro in Carcere, ii 153
SS. Pietro e Marcellino, ii. 122
S. Pietro in Montorio, ii. 449
    in Vincoli, ii. 54
Sta. Prassede, ii. 65
Sta. Prisca, i. 367
Sta. Prudenziana, i. 469

Churches of—*continued.*
SS. Quattro Incoronati, i. 340
SS. Rocco e Martino, i. 60
S. Sabba, i. 369
Sta. Sabina, i. 356
S. Salvatore in Lauro, ii. 224
S. Salvatore in Torrione, ii. 280
Il Santissimo Redentore, ii. 71
S. Sebastiano, i. 203
S. Silvestro a Monte Cavallo, i. 459
S. Sisto, i. 381
S. Stefano, ii. 278
S. Stefano Rotondo, i. 333
Sta. Susanna, ii. 44
on the site of Sylla's tomb, i. 37
S. Sylvestro in Capite, i. 74
S. Teodoro, i. 223
Sta. Teresa, ii. 45
S. Tommaso dei Cenci, i. 260
S. Tommaso degli Inglesi, ii. 170
the Trinità de' Monti, i. 52
Trinità dei Pellegrini, ii. 181
S. Urbano, i. 413
SS. Vincenzo ed Anastasio, ii. 400
S. Vitale, i. 474
S. Vito, ii. 71
Ciampelli, Agostino, ii. 75
Cicero, House of, i. 301; place of reception on return from banishment, 375
Cignazi, ii. 445
Cigoli, i. 69; ii. 88, 225
Cimeterio dei Tedeschi, oldest Christian burial-ground, ii. 278
Circus of—
Caligula, ii. 283
Flaminius, site of, i. 268
Maxentius, i. 422
Nero, ii. 283
Claude, i. 40
Clement, St., Church of, i. 342; house of, 347; exile of, 347
Clivus Capitolinus, i. 170, 172
Martis, i. 388
Victoriæ, i. 292
Cloaca Maxima, celebrated drain, i. 230
Cloisters—
of the Convent, ii. 165
of the Monastery, ii. 105, 144
of the twelfth century, ii. 405
Villino, Casino of Papa Giulio, ii. 418
Clovis, G., Tomb of, ii. 56
Club, French Military, i. 77
Cœlian Hill, its extent, and origin of name, i. 316; Parco di San Gregorio, 319; world-famous inscriptions, 319; Church of St. Gregory, 322; Church of SS. Giovanni e Paolo, 329; the Navicella, 330; S. Stefano Rotondo, 333; frescoes recording martyrdoms, 334; SS. Quattro Incoronati, 340; S. Clemente, 342

Coliseum, building of, i. 207, 208; architect unknown, dedication, 209; gladiatorial combats in arena of, 210; death of Christian martyrs in, 211; its size, grandeur, and extensive view, 215; history of its destruction and present preservation, 217, 218; ecclesiastical legends connected with it, 219; origin of name, 220

Collatia, ruins of the, ii. 135
Colle, Raffaello da, ii. 337, 339, 340
College for English missionaries, ii. 171
Collegio di Propaganda Fede, object of, i. 58
Collegio Romano, i. 87
Colonna, Agnese Gaetani, funeral urn of, ii. 273
Gardens, i. 458
Lorenzo, murder of, ii. 224
Oddone, tomb of, ii. 100
Palazzo, i. 98; Picture Gallery in, 99
Piazza, i. 77
Princess, tomb of, ii. 213
Vittoria, death of, ii. 387
Colonnades, of St. Peter's, ii. 238
Columbaria, i. 385, 386, 390
of the Arruntia family, ii. 77
of the Freedmen of Octavia, i. 385
Columna Lactaria, i. 242
Columns—
Colonna delle Virgine, ii. 80
Corinthian, sixteen, from Hadrian's Villa, ii. 317
Corinthian, sixteen, of the Pantheon, ii. 206
Corinthian, twenty-four marble, i. 357; ii. 63
Ionic, in S. Lorenzo, ii. 141
Ionic, of Temple of Saturn, i. 172
Ionic, twenty-two ancient, ii. 384
marble, twelve ancient, i. 233
in front of Palazzo di Spagna, i. 57
from Palestrina, twenty ancient, ii. 319

Columns—*continued.*
Pavonazzetto, ii. 118
of Phocas, i. 179
in Piazza Colonna, i. 77
relics, to which Peter and Paul were bound, ii. 236
relic, to which our Saviour is reputed to have been bound, ii. 68
of Temple of Castor and Pollux, i. 175
of Temple of Minerva, i. 165
of Temple of Vespasian, i. 171
in Theatre of Marcellus, i. 244
of Trajan, i. 160
Connell, Daniel O', monument of, i. 462
Constantine, statue of, i. 118; basilica of, 184; arch of, 206; frescoes representing the conversion of, 341; baths of, 458; last remaining column of basilica of, ii. 80; frescoes of legendary history of, 99; erection of a basilica on the site of St. Peter's, by, 242; Cimeterio dei Tedeschi, set apart by, 278; Saxe Rubra, site of decisive victory by, 425
Contadino, i. 386
Conte, Giacomo del, ii. 200
Conti, extinction of the family of the, ii. 54
Convents of—
Sta. Agate in Suburra, i. 461
S. Alessio, i. 362
Ara-Cœli, i. 153
Augustine, temporary residence of Luther, i. 42
S. Bartolomeo, ii. 363
S. Bernardo, ii. 45
the Buon Pastore, ii. 439
S. Buonaventura, i. 204
Camaldolese monks, i. 326
Carthusian, ii. 42
Sta. Caterina, i. 460
Sta. Cecilia, ii. 370
Cloister of the, ii. 165
the Minerva, ii. 122
S. Eusebio, ii. 77
Sta. Francesca Romana, i. 198
S. Francesco a Ripa, ii. 379
the Gesù, i. 107
Group of, ii. 65
Maronites monks, ii. 62
Monache Polacche, ii. 72
the Noviciate of the order of Jesus, i. 445

Convents of—*continued.*
S. Onofrio, ii. 435
the Oratorians, ii. 166
S. Pancrazio, ii. 452
S. Paolo, ii. 387
S. Pietro in Vincoli, ii. 53
Poor Clares, ii. 388
the Pregatrici, ii. 12
Sta. Sabina, i. 355
Sacré Cœur, i. 53
Santi Quattro Incoronati, i. 340, 342
Sepolte Vive, of the Farnesiani nuns, i. 465
S. Silvestro a Monte Cavallo, i. 459
S. Sisto, i. 381
S. Tommaso in Formis, i. 331
Tor de' Specchi, i. 270
Ursuline, i. 64
Visitandine nuns, i. 304
Coppi, Jacopo, ii. 56
Cordieri, Niccolo, i. 325, 326; ii. 99, 214
Cordonnata, La, i. 118
Cornacchini, ii. 246
Correggio, i. 68, 96; ii. 359
Corsini, Palazzo, the residence of distinguished personages, ii. 439
Corso, the, i. 36, 58, 60, 105; ii. 222
Cortile del Belvidere, ii. 308
S. Damaso, 337, 347, 359
Cortona, Pietro da, i. 69, 188, 268, 438; ii. 8, 75, 163, 166, 167, 183, 196, 224, 238
Cosmati, Deodatus, ii. 113
Giovanni, ii. 216
Costanzi, P., ii. 41, 261
Cranach, Lucas, i. 72, 82
Credi, Lorenzo di, i. 67
Crivelli, Carlo, i. 67, 105; ii. 120, 348
Cross, formed by cannon reversed, ii. 78; in form of Corsini Chapel 103
Crypts—
of S. Alessio, i. 364
in catacomb of St. Pretextatus, i. 405
only remains of the basilica on the site of St. Peter's, ii. 243
of St. Peter's, ii. 267
Crypto-Porticus, i. 281
Cubiculum of Sta. Cecilia, i. 397
of Pope St. Eusebius, i. 398
Cybele, Temple of, i. 294; Sacred Stone, 294; place of washing of the statue of, ii. 408

INDEX. 465

D.

Dalmatica di Papa San Leone, in Treasury of St. Peter's, ii. 276
Damasus, Pope St., inscriptions of, i. 396, 407, 418
David, i. 445
Diana, Temple of, i. 353
Diavolo, Casa del, ii. 124
Diocletian, Baths of, ii. 36, 38
Doctors in Rome, i. 28
Dolce, Carlo, i. 69; ii. 443
Domenichino, i. 69, 140, 203, 267, 268, 325, 439, 455, 458, 459; ii. 8, 15, 41, 43, 57, 61, 120, 174, 183, 200, 349, 384, 385, 435, 444
Dominic, St., Convent of, i. 355; orange-tree of, 356; vision of, 358; legends of, 359, 360; first residence of, 381; Divine mission of, 382; place of first meeting with St. Francis, ii. 105
Domitian, Palace of, i. 312; tyrannical vagaries of, 312; murder of, 313; martyrs under, 334
Doria, Palazzo, i. 93; Picture-Gallery in, 93—98; memorial of Princess, 455
Dorotea, Sta., legend of, ii. 390
Drawing, materials, shops for, i. 29; list of subjects for, for artists, 34; best months for, in Rome, 35
Dossi Dossi, i. 68
Durante, Alberti, ii. 167
Dürer, Albert, works of, i. 72, 84, 439; ii. 443

E.

Easter benediction, ceremony of the, ii. 240, 241
Egeria, Fountain of, i. 375; Grotto and grove of, 413
Emelingk, i. 97
Esquiline Hill, derivation of name, situation of, ii. 46; Cispius, and Oppius, 47; Carinæ, 47, 49; Suburra, 49; Tigellum Sororis, 49; residences of poets on the, 50; Septimius, 51; Nero's Golden House, 52; S. Pietro in Vincoli, 54; S. Martino al Monte, 63; Sta. Prassede, 65; Arch of Gallienus, 71; residence of Madre Makrena, 73; Sta. Bibiana, 74; Temple of Minerva Medica, 77; S. Antonio

Abbate, 78; Sta. Maria Maggiore, 81—92; Obelisk, 93
Eustace, St., legend of the conversion of, ii. 204

F.

Fabii, site of the destruction of the, ii. 424
Fabris, de, ii. 246, 257, 436
Faenza, Marco da, ii. 337
Farnese, Palazzo, paintings and frescoes of, ii. 174; Palazzetto, 178
Faustulus and the Sacred Figtree, Hut of, legend of, i. 238
Ferrari, Gaudenzio, i. 82
Ferrata, Ercole, ii. 194, 261
Festa, i. 444
Festa degli Artisti, ii. 135
Fiamingo, Arrigo, ii. 40, 287
Fiesole, Fra Angelico da, ii. 348
   Mino da, ii. 221, 273, 384
Filarete, Antonio, ii. 100
Filomena, Sta., popular saint, ii. 22
Fiori, Mario di, ii. 442
Fontana, ii. 89, 93, 96, 114, 238, 257, 391
Fontana Paolina, ii. 451
Footprint of our Saviour, i. 389, 417
Forums—
   of Augustus, i. 164
   Boarium, i. 227
   of Nerva, i. 165
   Romanum, origin and formation of, i. 168, 169; historical sites and remains of, 170—185; modern name of, 185
   of Trajan, origin and construction of, i. 159, 160
Fountains—
   antique, 388
   in Carthusian Convent, ii. 41
   of Egeria, i. 375
   Lacus Orphei, ii. 51
   near Sta. Maria in Cosmedin, i. 235
   of the Mascherone, ii. 175
   of Palazzo Aldobrandini, i. 461
   in Palace of the Senator, i. 120
   in Piazza Navona, ii. 196
   in Piazza Pia, ii. 236
   in Piazza delle Tartarughe, i. 267
   of the Ponte Sisto, ii. 391
   attributed to the prayers of Peter and Paul in prison, i. 156
   of the Termini, ii. 42
   of Trevi, i. 79

Fracassini, ii. 141, 345
Francia, Francesco, i. 67, 68, 82, 94, 96, 140, 439; ii. 348
Francis, St., relics of, ii. 379; celebration of Christmas by, 380
Frangipani family, castle of the, i. 217; fortress of the, ii. 62
Frescoes, i. 39, 53, 54, 86, 99, 137, 139, 149, 153, 203, 231, 268, 270, 276, 286, 292, 325, 326, 329, 334, 341, 342, 343, 346, 382, 384, 412, 438, 446, 453, 455, 456, 457, 459, 462, 466, 474; ii. 8, 15, 19, 26, 30, 43, 44, 53, 56, 62, 63, 65, 68, 75, 78, 88, 96, 99, 100, 104, 111, 118, 124, 128, 138, 141, 158, 160, 163, 183, 200, 204, 215, 220, 232, 276, 285, 286, 313, 324, 326, 337, 340—346, 374, 384, 388, 400, 407, 416, 423, 426, 435, 436, 446, 452
Friezes, i. 139, 165, 172, 201, 257, 259, 332, 358, 379, 384, 422, 424, 455, 457, 460; ii. 98, 99, 104, 137, 224, 372, 383, 448
Fuga, ii. 439
Funeral, Roman, ii. 145
Furino, i. 69

G.

Gaetani, Scipione, i. 440, 459; ii. 102, 166, 323
Gagliardi, ii. 224
Galiardi, ii. 407
Galileo, place of trial of, ii. 222
Galleria—
  degli Arazzi, ii. 321
  dei Candelabri, ii. 320
  Lapidaria, ii. 300
  delle Statue, ii. 313, 315
Gallery. See Picture.
Garbo, Raffaelino del, ii. 215
Gardens—
  of Adonis, i. 203
  of Barberini Palace, i. 443
  Botanic, ii. 439
  Colonna, i. 458
  containing Columbaria, i. 386
  Government, i. 379
  Hill of, i. 38
  on the Janiculan, ii. 445
  Monastery, i. 329
  of the Pincio, i. 46
  Priorato, i. 365
  of the Quirinal, i. 455
  of Servilia, i. 353
  of Sta. Silvia, i. 324

Gardens—*continued*.
  of Sallust, ii. 12
  of Villa Medici, i. 49
  of Villa Wolkonski, ii. 123
Garofalo, i. 67, 68, 82, 95, 96, 140; ii. 444
Genga, Girolamo, ii. 224
Germale, the, i. 279
Gesù Narazeno, miracle-working picture, ii. 182
Ghetto, the, i. 250; first used as place of captivity, 252; limits of, removed, 254; population and mortality of, 255; merchandise in, 256; division of parishes, 256; chief synagogue, 257; sketch of life in, 257; burial-ground for, 355
Giacometti, ii. 110
Giardino della Pigna, ii. 305, 333; relics preserved in, 333; celebrated Pigna, 334
Gimignano, ii. 96
Giordano, Luca, i. 269, 474; ii. 444
Giorgione, i. 70, 96, 97, 100; ii. 444, 445
Giotto, ii. 104, 215, 246, 277, 324
Giovanni di San Giovanni, i. 341
Gobelin tapestries, i. 454
Gozzoli, Benozzi, ii. 120, 213, 348
Græcostasis, i. 171
Grandi, Ercole, ii. 444
Gregory, St., legend of, i. 322; Church of, 322; monastic cell of, 324; statue of, 326; family to which he belonged, 363
Gros, Le, i. 86, 446
Grottoes of Cerbara, ii. 135
Guercino, i. 69, 83, 94, 95, 140, 141, 267, 455; ii. 15, 43, 57, 157, 168, 348, 355, 356, 442, 444
Guidi, antiquity vendor, i. 379
Guido, i. 140, 167, 325, 455, 456; ii. 7, 43, 62, 88, 103, 166, 174, 181, 183, 200, 359, 374, 443

H.

Halls—
  in Barberini Palace, i. 438
  discovered in ruins of Baths of Caracalla, i. 377
  of Busts, in the Vatican, ii. 315
  in Casino of Villa Borghese, ii. 413
  of the Conservators, i. 137
  of the Dying Gladiator, i. 133
  of the Emperors, i. 126

Halls—*continued*.
 of the Faun, i. 133
 of Illustrious Men, i. 131
 in Library of Vatican, ii. 323
Heads of Lions, on bank of Trastevere, i. 239
Heintius, ii. 454
Hermitage, i. 330
Holbein, i. 72 ; ii. 443, 444
Horti Lamiana, ii. 76
Hospitals—
 for aged women, i. 64
 Foundling, ii. 237
 Sta. Galla, i. 239
 S. Gallicano, ii. 382
 German, ii. 161
 of S. Giovanni Calabita, ii. 365
 for incurable diseases, ii. 370
 S. Michaele, ii. 376
 for receiving and nourishing Pilgrims, ii. 181
 of San Rocco, i. 60
 of Santo Spirito, ii. 237
 Surgical, i. 61
 for Women, ii. 95
Hotels, i. 27
 Costanzi, ii. 12
 del Globo, ii. 12
Houses—
 of Aquila and Priscilla, i. 368
 Cicero, i. 301
 Claude Lorraine, i. 54
 S. Clement, i. 347
 Drusus and Antonia, i. 292
 the Fornarina, ii. 368
 Hortensius, i. 304
 Lucrezia Borgia, ii. 62
 Marchese Campana, ii. 95
 Mark Antony, i. 303
 Nero's Golden, ii. 52
 of Nicholas Poussin, i. 54
 Octavius and Afra, i. 277
 Palestrina, i. 339
 Patrician families, i. 299
 Poets, ii. 50
 Pompey, ii. 48
 Pomponius Atticus, i. 435
 Raphael, ii. 225
 Rienzi, formerly of Pilate, i. 236
 Sta. Silvia, i. 321
 Spurius Mælius, i. 272
 the " Violinista," ii. 225

I.

Ignatius, St., rooms in which he lived, i. 107; his martyrdom, 211

Imola, Innocenza da, i. 82, 99
Inquisition, Palace of the, Inquisition established at, ii. 278 ; abolished and re-established, 279
Inscriptions—
 ancient, in S. Alessandro, ii. 33
 in Catacomb of S. Sebastian, i. 417
 ancient, in Crypt of St. Peter's, ii. 268
 in Cloister of the Monastery, ii. 144
 Early Christian and Pagan, ii. 121, 300, 384
 in Garden of Barberini Palace, i. 443
 in Jewish Catacomb, i. 408
 in. St John Lateran, ii. 99
 on Lunatic Asylum, ii. 439
 on Pantheon, ii. 204
 in S. Paolo fuori le Mura, ii. 405
 St. Peter and St. Paul, commemorating the farewell of, ii. 398
 on Ponte S. Bartolomeo, ii. 367
 on Ponte Sisto, ii. 399
 of Pope St. Damasus, i. 396, 407, 418
 on Porta Maggiore, ii. 132
 on remains of Pons Fabricius, ii. 360
 remarkable, in Portico of St. Peter's, ii. 247
 in S. Sisto, i. 382
 on Tomb of Baker Eurysace, ii. 132
 World-famous, i. 319
Intermontium, the, i. 116
Island in the Tiber, the, tradition of its formation, its ancient name, ii. 361 ; temples on, 362 ; use of, in early and middle ages, ii. 362

J.

Janiculan, the, situation, formation, and early history of, ii. 432—434 ; S. Onofrio, 434 ; Palazzo Corsini, 439 ; Farnesina Villa, 445
Jesuits, Order of the, established, ii. 262 ; re-established, 264
Jews, quarter of the, i. 250 ; history of, in Rome, from early times, 250 ; persecution of, 251, 252 ; terms of occupation of houses by, 253 ; revocation of laws against, 254 ; their population, government, and mor-

tality, 255; Synagogue of, 256;
burial-ground of, 355; cupidity
of, 355; catacomb of, 407; custom of, on the election of a pope,
166
Jupiter, Capitolinus, temples of, i.
111; ii. 366; — Tonans, — Feretrius, — Pistor, temples of, i. 115;
Statue of, 115; — Stator, temple
of, 247, 278; — Redux, temple of,
330; — Inventor, temple of, ii. 392

K.

Kircherian Museum, i. 88

L.

La Madonna Consolatrice degli afflitti, miraculous picture, ii. 221
Lace-shop, well-known, i. 267
Lake of Juturna, i. 176
    Servilius, i. 174
Landini, ii. 97
Lanfranco, i. 267, 268; ii. 88, 183, 225; tomb of, 385; works of, 443
Laocoon, the, in the Vatican, ii. 309
Lares, Shrine of the, i. 382
Lateran, the, i. 207; obelisk of, ii. 95; baptistery of, 96; oratory, 97; basilica, 98; derivation of name of, 98; coronation of popes in, 99; tabernacle, 100; Tabula Magna Lateranensis, 102; Cappella del Coro, 102; Corsini Chapel, 103; cloisters of, 104; five General Councils held at, 105; ancient Palace of, 108; Santa Scala, 110; modern Palace of, 114; objects of interest in, 114—117; Christian Museum, 117; Picture Gallery, 118; School of Music, 121
Leyden, Lucas van, i. 72, 97
Library, i. 29
    Barberini, i. 413, 437
    Bibliotheca Casanatensis, ii. 222
    of Cistercian Monastery, ii. 131
    in Collegio Romano, i. 88
    Corsini, ii. 445
    in Monastery of the Chiesa Nuova, ii. 167
    in Palazzo Chigi, i. 76
    Papal, ii. 322
    in the Vatican, ii. 300; entrance of, 322
Ligorio, Pirro, ii. 335
Lippi, Fil., i. 94, 99; ii. 120, 215

Locanda dell' Orso, ii. 223
Loggie of Raphael, ii. 337
Lorenzetto, i. 41; ii. 354
Lorenzo, St., sketch of life of, ii. 137; and St. Stephen, burial-place of, 143; cemetery of, 144
Lorraine, Claude, works of, i. 82, 95—97, 439, 440
Lottery, Roman, weekly drawing of the, ii. 198, 199
Lotto, Lorenzo, i. 71, 100
Loyola, Ignatius, residence of, i. 107; picture of, 445; church where he was wont to preach, ii. 170
Lucenti, ii. 82
Lunatic Asylum, ii. 439
Lunghezza, ii. 135
Lunghi, i. 64, 72; ii. 160, 378
Lupercal, the, i. 290
Luther, residence of, in Rome, i. 42
Luti, Benedetto, ii. 443

M.

Macellum Magnum, i. 334
Maderno, Carlo, i. 436, 455; ii. 43, 44, 225, 244, 407
Maderno, Stefano, ii. 373
Maini, ii. 194
Malaria, parts infected by, i. 21, 354, 381; ii. 387, 399, 408, 413
Maldacchini, Olympia, influence of, over Innocent X., ii. 197; villa built by, 455
Mamertine Prisons, i. 153; account of prisoners in, 155, 156
Mantegna Andrea, ii. 348
    Scuola di, i. 94
Manufactory, Papal, of Mosaics, ii. 359
Maranna, i. 375
Maratta, Carlo, i. 95, 99, 106, 445; monument of, ii. 40; works of, 41, 216, 267, 443
Marmorata, the ancient, ii. 393
Mars, temples of, i. 164, 373, 388
Martyrdoms—
    best authenticated, i. 334—338
    of Christians, place of, ii. 390
    graves of Martyrs, i. 396, 420
    paintings representing, i. 474; ii. 141, 201, 225
    of St. Paul, scene of the, ii. 395, 399, 402
    Pietra di Paragone, used in the, ii. 278
Marucelli, ii. 167

Masaccio, i. 343, 439
Massei, ii. 201
Matsys, Quentin, i. 94
Mausoleum of Augustus, i. 62; Statues at entrance of, 447
of Hadrian, ii. 334
Mazzolino, i. 67, 68, 95, 97
Medici, Villa, i. 49; view from, i. 51
Leo X. Giovanni de, and Clement VII., Giulio de, tombs of, ii. 218, 219
Melozzo da Forli, i. 453; ii. 276, 357
Memento Mori, tomb awaiting the living Pope, ii. 266
Mengs, i. 439; ii. 77, 324
Mentana, ii. 33
Meta Sudans, i. 206
Michael Angelo, i. 117, 119, 332, 334, 389; ii. 42, 58, 60, 163, 174, 210, 218; design of, for St. Peter's, 244; statue by, in St. Peter's, 256; frescoes by, 285; his most perfect work, 288; drawing of, 449
Milliarium Aureum, i. 173
Mills, floating, ii. 366
Miserere, of Passion Week, ii. 296
Modena, Pellegrino da, ii. 337, 338, 339
Monastery—
of St. Andrew, i. 321
of St. Anna, ii. 387
of the Chiesa Nuova, ii. 167
Cistercian, ii. 131
Cloister of the, ii. 105, 144
of S. Eusebio, ii. 77
of the Order of Passionists, i. 329
Monot, Etienne, ii. 265
Mons Sacer, ii. 32
Monte Caprino, i. 117
Cavallo, ii. 34
Giordano, ii. 166
del Grano, ii. 124
Mario, ii. 427
Parione di Pietà, ii. 181
Rotondo, ii. 19, 34
Sacro (Mons Sacer), ii. 32
Testaccio, view from, ii. 397
Morrà, national game of the Trasteverini, ii. 367
Mosaics—
best of ancient Christian, i. 471
in Sta. Cecilia, i. 374
in S. Cesareo, i. 407
in Chapel of Sant' Agnese, ii. 165
S. Antonio, ii. 79
Caetani family, i. 470
Sta. Helena, ii. 130

Mosaics—*continued.*
in S. Clemente, i. 345
in Convent of Redemptorists, i. 331
of SS. Cosmo and Damian, i. 192
in Crypt of St. Peter's, ii. 268, 273
fragments of ancient, ii. 405
in Sta. Francesca Romana, i. 198
in Gabinetto delle Maschere, ii. 316
in Jewish Catacomb, i. 407
in Lateran, ii. 100
in S. Lorenzo, ii. 138
in Sta. Maria in Cosmedin, i. 233
in Domenico, i. 333
Maggiore, ii. 82, 83
Scala Cœli, ii. 400
in Trastevere, 383, 385—387
in S. Martino ai Monte, ii. 64
of the Navicella, ii. 246
in SS. Nereo ed Achilleo, i. 380
in Oratory of S. Venanzio, ii. 97
in the Orto del Paradiso, ii. 67
in S. Paolo fuori le Mura, ii. 405, 406
Papal Manufactory of, ii. 359
in St. Peter's, ii. 252, 256, 259, 260, 261, 263, 264
in S. Pietro in Vincoli, ii. 57
in Sta. Prassede, ii. 70
in Quirinal Palace, i. 454
in Sta. Sabina, i. 357
in Sala Rotonda, ii. 318
in Sancta Sanctorum, ii. 113
in S. Stefano Rotondo, i. 339
in S. Teodoro, i. 223
at Torre Nuova, ii. 414
in Triclinium of Palace of Lateran, ii. 109
Mosca, Simone, ii. 62
Murano, Antonio da, ii. 121
Murillo, ii. 348, 444
Muro-Torto, description of, i. 46
Museo, Chiaramonte, ii. 300, 305, 333
Pio-Clementino, ii. 305, 331
Museums—
Christian, ii. 117
of Christian Antiquities, ii. 324
Egyptian, ii. 305, 332
Etruscan, ii. 327—331
Kircherian, i. 88
of Relics of art and history, ii. 212
of Statues, ii. 300
Muziano, ii. 41, 213, 276

N.

Navicella, i. 330; Mosaic of, ii. 246; Terrace of the, 334
Navona, Piazza, used as a market, ii. 197; custom of occasionally converting it into a lake, 198; tournament held in, 198
Naumachia, remnant of the pleasures of the, ii. 198
Nebbia, Cesare, ii. 89, 167, 323
Neri, S. Filippo, chapel of, ii. 166; library founded by, 167; foundation of Oratorians laid by, 169; hospital founded by, 181; portrait of, 181; resuscitation to life by, 187
Nero, Tomb of, i. 38; Statue of, 200; Palace of, 311; Aqueduct of, 330; Martyrs under, 335; Tower of, 459; house in which he died, ii. 20; Golden House of, 52; site of Baths of, 202
Nocchi, Pietro, ii. 120
Notte Vaticane, ii. 336
Nuit, Gerard de la, i. 445; ii. 444
Nymphæum, i. 413; remains of ancient, ii. 430

O

Obeliscus Solaris, i. 78
Obelisk—
of the Esquiline, ii. 93
in the Garden of the Redemptorists, i. 332
of the Lateran, ii. 95
of the Monte Cavallo, i. 446
Citorio, i. 78
of the Pantheon, ii. 211
of St. Peter's, ii. 238, 239
in the Piazza della Minerva, ii. 211
of the Piazza Navona, ii. 196
of the Pincio, i. 46
of the Piazza del Popopolo, i. 37
della Rotonda, ii. 211
of the Trinità de' Monti, i. 51
Observatory, celebrated, i. 88
Olivieri, Paolo, i. 470
Oratory, dedicated by Pius I., i. 472
of Sta. Galla, i. 269
of S. Venanzio, ii. 97
Orti Farnesiani, i. 276
Ortolano, i. 67, 68
Osa, Castello del, ii. 135

Osteria delle Frattocchie, i. 429; of Tavolato, ii. 125
Ostia, ii. 394; past and present condition of, 409
Ostian Gate, ii. 394, 399
Overbeck, i. 454; Studio of, ii. 45

P.

Paintings—
in S. Angelo in Pescheria, i. 248
in Appartamenti Borgia, ii. 324—326
in Ara-Cœli, i. 149
Architectural, ii. 448
in Barberini Palace, i. 439
in Baths of Titus, ii. 53
in Borghese Picture Gallery, i. 67—72
in Capitoline Gallery, i. 140
in Catacombs, i. 401, 410; ii. 21
in Catacomb of S. Ponziano, ii. 454
of Sta. Cecilia, i. 398
in Chapel of S. Sylvestro, i. 341
in the Chiesa Nuova, ii. 167
Communion of St. Jerome, ii. 349
in Crypt of St. Peter's, ii. 274, 276
in S. Francesco a Ripa, ii. 379
in S. Giovanni Decollato, i. 239
La Madonna del Rosario, i. 358
Last Judgment, the, ii. 293
in Loggie of Raphael, ii. 337—339
in S. Lorenzo in Lucina, i. 73
in S. Luigi dei Francesi, ii. 200
Madonna di Foligno, the, ii. 350
Madonna and Saints, ii. 355
in Sta. Maria sopra Minerva, ii. 213—222
in Sta. Maria del Popolo, i. 39
in Trastevere, ii. 384
Miracle-working, ii. 221
Miraculous, of the Crucifixion, ii. 122
in Palace of the Lateran, ii. 118
in Palazzo Albani, i. 443
Colonna, i. 99
Corsini, ii. 442
Doria, i. 94
della Regina di Polonia, i. 54
Sciarra, i. 82
Spada, ii. 180
in Picture Gallery of the Vatican, ii. 347—359
in S. Pietro in Vincoli, ii. 57

INDEX. 471

Paintings—*continued*.
  in S. Prassede, ii. 69
  Prophets and Sibyls, ii. 290—292
  Raphael's best work, ii. 164
  in S. Silvestro a Monte Cavallo, i. 459
  in Sistine Chapel, ii. 287
  Transfiguration, the, ii. 351—354
  in Trinità de' Monti, i. 52
  in Vatican Library, ii. 324
  in Villa Albani, ii. 19
Palaces—
  of Augustus, i. 280
  Barberini, i. 436
  of the Cæsars, i. 250
  of Caligula, i. 292
  of the Cancelleria, ii. 177
  of the Conservators, i. 135
  of the Consulta, i. 448
  Corsini, i. 388
  of Count Trapani, i. 459
  of Domitian, i. 312
  Farnese, i. 377
  Farnesina, ii. 388
  Giustiniani, ii. 202
  important to sight-seers, i. 32
  ancient, of the Lateran, ii. 108
  modern, of the Lateran, ii. 114
  of Nero, i. 311
  Orsini, ii. 360
  Papal, i. 435
  Patrizi, ii. 202
  of the Ponziani family, ii. 369
  of Pope Honorius III., i. 361
  of the Quirinal, i. 449
  of the Republic of Venice, i. 103
  of the Senator, i. 120
  of Tiberius, i. 291
  Venetian, i. 105
  of Vespasian, i. 281
Palatine, the, story of the Hill, i. 273; Palace of the Cæsars, 274; Orti Farnesiani, 276; guide in exploring, 276; the Velia, 277; Palace of Augustus, 280; Hut of Faustulus and the Sacred Fig-tree, 288; Cavern of Lupercal, 290; Palaces of Tiberius and Caligula, 291, 292; Temple of Cybele, 294; other temples, 298; site of houses of great patrician families on, 299—303; Convent, 304; Walls of Romulus, 305; Via Nova, 307; chambers once occupied by Prætorian Guard, 309
Palazzetto, Farnese, sometimes called Linote, ii. 178

Palazzos—
  Albani, i. 443
  Aldobrandini, i. 461
  Altemps, ii. 160
  Altieri, i. 107
  Bernini, i. 73
  Borghese, i. 65; gallery in, 66
  Braschi, ii. 188
  Buonaparte, i. 103
  Caëtani, i. 268
  Caffarelli, i. 142
  Cardelli, ii. 155
  Cenci, i. 259
  Chigi, i. 76
  Colonna, gallery in, i. 98
  Corsini, ii. 439
  Costaguti, i. 267
  Doria, i. 93; gallery in, 94
  Falconieri, ii. 175
  Farnese, ii. 174
  Gabrielli, ii. 166
  Galitzin, ii. 155
  Giraud, ii. 236
  del Governo Vecchio, ii. 165
  Lancellotti, ii. 197
  Madama, ii. 198
  Margana, i. 270
  Massimo alle Colonne, ii. 186
  Mattei, i. 268
  Moroni, ii. 387
  Muto-Savorelli, i. 103
  Odescalchi, legend relating to, i. 98
  Pamfili, ii. 196
  Parisani, i. 76
  Poli, famous jeweller's shop in, i. 81
  Pio, ii. 184
  della Regina di Polonia, i. 54
  Rospigliosi, i. 434, 456
  Ruspoli, i. 72
  Sacchetti, ii. 176
  Salviati, ii. 439
  Santa Croce, ii. 182
  Sciarra, gallery in, i. 82
  Spada alla Regola, the porter at, ii. 178, 179
  di Spagna, i. 57
  Torlonia, i. 104
  del Santo Uffizio, ii. 278
  Valentini, i. 98
  Vidoni, ii. 185
Pantheon, the, ii. 204; its early history, 205; its present state, 206; its interior, 206; burial-place of painters in, 209; service held in, on day of Pentecost, 210

Paolo, ii. 385
Parco di San Gregorio, i. 319
Parmigianino, i. 68
Pasquinades, ii. 188—192
Pasquino, ii. 188
Passignano, i. 367
Paul, St., house in which he lodged, i. 89; trial of, in Basilica, 284; chambers in which he was confined, 309; burial-place of, 419; the aspect of Rome to his eye, 430, 431; picture of, 455; relic of, ii. 100; statue of, 226; shrine of, 273; only existing witness of the martyrdom of, 395; parting of, with St. Peter, 398; martyrdom of, 399, 402; authenticated, i. 335; pillars to which he was bound, ii. 401; festivals of, 408
Penni, Francesco, ii. 276, 337, 338, 340, 356, 446
Perretti, Cardinal, relic of residence of, ii. 35
Perugino, i. 53, 67, 83, 196; ii. 19, 159, 286, 287, 345, 348, 356, 387
Peruzzi, Baldassare, ii. 160, 162, 165, 178, 186; tomb of, in the Pantheon, 209; design of, for St. Peter's, 244; frescoes by, 448
Pescheria, the, i. 249
Pesellino, i. 94
Peter, St., dungeon occupied by, in Mamertine Prisons, i. 153; legend relating to, concerning Simon Magus, 197; martyrdom of, authenticated, 335; tradition of, 379; legend relating to persecution of, 389; burial-place of, 419, ii. 242; picture of, i. 455; preservation of his chains, ii. 54, 61; bas-relief of, 57; relics of, 61, 100; fresco of, 204; statues of, 226, 254; episcopal chair of, 261; shrine and sarcophagus of, 273; parting of, with St. Paul, 398; crucifixion of, 451
Pettrich, ii. 40
Phidias, i. 447
Photographers, i. 29
Pianta Capitolina, i. 123
Piazzas—
 Barberini, i. 436
 of S. Benedetto a Piscinuola, ii. 368
 Bocca della Verità, ii. 392
 Borghese, i. 66; ii. 223

Piazzas—continued.
 del Campidoglio, i. 119
 di Campitelli, i. 269
 Campo di Fiore, ii. 176
 Capitoline, i. 135
 Capo di Ferro, ii. 178
 of the Cappuccini, ii. 7
 Colonna, i. 76
 di S. Eustachio, ii. 202
 del Gesù, legend of, i. 10
 di S. Giovanni, ii. 95
 della Guidecca, i. 259
 of Sta. Maria Maggiore, ii. 80
  in Monti, i. 464
 della Minerva, ii. 211
 Montanara, i. 242
 of the Monte Cavallo, i. 446
 Monte Citorio, i. 78
 of the Navicella, i. 330
 Navona, ii. 187, 196, 198
 del Orologio, ii. 166
 of St. Peter's, ii. 225, 240
 Pia, ii. 236
 del Popolo, i. 36; obelisk of, 37
 della Rotonda, ii. 211
 Rusticucci, ii. 225, 238
 Scossa Cavalli, ii. 236
 della Scuola, i. 256
 di Spagna, i. 56, 58
 delle Tartarughe, i. 267
 del Tritone, i. 436
Picture Galleries—
 in Barberini Palace, i. 439
 Borghese, i. 66
 Capitoline, i. 140
 in Sta. Maria degli Angeli, ii. 40
 Palace of the Lateran, ii. 118
  Quirinal, i. 455
 Palazzo Colonna, i. 99
  Corsini, ii. 442
  Doria, i. 94
  Mattei, i. 268
 the Vatican, ii. 347—359
Pierleoni, fortress of the, i. 245
Pietà, in Sta. Croce, ii. 130
 in Lateran, ii. 103, 104
 in Sta. Maria dell' Anima, 163
Pietra di Paragone, ii. 278
Pietro in Montorio, St., hill of, ii. 388
Pig-Market, Roman mode of killing pigs, ii. 417
Pigna, in garden of the Vatican, ii. 334
Pincio, description of, i. 43; fashionable resort, 44
Pinturicchio, i. 39, 67, 139, 149; ii. 128, 313, 325, 356, 436

Piombo, Sebastian del, i. 41, 69, 97; ii. 102, 293, 355, 448, 449
Pisanello Vittore, i. 94
Piscina Publica, i. 383
Plautilia, legend of, ii. 398, 399
Podesti, ii. 407
Pollajuolo, Antonio, i. 67; ii. 61, 258
Pomarancio, i. 69, 268, 329, 334; ii. 41
Pompey, statue of, ii. 179; theatre of, 184
Ponte—
S. Angelo, ii. 225, 226
S. Bartolomeo, ii. 366
Molle, ii. 421, 424
Nomentana, ii. 31
di Nono, ii. 134
Quattro Capi, ii. 360
Rotto, i. 237; ii. 369
Salara, i. 19
Sisto, ii. 390
Sublicius, i. 238
Pontecello, stream of, i. 429
Popes, eight, educated at Collegio Romana, i. 88; latest miracle of the Romish Church, 98; desecration and restoration of the Coliseum by, 218; Chapel of the, 395; graves of early, 396; election of, 451; Private Chapel of the, 455; Pallium of the, ii. 28; place of coronation of, 99; favourite walk of mediæval, 107; the residence of, at Palace of the Lateran, 108; Sancta Sanctorum of, 111; monument of Papal history of the tenth century, 129; custom of newly-elected, in relation to Jews, i. 203, ii. 166; passage intended for the escape to St. Angelo of the, 234; the Borgo, or sanctuary of the Papacy, 235; the Easter benediction, 240; additions to the building of St. Peter's by, 244; ceremony of destruction of the Wall of Porta Santa, 248; Memento Mori, 266; Sarcophagi of, 270—274; the Vatican, built by successive, 283, 284; Papal residence at the Vatican, 283, 298; prophecy respecting the line of, 299; daily walk or ride of the, 335; inscription commemorating the pope who defended Rome against Attila, 406; toleration of the Papal government in religion, 411

Popes—
Adrian VI., tomb of, ii. 161
Alexander VI., Rodrigo Borgia, grave of, ii. 170; paintings representing the life of, 325; pasquinade against, 189; empty tomb of, 269; death of, 428, 429
Alexander VII., his humility, i. 77
Boniface VIII., life and character of, ii. 269, 270; double crown first worn by, 270
Clement, St., exile and death of, i. 347
Clement VII, pasquinades against, ii. 190; "the Transfiguration" painted by order of, 351
Clement VIII., torturer and executioner of the Cenci family, i. 260, ii. 87; builder of the new palace of the Vatican, 87; punishment of parricides by, 183
Clement XII., founder of Corsini Chapel, ii. 103
Clement XIII., Order of the Jesuits attacked in the reign of, ii. 260
Cornelius, St., tomb of, i. 399
Damasus, St., inscriptions of, i. 396, 399, 407, 418, 419; ii. 21
Gregory I. (the Great), founder of Church music, ii. 122
Gregory XI., restoration of the Papal Court to Rome by, i. 196
Gregory XIII., New Calendar invented in the reign of, ii. 258
Gregory XVI., frescoes representing the life of, ii. 326; statue of, 405
Hilary, Chapels built by, ii. 96
Hildebrand, seizure of, ii. 92
Innocent X., pasquinade against, ii. 191, desertion of, at his death, 194; sale of bishoprics and benefices in the reign of, 197
Innocent XI., pasquinade against, ii. 191
Innocent XII., last pope who wore beard and moustache, tomb of, ii. 257
Joan, life, and legend of, ii. 94
Julius II., magnificent tomb of, ii. 59; introduction of the beard by, 60; destruction of the Old Basilica, and commencement of the building of St. Peter's, by, 244; grave of, 258
Julius III., Villa of Papa Giulio, designed and built by, ii. 418

Popes—*continued*.
Leo X., pasquinades against, ii. 190 ; early destination to the Papacy of, 218 ; tomb of, 218 ; his share in the building of St. Peter's, 244 ; St. Peter's statue cast by, 254 ; brilliant reign of, 336
Leo XI., short reign of, ii. 265
Leo XII., Vatican Picture Gallery built by, ii. 284
Martin V., tomb of, ii. 100
Nicholas V., Vatican Library founded by, ii. 271, 322
Paschal I., his account of his finding the burial-place of Sta. Cecilia, ii. 373
Paul II., remarkable beauty of, ii. 271 ; remains of his tomb, 271, 272
Paul III., Order of Jesuits founded in the reign of ; his character, ii. 262 ; Inquisition established by, 278 ; Sala Regia of the Vatican built in the reign of, 285
Paul IV., imprisonment of the Jews by, i. 252 ; his aspect and character, ii. 215
Pelagius II., Basilica of, ii. 142 ; his munificence, 143
Pius II., tomb and epitaph of, ii. 185 ; instance of relique-worship in the reign of, 421
Pius IV., his retiring nature ; Villa Pia built by, ii. 335
Pius V., eventful reign of, ii. 89
Pius VI., pasquinades against, ii. 191, 192
Pius VII., exile of, i. 449 ; return of, to the Quirinal ; re-establishment of the Order of Jesuits by, ii. 264 ; collection of pictures in the Vatican formed by, 347
Pius VIII., tomb of, the, last erected in St. Peter's, ii. 264
Pius IX., escape of, in the revolution of 1848, i. 450 ; preparation of his own monument, ii. 84
Sixtus IV., political reign of, ii. 258 ; Sistine Chapel built by, 284 ; Vatican Library increased by, 322
Sixtus V., eventful life of, ii. 90 ; the enemy of antiquities, 108 ; completion of the building of St. Peter's in the reign of, 244 ; Vatican Library increased by, 322
Sylvester II., memorial slab of, ii. 103

Popes—*continued*.
Urban II., refuge of, i. 201 ; ii. 363
Urban VI., his cruelty, and death, ii. 272
Urban VIII., ambition and magnificence of, i. 437 ; curious Will of, 438 ; pasquinade against, ii. 190 ; his passion for building, and his tomb, 261
Popolo, Piazza del, starting-point for exploring Rome, i. 36
Porta del, i. 37 ; ii. 422
Church of Sta. Maria del, i. 39
Pordenone, i. 70, 71, 96, 454
Porta, Giacomo della, ii. 174, 244, 251, 400, 401
Giuseppe, ii. 285
Guglielmo della, ii. 262
Porta—
Angelica, ii. 427, 430
Asinaria, ii. 107
Capena, i. 373
Carmentalis, i. 239
Cavalleggieri, ii. 280, 456
Collina, ii. 16
Furba, ii. 124
S. Giovanni, ii. 107
Latina, i. 384
S. Lorenzo, ii. 35
Maggiore, ii. 132
S. Marta, ii. 264, 278
Mugonia, i. 274
Nomentana, ii. 24
Ostiensis, Ancient, ii. 394
Palatii, i. 279
S. Pancrazio, ii. 452
S. Paolo, i. 368 ; ii. 393
Pia, ii. 24
Pinciana, ii. 16
Portese, ii. 377
Romana, i. 274
Salara, ii. 16
Salutaria, i. 435
Santa, ii. 83 ; ceremony of the destruction of the wall of, 248
S. Sebastiano, i. 387
Settimiana, ii. 388, 448
Sto. Spirito, ii. 434
Trigemina, ii. 392
Porticos—
of Baths of Constantine, i. 458
Doric, ii. 421
of St. John Lateran, ii. 99
Leonino, ii. 102
of Livia, i. 198
of S. Lorenzo, ii. 138

INDEX. 475

Porticos—*continued.*
  of Octavia, i. 247
  of Pallas Minerva, i. 165
  of the Pantheon, ii. 206
  of S. Sabba, i. 369
  of Temple of Mars, i. 388
    to Romulus, i. 435
  in Theatre of Pompey, ii. 184
Post-office, General, ii. 199
Potter, Paul, i. 72
Poussin, Gaspar, ii. 63, 442, 444
Poussin, Niccolas, i. 52 ; house of, 54 ; tomb of, 73 ; works of, 95, 167, 440 ; ii. 63, 326, 358
Pozzi, Giobattista, ii. 89
  Padre, i. 86
Prata Quinctia, i. 59
Praxiteles, i. 447
Presepio, origin of the, ii. 380
Pretorian Camp, remains of, ii. 34
Prima Porta, ii. 423
Prisons—
  Carceri Nuove, ii. 176
  in Castle of St. Angelo, ii. 234
  the Island in the Tiber used as, in imperial times, ii. 362
  for Women, ii. 42
Promenade, ancient Papal, ii. 127
Propaganda, the, i. 59
Protestant Cemetery, ii. 395
    Churches, ii. 410
Protomoteca, i. 136
Pseudo-Aventine, i. 368
Pyramid, site of, ii. 236
  of Caius Cestius, ii. 394

Q.

Quattro Fontane, ii. 34, 45
Quirinal, parish church of, i. 81 ; hill, limit of, 433 ; origin of name, temple to Romulus, 434 ; houses of great families on, 436 ; Palace, 444 ; residence of popes, 449 ; Gardens of the, 455

R.

Raggi, Antonio, ii. 194
Railway Station, ii. 35
Raphael, painter, sculptor, and architect, i. 41 ; Works of, 67, 83, 96, 167, 305, 439 ; ii. 102, 158, 164, 185 ; tomb of, in the Pantheon, 209 ; house of, 225 ; design of, for St. Peter's, 244 ; cartoons of, 321 ; Loggie of, 337 ; frescoes by, 338, 340—343, 345, 446, 448 ;
pictures by, 348, 350, 356 ; his last, 351 ; Villa of, 416
Regia, site of, i. 78
Relics—
  of St' Agnese, ii. 31
  of Ancient Basilica, ii. 407
  of Ancient Basilica of Lateran, ii. 102
  Architectural and traditional, ii. 105
  Arm of St. Thomas à Becket, ii. 172
  of Art and History, ii. 212
  of the Barberini family, i. 437
  Brains of St. Thomas à Becket, ii. 92
  Body of St. Bartholomew, ii. 364
  in Catacomb of Sta. Priscilla, ii. 23
  Chains of St. Peter, ii. 61
  ancient Chair of St. Peter, ii. 261
  Column to which our Saviour is reputed to have been bound, ii. 68
  Earliest architectural, i. 170
  of S. Francesca Romana, i. 270
  of St. Francis, ii. 379
  in Giardino della Pigna, ii. 333
  of Ignatius Loyola, i. 107
  list of, in Lateran, ii. 102
  in S. Martino al Monte, ii. 64
  in Monastery of the Chiesa Nuova, ii. 167
  in Sta. Prassede, ii. 71
  Pedestal of the Column of Antoninus Pius, ii. 334
  of St. Peter's, exhibition of, ii. 253, 254
  of Republican times, i. 105, 307
  in Sancta Sanctorum, ii. 112, 113
  Sancta Culla, ii. 91
  Santa Scala, ii. 110
  of Tasso, ii. 437
  Title of the True Cross, exhibition of, ii. 129
  in Treasury of St. Peter's, ii. 276
  of works of Art from the Basilica on the site of St. Peter's, ii. 243
Rembrandt, ii. 444
Remus, temple of, i. 191 ; and Romulus, legend of, 288
Reni, Guido, i. 69, 73, 83, 84, 95, 140, 141, 440 ; ii. 358, 443, 444
Ribera, i. 70
Ricciolini, ii. 40
Rinaldi, ii. 407

Ripetta, the, i. 37 ; Quay of the, 59
Ripresa dei Barberi, i. 105
Roman Pearls, i. 29
Romana, Sta. Francesca, favourite saint of the Romans, i. 148 ; ii. 136 ; her death, i. 195 ; ii. 370 ; miracle attributed to, 378 ; vineyard of, 398
Romanelli, i. 139, 267 ; ii. 41, 266
Romano, Guilo, i. 67, 68, 82, 305, 332 ; ii. 19, 71, 118, 161, 244, 276, 337—340, 345, 354, 356, 378, 425, 426, 443, 446, 452
Rome, statue called by that name, ii. 35
Rome—
Description of neighbourhood, i. 17 ; first view of city, 17 ; Madame de Staël's impression concerning, 18 ; climate, 20 ; life agreeable in, 21 ; Museums, 22 ; scarcity of Pagan ruins, 23 ; Mai's monumental record of, A.D. 540, 24 ; facilities afforded to strangers, 24 ; objects of attraction in the neighbourhood of, 26 ; Hotels, Pensions, Apartments, 27 ; Trattorie (Restaurants), English Church, Post-office, Telegraph-office, Bankers, Conveyance of goods to England, Doctors, English and Homœopathic, Dentist, Sick-Nurses, Chemists, English House-Agent, English Livery-Stables, 28 ; Library, Booksellers, Italian Masters, Photographers, Drawing Materials, Engravings, Antiquities, Bronzes, Cameos, Mosaics, Jewellers, Roman Pearls, 29 ; Bookbinder, Engraver, Tailors, Shoemakers, Dressmaker, Shops for Ladies' Dresses, Roman Ribbons and Shawls, Gloves, Carpets, and small Household Articles, German Baker, English Grocer, Italian Grocer and Wine-Merchant, Oil, Candles, and Wood, &c., English Dairy, 30 ; Artists' Studios, 31 ; Sculptors' Studios, 31, 32 ; Churches, Palaces, Villas, Ruins, Sights for each day in the week, 32, 33 ; Guide for travellers in, 36 ; favourite resort for Models, 56 ; English colony, 58 ; first English service in, 64 ; pious whippings, 85 ; celebrated Observatory, 88 ; Jesuit College, eight Popes edu-

Rome—*continued.*
cated at, 88 ; Church in which St. Paul lodged, 89 ; Capitoline Hill, 109 ; Forum Romanum, great historical interest attached to, 168 ; interesting sites and classical remains, 170—185 ; description of Mosaics, 192 ; decadence of Art in, 232 ; Mediæval gem of, 234 ; sketch of Jewish history in, 250—255 ; rich merchandise in Ghetto, 256 ; Palatine Hill, 273 ; recent discoveries among the ruins of the Palace of the Cæsars, 276 ; St. Paul's trial in Basilica, 283 ; Seven Hills of, 298 ; houses of great patricians of, 299 ; earliest pagan caricature of our Saviour's death, 308 ; Cœlian Hill, 316 ; place of departure of St. Augustine from, 319 ; grand view of Palatine, 324 ; ideal garden, 332 ; frescoes representing best authenticated martyrdoms in, 334—338 ; influence of Byzantine upon Roman Art, 341 ; ancient ecclesiastical architecture, 343 ; the Aventine, 348 ; Malaria, 21, 354, 356 ; Appian Way, course of, 372, 430 ; Baths of Caracalla, largest mass of ruins in, 376 ; Columbaria, 385 ; rare parisitical plants, 390 ; Catacombs, 390—411, ii. 20 ; paintings in Catacombs, symbolical, allegorical, and liturgical, i. 401 ; oldest Christian cemetery, 409 ; graves of Christian martyrs, 420 ; extensive view, 424 ; the appearance of, to St. Paul, 430, 431 ; the Quirinal and Viminal, 433 ; Saint most reverenced by people of, 463 ; spot of historical interest, 468 ; most ancient church in, 469 ; loveliest view in, ii. 17 ; Railway Station, 35 ; Esquiline Hill, 46 ; St. Peter's chains, 61 ; tallest palmtree in, 62 ; one of the principal objects of pilgrimage in, 68 ; memorials of middle-age warfare, 72 ; unique doorway, 78 ; consecration of animals after the feast of St. Anthony, 79 ; Obelisk, oldest object in, 95 ; beautiful view, 105 ; principal receptacle for antiquities in, 114 ; fine specimen of Roman scenery, 127 ; residence assigned to Patriarchs of Jerusalem visiting, 144 ; modern burial-ground of,

INDEX. 477

Rome—*continued.*
144; Roman funeral, 145; Roman Catholic Meeting-house for the lower orders, 158; Government establishment for the lending of money, 181; haunted house, 183; first printing-office in, 187; finest staircase in, 188; unique window, 197; most perfect pagan building in, 204; resort of bird-fanciers, 211; largest library in, 222; relic of siege of, 226; effect produced by the entrance of St. Peter's, 249; one of the few examples of Gothic architecture in, 280; view of, from balcony in the Vatican, 307; results of excavations, 327, 393; peculiar beauty of the Vatican Garden, 335; supply of water during the siege, 366; character of Trasteverini in contrast to the other Romans, 367; house of temporary retirement for young men, 369; principal remains of mediæval architecture, 379; first Church dedicated to the Virgin, 382; fine views from Ponte Sisto, 390; interest attached to the Pyramid of Caius Cestius, 395; facilities afforded for Protestant worship in, 410; view across the Campagna, 420; magnificent view of, 428; evening scene in the streets, 431; unrivalled view, 451; only perfect extant specimen of primitive subterranean baptistery, 453
Romulus and Remus, legend of, i. 288; walls of, 305; connection with Aventine, 349; temple to, 434
Rosa, Salvator, i. 94, 95; monument of, ii. 40; works of, 225, 442, 445
Rospigliosi, Palace of, i. 456; collection of pictures in, 457
Rosselli, Cosimo, ii. 287
Rossi, ii. 261, 263, 413
Rubens, i. 96, 140; ii. 167, 444
Ruins—
  of Agger of Servius Tullius, ii. 38
  Aqua Marcia, ii. 95
  Arco di Ciambella, ii. 211
  Basilica of Constantine, i. 184
  Basilica of S. Stefano, ii. 124
  Bath built by Augustus, ii. 77
  Baths of Caracalla, i. 375
  Baths of Constantine, i. 436, 458
  Baths of Diocletian, ii. 38

Ruins—*continued.*
  of Baths of S. Helena, ii. 132
  Baths of Titus, ii. 52
  Campus Martius, ii. 155
  early Christian cemetery, ii. 29
  Circus of Maxentius, i. 422
  Circus Maximus, i. 225
  Coliseum, i. 213
  Colonnace, i. 165
  Emporium, ii. 393
  Forum Boarium, i. 227
  Forum of Trajan, i. 161
  Gabii, ii. 134
  S. Giacomo degli Spagnuoli, ii. 197
  house of Mother of St. Gregory, i. 321
  Mausoleum of Augustus, i. 62
  Meta Sudans, i. 206
  Milliarium Aureum, i. 173
  Modern Capitol, i. 170
  Nero's Golden House, i. 52
  Palace of the Cæsars, i. 274
    Domitian, i. 312
    Lateran, ii. 109
    Nero, i. 311
  Palaces of Augustus and Vespasian, i. 280, 281
  Palazzo Cenci, i. 259
  Palazzo Margana, i. 270
  Pescheria, i. 249
  Pons Æmilius, i. 237
  Pons Fabricius, ii. 360
  Pons Sublicius, i. 238
  Ponte Salaria, ii. 19
  Porticus Octaviæ, i. 246
  Pretorian Camp, ii. 34
  Principal, in Rome, i. 32
  in Priorato Garden, i. 365
  of Regia of Julius Cæsar, i. 305
  Roma Vecchia, i. 427
  Sette Bassi, i. 124
  Sette Sale, ii. 53
  Studio of Canova, i. 61
  Tabularium, i. 122
  Temple of Antoninus and Faustina, i. 182
  Temple of Concord, i. 171
    Mars Ultor, i. 163
    Neptune, i. 79
    Saturn, i. 172
    the Sun, i. 436
    Venus and Rome, i. 198
    Vesta, i. 176
  Temples on the Aventine, i. 351

Ruins—*continued*.
  of Temples of Castor and Pollux, i. 175
  Theatre of Balbus, i. 259
  Tomb of the Cæcilii, i. 395
  Tor di Quinto, ii. 423
  Torre dei Schiavi, ii. 133
  Villa of Emperor Commodus, i. 427
  Villa of Flavia Domitilla, i. 408
  Villa of Livia, ii. 423
  Walls of Romulus, i. 305
  Walls of Servius Tullius, i. 368
Russe Tarpeia, i. 142
Rusconi, Camillo, ii. 259

S.

Sabbatini, ii. 337
Sacchi, Andrea, i. 439; ii. 12, 96; tomb of, 104; works of, 183, 358, 359
Sacer, Mons, ii. 32
Sala degli Animali, ii. 313
  della Riga, ii. 319
  di Constantino, ii. 340
  a Croce Greca, ii. 319
  Ducale, ii. 398
  delle Muse, ii. 317
  Regia, ii. 285
  Rotonda, ii. 318
Salita di S. Onofrio, ii. 434
Salviati, ii 163, 224, 287
Sancta Sanctorum, in Palace of Lateran, ii. 111
Sangallo, Antonio di, ii. 174, 244, 285
Sansovino, Andrea, ii. 158
Santa Scala, ii. 95, 110; picturesque scene on, 111
Santi, Tito, ii. 225
Sanzio, Giovanni, i. 99; ii. 121
Saraceni Carlo, ii. 162, 442, 443
Sarcophagi, i. 458, 471; ii. 18, 68, 103, 114, 118, 141, 174, 257, 263, 269, 270—273, 300, 405, 426
Sarto, Andrea del, i. 67—69, 82, 95, 440; ii. 120, 442
Sarzana, Leonarda da, ii. 84
Sassoferato, i. 69, 70, 95; ii. 120, 356, 443
Scannabecchi, ii. 425
Scarsellino, Ippolito, i. 94
Schiavone, And., i. 71
Schnorr, Paul, ii. 337
Schools—
  Castigliana, i. 256
  Catilana, i. 256

Schools—*continued*.
  for Music, in the Middle Ages, ii. 121
  Scuola Nuova, i. 256
  Siciliana, i. 256
  del Tempio, i. 256
Sciarra, Palazzo, Picture Gallery in, i. 82
Scipios, Tomb of the, i. 385
Sculptors, studios of, i. 31
Sculpture—
  Arch of Septimus Severus, on, i. 232
  Capitol, on the steps of the, i. 117
  Casino of Villa Borghese, in, ii. 413
  Castle of St. Angelo, in, ii. 234
  S. Cesareo, in, i. 383
  Collection of, ii. 14, 18
  Crypt of St. Peter's, in, ii. 273
  Gallery of, in the Capitol, i. 123 —136
  Jewish Synagogue, in, i. 257
  Madonna and Child, ii. 158
  Sta. Maria sopra Minerva, in, ii. 218
  Sta. Maria del Popolo, in, i. 39
  Michael Angelo, by, ii. 59
  Palazzo Mattei, in, i. 268
  Palazzo Spada, in, ii. 180
  Santa Scala, on, ii. 110
  Tomb of Adrian VI., on, ii. 162
  Tor di Babele, of, i. 460
  Trastevere, fragments of, in the, ii. 367
  Vatican Galleries, in the, ii. 300 —322
  Via Appia, among ruins of, i. 424
Sebastian, St., place of martyrdom of, i. 203; fresco, relating to legend of, ii. 56; statue of, 194
Seminario Romana, ii. 159
Septizonium of Severus, i. 312
Sermoneta, ii. 104, 165, 337
Sesto, Cesare, ii. 359
Seven Hills of Rome, i. 298
Shops—
  for Antiquities, i. 29
  Arvotti's, the famous Roman-scarf shop, ii. 198
  Bookbinder's, i. 30
  Booksellers', i. 29
  for Bronzes, i. 29
  for Cameos, i. 29
  for Carpets and small house articles, i. 30
  for Drawing materials, i. 29

INDEX. 479

Shops—*continued*.
English Grocer's, i. 30
Engraver's, i. 30
for Engravings, i. 29
German Baker's, i. 30
for Gloves, i. 30
Italian Grocer and Wine-Merchant's, i. 30
Jewellers', i. 29
for Lace, well-known, i. 267
for Ladies' dresses, i. 30
for Mosaics, i. 29
for Oil, Candles, and Wood, &c., i. 30
for Roman Ribbons and Shawls, i. 30
for Roman Pearls, i. 29
Shoemakers', i. 30
Tailors', i. 30
Sicciolante, Girolamo, ii. 200
Siena, Berni da, ii. 100
Siena, Gherardesco da, ii. 445
Signorelli, Luca, ii. 19, 120, 287
Simone, i. 345
Sirani, Eliz., ii. 442
Sodoma, i. 68, 203, 439; ii. 342, 448
Solario, i. 68
Spagna, i. 99; ii. 356, 445
Spagnoletto, i. 455; ii. 90, 356, 443, 444
Spoleto, Guido da, ii. 324
St. Peter's, first sight of, i. 17; view of, from the Pincio, 44; distant view of, from Villa Medici, 51; "View of, through the Keyhole," 365; the approach to, ii. 238; early history of buildings on the site of, 242; the building of, 244; expenses of building, 245; façade, 245; vestibule, 246; entrance of the Cathedral, 249; nave, 251; dimensions of building, 251; cupola, 252; Baldacchino, 252; relics, 253; statues, 254, 255; chapels, 256—258; monuments, 259—266; tribune, 261; ancient chair, 261; confessionals, 267; crypt of, 267 —274; sarcophagi, 270—274; dome of, 275; sacristy of, 275; treasury of, 276; archives of, 277; best view of, 454
Stanza, d'Eliodoro, ii. 341
of the Incendio del Borgo, ii. 345
della Segnatura, ii. 342
Statues—
Abbate Luigi, of, ii. 186
Sta. Agnese, of, ii. 194

Statues—*continued*.
Agrippa, of, ii. 206
Sta. Anastasia, of, i. 224
Antinous, the, ii. 308
Aristotle, of, ii. 180
Augustus, of, ii. 206, 424
Barberini Palace, in, i. 438
Baths of Caracalla, discovered in ruins of, i. 377
Benedict XIII., of, i. 363
S. Bruno, of, ii. 40
Calumny, of, i. 75
Capitoline Gallery, in, i. 123—135
Castor and Pollux, of, i. 118
Sta. Cecilia, of, ii. 373
Chapel of the Sacrament, in, ii. 89
Christian Museum, in, ii. 117
Clœlia, of, i. 199
Collection of, in Palazzo Sacchetti, ii. 176
Colossal, of Minerva, ii. 35
Constantine, of, ii. 106
Corsini Chapel, in, ii. 103
Discobolus, of the, ii. 186
Domitian, of, i. 179
Drusus, of, i. 387
Egyptian Museum, in, ii. 332
Gregory XVI., of, ii. 405
Hall of the Senators, in, i. 121
Henry IV., of, ii. 99
St. Jerome, of, i. 60
St. John the Baptist, of, i. 344
Julius II., on tomb of, ii. 59, 60
Juno, of, i. 112
Jupiter, of, i. 112
Justice of, i. 378
S. Lorenzo, of, ii. 137
Marcus Aurelius, of, i. 119; ii. 186
Mars, of, ii. 14
Sta. Martina, in, i. 188
Mausoleum of Augustus, at, i. 447
Minerva, of, i. 112
Moses, of, ii. 42
Nile, of the, i. 184
Orpheus, of, ii. 51
Pasquino, of, ii. 188
Peter and Paul, of, ii. 130
St. Peter's, on balustrade and steps of, ii. 245, 246; in nave of, 254; in Crypt of, 268, 273
Philip IV. of Spain, of, ii. 82
Pincio, on the, i. 43
Pompey, of, at the foot of which Cæsar fell, ii. 179

Statues—*continued*.
  Porta Pia, ii. 24
  Raphael, by, i. 41
  S. Sebastian, of, ii. 194, 221
  Sta. Silvia, of, i. 325
  Torso Belvidere, ii. 306
  Trajan, of, i. 161
  Vatican, in the, ii. 300—322
  Vatican Library, in the, ii. 324
  Villa Albani, in, ii. 18
  Villa Borghese, in, ii. 414—416
  Villa Pamfili Doria, in, ii. 454
Stern, Louis, ii. 69
Stone, on which Abraham was about to offer Isaac, ii. 237
  Sacred, legend of, i. 294
Strada del Borgo Sto. Spirito, ii. 237
Streets—
  Babuino, i. 36
  Clivus Capitolinus, i. 170, 172
  Corso, i. 36, 60
  Gregoriana, i. 54
  Sta. Lucia in Selci, ii. 65
  Ripetta, i. 37
  Sistina, i. 54
Studios—
  Artists', i. 30
  of Overbeck, ii. 45
  Sculptors', i. 31
Subleyras, ii. 41
Suburra, the, ii. 49
Summa Via Nova, i. 277
Sun, Aurelian's Temple of the, i. 436, 458
Superstition, modern, i. 223
Sustermanns, i. 100
Sylvester, ancient Chair and Mitre of, ii. 64

T.

Tabernacle, Gothic, ii. 385
Tadolini, ii. 246
Tarquin, site of camp of, ii. 378
Tasso, Monument of, ii. 436; death of, 437; remains of oak planted by, 438; annual commemoration of, at the Accademia, 439
Teatino, Don Gaëtano di, founder of the Order of the Theatins, ii. 388
Tempesta, i. 334, 457; ii. 226, 337
Tempietto, on site of St. Peter's crucifixion, ii. 451
Temples—
  of Æsculapius, ii. 364
  Antoninus and Faustina, i. 182
  Apollo, i. 296; ii. 134

Temples—*continued*.
  of the Aventine, i. 351—353
  Bacchus, i. 412
  Castor and Pollux, i. 175
  Ceres, i. 227
  Cybele, i. 294
  Fides, i. 114
  Fortuna Virilis, i. 235
    Muliebris, ii. 125
  Fortune, i. 228
  Health and Fever, i. 435
  Honour and Virtue, i. 115
  on "the Island," ii. 363
  of Janus Quirinus, i. 180
  Julius Cæsar, i. 183
  Juno, i. 247
    Moneta, i. 115
    Sospita, i. 298
  Jupiter Capitolinus, i. 111—114
    Feretrius, i. 115
    Stator, i. 247, 278
    Tonans, i. 115
  Liber, i. 227
  Libera, i. 227
  Mars, i. 114
    Ultor, i. 163, 164
  in Memory of the French who fell in the siege of Rome, ii. 455
  of Minerva, i. 298
  Moonlight, i. 298
  Neptune, i. 79
  Peace, i. 184
  Piety, i. 241
  Remus, i. 191
  Romulus, i. 434
  Saturn, i. 172
  the Sun, i. 117
  Tellus, ii. 48
  Venus Erycina, i. 114
  Venus and Rome, last Pagan, in use, i. 199
  Vespasian, i. 171
  Vesta, i. 176, 235
  Victory, i. 294
Tenerani, ii. 221, 264, 407
Teniers, i. 71, 82; ii. 445
Termini, ii. 34
Terraces of—
  the Navicella, ii. 334
  the Pincio, i. 43
  the Villa Albani, view from, ii. 17
    Medici, i. 49
Theatres of—
  Apollo, ii. 224
  Marcellus, i. 244
  Pompey, ii. 184

Thorwaldsen, i. 188, 455; ii. 210 264, 300
Throne, ancient Episcopal, ii. 386
Tiber, inundations of the, i. 222;
 Island in the, ii. 361; picturesque views on the banks of, 421; seven-branched Candlestick of Jerusalem embedded in the, 422
Tiberius, Arch of, i. 173; Palace of, 291
Tigellum Sororis, ii. 49
Tintoret, i. 100, 140; ii. 444
Titian, i. 70, 71, 82, 83, 95, 96, 99, 167, 437, 439; ii. 355, 357, 443, 444
Tito, Santi di, ii. 335
Titus, Arch of, i. 200
Tojetti, Domenico, ii. 26
Tombs—
 of Adam of Hertford, Bishop of London, ii. 372
 in Ara-Cœli, i. 147, 148
 of the Baker Eurysaces, ii. 132
 Bastari, ii. 385
 Bernardino Capella, i. 339
 Bibulus, i. 105
 the Cœcilii, i. 395
 Caius Cestius, ii. 394
 Camillo Borghese, ii. 87
 in Campus Esquilinus, ii. 36
 of Carlo Maratta, ii. 40
 Cardinals, ii. 216—222
 Cardinal d'Alençon, ii. 385
  Barberini, ii. 9
  Fortiguerra, ii. 372
  Gonsalvi, i. 87; ii. 90
  Mai, i. 225
  Pacca, i. 269
  Rovarella, i. 344
 Casale Rotondo, i. 428
 of Cecilia Metella, i. 422
 in Chapel of the Rosary, i. 359
 Cinque-Cento, ii. 215
 of Clement VII., ii. 219
  IX., ii. 84
  XIV., i. 101
 Sta. Constantia, ii. 28
 Cosmo and Damian, i. 191
 destruction of, in old Basilica, on the site of St. Peter's, ii. 257 —266
 Doric, relic of republican times, i. 105
 of Emmanuel IV., i. 444
  Francesca di Ponziani, i. 195
  eminent Frenchmen, ii. 200
  Geta, i. 388

Tombs—*continued*.
 of Gibson, the sculptor, ii. 397
  Gregory XI., i. 196
   XIV., i. 85
  the Historian of the popes, ii. 92
  the Horatii and Curiatii, i. 427
  John Lascaris, i. 463
  Julius II., ii. 59
  Knights of Malta, i. 365
  Lanfranco, ii. 385
  Leo X., ii. 218
 in S. Maria del Popolo, i. 39—42
 of Martha Swinburne, ii. 171
  Sta. Martina, i. 188
  Martyrs, i. 420
  Nero, i. 38
  Nicholas IV., ii. 84
  Nicholas Poussin, i. 73
  Painters, in the Pantheon, ii. 209, 210
  Paul IV., ii. 215
  Pius V., ii. 89
  Pompey, i. 429
  Pope St. Cornelius, i. 399
   Melchiades, i. 398
 in S. Prassede, ii. 69
 of Prince Altieri, i. 269
  Princess Colonna, ii. 213
  Ruins of, i. 426, 428, 429
  of Salvator Rosa, ii. 40
  the Scipios, i. 385
  Sixtus V., ii. 89
  the Stuarts, ii. 266
  Sylla, i. 37
 Temple of Divus Rediculus, i. 416
 of Torquemada, ii. 213
Tor—
 di Babele, i. 460
 Marancia, i. 408
 Nona, ii. 223
 Quinto, ii. 420, 423
 Selce, i. 429
Torre—
 degli Anicii, ii. 362
 dei Conti, ii. 48, 54
 del Grillo, i. 460
 Mellina, ii. 193
 Mezza Strada, mediæval fortress, i. 427
 delle Milizie, i. 460
 Nomentana, ii. 32
 Nuova, ii. 133, 414
 Pernice, ii. 133
 Pignatarra, ii. 133
 Sanguinea, ii. 100

Torre—*continued*.
 dei Schiavi, ii. 133
 della Scimia (Hilda's Tower), ii. 156
 Tre Teste, ii. 134
Torretta del Palatino, view from, i. 298
Towers—
 Capitol, of the, i. 121
 Frangipanni, ii. 62
 Mecænas, of, ii. 65
 Mediæval, of S. Lucia in Selce, ii. 65
Trastevere, the, i. 237; its present condition, characteristics of its inhabitants, its national games, ii. 367
Trattorie, resort of lower orders to, ii. 422
Travellers, hurried, scheme for, in visiting Rome, i. 32; first lesson in Roman Geography, for, 36; interesting excursions for, ii. 426; objects of interest for Irish, 450
Tre Fontane, condition of, ii. 399
Trevi, Fountain of, i. 79
Trophies of Marius, ii. 74
Turrita, Jacopo da, ii. 83

U.

Udine, Giovanni da, ii. 300, 324, 426, 448
Umbilicus Romæ, i. 173
University of the Sapienza, ii. 202

V.

Vaccine, herds of, ii. 424
Vaga, Pierino del, i. 53, 68, 87, 332; ii. 204; tomb of, in the Pantheon, 209; works of, 324, 337, 339, 342, 343, 345, 443
Val d'Inferno, ii. 430
Valadico, ii. 96
Valca, ii. 424
Valentin, i. 70, 82, 94; ii. 357
Valle Caffarelle, i. 390
 Filippo, ii. 257
Valleys—
 of the Almo, i. 388
 between the Palatine and Capitoline Hills, i. 222
 between Palatine and Aventine, i. 225, 365
Vallis Quirinalis, site of, i. 464
Vandyke, Works of, i. 71, 72, 96, 100, 140, 141; ii. 444

Vanni Francesco, ii. 40, 264
Vasari, ii. 285, 418, 449
Vatican, the, i. 467; history of the quarter, and of the foundation of the Palace, ii. 282—284; Sala Regia, 285; Sistine Chapel, paintings of, 286—295; residence of the pope in, 298; Museum of Statues, 300; Braccio-Nuovo, 300; Cabinets of Sculpture, 308—311; Gabinetto delle Maschere, 316; Library of the, 271, 322; portraits of librarians, 323; Appartamenti Borgia, 324; inner Garden of the, 333; larger Garden, 335; Golden age of the, 336; Loggie of Raphael, 337; Stanze, frescoes in the, 340—345; Picture Gallery, 347; Wine of the, 430
Vecchi, Giovanni de', ii. 216
Vecchio, Palma, i. 71, 100, 439
Velabrum, the, i. 222; derivation of name, 223
Velasquez, works of, i. 97, 140, 167; ii. 445
Velia, i. 277
Veneziano, Carlo, i. 82
Venusti, M., i. 141; ii. 216
Verlosi, Giuseppe, ii. 263
Vespasian, Palace of, i. 281; favourite residence of, ii. 12
Vesta, Temple of, i. 235; Shrine, of, 298
Via—
 S. Agostino, ii. 160
 Alessandrina, i. 165
 dell' Anima, ii. 193
 S. Antonio dei Portoguesi, ii. 156
 Appia, i. 206, 369, 390
 Appia Nuova, i. 412, 429; ii. 107
 Ardeatina, i. 389
 Babuino, i. 54
 di Banchi, ii. 224
 S. Basilio, ii. 12
 de' Baullari, ii. 178
 del Borgo Nuovo, ii. 236
 delle Botteghe Oscure, i. 268
 Calabraga, ii. 170
 della Caravita, i. 85
 Cassia, ii. 426
 S. Claudio, i. 76
 del Colosseo, ii. 47
 Condotti, i. 65
 della Consolazione, i. 174
 delle Convertite, i. 74
 dei Coronari, ii. 223
 della Croce Bianca, i. 165

INDEX. 483

Via—*continued.*
dei Crociferi, i. 464
Crucis, ii. 449
della Ferratella, i. 382
dei Fienili (Vicus Tuscus), i. 176, 221
Flaminia, great Northern road of Italy, ii. 423
delle Fornaci, ii. 449
S. Giovanni, ii. 94
Decollato, i. 239
de' Fiorentini, ii. 225
Giulia, ii. 175, 391
del Governo Vecchio, ii. 165
S. Gregorio, i. 375
Immerulana, ii. 122
Latina, ii. 124
Longarina, ii. 368
Lungara, ii. 434
Lungaretta, ii. 379, 382
de Macao, ii. 34
Maganaopoli, i. 461
Maggiore, ii. 72.
Margutta, i. 54
della Marmorata, ii. 392
Mazzarini, i. 461
de Mercede, i. 75
Monserrato, ii. 170
del Monte Tarpeio, i. 272
Morticelli, ii. 379
S. Niccolo in Tolentino, ii. 12
Nova, i. 307
Ostiensis, ii. 409
Pane e Perna, i. 466
S. Pantaleone, ii. 186
in Parione, ii. 165
della Pedacchia, i. 117
del Piè di Marmo, ii. 222
de' Pontefici, i. 61
della Porta Pia, ii. 43
delle Quattro Fontane, i. 474
del Quirinale, i. 444
Sta. Sabina, i. 355
Sacra, i. 205
della Salita del Grillo, i. 165
Savelli, ii. 360
della Scala, ii. 388
della Scrofa, ii. 155
S. Sebastiano, i. 375
della Sediola, ii. 197, 202
dei Serpenti, i. 463
di San Sisto Vecchio, i. 375
Sterrata, i. 443
Tor de' Specchi, i. 270
Tordinona, ii. 223
Triumphalis, i. 206
Urbana, i. 468

Via—*continued.*
della Vale, ii. 185
dei Vascellari, ii. 369
S. Vitale, i. 435, 466
della Vite, i. 74
Vittoria, i. 64
Vicus, Corneliorum, i. 436 ; Cyprius, ii. 49
Vigna, Codini, i. 386
dei Gesuite, i. 368
Marancia, i. 389
Vignola, ii. 418, 421
Villa Mills, i. 304, 311
Villas—
Albani, ii. 17
Altieri, ii. 132
Borghese, unhealthiness of, i. 21 ; resort of foreigners to, 35 ; description of entrance to, ii. 411 ; sculpture in, 413—416 of Claude Lorraine, ii. 419
Doria, unhealthiness of, i. 21 ; resort of foreigners to, 35
Esmeade, ii. 417
Farnesina, ii. 446
Lante, ii. 452
Lezzani, ii. 25
List of most important, i. 32
of Livia, ii. 423
Ludovisi, ii. 13
Madama, ii. 426
Massimo Arsoli, ii. 122
Negroni, ii. 35
Rignano, ii. 12
Mattei, i. 332
Medici, i. 49
Mellina, extensive view from, ii. 427, 428
Negroni, i. 473
Olgiati, once, of Raphael, ii. 416
Palombara, ii. 74
Pamfili Doria, ii. 454
of Papa Giulio, ii. 418
Patrizi, ii. 25
of the Servilii, ii. 124
Spada, ii. 20
Torlonia, ii. 26
Triopio, i. 414
Wolkonski, ii. 123
Viminal Hill, its limits, i. 433 ; derivation of name, 466
Vinci, Leonardo da, i. 67, 83 ; ii. 348, 437
Vineyards, i. 368, 370, 375, 395 ; ii. 53, 393, 398, 428
Virgin, one of the earliest representations of the, ii. 21

Vite, Timoteo della, i. 459
Vivarium, i. 329
Viviani, i. 326
Volterra, Daniele da, i. 52, 53, 137, 139, 458; ii. 119, 158, 174, 187, 295, 448, 450
Vouet, Simon, ii. 379
Vulcanal, site of the, i. 171

W.

Walls of—
    Aurelian, i. 385
    Romulus, i. 305

Walls of Servius Tullius, 368
Well, picturesque marble, i. 384
Whippings, pious, i. 85
White Mule, procession of the, ii. 212
Wine of the Vatican, ii. 430

Z.

Zuccari, F., i. 53, 69
Zucchero, Federigo, ii. 285, 400
Zucchero, T. ii. 15, 174; tomb of, in the Pantheon, 210; works of, 285, 335, 378, 385, 418

Works by C. J. Vaughan, D.D.

MASTER OF THE TEMPLE.

Family Prayers.
Crown 8vo. 3s. 6d.

The Presence of God in his Temple.
Small 8vo. 3s. 6d.

Sundays in the Temple.
Small 8vo. 3s. 6d.

Half-hours in the Temple Church.
Small 8vo. 3s. 6d.

Last Words in the Parish Church of Doncaster.
Crown 8vo. 3s. 6d.

Earnest Words for Earnest Men.
Small 8vo. 3s. 6d.

Voices of the Prophets on Faith, Prayer, and Human Life.
Small 8vo. 2s. 6d.

Characteristics of Christ's Teaching.
Small 8vo. 2s. 6d.

Christ the Light of the World.
Small 8vo. 2s. 6d.

Plain Words on Christian Living.
Small 8vo. 2s. 6d.

W. ISBISTER & CO., 56, LUDGATE HILL, LONDON.

Works by the late Henry Alford, D.D.

The Book of Genesis and Part of the Book of
Exodus. A Revised Version, with Marginal References, and an Explanatory Commentary. Demy 8vo. 12s.

The New Testament.
Authorised Version Revised. Long Primer, crown 8vo, 6s.; Brevier, fcap. 8vo, 3s. 6d.; Nonpareil, small 8vo, 1s. 6d.

Essays and Addresses.
Chiefly on Church subjects. Demy 8vo. 7s. 6d.

The Year of Prayer;
Being Family Prayers for the Christian Year. Crown 8vo, 3s. 6d.; 12mo, 1s. 6d.

The Week of Prayer.
An Abridgment of "The Year of Prayer," intended for Use in Schools. Neat cloth, 9d.

The Year of Praise;
Being Hymns with Tunes, for the Sundays and Holidays of the Year. Large type, with music, 3s. 6d.; without music, 1s. Small type, with music, 1s. 6d.; without music, 6d. Tonic Sol-fa Edition, 1s. 6d.

How to Study the New Testament.
Part I. The Gospels and the Acts. II. The Epistles (first section). III. The Epistles (second section) and the Revelation. Small 8vo. 3s. 6d. each.

Eastertide Sermons,
Preached before the University of Cambridge. Small 8vo. 3s. 6d.

Meditations:
Advent, Creation, Providence. Small 8vo. 3s. 6d.

The Queen's English.
A Manual of Idiom and Usage. Enlarged Edition. Small 8vo. 5s.

Letters from Abroad.
Crown 8vo. 7s. 6d.

Poetical Works.
Enlarged Edition. Crown 8vo. 5s.

W. ISBISTER & CO., 56, LUDGATE HILL, LONDON.

New Books.

The Autobiography of Thomas
GUTHRIE, D.D.; with a Memoir by his Sons, the Rev. DAVID K. GUTHRIE and CHARLES J. GUTHRIE, M.A. Vol. I. post 8vo. 10s. 6d.

Ivan de Biron;
Or, The Russian Court in the Middle of the Last Century. By SIR ARTHUR HELPS, K.C.B., Author of "Friends in Council." 3 vols. post 8vo.

The Huguenots in France, after the
Revocation of the Edict of Nantes; with a Visit to the Country of the Vaudois. By SAMUEL SMILES, Author of "The Huguenots; their Settlements and Industries in England and Ireland," "Self-Help," &c. Second Edition. Crown 8vo. 10s. 6d.

The Alton Sermons.
By the late AUGUSTUS WILLIAM HARE. New Edition, in one volume, uniform with "Memorials of a Quiet Life." Crown 8vo. 10s. 6d.

Jewish History and Politics in the
Times of Sargon and Sennacherib. By SIR EDWARD STRACHEY, Bart. New Edition, carefully revised, with large Additions. Post 8vo.

Wilkes, Sheridan, Fox: the Oppo-
sition under George III. By W. F. RAE, Author of "Westward by Rail," Translator of "Taine's Notes on England," &c. Demy 8vo. 18s.

The Great Ice Age, and its Rela-
tion to the Antiquity of Man. By JAMES GEIKIE, F.R.S.E., F.G.S., &c., of H.M. Geological Survey. With Maps, Charts, and numerous Illustrations. Demy 8vo. 24s.

W. ISBISTER & CO., 56, LUDGATE HILL, LONDON.

New Books.

National Education in Greece in
the Fourth Century before Christ. By AUGUSTUS S. WILKINS, M.A., Professor of Latin in the Owens College, Manchester. Crown 8vo. 5s.

The Period of the Reformation,
1517 to 1648. By LUDWIG HAUSSER. Edited by WILHELM ONCKEN, Professor of History at the University of Giessen. Translated by Mrs G. STURGE. 2 vols. post 8vo. 18s.

Complete in three Volumes.

Religious Thought in England,
from the Reformation to the End of Last Century By the Rev. JOHN HUNT, Author of "An Essay on Pantheism." 3 vols. demy 8vo. 21s. each.

Town Geology. By the Rev.
CANON KINGSLEY. Fourth thousand. Crown 8vo. 5s.

The Character of St Paul. By
J. S. HOWSON, D.D., Dean of Chester. Crown 8vo. 5s.

The Tragedies of Æschylos. A
New Translation, with a Biographical Essay and an Appendix of Rhymed Choruses. By E. H. PLUMPTRE, M.A., Professor of Divinity in King's College, London. Crown 8vo. 7s. 6d.

The Reign of Law. By the DUKE
OF ARGYLL. People's Edition. Limp cloth, 2s. 6d.

Revelation considered as Light:
a Series of Discourses. By the late Right Rev. ALEXANDER EWING, D.C.L., Bishop of Argyll and the Isles. Post 8vo. 7s. 6d.

W. ISBISTER & CO., 56, LUDGATE HILL, LONDON.

www.ingramcontent.com/pod-product-compliance
Lightning Source LLC
Chambersburg PA
CBHW021426300426
44114CB00010B/666